PRAISE FOR *NATURE AND THE HUMAN SOUL*

"Is it possible to discern and describe the entelechy of the human soul: the internal and eternal map to which we all are in service — whether we know it or not, whether we cooperate with it or not? In *Nature and the Human Soul*, Bill Plotkin draws from myth, diverse cultural forms, and personal insight, and produces a convincing map of our psychosocial life stages. To understand these developmental phases of our journey is to better appreciate their differing tasks, and perhaps better cooperate with their archetypal agendas."

— James Hollis, PhD, Jungian analyst and author of
Finding Meaning in the Second Half of Life

"Bill Plotkin enhances our grasp of the stages of life we are born to pass through by weaving into them themes of meaning, soul, and spirituality. This is a rich offering not only to the field of psychology but to a world torn from its roots."

— Chellis Glendinning, PhD,
author of *My Name Is Chellis and I'm in Recovery from Western Civilization*

"Brilliant, accessible, respectful, and compassionate, *Nature and the Human Soul* weaves a practical path for anyone from any culture to become whole, leading a soul-centered life that will benefit themselves and everyone and everything around them. Science, as currently practiced, can only tell us what is. *Nature and the Human Soul* shows what could (and should) be. There is an old adage that when the student is ready, the teacher will appear. The publication of *Nature and the Human Soul* may well signal that humanity is ready to learn a better way. It should be read by everyone, particularly those who choose to be parents, educate our children, guide our cultures and communities, and envision a better world."

— Dan Popov, PhD, cofounder of the Virtues Project
and coauthor of *The Family Virtues Guide*

"C. G. Jung, Joseph Campbell, Mircea Eliade, Father Thomas Berry, Julia Butterfly Hill, Joanna Macy. These are but a few of the bright visionaries who have helped us to understand the territory of the human psyche in its relation to the realm of myth, the profundity of cosmology, and the ancient human love affair with the natural world. In *Nature and the Human Soul*, Bill Plotkin joins their ranks by masterfully weaving luminous streams of insight and guidance, offering us new tools and maps. These potent maps not only hold the promise of personal transformation, but they may very well be a path toward our survival as a species."

— Frank MacEowen, author of *The Celtic Way of Seeing*

PRAISE FOR *SOULCRAFT* BY BILL PLOTKIN

"As we enter a future where humans and the natural world are more intimate with each other, we will surely be powerfully influenced by this new guide into the mysteries of nature and psyche. In *Soulcraft*, Bill Plotkin gives us an authentic masterwork. In the substance of what he has written, in the clarity of his presentation, and in the historical urgency of the subject, he has guided us far into the new world that is opening up before us. We will not soon again receive a work of this significance."

— from the foreword to *Soulcraft* by Thomas Berry, author of *The Dream of the Earth* and *The Great Work*

NATURE
and the
HUMAN SOUL

NATURE
and the
HUMAN SOUL

Cultivating Wholeness and
Community in a Fragmented World

BILL PLOTKIN

New World Library
Novato, California

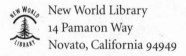

New World Library
14 Pamaron Way
Novato, California 94949

Permission acknowledgments beginning on page 495 are an extension of the copyright page.

The material in this book is intended for educational purposes only. No expressed or implied guarantee as to the effects of the use of the recommendations can be given nor liability taken. The publisher advises such activities as fasting or wilderness excursions not be attempted or practiced without appropriate guidance and support.

Text design by Tona Pearce Myers

Library of Congress Cataloging-in-Publication Data
Plotkin, Bill.
  Nature and the human soul : cultivating wholeness and community in a fragmented world / Bill Plotkin.
     p.   cm.
Includes bibliographical references and index.
ISBN 978-1-57731-551-3 (pbk. : alk. paper)
1. Developmental psychology. 2. Nature—Psychological aspects. I. Title.
BF713.P585 2008
155—dc22   2007038812

First printing, January 2008
ISBN: 978-1-57731-551-3
Printed in Canada on 100% postconsumer-waste recycled paper

g New World Library is a proud member of the Green Press Initiative.

10   9   8   7   6   5

To my beloved parents, Betty and Bernard Plotkin.

And in grateful memory of my inspired and inspiring teachers
Dorothy Wergin, Steven Foster, Dolores LaChapelle, and Peter G. Ossorio.

CONTENTS

CHAPTER ONE

CIRCLE *and* ARC

The Wheel of Life and the Great Turning

We must go far beyond any transformation of contemporary culture. We must go back to the genetic imperative from which human cultures emerge originally and from which they can never be separated without losing their integrity and their survival capacity. None of our existing cultures can deal with this situation out of its own resources. We must invent, or reinvent, a sustainable human culture by a descent into our pre-rational, our instinctive resources. Our cultural resources have lost their integrity. They cannot be trusted. What is needed is not transcendence but "inscendence," not the brain but the gene.

— THOMAS BERRY, *THE DREAM OF THE EARTH*

it's 3:23 in the morning
and I'm awake
because my great great grandchildren
won't let me sleep
my great great grandchildren
ask me in dreams
what did you do while the planet was plundered?
what did you do when the earth was unraveling?

surely you did something
when the seasons started failing?

as the mammals, reptiles, birds were all dying?

did you fill the streets with protest

when democracy was stolen?

what did you do
once
you
knew?...

— DREW DELLINGER, "HIEROGLYPHIC STAIRWAY"

CRISIS AND OPPORTUNITY

In our moment of history, perhaps the most sweeping and radical transformation ever to occur on Earth is under way. This "moment" is the twenty-first century, a lifetime from a human perspective, yet a mere dust mote of duration within our planet's 4.5 billion years of exuberant evolution.

As is so often the case, the opportunity at the heart of this moment arises from a great crisis. Over the past two hundred years, industrial civilization has been relentlessly undermining Earth's chemistry, water cycles, atmosphere, soils, oceans, and thermal balance. Plainly said, we have been shutting down the major life systems of our planet.

Compounding the ecological crisis are decaying economies, ethnic and class conflict, and worldwide warfare. Entwined with, and perhaps underlying, these devastations are epidemic failures in individual human development.

True adulthood, or psychological maturity, has become an uncommon achievement in Western and Westernized societies, and genuine elderhood nearly nonexistent. Interwoven with arrested personal development, and perhaps inseparable from it, our everyday lives have drifted vast distances from our species' original intimacy with the natural world and from our own uniquely individual natures, our souls.

But if we know where to look, we uncover great opportunities spawned by these crises. All over the world, we are witnessing a collective human response to exigency, an immensely creative renewal, addressing all dimensions of human activity on Earth — from the ecological, political, and economic to the educational and spiritual.

This book is my contribution to the global effort to create a viable human-Earth partnership.

My beginning premise is that a more mature human society requires more mature human individuals. For twenty-five years, I have been asking how we might raise children, support teenagers, and ripen ourselves so we might engender a sustainable human culture.

My second premise is that nature (including our own deeper nature, soul) has always provided and still provides the best template for human maturation.

In these pages, you'll find a narrative of how we might grow whole, one life stage at a time, by embracing nature and soul as our wisest and most trustworthy guides. This model for individual human development ultimately yields a strategy for cultural transformation, a way of progressing from our current *ego*centric societies (materialistic, anthropocentric, competition based, class stratified, violence prone, and unsustainable) to *soul*centric ones (imaginative, *eco*centric, cooperation based, just, compassionate, and sustainable).

In contrast to those presented in most other developmental models, the stages of life portrayed here are essentially independent of chronological age, biological development, cognitive ability, and social role. Rather, the progression from one stage to the next is spurred by the individual's progress with the specific psychological and spiritual tasks encountered at each stage.

This, then, is an ecopsychology of human maturation, a developmental psychology with a unique angle: it's a portrayal not of typical or "average" human development but of exemplary development as it occurs in the healthiest contemporary people — and as it *could* occur for everyone.

A third premise is that every human being has a unique and mystical relationship to the wild world, and that the conscious discovery and cultivation of that relationship is at the core of true adulthood. In contemporary society, we think of maturity simply in terms of hard work and practical responsibilities. I believe, in contrast, that true adulthood is rooted in transpersonal experience — in a mystic affiliation with nature, experienced as a sacred calling — that is then *embodied* in soul-infused work and mature responsibilities. This mystical affiliation is the very core of maturity, and it is precisely what mainstream Western society has overlooked — or actively suppressed and expelled.

Although perhaps perceived by some as radical, this third premise is not the least bit original. Western civilization has buried most traces of the mystical roots of maturity, yet this knowledge has been at the heart of every indigenous tradition known to us, past and present, including those from which our own societies have emerged. Our way into the future requires new cultural forms more than older ones, but there is at least one thread of the human story that I'm confident will continue, and this is the numinous or visionary calling at the core of the mature human heart.[1]

THE GREAT TURNING

What shape or pattern will the human story take in the future?

As of this writing, we cannot predict with any certainty the outcome of our current planetary cataclysm. In this tiny interval of the twenty-first century, we, the human species, will either learn to become a life-enhancing element within the greater Earth community... or we will not. If we fail, humanity will be reduced to a small number, we will have forsaken our potential as a species (this time around, at least) and we will have perpetrated the extinction of many thousands of species, perhaps millions — beyond those that have already perished at our hands.

And yet we now behold the possibility of a radical and foundational shift in human culture — from a suicidal, life-destroying element to a way of life worthy of our unique human potential and of Earth's dream for itself. What lies before us is the opportunity and imperative for a thorough cultural transformation — what eco-philosopher Joanna Macy calls the Great Turning, the transition from an egocentric "Industrial Growth Society" to a soulcentric "Life-sustaining Society," or what economist David Korten in *The Great Turning* calls the transition "from Empire to Earth Community." The cultural historian Thomas Berry refers to this vital endeavor as the Great Work of our time.[2] It is every person's responsibility and privilege to contribute to this metamorphosis.

Transformational progress is already under way through the creative initiatives of countless *ecocentric*[3] people and groups the world over. The Great Work has been launched in all realms of society, including technology, science, the arts, economics, education, government, and religion. A few examples: Major technological breakthroughs in clean, safe, local, renewable energy (wind, solar, small hydroelectric, and biofuels) and innovations in energy conservation methods. The science-rooted "new cosmology" — the sacred telling of the evolution of the universe and life on Earth. Local, human-scale economies and food systems that honor the "triple bottom line": people, planet, and profits. Primary and secondary education curricula rooted in ecoliteracy — the study of our relationship to nature, our first and foremost membership. The popular recent movements in South America that suggest the emergence of true Western democracies. The widespread longing for a more intimate relationship to the inscrutable mysteries of life as evidenced, for example, in the huge wave of renewed interest in nature-based and alternative spiritualities, from Celtic, goddess-oriented, and shamanic to Buddhism, Taoism, and Sufism. The burgeoning popularity and power of the environmental movement (the one movement that is surely not a "special interest"), the creation and widespread adoption of the Earth Charter (an international declaration of interdependence of all species and habitats), and the appearance of new laws (the "wild laws" of the new Earth jurisprudence) that grant essential rights to noncorporate nonhumans.[4]

These efforts and many others are unfolding largely outside the interest and coverage of mainstream media. Yet there are numberless groups, organizations, and communities around the globe creating the infrastructure of not only a new society but also a fundamentally new mode of being human. If we succeed, this century might be known in the future as the time Earth shifted from the geological epoch of the Cenozoic (now some 65 million years old, having begun at the time of the mass extinction that ended the reign of the dinosaurs) to what Thomas Berry calls the Ecozoic Era.

Will the twenty-first century turn out to be the Great Ending or the Great Turning? Will we succeed at the Great Work? It's up to us...you and me and all others who are waking up to the extraordinary challenge, opportunity, and imperative before us. As poet Drew Dellinger asks, "What did you do...when the seasons started failing?"

THE WHEEL OF LIFE

In this book you'll find a model of human development that is both ecocentric and soulcentric — that is, a nature-based model that fully honors the deeply imaginative potentials of the human psyche. I think of this model as a new natural history of the soul, a description of the organic, indigenous process by which a human child grows into a soul-initiated adult. Other times I've overheard myself say that this is a field guide for growing a genuine elder, starting, that is, at birth. This book asks the question, What do the stages of modern human development look like when we grow, in each stage, with nature and soul as our primary guides?

Twenty-five years in the making, this eight-stage model shows us how we can take root in a childhood of innocence and wonder; sprout into an adolescence of creative fire and mystery-probing adventures; blossom into an authentic adulthood of cultural artistry and visionary leadership; and finally ripen into a seed-scattering elderhood of wisdom, grace, and the holistic tending of what cultural ecologist David Abram calls the more-than-human world.[5]

The model, which I call the Soulcentric Developmental Wheel, the Wheel of Life, or simply the Wheel, is ecocentric in two respects. First, the eight life stages are arrayed around a nature-based circle (as opposed to the familiar Western linear timeline). Beginning and ending in the east and proceeding clockwise (which is sunwise), the stages and their attributes are based primarily on the qualities of nature found in the four seasons (east-spring, south-summer, and so on) or, alternatively, the four times of day (sunrise, midday, sunset, and midnight).

Second, the developmental task that characterizes each stage has a nature-oriented dimension as well as a more familiar (to Westerners) culture-oriented dimension. Healthy human development requires a constant balancing of the influences and demands of both nature and culture. For example, in middle childhood, the nature task is learning the enchantment of the natural world through experiential outdoor immersion, while the culture task is learning the social practices, values, knowledge, history, mythology, and cosmology of our family and culture.

In industrial growth society, however, we have for centuries minimized, suppressed, or entirely ignored the nature task in the first three stages of human development, infancy through early adolescence. This results in an adolescence so out of sync with nature that most people never mature further.

Arrested personal growth serves industrial "growth." By suppressing the nature dimension of human development (through educational systems, social values, advertising, nature-eclipsing vocations and pastimes, city and suburb design, denatured medical and psychological practices, and other means), industrial growth society engenders an immature citizenry unable to imagine a life beyond consumerism and soul-suppressing jobs.

This neglect of our human nature constitutes an even greater impediment to personal maturation than our modern loss of effective rites of passage, and it has led to the tragedy we face today: most humans are alienated from their vital individuality — their souls — and humanity as a whole is largely alienated from the natural world that evolved us and sustains us. Soul has been demoted to a new-age spiritual fantasy or a missionary's booty, and nature has been treated, at best, as a postcard or a vacation backdrop or, more commonly, as a hardware store or refuse heap. Too many of us lack intimacy with the natural world and with our souls, and consequently we are doing untold damage to both.

But it is not too late to change. This book suggests how we might embrace the nature task in each stage of human development and how we can address the culture task much more thoroughly and fruitfully than we do in industrial growth society. By devoting ourselves to both tasks, we can reclaim our full membership in this flowering planet and animated universe, and become more fully human, both as individuals and as societies. We can grow unimpeded into adulthood and, eventually, elderhood, and create twenty-first century life-sustaining societies.

BECOMING FULLY HUMAN

Joanna Macy and Molly Young Brown explain that the Great Turning is happening simultaneously in three areas or dimensions that are mutually reinforcing and equally necessary. They identify these as

- "holding actions" to slow the damage to Earth and its beings;
- analysis of structural causes and the creation of alternative institutions; and
- a fundamental shift in worldview and values.[6]

The first dimension includes a great variety of endeavors to defend life on Earth, including campaigns for progressive legislation and regulations, political actions and lawsuits that slow down the destruction of Earth's life systems, and direct actions such as boycotts, blockades, whistle-blowing, protesting, and civil disobedience. This is the more immediate, short-term work that provides time for the other two dimensions of building a life-sustaining society.

The second dimension asks us to deeply understand and demystify the dynamics of the industrial growth society so that we truly know how it works and why it is both seductive and destructive, and then to create alternative structures and practices in all our major cultural establishments, including economics, food and energy systems, government, and education. This book highlights some of these alternatives, especially in the realms of parenting and education.

The primary focus of this book, however, is on the third dimension of the Great Turning, which Joanna and Molly deem "the most basic."[7] They note that, in order to take root and survive, the alternative institutions created as part of the second dimension must be sourced in a worldview profoundly different from the one that created the industrial growth society. They see such a shift in human consciousness emerging in the grief that so many of us are feeling for a plundered world; in our new understandings from ecology, physics, ecopsychology, and other fields about what it means to be human on an animate planet; and in our deepening embrace of the mystical traditions of both indigenous and Western peoples.

The Wheel of Life provides a means to support and quicken this foundational shift in worldview and values; it offers a set of guidelines for actualizing our greater human potential. As Thomas Berry tells us in this chapter's epigraph, "We must go far beyond any transformation of contemporary culture.... None of our existing cultures can deal with [our current world] situation out of its own resources." In addition to creating new cultural establishments, we must enable our very mode of being human to evolve.

But I do not mean something implausible or fanciful. I mean what simply amounts to growing up. Rather than become something other-than-human or superhuman, we are summoned to become *fully* human. We must mature into people who are, first and foremost, citizens of Earth and residents of the universe, and our identity and core values must be recast accordingly. This kind of maturation entails a quantum leap beyond the stage of development in which the majority of people live today. And yet we must begin now to engender the future human.

Consequently, the question of individual human development becomes critical. How can we grow whole so that an ecocentric identity becomes the rule rather than the exception? How can we foster a global ecological citizenry?

There are three reasons that enhanced human maturation is essential to the Great Turning. First, we live in a largely adolescent world. And it is, in great measure, a pathological adolescence. There is absolutely nothing wrong with (healthy) adolescence, but our cultural resources have been so degraded over the centuries that the majority of humans in "developed" societies now never reach true adulthood. An adolescent world, being unnatural and unbalanced, inevitably spawns a variety of cultural pathologies, resulting in contemporary societies that are materialistic, greed-based, hostilely competitive, violent, racist, sexist, ageist, and ultimately self-destructive. These societal symptoms of patho-adolescence, which we see everywhere in the industrialized world today, are *not* at the root of our human nature, but rather are an effect of egocentrism on our humanity.

The Great Work cannot be completed as long as there are billions of people living a patho-adolescent lifestyle of conspicuous consumption — or aspiring to one — while billions of others live in abject poverty, or as long as there remains a majority of voter support for politicians (from either the right or left) with patho-adolescent ambitions and agendas, or as long as we live within political and corporate systems that suppress all alternatives to the industrial growth society.

As soon as enough people in contemporary societies progress beyond adolescence, the entire consumer-driven economy and egocentric lifestyle will implode. The adolescent society is actually quite unstable due to its incongruence with the primary patterns of living systems. The industrial growth society is simply incompatible with collective human maturity. No true adult wants to be a consumer, worker bee, or tycoon, or a soldier in an imperial war, and none would go through these motions if there were other options at hand. The enlivened soul and wild nature are deadly to industrial growth economies — and vice versa.

The second reason that human maturation is essential to the Great Turning is that the most potent seeds of cultural renaissance come from the uniquely creative work of authentic adults. All such adults are true artists, visionaries, and leaders, whether they live and work quietly in small arenas, such as families, farms, and classrooms, or very publicly on grand stages. They are our most reliable agents of cultural change. This book suggests a set of guidelines for restoring and refining the process of human maturation so that increasing numbers might grow into true twenty-first-century adults, into mature transformers of culture.

Thomas Berry writes, "We must invent, or reinvent, a sustainable human culture by a descent into our pre-rational, our instinctive resources. . . . What is needed is not transcendence but 'inscendence.' "[8] This descent, this inscendence, is the journey of soul discovery, which can be engaged only by those who have moved beyond the early adolescence in which our society has stalled. Through an individual's initiatory time in the underworld of soul, she uncovers a dream, a vision, or a revelation that will "inspire, guide, and drive the action" for the rest of life, as Thomas says. "The dream provides the energy for adult action."[9]

The most inspiring work in the world today is being performed by those who have undergone this initiatory passage, those who have returned with precious resources for a soulcentric or life-sustaining society. This is the descent of which Thomas writes, the mature hero's journey described by mythologist Joseph Campbell, the descent to the goddess portrayed by Jungian therapist Sylvia Brinton Perera, the process of individuation identified by Carl Jung and other depth psychologists such as James Hillman and Marion Woodman, and the subject of my first book, *Soulcraft: Crossing into the Mysteries of Nature and Psyche.*

We cannot simply think our way out of our current planetary impasse — not even with blue-ribbon panels of the world's best minds. As Albert Einstein noted, "No problem can be solved from the same level of consciousness that created it."[10] A viable plan for transforming our culture will not come from the worldview or the values that produced it. Viable cultural systems have always been sourced in the soul-rooted revelations, visions, and dreams of those with the courage to wander across borders into exotic psychospiritual realms, those like Crazy Horse, Gandhi, Jesus, and Buddha, and the equally inspiring but (in a patho-adolescent society) less-celebrated visionary women such as Mother Teresa, Hildegard von Bingen, and Wangari Maathai.

Mature revelation demands mature people. Positive cultural change is the natural outcome of healthy individual development, because mature people vitalize culture through their individual and collective actions. Cultural health and individual health engender one another. This book explores nature's ways — and every vital culture's ways — for raising healthy children; preparing adolescents for the initiatory adventure that opens the way to mature, authentic adulthood; and enhancing the cultural artistry and fulfillment of adult and elder lives.

The third reason individual maturation is essential is that, to succeed, the Great Turning must be overseen by true elders like Thomas Berry and Joanna Macy and tens of thousands of others like them. In its largest scope, the human venture must be guided not by assemblies of adolescent politicians and corporate officers, not even by mature, initiated adults, but by genuine councils of wise elders.

A PATHO-ADOLESCENT SOCIETY

In current Western and Westernized societies, in addition to the scarcity of true maturity, many people of adult age suffer from a variety of adolescent psychopathologies — incapacitating social insecurity, identity confusion, extremely low self-esteem, few or no social skills, narcissism, relentless greed, arrested moral development, recurrent physical violence, materialistic obsessions, little or no capacity for intimacy or empathy, substance addictions, and emotional numbness.

We see these psychopathologies most glaringly in leaders and celebrities of the Western world: Politicians blatantly motivated by image preservation, reelection prospects, power, wealth, and privilege. Moralizing religious leaders caught with their moral compasses askew. Entertainment icons killing themselves with alcohol, drugs, eating disorders, and cosmetic surgeries. Captains of industry reaching unprecedented nadirs of greed and power obsessions.

When we take an honest look at the people in charge of the governments, corporations, schools, and religious organizations of industrial growth societies, we find that too many are psychological adolescents with no deep understanding of themselves or the natural environment that makes their lives possible.

Many Western men spend their lives aspiring to the adventures of early-adolescent heroism — whether on elite playing fields, in the fastest cars, the highest summits, the most beds, or the most exclusive boardrooms. Many women hope to land the best male exemplar of that adolescent hero — or become a female version of him.

With so few ripened leaders, our communities have become caravans astray in a cultural wilderness. We've lost our bearings and forgotten where we were headed in the first place. When we arrive at a difficult crossing — say, a river or a chasm — having no boats or ropes, we sadly stare and then turn away to try another direction, perhaps hoping a god or a genie might someday come along to rescue us.

Although many of our social and psychological problems surface as early as the preschool years, our cultural disorientation becomes most evident in our remarkable failures with the life passage of puberty and the stage of life that follows it. As a society, we're profoundly confused about adolescence. We don't know if it is a form of early adulthood, late childhood, a blending of both, or something else entirely. We're not sure if we should treat a thirteen-year-old as an adult or a kid; we're not even sure *how* to do either. Parents of teenagers toss up their hands in mutual despair and resignation. An increasing proportion of teens feel lost and confused and cannot find someone trustworthy and wise to whom they can turn.

These confusions about adolescence are reflected in how we have collectively responded to puberty, which is, other than birth and death, perhaps the physically most obvious human transition. As a whole, Westernized societies don't seem to have a clue about how to prepare a young person for sexual flowering, social independence, authentic personal expression, soul discovery, or a lifetime of interdependent relationships in the more-than-human world of nature. Traditional rites of passage, stripped of their vitality centuries before, have become empty shells, like the long-discarded husks of departed souls.

Consequently, we are seeing the most alarming signs of cultural pathology in teenagers and children. We are witnessing an increasingly high percentage of teens who are drug addicted, violent, plotting to take their own and others' lives (and often following through), imprisoned, diagnosed with severe psychological disorders, and routinely prescribed mind-altering and emotion-numbing drugs.

And almost inconceivably, some *prepubertal children* are exhibiting adolescent pathologies. We are witnessing seven- and eight-year-olds involved in sex and drug addictions, homicides, and gang warfare. This is perhaps the clearest and most alarming symptom of a patho-adolescent society in the terminal stages of degeneration: even childhood is robbed of its wholesomeness.

A healthy childhood is rooted in nature and a supportive family, but many children in the Western world have been uprooted from both and given sexuality and trifles instead. Having lost the training and rites that prepare a girl for becoming truly queenly, a mature woman, we have instead beauty-queen contests for five-year-olds.

THE PROMISE AND HOPE OF ADOLESCENCE

But adolescence itself is not the problem. In fact, adolescence — healthy adolescence — holds our master key to both individual development and human evolution. Adolescence, at this time, is the locus of both our crisis and our opportunity. The crisis of adolescence and the crisis of our culture are two facets of the same impasse. Seizing the opportunity in one quickens the opportunity for the other. Once enough people embrace the true nature of adolescence — its promise and potential — Western culture will transform and again become life sustaining. To the extent that we don't know what adolescence is for, we don't know what *humans* are for.

It is likely that people who don't understand teenagers are the same people who, in their teen years, were not understood by *their* parents and teachers. Consequently, in each generation the promise of adolescence goes unrealized. This is our cultural dilemma.

A fourth premise of this book is that this dilemma — which has its roots in cultural changes associated with the advent of agriculture six to ten thousand years ago — is not accidental or due to bad luck. Rather, it is an intrinsic feature of what it is to be human: it has been, and is, unavoidable. This is a quandary hundreds of generations old, one so tangled and complex that we can't be surprised that humanity is just discovering means to resolve it.[11]

I believe our dilemma arises from the innate vulnerability, or Achilles heel, of the human species, a "sacred wound" that derives from our uniquely human mode of consciousness and that holds the secret to our destiny, our collective human soul.[12] Our distinctive ego-based consciousness — made possible by our reflexive self-awareness — engenders both our crisis and our opportunity. Ego consciousness is our greatest liability as well as our greatest power.

The symptoms of our human wound become most apparent in adolescence. This is the phase of life in which most contemporary people get stuck and the phase in which most need the greatest support. Adolescence holds the key to our becoming fully human.

Genuine adulthood is not obtained merely by reaching a certain age, birthing or raising children, or accepting certain responsibilities. The adolescent must undergo an initiation process that requires letting go of the familiar and comfortable. She must submit to a journey of descent into the mysteries of nature and the human soul. She must plunge to the depths, in a sense to "hell," but not at all in the way mainstream society has come to understand — and to fear. The descent that adolescents must undergo is what most scares people about teenagers (including teenagers themselves). But this is also what grieves many older people, because, somewhere inside, they know this is where *they* needed to go as teens but didn't, and the question still hovers in the air in front of them as to whether it is too late.

Through psychospiritual adventure, the adolescent comes to know what she was born to do, what gift she possesses to bring to the world, what sacred quality lives in her heart, and how she might arrive at her own unique way of loving and belonging. Entry into the life of the soul demands a steep price, an ordeal, a psychological form of dying. The uninitiated adolescent does not easily give up her claim on "the good life." Grasping this, we must invent, or reinvent, forms and methods for soul initiation.

A deeper understanding of adolescence is where our hope lies.

INVENTING THE WHEEL

Through my work as a depth psychologist, wilderness guide, and ecotherapist, I've had the privilege of observing how people grow into vibrantly creative, socially engaged, deeply fulfilling adulthood. I began with a great curiosity about how people uncover their destinies, their place in the more-than-human world. In 1981, as a complement to my psychologist hours, I plunged into guiding a contemporary Western version of the age-old cross-cultural vision quest. This was a ten- to fourteen-day experience that included four days of fasting in wilderness solitude.

Most participants came away with heart-rending or soul-stirring experiences, but by no means a single variety. I began to keep track of the many experiential themes, and over time, about eight groupings became evident, some centered on emotional healing or heart opening, some involving intimate communion or bonding with nature (often the first of a lifetime), and some featuring encounters with profound mysteries.

I wondered what factors influenced people's experiences on their vision fasts. I gathered notes from my own programs as well as the observations of dozens of other guides I knew. Gradually, a pattern emerged: personal response to a vision fast seemed foremost a function of psychological maturation, and secondarily a combination of the individual's intent for his fast and the guide's understanding of the meaning and potential of the experience.

During my programs, on the day before the fast began, my coguides and I began to predict — privately between us and solely for our own learning — the category of experience each participant would have on his or her upcoming fast. We based our conjectures mostly on a rudimentary model of developmental stages. To our own astonishment, we were correct at least 80 percent of the time.

Those who returned from their fasts with the most mysterious and world-shifting experiences — which we began to call soul encounters (revelations of the images, symbols, or themes of personal destiny) — were the ones who, at the outset, seemed to us most mature psychospiritually. Most always, these same folks were also the ones most at home in nature. Not surprisingly, the latter fact turned out to be correlated with a childhood history of ample unsupervised time in the wild world. I found it exceptionally interesting that these three things seemed so closely associated: a childhood immersed in nature, personal maturity, and the depth of experience on a vision quest.

So I became absorbed, almost obsessed, with the question of how we humans grow whole... or don't. I wondered why there appeared to be such disparate levels of development among people uniformly considered "adults."

For example, some of my colleagues who were guiding what we called "contemporary rites of passage" spoke of their programs as facilitating the grand shift from childhood to adulthood, as if that transition happened in one fell swoop courtesy of a two- to ten-day wilderness experience. They spoke as if you could take *any* child or teenager (or even an older person) and put him through a rite of passage and, presto-change-o, you'd have an adult. This led to troubling questions: What about that alleged stage of adolescence between childhood and adulthood? When do the passages into and out of *that* stage happen? Does someone — either a child or an adolescent — become an adult by merely undergoing a rite of passage? Isn't some kind of developmental preparation necessary? And what do we mean by *adulthood* anyway?

It became evident to me that the day-by-day process of personal development was a much bigger factor in maturation than the ritual marking of passages between stages. You might say this was a challenging realization for a person who had previously thought of himself as a rites-of-passage guide.

As you'll see throughout this book, I remain greatly encouraged that the more progressive elements of our society have become reattuned to the importance of rites of passage at times of major life transition. Indeed, one of the signs of a healthy society is that it provides its members with such rites at many of the major life transitions. But I am even more encouraged that we are beginning to learn that what happens during the life stages themselves is a good deal more essential to our development. A transitional ritual can have its intended effect only when the individual has made sufficient progress with the developmental tasks of the preceding life stages.

So, without intending it or desiring it, I became a developmental psychologist ... but with a twist. Rather than taking the conventional approach of studying current theory, or contributing research about "average" people in everyday American life, I spent very intimate time — eight to fourteen days at a stretch — in wilderness settings with small groups of exceptional people experiencing extraordinary personal, interpersonal, transpersonal, and terrestrial events. I was, of course, deeply and personally rearranged myself, both through my experiences of assisting others with their soul discovery and through my own wanderings in the wild realms beyond the familiar borders of the Western mind.

I began to create and flesh out a life-cycle model for what I was discovering, and named it the Soulcentric Developmental Wheel.

THE DANCE OF NATURE AND CULTURE

For approximately two million years, we humans have evolved within a matrix woven equally of nature and culture. However, since the beginning of Western civilization some five to ten thousand years ago, and certainly in modern times, our lives have become increasingly less attuned to nature and more solely to culture. And because of this, many modern cultures have diverged from their origins in nature, resulting in billions of modern lives radically alienated from the natural world and cultures devoid of the integrity and survival value implicit in natural systems.

Given this understanding of our human story, my first design principle for the Wheel was that each life stage must be envisioned from the perspective of nature as well as from that of (healthy) culture. To my knowledge, there are no other developmental models in the fields of Western psychology and contemporary Western spirituality that embrace nature as a core design element. (This absence of nature-based thinking and practice is itself revealingly diagnostic of both Western psychology and Western culture.)

The first choice to be made was which common parameter to use as the central characterization of each stage. I settled on the *developmental task*, because of what I had learned about the new rites of passage. If I had surmised correctly — if a rite of passage effected a true developmental shift only for people whose earlier life experiences prepared them for it — then we could say that readiness for a passage was a significant type of achievement. And if we were to speak of developmental achievements, there ought to be associated tasks in every stage that provide the opportunity to succeed (or fail) at those very achievements. Consequently, you'll find that each of the eight stages described in this book — two each for childhood, adolescence, adulthood, and elderhood — are characterized by tasks that the individual must address in that stage.

My understanding of the specific nature of each task arose largely from viewing each stage through the lens of nature — its cycles and rhythms as embodied in the progression of the seasons and the times of day. I kept returning to a specific question: "Given that we humans are as natural as anything else, what might these archetypal patterns — the rhythms of Sun and Earth — suggest about how a human life is meant to unfold?" (Several other design influences, in addition to nature's template, asserted themselves along the way, as I describe in chapter 3.)

As the model took shape and ripened, it became apparent that there was not one but two tasks in each stage, or in some cases, one task with two dimensions. For years, I found this duality merely interesting and ascribed to it no special significance. Then one day I noticed to my astonishment that there was indeed a deeper and unvarying motif. For each stage, one task (or one dimension of the single task) had to do with nature — with growing deeper into our human nature and our membership in greater nature — and the other with our relationship to culture. And furthermore, there was a dynamic tension, a necessary push-pull, between the nature and culture tasks of each stage. Immediately I realized it could not have been otherwise. Still, it amazed me it had taken so many years to see this, especially given that, from the start, I had intended the Wheel to be faithful to both nature and culture.

What has become clear is that the always-shifting dance between nature and culture is one of the principal dynamics that make us human. This appears to be true both for our individual development and for our species' collective evolution. Human ontogeny is shaped significantly more by cultural influences than is the ontogeny of any other life-form we know. And yet, as we've seen, a thorough experiential grounding in nature is equally essential for us: without it, pathology and self-destruction result.

This discovery of the twofold nature of the developmental tasks was followed by a second, even more surprising realization that, in hindsight, seemed equally obvious: contemporary Western society minimizes, suppresses, or ignores the nature task in every life stage, especially the first three. We no longer grow into our natural wildness, our true human nature. Rather, we retreat from it. For the majority of people in the world today, personal growth becomes arrested in the third stage of eight due to our alienation from nature — from both our human nature and greater nature. Furthermore, this alienation is the cause as well as the effect of dysfunctional culture. Each generation has a more difficult time maturing, resulting in cultures less capable of facilitating the maturation of subsequent generations — an ever-sinking spiral.

The Wheel of Life explores the nature task and the culture task in every life stage and suggests how we can get back on track with what nature intends for us as humans.

HOMO IMAGINENS

My third major realization was that nature's intention for us is not static. This intent itself has been evolving from the very beginnings of the human story: how we are presently designed to grow whole is not quite the same as how we were designed to grow whole in the past.

For example, one of the things I've learned from Thomas Berry is that modern science and cosmology require us to think about the world as not only unfolding in ever-repeating cycles but also as on a one-way, progressive, nonrepeating trajectory of evolution and transformation. Everything in the universe is steadily moving into entirely new terrain, entirely new sequences of development. There is a panoramic arc to our own existence as well as a replicating pattern.

This is a relatively new idea on the human scene, and a revolutionary one. The older, ever-renewing cycle model — for example, the repeating rhythms of the day, the Moon, the seasons, and the stages of plant and animal growth — is what we find in the traditional, classic, and indigenous views. In contrast, the irreversible trajectory model — for example, the universe originated in a big bang about 14 billion years ago and is still expanding, and birds evolved from dinosaurs, humans from apes, and all life ultimately from primordial single-celled organisms — is the perspective we find in modern cosmology and biology. Thomas refers to the latter perspective as "the time-developmental model."[13] His larger point is that our approach to the development of anything must now embrace both models — both circle and arc (in a sense, both feminine and masculine), which together describe a spiral progression through space and time.

Applying this pivotal insight to human evolution, we must recognize that, although our individual lives still unfold in a familiar nature-rooted cycle (as in the Wheel), we are nevertheless, as a species, collectively evolving in ever-new ways. The human life cycle itself is evolving. So although the Wheel takes the shape of a circle, this does not imply that we are now the same humans we were fifty thousand, ten thousand, or even two thousand years ago. We are developing as a species, too. We are still very much on an evolutionary adventure.

One of the recent developments we can identify in our evolution as a species — a phenomenon central to the design of the Wheel — has to do with the curious season of life we call adolescence. In a certain way, adolescence is a relatively new occurrence. The word *adolescence* itself was not used to refer to a stage of human development until 1900, by the first American to earn a doctorate in psychology, Stanley Hall. I have come to believe that modern adolescence represents a potential evolutionary advance, but one that we have not yet begun to fulfill.

Microbiologists tell us that our genetic coding is 98.6 percent identical to that of chimpanzees and that the other 1.4 percent mostly dictates the duration (that is, the slowness) of our juvenile development (neoteny). In other words, a major part of what differentiates us humans from other primates is the relatively long, pre-adult phase of our individual development.

It appears that adolescence is an evolving stage of growth, a stage gradually distinguishing itself from both childhood and adulthood. As the millennia unfold, we humans are each maturing slower and, on the average, living longer. Rather than a sign of psychological regression or biological error, modern adolescence might be evidence of an evolutionary trajectory, a momentous advantage we have not yet understood or benefited from. Longer juvenility allows for, but does not compel, fuller maturation. It is possible that, over the past ten thousand years, we've been evolving as a species but becoming less mature as individuals. Now we have the opportunity to mature as well.

As for our evolution, we might go so far as to speculate that a new dimension of the human species is in the process of emerging, or that the present human species is collectively mutating, and that the new wrinkle is not in our visible anatomy so much as an alteration in our mode and capacity of consciousness. Most significantly, at the heart of this postulated shift in human consciousness is our notably expanded and amplified capacity for imagination, a capacity that requires a healthy modern adolescence for its full realization.

To grasp the importance of an amped-up imagination, first recall that the human is the only creature we know of who has the ability to imagine alternative futures (and create them, using symbolic language and opposable thumbs).[14] This has been true of humans from the beginning, but now this faculty acquires a significance more pivotal than at any previous moment in Earth's evolution and, conceivably, in the universe's. In the twenty-first century, humanity must learn to use its forward-seeing imagination not only for its own sake but for the sake of all other species as well. As Thomas writes, "We now in large measure determine the earth process that once determined us. In a more integral way we could say that the earth that controlled itself directly in the former period now to an extensive degree controls itself through us."[15] For better or worse (and so far it is unmistakably for worse), humanity has become the dominant presence on this planet, as great as any geological force of the past or present.[16]

For this reason, our capacity to imagine the numberless facets of a viable future has far greater consequences and opportunities than ever before. We are now imagining not only for ourselves but for all Earthly creatures. A highly skilled and nuanced imagination — exercised by not just a few but the majority of humans — now acquires the most fundamental significance for survival. As a species, we must go beyond all previous functioning of our uniquely human imagination.

"*We cannot intentionally create unless we are able, first, to imagine,*" writes my colleague, the author and wilderness explorer Geneen Marie Haugen. "Imagination may be the most essential, uniquely human capacity — creating both the dead-end crises of our time and the doorway through them." She coined the appellation *Homo imaginens* many years ago to refer to our evolving consciousness, our way into the future. "*Homo, human,* and *humus* are thought to arise from a shared root — of the Earth. Thus, *Homo imaginens* might translate not only as the imagining human, but as the imagining Earth."[17] We might speculate that Earth is trying to imagine its own future through us. Psychologist Thomas Moore has more recently employed the almost identical *Homo imaginans.*[18]

We know that the geo-biological community of Earth excels in its ability to engender countless new forms and species to fill opportunities and needs within its constantly evolving and self-organizing web of life. This occurred, for example, 2 billion years ago when most terrestrial life took the form of primordial, single-celled, anaerobic bacteria (prokaryotes) living in the oceans. A by-product of their metabolism was oxygen, which, for them, was a poison. They generated such prodigious volumes of it that Earth's atmosphere became significantly altered and the prokaryotes were beginning to suffocate in their own waste. It was then that a new form of life appeared — bacteria that fed on oxygen (eukaryotes). Without such a transformational moment, life on Earth might have ended right there.

And now we find ourselves at a similar juncture. The human species is creating so much toxicity and pollution — and again radically altering Earth's atmosphere (and land and waters) — that its own survival is very much in question. If ever Earth, in its fecund generativity, were going to bring forth a new human species, now would be the time.

In 1988, Thomas Berry also suggested this possibility of a new species: "Because we are moving into a new mythic age, it is little wonder that a kind of mutation is taking place in the entire earth-human order. A new paradigm of what it is to be human emerges."[19]

Three of the most likely indicators of a new emerging human paradigm are as follows, features found in neither the contemporary Western human (yet) nor the traditional indigenous human.

- Universal awareness of an evolutionary arc to the unfolding of the world. This is the time-developmental perspective inherent in the science-informed universe story. Not only will the world change, but we will be transformed as a species when we collectively grasp and learn to live from the knowledge that (a) the universe is continuing to evolve, (b) we humans are both a part of and an essential mode of this evolution, and (c) relative to Earth, at least, we humans now have a determining role in this evolution. Humanity as a whole has never before confronted such a psyche-shifting idea or such an awesome, Earth-shaping responsibility.
- Universal visionary capacity. For most of human history, the highest development of visionary skill was limited to a few exceptional individuals in each community (shamans, prophets, visionaries, and so on). Now this capacity of deep imagination must be cultivated by all adults if we are to create sustainable cultures.
- Healthy modern adolescence. As I've suggested, we've not yet understood the potential and benefits of this new developmental period, which encompasses not one but two distinct stages with different, even divergent, tasks. Modern adolescence makes possible the more complete and destined development of the deep human imagination, our visionary capacity. This possibility is a central feature of the character of stage 4 on the Wheel of Life (as we'll see in chapter 7). Imagination might very well be the single most important faculty to cultivate in adolescence. Without this cultivation, true adulthood might never be reached.

My first book, *Soulcraft*, is a somewhat elaborate description of stage 4 (the Cocoon), which I think of as late adolescence, the period in which we intensively explore the mysteries of nature and psyche in preparation for initiation into true adulthood. In the Cocoon, if all goes well, we're granted a vision or revelation of our unique place in the world. When we commit to the practical embodiment of that vision, we enter adulthood.

FIVE FACETS OF THE WHEEL

The Wheel of Life represents not one but five things:

- A map or story of optimal human development
- A set of guidelines for individual psychological healing and wholing[20]
- A design tool for creating healthy human communities and life-sustaining societies
- A deep cultural therapy — a way to heal and transform our existing human cultures
- A portrait of the emerging stage of human evolution

A Map or Story of Optimal Human Development

The human life cycle is best understood as a story. The Wheel tells a story, in eight acts, of becoming fully human, and it offers a map for reaching that destination. It is at once a model of how human development would unfold in a modern, soulcentric, life-sustaining society — a hypothetical one — and of how it *can and does* unfold now in our existing egocentric society when there is sufficient support from soul-centered parents, teachers, extended family networks, schools, religious organizations, and social programs.

The Wheel is *eco*centric in that it models individual human development from the perspective of nature's cycles, rhythms, and patterns. Not only does the natural world feed us, clothe us, and shelter us; not only does it offer us communion with sacred mysteries; not only does it present us treasures such as flowers, gems, and seashells that we can offer to each other as gifts; not only does it inspire our music and art, but it also informs and guides every chosen step of our maturation, if we let it. The Wheel is, in essence, a biomimetic model of human development. Half the time, I call it the Ecocentric Developmental Wheel.

The Wheel is also *soul*centric, in two ways. First, it shows how soul attempts to guide our individual development. Second, it envisions the principal goal of maturation to be the conscious discovery and embodiment of our souls. It can equally well be called the Soulcentric Developmental Wheel.

Given that the human soul is the very core of our human nature, we might note that, when we are guided by soul, we are guided by nature. Both soul and greater nature *do* guide us in our individual development, whether or not we ask for this guidance. But if we know how to listen, we can benefit much more. Living in an adolescent culture does not banish us from soulcentric development. The assistance of nature and soul is always and everywhere available. In our own society, a large minority of people develop soulcentrically despite the cultural obstacles. The soul faithfully comes to our aid through dreams, deep emotion, love, the quiet voice of guidance, synchronicities, revelations, hunches, and visions, and at times through illness, nightmares, and terrors.

Nature, too, supports our personal blossoming (if we have any quiet exposure to her) through her spontaneities, through her beauty, power, and mirroring, through her dazzling variety of species and habitats, and by way of the wind, Moon, Sun, stars, and galaxies.

If we look at the biographies of our society's most celebrated geniuses, artists, and visionaries, we find that most of them had regular immersions in the wild, especially in childhood, and that all of them had great sensitivity to the stirrings of the soul's deep imagination.[21]

Although the Wheel resonates with the life ways of many traditional peoples, it is not a description of their approach to individual development.[22] Rather, it is a model of the underlying structure of healthy life stages traversed by contemporary people from any culture, including the healthiest and most creative Westerners.

The eight developmental stages together constitute a single story, the story of a deeply fulfilling but nevertheless entirely human life. The story the Wheel tells is very different from the one that most contemporary people live. What we need now are new stories to share with each other, new tales to live into the world, which is to say, stories to make real by living our own versions of them. As David Korten suggests, the most difficult and essential aspect of the Great Turning might be to change our stories. The Wheel provides guidance for shifting the stories of our individual and collective lives.

A Set of Guidelines
for Individual Psychological Healing and Wholing

There are two general approaches to alleviating psychological problems: pathology-centered and wholeness-centered (holistic). (This is also true for medical problems more generally.) Using the pathology approach, we ask, "What symptoms of dysfunction is this person exhibiting, and what can be done to eliminate these symptoms and/or this dysfunction?" Common psychological symptoms include anxiety, depression, obsessions, eating disorders, addictions, and mania. A shallow version of the pathology approach simply attempts to eliminate or suppress the behavioral, somatic, or emotional symptoms. A deeper approach tries to understand the psychodynamics of the dysfunction and then foster healing by addressing the deeper causes.

All pathology approaches begin and end with a symptom focus: you don't know what, if anything, is needed until symptoms appear, and you don't know your intervention has succeeded until the symptoms diminish.

Some pathology approaches attend only to the individual, and others consider the individual's difficulties to be symptoms of the larger system in which the individual is a member (his family, school, or community). The system perspective with the widest lens, found among ecopsychologists, conceives of individual pathologies as symptoms of environmental illness, illness generated by human activity; as symptoms of our disordered human relationship with nature.

With the holistic approach, in contrast, dysfunction is not a central focus. We ask instead, "What qualities or capacities are missing from this person's embodiment of wholeness, and what can be done to cultivate these qualities or capacities?" The goal is to encourage and foster something functional and fulfilling rather than to remove something dysfunctional and deadening. Missing psychological qualities might be, for example, innocence, wonder, body awareness, nature reverence, creativity, and the development of values and virtues. Capacities of wholeness include social skills, cultural knowledge, emotional and imaginal skills, conflict resolution, and self-reliance.

Although the identification of symptoms can be useful in the holistic approach, there's no need to wait for signs that something has gone "wrong" before making an assessment of your own or another's embodiment of wholeness. When symptoms *are* observed, the holistic approach views them as indicators of the qualities of wholeness that the psyche is attempting to activate — as opposed to something dysfunctional that needs to be removed. The symptom is honored as a message from the person's wholeness and becomes a guide for identifying what needs to be encouraged and cultivated.[23]

The holistic premise is that most dysfunctions and their symptoms are resolved in the course of restoring or engendering wholeness, which is far more than a cure. Any dysfunction is itself viewed as a symptom — of compromised or unrealized wholeness. In a successful pathology-approach, in contrast, pathology is cured but wholeness is rarely achieved or even attempted.

For example, with a holistic approach to depression (by which I mean, not sadness, but unassimilated emotions), not only is it rare to use antidepressants (which the holistic perspective views primarily as symptom blockers), but also the experiential release and assimilation of the emotions — say, grief following a major loss — would be considered only a partial treatment. The holistic practitioner would, in addition, coach the bereaved in fully developing his emotional skills (including emotional access through bodily experience, followed by intrapsychic insight and adaptive action or affective expression), since such skills are an essential component of every person's wholeness.

The pathology approach is reactive (eliminating dysfunctions when they appear), while the holistic approach is proactive (cultivating wholeness, whether or not there are observable symptoms) and can be employed anytime, on a regular basis, and by most anyone.

A crucial component of a holistic approach to individual development is a map or model of psychological wholeness. Without one, there's no systematic way to assess what elements of wholeness are missing. We need a map or model that is sensible, functional, sufficiently differentiated and nuanced, and both realistic and inclusive of the exceptional. With such a map or model, we can assess a person's wholeness independent of symptoms — in fact, without identifying symptoms at all.

The Wheel is a model of human wholeness differentiated into eight life stages. For each life stage, there is a set of qualities and capacities that a healthy person in that stage would be expected to develop. The Wheel, then, can be used as a tool for assessing deficits in wholeness. In describing how each of the developmental qualities and capacities is cultivated, the Wheel also provides specific guidelines for addressing developmental deficits. It is specifically an ecopsychological version of the holistic approach to individual development that looks at human wholeness through the lens of nature's patterns and cycles, which themselves always function holistically.

The Wheel suggests that the most common psychological symptoms result from neglecting developmental tasks in the first three stages of life. The ideal response is to, when possible, address these tasks with or without professional support. (Severe symptoms, like suicidal thinking or acute emotional trauma, must, of course, be attended to first, preferably by a well-trained professional.)

A holistic approach provides options well beyond prevention methods. Consider teen drug use, for example. Common prevention efforts include drug education, tellings teens to "just say no," teen-center drug-alternative activities, addiction counseling, positive and negative reinforcement (bribes and threats), and incarceration. All of these "treatments" are reactions to the symptom of drug use itself; they are attempts merely to eliminate the symptom, to get teens to stop using drugs. A holistic approach to drug use, in contrast, does not focus primarily on drugs but offers teens the opportunity to address their developmental deficits through a great variety of experiences, deficits that might have no obvious relationship to drug use or abuse. For example, one of the common wholeness deficits among drug-abusing teens is the unfulfilled and utterly natural longing to directly experience the mysteries of life. This is a common deficit in Western societies due to the near absence of cultural practices for fulfilling this normal feature of teenage wholeness. An adequate holistic approach to teen drug use must include, among other things, instruction in effective and suitable methods for altering consciousness and exploring the mysteries of nature and psyche.

Another example concerns the current epidemic in childhood depression, obesity, and attention deficit/hyperactivity disorder (ADHD). All three are most commonly treated with drugs and behavior therapy, with very limited genuine success. Recent research suggests that these dysfunctions are symptoms of wholeness deficits, especially of those qualities awakened by free-play time in nature, qualities like wonder, imagination, creativity, the love of learning, intimacy, and joy. This research shows that children with these dysfunctions, when allowed regular unstructured time in nature, show a rapid decrease in depression, obesity, and ADHD. (More on this in chapter 5.)

A core hypothesis stemming from the holistic use of the Wheel is that the "mental health" needs of a large percentage of troubled children, teens, and older persons would be much better addressed by helping them with their unfinished developmental tasks from the first three life stages than by pathology-centered psychotherapies or symptom-suppressing medication.

Another hypothesis is that the reason for the demonstrated effectiveness of the increasingly popular wilderness-based therapies is that they cultivate specific dimensions of human wholeness that contemporary societies neglect. Chief among these dimensions is the visceral, emotional, and imaginative discovery of nature's enchantment, something normally achieved in a healthy middle childhood (stage 2 on the Wheel). This sort of nature learning calls for regular time outdoors in natural environments but does not require a full-on wilderness setting. Other dimensions include value clarification, the development of affective and self-reliance skills, and the acquisition of ecological responsibility — all normally achieved in a healthy early adolescence (stage 3 on the Wheel), and all of which can be fostered perfectly well outside wilderness settings.

A third hypothesis that follows from developmental holism — there are many possible — is that the demonstrated effectiveness of meditation as a psychotherapeutic complement derives from the fact that it restores a dimension of wholeness that is ideally preserved and protected in early childhood (stage 1 on the Wheel) but rarely retained by people in patho-adolescent societies, namely, the capacity for present-centeredness or innocence.

A Design Tool for Creating Healthy Human Communities and Life-Sustaining Societies

This is the third of the five facets of the Wheel.

A healthy society is, among other things, sustainable, just, and compassionate. It is sustainable because it is expressly organized as an integral component of the greater community of Earth; it establishes a niche for itself that benefits both its people and the greater geo-biological community of which it is a member. It is a just society because it provides equal opportunities *and* benefits for *all* persons. It is compassionate because it shares its wealth with all other societies and with the greater web of life; it does not exploit other peoples or species. A healthy society also embraces and celebrates our enchanted human senses, bodies, and emotions and encourages our imaginative exploration of the mysteries of psyche and nature.

As a design tool, the Wheel does not dictate any specific versions of a life-sustaining society. To the contrary, any community — whether a family, village, or nation — can use it to help create its own version of an ecocentric culture. To cultivate an authentic, viable society, the specific design of its component establishments must be rooted in the revelatory experiences of its individual members as well as in the dreams shared by the majority of its people.

Such a society cannot be created by simply sitting down and planning one, no

matter how enlightened the designers or design principles. It arises only through a natural process of cultural evolution galvanized by soul-infused actions. The specific form
the society will take is unpredictable. Being transcultural, the Wheel both respects and
requires cultural diversity.

The primary way the Wheel functions as a design tool for healthy societies is by
assisting communities in creating and implementing developmental practices —
especially parenting, educational, and initiatory practices for children and adolescents
— that allow for optimum individual maturation. In doing these things, the community begets true adults and elders, who in turn engender, through their lives and
work, specific cultural forms that are authentic, vital, and effective because they arise
from soul, which is to say, from nature. In other words, the Wheel has an indirect function in creating healthy cultures. It can help communities establish the conditions for
the growth of mature individuals who, in turn, establish life-sustaining cultural practices and customs (including those that go into making schools, governments, spiritual organizations, and economies).

The Wheel, then, is a deep-structure model designed to be transcultural. It is deep-
structural in that it characterizes the stages of life, and the transitions between them,
in terms of their essence, depth, or significance, not in terms of their specific cultural
practices, traditions, myths, or ceremonies. What makes for developmental progress
within any stage is the intrapsychic and interpersonal significance of what the individual and her community does, as opposed to the specific cultural practices in which
she engages. It is the meaning and developmental consequences of her actions that
count, not the particular cultural forms or styles through which she achieves them.

Readers familiar with biologist Rupert Sheldrake's work might recognize that the
Wheel is a description of the "morphic field" underlying human psychospiritual
development.[24] A morphic field is the underlying formative pattern of a self-organizing
system, such as an oak, a bear, a human, an ecosystem, Earth, the Milky Way, or the
universe. The morphic field depicted by the Wheel gives the entire human life cycle
its distinguishing properties. In Buckminster Fuller's terms, the Wheel identifies the
nature-generated "pattern integrity" of human development. And to borrow an idea
from the physicist David Bohm, the Wheel corresponds to the "implicate order" of
human maturation. Bohm's term refers to the generative field underlying specific manifest forms, from atoms to humans to galaxies.[25]

As one example, in the fourth stage of the Wheel, developmental progress requires
a person to wander far from the familiar "home" of his adolescent ways of belonging,
doing, and being. He must, as poet Mary Oliver puts it, "[stride] deeper and deeper
into the world."[26] His culture will greatly influence the *manner* in which he wanders,
as will his gender, physical constitution, psychological temperament, age, and bioregion. In one culture, his wandering might take him geographically far from his hometown or village. In another culture, geographic movement will have little importance

for the true depth of his wandering. What is critical is not whether he engages in this practice or that, or undergoes this ritual or another, but that his wandering changes his relationship to the world, that he leaves the home of his adolescent identity, and that his border crossings usher him into the mysteries of nature and psyche. These deep-structure changes are necessary to maintain the pattern integrity of stage 4 and, thereby, of the entire Wheel and of the whole human-Earth relationship.

Only a deep-structure model of human development can approach the goal of be-ing transcultural. Another way to say this: The Wheel itself is not a spiritual path but is designed to be compatible with most. A specific spiritual discipline is a tradition-based method to meet one or more spiritual goals. The Wheel makes room for all spir-itual goals without identifying particular traditions for reaching them (except by occasional illustration) and illuminates the relationship between spiritual goals and other developmental goals, stages, archetypes, and so on.

Another example: What really makes a person an elder has nothing to do with, say, chronological age, number of grandchildren, retirement, or even achievement in a certain craft or career. Rather, it has to do with a way of belonging to the world that is consciously centered on the soul of the more-than-human community.

In addition to being transcultural, the Wheel is gender-neutral, a portrayal of the deep structure of both male and female development. While there are obvious differ-ences between masculine and feminine humans and the way they develop, these dif-ferences are either on the surface (different styles) or in the middle depths (the social practices and psychological dynamics by which the deep-structure outcomes are reached). The surface and middle-depth differences between masculine and feminine are greatest in early adolescence (stage 3). Because this is the stage in which Western societies have stalled, and because our societies are not informed by the deep struc-ture of human development, gender differences have seemed bigger and more defin-itive to us than they really are.

With the social advances brought by feminism in the late twentieth century, some have contended that healthy female development differs from that of male de-velopment, and that the imposition of male patterns on women continues the centuries-old oppression by the patriarchy. While I agree, my perspective is somewhat different. There is no question that women have been economically, educationally, and politi-cally oppressed in patriarchal societies (as have most minority and lower-class men), but both men and women have been cut off from soul and nature, and both have con-sequently faced great difficulties in maturing. Although healthy female development is different from patho-adolescent masculine development, this is equally true for healthy male development.

The essential issue concerning oppression is not gender-based or race-based but ego-centric versus soulcentric. In my view, the core problem with patriarchal (and matriar-chal) societies is their patho-adolescent egocentrism, which generates economic-class oppression, not their conspicuous suppression of the feminine or glorification of the (immature) masculine. Men have no monopoly on egocentrism. Men and masculinity are no more the problem than are women and femininity. I believe that most people would agree that we will not create a healthier society by affording women the equal right to be as pathologically egocentric as a large proportion of men have been for millennia, to acquire the equal opportunity to excel in the patho-adolescent, class-dividing world of prestige, position, and wealth, academic and corporate ladder-climbing, and power broking. Rather, mature men and women must join together to foster soulcentric development for both genders and for all races and cultures.

A Deep Cultural Therapy — a Way to Heal and Transform Our Existing Human Cultures

Speaking bluntly, Thomas Berry, a lifelong student of world cultures, refers to the current, near-universal commitment to industrial progress, unlimited growth, and a consumer society as "the supreme pathology of all history."[27] A valid response to such a pathology, he says, must include remedial treatment:

> The entrancement with industrial civilization . . . must be considered as a profound cultural disorientation. It can be dealt with only by a corresponding deep cultural therapy. . . .
>
> At such a moment a new revelatory experience is needed, an experience wherein human consciousness awakens to the grandeur and sacred quality of the Earth process. This awakening is our human participation in the dream of the Earth, the dream that is carried in its integrity not in any of Earth's cultural expressions but in the depths of our genetic coding. Therein the Earth functions at a depth beyond our capacity for active thought. We can only be sensitized to what is being revealed to us. We probably have not had such participation in the dream of the Earth since earlier shamanic times, but therein lies our hope for the future for ourselves and for the entire Earth community.[28]

Thomas is suggesting that the cultural therapy we need springs from revelatory or visionary experience, an awakening to the dream of the Earth. Given that such an awakening calls for the journey to our individual depths, then our cultural healing requires a means to facilitate that descent — a contemporary methodology corresponding to what we had in "earlier shamanic times." The Wheel proposes a means to galvanize a human awakening to the dream of the Earth, an awakening impelled by an identifiable series of developmental experiences, starting at or before birth, evoked and guided by parents, educators, initiators, mentors, and elders.

If it is true, as the human ecologist Paul Shepard and others have observed, that our environmental crises are due to a widespread failure of personal development, especially among the people in power in industrialized nations (mostly wealthy males), then a radical overhaul in our way of parenting and educating children is in order. How do we raise children to become compassionate, nature-revering, visionary, actively engaged adults? And how do we enable these adults to become, in time, true elders with the capacities of heart and mind to care for the soul of the more-than-human community?

The deep cultural therapy we need and seek requires profound changes in the way we embody and support every stage of human growth. The Wheel suggests the broad outlines of such a therapy.

A Portrait of the Emerging Stage of Human Evolution

Thomas Berry refers to the great transformations in the evolution of the universe as "moments of grace." These are "privileged moments" in which "the future is defined in some enduring pattern of its functioning."[29] The supernova that gave birth to our solar system is one such moment of grace. Others include the appearance on Earth of the first living cell and, later, the emergence of a cell capable of metabolizing oxygen. The advent of humans — primates with conscious self-awareness — is another such moment.

We might think of these junctures as moments of grace because, in them, the unutterably creative and mysterious imagination of the cosmos manifests itself most profoundly. Each of these extraordinary turning points is one of both crisis and opportunity. Says Thomas, "The catastrophic moments are also creative moments."[30]

And now we, both as a species and as a planet, have arrived at another crisis, a most dangerous and unique opportunity that requires what Thomas calls "a comprehensive change in consciousness."[31] Will we cooperate with grace, with the imagination of the cosmos, during this potential turning point? I say "cooperate," because, unlike any previous transformation known to us in the unfolding story of the universe, this one, if it is to happen, will require the conscious and deliberate cooperation of a sentient life-form. The cooperation with grace needed here is beyond anything humanity has previously achieved. It requires not only worldwide collaboration between individuals, communities, and nation-states but also, more daunting, something akin to the collectively activated human imagination, as suggested earlier in the idea of *Homo imaginens*. Innumerable new, generative images must be retrieved from the depths of the individual psyche and of Earth's own dream, images that are the seeds of cultural renaissance. And then, as a grand network of cooperating communities, we must come together to build a new world from those images.

The Wheel, then, is a portrait of this emerging stage of human evolution, a planetary moment when humanity develops, as Thomas writes, "a profound mystique of the natural world" and experiences "the deep mysteries of existence through the wonders of the world about us."[32] Collectively, the eight stages of the Wheel present a profile of the future human, a human capable of consciously cooperating with grace — the deep imagination of the cosmos.

Just as the universe evolves through moments of crisis, so do individual humans. Each of the nine life-stage passages on the Wheel evokes a crisis, a death-rebirth transition. And just as grace is an element in the universe's evolution, so it is in our personal unfolding. Our conscious cooperation with grace makes all the difference at our life passages, especially after early adolescence (stage 3). I believe that learning to cooperate consciously with grace — as individuals and as a species — is one of the essential elements in our current evolutionary opening.

CHAPTER TWO

THE POWER *of* PLACE

Stand still. The trees ahead and the bushes beside you
Are not lost. Wherever you are is called Here,
And you must treat it as a powerful stranger,
Must ask it permission to know it and be known.
The forest breathes. Listen. It answers,
I have made this place around you.
If you leave it, you may come back again, saying Here.
No two trees are the same to Raven.
No two branches are the same to Wren.
If what a tree or bush does is lost on you,
You are surely lost. Stand still. The forest knows
Where you are. You must let it find you.

— DAVID WAGONER, "LOST"

In this chapter, I clarify my use of several words central to all that follows in these pages, namely, *soul, spirit, mystery, ego, upperworld, middleworld, underworld, egocentric society*, and *soulcentric society*. Some might be new to you, and it's possible I use others differently than you or the traditions you're familiar with. I make no claim that my definitions are "correct" or "better," but if at the outset I am clear about my meanings, you'll better understand thereafter what I mean.

Some readers are naturally more intuitive than analytical and so will be less concerned with precise meanings. Others might simply be eager to dive into the Wheel.

In both cases, feel free to leap ahead to chapter 3. Yet other readers, before moving on, will wish to review the subsections of this chapter whose titles arouse their curiosity. Whether you read this chapter now (recommended) or later, please remember that you can always return here should you get lost as to my meanings.

SOUL
Ultimate Place

By *soul*, I mean a thing's ultimate place in the world. I use the word *thing* to embrace the fact that *every* thing has a particular place in the world and therefore has a soul — all creatures, objects, events, and relationships. More on this later.

By *place*, I mean not a geographical location but the role, function, station, or status a thing has in relation to other things.[1] A thing's place tells you how it fits in the world. A particular elder, for instance, might have the place of your grandmother, teacher, or congresswoman. Elders, in general, might be said to have the place of guardians of nature and culture. The stage of life we call adolescence can be imagined as having the place of a grand cultural crisis and opportunity, and Earth the place of the blue-green jewel of our solar system and perhaps even of the Milky Way. The twenty-first century might turn out to have the place of either the Great Turning or the Great Ending; we don't know which yet.

A thing's place corresponds to the set of relationships it has with other things in the world.[2] For example, to identify the place of the ocean, you might note such relationships as these: the ocean receives all the freshwater that flows off the land, it is the birthplace of all Earth life, and its currents and temperatures greatly influence global weather patterns. To identify the place of the Soulcentric Developmental Wheel, I might refer to its relationships to human development, the concept of a model (versus a theory), the circle, the number four, certain patterns in nature, the cross-cultural myth of the hero's journey, and the Great Work — as I will, in fact, in the next chapter.

An individual person's place is usually identified by social relationships or roles: for example, the relationships identified by the phrases "Adam's wife," "Mary's (or God's) only son," or "the man who reads the meter"; and roles such as prime minister of England, baker, mediator, or master of ceremonies. To identify a person in any of these ways is to state or imply something about the kinds of relationships she has with other people and things, and the kinds of behaviors she is eligible to engage in. In common vernacular, we'd say that a person's place identifies who she is or "where she is at."

A thing can be said to have multiple places, depending on the context. For example, a certain book might have the place of a novel, a long essay on human development, a revelatory scripture, or (hopefully not in the case of *this* book) a doorstop. I intend the Wheel of Life to have the place of a map of optimal human development or of a template for deep cultural therapy, to name two of five.

A thing's "ultimate place" is its place in the great scheme of things, its quintessential place in the world or the universe. Soul is the place that most centrally and comprehensively identifies a thing — a thing's *truest* place.

A thing's ultimate place corresponds to the set of relationships that this thing has with *all* other things in the world. But obviously, to identify a thing's ultimate place, you couldn't name each and every one of those relationships, or even a fraction of them. Rather, you use expressions that encapsulate or summarize those relationships, or you note a few of the principal ones.

When we say "ultimate place" — which is to say, when we are speaking of soul — we are calling attention to the very core or heart of a thing's identity, its decisive meaning or significance, its raison d'être.

Keeping in mind that the identity of the soul of a person or thing is always a matter of opinion, here are a few opinion-examples. The soul of humanity is the conscious celebration of the universe's grandeur. The soul of the U.S. Declaration of Independence is the affirmation of universal human equality. The soul of a possible future biocracy is the affirmation of the inalienable rights of all species and all habitats. The soul of Jesus is love, and the soul of the Buddha is emptiness. You might disagree with any of those soul-identifications, but you can see nonetheless that each uses the word *soul* in the sense of "ultimate place."

Using that definition, *every* thing has a soul, not just humans, not just animals, but also plants and trees, minerals, geological formations, mountains, rivers, skies, sunshine, planets, galaxies, and all things human-fashioned, including books, buildings, blouses, Buicks, bongos, and ball games. Collectives and categories of things have souls, too. Like the soul of a specific herd of elk. Or the soul of our solar system. Or a whole species, as in the soul of humanity.

The set of relationships a thing has with all other things is a *unique* set: each thing occupies a unique place, a particular node in the web of life. Therefore, the soul of each thing is unique.

The human soul is a person's ultimate place in the more-than-human world.

Psycho-Ecological Niche

Given that *nature* can be a synonym for *world*, the definition of *soul* used in this book implies that you were born to occupy a particular place in nature — a place in the Earth community, not just in a human society. You have a unique ecological role, a singular way you can serve and nurture the web of life either directly or through your role in human society. You have a specific way of belonging to the biosphere, as unique as that of any birch, bear, or beaver pond. What makes you the individual you are is not your autonomy but your interdependent and communal relationship with everything else in nature.

But having a specific and unique way of belonging to the world in no way implies that you necessarily know what that place is. Although you were born with the potential to occupy that place, you were not born with conscious knowledge of it. It's possible, in fact, that you might never come to consciously comprehend that place.

Notice that, as your ultimate place, your soul is both yours and the world's. Yes, it's *your* place, but it's also a distinctive place in the world, like a vibrant space of shimmering potential waiting to be discovered, claimed,...occupied. Your soul is in and of the world, like a whirlpool in a river, a wave in the ocean, or a branch of flame in a fire. As the anthropologist, biologist, and ecologist Gregory Bateson avers, psyche is not separate from nature, it is *part of* nature. Many contemporary depth psychologists maintain that nature *is* psyche.

Brian Swimme and Thomas Berry propose that everybody — and everything — not only has a unique place in the world but *is* a unique place or space: "Walt Whitman did not invent his sentience, nor was he wholly responsible for the form of feelings he experienced. Rather, his sentience is an intricate creation of the Milky Way, and his feelings are an evocation of being, an evocation involving thunderstorms, sunlight, grass, history, and death. Walt Whitman is a space the Milky Way fashioned to feel its own grandeur."[3]

If your soul is your ultimate place in the world and you need to live from that place to be fully yourself, then the world cannot be fully itself until you become fully *yourself*.

What I mean by *place* is similar to what ecologists mean by *niche*, which refers to the position or function of an organism within a community of plants and animals. A niche consists of a set of relationships with other creatures and with the land and sky and the waters. It's a particular node in a living web. But in the case of the human soul, a niche is highly differentiated both psychologically and ecologically. The human soul is a *psycho*-ecological niche, a niche whose essential features include the capacity for conscious self-awareness as well as social and ecological attributes. We humans occupy both a noosphere and an ecosphere. This is an essential feature of the soul of humanity.

As individual humans, we must, when developmentally ready, wander deeply into the world in search of our ultimate place, a place that may or may not have anything to do with a particular geographical location. Then we must learn to inhabit that psycho-ecological niche.

The human soul, like any soul, cannot be separated from nature. Our souls are of nature. If psychology is the study of the human soul, then an integral psychology must be an ecopsychology or, better, an eco-depth psychology.

The Privilege to Refuse Our Flowering

...I look out
at everything
growing so wild
and faithfully beneath
the sky
and wonder
why we are the one
terrible
part of creation
privileged
to refuse our flowering. ...

— DAVID WHYTE, FROM "THE SUN"

More often than not, we cannot identify a person's soul with any certainty or precision. We have only our opinions. This is all right. It is, in fact, why the word *soul* is so handy. When we use it, others know we are talking about the essential nature of a thing, even when we can't specify exactly what that is. One of the most valuable uses of the word *soul* is to be able to say, "I am seeking my soul."

I, like every person, can know without doubt that I have an ultimate place, without being able to tell you exactly what that place is — in fact, without being able to tell you anything at all about it. And if, on the other hand, I do understand something about my soul, then I can give you at least a sketch of what I believe about my ultimate place.

As far as we know, only humans can fail at embodying their souls. All other creatures seem to take their ultimate place instinctively, unself-consciously, and without struggle (with the possible exception of animals and plants we humans have domesticated or genetically modified). Everything in the universe seems to have been brilliantly designed to take just the place that it does. Humanity's apparent exception to this rule has led poet David Whyte to wonder "why we are the one / terrible / part of creation / privileged / to refuse our flowering."[4] I believe the reason we have this curious privilege has to do with our apparently exclusive possession of conscious self-awareness, the ability to know that we know.[5]

A necessary feature of our conscious self-awareness is the fragment of our psyche (the ego, the conscious self) that functions as the locus of this capacity to know that we know. Before we were human, we had no way to observe our *selves* and know what, or who, we were observing. Later, it was as if we became human by taking a part of ourselves and extending it some distance, so that this part could look back at itself. This is perhaps akin to what we humans collectively experienced when we gazed upon the first photographs of Earth taken from the Moon.

The ego — a fragment of the psyche observing the rest of itself from a psychological distance — has limited knowledge about the psyche as a whole. A virtually universal component of what our ego does not know, at least when we are young, is our ultimate place, our soul. Our immature ego rarely knows the soul because that knowledge is hidden in the depths of the psyche and the wilds of the world, and it takes a mature ego to find and comprehend it.

If it weren't for the existence of the ego, we wouldn't wonder about our true place. We would simply take it. It's our egos that do the wondering. Without egos, we would take our place instinctively, as everything else does, and like everything else, we would not know that we knew our place. And yet, if we didn't wonder about our place, if, that is, we didn't have egos, we wouldn't be human. We wouldn't have the place or soul of the human. Conscious self-awareness, in other words, appears to be the source of both our greatest failings and greatest potentials — our pivotal crises and opportunities.

Being capable of consciously observing ourselves makes us vulnerable to tripping ourselves up, as anyone knows who has ever performed or spoken publicly. Self-consciousness gives us the capacity to wonder about our true place, and the possibility of not finding it. The hazard, then, of possessing the capacity to know that you know is the vulnerability of becoming truly lost in a way no other creature can — unable to find your place and therefore unable to flower.

If we can agree that conscious self-awareness is a liability, let's take a look at the flip side. What's so good about it? What's so great about being human? It might be this: The ability to know that we know gives us the ability to know ourselves, the ability to know that we exist and that we exist in an astonishing universe. It gives us the ability to fall in love with every thing and with eternity. If we are the only beings who know that we know, then we are the only ones who can admire the universe *as* a universe or consciously know our place in the universe. Without conscious self-awareness, there would be nothing or no one to appreciate the universe. In effect, as Thomas Berry says, there would not be a universe. If the human is the only self-aware creature that exists, then we can say, as Thomas does, that the human allows the universe to exist. This is indeed a privilege. And it is why it's tempting to say that the ability to appreciate the universe as a universe might be the ultimate collective place of the human, the soul of humanity.

Perhaps the journey to self-knowledge that we each must take — the conscious discovery of our ultimate *individual* place — is the prerequisite or path to full human consciousness and to the ability to fully savor the grandeur of this world. Perhaps this journey is the only way to build that particular talent of savoring. If the adoration of creation is our collective human destiny, then we need only note that, to realize our destiny, we have to be capable of failing at it. As a result, we are necessarily the one part of creation *privileged* to refuse its flowering.

The process of becoming a true adult is the process of coming to know one's ultimate place as an individual. I think of this as the process of soul initiation, which makes up the first half of the Wheel of Life. It's not an easy path, and it rarely succeeds without guidance from initiators and elders.

The Language of Nature: Soul's Way of Identifying Itself to Us

We cannot meaningfully identify an individual human soul in terms of social or cultural roles or careers. For example, a person (like me) might be a writer, a depth psychologist, or a wilderness guide, but none of these roles identifies his soul. In other words, none of these designations gets at the mysterious core of his identity. They merely enumerate some of the delivery systems he uses to embody his soul, to inhabit his ultimate place.

To speak of soul as an ultimate place, we need a means of characterizing identity that is transcultural and independent of human creations. And we in fact have such a means: the natural world — its images, roles, patterns, processes, events, and animate beings. The language of nature is how soul identifies itself to us.

For example, my current, abbreviated articulation of my soul is: *the one who sits at Love Lake weaving cocoons of impossible dreams for his people.* What this means to me would require many pages (or conversational hours) to explain. It points to and gathers within it dozens of numinous experiences that together weave a single story, a soul story. The abbreviated expression is not simply a mysterious name given to me that I may or may not feel I understand. Rather, it's my own distillation of many encounters whose collective significance I believe I do in fact understand. (This allows for the possibility that I'm wrong, in whole or part!)

Or you could say that my shorthand articulation hints at how, at any given moment, I *experience* my place in the world. For example, when others see me doing things that they might encapsulate as "being a depth psychologist" or "guiding a vision quest," I am likely to be experiencing what I'm doing quite differently. I might say that, at those moments, I am weaving cocoons — by the way I do the things a depth psychologist or vision quest guide might do. Weaving cocoons is the significance of what I'm doing, and it is the conscious reason I'm doing it.

Here's another example. It's often said that highly creative people possess an uncommonly deep understanding of their own behavior. Consider a virtuoso concert pianist. We might say she is performing a Bach concerto, but she might declare that, while this is true on one level, at a deeper stratum she's carrying on a love affair with the dark mysteries of a luminous cosmos. It might well be that this is what makes her performances sublime.

In my first book, *Soulcraft,* I offer several other examples of personal soul articulations from a host of colleagues. Each one employs a metaphor from nature to point to an ineffable mystery — the unique way in which each person belongs to the wild world.

Rescuing Soul from Cartesian Matter and Ether

Of all the possible ways to identify what we mean by soul, I prefer "ultimate place" because it extracts us from the troubling and messy implication that the soul is something material or, just as unworkable, that it is something private, "inner," invisible, ethereal, or celestial. The soul of a thing, although certainly not a tangible object, is, nevertheless and in principle, publicly observable in the same sense that a love affair is observable (and usually not inner, invisible, or ethereal), or in the same way a theatrical performance, a touchdown, a faux pas, an embarrassment, or a victory is observable. We wouldn't say that any of those things is merely a physical object or an "inner" event, and yet we have no doubt about their existence and their significance to us. When you know a mature person well enough — someone who has consciously uncovered her soul to some degree and is consciously living it — you can see her doing it right here on Earth. Her soul is not "inner," invisible, or private.

My reason for wanting to rescue soul from the material and the ethereal is that both these notions about the soul buy into the profoundly unfortunate and unnecessary Cartesian split between inner and outer, between mind and matter. "Material" reduces psychology to neurology, and "ethereal" might as well be "*un*real."

For four hundred years now, Cartesian thinking and language have gotten us into all sorts of difficulties — scientific, religious, spiritual, and educational. I'm joining the many others who are practicing an alternative way of thinking and speaking within psychology, philosophy, and ecology.[6] So, for example, rather than say that we humans are physical organisms with "inner," invisible minds or souls, we instead might note that we are persons with ordinary person qualities, such as values, attitudes, interests, abilities, opinions, and knowledge. And consciousness. And souls.[7]

Ever since Descartes, it has been increasingly common to speak of the soul as something that is "in" us, like a ghost, a spirit, or an ether. But I prefer to say that a person is *in* her soul, or at least potentially can be, rather than saying that her soul is in *her*. If I am living from the place of my soul, then I am tenanting my true place in the world. If I am not living from that place, then not only am I out of my soul but I might also be out of my mind. If I am not living from the place of my soul — if, in fact, I don't know what that place is — then I have lost my soul or I have never found it, but, by *soul*, I mean a place, not an object.

Conversations, Stories, and Deep Structures

There are a few additional ways I enjoy imagining the soul, all of which, in the end, are alternative ways of saying *ultimate place*. David Whyte speaks of soul as "the largest conversation a person is capable of having with the world." Here "conversation" is the poet's way of saying *relationship*. You can see that the largest relationship a person can have with the world is the same as his "ultimate place" if you recall that the concept of *place* corresponds to the totality of relationships a thing has with other things in the world.

But a conversation is not just any kind of relationship. It's continuously evolving through a back-and-forth exchange. Both the person and the world are changed through this conversation. The kind of place we mean by *soul* is not only not geographical; it's also not static. The way we find and then occupy our ultimate place is through an ongoing conversation with the world in which we grow gradually clearer about what that place is.

David also writes of the "one life you can call your own," another striking image for soul.[8] A *life* in this sense is your way of being in the world — your place in the world. The *one* place you can call your own is your unique and ultimate place.

Another useful way to speak of soul is as story. Psychologist Jean Houston, for example, speaks of the larger story each person is born to live. This larger story — much deeper than your prosaic personal history — expresses the ultimate meaning of your life, its true significance, in the same way a myth communicates truth or gnosis. To be living that larger story is to be a particular character in a web of relationships and meanings, to have a particular place in the story we call the world. Because it's your larger story, that particular place is your ultimate place.

Yet another way to define soul is as the deep structure of a thing, its primary organizing or unifying principle. Similar to my earlier suggestion about the relationship of the Wheel to human development, we might say that the human soul is the "morphic field" (Rupert Sheldrake's term) of a person, or his "implicate order" (David Bohm's), his "pattern integrity" (Bucky Fuller's), or his "blueprint" or "primal pattern" (Robert Johnson's.[9]) Thomas Berry defines soul as "the primary organizing, sustaining, and guiding principle of a living being."[10] These are all various ways of saying *deep structure* or *deep pattern*. A person's ultimate identity, in other words, is seen in the deep structure of his psyche, the way he operates at his core.

The caution about this deep-structure perspective is that it can tempt some people, especially reductionistic scientists, to speculate about "mechanisms" that "make" a person do what he does. But the deep structure is not a way of referring to, nor will it be found in, a person's neurology or genes. It's a way of summarizing the deep patterns of his actions or, at least, of his potential actions, his destiny. For example: "My pattern integrity is one of cocoon weaving" is a pattern summary. To summarize a person's actual or potential behavior pattern is a way to identify his place. So, to speak of a person's deep structure is to speak of his ultimate place.

One final example. Geneen Marie Haugen thinks of the human soul as "our personal puzzle piece of the great mystery, somehow given to us from the undulating cosmos as we came from formless to form."[11] Every piece of a jigsaw puzzle, for example,

is the piece that it is by virtue of its unique place in that puzzle, its relationship to all
the other pieces. The great mystery that is this world, like a jigsaw puzzle, cannot assume its ultimate form unless every piece takes its true place. Each human is born to
take his or her ultimate place. We are born as the piece that can take that place. To be
born is to take form as a particular piece with a particular place.

The ultimate place of all the above articulations of *soul* is *ultimate place*.

Ways of Embodying and Discovering the Soul

There are several other things we might say about soul that identify how we embody
our souls, ways we discover our souls, or methods of listening to our souls. These are
all essential ingredients in our discussion about soul but are not definitions of soul.

Consider, for instance, the concept of personal powers, which divides into three
categories — abilities, knowledge, and values — each of which enables us to do things
we could not otherwise, which is what renders them personal *powers*.[12] Our soul powers are the ones that enable us to take our ultimate place. For me, the ability to weave
cocoons is a soul power. I require this ability in order to occupy my ultimate place, but
having this ability is not the same as having that place. The ability is part of what I need
to *embody* my soul (my place). It's possible to have the ability without having that place.
And it's possible to have that place without yet having honed the ability.

To successfully live from my ultimate place, I also require a certain physical embodiment, a certain biology, anatomy, and neurology, and this is, in part, my genetic
endowment. You might say that my genes provide the organizing instructions for my
embodiment. If you were to think of soul as the underlying, organizing principle of
my embodiment, then it would be tempting to say that my genes are my soul. But I prefer to say that my genes are one of the factors that make it possible for me to take my
ultimate place, for me to embody my soul.

We can also speak about the many ways we *discover* our ultimate place in the world.
These are not the same as soul itself. David Whyte, for example, writes of "the truth
at the center of the image you were born with." That image can be experienced in moments of soul encounter, and the truth at its heart reveals to you your ultimate place.
But this truth — knowledge about your soul — is not the same as your soul itself. Or,
in another version of soul encounter, you might at long last hear your one true voice,
an experience Mary Oliver describes: "... and there was a new voice, / which you
slowly recognized as your own, / that kept you company / as you strode deeper and
deeper / into the world...." Or, to borrow from David Whyte again, you might uncover
the "... shape / [that] waits in the seed / of you to grow / and spread / its branches /
against a future sky...."[13] Or you might begin to sense the shape of the story you have
been called to live. These are all means or paths to discovering your ultimate place in
the world — as distinct from that place itself.

Finally, there are the many ways we *listen* to soul. The soul speaks to us in images (visual, auditory, or kinesthetic), in symbols, and in metaphors — for example, through dreams, deep imagery, visions, and revelations. These ways of attending to soul are not the same thing as soul.

I just wrote that the soul *speaks* to us, and I use that same expression elsewhere in this book. You might wonder, "If the soul is a kind of place, can it really speak to us? Can it want things?" Yes. At the very least, poetically or metaphorically, yes. You probably have been to one or more extraordinary natural places — say, a waterfall, volcano, cave, or wildflowered meadow — and felt an astonishing response evoked from you there. You were sure that this place wanted or expected something from you or that it spoke to you. Or think of a role in a theatrical play, a role being a type of place. As an actor gets to know his role, he begins to sense what it wants of him. It speaks to him. All places and all things and all roles speak to us, if only we have the ears to listen. Likewise, your soul, your ultimate place, evokes something from you, wants something from you, speaks to you, sometimes in a quiet voice, sometimes in a roar.

The Power of Here

Wisdom traditions worldwide say there's no greater blessing than to live the life of your soul, the source of your deepest personal fulfillment and of your greatest service to others. It's what you were born for. It's the locus of authentic personal power — not power *over* people and things, but rather the power of partnership *with* others, the power to cocreate life and to cooperate with an evolving universe.

Before you find your ultimate place, you are, in a sense, lost. You have a particular destiny but don't know what it is. It's like being lost in a forest, as in poet David Wagoner's image at the opening of this chapter.

You can begin or deepen your relationship to soul in the same way the poet advises you to commune with the forest. None of the nonhumans in the forest — or the world, more generally — are lost. Each one is precisely in its true place, and each one knows every place in the forest as a unique place. They are doing something you do not yet know how to do. You could apprentice yourself to them. The forest, the world, knows where you are and who you are. You must let it find you.

If you don't yet have conscious knowledge of your soul, you haven't yet learned the power of place — or the power of Here. To acquire this power, which is the goal in the first half of the Wheel of Life, you must first get to know more thoroughly the place in life you already inhabit. This place consists of your relationships and roles in both society and nature. This is the place in which you are lost, in which you find yourself to be, and from which you can, eventually, find your *self*. You must treat this place you're in as a "powerful stranger," as Wagoner suggests, and educate yourself more fully about what it is to inhabit *any* place. To inhabit a particular place is to have the potential to do and observe the specific things that one can do and observe in that place. This knowledge about inhabiting a place will help you shift to other places in life (which is done by changing your relationships and roles) and to get to know what it's like to inhabit *those* places. You'll discover that some places feel more like your true place, closer to your ultimate place. By developing your sensitivity about place in this way, you can gradually move to your ultimate place. This is what you do in stage 4 of the Wheel. I think of this process as *wandering*.

Your soul is your true home. In the moment you finally arrive in this psycho-ecological niche, you feel fully available and present to the world, unlost. This particular place is profoundly familiar to you, more so than any geographical location or any mere dwelling has ever been or could be. You know immediately that *this* is the source, the marrow, of your true belonging. This is the identity no one could ever take from you. Inhabiting this place does not depend on having anyone else's permission or approval or presence. It does not require having a particular job — or any at all. You can be neither hired for it nor fired from it. Acting from this place aligns you with your surest personal powers (your soul powers), your powers of nurturing, transforming, creating; your powers of presence and wonder.

The first time you consciously inhabit your ultimate place and act from your soul is the first time you can say, "Here" and really know what it means. You've arrived, at last, at your own center. As long as you stay Here, everywhere you go, geographically or socially, feels like home. Every place becomes Here.

This is the power of place, the power of Here.

Before soul initiation, wherever you go, there you are. After soul initiation, wherever you go, *Here* you are.[14]

The Soulcentric Developmental Wheel

Keeping in mind this notion of soul as ultimate place, it's possible now to understand more fully what the Wheel of Life is and in what way it's soulcentric.

- The human soul is precultural and prelinguistic. A person's ultimate place is what it is before he is acculturated or acquires a human language. He is born with it. It's his potential. His *destiny* is to live from that place, but there is no guarantee he'll succeed.
- In childhood and early adolescence, a person is almost never conscious of or concerned about her destiny. Nor should she be. She has other, urgent developmental tasks, tasks that will prepare her for her future discovery of destiny.
- Genuine elders might be able to discern a child's or adolescent's destiny and explain it to her, but there is no value in this knowledge apart from the labor of retrieving it independently.
- A person must be psychospiritually prepared for the underworld journey, the

·descent to soul. The first three of the eight life stages constitute this preparation. Embarking·upon the journey unprepared is particularly risky and likely to result in failure.

- For most people, the journey of soul discovery is complex, challenging, and longer than we would have hoped.

- To succeed at soul encounters, most people need practices and methods specifically designed for this purpose. These are the psychospiritual technologies of which mainstream Western societies have lost nearly all knowledge, but which can still be found in vital indigenous traditions and in the mystery schools of the West. I name these technologies *soulcraft* in my book of that title.

- An adult is someone who has encountered her soul, retrieved some knowledge of her ultimate place in the world, acquired some practical means for occupying this place among her people, made a commitment to doing so, and is doing it.

- An elder is someone who, after many years of adulthood, consistently occupies his ultimate place without any further effort to do so. This frees him for something with yet greater scope and depth and fulfillment, namely, caring for the soul of the world. He does this by assisting others to prepare for, discover, and embody their souls, and by supporting the human-Earth system in the evolution of *its* soul.

- The Wheel portrays human development as the process of preparing to discover soul, cultivating a relationship with soul, and embodying soul. This is why I call it the Soulcentric Developmental Wheel.

SPIRIT AND MYSTERY

By *spirit*, I mean the single, boundless, and eternal mystery that permeates and animates everything in the universe and yet transcends all. Spirit has many names, commonly capitalized, including the Absolute, the Divine, the Tao, the One, God, Allah, Buddha nature, and the Great Mystery. Plato referred to it as the world-soul or the *anima mundi*, that which gives a living unity to the entire universe. The idea of *spirit* points to what all people and all things have in common: our shared membership in a single cosmos, each of us a facet of the One Being that contains all.

It would be tempting to say that spirit is the soul of the universe, the "ultimate place" of the universe — and this, in a way, is correct, except that the ultimate place of the universe is the universe itself. It has no further context of existence. The universe is the one thing that is entirely self-referent and self-normative.[15]

Spirit both transcends all things and is immanent in all things. Spirit can·be thought of as something "out there," something removed from ordinary life, but it is simultaneously that which infuses and animates all and everything — the land, the air, the animals, all peoples, our human creations, and our own bodies and selves.

While soul calls us toward our individual and unique relationship to the world, spirit constellates what is most universal and shared throughout the cosmos. In this sense, *soul* and *spirit* suggest opposites — the unique versus the universal. Ultimately, however, each soul (each thing in its soul aspect) exists as an expression of spirit and serves as an agent or emissary for spirit.

Our individual relationships with spirit and soul are not contradictory but complementary. A complete spirituality must embrace our relationships to both spirit and soul, not just one or the other. Together these two realms of spirituality form a whole. Either one alone is incomplete.

Spirit is independent of any beliefs or knowledge you have about yourself, no matter how shallow or deep, ridiculous or sublime. Rather than calling you to your individual life path, spirit invites you to return to the universal essence of your psyche through a surrender to the present moment.

Cultivating a personal relationship to spirit (unmediated by priests, priestesses, or other clergy) is essential to our individual development. The most common practice for doing so is some form of meditation, prayer, or contemplation, disciplines that quiet the mind and cultivate stillness and centeredness in the present.

While our relationship to spirit evokes "the power of now," as Eckhart Tolle puts it,[16] our relationship to soul evokes the power of Here. Together, you might say, they are an unbeatable combination. Here and now.

Perhaps the easiest way to grasp the relationship between spirit and soul is to imagine a web made up of a multitude of nodes (places where two or more strands intersect). Each node is a place in the web, like the soul is a place in the world. Spirit corresponds to the whole web (or the dynamic patterning of the web); it subsumes every node (soul) and the strands (relationships) that connect them. Like a node to a web, there's a part-whole relationship between soul and spirit. Imagined this way, it's easy to see that you can't have spirit without souls, and vice versa.

Both spirit and soul are transpersonal (beyond the personal) because they are spiritual realities greater than the personal conscious self (the ego or personality). As transpersonal realities, they are both mysterious to the conscious self.

Sometimes it's convenient to refer to the transpersonal without distinguishing between spirit and soul. In this book, I use the word *Mystery* (capitalized) to do that. Mystery is the undifferentiated realm of spirit and soul.[17]

EGO

By *ego*, I don't mean an undesirable or detrimental thing or something that should (or could) be done away with. Rather, I mean a person's everyday conscious self or personality — our normal way of experiencing ourselves and the world. The word *everyday* is key: I mean the conscious self while in its normal, everyday state of consciousness. Our state of consciousness can and does change, sometimes becoming significantly deepened or heightened or otherwise shifting. The conscious self in a nonordinary state lies outside what I mean by *ego*.

As you see, I am not using the word *ego* in a disparaging way — as in "He's got a big ego" or "She's on an ego trip"; I don't imply selfishness, self-importance, fixation, vanity, or conceit. Although people with immature egos are indeed often selfish, those with mature egos are genuinely loving, most of the time anyway.

An ego, in this sense, is a normal and essential feature of being human, one element of the greater human psyche. Having an ego, a conscious self with some degree of day-to-day stability, is what makes us human, for better and worse. If all goes well in our early development, a healthy first ego develops by age four, and then, over the years, it gradually shape-shifts as it matures and sees us through a lifetime of adventures.

It is primarily the ego that develops and matures through life, not the soul. The Wheel is a map of soulcentric ego development.

One of the major milestones in ego development occurs at the time of soul initiation. Before initiation, the ego has little or no understanding of the soul and is an agent for itself. At soul initiation, the ego accepts its role as an agent or handmaiden for the soul. In some traditions, it is said that the mature ego and the soul are lovers. Each provides the other with something essential and of ultimate value. Only the soul knows what the ego might find most fulfilling in life. Only the ego is capable of manifesting in the world the soul's desires. But even after soul initiation, the ego remains an ego, still "me."

The ego obstructs personal development when it gets stalled, lost, or entrenched at any life stage — when it resists change, loss, grief, or radical transformation at the hands of the gods and goddesses (personifications of the Mystery). A mature ego, in contrast, understands the occasional necessity of surrendering to or being defeated by a force greater than itself — for example, during the death-rebirth of the underworld journey, when ego surrenders to soul, or during ego transcendence, when ego surrenders to spirit. Just as each soul is an agent for spirit, each soul-initiated ego is an agent for soul and, by this means, for spirit as well.

THE THREE WORLDS

By *upperworld, middleworld,* and *underworld,* I don't mean geographical or cosmological locations but three realms of consciousness, or three domains of human life or identity, roughly corresponding to spirit, ego, and soul, respectively.

Upperworld denotes transpersonal states of consciousness identified with spirit and characterized by unity (or nonduality), grace, bliss, transcendence, emptiness, light (often golden), enlightenment (identified, for example, as Buddha mind, nirvana, satori, or Self-realization), the celestial realm, and pure awareness (consciousness without an object). During upperworld experiences, consciousness communes with or merges with spirit, in this way disidentifying from all personal and cultural beliefs, goals, desires, and attachments. Here the conscious self is transcended.

Meditation, prayer, contemplation, and yoga are common practices for cultivating a relationship with the upperworld.

Middleworld refers to our everyday, waking identity and state of consciousness — the "dayworld," the personal and interpersonal world of ego. This is the domain of family and community life, in which we procure food (whether through gathering, growing, hunting, or shopping), prepare meals, make a living, raise and educate children, build homes, cultivate relationships, socialize, recreate, and conduct the affairs of politics and civic society, including the practical embodiment of our soulwork. Here the conscious self is differentiated.

The middleworld is the realm of ego growth, which includes the healing of emotional wounds, the development of personal bonds, the cultivation of physical grace and emotional expression, and the blossoming of empathy, intimacy, and personality-level authenticity. A healthy ego is skilled in imagination, feeling, intuition, and sensing, in addition to thinking. In contemporary society, when ego growth has faltered or stalled, we seek help from psychotherapy and related disciplines such as personal coaching, art and movement therapies, and bodywork.

Underworld signifies transpersonal states of consciousness and identity associated with soul and characterized by depth, darkness, demons, the daemon, the subconscious, sacred woundings, dreams (the "nightworld"), the unknown or not-yet-known, shadow, death, and visions of personal and cultural destiny. This is Hades, the domain of soul encounter, the realm in which the conscious self is deepened and matured.

Underworld experiences deepen individuality through the discovery of our ultimate place in the world. This is facilitated by practices that I refer to collectively as *soulcraft* and that include dreamwork and deep imagery journeys, wandering in nature, and communicating with birds, trees, the winds, and the land itself. Many of these practices are found in the ancient (and continuing) traditions of nature-based peoples. Currently, soulcraft is finding its way back into contemporary Western life through modern mystery schools, through individual disciplines (such as trance dancing and drumming, council work, storytelling, symbolic artwork, soul-oriented poetry, and shadow work), and through the work of depth psychologists such as Carl Jung and James Hillman.

The shared purpose of transcending the conscious self (upperworld), differentiating the conscious self (middleworld), and deepening the conscious self (underworld) is personal development or maturation, which fosters cultural vitality and evolution, which in turn promotes ecological and planetary vitality and evolution.

SOULCENTRIC AND EGOCENTRIC: TWO TEMPLATES OF HUMAN DEVELOPMENT AND CULTURE

The Wheel is a deep-structure portrait of nature-and-soul-oriented cultures, a portrait that encompasses child-raising practices, core values, stages of growth, rites of passage, community organization, and relationship to the greater Earth community. I name such cultures *soulcentric* because they are designed to assist all members in discovering and living from their deepest and most fulfilling potentials (their individual souls), in this way contributing their most life-nourishing gifts to their community and environment and, in doing so, actualizing the culture's potential (the cultural soul) and supporting its ongoing evolution.

The first three stages of soulcentric life, early childhood through early adolescence, focus on the development of an ego capable of healthy communion with self, others, culture, and nature — an ego prepared, in other words, to enter the process of soul initiation. Then, soul discovery and embodiment compose the primary agenda of the next three stages, late adolescence through late adulthood. Elderhood focuses on the integrity of the Earth-human relationship, the soul of the more-than-human community.

A society that is soulcentric is necessarily ecocentric. A soulcentric society supports each person in discovering and inhabiting her ultimate place, which is her place as granted and revealed by nature. In so doing, that society roots itself in the natural world. The greater Earth community is accurately understood as the locus of every person's first membership. Because a soulcentric person consciously *experiences* this membership, she is naturally aware of her interconnectedness with everything else.

Soul-initiated adults serve both nature and culture by serving their souls. In fact, the experiential encounter with soul is nature's way of showing individual humans how to take their place in creating or sustaining a viable culture. When most people in a society take their ultimate place, individually, the society itself becomes soulcentric — it occupies *its* ultimate place in the Earth community and, consequently, is ecocentric.

In this book, I sometimes refer to a mature culture or a healthy developmental sequence as *soulcentric* and other times as *ecocentric*, depending on the context, and sometimes I use a composite: *eco-soulcentric*.

To say that a culture is ecocentric is to say that its customs, traditions, and practices are rooted in an awareness of radical interdependence with all beings. The individual in an ecocentric society perceives the world as an organic web of relationships and recognizes each living thing as an integral participant in this evolving web. Everyone in such a society knows that each thing, including each person, is what it is by virtue of its relationships with everything else. Every thing is praised and held as sacred.

Sadly, it has become rare in contemporary society to meet soulcentric men and women, those who are clear and passionate about life purpose, who know deep down in their bones the treasures they possess for their people, who truly know *who* their people are, who most every day can be found joyously engaged in their soulwork, who derive deep satisfaction from their efforts in making our world a more vital and beautiful place, and who experience deeply and abundantly their interdependent membership in the natural world. These are the surefire signs of a soul-initiated person, a genuinely adult human.

Soulcentric cultures contrast with *ego*centric ones, those that prioritize the lifelong comfort, security, and social acceptance of the early-adolescent ego. An egocentric culture has a dysfunctional notion of the self, which it sees as an isolated, competitive entity, a free and autonomous agent. An egocentric ego is ego-identified: it believes it represents only itself.

Most people in egocentric culture experience themselves as separate from the natural world, in it but not of it, a visitor to or proprietor of the planet with no deep-rooted membership in or responsibilities to the Earth community. Most relate to a highly restricted slice of life: their personal possessions, a job, a few amusements, their own body, and a small band of acquaintances and loved ones.

An egocentric culture is unavoidably anthropocentric rather than ecocentric. Such a culture is founded on human chauvinism, the belief that what is best for humans — in the narrowest imaginable sense, and often only humans of a certain race, gender, class, or nation — is what is morally right. This belief is held tightly despite its destructive results for those who hold it, other species, and the very environment that supports all life. Individual egocentrism ("I'm the center of the world") is a type of arrested development that makes an anthropocentric society possible. Likewise, cultural anthropocentrism ("the world was created for the use of us humans, especially my class, gender, religion, or nation") encourages each citizen to cultivate a use-relationship with things and other people (egocentrism). Thinking of oneself and others as "consumers" becomes a reasonable idea despite its profoundly deranged implications. In a *soul*centric world, egocentrism after a certain age would be considered an aberration or a pathology.

The problem with an egocentric society is not that it contains too many egos but rather that the early-adolescent values of the *uninitiated* ego are prioritized throughout society — it is an ego-*centered* society that contains too many *unhealthy* egos.

The primary values of an egocentric society are safety, comfort, middleworld pleasures, and enhancement of socioeconomic status. The safety that is sought includes physical and medical safety, but primarily it is a social safety derived from acceptance and belonging. There is nothing wrong, of course, with adequate amounts of safety and economic comfort or with ample measures of affiliation and pleasure. The point is that these goals are as high and as wide and as deep as they get for most people and for the culture as a whole in an egocentric society. These are the central and defining goals, the primary currency. The problem is not these goal themselves but what is missing.

The endless pursuit of security, comfort, and pleasure — in the absence of soul — leads, at best, to the accumulation of wealth (for the middle and upper classes). Wealth without soul leads to its inevitable pathological outgrowths: power differentials, socioeconomic (class) stratification, and exploitation of minorities, women, children, the poor, and all the "resources" of the natural world. For the presumably fortunate ones with adequate wealth, the pursuit of egocentric values often leads to boredom, addiction, alienation, and meaninglessness. For the lower classes, even basic security is rare. And for everyone, an illusory sense of autonomy ("freedom") tends to breed an amorphous fear, a sense of alienation and vulnerability.

A partnership with soul, spirit, and nature is the heart of any culture and of each of its members. The egocentric society cuts out its own heart and attempts to live without it.

There are other notable classifications of culture that parallel my distinction between soulcentric and egocentric. Three that strongly resonate with the Great Turning and with the ideas in this book are those of Joanna Macy, David Korten, and Riane Eisler.

Macy, as previously noted, contrasts the industrial growth society with a life-sustaining society. Eisler differentiates cultures organized around the principle of domination from those organized around the principle of partnership. The dominator model glorifies "the lethal power of the blade," while the older (original) partnership model reveres the chalice, "the life-generating and nurturing powers of the universe."[18] Korten refers to the former, hierarchically ordered societies as "Empire" and the latter, egalitarian and democratically ordered societies as "Earth Community":

> The mentality of Empire embraces material excess for the ruling classes, honors the dominator power of death and violence, denies the feminine principle, and suppresses realization of the potentials of human maturity.
>
> ... The mentality of Earth Community embraces material sufficiency for everyone, honors the generative power of life and love, seeks a balance of feminine and masculine principles, and nurtures a realization of the mature potential of our human nature.[19]

While the similarities in analyses are evident here, I prefer the labels *egocentric* and *soulcentric* simply because these concepts identify the root of the problem beyond their observable forms. Egocentrism is why industrial growth societies are greedy, empires are imperial, and dominator societies are violent. Soulcentrism is why life-sustaining societies and Earth communities serve the greater whole and why partnership societies are life-nurturing.

Patho-adolescence (life centered in violence, greed, self-centeredness, shame, and addiction) is not normal for humans; it is, rather, the effect egocentric society inflicts on many of its citizens.

Throughout this book, I differentiate soulcentric *society* from soulcentric *development* because the latter is possible even within our egocentric society, although more difficult to achieve and less common here. The Wheel portrays the soulcentric stages as they look in a soulcentric society, as well as their somewhat different appearance in an egocentric society. Having a map for soulcentric development in an egocentric society is essential because, if we are to succeed at engendering a soulcentric world, we must start from where we find ourselves. This is precisely what the Great Turning and the Great Work are all about.

My foremost goal in this book is to support people in reaching stage 5 (the Wellspring, the start of genuine adulthood), because initiated adults, and the elders they grow into, are the ones who are leading, and will lead, us to an ecocentric, sustainable future. The key to engendering new soulcentric cultures is to raise our children soulcentrically in the midst of our egocentric societies. In addition to making changes in child-rearing practices (this is relatively easy), we must radically transform our educational systems (much more challenging, but there are already some outstanding models). The transition to a soulcentric society might take several generations to complete, and we must begin now.

The Wheel is *not* a model of utopia or for creating perfect humans. As Carl Jung repeatedly declared, our goal is wholeness, not perfection. People living soulcentrically are not untroubled or unchallenged. They are not beyond experiencing times of confusion, mistakes, and tragedies. They have by no means healed all their wounds. They are simply on a path to wholeness, to becoming fully human — with all the inevitable defects and distresses inherent in any human story and with all the promise held by our uniquely human imagination.

CHAPTER THREE

OVERVIEW *of the* WHEEL *of* LIFE

There's a thread you follow. It goes among
things that change. But it doesn't change.
People wonder about what you are pursuing.
You have to explain about the thread.
But it is hard for others to see.
While you hold it you can't get lost.
Tragedies happen; people get hurt
or die; and you suffer and get old.
Nothing you do can stop time's unfolding.
You don't ever let go of the thread.

— WILLIAM STAFFORD, "THE WAY IT IS"

CIRCLES OF WHOLENESS
AND FOURFOLD TOTALITIES

On the Wheel, the journey through the stages of life proceeds in a circle, in contrast
to a linear life line with birth and death on distant and opposing shores. Where we
end up has some striking and meaningful features in common with where we begin.
All the diagrams of human development you'll find in this book are circles, each beginning and ending on the right side (the east) and progressing clockwise (sunwise).
More specifically, the Wheel's template is the quadrated circle, found in innumerable
traditions from all corners of the world and from all epochs known to us. It is composed of two elements: the circle itself and the number four.

Carl Jung and his associates, based on their research of world traditions, proposed that the circle is a universal archetypal symbol of wholeness, completeness, and total- ity. Aniela Jaffé, for example, notes that the circle "expresses the totality of the psyche in all its aspects, including the relationship between man and the whole of nature. Whether the symbol of the circle appears in primitive sun worship or modern religion, in myths or dreams, in the mandalas drawn by Tibetan monks, in the ground plans of cities, or in the spherical concepts of early astronomers, it always points to the sin- gle most vital aspect of life — its ultimate wholeness."[1]

People of nature-based oral cultures experience and understand all of life, even time itself, in terms of the endless cycles and circles of nature. The circle is found in their dances, their art, and the shape of their dwellings. The Lakota spiritual leader Black Elk, for example, observes,

> Everything the Power of the World does is done in a circle. The Sky is round and I have heard that the earth is round like a ball and so are all the stars. The Wind, in its greatest power, whirls. Birds make their nests in circles, for theirs is the same religion as ours. The sun comes forth and goes down again in a circle. The moon does the same, and both are round.
>
> Even the seasons form a great circle in their changing, and always come back again to where they were. The life of man is a circle from childhood to childhood and so it is in everything where power moves.[2]

Four-part patterns and motifs (such as the cardinal directions or the four corners of the world) are a second common cross-cultural strategy for symbolizing wholeness, including that of psychological development.[3] In addition to the psyche, the world it- self is commonly divided into four dimensions or some multiple of four, especially eight, twelve, and sixteen. This theme is found in our own mainstream Western tra- ditions as well as those of Eastern cultures.[4]

The number four and the circle are often integrated as a single symbol. In the Americas, the indigenous people have long employed a quadrated circle to map out their values, traditions, and spiritual perspectives.[5] In Western mysticism, too, the four- fold and the circle appear together. One of the central symbols of the tenth-century alchemists, for example, was the *quadratura circuli* — the squaring of the circle.[6]

Quadrated circles also show up in mainstream Western traditions, including those of Christian heritage. Jaffé offers examples such as the rose windows of the great European cathedrals, the halos of Christ and the Christian saints in religious paintings (sometimes Christ's halo is divided into four), Christ surrounded by the four evan- gelists (a scenario that originates in the ancient Egyptian representations of the god Horus and his four sons), and, of course, the cross or crucifix itself.

Although the quadrated circle is found in both ancient and contemporary cultures, each tradition employs the symbol in its own ways. Yet each rendering of the quadrated circle can be understood as a culture's way of saying, "This is what wholeness looks like *to us*."

One of the popular cross-cultural uses of the quadrated circle is as a template for individual human development. My own early exposure to these developmental maps consisted of several indigenous versions, especially Native American circles commonly referred to as "medicine wheels," each one somewhat different from the next.[7] In the early 1980s, the model I studied most closely was created by Steven Foster and Meredith Little, whose approach has roots in Native American teachings but is also drawn from other world traditions and their own extensive field experience.[8]

The Soulcentric Developmental Wheel, however, bears only cursory similarity to other models I know — Western or indigenous, ancient or modern. Rather, it is drawn from my own experience as a psychotherapist and nature-based soul guide and more than twenty other design influences identified later in this chapter.

NATURE'S TEMPLATE FOR THE WHEEL

The Wheel's most significant design influence is nature. Every feature of the Wheel is thematically tied to the readily observable qualities of the natural world associated with the four compass directions, the diurnal cycle (sunrise, noon, sunset, and midnight), and the four seasons.[9] Diagram 3-1 shows these four sets of qualities and our most common human associations to them.

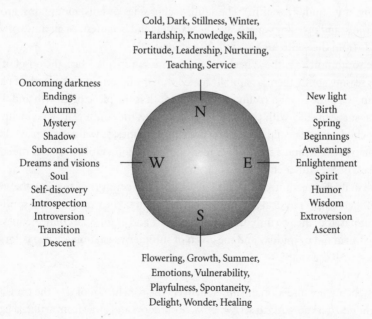

Cold, Dark, Stillness, Winter,
Hardship, Knowledge, Skill,
Fortitude, Leadership, Nurturing,
Teaching, Service

Oncoming darkness	New light
Endings	Birth
Autumn	Spring
Mystery	Beginnings
Shadow	Awakenings
Subconscious	Enlightenment
Dreams and visions	Spirit
Soul	Humor
Self-discovery	Wisdom
Introspection	Extroversion
Introversion	Ascent
Transition	
Descent	

Flowering, Growth, Summer,
Emotions, Vulnerability,
Playfulness, Spontaneity,
Delight, Wonder, Healing

DIAGRAM 3-1: QUALITIES OF THE CARDINAL DIRECTIONS

The east is where the Sun rises. Granting us light after the long night, the east is commonly affiliated with beginnings, origins, and birth. The east is also coupled with the spring equinox, the advent of the season that gives birth to the annual round of life for most plants and animals. In the cycle of plant growth, the east represents the seed, the beginning.

Because the dawn is also the end of the night, the transition from dark to light, the east is linked with illumination and enlightenment and, as a consequence, with spirit, too.

With the return of the light each morning, we can again appreciate the big picture, our world expanding beyond the immediate fears and concerns of our contracted night-selves. The east, then, is allied with qualities that expand our perception and understanding, in particular, humor ("lightening up"), innocence, wisdom, and perception or sensing itself.

With the light of the new day, we step out into the world — into public places and into our more communal roles. The east, accordingly, is coupled with extroversion — the directing of our attention and intention beyond ourselves.

Because the morning Sun rises, the east is paired with the upperworld and with ascent, as in the ascension to spirit. The yellow-gold hue of the rising Sun is commonly partnered with the east.

The south (in the Northern Hemisphere) is the place of greatest warmth and light, the Sun being at its midday zenith.[10] The south-facing sides of hills, mountains, groves, canyon walls, and dwellings are always the warmest and brightest. At all times of year, the winds from the south are generally the mildest.

The south notch on the Wheel also marks the summer solstice, the onset of the summer season. South, then, is naturally mated with the flowering and growth of plants and animals. In the human realm, as well, the south is the place of growth and flowering, most specifically with puberty. More generally, the south is matched with the growing child, with the child's emotions and vulnerabilities, as well as with playfulness, spontaneity, delight, and a sense of wonder. Some psychotherapists say that the south is the place of the "inner child."

Due to its direct connection with the warmth and comfort of the Sun, the south is also affiliated with physical and psychological healing. The warmth of the southern Sun connotes, too, the warmth of the human heart and emotional connectedness.

The warm red of midday and the green of summer vegetation are two colors often linked with the south.

The west, being the direction of sunset, delivers the conclusion of day, the transition from light into darkness. At sunset, when we're outdoors and away from artificial lights, we are often struck by a sense of culmination and by the inevitable movement into the dark. The west is all about this entrance into the shadows — sometimes frightening, sometimes bewitching or enchanting, sometimes glamorous. The west resonates with all life transitions that carry us into the unknown.

Because it is in the west that the Wheel diverges from most other contemporary developmental models, I offer here a more thorough exploration of the symbols of this direction.

In terms of seasons, the west is partnered with the autumn equinox, the commencement of fall, and the end of the growing season, the waning of green things. It is also, however, the start of the harvest, the reaping of the fruits of the Earth. An interesting mixture, this: the west at once a time of dying and a time of reaping. This is the way it is with human development, too, on the Wheel.

Ushering us into night, the west is the domain of mystery and shadow — the ambiguity of the hidden, the fear of the dark, the danger of specters. The west, however, is more about shadow than it is about full-on darkness. As day falls, shadows lengthen, reaching their greatest extension at sunset. The west, then, is often paired with the occult, esoteric, and secret. And because the evening Sun descends, the west becomes our doorway to the underworld, or Hades, into which we must dive in search of soul.

The west evokes the hidden places in nature: caves, holes, springs, dark forests and thickets, the nonvisible, the back side of things, as well as the impending night. Likewise, the west evokes the hidden dimensions of the psyche — the blocked, repressed, censored, forbidden, obscured. Carl Jung employed the term *shadow* to identify those aspects of the self that the ego insists are *not*-self, our rejected and denied personal characteristics. More generally, the west represents the unconscious or the subconscious — the domain of sleep and the realm of imagination, dreams, visions, and other numinous experiences arising from the shadowy depths.

The west, significantly, is the direction wedded to the soul itself. It is the direction of self-discovery, of introspection and introversion.

The west is also associated with the "little deaths" of life — the unavoidable traumatic endings and losses. (Our final, corporeal death is more commonly associated with the east.) The west is coupled with both the crypt and the cryptic.

The color connected with the west is frequently the black of mystery and shadow.

The north (in the Northern Hemisphere) is, implicitly, where the Sun goes after it sets and disappears — a place of cold, decisive dark, and stillness. Even during daylight hours, the north-facing side of things is the darker, colder side. At most times of year, the winds from the north are the colder and mightier winds.

The north is partnered with the middle of the night, the time of least light and least plant growth, the winter solstice, and, consequently, the beginning of winter.

As with winter, the north is a place of hardship, but hardship that has become familiar and accustomed (unlike the west, which is a transition zone into the long night). By the time the Sun is in the north — by the middle of the night, with its dangers and challenges — we have usually adapted to darkness and found ways to manage competently. It takes knowledge, skill, and fortitude to thrive in the cold and dark, so the north is linked with intelligence, competence, endurance, and strength. As Black Elk says, "The north with its cold and mighty wind [gives us] strength and endurance."[11]

The north, then, is affiliated with the leader, teacher, and parent, the protector and nurturer. The north is paired with the human faculty of caring, intelligent thought. Most generally, the north is associated with service. It is the place of the generative adult.

The white of winter is a common color symbolizing the north.

When we come full circle and return to the east, we're at the end of the day, the end of the seasonal cycle, the end of a lifetime. And yet the end flows seamlessly into the beginning. At the end of life, we return to the same invisible place from which we emerged, spirit. We go to seed, and in doing so, seed the next cycle. The east is yoked with our final and physical death as well as with our birth. It bonds the newborn and the elder.

The east and west have a complementary relationship. East is perception and extroversion. West is introspection and introversion. East is light, west is shadow. East beginning, west ending. East is the upperworld gateway, west the underworld portal. East is ascent, west is descent. East is linked with spirit, west with soul.

Notice, too, what east and west have in common: together they are the spiritual directions, embracing the otherworlds, the underworld of soul and the upperworld of spirit. *East-west is the transpersonal axis of the Wheel.*

North and south also have a polar relationship: North is survival, south is growth. North is parenting and leadership, south is childhood and play. North is knowledge and acquired skill, south is emotion and spontaneity. North is service, south is delight.

North and south, too, have something essential in common: together they embrace the personal and interpersonal — the middleworld. *North-south is the personal axis of the Wheel.*

THE MATURE FORM OF THE HERO'S JOURNEY

The feature of the Wheel that might seem most radical or controversial to the contemporary reader is its portrayal of the passage from psychological adolescence to adulthood. Although mostly foreign to modern culture and consciousness, the Wheel's depiction of this developmental sequence is consistent with what we find almost everywhere across the broad sweep of time and human traditions. This passage to maturity is anchored in the cross-cultural archetype of the hero's journey, a pattern often diminished or misunderstood in recent times.

Jungian psychologist Joseph Henderson introduces the hero archetype this way:

> The myth of the hero is the most common and the best known myth in the world. We find it in the classical mythology of Greece and Rome, in the Middle Ages, in the Far East, and among contemporary primitive tribes. It also appears in our dreams. It has an obvious dramatic appeal, and a less obvious, but nonetheless profound, psychological importance.
>
> These hero myths vary enormously in detail, but the more closely one examines them the more one sees that structurally they are very similar. They have, that is to say, a universal pattern, even though they were developed by groups or individuals without any direct cultural contact with each other.[12]

The hero's journey is an intricate interlude, often unfolding over a period of several months or years. It is the labyrinthine adventure of entering the mysterious depths of psyche and nature, experiencing there a psychospiritual death and rebirth, and returning with a new maturity and a life-enhancing vision. Mythologist Joseph Campbell proposed that the innumerable myths and sacred stories found in world cultures and religions exemplify the various stages of the journey. This is a pilgrimage that all of us are meant to undertake, each in our own way, in search of the holy grail of soul, the revelation of adult life direction. The hero's journey, in essence, transforms an adolescent into an adult:

> The hero ... is the man or woman who has been able to battle past his personal and local historical limitations to the generally valid, normally human forms. Such a one's visions, ideas, and inspirations come pristine from the primary springs of human life and thought. Hence they are eloquent, not of the present, disintegrating society and psyche, but of the unquenched source through which society is reborn.[13]

In designing the Wheel, I've attempted to flesh out and clarify the sequence of stages in the adolescence-to-adulthood transition, and to do so in a manner both more detailed than Campbell's and more applicable for contemporary people of both genders.

In recent decades, pop culture has diminished the mature form of the hero's journey by confounding it with an egocentric, adolescent caricature. We're all too familiar with the Hollywood story in which the valorous "hero" or "heroine" — from John Wayne to James Bond, from Superman to Mighty Mouse, from Batgirl to Bionic Woman — risks his or her life, health, or wealth, whether in sports, combat, espionage, or an impossible mission, in order to save the day, the damsel, or the planet and reap the rewards of personal triumph and acclaim. In this immature rendition of the hero's journey, the protagonist goes forth to cheat death and becomes a "man" or "woman," or flaunts machismo or machisma, more in the manner of a celebrity icon or a teen idol than a true adult. The adolescent hero returns with a few scratches but is essentially unchanged as a person. Although often entertaining, this is Dungeons and Dragons, not a mature hero's journey.[14]

Both men's and women's paths to genuine maturity are distinct from juvenile, usually masculine, heroism. The mature hero endures a descent to the underworld, undergoes a decisive defeat of the adolescent personality (a psychospiritual death or dismemberment), receives a revelation of his true place in the world, and returns humbly to his people, prepared to be of service according to his vision. This is equally true of the mature heroine.

When understood in a soulcentric manner, the basic dynamics and principles of the hero's journey are gender neutral. The journey is soul-defined rather than self-defined, and service focused rather than conquest obsessed. Although youth must first develop a healthy adolescent ego before surrendering it, the eventual defeat of the adolescent personality is essential.

DESIGN INFLUENCES

One of the most common questions I'm asked about the Wheel is, "Where did it come from, anyway?" Beyond the four-direction qualities of nature, the panhuman archetype of the hero's journey, and my own experiences, there were some twenty other categories of sources that inspired me. Some of these influenced the overall structure of the Wheel; some informed my understanding of only one parameter of each stage (such as the nature of personal identity); and others filled out my rendering of an archetype or a stage transition. I developed the Wheel by incorporating insights from all these influences into a single model. The Wheel has undergone quite a bit of stretching and shifting over its twenty-five years of development, and will undoubtedly continue to do so.

Because I constructed the Wheel as a model — as opposed to a theory — my primary design objective was to fashion a useful language, a way of talking about optimum human development, especially concerning the relationship between the ego and the soul. My goal has been to create a means of systematically articulating and discussing all the possibilities of soul-infused maturation, as opposed to championing a single theory or path. In appraising the merit of any model, the primary question to ask is not whether it's true but whether it's a valuable tool of description, discussion, and action.

Inventing the Wheel was comparable to solving a mathematical equation containing more than twenty variables. These variables correspond to the following design influences, which are ordered here more or less according to importance, from greater to lesser, but all of them are significant. (The nonscholarly reader should feel free to jump to the next section.)

- The characteristics of nature embodied in the four cardinal directions and observable in the qualities of the diurnal and seasonal cycles
- The symbols and themes of the universal hero's journey (the initiatory descent to the underworld) as found throughout world mythologies, especially as catalogued by Joseph Campbell
- My personal experience, since 1975, as a maturing human and a psychotherapist, ecotherapist, and soul guide — in particular, what I've learned from the life stories of individuals who have reached genuine adulthood
- The verse of soul and nature poets, especially Rainer Maria Rilke, Mary Oliver, David Whyte, W. B. Yeats, Antonio Machado, Adrienne Rich, T. S. Eliot, and William Stafford
- The work of ecopsychologists, ecophilosophers, and deep ecologists, especially Joanna Macy, David Abram, Dolores LaChapelle, Arne Naess, Ralph Metzner, Ted Roszak, Chellis Glendinning, Molly Brown, John Seed, Aldo Leopold, and Andy Fisher
- Human archetypes (especially the Innocent, Orphan, Wanderer, Visionary, Martyr, Warrior, Fool, and Sage), with special gratitude to Carol Pearson[15]
- Thomas Berry's work in cultural and religious history, and his work with Brian Swimme on the new cosmology, the resacralizing of the universe story
- Ecoliteracy advocates such as David Orr, Richard Lewis, David Sobel, Fritjof Capra, Zenobia Barlow, Richard Louv, and Jeannette Armstrong
- Human development models, values, and social practices from a selection of nature-based peoples, especially as discussed by Dolores LaChapelle, Martín Prechtel, Malidoma Somé, and Gregory Cajete
- Thomas Berry's and Joanna Macy's great-hearted perspectives and personal stories about elderhood
- The perception-shifting ideas and images of ecological imagineer and wilderness explorer Geneen Marie Haugen[16]
- The understanding of human development found in the works of Carl Jung and other depth psychologists, especially James Hollis, Marion Woodman, and Robert Johnson
- James Hillman's archetypal psychology
- Humanistic psychologist Abraham Maslow and his findings about self-actualizing people and his distinction between exceptional and average human development
- Peter G. Ossorio's Descriptive Psychology and his articulation of the concepts of person, behavior, language, and world
- The research and perspectives of cultural anthropologists and ethnologists concerning human development in oral cultures, especially Paul Shepard, Stanley Diamond, and Joseph Meeker

- The work of scholars and writers who have illuminated our human prehistory and the less-than-wholesome roots of Western civilization, including Riane Eisler, Derrick Jensen, Andrew Schmookler, and Daniel Quinn
- The four-directions-based model of human nature developed by the pioneering rites-of-passage guides Steven Foster and Meredith Little
- Research and models (some of my own from the 1970s) of nonordinary states of consciousness, including trance, hypnosis, psychedelic states, sleep and dreams, and meditative states
- The qualities of the lunar cycle, especially as articulated by Marilyn Busteed and Dorothy Wergin[17]
- Cross-cultural commonalties in the enactment of rites of passage
- The perspectives of the Mystery schools from European traditions, including the mystical traditions of Taoism, Hinduism, Buddhism, Judaism (the Kabbalah), Islam (Sufism), and Christianity (Gnosticism)
- Developmental models from Western psychology (for example, those of Erik Erikson, Jean Piaget, Wolfgang Köhler, and Rudolf Steiner)

OVERVIEW OF THE FOUR-STAGE WHEEL

To get a first impression of the Wheel, we'll consider a four-stage version before we explore the full eight-stage model.

Diagram 3-2 shows the four seasons of soulcentric life — childhood, adolescence, adulthood, and elderhood — separated by five transitions. On the Wheel, the life transitions are placed on the compass points and the stages are between them. *East* designates the first transition and also the last. Each transitional event is an initiatory experience, whether or not formally marked by a rite of passage.

Birth is located in the East because, as we've seen, this is the place of the rising Sun and of beginnings.

In childhood, we awaken to a wondrous world as we learn the fundamentals of nature and culture.

Puberty is the transition of sexual, social, and psychological flowering. It appears in the South because, being the place of greatest warmth, the south is linked with the flowering and growth of plants and many animals.

In adolescence, we acquire the social and psychospiritual capacities that prepare us for the experience of Soul Initiation.

Soul Initiation is the radical transformation in life orientation in which we shift from a focus on social belonging and soul discovery to the active embodiment of soul in our community. Soul Initiation is positioned in the West because this is where darkness blossoms, where the luminous gives way to the numinous, where the dayworld

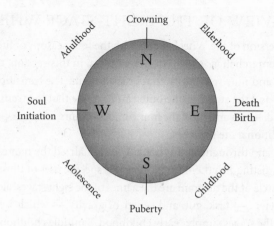

DIAGRAM 3-2: THE FOUR SEASONS OF ECO-SOULCENTRIC LIFE

luster of youth fades into the risky nightworld allurement of soul, the domain of dreams and visions that usher us into true adulthood.

In adulthood, we acquire and hone our unique ways of serving our community through soulwork.

The North is the site of the transition I call Crowning, where elderhood begins. At this transition, we relinquish our conscious attachment to the embodiment of our individual souls — the definition of adulthood — and turn toward the tending of a more expansive domain, the soul of the more-than-human community.

I adapted the term *Crowning* from contemporary women who refer to elderhood as the stage of the crone, a mature woman of wisdom and power. Sometimes women's groups enact a menopausal initiation ceremony called a "croning." This word seemed exactly right to me for the name of that life transition, but it only works for women. Then I realized that, if you simply add a "w" to make it "crowning," it implies the right thing for both genders — a coronation.

With its implication of royalty, Crowning marks the transition into the highest social status, true elderhood. Crowning poignantly contrasts with retirement, which, in our adolescent culture, means the commencement of the social status considered to be, despite rhetoric to the contrary, the lowest — "senior citizen."

Crowning occurs at the North because this is the cold and dark place of hardship to which we must proficiently adapt, and which, if we do, gives us strength and endurance.

Finally, the fifth transition, Death — the return to spirit — brings us back to the East. The realm to which we return is that from which we were born.

OVERVIEW OF THE EIGHT-STAGE WHEEL

The unabridged version of the Wheel begins with the four seasons of life as above but divides each of them in half, as shown in Diagram 3-3. In this version, there are eight soulcentric stages and nine transitions that bracket them. The transitions are shown in the inner circle and the stages in the outer. You can see that the transitional events from the previous diagram are still at the four compass points, but interspersed between them are four additional life passages.

On this map, and throughout this book, I've capitalized the names of the stages and transitions to distinguish them from other, less specific uses of those same words.

In the outer circle of the diagram are the names of the eight stages, along with three additional parameters — task, gift, and center of gravity — which I explain below. Rather than label the stages simply "early childhood," "middle childhood," and so on, I chose more evocative names that combine a human archetype with an Earth archetype to suggest the essential characteristics of each stage. This also reminds us to distinguish developmental stage from chronological age.

In this book, I ask the reader to think in a new way about what constitutes a stage of life. The timing of the transitions between soulcentric stages is independent of chronological age and social role and, for the most part, independent of biological and cognitive development. An individual doesn't pass from one stage to the next just because he reaches a certain age (such as thirteen, twenty-one, or sixty-five), or obtains a certain social status (such as schoolboy, bar mitzvahed, eligible for dating, worker, father, or grandfather), or has certain hormonal releases begin or end. Rather, the movement from one stage to the next is spurred by progress made with the specific developmental tasks encountered at each stage. The life passages occur when (and if) the individual's center of psychospiritual gravity shifts from one locus to the next.

In a soulcentric community, it is not considered "better" — either for the individual or society — for a person to be in a later stage than an earlier stage. Every stage provides fulfillment for the individual and an invaluable gift to the community when a person is in a healthy version of that stage. The only way to cooperate with the process of maturation is to embrace fully the stage you're in (and its tasks). Paradoxically, you have to love the stage you're in, in order to (eventually) leave it.

But every transition between life stages is painful, involves loss, and entails a crisis for the conscious self. Not only do you usually regret leaving a stage, the leaving itself has challenging and unpleasant features. But the next stage always brings new and greater opportunities for fulfillment and for growing more fully human, and soon enough you fall in love with that stage, too.

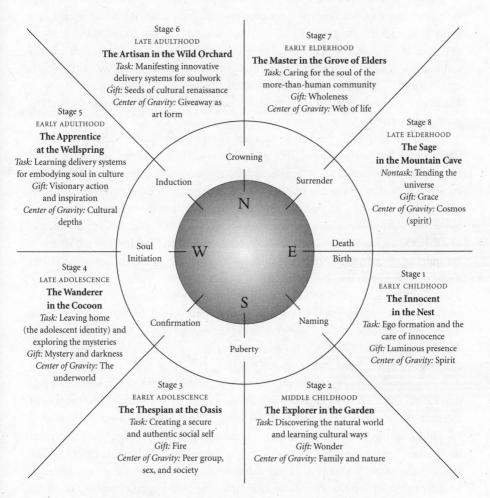

Stage 6
LATE ADULTHOOD
The Artisan in the Wild Orchard
Task: Manifesting innovative
delivery systems for soulwork
Gift: Seeds of cultural renaissance
Center of Gravity: Giveaway as
art form

Stage 7
EARLY ELDERHOOD
The Master in the Grove of Elders
Task: Caring for the soul of the
more-than-human community
Gift: Wholeness
Center of Gravity: Web of life

Stage 5
EARLY ADULTHOOD
**The Apprentice
at the Wellspring**
Task: Learning delivery systems
for embodying soul in culture
Gift: Visionary action
and inspiration
Center of Gravity: Cultural
depths

Stage 8
LATE ELDERHOOD
**The Sage
in the Mountain Cave**
Nontask: Tending the
universe
Gift: Grace
Center of Gravity: Cosmos
(spirit)

Crowning

Induction

Surrender

N

W   E

S

Soul
Initiation

Death
Birth

Stage 4
LATE ADOLESCENCE
**The Wanderer
in the Cocoon**
Task: Leaving home
(the adolescent identity) and
exploring the mysteries
Gift: Mystery and darkness
Center of Gravity: The
underworld

Stage 1
EARLY CHILDHOOD
**The Innocent
in the Nest**
Task: Ego formation and the
care of innocence
Gift: Luminous presence
Center of Gravity: Spirit

Confirmation

Naming

Puberty

Stage 3
EARLY ADOLESCENCE
The Thespian at the Oasis
Task: Creating a secure
and authentic social self
Gift: Fire
Center of Gravity: Peer group,
sex, and society

Stage 2
MIDDLE CHILDHOOD
The Explorer in the Garden
Task: Discovering the natural world
and learning cultural ways
Gift: Wonder
Center of Gravity: Family and nature

DIAGRAM 3-3: THE EIGHT STAGES OF
ECO-SOULCENTRIC HUMAN DEVELOPMENT

(For a larger-format version of this diagram that you can download and print,
please visit www.natureandthehumansoul.com.)

In soulcentric development, each stage of growth has an essential relationship to soul:

Early childhood (the Nest) forms the foundation for later soul discovery through the preservation of our original innocence and our innate relational intelligence and through the development of a healthy culture-rooted ego. The transition of Naming celebrates the appearance of this conscious self. Middle childhood (the Garden) affords us the opportunity to learn the enchantment of the natural world as well as the intricate cultural ways of our people — requirements, too, for Soul Initiation.[18] Puberty marks our sexual awakening and our readiness to move fully into the social life of the greater community.

Early adolescence (the Oasis) teaches us to balance authenticity with social acceptance, allowing us to be in the world with integrity, another prerequisite of Soul Initiation. The passage of Confirmation indicates adequate completion of our adolescent personality and our readiness to explore the mysteries of psyche and nature. Late adolescence (the Cocoon) is a time of withdrawal from the everyday social world as we leave behind our adolescent beliefs about self and world and seek our unique gift of soul to bring to our community. Adolescence ends with Soul Initiation,[19] when we commit ourselves to living that found gift, and our primary life-orientation shifts from social positioning to soul embodiment.

In early adulthood (the Wellspring), we apprentice in a specific form of soulwork and learn the art of bringing our particular gift into the world. Induction confirms the mastery of our early-adult soulwork. During the second half of adulthood (the Wild Orchard), we learn to embody our soul in ever more creative, abundant, and generative ways — through forms of our own creation.

Crowning ushers us into the first half of elderhood (the Grove), in which our primary focus shifts from the embodiment of our particular gift to caring for the soul of the more-than-human community. We do this, in part, by mentoring and initiating the youth, and by helping to maintain the delicate balance between the human and more-than-human worlds. Surrender marks the release of the goal-oriented ego, opening the way to the final stage, late elderhood (the Mountain Cave), in which our impulse turns toward the mysterious tending of the evolving universe itself.

In the first half of life, childhood and adolescence, we're not solely responsible for our own personal development. During early childhood (the Nest), in fact, parents have all the responsibility for accomplishing the tasks of that stage. Later, in middle childhood (the Garden), we come to equally share that responsibility with our parents and teachers, but the adults still must create the contexts for our growth and learning. In early adolescence (the Oasis), we become more independent and responsible for our own learning, yet now the larger community, beyond our parents and teachers, creates and provides the opportunities for maturation. In late adolescence (the Cocoon), we move close to full self-responsibility as we enter the time of the solitary wanderer. Yet still there are others — the elders and initiation guides — who assist us.

Although the Wheel is a model of optimal (soulcentric) development, I believe that all these maturation opportunities are entirely available to us now. Every day we are rediscovering more of the knowledge, skills, and values that can create soulcentric communities (from families to schools to towns) in the midst of an egocentric world. This knowledge is what I've endeavored to outline in this book. The skills can be acquired through a variety of existing programs, curricula, services, relationships, and experiences, some of which are referenced in these pages. The values are up to each one of us. Given the indomitable power of the soul's call and the resources available even in our contemporary world, it's entirely possible to begin or continue our soul-infused development and to create sound environments for our children and teens.

INTRODUCTION TO STAGE PARAMETERS

The next eight chapters of this book — one for each stage of the Wheel — are organized in a more or less uniform sequence of sections corresponding to a dozen parameters or features common to each stage of development. Here's an introduction to each parameter:

Wheel Math

Near the outset of each stage-chapter, you'll find a brief description of the "wheel math" of that stage. This curious term — which has nothing to do with numbers or arithmetic — refers to a method of deducing the fundamental qualities of the stage solely by noting the quadrant and hemispheres of the Wheel within which the stage lies.

You can see in Diagram 3-3 that stages 1 and 8 make up the East quadrant, while stages 4 and 5 are in the West, and so on. Stages 3 through 6 compose the West hemisphere, stages 5 through 8 make up the North hemisphere, and so on.

The wheel math for stage 1, for example, reveals the significance to human development of the fact that this stage is located within the East quadrant, the South hemisphere, and the East hemisphere.

I've already described the qualities of the quadrants (the four directions). The essential natures of the hemispheres are as follows:

- In the East half of the Wheel are the stages of being. People in these stages (childhood and elderhood) experience an *appreciation* of the world-as-it-is more than a desire to change it.
- In the West half are the stages of doing. These stages (adolescence and adulthood) are about reaching, *accomplishing*, changing, and producing.
- In the South half are the stages that highlight the individual. In these stages —

the first half of life (childhood and adolescence) — the emphasis is on individual needs and potentials, on personal growth with a focus on the *ripening* individual.

• In the North half are the stages that center on the collective. Here, in the second half of life (adulthood and elderhood), the emphasis is on collective needs and potentials, on personal growth with a focus on *serving* the whole.

Every stage transition represents either a quadrant change (Naming, Confirmation, Induction, and Surrender) or a hemisphere change (Birth, Puberty, Soul Initiation, Crowning, and Death), but never both. Notice that the second set of transitions is closer to what we would think of as major life changes.

In developing the Wheel, I found that observing wheel math was a principal way to maintain allegiance to the deep-structure logic of the quadrated circle and of the cycles of nature sung through it.

Psychospiritual Center of Gravity

Also near the start of each stage-chapter, there is a reference to the psychospiritual center of gravity (PCG) indicative of that stage.[20] PCG, also shown on Diagram 3-3, identifies the hub of a person's life, what her day-to-day existence revolves around. For example, in early childhood (stage 1), PCG is spirit. In late adolescence, it's the mysteries of nature and psyche, and in late elderhood, it's once again spirit. PCG is important to understand because it illuminates the deep structure of that stage, helping us understand what people in that stage find most compelling.

PCG is also important because it's the principal means of knowing what stage a person is in. What's more, you can tell that a person — you or someone else — is about to pop into the next stage because her PCG begins to shift. More on these two points later.

Passages and Rites of Passage

An early section in each stage-chapter describes the nature of the transition into that stage, gives a name to that passage, and suggests some of the principal features of a *rite* of passage that might mark or facilitate the transition.

The passage between any two life stages amounts to a psychospiritual trauma, a death-rebirth experience. There's both a loss and a gain — for the community as well as for the individual. The individual acquires new eligibilities and relationships, but leaves behind old comforts and joys and a familiar world. The community gains a more mature member but suffers a diminishment in the cherished qualities that the less-ripened person had conferred upon family and community. At Naming, for example, a more self-reliant school-age child emerges, but the precious innocence of early childhood wanes. At Crowning, the community gains a wise elder, but the active, cultural creativity of the adult fades.

Because of the trauma and loss inherent in major life passages, few people are wholly positive about their developmental transitions. We might look forward to "progressing," but as our center of gravity begins to shift, we're bound to experience some discomfort with the lurching ground, the anticipated life changes, and the developing grief inherent in leaving familiar territory. There's often, then, a hesitation — a sense of obstacle, crisis, or ordeal — because the transition forebodes an overthrow of our accustomed orientation to self and life.

This is where rites of passage can help. Every passage feels something like a change in state of matter, from solid to liquid, or liquid to gas. The Mystery is always the chief agent of transformation, but some human-added prod or quickener can help catalyze the transition. A rite of passage can be analogous to the addition of a seed crystal to a supersaturated solution — a fluid that is ready to form crystals but needs a catalytic agent to get it started — but it's the Mystery that readies the solution and empowers the catalysis.

A rite of passage does not, for example, turn a child or adolescent into an adult. Rather, it can supply the last spur an adolescent needs to turn the corner, a corner he has reached only after a long developmental journey. The initiators and elders might look like they have the power to convert an adolescent into an adult, but in truth, "all" they are good at is helping a youth prepare over a period of years, recognizing when he's at last ready, and knowing how to toss into the mix a seed crystal in the form of a dazzling ritual.

The key to timing a developmental rite of passage is to be able to tell when the Mystery is poised to relocate the person's center of gravity. The imminence of Birth, Naming (the appearance of an integral conscious self), and Puberty is obvious to most anyone, but after those three passages, the elders and initiators are the ones who can best tell when a person is about to be propelled into the next stage. They detect the subtle seismic stirrings of the individual's center of gravity as it starts to shift — rumblings that most other people miss.

A rite of passage, then, is never necessary in order for a person to progress between developmental stages. But sometimes the rite helps a little, sometimes it's a significant catalyst, and always it provides the opportunity for a family or community to celebrate or formally mark the transition.

Separate from its occasional and minor role as a passage facilitator, a passage rite most always serves as a potent social accreditation of the transitioning individual, psychologically supporting him and his family to openly act in accordance with his new status, something he might be reluctant to do otherwise. The rite publicly confirms the passage and sanctions new behaviors that accompany the new stage. Also, by signaling to the community that an individual has made a significant life transition, the rite serves as a tacit reminder for everyone to support this person during the initial weeks and months of his new status, which can feel like a disorienting interlude of psychospiritual homelessness. This social support can make all the difference for a successful launch into a new stage. In these ways, the rite has great value for both the individual and the community — even when it's enacted after the individual's center of gravity has already shifted.

I suspect that Confirmation and Soul Initiation are the two transitions for which rites of passage are most likely to occasionally serve as supplementary facilitators, in addition to being supportive and celebratory events. Obviously, Birth happens with or without a social ritual. Likewise with Naming and Puberty. But the next two passages, Confirmation and Soul Initiation, are the ones we need the most help with in making the shift, even when we're otherwise ready. Rites of passage at these two transitions utilize significant cultural forces to generate the momentum that can propel a youth through the long, risky, and multifaceted odyssey into adulthood. It's probably not a coincidence that these two transitions are the ones partnered with the ominous West quadrant of the Wheel — Confirmation ushering us into the West for the first time, and Soul Initiation plunging us even deeper.

After Soul Initiation, passage rites become a less significant factor in helping people make developmental shifts. But again, *every* life transition is abundantly supported, marked, and celebrated when accompanied by a ritual observance, and this is reason enough to have one.

Rites of passage are only the most visible aspect of a much longer, comprehensive, and integrated developmental unfolding from birth through death. What lies between the passages, although less dramatic, is considerably more important than the passages themselves or the rites that mark them. In recent decades, we've rediscovered passage rites but have overlooked the essential incremental progress that must be gained each day by skillfully tending personal development. It's as if we thought that failures in child-raising and our great variety of cultural pathologies could be overcome or erased by a single magic pill. Healthy development depends on progress with the tasks of each stage. Even the most powerful rites cannot make up for gaps and failures in psychospiritual development.

We're also just beginning to rediscover that there are several more major passages in life than most contemporary people suspect. Between childhood and adulthood, for example, we used to conceive of only one passage (and no intervening stages). The Wheel, in contrast, suggests three passages and two entire life stages between the end of childhood and the commencement of adulthood.

The French anthropologist Arnold van Gennep posited that the rites of passage found in all cultures tend to be structured in three major phases or acts. First is the *separation* from the old stage or status, then comes the *transition* phase, when the individual has no or indeterminate status, and finally the *incorporation* phase, in which the new status is bestowed or taken on. Joseph Campbell parsed the hero's journey into these same three phases but called them *departure, initiation,* and *return.*[21]

We might think of each of the nine transitional events on the Wheel as having these same three phases — separation, transition, and return — whether or not a rite of passage is involved. Each life passage involves a type of leave-taking, the leaving of a smaller home for a larger one. Each developmental transition begins with an ending, the death of the old stage, and ends with a beginning, the birth of the new. In the middle occurs that dynamic, precarious shifting of center of gravity.

One life transition in particular — Soul Initiation — is so demanding and difficult that we could think of the entire stage that proceeds it (the Cocoon) as an extended preparatory period of separation, while the stage that succeeds it (the Wellspring) could be envisaged as an extended period of incorporation.

Stage Name

The stage-name section of the next eight chapters introduces the name of the stage (Nest, Garden, Oasis, and so on) and explains how that name evokes the central qualities and opportunities of that stage. In keeping with the Wheel's ecocentricity, all stage names refer to natural environs — ecological habitats or settings. Each name refers to a *place*, reminding us that each life stage is an arena as much as it is a process. Each stage has a certain feel or atmosphere, a milieu.

Only after I'd chosen the stage names, based on the psychospiritual qualities of the stage, did I notice the intriguing relationship between those names and the cardinal directions. This discovery felt like an astonishing confirmation. It turns out that the stages in the East, linked with the rising Sun, are places at a height. South stage names refer to locations that are comfortable, warm, boundaried, and cultivated, as suggested by the qualities of the South. West stage names are places that are dark or that emerge from the depths. North stage names are settings that are productive or mature. If you look at Diagram 3-3, you'll also see some interesting relationships between the stage names opposite one another on the Wheel, perhaps suggesting (or confirming) a natural affinity between people half a lifetime apart. These multifaceted resonances illustrate the many moments of serendipitous corroboration that occurred during the Wheel's design process.

Stage and Quadrant Archetypes

Each stage is matched with two human archetypes — one specific to that stage and another that characterizes the whole quadrant. Diagram 3-3 includes the stage archetypes, and Diagram 3-4 (see p. 68) shows the archetypes for both the stages and quadrants. The archetypes illustrate additional qualities of the stages and of the Wheel more generally.

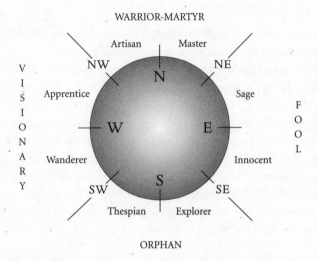

ORPHAN

DIAGRAM 3-4: THE ARCHETYPES

The quadrant archetypes work on a more mysterious level than the stage archetypes. They reveal more of the deep structure of the Wheel and, at first glance, seem enigmatic — perhaps even wrong. For example, you might wonder how the archetype of stages 2 and 3 (the South) could be the Orphan when these are such family-oriented stages. Good question. Arriving at an answer (and the stage-2 chapter offers a good one, I think!) requires us to delve more deeply into the nature of the human psyche. The quadrant archetypes have to hold a wider expanse of meanings than the stage archetypes. They must embrace half of one season of life (for example, childhood) and half of the next. To do this, they have to function in a more abstract and nonrepresentational manner. To identify an archetype that embraces both the Artisan and the Master, for example, we must descend to a more mysterious plane, that of the Warrior-Martyr.

Gift to Community

Given our society's prevailing bias that "progress" is the primary measure of goodness — as if, for example, it's better to be in a later developmental stage than an earlier one — some readers might get the impression that the first half of life holds nothing more than promise and potential. You might wonder if a person has any consequential value to his community before the second (North) half of life, when true soulwork becomes possible. Foundational to the Wheel, however, is the principle that every healthy person in every stage offers an essential gift of value to his community and to the world, a gift derived simply from his being in that stage. These gifts, collectively, are shown in Diagram 3-5.

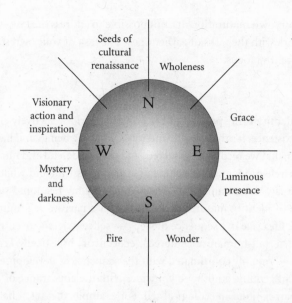

DIAGRAM 3-5: GIFTS OF THE STAGES (CONTRIBUTIONS TO COMMUNITY)

Maturation is beneficial, not because more mature people are better than less mature people, but because a society is healthiest when it contains a fair share of (healthy) people in each of the eight stages.

Every stage is the best one to be in. Having healthy people in every stage makes a society whole, which in turn allows each person to be fully in his stage and to move to the next stage when ready.

The best way to get to the next stage is to more fully address the tasks of your current one. By falling in love with the stage you're in, you move through it and toward the next. By yearning for the next stage, you fail to be fully in your present stage, and so you get stuck right where you are.

Developmental Tasks

This section is the centerpiece of every stage-chapter because personal development is served by addressing the tasks of your stage. Diagram 3-3 identifies the stage tasks but gives them only the briefest descriptions. The Appendix lists all the tasks and subtasks of all the stages in one place (in addition to the stage names, archetypes, passages, and gifts).

No developmental task is ever fully completed. Working on them is simply how you support your own maturation. It's not possible to address the tasks of later stages but you *can* work with the tasks of earlier ones. The task of your own stage, however, is always your central focus.

Circle of Identity

Our circle of identity is the portion of the animate world we actively embrace as essential to our existence. It's the breadth and range of living beings and habitats that we empathize with, that we recognize as sacred, and that we defend and nurture with our own life. Our circle of identity, or sphere of empathy, is who and what we earnestly mean when we say, "my community," "my people," "all my relations," or "my world."

Our circle of identity matures as we do. From a narrow beginning, it expands throughout the life cycle in a sequence of steps — selfcentric, sociocentric, ethnocentric, worldcentric (all-humanity-centered), ecocentric, holistically ecocentric, and cosmoscentric — roughly coordinated with the sequence of developmental stages.

The onset of genuine adulthood coincides with the appearance of ecocentricity. A mature human exhibits an ecological self. For example, the Australian deep ecologist John Seed, founder of the Rainforest Action Network, does not think of himself as protecting the rainforest. Rather, he says, "I am part of the rainforest protecting myself. I am that part of the rainforest recently emerged into thinking."[22]

Our circle of identity is not merely intellectual belief or professed values about community and interdependence, but a viscerally experienced and actively embodied value system. It refers to a quality of being deeper than what might be evidenced by occasional experiences of empathy. It is a reality lived more often than not — a stage, not a state. It's possible, for example, to experience states of trans-species empathy — a profound, I-thou moment of communion with a whale or wolf — without having achieved an ecocentric identity (one that encompasses all of nature). Experiences of trans-species empathy are common even for stage-2 children — when they have ample access to the wild world — despite their having only a stage-2 circle of identity (sociocentrism).

The more mature the self, the wider the web of life in which we feel our membership. As our way of belonging to the world becomes more particular (unique), our sense of community becomes less particular. We fall in love, outwardly and progressively, with the universe.

The Egocentric Stages

This book actually explores two Wheels, one soulcentric and the other egocentric. A section of each stage-chapter describes the egocentric counterpart to the soulcentric stage. For the sake of clear contrast, these sections assume a thoroughly egocentric environment, equivalent to the least wholesome dimensions of our contemporary societies.

The egocentric stages, and the transitions between them, have their distinctive names, as shown in Diagram 3-6. In a sense, there are only three stages of egocentric development — unsound versions of the Nest, Garden, and Oasis. The remaining five divisions are amplifications or extensions of egocentric stage 3a and are accordingly numbered 3b, 3c, 3d, 3e, and 3f.

Dear reader, fair warning: These unsavory and sorrowful portraits of human misadventure have too many similarities to what we observe in our contemporary world every day, in our own communities and on our mainstream news and entertainment networks. These sections can be oppressive or heartrending to read and fully absorb. Alternatively, you might find yourself vigorously resisting the suggestion that *any* segment of our society could possibly be so depraved.

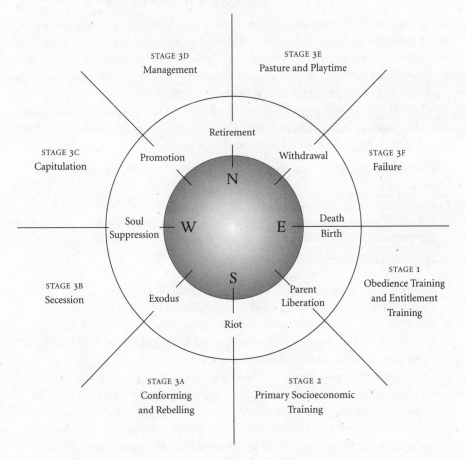

DIAGRAM 3-6: THE EGOCENTRIC STAGES
OF DEVELOPMENT

Suggestions for Cultivating Soulcentric Development
in an Egocentric World

My foremost goal in this book is to contribute to the creation of healthier societies. To succeed at this Great Work, we must transition from our current egocentric societies to soulcentric and ecocentric cultures. We must begin with the reality we have. Therefore, a section in each stage-chapter explores how we can actualize the soulcentric potentials of that stage within our current social, psychological, educational, political, religious, and economic realities.

OPERATING GUIDELINES

The Wheel's basic assumptions, or ground rules, are, in essence, operating guidelines, like those you might find in an owner's manual. The consistent use of these guidelines was key to my design and development of the Wheel. Likewise, when *using* the Wheel, these guidelines help us to speak more clearly and effectively about developmental possibilities and to ask and answer relevant questions, both our own and others'.

The Wheel's operating guidelines are listed below. A few of them are restatements of points made earlier. I suggest that you take a look at these now, and a few more times as you read through the chapters on the eight stages.

- People develop stage by stage through the sequence of eight stages. No stages can be skipped.
- You can be in only one stage at a time. You can, however, work on the unfinished tasks of any earlier stage in addition to those of your current stage. Your psychospiritual center of gravity is the primary indicator of your stage.
- You do not make progress through the stages merely by getting older. It's possible to stall in any stage along the way.
- Regressions to an earlier stage are possible but exceedingly rare.
- Each stage exceeds but encompasses the capacities of early stages.
- You don't get to choose when you move from one stage to the next — the Mystery chooses. Your parents, initiators, and elders don't get to choose either. Stage transitions are not based on your age.
- You must do your part, however. The way to facilitate your movement through the stages is to work on the tasks of your current stage. By doing so, you progress deeper into your stage and approach the next. Also, how fully you occupy the next stage (if and when the Mystery moves you there) is a function of how well you've done with the tasks of your present and previous stages.
- You never fully complete the developmental tasks of any stage. Until stage 8, you continue to receive opportunities to work on the unfinished tasks from previous stages.

- Ultimately, you pass from one stage to the next when your center of gravity shifts, which is brought about by your progress in the tasks of your current stage and by the unpredictable, mystical intervention of the Mystery.
- Sometimes the Mystery has reasons to move you "prematurely" to the next stage. But your ability to fully inhabit that next stage (when you get there) will be limited by your progress with the tasks of your current and previous stages. Working on the tasks of the next stage does not help you get there. In fact, it's not actually possible to do this (see below). You must learn to love your current stage and its tasks. Once you do, you'll soon enough be cast out of it by the Mystery.
- A rite of passage can sometimes supply the final jolt you need to move to the next stage, but only when the Mystery is ready for you to make the transition anyway. Most often, a rite of passage is a means of formally marking or celebrating a passage that has recently occurred.
- The way to more fully occupy or flesh out your *current* stage is to work on your unfinished tasks from *earlier* stages. If you aren't well embodied in your current stage, it's because you have a great deal of unfinished work from one or more previous stages.
- You experience and approach the tasks of previous stages differently than you did when you were *in* that stage. (Specifics are explored in the stage-chapters.) This is because your psychospiritual center of gravity has shifted from where it was while you were in that earlier stage; your center of gravity makes all the difference.
- It's not possible to work on the tasks of later stages because your center of gravity is not yet there.[23]
- The less work completed in a given stage, the less of you there is to bring to the next. This pattern can continue throughout life. It's possible to reach stage 8 conscious of, and able to express only a small portion of, who you truly are (but only if the Mystery has rushed you along for its own reasons). In the following chapters, I describe these not-fully-fleshed-out stages as "thin." Due to the egocentric character of our current societies, it's common for people to be in thin stages.
- The identifying signs of your stage (more or less from the most definitive to the least) are:
  - your current psychospiritual center of gravity (PCG)
  - the primary tasks you find yourself working on
  - the developmental archetypes with which you and your behavior most fully resonate
  - the primary psychosocial gift to community that you manifest without trying (simply through your presence)
  - your circle of identity[24]

The Wheel portrays the odyssey of the ego's developing relationship to soul throughout the life cycle. In this sense, the Wheel is actually a model of soulcentric ego development, not soul development. We descend into this world from spirit and develop a functional first, or primary, ego in stages 1 through 3, an ego that is grounded primarily in human society. Then our ego further matures as we align it with soul in stage 4, in time giving birth to a second-stage (soul-rooted) ego at Soul Initiation. Our second-stage ego carries us through stage 7. At Surrender, we release our soul-rooted ego and achieve a third-stage (spirit-rooted) ego in stage 8.

CHAPTER FOUR

THE INNOCENT *in the* NEST

Early Childhood (Stage 1)

God speaks to each of us as he makes us,
then walks with us silently out of the night.

These are the words we dimly hear:

You, sent out beyond your recall,
go to the limits of your longing.
Embody me.

Flare up like flame
and make big shadows I can move in.

Let everything happen to you: beauty and terror.
Just keep going. No feeling is final.
Don't let yourself lose me.

Nearby is the country they call life.
You will know it by its seriousness.

Give me your hand.

— RAINER MARIA RILKE

Stage 1: Early Childhood

Passage into this stage: Birth

Stage name: The Nest (a loving and protective environment that nurtures the infant and young child while he or she undergoes the earliest phases of physical and psychological development)

Tasks (managed by parents or caregivers): The preservation of innocence and the formation of a healthy, intact, culturally viable ego

Quadrant: East (spirit, light, innocence, and wisdom)

Hemispheres: South and East (individual being)

Stage archetype: The Innocent

Quadrant archetype: The Fool

Gift to community: Innocence, luminous presence, and joy

Circle of identity: None/infinite to selfcentric

Center of gravity: Spirit

Passage out of this stage: Naming

BIRTH: MYSTICAL PASSAGE INTO BEING

At birth, we tumble out of the great night womb into the daylight and into our frail human lives. This mysterious passage from spirit into Earthly life occurs at the Wheel's East point — the house of the rising Sun, the dawn — symbolizing not just birth but all of life's dark-to-light transitions and all its beginnings.

Birth is a mystery at least as great as any other we encounter thereafter. Somehow from the unknowable vastness of spirit descends a unique soul with an animated form. Where *were* we — and *what* were we — during the infinity of time before that sudden flood of birth?

Although she is now among us, the newborn's center of gravity abides very much in spirit. It remains her home, the hub of her existence throughout this first stage of life. Not until the end of this stage will there be a fully formed ego, a consciousness distinct from the integral mystery from which the child has emerged.

The East is not only the point at which the Wheel of Life begins; it is also where it ends, and birth is an ending, too. Author Terry Tempest Williams notes that our birth amounts to a type of death:

When we outgrow our mother's body, our cramps become her own. We move. She labors. Our body turns upside down in hers as we journey through the birth canal. She pushes in pain. We emerge, a head. She pushes one more time, and we slide out like a fish. Slapped on the back by a doctor, we breathe. The umbilical cord is cut — not at our request. Separation is immediate. A mother reclaims her body, for her own life. Not ours. Minutes old, our first death is our own birth.[1]

Every life transition includes the death of the previous stage and the birth of the new one. This is true for the transitions of birth and death themselves. Every passage begins with an ending and ends with a beginning.

Birth is a many-dimensioned miracle, an enigma with biological, psychological, social, mythological, and spiritual qualities. The astounding biological realities alone render birth its own rite of passage for the mother and family as well as for the newborn.

Birth as a rite of passage has three phases: *Severance* commences with the onset of labor, the process of separating from the womb. The journey through the birth canal constitutes the *transition*. Delivery, the first breath, and the cutting of the umbilical cord embody the *incorporation* — literally, in the case of birth, into independent corporeal life.

First-time mother Laura Cooper, in describing the birth of her son, Ian, at home in a birthing tub, echoes the theme of birth as a simultaneous death, as a joy and a grief:

After a final push, a baby came rushing out of me into the water. The baby swam up, around the umbilical cord, and I scooped this little being up and held his face out of the water. I marveled at the little body, warm and pulsating with life as he breathed and cried. We started calling him by his name, Ian. He looked at us, looked and looked, and we gazed back. There was a sense in the room of incredible rejoicing but also, at the same time, of deep, tender grief. This must come from the liminal quality of birth — both a beginning and an ending. The mother-child dyad is now two separate people, even when the cord is still connected between them. This is the death of the being that was mother-with-child-in-womb. I felt grief simultaneously with such joy. These two emotions touch for me, in extremis.[2]

Although the process of birth generates its own rite of passage, in many societies and traditions it is supplemented by ceremonies, the rites of childbirth.[3] Those of us who have lost the old ways can envision and engender new rituals for the start of life. In addition to rituals performed during the birth itself, other ceremonies can help incorporate a newborn into the community. These rites might involve the binding of the cord; the ceremonial handling, bestowal, or burial of the placenta and/or cord; the first bath; circumcision and the treatment of the foreskin; naming; or the presentation of the newborn to the community, Earth, and cosmos.[4]

The practices still used by the Tuareg, an indigenous people of the Sahara, illustrate a nature-centered approach to childbirth and how an entire community can support the mother, child, and family.[5] Early in her pregnancy, the expectant mother occasionally wanders in the nearby desert with the intention of finding — or being found *by* — a special site, where she will go when the time comes to give birth. After finding the birthing place that calls to both her and her unborn child, she visits regularly. She gets to know its particular plants, animals, winds, and invisible presences. While there, she also communes with the life growing within her.

Then, when labor begins, the mother goes to her sacred site in the desert. She goes alone — that is, without any other humans. She doesn't *feel* alone, because she's in relationship with the other-than-humans living there. How could she feel alone when wild nature surrounds her and moves through her as the very mystery that renders her a channel for birth?

Giving birth outdoors without human helpers is difficult to imagine for those of us who have forgotten how to fully trust and belong to the natural world. Independent of the fact that few Western women would consider it for themselves, the Tuareg's solo birthing practice dramatically illustrates for us that, even in a culture like theirs — one filled with sacred rites — the physical events of childbirth are so powerful and numinous that they require no ritual enhancements.

After delivering her child, the mother, perhaps with the help of other women, returns to her tent with her newborn protectively wrapped in her long, flowing robes. Mother and child remain in the tent for seven days and nights, accompanied only by other women. Not even the father is allowed in the tent during this time. The Tuareg believe that women are much more tenderly connected to the world of spirit from which the child has just come, and these seven days of seclusion allow the baby's soul to arrive as gently as possible in his little body and on this turbulent Earth. During these seven days, the mother is completely cared for by the other women.

On the eighth day, the whole community comes and surrounds the tent. Then the mother emerges with her baby and, with extended arms, joyfully presents her child to the people and to the whole world for the first time as she walks four slow circles around the tent — one revolution for each of the four directions. The delighted, marveling community praises the new child and welcomes her with love.[6]

Immediately upon the mother's completion of the fourth circle, the ceremony of first name-giving begins. Playfully or fervently, people start to toss out ideas based on intuition, feeling, or omens observed near the time of birth. This jubilant free-for-all continues until one particular name strongly resonates with the whole community, and everyone knows that that's it. In this way, something of the soul of the child — her essence — comes to be recognized in her name. Because the Tuareg view the child, in a fundamental sense, as belonging to the entire community, and not to her parents alone, it is only fitting that all the people join together to serve as the channel through which the baby's name arrives. Besides, like many nature-based peoples, the entire Tuareg village cooperates in raising each child. Each infant is received as a gift to the whole community.

For those of us in Western societies, rites of childbirth — whether traditional or newly designed — can ease, applaud, and bless the very significant changes in social roles for all family members at the time of a birth, changes that can be rocky for siblings and parents. First-time mothers, especially, benefit from ritual help in reintegrating into their community in their new role. Rites of childbirth also allow the extended community to celebrate the arrival of a new member and to provide social, material, and spiritual support for a suddenly enlarged family.

Birth, of course, initiates the first stage of life, which, if the parents have soulcentric values, constitutes a kind of nest.

THE NEST

A nest — the bed prepared by a bird for holding its eggs and for incubating, hatching, and rearing its young — serves as a womb for the first stage of avian life, in which the chick undergoes a complete transformation from shell-encapsulated mystery to flying juvenile.

Likewise, the Nest fashioned by human parents provides a loving and protective environment composed of the family and the nearby natural world, an environment of people and wild things that nurtures the human infant and young child while he undergoes the earliest phases of physical and psychological development. And like a hatchling, a human being in infancy and early childhood experiences a profound transformation, a metamorphosis from a being of spirit and primal innocence into a creature who possesses conscious awareness of itself and its world. This appearance of conscious self-awareness marks the end of the Nest stage and is, in essence, the birth of psychological personhood.

A healthy Nest calls for devoted, soulcentric parents or caregivers — and other community members — who understand the developmental needs of infants and preschool children, an understanding that is not nearly as common in our society as one might hope. The all-important tasks of the Nest, unlike those of any other stage, are not the conscious responsibility of the individual in this stage but belong instead to the parents and other community adults.[7] These tasks are the preservation of innocence and the formation of a healthy, intact, culturally viable ego. The principal accomplishment of this stage is a conscious, relational self still connected with wildness —. its own and Earth's.

THE ARCHETYPE OF EARLY CHILDHOOD:
THE INNOCENT

At the beginning of life, having no conscious self or conscious responsibilities, we are more innocent than we will be at anytime later. I imagine two versions of childhood innocence. The first is hypothetical — who knows if it ever really occurs? Containing no doubt or fear, it is a state of uncompromised love and perfection, because the separation from spirit has not yet occurred. Mythically, this state corresponds to the Garden of Eden before the Fall. We have not yet tasted the fruit of the Tree of Knowledge of Good and Evil.

The people of Bali have a related belief. They consider both infants and the most elderly to be more "of God" than human. The newborn has just emerged from the spirit world and the oldest ones have in some ways already returned. (This perspective is exactly what the Wheel suggests — when we look at life as a circle, the first and last stages adjoin, together forming the East quadrant of the Wheel, the place of spirit.) Before birth we are something universal — "of God" — and then, after birth, we become something that, although more differentiated, is actually lesser, namely, human. This Balinese-soulcentric idea contrasts with the notion, more typical of Western culture, that we start as something less (an animal, a blank slate, or a mere biological organism), and that, by "growing up," we become something more (human).

Taken literally, the state of perfect innocence doesn't last long, if it ever exists at all. Some might identify it with an early infancy of perfect nurture. Others would say it exists only in the womb. Still others would insist that even the womb is far from a perfect place.

A second, less radical approach understands childhood innocence as a type of present-centeredness — being here now, fully and simply. Infants are in relationship to each thing wholly in the way they sense and feel it in the moment. In the words of the developmental psychologist Jean Piaget, the infant exhibits "an unquestioned acceptance of the given."[8]

The newborn is the very embodiment of receptivity (as is the stage-8 elder, too). She is permeable, completely open to the world. She is not ruminating on the past or future because, as an infant, she is unaware of both. The newborn's innocence precedes her cognitive ability to criticize or to compare what is present with things from other places or other moments. An infant radiates such an extraordinary presence precisely because of her innate capacity to be so purely present. Most all people smile when they see a baby animal of any species. Such pure innocence perhaps reminds us of our own dormant capacity.

The innocence of a child springs both from her closeness to spirit and from her natural ignorance — her lack of awareness of the possible outcomes of her actions or those of others. She doesn't yet understand consequences. She doesn't know about hot stoves, toxic chemicals, or social expectations. She needs to learn about these things in the Nest, but — and this is the major point — it need not be at the expense of her innocence, her capacity to be fully and delightfully present to the world around her.

Although the child experiences fear and frustration at times, she reacts as if the world is *supposed* to take care of her. (It is.) This is an additional sense in which she is innocent.

Laura Cooper offers a portrait of both childhood and maternal innocence:

Watching my son, I often think of Mary Oliver's counsel: "You only have to let the soft animal of your body love what it loves." Ian does this as easily as breathing, while I struggle with it most of the time and every once in a while experience it as unbidden grace. I look on Ian as my teacher in this way. Also, I take my own mothering instincts as teachers. I look upon his body and my mother's heart loves it and marvels at it. So I turn this same quality of vision on my own body, on my own yard, on the Earth, and love them and marvel at them in the same way. They are equally holy and beloved.

INNOCENCE THROUGHOUT THE LIFE CYCLE

Innocence is essential to our psychological health throughout the life span. From infancy onward, innocence provides the foundation for our natural openness to the world, to other beings, to cooperative relationships, to new life experiences, to deep learning and creativity. Innocence is akin to what Buddhists call "beginner's mind"; it allows us to see with fresh eyes, respond with a young heart, act without guile or deception, love like we've never been hurt, dance like nobody's watching, and celebrate the joy of existence. Innocence is the newness of the East that, regardless of our age or stage, can blossom all through our lives.

In egocentric society, the original gift of innocence often atrophies or disappears during our early school years. Yet childhood innocence *can* be renewed and *can* mature from a birthright into an ability: the ability, at chosen times, to devote ourselves fully to the present moment without attention to past hurts or successes or to future consequences or aspirations. With preserved or restored innocence, we can plunge ourselves into the now — in a spring meadow or a desert canyon, during an intimate embrace with a lover, while absorbed in a work of art or music, or simply in the pleasure of being alive and sharing time with a friend. We can choose to give ourselves to others and to the world in this way, knowing what it might cost and yet not protecting ourselves.

When immersions like these occur in middle childhood or later in life, a secondary part of the psyche outside of awareness scans widely for dangers or opportunities. In infancy, because the psyche is not yet capable of such scrutiny, parents scan on behalf of the child while also teaching her, gently and gradually, how to do this for herself.

We tend to think of innocence as being opposed to experience, as if, through living, we inevitably lose our innocence. But in fact, we can keep our innocence alive and accessible if we develop soulcentrically. And we must. Innocence, after all, is the foundation of our capacity to cooperate, and cooperation is essential to a soulcentric society, what Riane Eisler calls a "partnership society."

According to the natural historian Elisabet Sahtouris, cooperation is also a necessary foundation for survival and success at the species level. After a period of hostile competition occurring between young species (young in the evolutionary sense), those species learn to negotiate differences and work out a cooperative relationship to their mutual benefit. Interspecies cooperation is necessary for the sustainability of species and ecologies.[9] Likewise, interpersonal cooperation is necessary for the sustainability of individual humans and their societies. Individual interest (competition) and collective interest (cooperation) must always be balanced. Collective *human* interest (our species' sustainability) is enabled by our human capacity for cooperation, which grows out of innocence. The dream of human peace and harmony, then, begins with a soulcentric early childhood.

Childhood innocence is foundational to other developmental milestones, too. For example, the experience of soul encounter, as we will see, requires a natural openness to the world that is grounded in innocence. And the life passage of Soul Initiation coincides with a deepening of innocence — our conscious presence to each moment, which is bedrock to performing our soulwork.

THE FOOL

The Fool — about whom I'll say more when we explore the final stage of life — is the archetype of the Wheel's East quadrant, which encompasses both early childhood and late elderhood. The Fool doesn't notice or follow the rules that govern society. We see him as absurd or ignorant because he doesn't conform to convention, doesn't care what others think about him, and isn't trying to impress or get ahead. But, from his perspective, there's never a better place than where he already is. Here and now is always more than enough. Although he loves his life, he's not attached to it. He's in constant celebration of existence. It is as if he's from another world — a world of joy, delight, and light. The Fool, then, is an archetype of the sacred. He teaches us nonattachment, simplicity, and joy in the moment.

The small child and the most ancient of elders both embody the qualities of the Fool.

THE INNOCENT'S CONTRIBUTION TO THE WORLD: LUMINOUS PRESENCE

For the young child in the Nest, the gift that radiates from his being is, of course, his innocence, the luminous presence of spirit that shines through him. It is hardly possible for an emotionally alive person to be in the company of a well-nurtured infant and not be flooded with joy, delight, and intimations of the divine. Imagine a society, if you can — even an otherwise healthy society — in which people are somehow born with adolescent psyches. That would make for a forlorn world without innocence for anyone of any age. The very young child not only embodies but also *anchors* innocence in our human world. His innocence proceeds from his being, uplifting everyone who comes in contact with him, pervading the entire community. He is an emissary from spirit, a gift of pure love in the world. All the more reason for the family to adequately care for his precious innocence.

THE DEVELOPMENTAL TASKS OF THE NEST

The preservation of innocence is, in fact, one of the two tasks of the Nest. The second is the development of a healthy, intact, and culturally viable ego. Success with these two developmental tasks in early childhood lays the psychological groundwork for a healthy middle-childhood, adolescence, and adulthood.

It bears repeating that the conscious responsibility for accomplishing the tasks of the Nest, unlike the arrangement we find in all other life stages, rests entirely with the parents or caregivers. Consequently, to fully grasp the nature of early childhood, we must first understand something about stage 5, the Wellspring (early adulthood), which is on the far side of the Wheel, half a lifetime away. This is because the tasks of the Nest are best carried out by parents who are soul-initiated — Soul Apprentices — at the time they begin parenting.

As we'll see in chapter 8, initiated adults are people who have discovered their soul qualities or the larger story they were born to live. These are people who experience themselves primarily as agents for soul and as members of a more-than-human community; they're in service to the whole, not merely to their limited self-interests. If they also have children, they embrace parenting as soulcraft — the privilege and challenge of assisting a young person to grow into a soul-embodying adult. They think of their child not as something they own or as raw material to be shaped as they wish but as a unique individual with a particular destiny. They know their opportunity and responsibility is to create a Nest within which their child can sustain and develop her natural trust of self, parents, village, and world as she learns to belong to both her human society and her more-than-human world.

Sam Keen, in *Fire in the Belly*, writes of the time he was a young man going through the anguish of a divorce. His mentor at that time, Howard Thurman, told him that there were two important questions in life, and that it was essential not to get them in the wrong order. The first is "Where am I going?" and the second is "Who will go with me?"

We must discover first where our souls intend for us to go before we can truly know if we are meant to be parents or choose wisely a partner with whom to conceive or raise a child. Stage-5 adults are people who have discovered where they are going and have made a commitment to that destination and to that destiny. Child development goes best when the parents' choice to raise a family is in keeping with their soul discoveries in the Cocoon (stage 4). This is the primary reason why it's best that young men and women not conceive or adopt children until after they know where they're going.

To help their youth unravel the mysteries of destiny, a soulcentric society provides ample resources in the form of initiators, elders, sacred stories, engaging developmental challenges, and initiatory education. When people make a clear-headed and heart-centered decision to raise children and a wise choice of life partner, parenting is more likely to be fulfilling and successful, and consequently the whole society is more likely to be just, sustainable, and compassionate.

Although the Nest generally unfolds best when parents are in stage 5, people in stage 3 or 4 can be outstanding parents if their values are soulcentric. The primary desire of a soulcentric parent is to provide his child with the experiences and opportunities she'll need to become a soul-initiated adult, someone who has discovered the gifts that are hers alone to bring to the world. His fondest wish for his child is that, in time, she will experience the joy derived from contributing meaningfully to the evolution of the culture and the health of the more-than-human world. Her capacity for eventual economic self-reliance is important in a foundational way but not primary. Economic *excess* is of no interest at all. Even in our egocentric society, there are many stage-3 and stage-4 parents with these kinds of soulcentric values and, consequently, the capacity to create a nurturing Nest.

In contrast, the foremost goal of a parent with egocentric values is that his child will succeed in egocentric society, an aggressively competitive society in which security and enhancement of socioeconomic standing are the primary ideals. That's as far as the egocentric vision goes. For all their boys and some of their girls, the most common desire of egocentric society is that they develop the skills to someday land a well-paying job that allows for the consumer items that make an egocentric life secure and enjoyable. For many of their girls — although this is becoming less so in much of middle-class America — the hope of egocentric society is that they develop the skills and appearance necessary to attract a man with that well-paying job or the potential for it.

Egocentric parents don't have a vision of life beyond stage-3 adolescence, while soulcentric parents, even if they're in stage 3 or 4, do.

In the remainder of this section, we'll look at the nature of stage-1 child development when parents have soulcentric values, regardless of whether they're in stage 3, 4, or 5 — and why stage-5 parenting is the ideal. Then, later in this chapter, in the

section titled "Stage 1 in an Egocentric Family," we'll take a look at the greatly contrasting course of early development when parents have entirely egocentric values.

The Preservation of Innocence

Preserving your child's innocence begins by simply opening your heart to her, to the
preciousness and miracle of her existence, taking in all of her as she is. This means
opening yourself to her fragility, her tenderness, the joy of her, and even to the potential
of losing her. In other words, you must allow *yourself* to be innocent. You must be utterly present with your baby, not wanting her to be anything other than what she is right
now, here, in your arms, not planning her future or hoping she turns out with one particular personality or talent over another. By being fully present with your child in the
Nest, you are making the best contribution you can toward her Soul Initiation and fulfillment many years down the road. By preserving your child's innocence, you also enhance her potential to one day become a mature parent for her own children.

The task of protecting and nurturing innocence, however, belongs to all (genuine)
adults in a community, not just the parents. Healthy innocence in all stages of life
requires consistent care, just as a communal garden does. Preserving innocence is a matter of assisting children, adolescents, yourself, and other adults in being fully present
with their experience as it is, not pushing any parts away. This is especially important
in moments that are unexpected, intense, or overwhelming, moments when people
would prefer not to be present, including occurrences of physical or emotional pain.
Children in particular need help learning how to manage disappointment and discomfort, including how to find some meaning and value in it. By caring for each other's
innocence, people in a soulcentric community cogenerate a psychosocial field that amplifies every parent's ability to protect his or her children's innocence. Later in this chapter, we'll consider several specific practices and principles for preserving innocence.

Childhood innocence is nature's foundation for a soulcentric adult life. Our original innocence serves as the seed for our sense of wonder, which becomes our core quality in
the Garden (stage 2). To wonder freely about a flower or a flute song requires that we
be innocently present with it. Our capacity for wonder, in turn, sets the stage for the social authenticity we'll need in the Oasis (stage 3). This is because developing an authentic
self necessitates that we wonder deeply about ways of social belonging. All three of these
qualities — innocence, wonder, and authenticity — provide the platform for our descent into the initiatory mysteries of the Cocoon (stage 4), which is the passageway to
adulthood.

The loss or contraction of innocence is all too common in our egocentric society
as a result of child-rearing practices and philosophies that emphasize obedience,
indulgence, or preschool academic achievement.

The paths of egocentric and soulcentric societies begin their divergence with the birth and early years of every child. The central distinction between egocentric and soulcentric parenting in the Nest is found in the different ways they relate to innocence.

From the egocentric perspective, one might legitimately ask, "What good is innocence, anyway? It makes a child more vulnerable, less competitive, less likely to make a killing as an adult, more likely to be left in the dust while his peers are getting ahead."

From a soulcentric perspective, in contrast, one might ask what value life has if we cannot be present for it and cooperative with it, if we cannot partner with others without having ulterior motives. Or one might look sadly at the egocentric achievers that abound in our society and ask, "How can we embrace these people who have such difficulty loving themselves and the world, who cannot cooperate, and who are a danger to themselves, others, and the environment that supports us all?"

A society's return to soulcentric life begins with the care of childhood innocence.

Ego Formation

The soulcentric parents' second, simultaneous task in the Nest is to support their child in developing an intact, healthy ego that is culturally viable — an integral, conscious self or personality that is functional in their society.

By *culturally viable*, I mean that, by the end of the Nest, the child has learned the basics of social skills and language so that people in her community continue to accept her as one of them. But we need to be careful with this criterion when the culture in question is egocentric, as is ours. The goal in soulcentric development is *not* a personality that an egocentric culture would consider exemplary or even average — a personality, that is, that might be detrimental to oneself, others, and the Earth. This first criterion of cultural viability is intended to be minimal: namely, that the child becomes sufficiently verbal and acquires enough of the basic cultural customs needed to function well socially.

By *intact*, I mean an ego that is integral — a conscious self that is singular, of "one mind." A child with an intact ego recognizes herself as a person and understands that she is essentially the same person from one day to the next, even though she is always developing and growing. She embraces most of her experiences as being her own (as opposed to her being prone to amnesia). In contrast, a child with a splintered ego is fundamentally confused about her identity, feels as if she's different people at different times, and is troubled in most relationships; by the time she reaches her teen years, she's likely to be diagnosed as having multiple personalities or a dissociative identity disorder.

By *healthy*, I mean a personality that, by the end of the Nest, can be self-directed, relational, and goal-directed, as well as present-centered, persevering, curious (about self, others, and the natural world), and reasonably resilient (much of the time able to respond flexibly, resourcefully, and persistently).

An intact, healthy ego — even at age four or five — has clear and yet permeable boundaries with others and the world, is able to delay gratification sometimes, and is capable of communion with other people and with the more-than-human natural world.

All this might sound like a tall order, an expectation that makes parenting nearly impossible. But in fact, an intact, healthy, culturally viable ego pretty much forms on its own during the first four years of life if parents provide a loving, respectful, and nurturing Nest. Although doing so is more challenging in an egocentric culture, it's still relatively easy for soulcentric parents. There's no need to *force* ego formation or even go out of your way to assure it. Forcing undermines child development. Over millions of years, nature has worked out the means by which human egos form, ways that are superior to anything we might invent. But in an egocentric culture in which initiated parents are the exception, there are a few things we must unlearn and a few pitfalls to guard against. Below we'll explore several guidelines for creating a Nest within which a healthy ego forms on its own.

Tension between the Two Tasks

The two tasks of the Nest — one focused on human nature (innocence) and the other on human culture (ego formation) — are in dynamic tension with one another, as is the case with the two tasks in every life stage. This tension, like that between nature and culture more generally, is ultimately beneficial to the child's development. But it also can make parenting in the Nest challenging, especially in an egocentric society. Parents must help their child develop social skills and, at the same time, preserve as much as possible of her original innocence. The former task requires that the child learn some boundaries and consequences, while the latter requires that she disregard those boundaries and consequences, even transcend them. The former serves the need for a gradual separation from her mother, while the latter serves the need for affiliation, permeability, cooperation, and connectedness with the world — a receptive communion with other people and with other-than-human nature.

But the two tasks also support each other. The more innocence is preserved, the fuller can be the child's communion with the world. This results in greater ego differentiation, because the ego develops by way of relationship. Both communion and separation are essential to becoming a healthy individual. Although the process of ego formation exiles our conscious self from our original oneness with the world, the preservation of innocence enables a person, later in life, to *consciously experience* that oneness and to deepen and widen her relatedness to the world.

The fact of this dynamic tension between the two tasks of the Nest is one reason why it's best when parents are stage-5 adults. Secure in their identities, soul-initiated parents can sustain an open, respectful, and empathic wondering about who their child is, who she was born to become, and what *her* way of learning and growing is. They can value equally their child's innocence and her need for enculturation.

In contrast, stage-3 parents are still in the process of forming secure and authentic social identities of their own. Even if they have soulcentric values, stage-3 parents are more liable to entangle their child in their own process of becoming and, in doing so, impair their child's innocence. They might ask themselves at times: How can I shape my child to make *my* life easier or happier or more secure, or to minimize parenting effort, or to please *my* parents or the church, or to "do parenting right," or to achieve my purposes (for example, to raise children who will take care of me when I'm older, to allow me to vicariously experience what I wasn't able to live myself, or to get others to admire me)?

Stage-4 parents (those in the initiatory upheaval of the Cocoon), whose attention is rightly riveted on the bewildering mysteries of the world, would be capable of doing as good a job as stage-5 parents if it weren't for the fact that they are wandering far from stable self-definitions and social arrangements. Their world is unraveling too much for them to be able to weave an optimal Nest for their child. On the other hand, being as attentive as they are to the mysteries, it's easy for them to embrace their own child as the unique magnificence that she is.

Our society's current approach to parent education is skill-based: it teaches strategies of nurturing and disciplining. But even the best parenting education, although helpful, is an insufficient substitute for genuine maturity. For stage-5 parents, creating a healthy Nest is second nature.

Preserving and Embracing Original Wildness

By preserving the child's innocence, the Nest safeguards something equally essential: the child's original, natural wildness — her instinctive, sensual, emotional, and imaginative qualities, those that exist before any cultural shaping. This aspect of the psyche is what Freud called the id. However, Freud's soul-suppressing agenda was to tame and supplant that wildness, not nurture it. "Where id was, there shall ego be," he advised.[10] In contrast, our hope is that, in the Nest, this dimension of the human psyche — what I call the Wild Self or Indigenous Self — will be celebrated, sustained, and incorporated in the developing personality.[11]

In author Theodore Roszak's terms, the Wild Self is "the protohuman psychic core that our evolution has spent millions of years molding to fit the planetary environment" and "our treasury of ecological intelligence."[12] We need to preserve and embrace this priceless resource of our individual wildness in order to become fully human. And, as a species, we need the wildness of the land, air, and waters in order that we might *remain* fully human.

In your child's first four years, then, rather than emphasizing social conformity and predetermined lessons, you'll want to encourage and celebrate her natural curiosity, her dogged and multisensory exploration of everything in her world indoors and out, the pleasure she takes in her own flesh, her unrestrained laughter, her full-bodied emotionality, her unfettered sensuality (including her love of mud and rain), and her thrill in wild movement. In her infancy and early childhood, say YES! to her impulses in every way you can. Reserve your use of NO! for those rare moments when you need to teach her to avoid real dangers. (In the next section, we'll consider how to make this possible.) In doing so, you'll help her funnel her original wildness into one of the countless personality types that have a welcome place in any family or community with a tolerance for diversity. There's a good chance her emerging personality won't end up looking overly much like either of her parents', and if that's how she was born to unfold, it's something to be celebrated.

Parenting is not meant to be a war against nature — the child's original nature — but rather a collaborative dance *with* that nature. This allows the child to learn her own dance of belonging, one that interweaves her original human nature and her cultural embodiment of self. Creating such a fusion is an aesthetic undertaking, a work of art, for both the child and her parents.

Human development is *meant* to be a work of art, and is so when we allow our deepest nature to guide our development. When our human growth is artful and natural, then the things we create in our maturity will themselves be works of nature as well as works of art.

Safety, Nourishment, Touch, and Play

Accomplishing the central tasks of the Nest — both ego formation and innocence preservation — requires a few preexisting conditions in the child's life. The family must provide for the infant's basic physical needs for safety, nourishment, and touch, and her basic psychological needs for play, variety, and belonging. These needs are foundational — bedrock to the two central tasks.

Meeting the child's basic needs begins before birth and includes the decision about the nature of the parenting partnership and the kind of birth desired. The mother, of course, must take care of herself by having a nutritious diet and regular exercise. A low-stress pregnancy is ideal, obviously. And the less invasive the birth, the better it is for mother and baby.[13]

One cannot overemphasize that infants and toddlers need to be physically touched, lovingly and often. They need to be regularly held, beginning at birth. The younger they are, the more often they need to be cuddled and warmly embraced. Nurturing touch through gentle massage calms infants and enhances their development. Many contemporary parents "wear" their baby, just as mothers have done in nature-based cultures since the beginning of the human story, by using soft carriers or slings that keep the baby close, amply meeting the child's need for physical contact, security, stimulation, and movement. "Baby wearing" promotes infant health in several ways. For example, it strengthens the emotional bond between baby and parents, and creates the stimulation that regular movement affords, promoting neurological development. Carried babies cry less too. Infants who receive nurturing touch through loving physical contact, such as massage and holding, gain weight faster, are calmer, and have better intellectual and motor development.

Breastfeeding is the most natural way to meet many infant needs, including optimum nutrition and physical contact. But parents who bottle-feed can also use "breastfeeding behaviors" such as holding their baby when feeding, making eye contact, and talking to their baby. As part of innocence preservation, infants should be fed when they are hungry rather than by the clock. Although weaning is a mutual process determined by the readiness of the baby and mother, the World Health Organization recommends breastfeeding until the child is at least two years of age.

The child-rearing philosophy called "attachment parenting" offers specific, research-based advice on nurturing touch, breastfeeding, and other topics.[14] "Attachment" refers to a strong emotional bond between a baby and her caregiver. Healthy parents bond with their babies during pregnancy or, at the latest, at birth, but babies don't experience attachment until six to nine months. Once attachment occurs, separation anxiety and wariness of strangers appear, too, because now the child emotionally distinguishes between her family members and others. Problems with attachment and bonding are signs of trouble in the Nest.

Bonding and attachment are most effective when they occur in a web of relationships wider than just the immediate family. When grandparents and others don't live nearby, surrogate grandparents, uncles, and aunts can be cultivated.

Play, too, of course, is essential to the small child's development. What we call play is simply the child's exuberant exploration of her world, an exploration that is naturally and thoroughly sensory. She wants to see, touch, hear, taste, and sniff everything. She wants to tactilely interact with each thing she encounters in the home and in nature. And she needs regular interactive play with her parents and other family members.

Because it's so important that a child be free to explore her world, it's essential that parents make this safe to do. Your home and outdoor play area ought to be one in which touching and tasting is okay. You want to rarely have to say NO! or DON'T! to your baby or young child, because this will confuse her, undermine her nature-programmed need to explore her world, and compromise her original innocence. Instead of spending the first four years of your child's life saying DON'T TOUCH!, support as much touching as she wants. You just need to make this safe enough, and once your child starts crawling and walking, you need to begin to gently establish boundaries and limits. Your child, after all, wants to know what those boundaries and limits are, and they can be established positively and nonviolently. The necessary ones are surprisingly few and help promote a sense of security and confidence in your child.[15]

Mirroring the Child's Personal Qualities

Beyond meeting the child's basic needs for safety, food, touch, and play, the art of parenting in the Nest requires careful observation and mirroring — something that un-
stressed, affectionate parents do naturally. The soulcentric parent mindfully attends to
his infant, with loving eyes and ears, and asks himself: What are my child's distinctive
ways of meeting her needs? What are her unique ways of feeding, receiving and seeking touch, absorbing or creating warmth, moving, playing, or expressing happiness or
frustration? Whatever the parent discovers about his child during early childhood he
accepts and celebrates, as long as it doesn't threaten her safety. The responsive, soulcentric parent follows the child's lead, feeds her when she is hungry, puts her to bed
when she's tired, and helps her to follow her curiosity and desires.

Each child, like every living thing, seeks to become a genuine version of him- or
herself, a being with a particular physical embodiment and an individual set of impulses, traits, interests, and styles. Soulcentric parents support their child in acquiring
a culturally viable personality *in the child's own way*. This is analogous to, and a developmental precursor of, the task that will be encountered later in life, in stage 5, when,
as an Apprentice to Soul, she will learn to embody her individual soul qualities by se-
lecting one or more culturally viable methods.

The best way to help your Innocent child become her authentic self is by observing, welcoming, and mirroring her emotions and emergent personal qualities. When
she's unhappy, empathize by giving her an embrace and compassionate sounds
or words. (It doesn't matter if she doesn't understand the words.) When she's angry,
let her know that you know, using words and gestures that convey that this is her
emotion, not yours, and that you feel compassion that she didn't experience something
she wanted. (And let her have what she wants if there's no reason not to!) When she
laughs, laugh with her. When she shows curiosity or delight in something, join her in
amazement.

Through your loving reflection, you're simultaneously engaging both tasks of the
Nest. You are helping your child grow into a true version of herself (first task), someone who can also function as a member of society (second task). Authenticity (naturalness or genuineness) is a goal of innocence preservation, and functionality a goal
of ego formation.

A soulcentric Nest is what some psychologists call "a healthy holding environment," a safe and effective place within which to grow. Through compassionate mirroring, the infant nonverbally receives the message "We *see* you. We see *you*. We're
delighted you're here. You *belong* here."[16]

The child's emerging ego takes shape through this mirroring by the parents
within the holding environment of the Nest. Through imitation, empathic responses,
and physical-emotional contact, parents (and other family members) reflect back and
engage the baby's smile, voice, emotions, and movements. Family members are, in

essence, saying YES! to the infant's incipient ego, welcoming that self, and helping her ego to form by means of recognition, mutuality, and communion.

In addition to touch and holding, the infant's social needs include preverbal exchanges of sounds and interactive play that the baby initiates as often as the others do. By engaging in these natural kinds of affectionate and responsive interactions, family members foster both ego formation and innocence preservation. Babies come to know themselves by reflection, by the way they are treated, and by their own efforts to be relational.

Nature, Stories, and the Nest

The more-than-human world of nature is the larger context for the holding environment — the Nest — that eco-soul-centered parents fashion. A holistic holding environment embraces all living things. The biosphere, after all, is everyone's primary caregiver. Together, parents and other-than-human beings — butterflies, brooks, and beavers — provide the interactive nourishment for the child's full development. With plenty of time in nature, the infant learns that her greater mother, the animate world, is always there.

The child's innocence enables her to greet everything in the natural world as alive and personal. Each thing has a presence and a voice and can be spoken to. In an eco-centric society, the child's instinctive animistic response to the world is the foundation for a lifetime of I-thou relationships with trees, flowers, animals, mountains, rivers, and stars.

Deep ecologist Dolores LaChapelle maintains that, in order for a child to acquire a basic trust in the world, she "must encounter nature as well as humanity,"[17] must learn that she can trust not only her parents, her culture, and herself but her natural environment as well. Even while the infant is still in her mother's arms, her development needs to be grounded in her experience of sunshine and rain, fresh air, the song and flight of birds, the feel of mud and tree bark, the audible movement of wind and water, and the voices of animals and humans. The eco-soulcentric parent naturally and faithfully presents her Innocent child to the more-than-human world.

Laura Cooper took great care to allow Ian, at eighteen months, to fall in love with the natural world:

> When Ian wants to touch things, I let him unless there is a danger to him or to what he wants to touch. In other words, he gets dirty a lot — he's fascinated with mud, rotting leaves, wet grass. Yesterday we had to undress him outside because he had a glorious time running in the windy rain and splashing in every puddle he found. I want him to have this early, delightful, sensual experience with the world. I want him to know his place in it, to feel his belonging to the "family of things." I want him to feel how precious and

enchanting a worm or spider is; how fascinating and necessary a dead lizard or a rotting log.

LaChapelle writes of "childhood nature mystic experiences" — timeless moments of bliss in nature — and notes that they are common in early childhood when children have the chance to play freely in nature. Through these encounters, "the child knows that he is part of the whole and that the whole of nature accepts him as part of it. Any time in life the child or adult can draw on this."[18] LaChapelle gives us an example from her own childhood, when she was five:

Just behind the house was a small field of meadow grass. I lay down there on my back to watch the clouds and moving leaves of the cottonwood trees above me. Then I noticed the seed pods of the grass, just above my face, waving in the wind. Suddenly I was enveloped in a feeling of complete happiness. There didn't seem to be any separation between me and the gently waving grass pods or anything else around me. That's the only way I can explain it now; then, of course, I had no words at all.[19]

Judy Hall, a fifty-year-old professional and mother, recalls:

I remember being a toddler in my mother's flower garden, toddling around while she was gardening nearby. I had this sense that the flowers and plants were my kin, that we were in this place together, that they were somehow playmates of mine. I felt connected to them and I wasn't afraid that my mother might not be able to see me. I could see her but was content to be covered, almost hidden by the stems of the flowers.[20]

Although a relationship to the natural world will not be an infant's or toddler's first developmental priority until the next stage (middle childhood), her safe introduction to nature is essential. Parents can get backpack-style kid carriers and take their infants on hikes in parks and the nearby wild. Or just allow them to nap and wake in the backyard and the garden where they can observe trees, flowers, birds, and small animals. Allow toddlers plenty of free-play time outside, take them for minihikes, and join them in unrestrained delight in the other-than-humans.

Laura Cooper describes one of Ian's first relationships formed in the more-than-human world, a communion that began when he was ten months old:

Ian loves the acorns that fall from our California oaks. I had never noticed acorns like I do now, despite growing up in these hills. Every day, we make at least one pilgrimage down the street to an oak where Ian gathers acorns. I hold Ian up and I ask the tree if we could pick an acorn. Ian then reaches up and grasps one. If the tree lets it go easily, then it's okay to take it. If not, we ask again for a different acorn. We always thank the tree when it gives us an acorn. Now that Ian is eighteen months old and combining words into two- or three-word sentences, he thanks the tree, too. Sometimes, after gathering, we walk to a bridge over the creek where Ian drops the acorns in the water, but mostly he just loves to hold them. Ian is learning to be in conversation with the tree — with the world — to ask and to listen.

Another way the Nest supports the preschool child's animated entry into the world is through the enchantment of stories. Cross-culturally, stories, especially fairy tales set in nature and populated by animal characters, help the child bring the pieces of his world together. Children instinctively experience continuity with the natural world. The work of the child psychologist Bruno Bettelheim demonstrates how stories of magical places and animals "educate, support, and liberate the emotions of children" and help them understand what is possible in life as they develop their earliest sense of what the world is and how it works.[21]

Traditional children's stories encompass all the human emotions, from rage and shame to love, not just the "positive" ones. By including the shadow side of human existence, these stories help the child to be present to all dimensions of his psyche and to grow toward his wholeness. People who know how to recognize their anger, for example, and act on it in ways compassionate to both self and other, are less likely to be violent or to support their nation's violence in their name. Put positively, they are better at partnership, diplomacy, and democracy.

CIRCLE OF IDENTITY:
FROM NONE/INFINITE TO SELFCENTRIC

The newborn is a special case when it comes to the circle of identity. Not having a conscious ego, he has a circle of identity that is zero. Curiously, we could also say the polar opposite about an infant. Without an ego, he is in open and innocent relationship with everything. Because he has not yet separated from spirit (his center of gravity remains there throughout the Nest), he is one with the entire world. His circle of identity, although unconscious, is infinite.

Toward the end of the Nest, however, as the conscious self begins to crystallize, the child starts to act as if his identity is limited to his own immediate person — "mine" becomes anything that occurs inside his skin and any object of interest that is immediately available to his senses. Other than that, the remainder of the world is, in essence, "not mine." In this sense, the individual's circle of identity becomes conscious and "selfcentric" by the end of early childhood.[22]

"Circle of identity" indicates the range of beings with which an individual empathizes. But is a stage-1 child (an Innocent in the Nest) capable of empathy? Here we need to distinguish what might be called preconscious and conscious empathy. In healthy families, Innocent children, beginning in their second year, are actually quite empathic behaviorally, but not consciously so (that is, they don't consciously understand that other people's experiences and feelings are different from their own). These kids share their belongings with others, make efforts to help others (like picking up a dropped item), and offer verbal sympathy. They provide physical comfort to others who are hurting — by hugging or patting, for example. They bring home small, injured animals to be healed. Even infants in their first year of life will cry in response to other infants' distress.[23]

I believe that early, preconscious empathy is a simple consequence of our original innocence, our natural tendency to affiliate, our innate desire (and capacity) to belong to a family, an initial community. This seems to be true for all, or nearly all, baby animals. We, too, are born with a desire to connect, to cooperate, to be a member. The adaptive, evolutionary significance is obvious.

But is the newly formed human ego — at the end of the Nest — naturally empathic? Or does the conscious self start out selfish and need to learn conscious empathy? In our egocentric societies, the latter seems to be the case; the ego starts out egocentric — reluctant to share and unable to consciously empathize. But some say that in partnership cultures or indigenous soulcentric societies, it is otherwise, or at least that egocentrism in four- or five-year-olds is less evident. In egocentric society, does a two-year-old's desire to help, disappear by age five because we don't honor it? ("No, sweetie, don't help now, I'm busy" or "Every time you try to help, you break something!") Or does empathy disappear because of a more general cultural dysfunction in egocentric society? More on this later.

CONCERNS ABOUT OVERINDULGENCE OF NEEDS

In the Nest, soulcentric parents consistently observe and respond to their child's physical, emotional, and social needs — not perfectly, but pretty well most of the time and well enough to preserve innocence. For example, a mother's and father's recognition, acceptance, and naming of their baby's emotions ("Oh, that frightened you!"), as well as their nurturing response to those emotions, communicates to the child that she is loved and that she is embraced as a particular individual. But because no family, no matter how devotedly attached, could mirror a child's emotions flawlessly, children become motivated to more clearly express their emotions and desires. Because expressive abilities are essential, some parental imperfection is necessary as well as perfectly natural.

The small child's efforts to get her needs met (by reaching, crawling, early verbalizations, smiling, crying, or otherwise physically reacting) are her necessary steps in the development of her will and a conscious ego. Need and desire strengthen the "I" that hungers.

The question that parents often ask is whether it's possible to overindulge an infant. More specifically, is it possible to respond too quickly or too completely to a baby's needs for food, physical comfort, touch, or belonging?

First, it's important to distinguish between needs and desires. A need is a requirement for well-being. A desire is a preferred outcome. If our true needs go unmet, physical or psychological illness results and, if not met at all, we die. If a desire is unmet, we might be disappointed or angry, but are not essentially harmed. If you accept these definitions, then you cannot overindulge a need. On the other hand, it is unquestionably harmful to *neglect* an infant's basic needs. If a child's needs are only partially met or met with great delay, the result is a decay of innocence, a weakening of attachment, and the accompanying development of mistrust, hypervigilance, anxiety, and, in the worst cases, a failure to thrive or even death.

And yet, with too *little* frustration of needs, there's no catalyst for differentiating the self from the world and consequently no incentive for ego formation. Some degree of frustration and some experience of separation lead to ego growth. With some lag, for example, between the infant's expression of hunger and the offering of nourishment, the baby begins to know herself as separate from her provider of food. However, there's no need to deliberately delay. It's not humanly possible for parents to consistently meet an infant's needs perfectly, or even always know exactly what those needs are. The caution by some psychologists against overindulging an infant's basic needs (as if that were easy or even possible to do) strikes me as an unconscious justification for neglect.

Because the mother is sometimes absent, the infant must look around and reach out for her. There's no need to manufacture special occasions of absence to assure that this happens. The infant's early looking and reaching are her initial moves in forming an ego. Separation milestones like crawling, walking, toilet training, and weaning hasten and support the development of the ego.

But attention to the timing and speed of separation is important. If weaning, for example, is harsh, too soon, or too abrupt, it can result in an insecure and anxious infant and, ultimately, an overly dependent personality. And weaning that is unnecessarily delayed hinders ego formation and reinforces dependency as much as the other extreme. If well timed and gradual, weaning is not a denial of basic needs but rather a natural separation process that helps the infant grow secure, self-reliant, and confident.

About the time children begin to walk (normally eleven to seventeen months), they have developed quite a few desires beyond their needs. Is it possible to overindulge those desires? Absolutely. We'll discuss this below as a feature of Entitlement Training, which is one of the egocentric versions of stage 1.

ANXIOUS PARENTING

Although one can't be too adept at meeting an infant's basic needs, it is possible for a mother or father to be so anxious and vigilant about those needs that the whole relationship becomes tinged with worry and a sense of jeopardy. Some parents, for example, live in fear of their baby falling, choking, or suffocating, and they attempt to cope with their anxiety by being overly protective. Other parents, afraid that infant frustration might lead to permanent emotional damage, become anxiously indulgent. The problem is never that the baby's needs are met, but that her parent is chronically jumpy or ruffled. Anxious overprotectiveness is an obsession with avoiding harm, while anxious indulgence is an obsession with providing satisfaction. Both fail at their intended goals.

The anxious, overly protective mother might be reluctant to let her baby touch the earth, try unfamiliar foods or new ways of playing, be held by others, or live much beyond the playpen or a rubber-cushioned playground. The child detects mother's persistent apprehension through the tension in her touch and her voice, in her too-frequent shouts of NO!, in her worried tears, and perhaps through fear-related enzymes in her milk. Mother's anxiety spawns chronic fear in her child and a disturbed attachment to mother and the world. The behavioral symptoms of anxious attachment — frequent crying, tantrums, illness — cause, in turn, an increase in mother's fear, and so on.

The anxiously parented child is likely to become fearful of unfamiliar people, objects, and events and find it difficult, later in life, to wander deeply into the world in the way that's necessary to progress beyond developmental adolescence.

Anxious parents are often hyperattentive to their child, reactive to every mishap in their child's day, eager to solve every problem for their child — and they mistakenly believe that this is good parenting. Parents who hover over kids and "protect" them from even minimally stressful experiences create anxious children.

Overprotectiveness and anxious indulgence are most likely to occur with parents who are too identified with their child, emotionally overinvested in their child's "success," lack trust in the world, or are unclear about their own deeper identities, a not uncommon scenario with stage-3 parents, less likely with stage-4 parents, and essentially inconceivable with stage-5 parents. It's easiest to foster confidence in stage-1 children when you possess the sort of confident self-identity that comes in stage 5.

When young children are doing something potentially dangerous, the appropriately protective parent educates the child by gently but firmly saying, "No, not that," and then redirecting her child's attention elsewhere or showing her how to do it safely. In contrast, the overprotective, anxious parent might become agitated, at one extreme, or, at the other, redirect her child without any instruction about dangers or safe-enough ways of proceeding. In the first case, the child's fear is amplified. In the second, the child doesn't learn how to cope with life's little day-to-day risks and as a result is less likely to develop competence, resiliency, or an appreciation for adventure.

Without challenges, children become afraid of risk, psychologically fragile, and anxious. This undermines their development of identity and a sense of accomplishment. It's important, then, for parents to not *overly* protect their small children from disappointment or discomfort. Through failure, we learn how to cope. By learning how to cope, we become adventuresome enough, later in life, to wander into the world in search of our souls.

STAGE 1 IN AN EGOCENTRIC FAMILY: OBEDIENCE TRAINING AND ENTITLEMENT TRAINING

Here we'll take a look at what stage 1 looks like when parents' values are strongly egocentric and fear based. As a reminder, egocentric values lead people to experience themselves primarily as agents for themselves and to maximize safety, personal comfort, and material satisfactions.

What you'll read in this section is highly unlikely to be a description of you or your children. My intention here is, in part, to underscore the essence of soulcentric parenting by contrasting it with its polar opposite. This section portrays something like a worst-case scenario, but one that I believe is all too prevalent in contemporary American society. This portrayal of the egocentric pole might also help some readers better understand their own childhood experiences, deepen their empathy for those raised in emotionally difficult circumstances, or appreciate the cultural changes needed to create a soulcentric society in the twenty-first century. The fact that you're reading this book makes it likely that you're already working for cultural change; you might even be active in the field of parenting and early childhood.

Although healthy ego formation is nearly effortless in a soulcentric setting, it can go terribly wrong when the family is highly dysfunctional. In the most tragic circumstances, pregnancy is unwanted and the infant is unloved. Or the child's basic needs are neglected or he is physically or emotionally abused. Such an Innocent is apt to suffer disorders of the most basic personality functions, forming an ego that is not at all intact.

Some egocentric parents treat their babies, even if they love them, partly as a ticket to social or economic betterment or as a shield against abandonment or loss. A new mother, for example, might become eligible for welfare, be treated better by her husband, be shown more respect in the community, or be excused, for a few years, from disagreeable work outside the home. The new father, too, might gain some added respect or acceptance. Or he might feel less likely to be abandoned by his wife.

In an egocentric society, many parents suffer from an absence of meaning or purpose in their lives and seek substitutes for, or distractions from, their emptiness. They might look to their children's achievements to render their own lives satisfying.

If a mother sees parenting as a way to fix what's wrong with her life, things will go poorly for both her and her child. The ways she wants her child to behave will often have little to do with the child's intrinsic unfolding. She might grow frustrated with her child's failure to conform to her expectations. She might come to resent her child's basic needs — for nourishment, touch, and play.

Virtually no parents consciously intend to be cruel to their children, but it can be challenging to become a healthy parent when raised within an egocentric family and society.

How can troubled families be helped? Family therapy (if soulcentric) can be beneficial, and, with support from others, parents can work on their incomplete tasks from the first three life stages and assist their kids with those same needs and tasks.

As we've seen, in a soulcentric setting, stage 1 is a nurturing Nest. But in an egocentric family, stage 1 could be more accurately, and sadly, labeled Obedience Training (OT) or Entitlement Training (ET), as shown in Diagram 3-6 (see p. 71).

In both OT and ET, parents, without intending it, neglect or minimize the first task of the Nest (innocence preservation) and, within the second task, emphasize only one dimension (the cultural viability of the ego) while neglecting the other two (the ego's psychological health and integrity). Egocentric families often live in a social environment in which the most viable egos are materialistic, self-absorbed, and much more competitive than cooperative.

Which kind of training an infant receives — OT, ET, or an amalgamation of both — depends on the parents' emotional wounds, fears, and beliefs.

Obedience Training

Some parents believe that obedience and conformity are the most important early-childhood factors in forming a culturally viable personality. For them, raising a child is a matter of teaching her the "right" way of doing things. This "right" way tends to be rather narrowly and egocentrically defined, perhaps based on religious, ethnic, or subcultural values.

One version of the "right" way consists, essentially, of the *safe* way. Most safety-obsessed parents are people who, from their own childhood on, never felt secure. As parents, their foremost question becomes "How must I train my child to behave and obey in order to keep her and my family safe?" They have not learned what philosopher Alan Watts called "the wisdom of insecurity"[24] — that life is a hazardous adventure (which is what makes it interesting and joyous), that an artificially secure life is a dull one, and that significant security is impossible because change is unavoidable, illness and injury are common, and death inevitable.

Other obedience-focused parents believe that, if you spare the rod, you spoil the child, or that all of us are born sinful or savage, and that the primary job of parents is to discipline and mold a child. In the most pathological versions, the goal is to break the child's will (so that "God's will" can take over), beat the devil out of her, or house-break her for her own good. Strict discipline is often imagined or justified as a way to keep the child safe or to support her in being successful.

Some parents simply have so little patience or aptitude for parenting that they mostly want to teach their kids to behave and obey in ways that minimize parental time and effort.

Obedience Training (OT) can take many forms. Most commonly, OT parents punish their child's unwanted behaviors — by slapping hands that reach too much, frequent NO!'s, spankings, loss of privileges, time-outs (emotional withdrawal), and demands for "proper" behavior even before a child is cognitively capable of under-standing the rules. Parents might follow strict feeding schedules, ignore or punish crying, and selectively reinforce "good" behaviors.

You might find it hard to believe that Obedience Training is a common occurrence in the contemporary Western world. If so, you might never have heard of James Dobson, a conservative Evangelical Christian and psychologist who has a daily radio show called *Focus on the Family*, which airs on more than six thousand stations worldwide in more than a dozen languages, and which airs on eighty U.S. television stations each day. In 1977, Dobson founded a nonprofit of the same name based in Colorado Springs. His organization sends and receives such an enormous volume of mail that it has its own zip code. In late 2006, he claimed that 200 million people heard his pro-grams every day in 164 countries.[25] From his website:

> According to Dr. James Dobson, it's best to start disciplining your children when they're young, approximately 14 months of age. Youngsters are more pli-able until they're around 4 years old. After that, the concrete hardens a little and you have to work harder at breaking it up.
>
> Dr. Dobson summarizes discipline like this:
>
> *At a football game when a guy jumps off sides, what does the referee do? He doesn't get red-faced and begin screaming about the virtues of keeping the rule. He drops the flag and he steps off the penalty.*
>
> In the same way, when your child messes up, don't break the peace of your home. Step off the penalty — and do it consistently. Don't reason with the little guy. Discipline him.
>
> ...The core of discipline...is to find a way to help the child experience negative consequences proportionate to his bad behavior....Parents would be wise to keep a large repertoire of disciplinary strategies in their hats.[26]
>
> It is not necessary to beat the child into submission; a little bit of pain goes a long way for a young child. However, the spanking should be of suf-ficient magnitude to cause the child to cry genuinely.[27]

> By learning to yield to the loving authority... of his parents, a child learns
> to submit to other forms of authority which will confront him later in his life
> — his teachers, school principal, police, neighbors and employers.[28]

In addition to strict-father parenting and dominator relationships more generally, Dobson is a resolute promoter of strict-husband patriarchal marriage, believing that men have the divine obligation to lead their families, and women have the divine obligation to submit to their husbands' authority. *This* is the counsel that millions of parents listen to every day.

With Obedience Training, as promoted by Dobson and others, parents undermine a meaningful relationship with their child even when they want the latter as much as they want obedience. Some parents genuinely believe their child's innate character doesn't matter or is an impediment to her development. The child is trained to suppress personal qualities and behaviors inconsistent with parental standards and conditioned to "emit" desired behaviors. To survive, the child begins to learn, even in infancy, to attend foremost to what others expect of her. She learns to be relational, but only superficially, in a submissive, compliant, and deferential way. She learns to fear or distrust her own wildness and innocence, her own desires, her original nature.

The primary principles of OT are prohibition, shame induction, fear generation, and punishment. The infliction of fear and emotional and physical pain sometimes masquerades as kindness: "I'm doing this for your own good," or "This hurts me more than it hurts you."[29]

Some parents who emphasize obedience training are more concerned with their social image than with their kid's behavior or welfare. Because they don't want to get caught looking like a "bad parent," they try to make their child conform to cultural expectations.

Most OT-raised children grow into conformists, rebels, or victims — or some blending of the three. Conformists are by far the most common, people who have an inordinate fear of sticking out, of being disobedient, of being abandoned, ostracized, criticized, fired, or punished for breaking the rules. As the final sentence of the Dobson quote above implies, creating fearful, submissive conformists (immature worker-consumers) is precisely the intention of OT. A plenitude of such conformists is a fundamental requirement for prolonging the industrial growth society.

Some children raised under a regimen of OT react with at least as much anger as fear. As they get older, they become irate at having been subjected to such oppressive parenting. These children become rebels.

A third subset will, like the first, react primarily with fear, but because of race, disability, or social handicap, will be excluded from the favorable social roles or jobs available to conformists. These children become the victims of society — the downtrodden, unemployed, homeless, suicides, imprisoned, and, in many cases, the mentally ill.

All three — conformists, rebels, and victims — will be poorly prepared to begin the journey of soul discovery. Conformists, if they've achieved success at the American dream, might have little motivation to surrender their materially rewarded lifestyle. Victims are unlikely to have the social skills or economic foundations that enable further maturation.

Of the three, rebels have the best chance of maturing beyond stage 3, because they are already alienated from the American dream and so don't have as much to lose as the conformists. But they need to get over being angry and merely railing against the establishment before they can enter the foreboding and ecstatic mysteries of their own lives.

Entitlement Training

Entitlement Training (ET) turns children into little princes and princesses. Like OT, ET minimizes innocence preservation and accentuates culturally viable egos, but instead of placing its emphasis on obedience, ET strives to satisfy the child's every desire. An ET stage 1 results, several years later, in stage-2 and stage-3 personalities adept at getting their self-centered personal desires met. By middle childhood and beyond, this becomes an interpersonal disability, an inordinate focus on deriving satisfaction from one's self and from activities independent of empathic relationships.

With ET, overindulgence begins in the child's second year, when toddlers develop desires beyond their needs and get better at communicating them. This increases the possibility for mom and dad to overindulge with toys, non-nutritious food, and entertainment. The more indulgence the parents offer, the less they offer heart-centered mirroring. Without mirroring and joy-filled interaction, the child is less likely to learn social skills such as requesting, sharing, and taking turns, or to develop the psychological skills of patience, conscious empathy, and accepting disappointment.

Parents who overindulge — and as a result unintentionally cause relational disorders in their kids — often do so because they don't know how to be deeply relational themselves. Self-centeredness is passed from one generation to the next.

Overindulgence is a type of neglect. There's little or no mirroring of the child's developing self (which is a genuine need in early childhood). For comfort, the psychologically unseen child learns to settle for material things and self-involvement. There's little or no innocence or present-centeredness preserved because the child learns that her gratification comes from the toys, food, and entertainment she can get in the near future as opposed to who or what she can relate to in the here and now.

ET teaches the child to be in control of the world (like a behaviorist, unscrupulous developer, or superpower president) instead of relational. It encourages her to "own" the world rather than to enjoy it, explore it, converse with it, or belong to it.

Whereas indulgence discourages genuine relationship, soulcentric mirroring cultivates authenticity and integrity by reflecting back to the child her physical, social, and emotional truths — including her desires, and her disappointment when those desires are not met. Mirroring helps the child grow and differentiate an authentic, relational self.

Indulgence, in contrast, pacifies the child and results in a superficializing of the ego, so that the self is experienced as a mere collection of immediate desires and vested interests. Indulgence makes it difficult for the child to learn that other people have their own independent worth, or that the world, which cannot be owned and in which every living thing shares, is a majestic wonder with fundamental intrinsic value.

With a variety of motivations, ET parents are too busy serving their children to actually get to know them and have a meaningful relationship with them. The ET-raised child is taught, implicitly or explicitly, that the goal of life is to be a consumer.[30] She is likely to become relational in a superficial, manipulative, and selfish fashion — a princess.

Compared to soulcentrically raised children, princes and princesses are relatively unlikely to embark upon the journey of soul initiation, because accepting deprivations will be anathema to them, and initiation always involves some significant challenges to the ego. But because the soul constantly calls to everyone, the prince or princess might yet be tricked into the journey.

As we've seen, one of the two tasks of stage 1 is the formation of a culturally viable ego. In a healthy society, a prince or princess personality does not make for a culturally viable ego. This way of belonging to the world is not tolerated, simply because it has little of value to offer.

Prince and princess personalities are culturally viable only when the culture-at-large is self-centered and consumer-oriented — a society in which people are obsessed with fulfilling materialistic desires. Before recent decades, prince and princess personalities were culturally viable only in upper-class egocentric subcultures, hence, the terms *prince* and *princess*. But more recently, we've seen an epidemic of self-centeredness around the world that has reached all the way through the middle-class in affluent societies. Consequently, ET is becoming increasingly common as a child-rearing practice. And humanity is becoming ever more class-divided between the entitled and the disenfranchised, the wealthy and the poor. In addition to being unsustainable, this polarization is socially, economically, and politically unjust. The root cause is the pervasive failure of individual human development, which, at its core, is a cultural failure. Solutions, then, are not merely economic or political; they are also psychological, cultural, and spiritual.

Behavior Modification

Obedience Training and Entitlement Training are sometimes combined and called behavioral conditioning or behavior modification, employing both punishment (OT) and rewards (ET) to shape behavior. The use of rewards and incentives to influence child (or adolescent) behavior often backfires by freezing personal goals at developmentally earlier levels. A child rarely comes to appreciate the pleasures of empathy and altruism when he's kept busy accumulating prizes provided by behavior-modifiers in the guise of adults, teachers, and mental health professionals.

"Positive reinforcement" by any name or euphemism is nonetheless bribery, just as "negative reinforcement" amounts to coercion, blackmail, or extortion, and "aversive conditioning" is still punishment.[31] A child subjected to behavior modification learns that life is a matter of ulterior motives, what's in it for him, who's willing to pay the most, who's got the power, how to hurt or threaten others to get what he wants, how best to manipulate the system and/or avoid punishment.

Recent research demonstrates that even the use of praise can be contrary to healthy parenting when it is self-consciously designed to reinforce what the child is doing as opposed to a genuine expression of gratitude and admiration.[32] Contrived praise does not raise a child's self-esteem or motivate him to do better; it merely trains him to seek more praise. Manipulation through praise is a poor substitute for cultivating a heart-centered relationship, in which there is genuine interest in what the child is doing and feeling.

SOULCENTRIC PARENTING
IN AN EGOCENTRIC WORLD

How can parents with soulcentric values raise stage-1 children in an adolescent, egocentric society? For many, this will actually be the easiest stage for both children and parents, because during infancy and early childhood — before the school years begin — it's possible to oversee most influences in your child's world. Your family's and friends' homes and your visits to relatively unpeopled nature will compose the vast majority of your child's domain. During her first four or five years, it's possible to insulate your child from most of the egocentric influences of the surrounding society. This definitely won't be true after the Nest. And it's impossible to overstate the importance of the Nest as a foundation for all that follows, all the more so when your child's future is an egocentric world.

For other parents, it might not be so easy. It might be an inescapable reality, for example, that you and/or your coparent must work outside the home, even during your child's infancy, and this inevitably reduces time and energy for touch, breastfeeding, holding, play, and mirroring. We all know about the maddeningly frenetic pace of most American lives in the twenty-first century.

Many mothers who stay mostly at home with their children during the first two years say that the boredom and social isolation from other adults nearly drives them crazy. Many other moms choose *not* to stay at home with their small children, even if they can afford it, because it would disrupt their career. It used to be, when we lived in small, close-knit villages, that mothers with stage-1 children would spend their days together. This allowed for parenting tasks to be shared and for mothers to socialize. The social isolation of mothers and infants is one of hundreds of reasons why we need radical cultural change, including in how we parent, where we live, and how we socialize.

One of the most potent ways to contribute to cultural transformation is for you and your family to become role models — *you* make a radical change in lifestyle, if you can, if you dare, and if it feels right and inspiring to do so. The soulcentric lifestyle choices that you make really do have a significant impact on your community. Others who are ready to make similar changes will be inspired by your example. Culture shifts one individual and family at a time.

Another egocentric influence in American culture is the escalating pressure on parents to make their stage-1 children learn ever earlier and ever more. It's pretty easy to see that in most cases this "early enrichment education" is serving egocentric values. It's designed to help your kid compete, get ahead, crawl to the top of the heap, and be first in line for that all-important egocentric award, trophy, or winning school application. If it's possible now for your child to be a computer whiz at eight, it's tempting to think it would be even better if she could get there by five.

Let the two tasks of the Nest be your focus in the first four years, set aside technological education until the school years, and banish coerced learning forever.[33]

Although you can make your own choices about how many and what sorts of toys to buy or make for your kids, what about the toys that your well-intentioned friends or family members deliver? And what about the potentially traumatizing behaviors of egocentric members of your own extended family you can't so easily ban from your home? You might need to set some limits and boundaries with your friends and family.

TV, of course, is another major egocentric influence. Despite your soulcentric values, have you surrendered to the use of the electronic babysitter? Research shows that overuse of TV, computer, and other media negatively affects the brain development of children.[34]

If any of the above scenarios sound like yours, I can offer only a few compassionate and, I hope, helpful questions. Remember, I'm assuming you have soulcentric values whether you're in stage 3, 4, or 5. These questions might be hardest to answer if you are in stage 3, easiest in stage 5.

Are you and your spouse or partner working more hours than necessary for the economic necessities of a nurturing Nest? If you were to stop purchasing most of the consumer items and services that don't deeply serve you and your children, could you work less and spend more time with your family, especially during your kids' first four years? (Do you really *want* to?) Could you move to a home or region that is less expensive, more accessible to wild nature, and closer to other parents with small children?

Have you taken a close look at your core values? Are you clear about your highest priorities and deepest desires for your children's future?

Might there be some wounds from your own childhood, not yet sufficiently addressed, that make it difficult for you to open your heart more fully to your children?

Added to the above concerns, you'll need to help your stage-1 child form a healthy personality that can survive and thrive in an egocentric society. Toward the end of the Nest, and during part of the Garden, you'll want to teach your child how to cope with common egocentric fare such as out-of-control materialism, ubiquitous advertising, sexist and racist remarks and customs, and educational systems and teachers that might be far from progressive or ecoliterate. On the positive side, doing this will also be your initial step in helping your child form a personality that will become transcultural and, eventually, culture-transformative, as well as culturally viable. The soul-initiated person you hope your child becomes must, after all, develop a personality that can function in egocentric culture without being solely *of* it.

RE-EMBRACING INNOCENCE LATER IN LIFE

Having grown up in an egocentric society, one day we wake up, perhaps in our twenties, thirties, or quite a bit later, suddenly and painfully mindful that our innocence disappeared many years earlier. Is it possible to regain what has been lost?

I am certain it is. We can, in fact, revisit the incomplete tasks of *any* earlier stage. The peculiar thing about working on the tasks of the Nest, however, is that in early childhood we never consciously worked on them at all. (Our parents did — or didn't.) Now, later in life, we get to invite innocence consciously, which makes this task look a lot different than it did in early childhood. Then the goal was to preserve someone else's innocence — innocence that had not yet been lost. Now the opportunity is to reclaim or re-embrace for ourselves what has at least partially disappeared. Here are seven practices for doing this in the Oasis or later:

Meditation is a time-honored and cross-cultural method for re-embracing innocence. Innocence regained is experienced as radiant presence. Present-centeredness can be cultivated through the contemplative arts from any cultural tradition, including Christian contemplative prayer, Buddhist vipassana, the silence of Quaker meetings, or more physically active forms such as tai chi, qigong, and yoga.

In meditation, we practice fully inhabiting our experience right now just as it is. We practice nonattachment or nonclinging to particular memories or desires. To be nonattached to the past and future is to be here now. The more we practice, the better we get at it, and the more natural it is. The more present we become, the more our senses come alive — and our emotions and imagination, too. We occupy our lives, our loves, and our land more fully. We can wander more deeply into the world and are more likely to consciously encounter there the astounding mysteries of our own souls.

It should not be surprising that, in addition to its other benefits, meditation offers a path to rejuvenated innocence. Meditation, after all, is more generally understood as a means to cultivate our relationship to spirit or emptiness or the nondual. The portal to spirit resides in the East on the Wheel. Both the Nest and innocence also abide in the East. "Zen mind, beginner's mind." Think of meditation masters you have known or read about — overflowing with a certain freshness, an innocence, yes?

Another proven resuscitator of innocence is solitude in nature. I mean full-bodied, multisensory, openhearted time in the wild in which you offer your attention fully and reverently to the land, the waters, and the sky and all that is alive in those kingdoms. You might wander on foot or skis or in a self-propelled boat, or sit very still for extended periods. The important thing is a joyful mindfulness to the wild world. Solitude in nature offers the opportunity "to fall in love outward," as poet Robinson Jeffers puts it.[35] Falling in love outward is, in essence, a contemplative art, an ecocentric one. Think of it as a nature-based variation of vipassana, the Tibetan Buddhist meditation practice in which awareness is constantly opened to what is present here and now, without attachment to past or future. Mindfulness in nature adds to vipassana the fact that you are attending to the fullness of the wild world, making it easier to be utterly here, now. You don't need to be someplace as wild as Alaska or southern Utah to do this. A nearby forest, streamside, or thicket works wonders. A city park or your backyard might do.

A third approach is the creative art process. Immerse yourself, for an hour or two at a time, in any of the arts. Previous experience unnecessary. This is not about creating "works of art" for anyone's approval or admiration, including your own. It's about surrendering to what is immediately present — your art media and whatever impulses and feelings arise within you. Use familiar and unfamiliar media: drawing, painting, sculpting, collage, music, poetry, short stories, or dance. Drop each imagined goal as it arises and instead expand into being fully at home with yourself and the creative process. Apprentice yourself to your intuition. Let yourself be surprised by what color attracts you, or what sound, shape, emotion, texture, movement, image, or word. Say YES to it.[36]

Innocence can also be rejuvenated through the kinds of psychotherapies and therapeutic practices that emphasize present-centeredness. In Gestalt therapy, for instance, the individual is steadily encouraged to experience his or her own feelings and behaviors in the here and now. Excessive focus on the past (memories) or on the future (plans) is considered an escape from your life, because your life happens only in the present. Gestalt therapists insist that you express everything within your field of awareness and be in full relationship to that. Your past, future, or fantasies can be made present by dramatizing them, using gestures, postures, and speech.

Other therapies, too, offer exercises and practices for enhancing presence. These include psychosynthesis, existential therapy, focusing-oriented psychotherapy, sensory awareness, and the expressive arts therapies.

A fifth method for restoring innocence, one that you can use almost anytime and anywhere (but selectively), is to consciously enter social occasions as openly as you can. Drop expectations. Don't hang on to memories. Let go of desired outcomes. This, too, is a practice. The situation might be a committee meeting, a rendezvous with a friend or lover, a solo walk in a (safe enough) neighborhood, or a social gathering, a workshop, a museum. Practice being fully present. Let your senses come alive. Allow yourself to be utterly curious about everything. Grant yourself permission to be amused, saddened, horrified, ecstatic. Trust your own unknowing. Say and do whatever comes to mind — unless you are quite sure it'll get you into the kind of trouble you'd rather not be in. You might notice how, unintentionally, you begin to protect yourself physically, emotionally, or socially. If you can, let it go, relax. Practice innocent presence.

Yet another approach to re-embracing innocence is to get in the habit of reviewing your day to find one or two situations in which you *could* have been more innocent and present had you been more mindful. These are the moments that did not require the degree of vigilance and protectiveness you adopted. Imagine yourself re-entering those circumstances one at a time, this time entirely centered, open, and observant. Notice how the scene unfolds differently. Doing this review sensitizes your psyche to the possibility and blessing of innocence in your life. You rehearse the attitudes, moves, and faith implicit in full present-centeredness. The next day, you'll be more likely to recognize the opportunities for innocence as they occur.

My final suggestion is to hang out with infants! Why not sit at the feet of a master? When he's awake, let your little teacher (eighteen months or younger) lead the way in play. He'll show you how to be, as well as what to do. Get down on the carpet with him — just you and him. (If you are alienated from your innocence, you might feel ridiculous apprenticing to a baby while other people are watching you.) Let him teach you some games. When he falls asleep, you'll notice that he's no less a teacher of innocence. Take some deep breaths and immerse yourself in the miracle of his existence. Practice being present with his luminous presence — and yours. (For additional exercises for addressing the tasks of the Nest — or the Garden or Oasis — later in life, please visit www.natureandthehumansoul.com. The website also includes exercises that help you experience the qualities of each of the subsequent stages.)

What if we suddenly wake up and realize we were brought up egocentrically in an egocentric society? The good news is that healing, recovery, and deepening are fully available even for those of us whose early childhood went terribly wrong. We've just seen, for example, how, in the Oasis and beyond, we can restore our original in-nocence. And in the next chapter, we'll see what we can do if we missed out on one or more tasks of the Garden (middle childhood). As I suggested in chapter 1, addressing our developmental deficits — restoring our lost innocence, for example — may have considerably more benefits than attempting to directly suppress or eliminate disturbing symptoms such as tobacco or food cravings, insomnia, or a social phobia.

In addition to addressing our developmental deficits, we also have the opportu-nity to experientially explore our psychological wounds. Every one of these wounds, including those engendered by an egocentric family or culture, can serve as catalysts for our renaissance and soul discovery. Carl Jung was fond of reminding us that, to the soul, the wrong way is always the right way. As you'll see in the chapter on the Cocoon, our deepest wounds and our soul are intimately related. If we journey far enough into the inner landscapes of our wounds, we discover there the mysteries of destiny. So, too, in encountering our souls, we learn how our wounds are essential facilitators of our soul lives.

The important thing, but often the most difficult step in an egocentric society, is simply to wake up! If you're reading this book, more than likely something has already happened in your life to arouse you, whether in recent days or long ago. If there are sleepers in your life whom you love and who are beginning to stir, you might jostle them a bit. This book suggests some ways.

Once awakened, we begin to remember the call of the soul and the song of the world, and we suffer the immense grief and hope gifted by those revelations. Grounded there, we can re-root our lives in soul and nature.

WHEN DOES THE CHILD LEAVE THE NEST?
THE EMERGENCE OF A CONSCIOUS SELF

Having no conscious responsibilities at birth, the child begins life in a symbiotic re-lationship with his primary caregiver, usually his mom. During the first six to nine months of his life, the child has no sense of self or identity apart from her. His actions are limited to the reflexes provided him by evolution. Then, sometime in the second half of his first year, a self begins to emerge, a prototypal sense of an *I* that gradually separates from his mother. He can begin to distinguish *in here* from *out there, I* from *not-I.* He begins to treat his fingers as part of him; his mother's breast as not.

Most developmental psychologists, however, agree that a good deal more needs to happen before a child has acquired a truly conscious self. In particular, the child needs the ability to distinguish the self *as a self* from other selves, and also some early language skills. For example, at twelve months, the infant has an *I* but still no sense of a *me* — no recognition of himself as a being in the world, someone that other people can be aware of and interact with. When he looks in a mirror, he doesn't recognize the baby who looks back at him. He doesn't think something like "That's me!" He continues to act as if it's another child, until he reaches eighteen to twenty-four months or more. Not coincidentally, he also begins then to use rules to combine two or more words into primitive sentences. He begins to speak in a human way.

Still, most psychologists would say that a fully conscious self, an ego, doesn't emerge until later — not until the appearance of autobiographical memory, the child's ability to tell stories in which she includes herself as a character. Now she can say "I" and be conscious of what that means. Most commonly, this ability is first observed when a child is about four years old. At this point, language (and brain) development enables the child to do extraordinary and unprecedented things — she can tell you about events in her life, appreciate what a story is, and begin to narrate her own experiences. Consequently, most people's earliest memories come from this age. Before this, children don't have the language abilities needed to weave their experiences into what we normally call memory.

When autobiographical memory appears, the child has acquired a fully conscious sense of self. This miraculous milestone signals the completion of the Nest.

Although parents are always proud and pleased to see their children grow, there's also something terribly sad about the end of the Nest. This precious stage of innocence, of original spirit-connection, and of primal parent-child attachment is over and can never be recaptured. In many ways, the Nest was the best stage of life to be in.

CHAPTER FIVE

THE EXPLORER *in the* GARDEN

Middle Childhood (Stage 2)

In our grasshopper and salamander days, who among us didn't ask why the grasshopper could jump so far — or why the salamander had black dots on its orange body? We trampled leaves with our feet just to hear what kind of sounds leaves made. We threw flat stones over the surface of streams to see how far the stones could skip. We listened to crickets cry in nights far beyond our grasp of what the darkness was. We slept, only to wake, with the strange sense of how could we be awake when we had only just been sleeping.

In those days we knew as much as we had to know in order to ask what we didn't know. Our ignorance wasn't just innocence but the foundation from which we offered ourselves the daily surprise of discovering another question, another way to uncover something mysterious, something we hadn't understood yesterday. We lived by wonder, for by wondering we were able to multiply a growing consciousness of being alive.

— RICHARD LEWIS, *LIVING BY WONDER*

Stage 2: Middle Childhood

Passage into this stage: Naming (celebrates the psychological birth of the child
　　— the emergence of conscious self-awareness)
Stage name: The Garden
Tasks: Learning the givens of the world and our place in it (discovering the
　　enchantment of the natural world and learning cultural ways)
Quadrant: South (emotions and body)
Hemispheres: South and East (individual being)
Stage archetype: The Explorer
Quadrant archetype: The Orphan
Gift to community: Wonder
Circle of identity: Sociocentric
Center of gravity: Family and nature
Passage out of this stage: Puberty

OPENING TO NATURE AND HUMAN NATURE

A healthy childhood overflows with wonder and with spontaneous learning that occurs most anywhere. Everyday encounters with natural things — grasshoppers, leaves, stones, streams, other children, darkness, dreams — enthrall and usher the child into an intricate sphere of mystery and enchantment. Children extend the boundaries of their known world through their explorations, grounding their lives in the blooming, buzzing world around them. The simple innocence of the Nest endures, forming a life-long foundation, but now gives birth to a more advanced, resourceful, and inventive quality — the wonder and prolific imagination that is the hallmark of a healthy middle childhood. The undulating, turquoise sea becomes the frolicking play of a huge invisible creature. The wispy sky becomes the tall trees' laughter. The worm, the tickle and touch of the Earth itself.

My fondest and most enduring memories of my New England suburban childhood in the 1950s restore me to the sensuality and surprise of early explorations. First the backyard: the scent and color of the crabapple tree in spring, the warmth and worth of summer mud, the crunch and concealment of fall leaves, the cold and depth of snow. Then the farther adventures to the spooky rock ridge at the end of the lane and the woods beyond, followed a few years later by exhilarating expeditions into the deeper forest and wandering even further into the unknown. My friends and I messed around by untamed creeks and in an abandoned quarry, discovered the scent and texture of pine and maple and oak, and found places to hide and ways to move both stealthily and with abandon. Animals held infinite fascination: birds, squirrels, and frogs; my pet rabbits and my friend Joseph's falcon, with its sharp beak, talons, and eyes.

My favorite activities with friends and siblings revolved around making a home together in nature, learning to *be* at home in the greater world that we had inherited: the fort of stone, logs, and discarded lumber that we built in the forest, the endless snow tunnels of winter, and the meandering corridors we made in the tall, dry hide-and-seek grass of my grandparents' New Jersey farm.

Surrendering to the enchantment of nature is absolutely essential to childhood, self-discovery, and to all healthy maturation afterward, including the process of soul initiation. And yet, that enchantment is sadly what we have most neglected in the course of raising and educating our children.

A healthy childhood also overflows with emotions — joy, sadness, fear, guilt, hurt, anger, love — experienced fully in the body, often acknowledged and mirrored by caring adults, each emotion potentially yielding a treasure that helps form a particular young self, the beginnings of an authentic way of belonging to the world.

When I was six, I was elected treasurer of my first-grade class. After school, I rushed home and gushed my great news to my mother's back as she stood at the kitchen counter. There was kitchen noise, maybe water running in the sink. Not really hearing me or the elation and pride in my voice, she responded, "That's nice." Shocked and deflated, I turned and ran into the next room, crying. My father, home early from work, had heard the exchange, and quickly came over to hold me and offer congratulations. Then he called to my mother and told her what happened — both at school and in the kitchen. Joining us, she apologized for not hearing, hugged me, and told me how proud she was.

Although I was unaware of it at the time, there were many things about self and world that I took in and incorporated from that event. There was the pride of accomplishment, the danger of a snub and the emotional pain that results, the sweetness of recognition, the importance of timing when speaking to others, the warmth of belonging, the possibility of redemption — all these, from just one small incident, informing and shaping the texture and possibilities of a self and a world.

Emotions happen. They happen to children (adults, too!) nearly constantly and entirely naturally. Some are as simple and innocent as the above story, others considerably more complex and difficult. Either way, they are gifts. As we'll see in these pages, emotions are vital in growing a child into a particular self, a self sufficient to embrace the mysteries of the soul later in life.

What do these two opening themes — the great outdoors and the emotional fabric of human life — have in common? Simply this: they are both part and parcel of nature. Human nature (including our emotions) and more-than-human nature are foundational to the world we are born into, and a full opening into each is vital to growing whole.

At the southeast point on the Wheel, the child leaves the East quadrant and enters the South while remaining in both the East and South hemispheres. His life continues to be one of individual being (East hemisphere = being; South hemisphere = the individually focused life), as it was in the Nest and will remain through this second stage of childhood, the Garden. But there is nevertheless a major shift in his life as he moves from the East quadrant (innocence and spirit) to the South quadrant (emotions and body). More specifically, his psychospiritual center of gravity moves from the Nest realm of spirit to the Garden domain of family and nature. Now the hub around which his life circles is no longer the great mystery from which he came but the animated Earth and the verbal human clan to which he has been delivered.

There's no precise age at which the Garden begins, although most children make this transition in their fourth or fifth year (that is, at age three or four). The way to tell if a child has entered the Garden is not by her age or by her physical or cognitive development but by her psychospiritual center of gravity. In the Nest, there was not yet a fully formed ego distinct from spirit. The Garden begins as the child's life becomes less centered in spirit and more about her conscious relationships to nature and family.

NAMING: PASSAGE INTO EGO CONSCIOUSNESS

Between the end of the Nest and the onset of the Garden lies a transitional event of profound consequence: the dawning of a conscious self, the moment when a human being first apprehends the wondrous, terrible, and potent meaning of the word "I." I call this singular passage, associated with the southeast point on the Wheel, Naming (see Diagram 3-3, p. 61) in accordance with the practice, found in many cultures, of giving a child a new or additional name at this time.[1] Naming celebrates the psychological birth of the child, the achievement of a conscious social presence, an intact ego.[2] When a child is renamed at this turning point, he is further individualized. He is embraced by society in a new way and ceremonially celebrated by his family and clan and perhaps also by his neighborhood, school, or village.

In a soulcentric society or clan, this life transition is often marked by a rite of passage for the child and family.[3] Whether or not this transition coincides with a birthday, there might be a ritual bath for the child, a distinctive haircut, a new set of clothes that symbolizes his psychological arrival in the family, a special meal or community feast, or a first outing to a sacred or awe-inspiring place. The child might also be given a new or auxiliary name during this ceremony or, as might be more common in some cultures, *choose* a name or nickname.

What kinds of names do four- or five-year-olds choose? Mysterious ones. Playful ones. Alter-ego tags from myths, nature, fairy tales, or other stories. Archetypal names. Sometimes names that seem to refer to past lives.

If his family gives the child a name at this time, it is likely to be nature-based. It might be one that embraces something of the natural world to which the child has been strongly drawn, or an animal that has been drawn to her, or nature elements that reflect her emerging personal qualities. One family I know nicknamed their four-year-old daughter Otter Girl because of her love for water and her playfulness. Or the child might be given a name of a totem animal that embodies her link with nature and that will accompany her as an ally through life.

Whether chosen or given, in some cases these names will rarely if ever be spoken by others, perhaps only during ceremonial occasions. In other cases, the new name will suddenly or gradually become the child's everyday tag, at least until puberty, or will perhaps last a lifetime.

However embodied, a Naming rite formally welcomes a new, psychologically present individual into the family and community.

Parents might take special care to note their children's dreams around the time of Naming, age three to five. "Big dreams" often arrive at this crossroads as the child emerges from the nightworld of spirit into the dayworld of society. A big dream is one with deeply mysterious and transpersonal themes, a dream that portends something of the child's destiny. It's as if the Mystery seizes this opportunity, the dawning of ego consciousness, to outfit the child with something like a guidebook for his deeper life. Carl Jung, for example, had (and remembered) at that age a life-informing dream of descending to an underground chamber and encountering there a holy and terrifying presence. I, too, had the great fortune to remember a dream from that time in my life, a dream of entering a cemetery and descending into a crypt where sacred rites were taking place.

The passage of Naming is a unique moment in the child's life. If a big dream had arrived earlier, the child might not have noticed it or been able to report or remember it. On the other hand, if it were to come later, his ego might already be too oriented toward the cultural world to be able to receive it or retain it. There is inestimable value for the soul life in recording these dreams and saving them for in-depth dreamwork in stage 4 (the Cocoon) and beyond.

THE GARDEN

With her newly wakened conscious self-awareness, the child begins to earnestly and energetically flesh out her world, in effect creating a world by exploring it, interacting with it, and discovering the other beings who coinhabit it. In middle childhood, she finds nature and culture to be equally fascinating. The world for her is a garden — both cultivated (shaped by culture) and wild (self-arising from nature). The Garden is an enchanted place in which she learns both the marvels that spring out of the world on their own (nature, the givens of life) and what she herself is capable of doing with them (cultivation). In this stage, she stays relatively close to home, both physically and psychologically. The Garden is a place and time of comparative safety and warmth. Like a springtime garden, the child herself is sprouting and growing in so many ways.

Sometimes frightening, sometimes comforting, the world as Garden is always a place of wonder. The healthy child *exists* in a state of wonderment. Through her explorations, she constructs a self, clothing herself in her discoveries. She is a natural creation of her world, but she is also, simultaneously, a cocreator of it, a being who both reflects upon her world and is reflected by it. The child and the world interact to create a "being-in-the-world," a term coined in the early 1900s by the German philosopher Martin Heidegger, implying that each person generates and defines a somewhat distinct world. It is an interaction, a relationship. Although each of us is as unique as our relationship with the world, we are similar to the extent that we share language, culture, and experience.

The paramount task in the Garden is to become a full member of one's family and of the natural world.

THE EXPLORER:
ARCHETYPE OF MIDDLE CHILDHOOD

The two archetypes associated with the Garden are the Explorer and the Orphan.[4] The Explorer is specific to this second stage of life, while the Orphan encompasses both the second and third (and thus the entire South quadrant of the Wheel). (See Diagram 3-4, p. 68.)

In the Garden, the child is a wide-eyed researcher, an incessant questioner of everything from the color of grass and sky and the twinkling of stars to the properties of magnifying glasses and magnets, from the flight of butterflies and the power of lions to the meaning of kisses and touchdowns. He is gathering his world. Whatever he does, exploration is at the center of his activities, whether he is at home, at school, playing outside, alone or with friends, attending a social event, or accompanying a parent to work. He is a learner, student, novice, a disciple of the wondrous and marvelous — in essence, an Explorer.

One of the ways the Explorer investigates his world is by altering his consciousness, his perspective on the world. He does this by, for example, spinning until he gets dizzy and falls, rolling down hills, hanging from a tree upside down, or deliberately surprising himself, scaring himself, or getting a bit lost. He wants to see the world from as many perspectives as he can. He is, by nature, inclined to explore the unknown, experiment with equilibrium changes, and face his fears.

These are precisely the sorts of things we'll continue to do in more elaborate ways when older — if, that is, we grow soulcentrically. By the same token, these are the very things our egocentric society teaches us to resist as "adults."[5]

The reason the Explorer archetype appears on the Wheel as we first enter the South quadrant, the midmorning of the Wheel, is because this is when the Sun begins its time of greatest brightness and warmth, the time when we are most fully and securely invited out to explore the world.

Of course, we might be Explorers later in life, whether on the high seas, in outer space, inner space, the boardroom, or our own backyard, but even the most accomplished of adult explorers can't rival *any* child in her degree of curiosity, persistence, purity, clarity of observation, or delight. A healthy adult always has a quality of the Explorer about him, but only the child enjoys a primary resonance with this archetype.

The Explorer archetype constellates what is exciting, engaging, and inspiring about middle childhood. The Orphan archetype, in contrast, reminds us of what is difficult and beneficially challenging about our youth (both middle childhood and early adolescence).

THE ORPHAN: ARCHETYPE OF THE SOUTH

Most of us were not literally orphaned, but all of us experienced, quite early in life, psychological abandonments — those moments of realizing we must fend for ourselves emotionally, socially, or physically. These abandonments, these unavoidable cataclysms of childhood, take place even within the healthiest and most fortunate of families.

It might seem odd at first for the Orphan to be designated the archetype for this family-based quarter of life, but the Explorer, on an existential level, is now in fact orphaned from his original home, from spirit, from his original paradise of innocence. All archetypes function in a subterranean realm of the human psyche as well as in our surface lives. The *quadrant* archetypes — each covering a full quarter of the life cycle — operate primarily on the deeper levels. The wider the influence, the deeper the source.

While most children are warmly enveloped within a loving family, they experience themselves, in another sense, as alone in the world — and in a manner they did not encounter in the Nest. What five-year-old child has not recognized that nobody can perfectly protect him from pain, embarrassment, fear, loss, or illness? The Explorer must begin to make his own way in the world despite the love and shelter provided by both family and nature.

The Orphan archetype begins to take hold of our lives the first time we feel let down by caregivers who have been less than perfect in their caregiving. At that moment, we feel forsaken. This experience of abandonment is a catalyst, perhaps an indispensable one, for the full emergence of the ego.

This is one of our first conscious experiences in life: being split off, tossed out of the Innocent's paradise, suddenly separated and needing to make independent decisions for our own welfare. The ego is launched not only *when* we first experience our separateness but also *because* of it. Aghast, we realize one day that we understand some of our needs better than our caregiver, a shocking revelation even when triggered by a minor disappointment. Despite intimate bonds with others, we recognize that we are independent beings, that on some level we are fundamentally alone in the world. Orphaned.

I remember, at age four, standing in the dining room with my mother, who, at five feet, one inch, towered far above me. As I looked up to find her face, I could see the underside of the table, how the dull unfinished wood there contrasted with the lacquered surface of the edging. I was asking for something — I don't remember what, but my sense now is that it was nothing unusual for a child to be asking, perhaps for food or a toy. She responded, but not in the way I had hoped. I asked again, perhaps rephrasing my request in an ardent attempt to get her to understand. Still clinging to the utter innocence of the Nest, I believed that my need should automatically lead to my gratification. She responded as before. A flush of panic or dislocation passed through me. My knees weakened. My stomach clenched. I felt my face beginning to contort into a cry but then it froze as a terrible and previously unthinkable realization arrived: There was something I knew about myself — what I required or desired — about which she had no clue. She misunderstood me and so could not help. Confronted with the incontrovertible fact of my aloneness, I was forever cast from her sphere of absolute safety and compelled to begin to fend for myself.

Following that moment, I knew more fully than before what the utterance "Billy" implied. That was the day I first lived and breathed the archetype of the Orphan.

As you can see, my fall from original innocence was rather innocent. For others, the watershed event at age four or five is a good deal more traumatic. For one child, the moment might arrive with the birth of a younger sibling and his parents' consequent shift in attention. Or, more traumatic yet, the onset of a child's psychological orphanhood might be triggered by her parents' divorce, the death of her mother or older brother, or the indelible wound of molestation.

As middle childhood unfolds, the inevitable disappointments and hurts will continue; but from a soulcentric perspective, some of these wounds are both inevitable and necessary as catalysts for maturation. They constitute an essential element that impels the soul search later undertaken in the West quadrant of the Wheel.

These traumas constitute one locus of the sacred wound that each of us will explore and partially heal during late adolescence and adulthood as part of the process of soul initiation and beyond. Among other benefits, our sacred wounds help us develop the powers and sensitivities that support our embodiment of soul. It is said, for example, that all parents, no matter how loving and skillful, inevitably wound their children. One might even think of it as a parental obligation. This is not to condone abusive acts or real neglect, travesties all too common in egocentric societies. Yet even in the healthiest families, children are orphaned by emotional woundings, although mostly unintentionally.

In the course of these woundings, the child learns to express her emotions. She learns to distinguish between people and circumstances that are trustworthy and safe enough and those that are not. Accepting her Orphanhood, she learns how to survive, if not thrive, in the world, usually with the help of family members, teachers, and other community allies.

The South quadrant is the province of the Orphan because the child, orphaned from the Nest, requires the safety and warmth of midday (South) in order to survive and grow at all. Human development from Naming through early adolescence — the Garden and Oasis — takes place in the relatively tranquil, sheltered, and day-lit zones of nature and society, like summer plants enjoying maximum growth beneath the Sun. In the South, we are no longer the newly sprouted seed of the East or of spring, but neither are we yet the fruit-bearing plant of the West or of autumn.

THE EXPLORER'S CONTRIBUTION
TO THE WORLD: WONDER

In a soulcentric approach to child development, the primary task of parents and teachers is to raise children who will grow into soul-rooted (initiated) adults, people who have discovered the gifts they were born to bring to the world. But during childhood the primary value of a child is not that she might become an initiated adult someday. Every child *as a child* contributes many precious qualities to her family, to her playmates, to her school, and to her more-than-human world. These qualities supplement and often surpass the important social roles the child fills, such as caring for younger children, pets, or farm animals, or working in the garden or kitchen.

The single greatest contribution that Explorers, as a "genus," bestow upon the world, just by existing, is, of course, the gift of wonder. There is no time in life, before or after, that brims more fully and naturally with amazement and awe. Within the orbit of a healthy child, an adult cannot help being caught up in the natural exuberance and thrill of discovery within which that child lives and breathes. She exudes wonderment in her fresh and provocative questions, in her wide eyes and open ears, in her ability to derive the greatest delight from the smallest or most subtle of phenomena, and in her constant readiness to celebrate discoveries with creative play, leaps of joy, shouts of exultation, and paroxysms of giggles. Surely, the world would not be so wondrous for the rest of us without the presence of imaginatively and emotionally healthy Explorers.

THE DEVELOPMENTAL TASKS OF THE GARDEN

In the previous stage, the Nest, the developmental task was not the child's at all, but the parents'. In the Garden, children still need a great deal of developmental help from parents, teachers, and other adults. In the post-Garden stage, the Oasis, the adolescent will need relatively little help from her parents. In the Cocoon and beyond, the parents' help will no longer be needed in any ordinary or everyday manner and might not even be possible.

The child's primary task in the Garden is to *explore and learn the givens of the world and his or her place in it*. For the young child, nearly everything is a given: all of nature and all of human culture, and the relationship between the two. The Explorer does not get to choose his parents or siblings, the shape of society, the traditions of his family, or the form and forces of Earth and the boundless universe.[6] Rather, these are the given actualities of the world, to be explored and marveled at, sometimes suffered and endured, and which constantly spark the young imagination and sense of wonder. For the most part, the child utterly delights in discovering these actualities and how he fits in among them. He needs to learn about his world in order to live in it. His natural desire is to make a home both in culture (primarily family, in this stage) and in nature, and so become a member of both, a true inhabitant of his world.

The most poorly adjusted children (and the adolescents and "adults" they become) are the ones who are at home in *neither* nature nor culture. These are the kids who remain Orphans for life, forever stuck in the lesser dynamics of that archetype — destitute, isolated, lost, wary, unfriended, homeless. It might be impossible for us to succeed at the challenges and tasks that will come in adolescence without first having established in childhood a solid sense of belonging to the world, of having a true home in our family, in our community, on the land, and in the cosmos as revealed to us by the Sun, the Moon, and the night sky.

A person at home only in culture will feel like prey or an alien when in wild places, at best a visitor. He is unlikely to uncover the depths of his own inner nature, the wilds of his own soul. And a person at home in nature but not among people will feel like a stranger in a strange land when among his fellow humans, unable to embody his creative, soul-infused self in society.

Exploring and learning the givens of the world and our place in it includes two subtasks: (1) discovering the enchantment of nature, and (2) learning the social practices, values, knowledge, history, mythology, and cosmology of our family and culture. These two subtasks share a common purpose: to enable the child to belong to the world as he finds it.

Despite their common purpose, there is an intrinsic tension between the nature and culture subtasks. Soulcentric parents want their child to be fully at home in both nature and culture. Most children want this, too. But the more the child emphasizes one realm, the less he might succeed in the other. Soulcentric parents and teachers must strike a healthy balance and help children do the same. Obviously, in contemporary egocentric society the mix has swung way too far toward the culture pole.

In reading the remainder of this chapter and the next, it will help if you keep in mind that, from a soulcentric perspective, the primary developmental goal in parenting is not raising happy, well-rounded, well-educated, physically sound children. We all want this, but there is a greater goal that reframes all other child-rearing intentions, and which actually enhances the chance of raising happy children. That greater goal is to *maintain the vitality of the culture*, which sometimes means, as it does now, to thoroughly transform the culture — and to do so in part by raising children who have the potential to become soul-initiated adults, people who will remake our world through their mature, embodied creativity.

Discovering the Enchantment of Nature: Wild Nature

By *nature*, I mean both our own human nature and the nature of mountains, meadowlarks, and the Moon. Humans, all of us, regardless of race or culture, are indigenous expressions of the natural world. We have our own instinctive and given nature as much as any bear or galaxy does. Three core aspects of our human nature are our bodies, our imaginations, and our emotions.

But first let's consider the other-than-human nature of the wild world — the original matrix that gave birth to our species — and the essential catalysts it provides for the healthy development of every human child.

INTIMATE CONTACT WITH THE WILD WORLD. At the outset of the Garden stage, the child is newly and keenly aware of herself as a separate person, an individual with a name, a gender, a membership within a particular family, a home, and a neighborhood. If her parents allow it, much of her attention now flows naturally toward the world outside her home, with its treasures, dangers, and exotic possibilities. She is fascinated by the more-than-human world of wild places, animals, plants, and the night sky. This is, after all, the world that she finds — or, at least, *used* to find — right outside her house, hogan, or yurt. It is membership in the greater world of nature that she discovers to be the other half of her birthright beyond family, school, and market. Given the chance, this child will take every opportunity to explore the backyard, the nearby woods and thickets, the ditch or creek, the prairie, the hill, or the beach, and the manifold forms and forces of nature she finds on her journeys. And she will, of course, have numberless questions about the sky, the Sun and the Moon, the stars, and the planets.

The child's need is not merely to be out-of-doors but to be immersed in nature and among other-than-human beings — sometimes alone, sometimes with peers, and sometimes with adults. Outdoor sports or a forced march to a predetermined destination — a lake or a summit — are not the same as spontaneous and unsupervised play in nature. Intimate contact with the wild world is essential to her development.

Many have written about the universal need for children to freely explore the natural world. For example, educator, parent, and deep ecologist Dolores LaChapelle writes, "The child must play outdoors as much as possible.... The best play places are similar to what humans have always preferred since we were primates newly out of the trees. Places to hide, safely, and look out at others, places to climb, simple natural items to make things out of — rocks, sticks, dirt, mud. At the same time the child needs to see nonhuman beings: animals, trees, mountains, rivers."[7]

"THE MYSTERY OF KINSHIP: LIKENESS BUT DIFFERENCE." Offering a model of healthy development in nature-based societies, ecologist Paul Shepard notes that, at the commencement of middle childhood, the child goes out to play on the fringes of the human zone:

> Play is an imitation, starting with simple fleeing and catching, going on to mimic joyfully the important animals, being them for a moment and then not being them, feeling as this one must feel and then that one, all tried on the self. The child sees the adults dancing the animal movements and does it too. Music itself has been there all the time, from his mother's song to the melodies of birds and the howls of wolves. The child already feels the mystery of kinship: likeness but difference.[8]

Through his interactions with wild nature, the child is granted the widest and deepest trove of resources with which to flesh out a self. Unself-consciously, he discovers some of his own possibilities in the animals: the grace and stealth of cat, the cunning of fox, the lighthearted spirit of butterfly, the rowdiness of coyote, the fluid grace of trout, the power and roar of bear, the joy and song of wren. He catches glimpses of his possible self in the rootedness, open arms, and tall-standing nature of tree, the beauty and delicacy of flower, the solidity and patience of rock, the enfolding of snow, the Sun's warm countenance, the shape-shifting of clouds, and the hope and endurance of stars.

Eco-philosopher and Earth elder Joanna Macy opens her memoir with a reminiscence of her childhood summer days in the 1930s on her grandfather's farm in upstate New York. The very first being we meet in her book, even before Joanna herself, is a tree — a maple that stood in front of her grandparent's house and into whose branches she climbed regularly. She writes of this maple in tones of tender reverence, gratitude, and mystery. Clearly the tree provided a grounding presence and place from which Joanna greeted the world and the world made itself known to her.

Did the maple mirror to Joanna her own core qualities? Did it introduce her to an authentic way to be in the world? Here's her description of the maple: "Tall and graceful. She did not live in a cluster of her own kind, as the fruit trees did; she seemed more self-reliant and self-contained. . . . She held her stillness and mystery right in the midst of things."[9]

When Joanna was high in the maple, she "entered a solitude that was more than my own. It was a protected solitude. . . . Here one single, living being was holding me." In the maple, she drifted into nonordinary consciousness, a nature-mystic experience, an I-thou communion with a nonhuman other, which is profoundly beneficial and surprisingly common for children granted times of solitude in nature.

> I only went there alone. It was a place to be quiet, a place to disappear into a kind of shared presence, the being that was tree and me, with the light coming through. The light is what I remember most of all; high and wide around me, it shaped a luminous, breathing bowl. It danced through the leaves, glowing them green and gold. It stroked the limbs with flickering shadows. When I sat very quiet, the play of light seemed to go right through my body, and my breath was part of the maple's murmuring. . . . She let me glimpse a wild serenity at the heart of my world.[10]

In passages like this one, Joanna's memoir offers us a rare and intimate record of a contemporary soulcentric life — from early in the Garden all the way through the Wild Orchard (stage 6). In each of the next four chapters, we'll visit a strand or two of her life story as it exemplifies soulcentric human development. Then, the chapter on the Grove (stage 7) features excerpts from my 2006 interview with Joanna in which she muses upon her experience of elderhood. Joanna's biography exquisitely illustrates how contemporary lives *can* unfold soulcentrically despite an egocentric cultural milieu, and even without an explicit personal focus on questions of soul or the underworld.

NATURE-DEFICIT DISORDER. Until recent history, most children grew up with intimate contact with nature, the kind that Joanna describes, an experiential grounding in the green world essential for physical, intellectual, emotional, and spiritual development. But in industrialized societies, this has become increasingly rare in the past thirty-five years. In our current culture of fear, most children are virtually imprisoned indoors.

In *Last Child in the Woods*, Richard Louv identifies several societal trends that in "countless [American] communities have virtually outlawed unstructured outdoor nature play."[11] These include "overdevelopment, multiplying park rules, well-meaning (and usually necessary) environmental regulations, building regulations, community covenants, and fear of litigation," with the result "that organized sports on manicured playing fields is the only officially sanctioned form of outdoor recreation."[12]

In recent years, researchers have documented the direct relationship between lack of contact with nature and some of the most disturbing symptoms, difficulties, and pathologies of childhood. Louv coined the phrase "nature-deficit disorder" to summarize what loss of nature does to children, including a dulling of the senses, obesity, attention deficit/hyperactivity disorder (ADHD), depression, and the attendant prescriptions of Ritalin and antidepressants. "Nature-deficit disorder is not a medical condition; it is a description of the human costs of alienation from nature. This alienation damages children and shapes adults, families, and communities."[13] The absence of free play in nature also breeds lifelong apathy toward the environment and ecological harm, so that, ultimately, loss of nature contact results in loss of nature. The innate tendency that humans have toward biophilia is replaced by alienation and biophobia.

However, on the positive side, research shows that regular free play in nature results in better concentration in ADHD children;[14] better coordination, balance and agility, and less illness;[15] more imaginative and creative play, which fosters language and collaborative skills;[16] improved problem solving, critical thinking, and decision making, and greater awareness, reasoning, and observational skills;[17] a reduction in the impact of life stress and better coping with adversity;[18] reduced antisocial behaviors such as violence, bullying, vandalism, and littering;[19] greater powers of observation and creativity; an enhanced sense of peace and being at one with the world;[20] and more positive feelings about playmates.[21] Instead of plying our children with amphetamines, other stimulants, and antidepressants, we could instead truly nurture them by encouraging free play in nature (along with less television, computer use, and video games and with more of the other forms of guidance and experience described in this and the preceding chapter). As Louv notes,

> If it is true that nature therapy reduces the symptoms of ADHD, then the converse may also be true: ADHD may be a set of symptoms aggravated by lack of exposure to nature. By this line of thinking, ... the real disorder is less in the child than it is in the imposed, artificial environment. Viewed from this angle, the society that has disengaged the child from nature is most certainly disordered, if well-meaning. To take nature and natural play away from children may be tantamount to withholding oxygen.[22]

EMPATHIC AND IMAGINATIVE NATURE PLAY. David Sobel, an educator, parent, and author, suggests that empathy between the child and the natural world should be a main objective for children aged four through seven (that is, those in the first half of the Garden).[23] He advises parents and teachers to encourage emotional responses to the animals and plant life that children discover in the natural world. Children, for example, are naturally drawn to baby animals. The sense of connectedness that develops during empathic interactions with animals builds an emotional foundation for the child's sense of belonging to the world, as well as for his later (mostly stage-3) study of botany, zoology, and ecology. When given the chance, children naturally form deep relationships with animals, experiences that enhance the development of selfhood, empathy, affiliation, and morality with respect to both animals and humans.

It is easy and enjoyable for parents and teachers to encourage and facilitate a heartfelt and hands-on form of nature education. Adults can share with children stories and songs about natural landscapes, weather, and animals, both real and imagined. Adults and children can move together like animals — run like deer or slither along the ground like snakes. They can celebrate the seasons with simple ceremonies and time enjoyed together outside. There is great pleasure in sharing with children the enchantment that the world unceasingly affords.

Long walks in nature provide some of the best parent-child interactions during middle childhood. Let the child set the pace and stop when she stops. Wander and wonder together, admire and explore. It's probably best not to volunteer information, but do answer her questions in a way that evokes further wonder — and ask her imaginative questions of your own.

Free play in nature fosters the imagination of the child, possibly the single most important dimension of growth in the Garden. Parents and teachers can encourage imaginative play not only by providing a variety of natural materials for children to explore and handle but also by suggesting that children take on the roles of other creatures. With a little encouragement and a few simple props, young children love pretending to be something else. While children often assume familiar human roles (for example, parent, teacher, firefighter, police officer), they also enjoy imitating animals they've seen or heard about. This dramatic play should usually be child-initiated and unsupervised, but caregivers can occasionally add richness by providing costumes or materials to make dens, cocoons, or nests. Adults might also suggest that children act out natural phenomena such as migration, hibernation, or metamorphosis.

If a child has spent too much of her young life indoors with books, computers, and other artifacts of modern society, her parents and teachers might need to coach her on how to see and hear natural things, how to feel their textures, and how to sense their dimensions and relationships with other things. Parents and teachers who aren't experienced with this themselves might seek out others who can help bring alive *their* senses and ecological awareness.[24]

David Sobel recommends that, during the second half of the Garden stage (approximately ages seven through eleven), the educational goal shift from empathy to a more far-ranging exploration of nature. The child's world now expands from the home and backyard into the larger neighborhood and community, and then into the region and beyond. The child's desired activities naturally turn to "making forts, creating small imaginary worlds, hunting and gathering, searching for treasures, following streams and pathways, exploring the landscape, taking care of animals, gardening, and shaping the earth."[25]

Do you remember your special places from childhood, your hiding-and-observing thicket, your secret alcove where you met with friends? Even the most urban childhood includes favorite habitats: little houses of blankets, a corner in a closet, a hedge, your own tree in a park, or that hidden niche behind a boulder. Children from more rural families have tree houses, a cubbyhole in an old outbuilding or abandoned farmhouse, haylofts, a miniature magical meadow, a hollowed-out tree trunk, or a little fort or cave in the woods. Regular visits to these special places allow a child to belong to the world in his own way, especially to the more-than-human world that mirrors his wildest possibilities, and to learn what it is to create a place of his own, an endeavor that takes on much wider and deeper significance later in life.

DREAMS, NATURE PLAY, AND SOUL. Special places of wonder also appear in your dreams — both your childhood dreams and those from more recent times. Can you remember that magical house or village or forest that you often visited in your dreams, where you felt so at home? Perhaps you found a secret room, meadow, trail, or hallway there. These are the wonderlands, never-never lands, and Narnias of your own childhood and nightworld.

As a human of any age, you have the natural desire to belong to the dreamworld of your own possibilities — your destiny — just as much as you want to belong to the dayworld places of home, school, neighborhood, park, forest, river, and canyon. The soul — through your dreams and your fascination with the wild world — is constantly nudging you to cross borders and step beyond your routine way of being in ordinary locales. It is best, and easiest, if this begins in childhood. By exploring the wild places outdoors and in dreams, children create the emotional and imaginative foundations for their later soul-rooted lives.

Parents and teachers can rouse and quicken the full rainbow spectrum of children's personalities and potentials by providing ample opportunity for the exercise of young bodies and imaginations in more-than-human places of diversity and wonder. Without an empathic and expansive bond with nature in childhood, or remedially, later in life, we end up handicapped when it comes time to encounter the mysteries of the soul.

FROM NATURE-AVERSION TO CARING FOR LIFE. Some Western children, however, seem to steer clear of wild nature — the boy who prefers the computer to camping, or the girl who refuses to get dirt under her nails. How should their parents and teachers think about their developmental needs in relation to wildness? The child who shows no interest in nature might be a child whose natural fascination has been suppressed by her early upbringing or by trauma. This child's fears need to be explored, her safety enhanced, and her natural interest in nature encouraged.

Other children are simply more oriented to the mind than to the body. They can be encouraged to begin their exploration of nature by taking a more intellectual approach: taxonomy, phenology, zoology, or astronomy. Walk out the door with them and explore the different birds, tree barks, or geological formations. Buy or borrow a telescope and learn the names, locations, colors, and cosmic stories of the planets, stars, and galaxies. Fastidious girls might be entranced by the beauty and scent of flowers. Once outside, when their wonder is let loose, their imagination and natural curiosity will blossom. With some children, you might begin by gardening, going to natural history museums, or drawing and painting flowers that the two of you gather and bring home.

The natural world in most places is mostly benign and always wondrous. But like life more generally, nature also has plenty of harmful things — stinging nettles and bees, poison ivy, cliffs, slippery slopes, and potentially fatal cold and heat. Time in nature, therefore, is also a child's opportunity, with adult instruction, to learn skills of self-care, discrimination, and broadband attentiveness.

The outdoors is also the place to learn to care for the "others," the other-than-human creatures and places — the butterfly, the birch, and the beach. The natural world, alive with so many beings in the plant, animal, and mineral communities, affords the child's best opportunity to widen and deepen her respect and care for life, for difference, for diversity.[26]

EXPERIENTIAL GREEN EDUCATION. Parents and teachers throughout the Western world and beyond are increasingly recognizing the need to raise a new generation of environmentally sensitive citizens. Significant strides are being made in "green" education, or ecoliteracy. David Sobel offers a wise approach for middle childhood.[27] He advocates the adoption of age-specific environmental curricula so that the educational content corresponds to the child's intellectual and emotional development.

In primary education, for example, Sobel advises teachers to avoid utilizing concepts and images of environmental degradation such as tropical deforestation and global warming. Exposing stage-2 children to such realities may cause them to fear the natural world rather than explore it joyfully. Expecting children to deal with global problems before they develop an experiential bond with nature in their own backyards and neighborhoods is counterproductive to the long-term goals of environmental education. "If we want children to flourish, to become truly empowered," writes Sobel, "then let us allow them to love the earth before we ask them to save it."[28]

Every child needs adults who can help him experience his full membership in the natural world so that he knows instinctively that he fully belongs here and that he is as wild as any animal, wildflower, or cloud. Nature must become (or remain) the child's friend, ally, and teacher — his home — as opposed to a threatening place full of hostile aliens. The healthiest, most unconditionally accepting family is not enough to enable the child to feel at home in the world. A deep-rooted sense of belonging-in-nature may even go a long way in making up for family dysfunction or a lack of social acceptance among peers. I have known many adolescents and adults whose psychological and social survival were made possible only by their extensive childhood time in wild places.

AN ECSTATIC INVOLVEMENT WITH THE UNIVERSE. The wild world, of course, extends far beyond the forests, rivers, and mountains of Earth; it stretches infinitely to the great mysteries of the farthest galaxies. Brian Swimme, cosmologist and author of *The Hidden Heart of the Cosmos*, reminds us of the utter importance of introducing children to their membership, not only in family and tribe, land and waters, but also in the unfathomably immense universe — the Moon, Sun, our solar system, our Milky Way galaxy teeming with billions of stars, each with its own solar system, and the greater wilderness beyond with a trillion of such galaxies, all flying away from each other at unimaginable speeds.

An essential component of the child's discovery of enchanted nature is learning the meaning of the universe and our place, as humans, in it. If the most pressing task of our times is the integration of our lives with the life of the planet, as Swimme suggests, then in childhood we must learn to live in our solar system as well as in our family system and our school system. We must initiate our children into an ecstatic involvement with the universe and the story of its unfolding. (I'll return to this theme later in discussing children's study of cosmology.)

SEEING NATURE FOR THE FIRST TIME: LIFTING THE VEIL. On the first day of the soulcraft programs I guide for adults, many people confess that they have never bonded with the natural world, that indeed they tend to experience wilderness as dangerous, rife with menacing animals and treacherous terrain. By the end of the program, however, most people have a remarkably shifted perspective.

One man in his midforties, an East Coast organizational consultant, vision-fasted with us among the high peaks of Colorado. He returned to base camp with a new light in his eyes, saying that a perceptual veil had lifted. He told us how he had begun to truly see nature for the first time, observing things (animals, flowers, creeks) and qualities (wildness, fragility, resilience) and relationships (prey-predator, symbiosis, decaying life feeding new life) that were in plain sight but which he had never before noticed. He hadn't known the veil was there until it lifted. On the final night of his fast, he had a dream: He is sitting on a porch holding a small boy. The man is pointing outside to the teeming and alluring world and telling the boy that the two of them would be exploring all of it... together. He is filled with elation and excitement.

Many people, especially those from urban centers, did not have even a single nature-bonding experience in childhood. But it is never too late to establish a personal, visceral relationship with the more-than-human world. In addition to inviting our children into wild places, we must remember, like the man who lifted the veil, to take ourselves there, too.

"IF WE LOSE THE FOREST, WE LOSE OUR SOULS." Thomas Berry elo-
quently articulates the essential relationship between childhood nature-exploration and
soulcentric development:

> Rather than instructing our children in biblical studies, their time would be
> better spent for the most part experiencing things of the natural world. Here
> in California, we discuss the question of cutting the old growth of the forest.
> We argue about the jobs issue, we argue about the rights of the owners. But
> the real problem is neither of those. The real problem is that if we lose the for-
> est, we lose our souls. If we lose the singing of the birds, we lose our souls. If
> we can no longer see the stars because of the artificial light of our cities, our
> children lose their souls; they lose their imagination. They're deprived of an
> inner development. It's not taking away from a higher vision; it's giving
> them a higher vision. So that this bonding of the child with the natural world
> is the finest thing we can do. If we devastate or distort the natural world, to
> that extent our inner world is distorted because our inner world is determined
> by our outer experience. What the child experiences, what we experience out-
> wardly, shapes our inner being.[29]

Thomas is one of our many cultural leaders currently illuminating how the outer
and inner worlds reflect each other and how nature, soul, imagination, and creative human vision are interwoven. The spontaneous interpenetration of psyche and nature
throughout childhood, when allowed, begets a healthy, ecocentric, soul-filled human.

Discovering the Enchantment of Nature: Human Nature

Nature can be defined as all that exists independently of human obstruction or invention, each thing according to its own spontaneities. In this sense, nature includes, of
course, most everything the child encounters in field and forest, but it also encompasses
much of what the child discovers to be *himself*, namely his body, his imagination, and
his emotions. In other words, the enchanted nature explored in the Garden includes
human nature — all that we discover ourselves to be without our having consciously
intended it to be that way, the "me" prior to, or independent of, our choices. We don't
choose our bodies — their general size, color, gender, race, basic capacities, constitu-
tional vitality, or disease proneness. We don't choose our deep imaginations — our
dreams, our waking imagery arising from subconscious springs, or our intuitions, visions, and revelations. And we don't, as a rule, choose our emotions. Bodies, deep imaginations, and emotions all "happen."

BODY. It's only natural for a child to explore — with head and hands and heart —
the organism through which his being is embodied: How does this body work anyway?
What's this part for? What does it mean when my skin turns red, or blue, or my nose

runs, or my stomach aches, or that it feels good when I move in this way? Why do my hair and nails grow? Why does my face look like my mother's but my body like my father's? Why does my body change the way it does as I get older? How and why is my boy's body different from girls' or from some other boys'? Why does it hurt when I do this? How do I enhance my strength, flexibility, balance, or coordination?

The body is an essential realm of the enchanted world. Its thorough exploration, befriending, and celebration with the child's own hands, eyes, nose, ears, tongue, thought, emotions, imagination, and movement is natural and essential for healthy development, and ought to be encouraged by parents and teachers.

For children in this stage, the honoring of their bodies can be assisted through stretching or yoga, education in self- and other-massage, eurythmics (or other neuromuscular coordination exercises), and healthy eating habits; team sports, dance, martial arts, tai chi, swimming, running, bicycling, hiking, backpacking, skiing, and so on; and basic information in anatomy, physiology, biology, and individual differences in body shapes and sizes.

IMAGINATION. It is natural and essential for the child to fully engage and enjoy her imagination, a most fundamental resource for exploring the world and the self. Through her imagination, the child can ask and answer questions such as: What are the different ways I can be in this world? What would it feel like for me to be that way? What are the different versions of me? What can I discover or create in this world, and how can I discover or create those things? How can I show others I love them or tell them about my desires or feelings?

A vibrant, active imagination is a requirement for healthy human development and, on the collective level, for the creation of a soulcentric society or a compassionate, just, and sustainable world. In addition to being an indispensable faculty for the realization of our individual and collective futures, imagination is also a vital resource for understanding what already exists. There are many features of the world we can fathom only through our imaginations, things like what another person or animal is feeling (empathy); what someone means by a certain gesture; what an infant, pet, or wild animal needs; what poetry conveys; what a story tells; the doors that can be opened with dreams; or what gift to choose or make for someone. There are things we can do with our imaginations that we cannot do well otherwise, like express to another what we are feeling; solve problems creatively; write a poem; create a ceremony; perform a piece of music insightfully (or even hear it fully); prepare a tasty and nutritious meal; communicate with an animal, tree, or mountain; express affection; make a house a home; or, most vitally, perform our individual and collective parts in creating a world that works for all beings. A healthy imagination is essential to growing up, becoming fully human, encountering our souls, and offering our unique and necessary gifts to the world.

We are each born with a wild and fertile imagination, but to maintain that creative current and allow it to reach its full potential, it must be encouraged and exercised throughout childhood. In our society, however, imagination has become an
endangered human capacity. Truly visionary creativity is one of the most suppressed
human qualities in contemporary politics, education, religion, and business. This is
deplorable and ruinous because deep creativity serves life, diversity, and freedom, and
foils paralysis, sameness, and slavery. With their imaginations animated and thriving,
people experience ample joy in their lives and instinctively protect and promote the
diverse flourishing of the more-than-human world.

To enhance cultural sanity, justice, and freedom, we must cultivate and celebrate
our deep imaginations and we must enable our children to never stop enjoying and
employing their own. As suggested throughout these pages, a widespread revival of the
contemporary imagination will require radical changes in our mainstream approaches
to education and child development.

There are two forms of imagination to distinguish: directed and deep. We use directed imagination when we consciously create or influence the content of our own or
others' imagery. When someone suggests, for example, that you imagine lying on a warm,
white-sand beach beneath the gently swaying fronds of coconut palms, this is directed
imagery. Deep imagery, in contrast, arises on its own, out of the depths of our instinctive human nature, without our conscious intention for it to be one way or another. Deep
imagery is the stuff our dreams are made of, as well as the waking imaginal offerings of
our subconscious selves that we might call intuitions, revelations, or visions.

Every child has a natural penchant and aptitude for exploring and enjoying her
deep imagination. In a soulcentric setting, her parents and teachers encourage her
imaginal explorations and celebrate her imaginary friends and worlds. These are not
an escape from the social or academic worlds but an enrichment of them.

The child's dream life also should be encouraged. Parents and teachers, for example, can invite children to tell their dreams, marveling at the sensory qualities (colors, sounds, textures) of the dreamworld, its emotions, and its story line and characters.
The goal with soulcentric dreamwork is not interpretation but rather the exploration
and feeling of the dream, allowing the dream to have its effect on *us*, as opposed to our
having our way with *it*.

Invite children to tell their dreams to you, each dream at least twice and without
interruption other than brief expressions of wonder and empathy. Then, encourage
them to fully feel whatever emotions are evoked by the dream as you actively empathize
with those feelings. Once their emotions subside, help them find adaptive ways to act
on these emotions. (In the next section of this chapter, you'll find additional suggestions for helping children with their emotions.) Encourage children to share their
dreams with friends and other family members, to draw them or dance them, or to
write them as stories.

Studies of the dreams of children younger than age six reveal that as many as 80 percent of their dreams are about animals.[30] This astonishing fact suggests the unsurprising conclusion that nature itself has designed us in such a way that our childhood dreams support the development of our relationship with animated nature. But it might very well be that this relationship must be nurtured in our earliest years if it is to become a foundation for life.

Imagination and wild nature are deeply and intricately related. The ecologist Edith Cobb asserts that imagination in childhood depends *wholly* on contact with the natural world, and that the inventiveness displayed by deeply creative adults is most always rooted in their early experiences in nature.[31]

Likewise, the depth psychologist James Hillman observes that

> the world is made less of nouns than of verbs. It doesn't consist merely in objects and things; it is filled with useful, playful, and intriguing opportunities. The oriole doesn't see a branch, but an occasion for perching; the cat doesn't see a thing we call an empty box, it sees safe hiding for peering. . . .
>
> Children, especially, recognize this nurturance and instruction offered by nature. . . . Imagination does not grow all by itself in the household, or even out of imaginative tales told by parents. Children are "by nature" at home in the world; the world invites them to grow down and take part.[32]

The educator and author Richard Lewis maintains that a rich imagination is essential to discovering our true human nature and to growing fully alive. He encourages his fellow educators "to engage children in a process which uses 'inner' seeing and imaginative envisioning as much as an ability to see 'outwardly.'"[33] In a second-grade classroom, he might begin by passing around a simple tree branch and asking the children to imagine where it came from and how it might have broken off a tree. Some respond with gestures of outstretched arms, some in words, and others in drawings. Lewis observes,

> The moment in which children relax into the presence of their imagination there is often a collective sigh of relief — of children smiling to each other, knowing that their inner world is not peculiar to one's self, but a vast gathering of information in everyone, like the richly populated voicing of the sea or a summer meadow. If not specifically articulated there is an intuited understanding that we all now speak the language of the imagination without being criticized. It is the sky each of us lives within.[34]

Imagination is a defining dimension of human nature, and all of nature is profoundly imaginative. The great eighteenth-century English poet William Blake remarked that "to the Eyes of the Man of Imagination, Nature is Imagination itself."[35]

EMOTION. This is a third dimension of human nature. Emotional development and emotional bonding with family members is essential in the Garden, when the child is learning the fundamental features of having and being a self and how that self forms a world and operates within it. Emotion is one of his primary guides. Although in the Nest he experienced and expressed emotions, he didn't yet have a fully formed ego that could take ownership of them. His emotions did not teach him about himself, since he did not yet *have* a self. Rather, his emotions, we hope, taught his parents something — something about *him*: what he needed (for example, sleep, food, touch, reassurance, boundaries, or instruction). In the Garden, however, the child, through his emotions, consciously learns about himself and about relationships.

Good or bad, emotions are not experiences he chooses. They occur in response to his ever-changing relationships to self and others, relationships that regularly and inevitably get out of balance. Through the information contained in his emotions, he discovers how to repair or refashion his relationships, especially with his family members.

Mad, sad, bad, glad, scared. Every emotion contains its own lesson. Each *type* of emotion (for example, mad versus sad) points to a particular kind of lesson about self or about relationship of self to others. Each type of emotion also points to particular kinds of action that can bring the world back into balance.

For example, what makes him mad or feel hurt? The lesson built into every instance of anger or hurt evokes questions, such as: What do I believe I deserve? What do I feel about how I should be treated by others? In what way might I be part of the problem? Each time an Orphan-Explorer feels angry or hurt, his parents, teachers, older siblings, or other adults can help him form these questions and find the answers. His answers will teach him about himself, his relationship to others, and what he must do to make things right again.

What the child believes he deserves is, of course, not necessarily an accurate assessment. The value of the questioning is to help the child understand himself — his own beliefs and attitudes — as well as the moral and social conventions of his people. Parents and others do not necessarily encourage the child to expect to get what he thinks he deserves. Sometimes he'll be helped to see that his beliefs were mistaken. Other times he'll receive agreement. In both cases, he can be coached in how to act on his anger and hurt — in particular, how to respond to others in a way that fosters healthy relationships.

When he is sad, these questions arise: What do I love or admire or desire — an important thing, person, relationship, or opportunity that I've lost? What does my love or desire say about who I am? What do I have that I cannot bear to lose? What can I do to keep the loss from happening or getting worse? If it's too late, how can I mourn and/or praise what I've lost?

When he feels bad — guilty or ashamed: What is expected of me? What do I expect of myself? What are the right ways for me to be and to act? How do I make things right again with others?

When he's glad: What makes my world better, more complete? What do I rejoice in? What does this say about who I am? How do I praise or celebrate?

When he's afraid: What is dangerous and therefore to be avoided, or approached cautiously? How do I take care of myself?

In the Garden, the child needs to be helped by his teachers, parents, and other family members to fully embrace his emotions. He learns, first, to experience his emotions thoroughly, beginning with precisely how they feel in his body. Then, he learns how to identify the different types of emotions, to discover what each tells him about himself, the basics of expressing his emotions to others in word and action, and, in particular, how to act on his emotional truth in a way that makes his social world right again. In this way, he learns, with the aid of his emotions, how to bring his outer world of relationships into alignment with his inner world of self-experience, and vice versa.

In the next stage (the Oasis), the adolescent will be developmentally ready and able to learn additional and more sophisticated emotional tools, and he will be able to employ these tools on his own, more often than not.

It's no surprise that each of the four domains of nature (emotion, imagination, body, and the wild outdoors) helps the child explore each of the other three, especially if parents and teachers guide the child in becoming conscious of these interactions.

Imagination and nature: Imagination helps the child explore the world of Earthly nature. What would it be like to be a bird, to stalk like a cat, to be that particular branch of that tree?

The body, nature, and imagination: To be in nature is to be a body in nature. The child does not just observe but interacts with all her senses. The wren is not just seen but also felt in the movement of the child's own arms and the lightness of flight in her stomach, and heard in the sound of the wind and the bird's song. Trees are for climbing. Water is for splashing or for diving into. And through her imagination, her body can merge with the life of the animals she encounters.

Emotions and nature: Her emotions can be clarified in the outdoors, especially when she is guided to consciousness by people who are in the Oasis and beyond. The rain can help her feel her loss; the warmth of the Sun, her hope; the storm, her fear.

Emotions and the body: Emotions, especially for the child, are experienced in the body and are of the body. When a child says, "Susan told me today her family is moving far away, and I cried," her father might help her make the body-emotion connection by responding, "You're really sad. You'll miss your good friend so much!"

"My stomach aches." "Are you afraid to go to school today?"

"I'm all smiles." "You're really happy!"

Imagination and emotions: Imagination, too, helps her explore her emotions. Her dream images, for example, embody her fears and her wishes, her hurts and her anger. Parents and older siblings can help her investigate her dream images in this way.

Her daydreams project what she longs for, what she lost, how she feels things ought to have been. By intentionally imagining how she would like things to be, she can discover what she feels now.

Imagination, the body, and emotions: Finally, her imagination helps her discover and practice the movements and gestures she can make with her body, like a queenly bow or a feline leap — gestures that will expand her vocabulary in dance, sports, play, theater, conversation, and socializing. And her body provides her with metaphors to express her imagination and emotions — "I'm going to stand up for myself," "This is a headache," "I want to hide my face," or "I'm jumping for joy!"

The imagination, body, emotions, and wild nature operate together and interact in complex and fascinating ways, a fact that underscores the necessity for children to be allowed, and to be encouraged to cultivate, a full relationship with all four of these dimensions of nature. Diminished opportunities in any dimension impair the child's relationship with each of the other three.

Learning the Social Practices, Values, Knowledge, History, Mythology, and Cosmology of One's Family and Culture

The second subtask of the Garden is cultural learning, the other half of the child's exploration of her more-than-human world and her place in it. For a child, her culture — the totality of practices, values, knowledge, and stories of her people — is as much a given as is wild nature.[36]

SOCIAL PRACTICES. In order to thrive socially and psychologically, to effectively belong to her world, the Orphan-Explorer must learn to participate successfully in the life of her family and, more generally, the practices of her people. She must acquire her people's sense of good manners, their ways of speaking, eating, playing, praying, grieving, celebrating, dancing, singing, and making music. She must be shown the acceptable ways of interacting with people of both genders and of different ages, clans, and social statuses. She must be taught how to argue, resolve conflicts, cooperate, tell stories, and acquire self-knowledge. She must develop skills in planning, counting, obtaining and preparing food, maintaining her health, learning, working, and relaxing. She must learn her people's way of treating sacred things properly and maintaining good relations with the spirits, gods, animals, and landforms.

To participate in the social practices of her people, the child must also learn how the material things of her culture work: how to make and shoot a bow, operate a vacuum cleaner, ride a bicycle, light a fire, pitch a tent, or surf the Net. Learning the social practices of her family and culture is an essential element of the child's education, which is provided by family and community members and fueled by the child's own natural desire to belong.

VALUES. If a child is to become a member-in-full-standing of her family and culture, then her parents and other adults in her life must model a coherent and consistent set of values, a system of ethics and principles for making choices, a system that is authentically lived by the family and its ethnic or social group. Although modeling values is most important, parents must also teach their children *about* values. A child must understand the values and choice-principles beneath the social conventions and actions, and he needs help in making his own value-based choices. But teaching values without modeling them is disastrous to the child's development and to family and cultural life.

In some "liberal" circles, parents believe it inappropriate to impart too many (or, sometimes, any) values to their prepubertal children, not wanting to impose their way of life on the next generation. But a child has to acquire a first set of values in order to understand what it is to have *any* set of values. Prepubertal children do not acquire value systems by being told that right or wrong is always a matter of opinion, and that all choices are equally valid. A child raised in a value-free or value-relative environment is in danger of lifelong confusion about what's important, and may be unable to decisively choose a life path, may rarely get inspired, and may be unable to criticize even the most heinous human acts, such as genocide or environmental destruction. Learning the relativity of values and evolving one's own value system are important components of education, but these are not developmentally appropriate until early adolescence (the Oasis).

Values are imparted primarily in the home, through conversations and the choices modeled by parents and siblings. Especially important and effective are the stories, legends, and myths told by elders, stories about relationships with people, animals, and plants.

But what set of values can be embraced in contemporary primary schools? What values can a wide range of parents and teachers agree on? Surprisingly, recent polls show broad agreement among people of all faiths and those of no faith. Gallup, for example, has found that more than 90 percent of Americans agree that teachers should emphasize honesty, democracy, moral courage, caring for friends and family, and the acceptance of people of all races and ethnicities.[37] We also know that the very survival of any human community requires a sustainable lifestyle, and so the values of cooperation, avoiding waste, and honoring all life are essential. Beyond these ecological foundations, each soulcentric family and school will embrace somewhat different sets of values. What is important, however, is to *have* a set and to integrate shared-value education into classroom activities and everyday family life.[38]

A child who acquires a coherent value system within a healthy community is more likely to mature into an adult able to modify or transform the set of values with which she grew up. Some shifting of value systems in adolescence and adulthood is inevitable and also necessary for the health of the culture. The community's way of life, after all, must evolve in response to changes in the environment, the size of the community, its relationship to the more-than-human world, generational shifts, and new cultural developments, both social and technological.

KNOWLEDGE. Every culture has a storehouse of facts about the world. Children need to learn some of these facts in order to become members of their culture. Among hunter-gatherer people, for instance, much of their knowledge revolves around the behavior and habitats of prey animals and the different species, properties, and uses of plants, and the methods of collecting them. Among circumpolar cultures, everyone needs to know quite a bit about snow and ice. All cultures have knowledge about their local weather, climate, water, and terrain. Contemporary Western culture divides *its* endless array of knowledge into compartments corresponding to the familiar university departments: physics, chemistry, biology, botany, zoology, psychology, anthropology, sociology, astronomy, business, math, the arts, and so on. At least as important as the knowledge sorted into these distinct disciplines, however, is an understanding of the dynamics of systems, of wholes — the patterns that connect the elements of the web of life.

Knowledge is one of the fundamental possessions of every culture. All other elements of culture depend on knowledge in some way. Every social practice (hunting, chess, cooking, building shelter, playing a guitar, midwifing) requires knowledge. Acting on values requires knowledge. History, mythology, and cosmology are themselves three special categories of knowledge.[39]

In the Garden, children need to acquire knowledge, but what kinds and how much? More knowledge has been accumulated by contemporary culture than anyone could ingest in a lifetime spent in libraries or in front of computers. Which facts are most important for any particular child? How do we keep from exposing children to too much knowledge or the wrong kinds (for example, irrelevant, boring, useless, value-free, or imagination-destroying) or at the wrong time? These are essential questions for parents and educators to ponder. The answers depend on our values. Each parent, and society as a whole, must ask: what are the most important goals in child development, and what kinds of knowledge must children acquire to reach these goals?

An important consideration about knowledge and childhood concerns the danger of computers. In 2001, the nonprofit Alliance for Childhood issued a report, *Fool's Gold: A Critical Look at Computers in Childhood*, supported by more than eighty-five experts in neurology, psychiatry, and education.[40] The report concludes that, after thirty years of research on educational technology, there is virtually no evidence to support the notion that computers aid childhood learning. The cosigners of *Fool's Gold* called for a moratorium on computer use in early childhood education based on their concern that computers might in fact be hazardous to the health of young children. We might surmise that the problem with computers is not merely the computer itself but also the overdependence on them that displaces other sources of knowledge acquisition, including free time in nature, socializing, the arts, storytelling, and family play and work activities.

Perhaps the most important area of study for Explorers is ecoliteracy. Ecoliteracy is knowledge about ecosystems — communities of plants, animals, and humans that make up the web of life, especially on one's own home ground. Ecoliteracy is commonly neglected in contemporary schools, but it is essential if the child is going to truly belong to the world.

Both at home and at school, children can be taught about animals and plants in the same manner that traditional land-based people accomplished this — through stories and songs that reveal the roles these beings play in their world. Children need to learn guidelines about how to be in relationship to and how to care for particular species of plants and animals. They need to appreciate, for example, the quality of different firewoods, the songs of birds, the distinctive floral fragrances, and the mammalian musks.[41]

Environmental education can be cultural education, too. Parents, educators, and elders can tell stories about how their ancestors, or perhaps the indigenous human inhabitants of their place, actually lived there. This ecological education is especially effective if conducted while actually playing or working on the land, while gathering wood or berries, for example, or while gardening, fetching water, or fishing.

And environmental education can also be psychological education. The personal qualities of animals and plants provide metaphors for our human aspirations. We might desire to become wily like a coyote, stalwart like an oak, swift like a falcon, or talkative like a mockingbird. Sharing these metaphors with children fires up their imagination concerning their own possibilities. Soulcentric development, after all, is the biomimicry of human maturation: we look to models from nature to help us see how we might best mature as humans.

As people grow more removed from personal contact with nature, awareness and appreciation of the environment declines. Eco-illiteracy breeds apathy about environmental fragility and, inevitably, leads to further degradation of habitat, the very habitat that human survival and imagination depends on. People who know about their environment care about it. People who care, conserve.

See this chapter's resource section in the back of the book for more on ecoliteracy and for suggested references for further learning in this area.

CULTURAL HISTORY AND MYTHOLOGY. Learning the most vital, emotionally provocative, and imagination-stirring stories of one's people is the fourth component of culture acquisition. We can divide these stories into three categories: histories, mythologies, and cosmologies. Let's consider histories and mythologies first.

Cultural history and mythology are not the same thing. The former recounts the lives and deeds of our ancestors, whereas the latter conveys stories from another

THE EXPLORER *in the* GARDEN

THE EXPLORER *in the* GARDEN 139

dimension, a time discontinuous with our historical time ("a time before time," "a time before the world began," "once upon a time"). Whereas history enumerates the facts of how we, as a people, came to live where we do, and how our social, religious, and economic traditions developed, our myths whisper of the psychospiritual possibilities of our individual lives, of the realizable mysteries of being a human, of our often veiled relationship to the transpersonal (to both soul and spirit), and of our sacred and reciprocal relationships with the other beings of nature.

The world of the Greek gods and goddesses, the Native American tales of Coyote, the Hopi stories of the three previous worlds, and the songlines of the Australian Aborigines are examples of mythology. These stories are populated not by our historical ancestors but by the gods, goddesses, and associated characters from other worlds (from Mount Olympus and Hades, the Hopi's Land at the Red Mountains, or the Aboriginal Dreamtime), by animals and rivers that speak human languages, or by people who live at the bottoms of rivers or on the other side of rainbows. You might say that mythologies are always true but never real, while histories are purportedly real but often not true. A historian might say, "These things really happened to our ancestors, although I might have gotten some of the facts wrong." A myth teller might begin by saying, "In a time long, long ago, and a place far, far away..." and then recount a tale that illumines the meanings, challenges, possibilities, and obligations of our human lives, including our deaths.

Mythology, sourced in the wilds of the collective human psyche, supports our wandering more deeply into our strange and astonishing world. Myths free our imagination from ordinary time and the everyday events of history. They open the door to mystery and to understanding our human place in the more-than-human world.

Myths help us pose the big questions of our individual and collective lives: Why am I here? What does it mean to be someone's child, parent, or sibling? How do I uncover my destiny? What is the nature of passion, love, marriage? What is death? What or who is rain, snow, salmon, bear, buffalo, corn, and ocean, and what is the nature of our relationship to these beings? How are we to properly behave in relation to them?

Unlike history, mythology ushers us into the realm of enlivening metaphors, symbols, archetypes, the uplifting possible as well as the inspiring *im*possible. In comparison, history is prosaic.

But a cultural history, too, is indispensable because it informs our collective or ethnic identity, our sense of who we are as a people, and it illumines the successes and mistakes of our ancestors, shedding light on how best to conduct our public affairs, our social, religious, economic, scientific, and political lives. Because our children are preparing to take their places in our culture, they need the historical stories. But rather than the all-too-common textbook tales of war and conquest, children need to hear the narratives that reveal what makes their people distinctive — how they ate and dressed, how they raised families, and what and how they celebrated and worshipped.

In addition to general histories, children need to hear or read inspiring stories of self-actualized individuals from their ancestry, biographies of Helen Keller, John Muir, or Eleanor Roosevelt, or of Black Elk, Sojourner Truth, Mohandas Gandhi, or Nelson Mandela. These personal accounts stimulate the child's imagination of how she herself might someday belong to the world; they serve as a beginning template of personal identity.

Being grounded in cultural history, and bonded to a specific place in nature, allows the child to make and believe a statement such as "We are the ones who are from *this* place and who have *this* relationship to each other, the land, and the other beings here. We belong here. I belong among us. I am one of us."

Human cultures of all times and places have had both mythologies and histories. Both seem to be necessary for a healthy human community. Until about five thousand years ago, mythology and history were independent enterprises. However, the Abrahamic religions (Judaism, Christianity, and Islam) blurred the distinction, framing their sacred stories as historical events from a time and place continuous with their own.[42] It then became possible to treat the sacred stories as nothing more than literal fact as opposed to life-guiding parables or metaphors for individual psychospiritual development.

History and mythology, however, have different purposes, and confounding the two enterprises diminishes both. The dangers of the entanglement are the literalizing of the self, on the one hand, and the counterfeiting of history, on the other. The possibilities of the self — our individual soul-infused destinies — as well as the possibilities of our collective human adventure, are far more diverse and astonishing than any literal history could encompass. By literalizing our mythologies, we literalize ourselves and thereby limit what we might become. To literalize ourselves is to understand who and what we are prosaically, unimaginatively. As commonplace, humdrum. Just the facts. No metaphors. No potential, destiny, or creative unfolding. Although some historical stories hold rich metaphors (as many in the Bible do, for example), their vital spiritual lessons are harder to extract or recognize when couched as literal facts. The diminishment of mythology impedes the developing selves of our children, who deserve to fully participate in the mysteries of the world and of their own ensouled lives.

Blurring the history-mythology distinction also prompts the distortion of history, because the religious historian can make the facts conform to his moral or religious aims, giving rise to fundamentalisms (the literalizing of spiritual metaphors). Genuine mythologies, in contrast, do not arise from what actually happened in the past, but rather from the vast, as-yet-unrealized potentialities found in the imaginative depths of the collective human unconscious, the realm of the archetypes, as embodied, for example, in the lives of the gods and goddesses.

Although genuine, potent myths in mainstream America are few in our everyday

family and cultural lives, we nevertheless have available to us an abundance of resources. A treasure chest of myths from diverse traditions has been carefully preserved.
Among the best sources are the works of Joseph Campbell, who spent a lifetime
studying sacred world tales, plumbing the multilayered depths of their meanings, and
sharing the fruits of his research in more than a dozen volumes, many audio and video
recordings, and the gifts of his own storytelling talents. Many of the myths that
Campbell recounts are from the European or Middle Eastern ancestry of mainstream
Americans — from the Greeks, Romans, French, Celts, Norse, Finns, Turks, Persians,
Hebrews, Egyptians, and ancient Babylonians. Others derive from indigenous Americans, Africans, and Aboriginals and from Hindus, Buddhists, Taoists, and others.

As children, we need to be immersed in tales such as those of Persephone's ab-
duction by Hades (an ancient Greek myth), Beowulf's descent into the abysmal
swamp to do battle with the mother of all monsters (from eighth-century England),
and Inanna's fatal visit to her underworld sister, Erishkigal (from Sumer, five thousand
years ago), three of the innumerable portrayals of the death-rebirth journey of personal initiation.

In contemporary culture, the rare myths that we share with our children tend to
be few and unimaginative. We have Disney movies that degrade archetypal stories into
sitcoms and shallow heart-warmers. We have Hollywood sci-fi and action films that
have traded the original richness of mythology for the endless portrayals of superficial male-adolescent heroism and the sexual objectification of women. We have taste-
less and insipid television stories and ads designed to raise profits, not children. The
enchantment of the world has been stifled and corrupted.

We do still have fairy tales, but all too often they are contemporary, sanitized
versions of ancient stories, the invaluable dark elements having been removed or minimized. Some of the deepest mysteries and keys to our individual destinies are hidden
in those shadowy places. Seek out, then, the older, original fairy tales such as those com-
piled by the brothers Grimm.[43]

It's best for children to read — or, better, hear — the genuine myths, including
fairy tales, as opposed to the commercial stories fabricated by trendy fiction writers.
Children need the imaginally and symbolically rich tales that spring from ancient wells.
They need stories fashioned from universal themes as old as humanity and that have
been told, generation after generation, by spellbinding storytellers. Children might consciously understand only the surface layer of these stories, but the stories will resound
within their psyches for a lifetime, providing doorways that can be opened only later.

We need authentic mythology for the same reasons we need untamed nature and
our own dreams. Indeed, these three realms — myths, nature, and dreams — are intimately related through their common feature of wildness. Mythology gathers our innate and collective human wildness and reflects it back to us in compelling images,
characters, and story lines, just as dreams do for the wildness of our individual psyches.

And the natural world, from which we are born, feeds and reflects the wildness of our deepest imaginations.

By inspiring children to dream the seemingly impossible for themselves and their people, myths cultivate the seeds of visionary consciousness that, in adulthood, blossoms into culture-transforming soulwork. If we teach only what we know and what we were, we fail our children. We must also enable them to imagine what we haven't — especially that which they might become.

COSMOLOGY. In addition to — and distinct from — both cultural history and mythology, children need a cosmology. A cosmology provides a story of the universe, one that tells how it all began, where it all came from, and the origin of humanity, other species, rivers, landforms, and heavenly bodies visible (or not) in the sky.

Traditional cosmologies range from the Judeo-Christian Genesis to Native American tales of Coyote or Spider Woman creating the world. Sometimes these are classified as mythologies or as components of religious cultural history, but these three kinds of stories (cosmologies, mythologies, and histories) serve distinctly different functions.

Thomas Berry explains the significance of cosmology:

> The cosmological narrative is the primary narrative of any people, for this is the story that gives to a people their sense of the universe. It explains how things came to be in the beginning and how they came to be the way they are. It provides the first sense of creativity in a story that is generally recounted at any significant initiation event of the community or a person. It is a healing story, a power story, a guiding story.[44]

One quality that traditional cosmologies — world-creation stories — have in common with myths is that they are imaginal. Arising from the collective unconscious of a people, traditional cosmologies are fictions, which in no way reduces their value. Indeed, much of their power and effectiveness stems from their imaginal nature. They are *true* fictions, in that they are sincere and provide vital meaning for the culture. Most people understand that the world was not literally created by a male god in seven days about six thousand years ago. Although not intended to be taken literally, the Genesis myth — whether we subscribe to it or not — has many sincere things to say about what kind of world this is and what it means to live in it.

Histories are couched in prosaic facts, mythologies in deeply imaginal fiction, and, until very recently, cosmologies were expressed as fiction, too. Then, something extraordinary began to unfold when, in 1543, Copernicus postulated that our planet was not the center of the universe but actually revolved around the Sun. Since then Galileo, Newton, Kant, Einstein, Hubble, and millions of other scientists have discovered an astonishing range of facts about the origin and structure of the universe, so that we now have a cosmology that, in its broad strokes, is universally accepted by scientists around the world, and that offers an astonishing empirical (nonfictional) story of the origins and evolution of the universe.

This modern cosmology arose not from the deep imagination of the human unconscious but, in a sense, from the deep imagination of the universe itself. This is a story in which the universe began some 13 billion years ago with an explosive primordial expansion that unfolded through a number of phases, resulting in a universe of a trillion galaxies, each populated by billions of stars and an untold plenitude of planets. It is a story of a universe still evolving and still expanding at an enormous rate.

Earth is one planet among many trillions in the universe. Its own evolution, during the 4.5 billion years of its existence, is, for us humans, an essential and more intimate chapter of cosmology. The Earth story recounts the progressive changes in our planet's oceans, atmosphere, and geology that enabled life to appear here and determined the shapes and diversity of Earth's living things. The facts are nearly too extraordinary to believe, which is to say they ignite our wonder, imagination, and sense of the sacred.

Cosmologist Brian Swimme and cultural historian Thomas Berry believe that the universe, in its sequence of transformations from its beginning, is best understood as a story. They call this the Universe Story in their book of that title. This nonfictional telling of the unfolding of the universe is at once scientifically derived and a sacred story as inspiring and spellbinding as the best yarn you've ever heard. Any child can easily understand a simplified version — and needs to.[45] The Universe Story provides the contemporary child with an essential catalyst for psychospiritual development. Thomas writes, "This story must provide in our times what the mythic stories of earlier times provided as the guiding and energizing sources of the human venture."[46]

In addition to the fact-versus-fiction distinction, another fundamental difference between modern cosmology and traditional world-creation myths is that the latter are ever-renewing cycles, while the former is an ever-transforming sequence. This is the same difference we noted, in chapter 1, between the Soulcentric Developmental Wheel and traditional-indigenous models of human development. The Wheel has been designed within the context of a time-developmental framework that recognizes that the human species itself and the human life cycle, in particular, continue to evolve. Due to our modern understanding of evolution, we must note that the traditional cosmologies are no longer sufficient. We humans are now the dominant power determining the near future of Earth. In the Garden, children must be exposed to the Universe Story so that they mature into adults who appreciate the full significance of being human at this time — and the awesome responsibilities entailed.

Many contemporary parents wonder if it's necessary or best to raise a child within the traditions of a mainstream religion, or even whether it's advisable. Perhaps the following ideas will help you choose: The Explorer is best served by a family environment with an authentic, consistent, coherent value system and by a generous exposure to stories of cultural history, mythology, and cosmology. Such values and stories are embedded within all religious traditions and can also be imparted to a child outside such traditions.

Part of the challenge is that most of our Western religious traditions bear upon a limited spectrum of life. They teach children about their relationship with other people and with a mostly distant, disembodied god, but rarely anything about their relationship with stars, soil, wind, frost, creeks, canyons, galaxies, or swans. Families with religious traditions that do not fully flesh out the human-nature relationship can supplement their children's education with ecocentric values, stories, practices, and ceremonies.

Concerning values, it's essential for parents to ask if the ones they actually live are consistent with those embedded in their religious tradition. Children invariably notice discrepancies between what their parents live and what is preached to them. These discrepancies weaken the family and undermine the child's acquisition of a functional value system.

As for the stories, it's vital to share all three kinds, honoring their differences in significance and intention. Some parents will need to supplement the stories they heard as children with mythologies and cosmologies from other sources and to tell some of the religious narratives with a new sensibility and understanding, recounting these sacred stories in ways that fire children's imaginations.

PRIMARY EDUCATION IN EGOCENTRIC VERSUS SOULCENTRIC SETTINGS

Many parents and educators today have a limited appreciation of the developmental needs of children in the Garden. Primary education curricula place nearly exclusive emphasis on reading, writing, math, and general knowledge. Other dimensions of learning (for example, nature, the arts, mythology, cosmology, self-care, emotional intelligence, and social skills) are commonly ignored or minimized.

We neglect whole spectrums of knowledge and social, emotional, and spiritual competence vital to being human — like the ability to grieve fully, make music spontaneously, resolve conflicts, engage in mutual storytelling, acquire self-knowledge, work with dreams, be at home in nature, cultivate relations with other-than-human beings, and cocreate the simple ceremonies that honor and revitalize our relationship to the seasons and to the Sun and Moon and stars.

Most of our schools impose significant limitations not only on what we teach but on how we go about teaching, relying on pedagogic methods of rote learning and thinking, to the near exclusion of the other essential modes of learning (discussed in the next section of this chapter). Most schools still utilize rows of uni-directed chairs and the associated learning hierarchy (as opposed to true learning communities in which everyone, from principal to preschooler, is both a student and a teacher). Still widespread are the rigid and regimented school-day schedules and the soulless linearity of school buildings. The award-winning American schoolteacher John Gatto, author of *Dumbing Us Down: The Hidden Curriculum of Compulsory Schooling*, argues that our contemporary school systems make learning *anything* difficult. They discourage the development of independent critical thinking and "stamp out the self-knowledge, curiosity, concentration, and solitude essential to learning. Between schooling and television, our children have precious little time to learn for themselves about the community they live in, or the lives they might lead. Instead they are schooled to merely obey orders and become smoothly functioning cogs in the industrial machine."[47]

Children have a difficult time learning about the natural world and about real community when they are isolated from both. It's as if the intention of our educational system were to shape children into industrial humans and consumers of things they don't need, rather than to help them become fully themselves, belong to a place, create a meaningful life, and contribute to the health of the biosphere and the creation of a sustainable society. Gatto observes,

> One . . . thing I know is that eventually you have to come to be part of a *place* — part of its hills and streets and waters and people — or you will live a very, very sorry life as an exile forever. *Discovering meaning for yourself*, and discovering satisfying *purpose* for yourself, is a big part of what education is. How this can be done by locking children away from the world is beyond me. (Italics in the original.)[48]

In contemporary America, we tend not to think of middle childhood as a time of bonding with nature or as a time to encourage imaginal, emotional, and social growth but instead turn it into a nearly full-time classroom regimen of "reading, writing, and 'rithmetic." From the perspective of nature and soul, these are not primary developmental needs in the Garden. Although language and math skills are important, they can be incorporated in ways germane to the childhood exploration of nature and to the affective, social, and creative arts. They need not be studied in abstract isolation as hypothetical preparation for some far-off world of work.

Many parents and educators believe that some children, judging by their school performance, simply do not enjoy learning. More likely, these kids are unable or unwilling to learn in standard classroom environments, about things that are alien to their lives, by means of limited learning styles. All young humans *love* to learn and are designed by nature to do just that. The question is not how to *make* children learn but how to allow them to exercise their natural curiosity and desire to belong to the more-than-human world.

Over the past twenty-five years in the United States, there have been enormously creative developments in soulcentric and ecocentric education for children, although, as of yet, these have been adopted by very few schools. See this chapter's resource section in the back of the book for a few highlights of methods and principles.

Transforming our educational system is essential, but it is important to remember that, during a healthy childhood, work and productivity are secondary to play and time in nature. The free exploration of self, relationships, and nature provides the best educational opportunities and the finest ways to nurture creativity.

This principle about learning is really not so different from what we find in a soulful adulthood. It is often said that play is the work of childhood, but we might equally well say that work is the play of true adulthood. In soulcentric development, craft and career become compelling and play-filled features of the world for the maturing individual. As Alan Watts has said, in his Taoist way, "The sensible person is one who gets paid for playing. All work can be transformed into play — if one is not in a hurry to be somewhere else."[49] How can we raise and educate children so that they maintain their nature-given innocence, wonder, and creativity and carry these qualities into their adulthood and elderhood?[50]

INTUITION AND THE FOUR WINDOWS OF KNOWING

Feeling, imagining, sensing, and thinking: together, these four modalities make up what psychologist Eligio Stephen Gallegos calls the "four windows of knowing," the four human faculties through which we learn about self and world.[51] Each of the four is of equal power and importance in the living of a full, balanced, and creative human life. Each is a distinct faculty not reducible to any other. Thinking allows us to know our selves and the world in a certain way and to a certain extent, but feeling, imagination, and sensing each allow us to know in ways that thinking is not able to encompass.

Let's say, for example, that you want to better understand an important personal relationship. You could think about that other person and about interactions the two of you have had, but this is going to get you only so far. If, in addition, you let yourself feel the full range of emotions evoked by the other and by your patterns of relating, you'll learn additional things you wouldn't have otherwise appreciated — often quite surprising and possibly more valuable and relevant to what you learned through thinking alone. Then, you might use your imagination to empathize with what it's like to *be* the other, to have that life with those difficulties and opportunities. Doing so will result in additional discoveries you'd never have had through thinking or feeling alone. Last, the next time you're with that other, you can open all your senses to her, look very carefully at her face and at the way she moves, listen mindfully to the sound of her voice, take in her scent. What do you learn that you didn't discover through thinking, feeling, and imagining? And what emotions, images, and thoughts are evoked by these new discoveries?

Gallegos understands thinking, feeling, and sensing in a manner similar to Carl Jung's, but where Jung wrote of intuition as the fourth "function of consciousness," Gallegos offers the insight that the fourth faculty is actually imagination. Gallegos explains that intuition is our ability to know things "beyond the present moment and circumstance and for which there is no immediate evidence."[52] Intuition, he notes, can operate through any of the four windows, although for any given person it tends to operate primarily through one in particular. In other words, for some people intuitions arrive in the form of an image, say of a loved one's face just before that person walks in the door. Other people intuit by way of a thought "out of nowhere" that enables them to understand more deeply something happening in the moment. Some people intuit by way of a feeling or emotion. A fourth group experiences intuition through sensory perception — say, the appearance of a certain bird, breeze, or blossom, which tells them that some specific event (such as a birth or a death) has just happened or is about to happen. Jung's own intuition, as it turns out, operated primarily through his imagination, which led him to identify the fourth function as intuition.

Intuition is an essential human capacity. Parents and teachers can help children grow whole by encouraging the cultivation and use of intuition, keeping in mind that it can occur through any one or more of the four windows of knowing.

In contemporary America, our schools tend to overvalue thinking and ignore the development of emotional, imaginal, and sensory intelligence. In fact, even genuine thinking is discouraged in our schools, most of which teach only memorization and mimicry. By overemphasizing shallow thinking and inconsequential strategizing, we shortchange indigenous human desires and developmental needs, such as the needs for exploration and celebration of the wondrous and beautiful, creativity and artistic expression, emotional growth and healing, healthy relationships, and personal fulfillment and meaning.

After shallow thinking, our schools place a secondary emphasis on sensing, but here the focus is mostly on seeing and hearing, with little attention to tasting, smelling, or touching. Even with sight and audition, there is little effort invested in helping children to see or hear clearly, to employ their full appreciation for nuance and depth in the play of light and sound.

Creative thinking and emotional, imaginal, and sensory experience should receive full attention in our classrooms and at home so that our children can grow into mature humans with full mastery of all four of their fundamental human faculties of knowing. Four-window learning in school and at home is facilitated simply by creating educational projects in which children are asked to use each of their four faculties of knowing to (1) gather information about the project, (2) design the project, (3) carry out the project, and (4) report on the results. Parents and teachers, of course, must use their imaginations, especially, to generate four-window learning opportunities!

Consider a creek restoration project undertaken by a fifth-grade class. The children will gather information about the project through thinking — for example, by reading about and then discussing and debating the effects of industrial waste on water quality, or about the effects of invasive plant species on wildlife, or about failures and successes with previous restoration projects. But they will also gather information through their senses. What is the odor of this creek mud, and what do the fish in this creek actually look like? What are the sounds of this creek in midday or evening compared to the sounds heard at a nearby healthy creek? Through their emotions, they'll explore how they feel after spending time at the two ecosystems. They'll also use their imaginations to picture how the creek would look or sound with two or three equally valid restoration approaches.

Later, the children might be guided on a deep-imagination journey to retrieve design possibilities for aspects of the project. On that journey, they might be asked, "What kinds of public-information signs do you see near the creek? Where are they placed? Where do you see the boulders in the creek, or the benches where people can sit and enjoy the restored ecosystem?" The possibilities generated in this way can later be checked against knowledge gathered by thinking, emotion, and sensing. At the end of the project, children can be asked to report the results using their senses, thinking, imagination, and their own and others' feelings about what they accomplished.

Learning itself is most complete when the four windows are equally engaged. Much of what we learn about the self and the soul — our emotions, dreams, possibilities, and destinies — is first acquired through feeling and imagination and perhaps later elaborated through thinking. Much of what we learn about nature and society is initially acquired through sensing (observation) and thinking, and later extended through imagination and feeling. Imagination, feeling, and sensing are at least as essential as thinking to establish and maintain relationships that are caring, cooperative, creative, fun, and gratifying.

COGNITIVE DEVELOPMENT IN THE GARDEN

Swiss psychologist Jean Piaget showed that, between ages five and nine, most children undergo a pivotal change in cognitive capacity that unfolds in two major steps. First, between five and seven, most children acquire the ability to think reasonably and logically about concrete objects (that is, things we can see, hear, and touch). For example, before this shift, they will believe that, when you flatten a ball of clay, you've changed the amount of clay, not just its shape. They will be quite sure that, when you pour water from a tall, thin glass into a short, wide one, there is less water. If they watch you play with a ball that is red on one side and blue on the other, and then place it between you so that they can only see the blue, they will have no doubt that both of you are seeing blue. In general, they are able to think about only one aspect of a situation at a time and can relate only to the qualities right in front of them. After the shift, however, they are no longer fooled by irrelevant changes in appearance, they can think about several aspects of a situation at once, and they can compare the way things are now with the way they were before or might be in the future. Piaget called these new abilities "concrete operations."[53]

The development of concrete operational thought profoundly affects the Explorer's relationship with both self and others. Now he begins to see the difference between his perspective and that of others — differences in motivations, values, and abilities. He develops the capacity to imagine or take the role of another person, to feel things from that person's perspective, and as a result to experience conscious empathy, a faculty more advanced than that which is exhibited in the simple helping behavior of Innocents in the Nest. And he becomes able to recognize his own characteristics in a way not possible earlier. He can understand, for example, that he might be more talkative or energetic than others, good at soccer, or poor with math.

These cognitive skills are necessary for him to consciously recognize and savor individual differences. Without an appreciation of the relativity of perspective and values — and a delight in the great variety of human personalities — he won't be able to participate successfully in the more nuanced social activities, such as the arts of conversation, teamwork, or loving.

Not until age eight or nine do most children take the next big step in concrete operations: being able to criticize *themselves*. Now the child can not only compare two perspectives, but she can also see how she personally stacks up against one perspective or another. She can now pass judgment on herself and might become harshly self-critical. This ability to judge the self results in, among other things, a more differentiated relationship to one's own emotions. Earlier, the child experienced and spoke of her emotions primarily as bodily shifts ("my stomach feels bad") or how she acted on her feelings ("I ran away"). Now she can more easily name her feelings ("mad, bad, sad, glad, scared"), express them directly, and grasp that it is possible to feel more than one emotion at a time. Furthermore, she's able to do something not previously possible: she can consciously hide or deny her emotions.

Concrete operational thought furthers the child's progress with the task of the Garden: exploring the givens of the world. It enables the child to more fully relish nature's constant unfoldings, such as the astonishing sequence of growth in a rosebush, bald eagle, or kitten; the changes in size, color, or form of a spring creek, the Moon, the winter snowpack, or an aspen in autumn; and the seasonal successions themselves. And it allows the child to appreciate the fine points in more complex and subtle social practices, such as making friends, resolving conflicts, admitting guilt or anger, sharing a precious object, playing a role, telling a joke, expressing gratitude or compassion, creating an intimate moment, or, eventually, conversing with his own soul.

The development of concrete operational thought appears to be hardwired into humans. But the fact that some children never acquire concrete operations leads us to wonder if egocentric child-rearing and educational practices can suppress or delay this and other normal developmental milestones. Conversely, we might investigate what practices can enhance and extend these developments.

CIRCLE OF IDENTITY: SOCIOCENTRISM

At the beginning of the Garden stage, the child has no capacity to imagine being in the position of another, a capacity necessary for conscious empathy. Although stage-1 toddlers commonly *act* empathically and altruistically — they'll help mom fold laundry — this is, as I've suggested, an expression of their innate desire to belong, not of an ability to experience the world from another's perspective. True empathy does not appear until the emergence of concrete operations. Before then, the child's interests are his own very personal ones, including his desire to be part of a community of others.

If all goes well in the Garden, the Explorer's circle of identity gradually shifts from self-centered to sociocentric (family-centered) in the course of this stage. This transition takes place in two phases. In the first, conscious empathy becomes possible as the child learns to imagine the perspective or take the role of another. Empathy develops not just because of neurology-enabled concrete operations, but more significantly as a result of the child's natural emulation of empathic adults and older children he observes, as well as his felt experience of being valued by others. Through imitation and his desire to be a part of his world, he learns to imagine being in the position of another. By developing conscious empathy, he becomes capable of genuine altruism — seeing another's needs as more important to the other than his own needs are to himself. And the "other" need not be human. For children who have plenty of free play in nature, experiences of trans-species empathy and altruistic acts are common — and profoundly beneficial to their soulcentric growth.

The development of conscious empathy and altruism, however, take us only halfway to a sociocentric circle of identity. The sociocentric child experiences his family as the primary realm of his existence and loyalty. His circle of identity grows beyond his own person to encompass others. Not only can he imagine the position of another (empathy) and act altruistically, but he can also make choices from the position of his family-as-a-whole. He's able to act in the best interests of his family even when those interests conflict with his own narrower desires. Moreover, the sociocentric child not only can *think* from his family's perspective but also can act from that identification instinctively, without coaching and without incentives.

Sociocentrism does not mean that a child necessarily considers his sister's rights, for example, to be more important than his own. Rather, it means that he has the ability to empathize with his sister and to consider the possibility that his *family* might be better served by supporting his sister's immediate needs or desires above his own. This isn't really an altruistic act; it is something even more mature: both he and his sister are benefiting from his choice, he by furthering the welfare of the family of which he is a member, and his sister through the support of her immediate needs. His effort on behalf of his sister is an act of self-love as much as it is love for another *if* his circle of identity has come to encompass his family.[54]

Sociocentrism, then, is more than empathy and altruism. Sociocentrism is putting one's family first. Sometimes a sociocentric person will put his own immediate needs above another family member's because doing so serves the family best. For a sociocentric person, this wouldn't be a selfish act.

In the Garden, however, the child's circle of identity rarely reaches beyond his family. From his perspective, his family (and often his religion, ethnic group, or country) is "in" and "right," while most others are "out" and possibly "wrong."

CHILDHOOD SURVIVAL STRATEGIES

In an ideal world, all children would be fully accepted by everyone for exactly who they are. But this is not the way the world works. Even if all children were unconditionally loved by all adults (not likely), there are the other children, especially siblings, who, given their immaturity, would be a good deal less than fully accepting. Moreover, even soulcentric parents cannot say YES to *everything* their own child does. After all, part of the parents' job is to help their child become an accepted member of society. The child must become human in one particular cultural way. Inevitably, some of the child's choices and behaviors are going to be deemed improper, and it's the parents' task to help him learn the ways that work. Soulcentric parents will give him as wide a range as possible within the limits of family and culture.

For the child, the difference between a soulcentric and an egocentric setting is not automatic social acceptance in the former; it is the fact that gaining it is rarely, if ever, traumatic.

In both the egocentric and soulcentric versions of stages 1 and 2, most children shape themselves into one of the particular social styles deemed acceptable by their families. This requires children to suppress some of their impulses and emotions and to modify some of their behaviors. I call the silent, private methods that children develop for self-shaping "childhood survival strategies" (CSSs). These are in fact the child's best option for psychologically navigating his early years. They can be extensive and severely self-hampering when the family is egocentric and highly repressive. But every child, even in the most loving soulcentric setting, needs at least some modest survival strategies.

The most common ones in egocentric society include self-criticism, codependent "helping" styles, perfectionism, and emotional suppression — each a method of conforming to expectations or rendering the self less visible or offensive and thereby, emotionally and socially safer. For boys, nonemotional macho personas or save-the-day heroism are common, especially in egocentric families. For girls, princess and coquette personas are more likely. Some children have no better options than to become the clown, the mascot, the oddball, or the victim.

A boy, for example, who grows up hearing from his divorced mother "It's a good thing you're not like your father, who never appreciated me!" is likely to develop a codependent survival strategy of paying more attention to his mother's desires (and later his girlfriend's and wife's) than his own.

Children who are indulged by affluent, egocentric parents — parents, for example, who work full-time, have largely abandoned their children to nannies or day-care workers, and attempt to assuage their guilt by giving their kids whatever they want — develop a special set of strategies. These children often close their hearts to all people, because the absence of their parents' genuine love is a pain too great to bear. Indulged children with little interest in social acceptance can end up as self-absorbed "adults" with little capacity to form meaningful relationships.

The intent of every CSS is to place self-imposed limits on behavior so as to enhance acceptance or minimize criticism, punishment, or abandonment. These strategies succeed by downsizing the self — making it small or narrow enough to conform to the expectations of parents and others, or to fly beneath their radar, or to be emotionally immune to their demands.

Significant self-suppression, which is common in egocentric society, often results in emotional depression and anxiety disorders and the withering of the child's innate and wild imagination. The emotional and social results become apparent in early adolescence, which we'll explore in the next chapter.

Childhood survival strategies from stage 1 work as well as they do because they are fashioned outside the child's own awareness — the child, after all, *has* no conscious self in stage 1. Moreover, these strategies are shaped by a part of the psyche that is older, more clever, and more self-protective than the conscious self, a part capable of taking survival matters into its own hands. The ego is not able to interfere with self-limiting choices of which it is unaware. This is also why CSSs are so difficult to stop — or to even recognize in oneself. I call this self-protective part of the psyche the Loyal Soldier because it does everything it can to secure our safety in the best ways it knows. It's similar to what Freud meant by the superego. We'll discuss it more in the next chapter.

The child, then, must divide himself internally and sometimes act in opposition to his true self. He must learn to behave in part as if he is someone he's not — the false self. Yet, under the circumstances, this is in fact the best choice, the healthiest option. Unlike an adult or even an adolescent, a child *must* fit into his immediate family and community. If he has no place there, he has no recourse — he literally has no place at all, and he will not survive, psychologically or physically. Despite their personal toll, CSSs are developmentally appropriate and often necessary, the alternative being far worse.

In an egocentric family, the child who fails to develop adequate CSSs as needed is likely to suffer serious psychological injury. She's the one who neither conforms nor goes invisible and so gets labeled oppositional, defiant, rebellious, hyperactive, or learning-disordered. She has not learned how to diminish herself for the sake of her own survival. As she becomes discouraged about ever being accepted in her world — her family — she is likely to rebel openly against those she sees as the perpetrators of her isolation. She might progress from power struggles with her parents and other authority figures to acts of revenge, both stemming from her increasing discouragement about belonging. She runs a high risk of chemical addiction, prison time for crimes of violence, homelessness, incapacitating mental illness, or dying young.

In both soulcentric and egocentric settings, childhood survival strategies, when successful, help the individual reach emancipation age psychologically intact — somewhat suppressed and depressed perhaps, but with personal potential still recoverable.

After leaving his parents' home, a youth will no longer need most of his childhood survival strategies, but these strategies will nevertheless remain on automatic pilot, deployed without his awareness or consent. If he is fortunate — perhaps with the help of an elder, an initiation guide, or a well-trained psychotherapist — he might (1) begin to consciously recognize his survival strategies, (2) learn to suspend or interrupt them, (3) begin to heal his old wounds by finally accepting and feeling the subterranean emotions that have been smoldering since the time of his early emotional woundings, (4) undergo the emotional, imaginal, and interpersonal learning that was delayed as a result of his old survival strategies, and (5) creatively choose less defensive, more effective and authentic ways of belonging to the world and of living at his own frontier. We'll explore these steps in more detail in stages 3 and 4.

PRIMARY SOCIOECONOMIC TRAINING: THE EGOCENTRIC COUNTERPART TO THE GARDEN

With their whole gaze
animals behold the Open.
Only our eyes
are as though reversed
and set like traps around us,

keeping us inside.
That there is something out there
we know only from the creatures' countenance.

We turn even the young child around,
making her look backward
at the forms we create,
not outward into the Open,
which is reflected
in the animals' eyes. . . .

— RAINER MARIA RILKE, "THE EIGHTH ELEGY"

When contemporary children are raised with little or no free play in nature and with-out the daily guidance of soulcentric parents and teachers, they're likely to experience a version of stage 1 very different than the Garden. Rather than experience a wonder-filled youth in field and forest and an irrepressible curiosity about creative cultural prac-tices explored with friends and family, they are more likely to spend their days at the mall, in front of TVs, computers, and video games, and in classrooms where they are force-fed facts with little relevance or interest. The worst-case scenario looks like a full-time apprenticeship in consumerism, competition, conformity, rote learning, fast food, and passive viewing — "turn[ing] even the young child around, / making her look backward / at the forms we create, / not outward into the Open," as Rilke laments in his elegy.

But with good fortune and a reasonably healthy family, many children in ego-centric society experience something not nearly so extreme or toxic. For the sake of a clear contrast, however, I describe here an egocentric middle childhood that is a far cry from the Garden and which might be more honestly called Primary Socioeconomic Training (PST). Although this might sound Orwellian to some readers, it will, alas, be all too familiar to others.

While contemplating this section, you might experience a good deal of grief that your childhood (or your children's) was more like the egocentric version depicted here than the soulcentric rendering described previously. If so, please remember that grief is virtually always the necessary doorway to major personal change, in general, and to the underworld journey of soul, in particular. We must open to our lacks and losses in order to find our deepest longings, which, in turn, form the path to our true way of belonging to this world. So, should you encounter grief here, please recognize and embrace it as the very doorway you need. If you cannot do this on your own, you might seek skillful help in falling into that grief, at the bottom of which you are sure to un-cover a treasure.

If guilt, shame, or anger should arise as you read, those emotions, too, when accepted, will become portals to your healing, because, in due time, they will bring you to your grief. If your psyche, unbeknownst to you, is now ready for an experience of healing and wholing, you might feel that the following description of PST is somehow blaming you when it is actually intended as a dispassionate portrayal of how egocentric society really functions. When viewed with an open heart and mind, such a society is experienced as unspeakably sad and tragic. But the way out is always through. Joanna Macy's work has demonstrated that the unrestrained experience of despair leads to empowerment. Similarly, grief, when fully felt, leads to personal transformation.

On the egocentric wheel of development, the first stage of life, Obedience and Entitlement Training, ends with the transition of Parent Liberation (see Diagram 3-6, p. 71). The child's enrollment in school signifies the parent's freedom from the near-constant task of child rearing. To the egocentric parent, this liberation is as significant as the commencement of the child's formal education.

Primary Socioeconomic Training continues where Obedience and Entitlement Training left off, but now both obedience and entitlement are promoted in concert by schools, advertising, egocentric religions, and government, as well as by egocentric parents. The implicit message (sometimes explicit) is: "You must unquestioningly obey your parents, teachers, minister, God, and president, and you must remember that you live in the greatest country that ever existed, that your religion is the only one that God endorses, that God is always on the side of your nation and against all its enemies, and that you are entitled to all the consumer items advertised to you." (Recall the parental advice on Dobson's website quoted in the last chapter.)

Stage-1 Obedience and Entitlement Training do not disappear, but are subsumed within PST and reinforced with new and more potent age-appropriate methods.

The covert goal of PST is the conditioning and indoctrination of the future workers, consumers, and soldiers needed to sustain a global industrial growth society and its extreme disparities of wealth between the elite class and the poor. PST drills the child in the knowledge, skills, values, and behavior patterns that support those kinds of roles in that kind of society. It creates an environment in which healthy natural faculties are suppressed or undermined — faculties such as imagination, wonder, independent thinking, the love of learning, deep feeling, vibrant sensing, cooperation, self-esteem, positive body-image, empathy, and intimacy. The child is bombarded with egocentric messages on TV, computers, video games, radio, and recorded music, in newspapers, magazines, and public buildings, and in the hallways, books, and curricula of his schools. PST is the child's initiation into a synthetic culture of dog-eat-dog competition, materialism, virtual relationships, violence, superficial and objectifying sex, and unfulfilling work.

PST prepares the child to make a life within the egocentric economic system, shaping him as an instrument for enhancing the gross national product or the nation's military might, the primary objectives of an egocentric-dominator society. In their personal lives, egocentric citizens (especially of the middle and upper classes) pursue individual versions of these same goals of wealth and security — material riches obtained through work or theft and personal security enforced by gated communities, insurance policies, lawyers, or guns.

In a highly egocentric family, childhood survival strategies are many and extreme. The child's genuine personal qualities are largely ignored or suppressed. In order to survive, the child learns to focus almost exclusively on what others expect of him. He becomes proactively adept at pleasing others — a codependent, caretaker, rescuer, or enabler. Having lost much of his innocence in his first stage of life — and thus his natural capacity for presence, affiliation, and belonging — he experiences little self-worth. Self-discovery, imagination, and enthusiasm are thwarted. He becomes increasingly unlikely to uncover a genuine identity rooted in nature or his own soul.

In an egocentric setting, the first two developmental stages and the transition between them are parent- and economy-centered, hence the names I've chosen: Obedience and Entitlement Training, Parent Liberation, and Primary Socioeconomic Training.

In a soulcentric setting, in contrast, a child-centered and community-centered perspective asks: In order to grow into the most authentic and wild (natural) version of himself, what are the child's most essential needs and how can the family and community meet those needs? In the Nest and Garden, and by means of Naming, how might we best welcome the child into the more-than-human community so that his life serves the whole?

In an egocentric world, a dehumanizing and nature-foiling cultural agenda stretches from childhood to the grave. Interpersonally, other people are seen primarily as objects, as mere extras in one's own self-important, nonrelational drama or as consumers in the nation's ever-expanding GNP. How can this person meet *my* needs or the economy's needs? Children are trained to see themselves this way, too — in other words, not in terms of their natural qualities but in terms of their social or economic worth. It is tragic enough that our society treats the nonhuman world — animals, forests, soils — as a collection of objects to be used, but people are also trained to do this with each other. This is the hidden agenda of the most degenerate dimension of egocentric society, and it is unutterably corrupt and heartbreaking — rewarding people for experiencing themselves as economically serviceable veneers.

Such materialistic values and lessons are embedded in contemporary culture and form the context in which children are raised. In addition to the competitive, authoritarian, and consumer-oriented programming inherent in our schools, films, and media, there are also the narrow gender roles modeled in games, sports, and socializing, and the ubiquitous social emphasis on material possessions and fashion, as opposed to the development of relationships, sensitivity, feeling, imagination, sensing, and creative thinking.

Primary Socioeconomic Training is embedded in many of our pastimes and is found as subtext in our churches and synagogues, the military, the business world, entertainment, and colleges and universities.

As one example especially relevant to stage-2 children, consider video games, some of which are designed and produced by the U.S. military to condition future recruits to think militaristically and to experience killing as natural. An often-cited selling point of video games is that they help develop strategizing abilities, which is to say, staying in your head and out-thinking your opponent — which, in turn, leads to greater success in business and the military. Video games also cultivate amoral conformity, which is an essential foundation of an enduring egocentric society. A recent review of video games discusses the rise of the "Organization Kid" and quotes a description of Princeton University students by the *New York Times* columnist David Brooks:

> "They're not trying to buck the system; they're trying to climb it," Brooks wrote of the respectful, deferential students he met. A Princeton sociology professor whom Brooks interviewed could have been describing ideal soldiers when he said of his students, "They're eager to please, eager to jump through whatever hoops the faculty puts in front of them, eager to conform." Brooks summarized the love-the-power worldview of the Organization Kid like this: "There is a fundamental order to the universe, and it works. If you play by its rules and defer to its requirements, you will lead a pretty fantastic life." That's a winner's ideology: Follow orders, and you'll be just fine.
>
> Whether you find the content of video games inoffensive or grotesque, their structure teaches players that the best course of action is always to accept the system and work to succeed within it.
>
> ... So don't worry that video games are teaching us to be killers. Worry instead that they're teaching us to salute.[55]

To the extent that PST succeeds, children's interests and circles of identity never grow beyond what is necessary to meet their immediate personal needs, and never embrace more than the economic or security needs of their nation. Other nations are perceived as actual or potential storehouses of slave-wage workers, as economic and military allies (when they share the same narrow and self-serving interests), as "evil empires" (when they don't), or as irrelevant. Other species and Earth's soils, waters, and air are perceived and treated simply as "resources." Empathy is poorly developed, genuine altruism rare.

In the end, I don't know what is more surprising: how often in egocentric society PST succeeds (namely, with more children than not) or how often it fails (a sizable minority). Given PST's power and prevalence in our society, its failures are one of the strongest arguments for the existence and survival of the human soul and of the animate and animating Earth.

CREATING A SOULCENTRIC FAMILY LIFESTYLE
IN AN EGOCENTRIC WORLD

How can you, as a soulcentric parent in an egocentric society, optimize the social, psychological, and educational environment in which your child learns and grows in the Garden?

There are two things you can do: protect your family from egocentric influences, and create a soulcentric lifestyle. When enough families have done this, our culture will shift fundamentally and radically — with or without the support of governments, large corporations, schools, or religious organizations.

Creating a Shelter from Egocentrism

Here are several examples relevant to prepubertal children (several helpful books are listed in the resource section at end of this volume):

- Minimize or eliminate children's exposure to TV. Most programming is bad enough, but the underlying message of the ads is worse (the way to personal happiness and social success is physical appearance, conformity, and commercial products). The best approach is to not have a TV in the house. If you own a TV and are not ready to toss it, begin by removing it from any central or visible location in your house. (Hide it in a cabinet or beneath an attractive fabric, or wheel it into a closet.) Yes, it's possible to live without TV. No, your child will not be socially disadvantaged if she cannot talk about popular shows and commercial products. She will have more intriguing things to talk about. If you choose to continue living with a TV, use it rarely or only for viewing selected videos or high quality programs that occasionally appear on PBS or other networks. If your children do view any programs, watch them together. Be aware of your desired outcome in watching the show and create a dialogue with your children around that theme. But beware the power of addiction! If there are any TV addicts of any age in your home, the TV will tend to stay on and on and on.
- Limit video games and movies watched at home, too, for the reasons listed above, and because your children need to have plenty of time to exercise their own imaginations with other children, you, nature, books, and the arts.
- Be selective about which movies children see, video games they play, and music they hear at home and, to the extent possible, elsewhere, and make it a habit to talk to them about the values implied in particular films, games, and songs.
- Have a few nights a week when computers are off-limits and activities are encouraged that creatively rely on imagination, emotion, the senses, and independent critical thinking.
- Be discriminating about the books your children read and the stories you read

or tell them. What sort of values and lessons are embedded? As Mary Pipher notes, "Most of the stories children hear are mass-produced to induce them to want good things instead of good lives."[56]

- Limit the amount of time your kids spend in organized, high-pressure, winning-obsessed sports (so they don't become preoccupied with aggressive competition and performance, and so they have time for all the other dimensions of growing).

- Are you caught in work that is stressful, unsatisfying, and that may or may not pay the bills? If so, your reserve of energy and creativity to spend on and with your children is likely to be limited. Is it possible to shift your lifestyle? Are you remaining in your current job merely to afford things that do not truly serve your family?

- When contemplating the purchase of the latest technological wonder, ask first not about its affordability but about its effect on family life and sound childhood development.

- Avoid gifting your children with commercial toys and products. As much as possible, allow their rewards to be experiences naturally engendered by interacting imaginatively with the world — with other children, with you, with nature, and the arts. When you do give them material things, let those be items that richly engage their imagination, senses, thinking, and feelings.

Creating a Soulcentric and Ecocentric Family Lifestyle

- Focus on the two subtasks of the Garden discussed in this chapter, especially giving your children lots of exploration time in wild places; helping them to cultivate their relationships with their bodies, imaginations, and emotions; and telling them stories rich with virtues, values, ecocentric moral lessons, and imaginative possibilities.

- Cultivate in your children an awareness and appreciation of all emotions — yours and theirs. Each emotion, when felt, respected, expressed, and explored holds a treasure, a gift, for the whole family.

- Hold regular family meetings to discuss important family issues — meetings in which authentic dialogue can take place. Learn and use a council format for these meetings. Begin this tradition around the time of your oldest child's Naming. This will work well only when you show up as a true adult — authentic, vulnerable, emotionally congruent, and compassionate. Never use these meetings to sabotage, manipulate, or covertly punish your kids. Poorly implemented councils are worse than none at all. See references on family councils and meetings in the resource section in the back of this book.

- There are many ways to spend time in nature with children: learn the different leaves, needles, seeds, fruits, and barks of trees; identify types and parts of flowers;

draw or paint flowers, trees, animals, lakes, streams, forests, mountains; or make up songs and dances that celebrate natural things. You can also watch birds and mammals (with and without binoculars); visit uncrowded beaches, forests, canyons, deserts; play hide-and-seek in those places; camp; or fish (it would perhaps be best if you fully honor the lives of the sentient fishes, keeping and eating those you catch — as opposed to catching and releasing and thereby traumatizing them — so that your children learn to appreciate the sacred gift of lives providing food for their own). Or you might collect feathers, bones, or stones where this is environmentally tenable; gather plants or fruit; or plant and tend a garden.

Real time in nature can be supplemented by visits to outdoor natural history museums and botanical gardens, or by pets and stuffed animals, nature films and books, and video libraries with nature themes. But nothing substitutes for frequent unmediated contact between children and wildlife in natural habitats, contact that is spontaneous, intimate, and visceral. The emphasis should not be on the rarely seen, aloof animals, but rather on the often smaller, more common wild beings — a flock of ducks, a swarm of termites, an army of leaf-cutting ants, a community of ground squirrels. This way, the child experiences the magic in nature everywhere, not merely in the exotic and rare. Also beware of traditional zoos that cage and traumatize animals, treating them as mere spectacles for human entertainment.

- Invaluable are nature stories told by elders with a lifetime of intimate relationships with the local plants and animals.
- The best learning environment for your child is the wild outdoors explored with other children. But if you have limited access to untamed nature, the next best thing might be "naturalized playgrounds" at schools. These contrast with most play areas found at schools, which are paved, flat expanses filled with manufactured climbing equipment, with neither shade nor shelter and no opportunity to interact with natural things and beings. Such playgrounds are designed to allow easy surveillance of kids and ease of maintenance, and to provide teachers a break from kids. You might join with other parents and teachers to transform the playground at your child's school.

The new naturalized playgrounds beginning to appear in North America are planted rather than built. They use the landscape — its vegetation and materials — as the play setting, and are designed to be as wild as possible and to stimulate children's natural curiosity, imagination, and wonder. Basic elements include water; indigenous vegetation; small animals; ponds and their aquatic life; butterflies and bugs; sand; natural places that children can sit in, on, under, lean against, and climb, and that provide shelter and shade; places that offer socialization, privacy, and views; and structures and materials that can be changed and manipulated by children, including lots of loose parts.[57]

- Encourage active life-making rather than passive life-watching. For example, support kids in making music rather than just listening to it.
- Find opportunities in the community for the family to volunteer its time and talents in support of other people, animals, or habitats. This helps children feel good about themselves because they experience their usefulness and connection to a bigger world.
- Create ceremonies and rituals that celebrate your family relationships, significant human passages, the seasons, dawn and dusk, your home bioregion and its more-than-human community, and Earth more generally.
- Develop ongoing relationships with sacred places — specific ones, both natural and cultural. Visit those places regularly as a family.
- Formal education: Over the past three or four decades, some public and private schools have remembered that the word *education* actually means to draw out (rather than fill up). These schools appreciate and accommodate different learning styles, invite children to think critically and creatively, emphasize project-based and place-based learning, and provide plenty of opportunities for feeling, imagining, and cultivating the senses (for more on this, see this chapter's resource section at the back of the book). If you have the economic resources as well as the educational options in your community, carefully select the schools to which you send your children. If there is not yet a desirable school in your community, seek out other parents who would join you in creating one. Some parents are able to provide part-time or full-time homeschooling. Those with limited financial means must supplement the education provided by their children's public schools. Meanwhile, those of us who are affluent have the obligation to do what we can to transform our society so that the quality and variety of education is not class-based. This is not merely a moral obligation but one of the most exciting and potent opportunities to cocreate an eco-soulcentric partnership society.
- Cultivate a true community with like-minded neighbors, a community that includes people in as many stages of development as possible. Gather with others and explore the roles of education, politics, religion, food, ceremony, mythology, and cosmology within your community. Only through community and united action can we create a more ecologically sustainable and culturally sound world.

REAWAKENING WONDER LATER IN LIFE

No matter how old we get or what stage we reach, we never grow out of our capacity for wonder. There's always, in life, infinite good cause for naïveté, curiosity, amazement, and exploration.

Yet, while reading this chapter, perhaps you've wondered how well your ability to truly wonder has survived. You might, in addition or instead, feel that you never, even in childhood, fully immersed yourself in the boundless enchantments of the natural world. The good news in both cases is that it's not too late. It never is. You can always devote yourself to the uncompleted tasks of previous developmental stages. Doing so strengthens the foundations of your current stage and enriches the possibilities of your unfolding life. In contemporary culture, most all of us have a good deal of unfinished business from middle childhood.

If you suspect this is true for you, here's what I recommend. Spend as much time as you can — either alone or with a prepubertal child — in wild or semiwild places. A city park, woodlot, or garden will do. If and when you can, get out of the city and into less tame places. Make a regular habit of it. Learn the names of plants and animals, if you'd like, but more important, learn through your own senses their habits, stages or cycles of growth, habitats, and needs. Don't forget about the water-dwelling and air-roaming creatures, in addition to those that favor land. Also, through your own observations, what can you learn about rocks, about their geological origins, textures, and hardness? For the time being, don't consult books, and do filter out your ideas about these others' "usefulness" or "nonusefulness" to humans. Get to know them on their own turf, instead. Observe them and respectfully interact with them with as much reverence and wonder as you can muster.

If you bring along a child, then once you arrive at your destination, let her bring you along. Let her set the pace and the focus. Get down to her level. It's your responsibility to keep the two of you safe enough, but other than that, let her be your role model, your guide to wonder and exploration.

Like a child, allow yourself to become a naturalist, something you'll find easy if you let yourself be curious. All humans are naturally naturalists. We humans evolved, after all, in the wild, and our survival and fulfillment depended on our having the ability and desire to get to know our world fully and subtly. Genetically, you are still one of those humans.

Visit field, forest, wetland, desert, and ocean as often as you can. Offer your attention with care. If you like, keep a journal of what you discover.

Here is a solo exercise you can use to reawaken and deepen your innate, childlike sense of wonder in nature: Go for a walk in a park, a rural area, the seashore, or some other wild place. Find your pace, a rhythm, some balance. After five minutes or so, let yourself travel back in time to childhood. Remember how it felt in your body when you were a child, as young as five or as old as ten, to be small and energetic and limber and to be outside with plenty of time. Let your center of balance shift downward. Allow yourself to walk like you did as the child you were, to see as you did, to *feel* as you did. Surrender your adult agenda. Look around, play in the sand, collect "treasures," hide in small places and peer out, build a "nest," draw with a piece of found charcoal, skip, talk to a tree, climb a tree, look down a hole. Explore, build, play. Go wild or be still. Allow the world to be new again. Take at least an hour to do this. A whole day would be better. Let yourself be surprised by what happens. Bring a couple treasures back with you (physical things, if their extraction or absence would in no way harm that place, or perhaps a story, sound, song, gesture, or movement) and share their wonder with someone you trust. This last step is especially important.

Hand in hand with nature, the wilderness of your imagination is the other realm within which to reawaken wonder. If you don't enjoy a robust relationship with the imaginal, especially your deep imagination — your dreams, deep imagery, and visionary capacities — consider taking courses in dreamwork, imagery journeys, art, dance, music, or creative writing.

Here are some additional suggestions:

- Allow yourself to play again! Play the way an Explorer does. Skip. Build sandcastles. Play fort or tag. Learn to skateboard or ride a mountain bike.
- Immerse yourself in one or more expressive arts, playfully.
- Try new forms of movement or dance, including Authentic Movement or five rhythms.[58]
- Become a gardener with an emphasis on wonder and play.
- Read a book on the Universe Story and let yourself feel the astounding and bewildering imagination of the cosmos.[59] On a clear night, go to a place far from city lights (ideally with an Explorer), lay on the ground, gaze deeply into the sky, and wonder. Perhaps learn to use a telescope.
- Watch for synchronicities in this playful universe!
- Learn a new language, just for fun.
- Lose yourself in poetry.
- Do something that is totally new to you (eat new food, travel, visit museums, dance).
- Go to a children's museum or an amusement park.

CHILDHOOD'S END

We might say that a child has completed the Garden stage at the commencement of puberty, but, by itself, that statement wouldn't be informative, for two reasons. First, there's no single identifiable moment at which puberty begins. No definitive bells, whistles, or fireworks. Second, it is *psychological* puberty that signals the end of the Garden. Psychological puberty and physiological puberty are distinct phenomena, even though either might quicken the other. So, saying that the Garden ends with puberty begs the question: How do you know when psychological puberty has begun?

It's not when the tasks of the Garden have been completed. Recall that, although working on the tasks of our current stage is what moves us through that stage, the transition is neither caused nor signaled by our completion of those tasks. After all, no developmental tasks are ever fully completed.

A principal theme of the Wheel is that the transition from one stage to the next is caused by a shift in the individual's psychospiritual center of gravity, a shift that is set in motion by the Mystery. With Puberty (the passage from the Garden to the Oasis), the shift is from a life centered in nature and family to one that orbits around a peer group, sexuality, and society. Mythologically speaking, what happens is that the child tastes the fruit of the tree of knowledge of good and evil and is thereby expelled from the Garden.

You know a child has moved into early adolescence — or is at least ready to move on — not by his physiological sexual awakening, which is neither necessary nor sufficient, but by his questions, choices, concerns, and preoccupations. His whole life begins to demonstrate that what matters most to him now are not the wonders of the fields and forests, nor his relationships with parents and siblings, but rather the intricate possibilities of peer relationships, the allure of sexuality, and the enhancement of his social status within the larger human community. It might seem to his parents (and sometimes even to him) that what he most wants is to get as far away as humanly possible from his parents and younger siblings, but what he really wants is to immerse himself as deeply as he can in social and sexual relationships that he can cocreate with his peers independent of his family's surveillance or interference. This, of course, is the subject of the next chapter.

The passage of Puberty usually holds a good deal of unavoidable sadness for both parent and child. Childhood is over — that blessed interval of play, wonder, exploration, unimpeded learning, and an essential simplicity and innocence relative to what's coming. Many would say that the Garden was the best stage of life.

CHAPTER SIX

THE THESPIAN *at the* OASIS

Early Adolescence (Stage 3)

This being human is a guest-house
Every morning a new arrival.

A joy, a depression, a meanness,
some momentary awareness comes
as an unexpected visitor.

Welcome and entertain them all!
Even if they're a crowd of sorrows,
who violently sweep your house
empty of its furniture, still,
treat each guest honorably.
He may be clearing you out
for some new delight.

The dark thought, the shame, the malice,
meet them at the door laughing,
and invite them in.

Be grateful for whoever comes,
because each has been sent
as a guide from beyond.

— JELALLUDIN RUMI, "THE GUEST HOUSE"

Stage 3: Early Adolescence

Passage into this stage: Puberty

Stage name: The Oasis (Social Individuation)

Task: Fashioning a social presence that is both authentic (the nature task) and socially acceptable (the cultural task)

Quadrant: South (emotions and body)

Hemispheres: South and West (individual action)

Stage archetype: The Thespian

Quadrant archetype: The Orphan

Gift to community: Fire

Circle of identity: Ethnocentric

Center of gravity: Peer group, sex, and society

Passage out of this stage: Confirmation (confirms the adequate completion of the adolescent personality and the consequent preparedness for the descent to soul)

IGNITING THE WORLD

Mysterious changes in the body. Hormonal flushes. Sudden, unbidden stirrings, softenings, and swellings. The longing to touch and be touched, and the terror of it too. Fire!

Puberty ignites many fuses, but they're not only physiological and sexual. We feel the explosive push and pull propelling us into the world to forge what seem like unconventional relationships. We begin to detect and then claim a niche we might call our own in the suddenly heated social and sexual scene.

The difference between the sexes now makes all the difference in the world, more than it will in any later stage. A grand tension develops between teenagers — both in the sense of conflict and in the sense of sexual charge, the one pushing us apart, the other pulling us together. We begin to orbit each other, close enough to suffer the passion and pain of the slow burn, but usually not yet close enough to be consumed and transformed in that fire.

A quick look at the Wheel of Life (Diagram 3-3, p. 61) shows us why puberty incites our fiery leap into the wider world. Puberty is the transition at the South point on the Wheel. With this shift from the Garden to the Oasis, we remain in the South quadrant (the quarter of life centered in body and emotional life), but a transition takes place here that has profound implications. At puberty, we are in the center of the warmest wedge of the Wheel (the South), but we are also emigrating from the East hemisphere to the West. We are crossing over from the *being* half of life to the *doing* half. In the soulcentric version of the previous stages (the Nest and the Garden), the child's life was not focused on getting ahead, winning, making a name for herself, or providing for others. (To the extent she *was* focused in that way, she was robbed of her childhood, a developmental tragedy that happens all too often in our egocentric society.) Rather, her childhood was more about innocence, growing, wondering, feeling — in short, *being*. Now, in the Oasis, everything shifts. We leave childhood behind forever and depart the East hemisphere for what might as well be forever. Entering the West hemisphere, we add impassioned action to the already established heat of the South. As a result, the world tilts and the matrix of life pitches forward. There's an urgency to make something of oneself, to plunge into the social world, to fire up new varieties of relationships, to leap into love and heroic adventures, to take on risky and unfamiliar responsibilities, to choose a direction in life, to seek a mate or a lover, to develop a style, a flair, a name, a gig, a special talent, a distinctive personality.

The world fairly *explodes* for us with all this running about and erotic heat. The root impulse of sex is creative action — not merely procreation but also the engendering impetus of life itself and of the very universe. As indigenous inhabitants of the cosmos, we're driven to merge with others and create never-before-seen wonders. In the flames of puberty, volcanic emotions and desires erupt. In a healthy (soulcentric) early adolescence, our strongest urge is not simply for sexual intimacy but also for the imaginative forging of innovative social forms. While culture was a given in childhood, now it becomes a fabric for us to refashion.

And for each of us, one of the newly forged social forms will be our own personality, an authentic social presence. Fashioning a genuine life is the central task of early adolescence and requires a refuge from the family matrix that defined the childhood self.

In the midst of her adolescence, Joanna Macy found such a refuge in Montaigne's tower. Being a student in a French lycée in New York City, she learned about Michel de Montaigne, the sixteenth-century French parliamentarian and essayist who built himself a tower for personal retreat. In her imagination, she regularly entered Montaigne's tower to be apart from the turmoil of her family life, to allow her mind to still and then to fill with her own genuine thoughts and feelings. Finding out what she really thought was Joanna's way of finding out who she was. In her memoir, she recalls her teacher saying that "self-portrayal forms a person, delineates his inner self, reveals *le moi profound*." "Immediately," Joanna writes, "I felt my own desire for precisely that: to find out what I really thought, to know my *moi profound*. That is why Montaigne needed his tower, and why I needed it too."[1]

The transition at puberty is as monumental as the one that will happen half a lifetime later, when we recross the same hemispheric boundary but in the other direction — from West to East, from doing to being.

It's important to keep in mind that, as in the first two stages of life, there are both soulcentric and egocentric versions of this third stage. Through most of this chapter, I describe the soulcentric (healthy) version, saving the egocentric (and actually more common) rendition for the section titled "Conforming and Rebelling."

PUBERTY: PASSAGE INTO ADOLESCENCE

Puberty refers not only to a cluster of sexually related biological blossomings but also to a host of cognitive, motivational, emotional, and social developments. Even from a purely physical perspective, puberty is not a single event but a long and gradual unfolding that can begin anywhere from age eight to age thirteen and end as late as age eighteen. A girl's first menses, for example, does not signal the start of puberty but instead occurs relatively late in the course of sexual maturation. The South point on the Wheel, then, represents not physical puberty but *psychosocial* puberty, a transition sudden enough to be considered an event, and betrayed by identifiable psychological changes.

The child reveals that she's on the brink of puberty neither by her age nor by observable changes in her body but by a profound alteration in her primary motivations and her understanding of what the world is. Her psychospiritual center of gravity — the hub of her world — shifts from family and nature (where it was during the Garden) to peer group, sexual identity, and the larger society beyond her family. Her motivational priorities migrate from wonder-filled explorations of nature and foundational cultural practices to creation of an authentic and socially accepted place, including a sexual place, among her peers. After this transition, she will still make discoveries about nature and culture — this will continue for the rest of her life — but these central concerns of childhood are no longer primary. Equally so, it's not as if, before puberty, she had no interest in her peer group, gender roles, and the greater society. It's just that these were secondary, forming a background or supplement to the central focus of her life — family and nature.

In a soulcentric adolescence, the natural world is not left behind or neglected. Wild nature itself becomes an essential generator of the heat that forges the healthy adolescent personality, especially its authenticity. Early adolescents need a testing ground, a place of healing, and a mirror other than, and wider and deeper than, the one provided by mom and dad or, for that matter, anything found in the village.

In preagricultural societies, puberty rites served not only as a passage into social and sexual maturity but also as an initiation into adulthood. Today, however, even in the healthiest of modern settings, no pubescent youth are even remotely prepared for true adulthood. Now they have the growth opportunities of adolescence to contend with and, potentially, to benefit from.

In this book's first chapter, I suggested that the relatively recent appearance of what we now call adolescence might confer a momentous evolutionary advantage, as the idea of *Homo imaginens* implies, but only if we take advantage of its growth opportunities. To do so, many radical changes in society are required. We've already considered several in these pages, and we'll explore more as we continue. But first let's consider how a rite of passage can get adolescents off to a heartier and more empowered start, while keeping in mind that a puberty rite alone can never make up for failures with the tasks of the Nest and Garden.

When parents notice the earliest signs of psychosocial puberty, they have the responsibility and pleasure of preparing, with the full participation of their child, a ceremonial rite of passage. Of the nine major life transitions on the Wheel, puberty is especially important to celebrate, because it is the first one in life in which the individual possesses conscious self-awareness on both sides of the passage. Consequently, a puberty rite provides the individual with an experiential template for all subsequent major life passages. A puberty rite also eases the transition and brings clarity for all family members, and the child is enabled to begin adolescence with less confusion and more pride and confidence. Parents have the opportunity to ceremonially conclude their role in parenting a largely dependent child, offer their blessings, and prepare for the very different role of parenting a much more independent youth — an adolescent.

It's crucial, however, to understand that a puberty rite is an initiation into adolescence, not adulthood. The latter is still two life stages away.

The best way for puberty to be ceremonially marked and celebrated depends, of course, on the individual's family and culture. In creating a puberty rite, it's essential that parents don't expect from their child a maturity she hasn't been prepared for, or that she doesn't see admirably modeled in the adults around her, or for which there is no satisfactory outlet in the social world as it exists.

A puberty rite in a modern soulcentric family might include the following elements:

- A period of preparation, perhaps as long as a year. Preparations might include:

  - Putting away childhood things. The child is guided in gathering her belongings and clothing specific to childhood. She divides these items into those she'll keep and those she won't. Before and/or during the puberty rite, the initiate will either give to younger children the items in the second group or ceremonially sacrifice them (either by recycling them or, for those items that are nontoxic and biodegradable, by burning or burying them or casting them in a river). These items symbolize the qualities of childhood that the initiate will leave behind — perhaps a security blanket or certain toys that imply a small worldview. (In a sense, the puberty rite is a funeral for the Explorer.) The first group of items symbolizes the childlike traits that the initiate intends to take with her into adolescence and adulthood, such as a prized collection of rocks or pinecones that speaks of her lifelong capacity for wonder.

- A number of instructional meetings with a group of adults of the same gender as the child (usually *not* including the child's parent, because the puberty rite as a whole constitutes the ending of the family's role as the hub of the child's life). This group might be made up of friends of the parents, aunts or uncles, grandparents, community elders, and/or others chosen by the initiate. The meetings might include more than one initiate. The purpose of these meetings is the transmission of fundamental principles concerning sexual maturity and social roles, illustrated with informative and engaging stories. Topics might include the biology and psychology of sexuality; the naturalness, goodness, and sacredness of sex; the physical, emotional, and spiritual nature of sexual relationships; what it means to be sexually mature; how to create and maintain a masculine or feminine role among peers; the nature of emotional intimacy; and what it will mean to become an initiated adult (two stages later).

  These meetings might also be the time to teach or remind the initiate(s) about the community's world story — stories that reveal the sacredness of the world and of all life — and its understanding of the psychospiritual stages of the human life cycle, perhaps while presenting a four-directions map such as the Wheel of Life. An introduction to the Wheel might happen outdoors, everyone sitting on the ground, with the map embodied in stones and other natural objects. There might also be a review of, or advanced instruction in, psychosocial skills, such as emotional access and expression, conflict resolution, and expression of empathy.

- Individual preparation activities, such as self-exploration and value clarification through creative writing, music, dance, drawing, and painting.

- Fashioning of adolescent symbols and implements. As the time of the puberty rite nears, the initiate might be assisted in crafting items that will either aid him during the rite or symbolize his community role during the next stage — perhaps a blanket, a knife, a basket, or an article of clothing. These items would be "officially" employed for the first time during the puberty rite. Boys and girls might choose different sorts of items that symbolize differences in gender roles.

- The puberty rite itself, lasting anywhere from several hours to a couple of days, with activities such as:

  - Purification rites — for example, bathing, water immersion, sweat ceremonies, smudging with burning herbs or incense, prayers, and blessings.

- Men's and women's circles open only to the initiate(s), initiated adolescents, and adults, for lively exchanges on the significance of puberty and the opportunities and obligations of adolescence, and for generating gender-specific ways to support and celebrate the initiate's transition.
- The initiate's ceremonial sacrifice, either private or witnessed, of some of the childhood objects and symbols.
- The initiate's giveaway, to younger children, of other childhood items.
- The initiate's gifts to parents, expressing gratitude for birthing and growing her as a child.
- Gifts to the initiate by members of the family and community — gifts that symbolize the end of childhood and the attainment of adolescence.
- Statements and symbolic enactments by parents, other adults, and older adolescents concerning the character of the initiate.
- Statements or symbolic enactments demonstrating that the initiate is leaving behind childhood.
- A ritual enactment with closest family members, perhaps witnessed by others, that symbolizes the cutting of the bonds of childhood that had kept her safe yet restricted within the womb of the family. One way I've seen this done begins with the family standing in a close circle. The initiate holds on to one end of a ball of twine and tosses the ball to another person in the family. The tossing of the ball proceeds from one family member to the next until there is a web of twine connecting each family member to every other. Here, then, is a visual and poignant embodiment of the intertwined heart connections. Then, the initiate cuts herself free with a knife, perhaps looking each family member in the eye as she makes the cut and thanking them for their part in growing her. This ritual ends with the initiate leaving the ceremonial site either alone or accompanied by adolescent, adult, and/or elder members of the same gender. As the initiate leaves, her family shouts words of love, encouragement, and their feelings of both sadness and pride in seeing her go.
- At some point, perhaps in the middle of the night, a meeting with one or more nonfamilial adults — *soul-initiated* adults — of the complementary gender. Everyone is seated on the floor or the ground, in a circle. The initiate is instructed in the psychosexual nature of the other gender and in the dynamics of sexual relationships from the perspective of that gender. The sacredness of sex is emphasized, and the initiate's natural curiosity about sexuality is encouraged to flow freely in questions. A nonfamilial adult of the initiate's gender, serving as witness and support, accompanies him or her. The initiate is given the opportunity to ask questions. This meeting might best take place outdoors around a campfire or inside a tent, yurt, teepee, or other small, ceremonial structure.

- Solo time outdoors, perhaps in a place held sacred by the initiate or the community. Either a long, wakeful night or a more extended period, by which the initiate demonstrates her willingness and ability to take care of herself; to be separate from the care and comfort of parents, siblings, and peers; and to encounter aloneness and personal demons.
- A ceremony, with symbolic objects and/or ritual actions, in which the initiate claims Earth as her primary mother and the Sun or sky as her principal father. This ensures that the initiate continues to be parented, but now by powers greater than just her mom and dad, who, during the ceremony, make a ritual enactment of surrendering a portion of their role as parents.
- A ritual to reintegrate the initiate, as an adolescent, into the family, emphasizing the different status that the initiate now occupies, using symbolically significant clothing, words (for example, vows and lists of new responsibilities and freedoms), gestures, and/or other actions.
- A community feast or celebration.

Other families create much simpler versions of puberty rites that still possess significant power. Soul guide Lauren Chambliss describes one of several ceremonies she enacted with friends or family to welcome her daughter into adolescence:

> When Cece was 11, we enacted a ceremony to deepen her connection to and understanding of her emerging womanhood. Four women friends gathered round and, while she lay on the Earth, the four of us massaged her young body and each of us talked of what it meant to be a woman. We could see her absorb every word, each touch of our hands, the oils, and the richness of the ceremony. I believe this initiation helped her view her coming transition into womanhood as a gift, a heritage, a possibility.[2]

Over the past three decades or more, creative families and communities around the world have developed many innovative models for contemporary puberty rites. Kia Woods, a psychotherapist and ceremonialist specializing in the dynamics of puberty, has worked in this field for over thirty years and has refined a powerful and artful ritual form that brings people from the wider community together with the initiate and family.[3] Other models are discussed in a compilation entitled *Crossroads.*[4]

EARLY ADOLESCENCE AS AN OASIS

I imagine a healthy (soulcentric) early adolescence as an oasis. After puberty, the teenager ventures from the family home, garden, and neighborhood and soon enough finds himself at a community gathering place, an oasis. Here he encounters people of all ages, personalities, agendas, styles, and, in most contemporary societies, races. The people here are diverse and often exotic to him. There is allurement and danger. The possibility of erotic attraction and liaison is everywhere in the air. The oasis is a marketplace as well, and there are foods, spices, clothing, intoxicants, and crafted items that delight, amaze, puzzle, and frighten him. There are people engaged in unfamiliar activities — businesses, gambles, social experiments, ventures, celebrations, rallies, and expeditions preparing to depart to points unknown. And nature is there, too, in the waters of life, the trees and bushes, the soil, the wind, and the constant, palpable presence of the wild that surrounds the oasis.

Although a relatively safe and contained space, the Oasis of early adolescence always has a storm on the horizon and, not infrequently, one sweeping through. A soulcentric adolescence is not a particularly peaceful time even in the healthiest families and communities. Unbidden disturbances are common — emotional tempests, hormonal hurricanes, relationship squalls, and courtship typhoons that sometimes feel like volcanic eruptions from hell.

Although occasionally stormy, the Oasis stage nonetheless eases the transition between the comparative safety of the Garden and the unconditional metamorphosis that occurs in the Cocoon. In this sense, the Oasis (a *soulcentric* adolescence versus one that is egocentric) is a temporary sanctuary, a refuge, a haven.

For the adolescent, the Oasis often feels like a talent show or a popularity contest. Everyone is checking out everyone else (usually covertly), and everyone is trying to appear attractive in one way or another. Everyone is busy individuating socially.

SOCIAL INDIVIDUATION AND THE OASIS

Carl Jung, who coined the term *individuation*, referred to "a slow, imperceptible process of psychic growth" that gradually results in "a wider and more mature personality."[5] Individuation, then, is the lifelong process of growing into wholeness. Marie-Louise von Franz, one of Jung's senior students, compared human individuation with the process by which a pine tree develops from a seed: "Thus an individual pine slowly comes into existence, constituting the fulfillment of its totality, its emergence into the realm of reality. Without the living tree, the image of the pine is only a possibility or abstract idea. Again, the realization of this uniqueness in the individual [person] is the goal of the process of individuation." Echoing the theme of soul, von Franz notes that "each of us has a unique task of self-realization. . . . The fact is that each person has to do something different, something that is uniquely his own."[6]

In the Oasis, we individuate primarily in terms of our social roles and relationships. Therefore, the Oasis can also be called the stage of *Social* Individuation, the period in life, whether a few years or a lifetime, when the individual differentiates herself within the horizontal, polymorphous, yet relatively superficial world of everyday society. In contrast, after Soul Initiation (that is, beginning in the Wellspring stage), the adult ripens herself in relation to the more mysterious, deeper, and diverse worlds of soul and greater nature.[7]

Adolescence is thoroughly misunderstood in egocentric society, in part due to the evolutionary recency of this stage and in part due to a profound misconception of the nature of adulthood. Egocentric society thinks of adolescence as "young adulthood," as an early version of maturity without full eligibility for adult opportunities, or as a pause on the threshold of the adult world. These ideas are not entirely wrong. Obviously, adolescence *is* a sort of preparation for adulthood. But in the contemporary world, the "adulthood" for which adolescence is said to be a preparation is conceived, and embodied, in a way that amounts to little more than an advanced version of adolescence. It's adolescence with all the trimmings. From such a perspective, teenaged adolescence is truly only a minor-league version of the subsequent egocentric adolescence that passes for adulthood.

From a soulcentric perspective, adolescence is not early adulthood but another thing altogether. With the onset of adolescence, the individual becomes the social adventurer who must learn the art of making his way in the world without the shield (or fenced garden enclosure) of his immediate family. The human community grants him eligibility to participate in new social activities and relationships. It's time for him to push the limits, try out his new social powers, see where and how he fits. Social belonging and loyalty mean everything at this stage. The world reveals itself as a fundamentally different place with a new set of attractions, opportunities, and problems to solve. Within and especially outside the family, the self takes on a social and sexual presence that did not exist previously.

The goal, and task, of Social Individuation is to fashion a self that is both authentic and socially acceptable, to find a genuine way of belonging and a group to be faithful to. When successful, the adolescent gradually differentiates a persona, a personality, an individuality, one that has an endorsed place in the social world — a place that is respected and deemed worthy by *both* self and others in a peer group or community.

The psychologically successful adolescent in the Oasis knows where she stands socially, knows which sorts of people she gets along with in what sorts of ways. She knows and appreciates her own developing personal style, interests, attitudes, and sensitivities. She knows and appreciates her most salient weaknesses and liabilities, as well as her most prominent talents and gifts. She is able to experience her own emotions and knows how to express them to others in a way that serves both self and other. She enjoys a good foundation of self-esteem while understanding that the self is always a work-in-progress, and she has acquired the basic skills of initiating and maintaining intimate relationships with family and friends. She has become comfortable with the fact of her gender and with the opportunities, joys, and responsibilities of sexuality.

Early adolescence is meant to be a kind of apprenticeship — not an apprenticeship to adulthood or to soul, but an apprenticeship in the art of differentiating a social self and of belonging to an extrafamilial social group. The adolescent's task in the Oasis is to compose one particular way of being human — her *own* way — that works well enough in her society. It is her first extended spin around the sociocultural block. As with all apprenticeships, she learns by doing. She learns what it is to consciously construct a social self by constructing a first one. Her mission is limited to the development of this first, provisional way of belonging to the wider human community. Her creation is not meant to be a final product to last the rest of her days. Starting in the next stage, the Cocoon, she'll begin the project of building a more deeply authentic self, an adult self — a self rooted in soul.

SOCIAL INDIVIDUATION
AT DIFFERENT TIMES IN LIFE

Up to this point, I've written as if everyone in the Oasis and everyone in early adolescence is a teenager. But in an egocentric society like ours, this is hardly the case. More people than not either remain in the Oasis (soulcentric stage 3) for the balance of their lives or, even more commonly, enter egocentric alternatives to the Oasis. The latter, egocentric trajectory begins with a teenage stage I call Conforming and Rebelling (described later in this chapter) and then continues through a sequence of five other egocentric stages (described in the next five chapters), each approximately a decade long.[8]

Many teenagers in egocentric society never reach the Oasis, because they have been in the egocentric sequence since birth. Instead of experiencing the Nest in early childhood, they were in Obedience and/or Entitlement Training. Rather than the Garden in middle childhood, they were in Primary Socioeconomic Training. Now they find themselves in Conforming and Rebelling rather than the Oasis. But I believe it's still possible to enter the Oasis from any of the later egocentric stages, beginning with Conforming and Rebelling (stage 3a), and that the most effective way is to work on the previously unaddressed or most incomplete tasks of the Nest and Garden. After entering the Oasis, a person can also work on the Oasis tasks and eventually reach the Cocoon, especially with the support of mature (adult) guides. But in contemporary societies, the Cocoon is rarely attained in the teen years and is more commonly reached in the late twenties through forties, or later still, if ever.

In contrast, in a hypothetical soulcentric society achieved later in this millennium, I would expect most everyone to make the transition from the Oasis to the Cocoon between the ages of sixteen and twenty.

Although the majority of people in contemporary societies remain in some version of stage 3 long past their teen years, it's important to emphasize that people in the Oasis (which is always soulcentric) are significant contributors, regardless of their age, to the health of human community. A healthy person in *any* soulcentric stage, from the Nest to the Mountain Cave, contributes to a sound society. My guess is that about 25 percent of all Americans over the age of thirteen are in a more or less healthy Oasis, about 25 percent are in the Cocoon or beyond, and the remaining 50 percent are in one of the six egocentric versions of stage 3 (that is, 3a through 3f — see Diagram 3-6, p. 71).

Given that so many in our society find themselves in stage 3 long after their teens, we need to think of two versions of Social Individuation as we continue in this chapter. The two versions have somewhat different sets of concerns.

With teenage and college-age Social Individuation, a major consideration is how parents and teachers can best relate to stage-3 youth, young men and women who might be in high school, college, or neither, and who are either in the soulcentric Oasis or in the contrasting egocentric stage of Conforming and Rebelling. Parents and teachers are still very much part of the everyday lives of most teenagers and many college youth, but how much the parents and teachers can assist the maturation process depends entirely on the mentors' own developmental stage.

The circumstances of most post-college-age stage-3 people are quite different from those of teenagers, because their parents and schoolteachers no longer play major guiding roles, or at least not in the same way. Most of these people in later-life Social Individuation are economically and socially independent. The question for them is how to relate to their *own* personal development and how to find their own soulcentric mentors and role models.

Underlying both sets of concerns is the question of where stage-3 people in an egocentric society can get help with the maturation process, whether they are in their teens or later years, and whether they are in the Oasis or one of the six egocentric versions of stage 3. Where are the mature guides, therapists, and elders? Given that the transition into the Cocoon — and then the Cocoon itself — is perhaps the most challenging time in life, it's no coincidence that this is where contemporary societies have run aground. Getting help with the tasks of the Oasis — from soul-initiated adults — ranges from invaluable to flat-out necessary. These mentors do indeed exist, even in our egocentric society, but you'll need to search a while to find one, exercising discernment along the way, because every next person seems to be offering one form or another of the "answer" or the "secret."

The most essential consideration when seeking an initiation mentor (or a psychotherapist, for that matter) is the mentor's developmental stage. This is far more important than the words or models the mentor uses. What can you detect about her deepest motivation? If she is truly an initiated adult, her principal life motivation is soul-rooted service, which means her conscious intention is to serve her more-than-human community as well as the desires of her own soul. (It's not possible to do one without the other.) Is this kind of motivation evident in the way she conducts her life, both privately and publicly? Or, like adolescents more generally, is she merely or primarily trying to carve her own socially acceptable and economically viable niche in the world?

THE THESPIAN: ARCHETYPE OF A SOULCENTRIC EARLY ADOLESCENCE

Shakespeare noted that *all* life's a stage and all of us merely players, but this is especially true in the Oasis. At this stage of development, society is the center of our life and often the full compass of our conscious concerns. We are first and foremost Thespians, dramatic actors on the social stage. Most important to us are our social scene, our job, our way of expressing our personalities, our relationships, and our human community. We're forever auditioning for new parts, polishing our familiar roles, scrutinizing other people for potential roles in our personal dramas, and giving stage directions to the current players in our life who, in our estimation, often seem to be getting their parts wrong. We are experimenting with new social styles and expressions, fabricating new sets and scenes. Sometimes believing in our act more than at other times, we know ourselves, in any case, as performers, dramatists, social joiners, and occasionally, quitters.

It's not that there's any time in life when we cease being interpersonal beings in a human community, but in the Oasis our social life is our *central* focus, the coin of the realm, our raison d'être. And our social life has a great significance to us independent of its relationship to anything deeper or greater — independent of soul or spirit, the greater mysteries of life. The primary context of our lives is the village, and our primary self-identification stems from our roles as actors — players — on that stage. We are continuously jockeying for more comfortable, rewarding, and authentic positions in relationships of all sorts — romance, sex, friendships, family, employment, cliques, and clubs — and in connection to all sorts of social endeavors, including sports, music, crafts, career, and games.

Thespian comes from Thespiae, an ancient city of Greece, where, according to mythology, the Muses — the nine daughters of Zeus and Mnemosyne — performed their many games, including the theatrical kind. Thespians, then, have a great variety of styles and genres generated by the musing feminine dimension of our humanity. Thespiae was founded by Thespius, who, in Greek mythology, was the father, by

Megamede, of fifty daughters, all of whom bore sons by Hercules. Hercules represents the epitome of the early-adolescent male hero — the enormously strong demigod who slays the dragon (actually the Thespian lion who attacked the flocks of Hercules's father), returns unscathed (and thus essentially unchanged), has sex with all the maidens (all fifty), engenders a great deal more macho masculinity (fifty sons!), and gains immortality as his reward for near-impossible feats. What a guy. Hercules is a fitting icon for male Thespians, just as the Muses, immersed in their many artistic pastimes, are for adolescent women (of any age).

The archetype of the Thespian does not imply inauthenticity. In fact, the cultivation of authenticity is one of the Thespian's top priorities. He's in the process of discovering which social roles are most fitting for his particular personality and worldly circumstances.

The Thespian is the archetype of all soulcentric stage-3 people of any age — in other words, people in the Oasis. Egocentric stage-3 people, in contrast, are ruled by the archetype of the Impersonator, which *does* imply willful inauthenticity for the purpose of social acceptance or self-aggrandizement. In the section on egocentric development later in this chapter, I'll further differentiate the archetype of the Impersonator.

Given that the differences in gender roles are greatest in the Oasis, we need masculine and feminine versions of the Thespian, at least for how they appear in Western culture. The more masculine rendition is the Societal Entrepreneur — someone focused on social advancement. The Societal Entrepreneur is looking for opportunities to make things happen (progress), arrangements that'll be interesting, profitable, and a contribution to society, or at least ones that will allow him to get by socially and financially. He — or she — wants to create a notable place for himself on the socioeconomic map, a way to compete in a healthy way, a way to obtain attention, admiration, sexual partners, or at the very least, a decent place in the world. Even the shy introvert can be a Societal Entrepreneur. He may not be gregarious or have hordes of friends, but you can bet that his greatest desire is to be admired by his peers. As in the business realm, the Societal Entrepreneur is an innovator, generating and experimenting with new roles and ways of being, new styles, and new social environments. He's looking for the authentic combination that attracts his fair share of social, sexual, and economic fulfillment.

A more feminine incarnation of the Thespian is one we might call the Communal Gatherer. She (or he) operates by cooperation more than competition. She's more sensitive to her connections with people and places and to what feels good in the moment. She's less interested in getting someplace new than she is in more fully inhabiting and enjoying where she already is. She is furnishing, adorning, and making comfortable the place she calls home. She is cultivating and gathering her clan, looking for the resonances that already exist and saying YES to them. She's more interested in creating something *with* others (a community, a sorority, a home) than in outcompeting anyone in her social group.

Beyond their differences, however, both the Communal Gatherer and the Societal Entrepreneur are busy designing and organizing, and most of their effort is in the social realm. Their common goals are social enjoyment, participation, and security. Any given Thespian, male or female, might function more like the Gatherer or the Entrepreneur, emphasize one style over the other in different settings and relationships, or combine both styles at once.[9] (We'll further explore gender differences later in this chapter.)

In our egocentric world today, most people over twelve are doing what both Thespians and Impersonators naturally do — attempting to improve their personal position (masculine) and environment (feminine) in social, aesthetic, and economic ways. This is true on the collective level, too.

In egocentric America, for example, the mainstream national conception of progress (usually, in fact, called "growth") refers to the egocentric-masculine goals of an ever-increasing gross national product and an expanding market overseas, and to the egocentric-feminine goals of secure borders (to keep out those who "aren't like us and don't belong here") and plenty of consumer goods for all real Americans. On the individual level, it's a matter of finding an emotionally safe spouse or social group, keeping up with the Joneses, one-upping the competition, and dying with the most toys.

In contrast, in the soulcentric culture beginning to emerge all across the globe, the Thespian version of collective societal progress promotes mature, soulcentric-masculine goals such as sustainable development and the triple bottom line of people-planet-profit. It also promotes mature soulcentric-feminine goals such as economic fairness and justice for all people, and basic rights for all species and habitats. Personal goals include the cocreation of an intimate, egalitarian relationship; forging a fulfilling and adequate livelihood; and contributing to the social, economic, and environmental health of the human community.

For those who mature past the Oasis, the Thespian — although no longer the primary archetype — forever remains an important component of a healthy personal constitution. The Thespian archetype always informs our way of cultivating new, authentic, and ever more fulfilling relationships and of celebrating community as the setting for soul-filled child-raising, human intimacy, mutual support, personal initiation, and our soul-rooted giveaways.

THE ORPHAN, PART II

The archetype of the Wheel's South quadrant, the Orphan, continues to have a powerful pull in the Oasis. In a sense, we are now doubly orphaned — from our family as well as from the womb and spirit, our place of origin. It doesn't matter that our own longing for independence contributed to this new stage of orphanhood. The fact remains that we now feel our aloneness all the more acutely and so, too, our longing for a more secure and authentic way of belonging to the world, of fitting in. As Thespians, our desire is to create a world and a self that works for us, one that provides a way of being that holds some promise, a future, the possibility of fulfillment and companionship, work, and love. Only for the Orphan does such a desire feel like the primary and all-consuming need.

Beyond the Oasis stage, the Orphan archetype continues to serve us whenever we need to create or maintain a safer or more functional place for ourselves in the social world, and certainly whenever we feel alone or abandoned, betrayed or afraid. It's the job of the Orphan dimension of our psyche to regenerate a secure world and an authentic self. The Orphan archetype operates in this way, either overtly or in the background, until the task is accomplished. In healthy development, the Orphan serves as a necessary and adaptive image, being neither unfortunate nor regressive — unless, like adolescence more generally, we get stuck there.

THE THESPIAN'S CONTRIBUTION TO THE WORLD: FIRE

Go into any reasonably healthy seventh or eighth grade classroom, and it will be obvious: The gift of the early adolescent to the world is fire! Healthy teenagers are ablaze, radiating warmth as intense as the midday Sun. Just as we receive most heat when the Sun is in the south, we humans emit most heat when we're in the South quadrant of the Wheel. Teens run a fever of enthusiasm, idealism, and sexual arousal. The world is to be tasted, consumed, pressed upon. Raw passion and willfulness fuel their fire. They crave extremes of experience, mobility, and volatility. They're ready for adventure, especially social and sexual research, in their energetic quest to find their unique place in the human community.

This gift of fire is a great boon to the larger community. By way of that fire, the Thespian is an extraordinary innovator. She's cooking up new styles in fashion, music, dance, language, games, and sports. She brings a fresh perspective and an enormous unquenchable desire. She shakes things up, like a hyperactive critic from a strange and exotic discipline; she has a fresh perspective and she's going to share it whether you ask for it or not. And god knows, she can show you some things you wouldn't have seen otherwise, because maybe you've become a bit overinvested in one particular way of being alive. So she keeps social life fresh, new, safe from calcification. She reminds you that, as important as essence is, style matters too. She's in your face, holding up a mirror to your social forms, showing you where you've begun to take yourself too seriously, showing you where you've forgotten to grow in style.

The Thespian's fire is hottest in the teen years, the years for which nature designed us to be at the Oasis. By our midtwenties, that social fire is beginning to cool. If we don't move on developmentally, we might find ourselves becoming a parody of a teenager, a flamer without heat, an aging, surgery-assisted Barbie doll or a knight in crumbling armor.

THE TASKS OF THE OASIS

The central developmental task of early adolescence — again, this refers to Thespians of any age, not just teens — is to create a secure and authentic social self, one that invites both social acceptance and self-approval. Either criterion alone is insufficient, which is why the Oasis is so challenging and stormy. Fashioning a socially acceptable self while ignoring authenticity is relatively simple — you just mimic whatever works for others and ignore your own impulses. Likewise, an authentic personality is not so difficult to shape. All you need do is whatever you feel like in each moment while disregarding social niceties, relationships, or those damned interpersonal torpedoes. But generating a social presence that is *both* secure and authentic is difficult for most people even under the best circumstances.

Authenticity is the nature-centered component of the task in this stage. Who you really are (your attitudes, interests, and so on) and how you really feel are not part of a strategic decision of your conscious mind. These are elements of your actual nature. At the Oasis, the Thespian's job is to uncover that nature and learn to enact it.

Social acceptability is the culture-centered component of the Thespian's task. What's acceptable and what's not, especially in this stage, is a matter of fashion, fad, cultural mores and styles, and social meanings and conventions.

Living each moment with the dynamic tension between the nature and culture dimensions of her developmental task, the Thespian must find a way to honor and incorporate both aspects of her humanity. Lauren Chambliss describes her teenage daughter's successful struggle with this tension as amplified by the intense peer pressure typical of egocentric America:

At age 13, Cece is a small, lithe, physically beautiful, athletic, and socially popular young woman. The "cool" boys at school are letting it be known that she would have a cool boyfriend if she acted more like "a girly girl." We have discussed what this would mean. She says, "Well, I would have to be less opinionated, not beat the boys in sports, and wear sexier clothes more often."

I asked her if she would be happier if she had a cool boyfriend. She thought for a moment and said, "I don't know. Sometimes I think so, but the cost of not being myself feels like it is too much."

Essentially this child is making conscious decisions about the limits to which she will mold herself to fit into her peer group. She is not blindly be-ing initiated by peers, but questioning and aware. She straddles both worlds — self and society — and it is not easy. I am astonished that she can find a way to listen to her authentic self in such a stifling social environment.

One factor that makes the task of the Oasis so difficult in contemporary society is the complexity of the social world. There are not only social roles and sexual relationships but also the intertwined dimensions of style and fashion, sports and music, clubs and cliques, drugs and alcohol, and political perspectives and social movements.

During the Oasis stage, the world becomes more personally *constructed* and *chosen*, as opposed to the given world of family and nature that was *discovered* and *accepted* in the Garden. This conscious and creative fashioning of an authentic social self — a self-in-a-world — lays the foundation for the passage of Soul Initiation some time in the future. Although our first personality — the one we flesh out in our teens — is meant to be provisional, its adequate development is essential for all that follows. We require a solidly grounded, well-rounded first personality before we can benefit from the rigors of the soul-initiation process.

The task of creating a socially acceptable and authentic self divides into eight sub-tasks pertaining to values and authenticity, emotional skills, conflict resolution, status assignment, sexuality, sustenance, human-nature reciprocity, and childhood survival strategies. These eight subtasks are explored in the following sections.

Acquiring some comfort with and appreciation of risk, especially social risk, is a built-in feature of all eight subtasks. For teenage Thespians especially, trying out new values, social personas, and authentic self-expressions can be perilous undertakings. Thespians of *any* age must develop proficiency with assessing risk and risk/benefit ratios, embarking upon ventures that might reap greater authenticity, intimacy, and cre-ativity. And they must learn to assimilate the emotional and social results after their leaps.[10]

Value Exploration and the Skills of Social Authenticity

In order to compose a sound social self beyond the boundaries of his extended fam-ily, the healthy Thespian at the Oasis (male or female, teenage and up) experiments with new values and the ways of life those values suggest. His new values might be derived from most anywhere within the widest bounds of society. He searches for a life he can call his own. He asks new, bigger questions and, at this stage, looks for answers out-side himself, in the greater community — answers that resonate with what he intuits inside: What is worth striving for? Who are my people? What principles will I fight to uphold? To whom and what will I be faithful? What is necessary for a decent life? What is the meaning of human existence? What, to me, is God, death, infinity?

The teenage Thespian now needs a type of support from his parents and teachers unlike anything he received or sought in the Garden. He needs the latitude and encouragement to explore new values. Grounded in his stage-2 family-membership, he must now evolve a modified set of values that fits his unfolding individuality. Teenagers in the Oasis need a good measure of psychological emancipation from their families and from any imposed loyalty to the value system of their childhood. If their time in the Garden went well, they won't stray terribly far from their family's values, anyway. If it did not go so well, they will most likely *need* to wander off quite some distance.

Parents can help by offering gradually extended freedoms within well-defined but liberal limits and by shifting most of their interventions from instruction (lectures) to questions — questions that help the healthy teenager explore the potentials and contradictions in his developing value system. Teachers can support the Thespian by offering courses that help him develop effective strategies for value clarification, without any discourses on the "right" values. Parents and teachers can also — often must — guide teens through their social and emotional obstacle courses as they try out their experimental values on the perilous terrain of peer relationships. Mature adults can give teens the enormous gift of mirroring who they are becoming as a consequence of their youthful choices, choices that sow the seeds of "failures" as well as "successes." Most important, parents and teachers must strive to be role models of personal authenticity themselves.

The tasks of Social Individuation absorb most of the attention of nearly all teens aged twelve through fifteen — which is only natural at this age. But in our society this preoccupation extends well beyond the teen years — which is not at all natural. Our society's egocentrism makes value clarification, for example, highly challenging at any age. Popular mainstream culture constantly broadcasts that the sole or foremost goal in life is socioeconomic advancement. Other dimensions of existence, such as psychological or spiritual self-development, service, art, sustainable living, and intimacy, are too often marginalized or ignored. Many people are motivated simply by the desire for psychological comfort, hoping in effect to not be challenged in any way by life. If comfort, security, and socioeconomic progress are the things that count, then authenticity, individuation, and love are secondary at best and, more often, irrelevant or detrimental. Most school curricula suppress the imaginative, emotional, sensory, and intellectual capacities needed to fashion a creative and fulfilling life, and there are few true adults and elders in the community to show our youth the way.

On some level, most teenagers recognize that our society is largely shallow, unjust, and inauthentic. They sense they will likely not find within mainstream America what they are looking for — an existing community worth belonging to and being faithful to. The world they were born into is not one that many of them really want to join, but they don't know what alternatives, if any, exist. Consequently, to find their own values and to succeed at psychosocial emancipation — even in a minimal way — a majority of teenagers in egocentric societies rebel against their parents, who, for them, are the primary representatives of the mediocre mainstream.

A second reason for the rebellion of so many Western teenagers is their profound ambivalence about emancipation. Teens naturally want freedom, but because most Western teens have had so little experience with real psychosocial risk, they are also terrified by genuine independence. Egocentric societies, with their emphasis on materialism, mechanical thinking, and conformity, do not engender much teenage risk-taking beyond the limited-run, hormone-goaded, adolescent antics, which, whatever results they might have, do not incite any psychological or interpersonal growth. Consequently, Western teens alternate between their dread of leaving home and their fear of being seen publicly under any circumstances with mom or dad. Many act out their ambivalence in exaggerated dramas of mostly symbolic rebellion. Nevertheless, given the options at this stage — rebellion or conformity — even shallow rebellion is a healthier choice. At least it gets them out the metaphorical door so they might begin their exploration and clarification of authentic values.

In egocentric society, stage-3 parents are as ambivalent as their teenagers about their teens leaving home. For sure they want to see their kids mature, but they're also grief stricken at the thought of "losing" them. They try to avoid their grief by attempting to delay the inevitable emancipation, convincing themselves that their teens are simply not emotionally ready for greater independence. To the extent parents succeed in delaying emancipation, they obstruct their teens' stage-3 development. Many of these parents are trying to postpone the daunting question of how they'll define *themselves* and shape their own lives when they're no longer everyday parents. By delaying their own self-examination and growth, they are perpetrating the same developmental crime against their teens.

Some stage-3 parents might also be jealous of or competitive with their child and, consciously or not, want to see their teenager fail at joining the larger world.

Many parents (in any stage) feel hurt by their teens' rebellions, and understandably so. They miss the warmth and regular family activities they enjoyed with their prepubertal children. Parents also feel the sting of their teen's not-so-veiled criticisms of mom and dad's personal traits and way of life.

But it's essential to see that, by rebelling, these teens are not trying to push their parents away. Rather, they're trying to push *themselves* away — to shove off from the launching pad (whether exemplary or shoddy) that their parents helped them build. Healthy early teens are ready to launch themselves into the wider social world — and they need to. Parents must stand firm so that their kids have something solid to push against.

Standing firm means holding on to yourself and your value system and acknowledging that your teenage child is becoming someone different from you, and that this is okay even though it evokes sadness and fear. (One example of how this might sound: "I see you're exploring a different way of life, and that you have some misgivings about the one you grew up with, the one I still choose. I'm sad about that, and somewhat afraid, but I'm also proud of you for taking risks and finding your own way. I see you're becoming different from me, and I want you to know I admire who you're shaping yourself to be.") Standing firm means telling your child about your feelings without implying that he must change what he's doing, or expecting him to do so. You can validate yourself and validate your child simultaneously. And it's important to celebrate his successes *and* failures at psychological and social independence: his courageous and imaginative explorations are more important than successful outcomes. Let him know you'll be there when he needs you. Set clear behavioral limits for your teen — limits that are as wide as he can responsibly handle on most days — and stick to them until it's time to widen them again. As always, and more than anything, standing firm means being a role model of authenticity, intimacy, and emotional transparency.

Given our imagination-numbing society, it's justifiable and probably necessary for teens to dress and behave in any way that helps them shove off from the mainstream and the styles of their parents' generation. This is normal, especially given our society's abnormality. (It might also be a normal form of self-exploration in soulcentric cultures.) The problem is the lack of genuine adults or elders showing teens how to develop true authenticity — as a complement to the acceptance-through-conformity that teens are practicing in their peer groups. Even parents who know how to help might be treated by their teens as ineligible to teach *anything*. In egocentric society, this is part of normal teenage pushing-away as they move into the larger community. With good fortune, teens will encounter an initiated adult or a true elder who can assist them with value clarification and social authenticity. That adult might even have teenagers of her own — and be regularly ignored by them!

In order to create an authentic social self, the Thespian of any age must be able to distinguish what is true about herself from what is not, becoming increasingly clear about her own genuine attitudes, interests, styles, desires, and emotions. This ability, like any, is developed through practice. Sometimes a person can benefit significantly from the help of a friend, mentor, psychotherapist, life coach, or elder. Here are some questions the Thespian might use to aid self-discovery:

Attitudes: where in fact do you stand in relation to the important issues of your place, time, and social group?
Interests: what social activities, music, art, and entertainment do you find most compelling and enjoyable, and what are your favorites among them?

Styles: what is *your* way of doing things?

Desires: at any given moment, what would you most like to do?

Emotions: what are you feeling right now? What problems in your life need to be addressed — or successes celebrated?

Getting to know ourselves in these ways is not easy and takes some focused effort. As learning proceeds, we notice that at any given moment it's possible to act in keeping with — or contrary to — our real self. Authenticity is a skill as well as a decision. We learn to distinguish authenticity from deception, and we gradually learn to spot our self-deception as well as our deception of others.

Although at the Oasis we acquire skills of authenticity, social acceptance properly takes developmental priority over authenticity when there's a conflict between the two. At such times, a stable base of social belonging promotes psychological survival and thriving even more than genuineness does. Belonging to the world is a fundamental, nonnegotiable need, and we won't be capable of a deeper, soul-rooted way of belonging until we reach the Cocoon. During the Oasis, we need only appreciate the difference between acceptance and authenticity and strive for both wherever we can.

In the previous stage, the Garden, social authenticity was not at issue. We only wanted — and needed — acceptance within the family. In a healthy family, acceptance is guaranteed. We rarely asked if we were being true to ourselves, and until late childhood we were not even cognitively capable of asking that question. In the stage that follows the Oasis, the Cocoon, authenticity becomes a *higher* priority than social acceptance. Thespian authenticity becomes a foundation for later asking the deeper questions of soul.

If you are undergoing Social Individuation (the Oasis) later in life — in your midtwenties or beyond — you, too, can use help in value exploration and social authenticity, but now it's not likely to come from parents or schoolteachers. Mature friends or mentors might help, or perhaps a psychotherapist. But primarily it's going to come from doing what healthy teenagers do. You're going to step away from what keeps you socially safe and insulated. And then you're going to roam the cultural world, open to new alliances and activities. You're going to sample a new and diverse set of relationships, pastimes, spiritual paths, foods, styles, social groups, political persuasions, sports, and jobs — as much as you can with as much variety as possible. All the while, you'll be keeping your eye open for what genuinely brings you alive, for what has heart for you and what doesn't. In this way, you'll uncover your more authentic self.

To make room for these explorations, you'll need to gradually — or sometimes suddenly — let go of existing roles and relationships that don't feel authentic, that do not truly serve both you and others. Although this is not a suggestion to shirk genuine responsibilities, beware the parts of you that are terrified of freedom. They will betray you by portraying you as indispensable to people who might in fact do better without your "help" or companionship. (On the other hand, your stage-1 and stage-2 children, for example, obviously *do* need you. If your relationship with them does not bring you alive, you need to look at why and how you've deadened yourself.) The odds are that you've designed your life to avoid your more authentic values because, should they be uncovered, they will propel you toward risky territory — your one true life — where you will be shorn of your safe and comfortable routines.

In 1945, in the midst of her teen years, Joanna Macy found herself questioning many of her foundational values. She was unable to make sense of the turmoil in her family — her father's abusiveness, her mother's codependency, and her own growing hatred of her father, all of which she judged harshly. Equally troubling to her was the measureless and seemingly meaningless death and destruction of World War II.

To find some clarity about values and her own way to belong to the world, and in the absence of real mentors and elders, she did what so many Thespians naturally do. On weekends, she roamed alone, courageously and aimlessly into the world, which for her was her hometown of Manhattan: "I walked for miles, not knowing where I was going or what I was looking for.... I was fifteen and three-quarter years old and all I knew was that I was ready to walk straight into the isolation and meaninglessness I had feared."[11] After some weeks of wandering, a pattern emerged. Joanna found herself regularly entering the Cathedral of Saint John the Divine. "The generous immensities of that huge unfinished structure soothed me. They surrounded me with mystery, received the turmoil and the aching emptiness I carried inside me."[12] There, in the cathedral, she simply touched things: stone and wood, intricate carvings, the texture of altar cloths. This was not a religious experience for Joanna, but a sensual, emotional grounding that led her, eventually, to "a kind of belonging that seemed somehow to hold me."[13]

A penetrating exploration of values is easiest in your teens (when it's supposed to happen) because you're not yet locked into a specific lifestyle anchored by career, marriage, and other midlife obligations. But by your midtwenties or later, you've achieved, more or less, "the full catastrophe":[14] a job, colleagues, deadlines, a mate, children, a mortgage, and no deep sense of what you might do with what Mary Oliver calls "your one wild and precious life."[15] To find out, you'll need to take some cues from healthy teenagers.

However, this formula — simplify your life, roam the cultural world, and notice what has heart for you and what doesn't — won't work for everyone in the Oasis stage. In particular, it won't work for those with significant developmental deficits from the

Nest and the Garden. For example, in order to simplify your life and explore the cultural world, you'll need a good foundation of psychosocial safety, the confidence of genuinely belonging somewhere. You'll need some sense of heartfelt membership either in your family, in your primary relationship, or in a small but tight network of intimate friends who'll support you in exploring whatever worlds you must. Or you'll need a rich and deep-rooted felt membership in the natural world that enables you to return there for nurturance no matter how rough the seas might get. The formation of these kinds of basic membership is one of the tasks of the Garden. If you haven't achieved this, you need to return to those Garden tasks (see chapter 5). Although not necessary, a skilled psychotherapist, if you can find one, might help.[16]

Perhaps you already have that — a foundational sense of belonging in the world — but you find it difficult to carry out the next step of discriminating what has heart for you and what doesn't. Doing so requires a good relationship with what, in the last chapter, I called your human nature — your body, emotions, and imagination. You need to be experientially in your body, be able to feel and integrate your emotions and have access to your lively imagination. To truly know what brings you alive, you need to be capable of *being* truly alive. This, too, is a Garden task, and you'll find some assistance with this task in chapter 5.

Noticing what has heart also requires you to be good at offering your attention — to the present moment, in particular. This is one of the gifts of innocence that your parents helped you preserve in early childhood — or didn't. If your parents didn't succeed, or didn't even try, you need to retrieve your original innocence, your capacity for presence. You'll find helpful suggestions for this at the end of chapter 4.

Finally, you might have had adequate success with the tasks of the Nest and Garden, but before you can explore the social world more widely, you might need to further develop some of your Oasis skills, in particular those involved with authenticity, emotions, negotiation, status-assignment, sexual relationships, and sustenance. If so, read on.

Emotional Skills

After puberty, maintaining and nurturing emotional health is especially important — and challenging. Both teenage and older Thespians begin with the affective foundations formed in the Garden, upon which they must build a more sophisticated set of emotional skills.

I've found it valuable to map emotional skills onto the four cardinal directions. This model, applicable to every emotion, describes five components of emotional integration. It begins in the East and circles around the Wheel clockwise, returning to the East. While in the grip of a strong emotion, it's possible to get stuck anywhere along the way. Until the cycle is complete, the emotion is not fully assimilated and soon enough will demand more attention. Some degree of emotional depression can be expected until all five steps are completed.[17]

1. *Somatic experience of the emotion.* Your first recognition of an emotion might be little more than "there's something going on in my body" — butterflies in your stomach, a burning of the nose, a facial flush, weakening of the knees, a lump in the throat. This bodily awareness is the threshold to the first step (corresponding to the East) of emotional integration. Upon noticing a change in your somatic experience, offer your full attention to that shift, allowing the sensation to expand in any way it wants as you get to know it. These uninterpreted sensations lead to the second step.

2. *Full psychological and bodily experience of the emotion.* This is the South step. Let the emotion have its way with your body. How does your body want to move? What postures open the doors to this emotion? What sounds does it want to make through you? What gestures? Let it happen. Perhaps you can draw it. What colors and shapes best express this emotion? Can you sing it? Express it poetically? What images arise? What memories? What metaphors occur? It often helps to name the emotion: begin with the Explorer's basic set of emotion categories (mad, bad, sad, glad, and scared) and elaborate it into something like: anger, hurt, guilt, shame, sadness, happiness, joy, fear, envy, jealousy, despair, and love. What you're feeling could be any one or a combination of these possibilities. Give your body full permission to have these feelings until you find yourself reapproaching equilibrium. Don't move on to the next step until that's happened.

3. *Insight.* Now ask about the meanings and significance of the emotion. This is the West step, in which you become fully introspective. Begin with this: What is your current emotion most directly *about*? If it is fear, for example, what is the danger? If it is joy, what are you celebrating? If sadness, what have you lost? If guilt, what do you believe you've done wrong? If anger or hurt, in what way do you feel you've been mistreated? Next ask this key question: What does the fact that this emotion occurred under those specific circumstances (which include any other person or people involved) tell you about *you*? The insights you're after here are all about you, not others. There's no requirement to put yourself down. Ask with self-compassion. Unless you get completely stuck, don't let anyone help you with this. In the Oasis, it's essential that you learn to understand yourself through your emotions. Look for your values revealed by this emotion, as well as for your desires, limitations, needs, hopes, loves, fidelities, beliefs, attitudes, sensitivities, inner conflicts, other emotions with which this one conflicts, childhood survival strategies, and your old scripts and stories about yourself and the world. Also ask: In regard to the situation that engendered this emotion, what do you most deeply want? If you could get what you *really* want, what would it be? Don't go to the next step until you've achieved some insight about yourself.

4. *Action.* Now you're ready to act on what you learned in the West. This North step is essential because the emotional cycle is incomplete until you've acted on your feelings. Given what you've learned about yourself in the previous step, what can you do to align your social world with your emotional world? Often, for example, it's appropriate to express your feelings to others. But more generally you must compassionately act on your emotions — and the qualities of self that they reveal — so that you honor both yourself and any others involved. This is essential — that your action is deeply respectful of everyone, even if (especially, actually) you felt hurt by an intimate other. When you become clear about what you need to do, go do it.

5. *Illumination.* Finally, after completing the action step, you come full circle, returning to the transcendent perspective of the East. Take the opportunity here to review the entire cycle of this particular emotion and notice the irony or humor in it. Gather any wisdom gained about yourself and your life — or about the human condition more generally. Your aim here is not detachment from the emotional experience, but, as Buddhists say, *non*attachment — neither clinging to the emotional cycle, nor rejecting it.

The emotional skills embedded in these five steps are key to the development of self-approval as well as to gaining genuine approval from others. If you're not able to honor your emotions — from experiential access all the way through to action and illumination — you'll fail to honor yourself. Low self-esteem and emotional depression are the results. Conversely, emotional self-honoring and authenticity compose the shortest path to positive self-esteem.

Developing your emotional skills is a key component of "Inner Child" or "Wounded Child" work. These five steps are your way of exercising emotional self-care as well as one component of your loving care of others. The part of your psyche you're developing with this practice is what I call the Nurturing Parent, a dimension of your wholeness that you need in order to truly love yourself and others.

The Art of Conflict Resolution

Conflict resolution or negotiation is another social skill that needs to be further developed in the Oasis. Interpersonal conflict is inevitable. Without negotiation skills, you can have social acceptability (if you always concede) or you can have authenticity (if you doggedly assert your position), but you can't have both. Conflict resolution encompasses a number of subskills:

- Clear and nonviolent expression, including the ability to make "I statements," in which you confess your own feelings, desires, and mistakes rather than enumerate the other person's shortcomings
- Openhearted listening, also termed active or reflective or empathic listening

- The ability to emotionally draw out another person, to help them discover and express their emotional truths
- The skill of legitimizing or validating another person's emotions, in which you make the case for how the other's emotions make sense, given your understanding of that person's expectations, needs, perceptions, beliefs, hopes, values, and other qualities. Validating another's emotions is not to be confused with affirming their beliefs, especially their beliefs about you, which you will often believe are mistaken
- The ability to modify your position
- The effective use of time-outs
- The ability to agree to disagree

As a Thespian, you must also acquire and hone the ability to resolve *inner* conflict — the internal collision of motivations to engage in two or more mutually exclusive courses of action.

The art of conflict resolution — and, more specifically, each of the above listed skills — requires the ability to empathize, a capacity that develops naturally in the Garden (explored in the chapter 5 discussion of circle of identity). However, if a child's natural empathic abilities were thwarted or suppressed, or if she lived in a family or attended a school where these capacities were too dangerous to use, then the person she became (as a teen or older) will need remedial help in cultivating empathy. To assist Thespians still at home or in school, parents and teachers would benefit by learning effective strategies for teaching empathy and for building a school or family culture of caring and compassion.[18]

Status-Assigning Skills

The ability to assign statuses effectively and wisely is a necessary skill for competent social maneuvering. By *status*, I don't mean the egocentric ranking of a person's social class or worth (as in "higher" or "lower" status). Rather, I mean the more general notion of a person's place-in-the-world, his social place, position, or role. (This is the same use of *place* employed in the chapter 2 discussion of soul as ultimate place.) "Boyfriend," "jock," "nerd," "girlfriend," and "confidant" are possible statuses that a teenage Thespian might assign to other people in her life. Statuses can be assigned to social activities, too. "Fun," "forbidden," "tweaked," "not for me," and "real" are examples of statuses she might give to different activities.

The Thespian of any age comes to understand that society is not simply a given, as it was for her in the previous two stages. She recognizes that she's a cocreator of her social world, and that she must learn to act accordingly. She must become imaginative and skilled at deciding what place specific people should have in her world — the role they might play, or ought to play, in her life. Likewise for the variety of social activities she might choose. And she must develop her capacity to treat people and activities in accordance with the place she's assigned them.[19]

If she is passive and allows others to determine what statuses she'll have in their lives and what statuses she will not, then achieving social authenticity will be nearly impossible for her. She must be both assertive and artful in shaping and claiming her place in others' lives, and she must know what brings her alive. On the other hand, if she has not yet developed empathy and compassion, and if she attempts to arrogantly assign statuses to others independent of their needs and desires, she will find herself socially isolated — or befriended only by sycophants, strays, and the most timid.

In romantic courting, for example, consider polar opposite ways of going wrong. One is the presumptuous "You're meant to be my girlfriend whether you want to be or not" or the more disarming but equally unappealing "I don't care if you don't want me, I'm yours!" The other is the overly passive "She'll never even notice I exist!" Successful courting is more a matter of making a clear, compelling, and nuanced invitation to the other to consider the status of "lover."

The Thespian must, in other words, learn to assign statuses that are appropriate to who she is and who others are. Rather than be at the mercy of everyone else, she must step up to the plate and become a cocreator of her world. She must decide, for example, that *this* person is a candidate for being her boyfriend or "just" a friend and *that* person is not; this one is a trusted adviser and that one isn't; playing music with these people is what I'm about, while playing golf is not; helping to keep the riverbank clean is important to me, while being on the cheerleading squad isn't, or vice versa. She must also, of course, become clear about the place in her social world *she* will occupy, how to act accordingly (that is, how to effectively let others know how she expects to be treated), and how to negotiate the inevitable conflicts between her self-status assignment and the status that others assign *to* her.

The world is a stage. The Thespian must learn to accede to that fact and proactively and collaboratively compose a social drama worth starring in.

Skills in Sex and Sexual Relationships

Being human and carnal, we are drawn, after puberty, to sensually and ecstatically merge with the body of another. Being human and soulful, we are also drawn to explore, through the dance of romantic bonding, the less tangible but no less potent mysteries of self and other. Sex and romance, distinct but related, are arousing and beguiling to all normal teenagers, even though a capacity to experience the full depths of both will not be reached till later years and life stages.

Naturally, the insistent fact of sex does not go away for teenagers when it's ignored, proscribed, or punished by parents or other professed authorities. Nor, of course, should it. Teens do not become skillful with sexuality through silence, prescribed limits, shame, or threats. At puberty and after, young people need help understanding and embodying their libido, their lust, their eros and eroticism. They need help from elders and initiators (or, at least, from more mature role models) with a number of eros-related matters. They need to know how to express sexuality in clothes, language, and behavior; how and when to flirt or court; how to determine one's own sexual orientation when there are doubts; how to accept or celebrate homosexuality or bisexuality, either one's own or another's; how to be sexual in a way that is safe enough both physically and emotionally; how to prevent disease transmission; how to decide where to draw the line; how to say NO clearly; how to use birth control; how to respect oneself and one's partner, both physically and emotionally; how to be skillful in sexually pleasuring oneself and another; how to deal with people and institutions that have sexual hang-ups and prejudices; and how to balance sexuality with all the other facets of social life.

The specific things learned in this domain are, of course, somewhat different for teenage boys and girls. Girls must learn what it means to be the sexually receptive gender, to wax and wane with the phases of the Moon, to contain the sacred vessel of the womb, and to be a mother. These dimensions of female sexuality are independent of culture, but girls must learn some version of their people's style of being feminine.

Boys, in addition to particular cultural practices and prohibitions, must learn what it means to be the sexually penetrating gender; to have a body that is generally taller, stronger, and faster; and to assume the sacred responsibility of fatherhood.

Each gender must learn about the normative strengths and vulnerabilities of the other and to appreciate the differences in biology that both must contend with and both get to celebrate.

Gay and bisexual youth must learn and appreciate the ways they are wired differently from their heterosexual peers, and how their way of embodying and celebrating sexuality carries its own set of puzzles, possibilities, problems, and pleasures.

If boys and girls (and, for that matter, older Thespian women and men) don't learn these things from mature, sexually vibrant role models, then for sure they'll learn juvenile substitutes from each other or, in an egocentric environment, from the unlimited number and variety of crude, sexist, and puerile images and stories available.

. And although it's too early, developmentally, for them to appreciate the enormous depths and subtlety of romance, teenagers need at least an introduction. They need to understand something about the relationship of the genitals to the heart, that sex, in addition to being a means to physical ecstasy and procreation, is also a doorway to the mysteries of love and soul, shadow and self, separateness and union, death and joy. At the Oasis, teenagers require an initiation into these realms even though they will not be fully prepared to embody them until the Cocoon or the Wellspring.

Developing Sustenance Skills

People in the Oasis must also develop skills of material self-reliance, the ability to earn a livelihood and define themselves culturally. The capacity to feed and shelter oneself (whether through employable skills, a craft, a socially valuable talent, a membership in a religious community, farming, or hunting and gathering) is necessary for achieving social and economic independence from one's parents or a spouse, and this sort of independence is necessary for moving beyond the Oasis in a meaningful way. Most economically dependent people don't possess the confidence and courage needed to descend into the mysteries that become both accessible and alluring in the Cocoon.

Acquiring sustenance skills does not require career training, planning out one's entire life, or sticking to a particular job. It only requires the development of skills and assurance that enable one to get by in the world, a livelihood that one might very well leave behind in the Cocoon or the Wellspring.

In egocentric Western society, sustenance activities often consume most of a person's energy and attention. This is usually not the individual's fault, but rather the way our society is designed — both in terms of how much time and effort it takes to make a living and in terms of the materialistic perception that you can never earn enough money or own enough things. This is not how it used to be or how nature designed us to be.

Studying Human-Nature Reciprocity and Ecological Responsibility

Learning about the natural world continues in the Oasis, but here the emphasis is on human-nature reciprocity, especially the responsibility of all mature members of society for the well-being of the greater Earth community. In the Oasis, our attention turns to nature's larger story, the web of relationships that connects all life, the ecology of Earth. Individual mentors and role models help us develop our own reciprocal and harmonious relationship with nature, so that we become good citizens (ecologically acceptable, in addition to socially) of the more-than-human community. Ideally, this accountability component of eco-education takes place in our early teen years, though many of us in egocentric society do not receive the opportunity until our twenties, thirties, or later — if ever.

In a soulcentric society and soulcentric human development, an essential relationship exists between the social and the ecological, a relationship that becomes salient and vital in the Oasis. We come to understand and experience the human (social) world as a component of the greater Earth community. We realize that fashioning an authentic way of social belonging requires us to study the systemic relationships that make up our more-than-human world. In an eco-soulcentric society, a personality is not acceptable to others if that person's values clash with the very environment that sustains him and his human community. Consequently, to belong to such a community — a healthy human village — the Thespian must learn how to become a full and responsible member of the larger biotic neighborhood. And this is what he naturally wants to do if he has had a soulcentric childhood.

A growing desire to study ecological relationships parallels the shift in the Thespian's center of gravity, in which his focus on individuals and relationships (in the Garden) is superseded by a fascination with the web of the larger social community (in the Oasis). The Thespian seeks to understand the relationships between his own individual life, the lives of the other-than-human beings with whom he shares his world, and the specific Earth processes of his bioregion. He learns where his water comes from and what he (and his village, city, state, or nation) does — or ought to do — to conserve and protect that water source. He does the same in regard to his food and air and the sources of his heat, clothes, and shelter. He learns to become a competent, proactive protector of nature, no longer passing these fundamental human responsibilities on to his parents and others as he did earlier. He learns not only how the human world is part of the larger Earth community, but also what his specific and immediate responsibilities are. His ecological study and participation immeasurably widen his sense of belonging and support his developing social confidence.

The Thespian's study of human-nature reciprocity also includes ceremonial practices that support his people in celebrating and expressing gratitude for the generosity and abundance of nature. These ceremonies include those associated with gardening, farming, hunting, eating, and observances of the seasonal cycle (anchored in the solstices and equinoxes). All these things are essential to his creation of a socially acceptable self that comes to belong to the more-than-human world.

Teens in an ecocentric society naturally desire to study ecological patterns and human-nature reciprocity, but in an anthropocentric-egocentric society there is little interest in such things among people of *any* age. To sustain its "profitable" but dead-end trajectory as long as possible, an egocentric society cultivates ignorance about Earth systems. It must generate fear of, arrogance toward, and even hatred for the natural world that constitutes human society's very foundation. Otherwise, people would naturally refuse to participate in the degradation of their own lives, habitats, and the lives of their children.

To form a transitional society, one shifting from egocentric to ecocentric, parents and educators must make it a priority to teach teenagers and college students the concepts and practices of human-nature reciprocity. These youth and *their* children, after all, will become the principal shapers of the twenty-first century, the moment of truth for our human future.

We can and must, for example, create curricula that place the human-nature relationship at the core of all secondary education. Much of this study ought to be experiential field research. Many progressive educators in America have taken precisely this path and created schools that cultivate language, math, and science skills within a core ecological curriculum.[20]

The Oasis study of human-nature reciprocity and responsibility, especially in a transitional society, might include an exploration of

- how nature supports every aspect of our human lives
- how there is only one economy — Earth's — of which all human economies are components
- how to design an individual lifestyle and a human economy with zero waste and emissions
- how to proactively care for endangered species and ecosystems
- how to care for abandoned pets
- how to restore damaged habitats
- how to cultivate intentional relationships in the more-than-human world
- how extractive industries have violated the human-nature balance, how to restore that balance, and what alternatives exist for meeting our genuine needs
- renewable and safe energy sources, processes, and economies
- rituals and practices for observing and deepening sacred reciprocity with the natural world
- how to see the natural world as our model, mentor, and inspiration for fashioning elements of human society and solving human problems (This is the new field of biomimicry; see the resources at the end of this book.)

In a transitional society, we must remember that the conscious discovery of the natural world's enchantment is never complete. Eco-soulcentric people regularly seek out immersions in nature in every life stage. Nature is the fundamental context and literally our home throughout life and with every breath we take. Environmentalism is not a special interest. It is a foundation to all else.

But our relationship to nature changes through the stages of the life cycle. We've already seen that, in a healthy, ecocentric childhood, the natural world is fascinating and generally benevolent and comforting. And except for the rare times when the child is physically endangered there (and knows it), he feels fully accepted and unconflicted in nature. It feels as much like home as the house he shares with his family.

The teenage Thespian, however, comes to experience nature not only as a home but also as a reflection of the self. His hopes and fears are freely projected there. The forest becomes the inscrutable maze of his own unfolding life. The mountaintop feels as distant as his own aspirations, the ocean as deep as his emotions, the desert plain as vast as his own heart. In the wild, he discovers and embraces the authenticities of his personality.

The masculine element within all Thespians comes to see nature, in part, as a context of danger and adventure in which the self can be thoroughly tested. In a complementary manner, the feminine element in Thespians experiences wildness as the standard of a fully fleshed-out self, an inspiration for personal growth. Healthy

Thespians of both genders see humanity as a part of nature, as opposed to seeing nature as a place without humanity. Their wish is for nature (including wild nature) to remain diverse and vital, and they form their position on the management of wild places from this perspective of diversity and vitality.

Welcoming Home the Loyal Soldier

Evolving an authentic and presentable social presence requires some reconciliation and rapport-building with a subpersonality, the Loyal Soldier, that each of us possesses. Subpersonalities are constellations of feelings, images, and behaviors that operate more or less independently from one another and often independently of our conscious selves. Earlier I mentioned another subpersonality, the Wounded Child, and a dimension of our Self (our wholeness) that I call the Nurturing Parent, our mature capacity for loving self and others. Unlike subpersonalities, the Nurturing Parent and other dimensions of the Self operate in cooperation with one another and most often consciously.

The Loyal Soldier subpersonality forms in our early childhood (stage 1), and its mission is to develop survival strategies necessary to assure our social, psychological, and physical survival and to minimize additional woundings.[21] This subpersonality sees his task as protecting us, but at a certain point in our personal development, his childhood survival strategies (CSSs) impede our growth far more than they provide a genuine service. This is why making peace with the Loyal Soldier is essential for people in the Oasis, and why this work will continue to be necessary, from time to time, through the Grove (stage 7).

The image of the Loyal Soldier derives from actual events of World War II. During the war in the Pacific, quite a few Japanese marines and soldiers found themselves stranded on deserted or sparsely settled islands after surviving shipwrecks or plane crashes. Some of them managed to endure, alone or in small bands, under primitive conditions and in total cultural isolation. Several were discovered many years after the war — some more than thirty years later. The astonishing thing is that each of these men retained an extraordinary loyalty to his military mission. Unaware that the war had ended, each one, upon being found, was keen to return to combat. They were told, of course, that the war was over, and that Japan had lost. But defeat was unthinkable. To them, the war could not be over because their loyalty to that cause was the psychological anchor that had kept them alive.

Upon returning home, however, they were held in no less esteem for upholding the by-then discredited aspirations for military empire. The Japanese people highly value the capacity to sacrifice personal agendas for a greater cause. So these loyal soldiers — unlike America's Vietnam-era veterans — were welcomed home with great honor and hailed as heroes.

Each one of us has a subpersonality that is a Loyal Soldier, a courageous, competent, stubborn, and self-sacrificing entity committed to assertive and sometimes drastic measures to survive the realities of our families, which, in our egocentric society, are often dysfunctional. His most common strategy was, and continues to be, a sort of psychosocial downsizing, suppressing our natural exuberance, emotions, and desires so that we might be what our parents and others expect from us, or so that we might be immune to others' hurtful opinions and behaviors.

To elaborate on the previous chapter's examples, childhood survival strategies include harsh self-criticism (to make the ego feel unworthy and less likely to make enthusiastic choices that could provoke punishment, abandonment, or criticism); focused self-flattery (to motivate the ego to adopt and maintain an agreeable but one-dimensional role such as heroic rescuer or brilliant confidant); placing one's own agenda last (to not displease anyone or arouse anger or envy); and other codependent behaviors (a focus on meeting everyone else's needs). Strategies also include the development of immature and inauthentic personas that are "pleasing" (clown, hostess, flatterer, flunky, handyman) or invulnerable and thus emotionally safe (thug, bully, king or queen, honcho, lunatic); partial or complete social withdrawal (to minimize hurtful contacts); efforts to protect ourselves from criticism by adopting an unpleasant or downtrodden appearance; and the suppression of our intelligence, talent, emotions, wildness, or enthusiasm. Whatever the strategy, the Loyal Soldier's adamant and accurate understanding is this: it's better to be suppressed or inauthentic than ostracized or emotionally crushed — or dead.

David Whyte offers a startling image of the Loyal Soldier — a dark presence who alleviates our fears in exchange for the suppression of our authenticity:

> ...you made that pact
>   with a dark presence
>   in your life.
>
> He said, "If you only
>   stop singing
>   I'll make you safe."
>
> And he repeated the line,
>   knowing you would hear
>   "I'll make you safe"
>
> as the comforting
>   sound of a door
>   closed on the fear at last.... [22]

The grave problem with having made such a pact is that, once adopted, the Loyal Soldier's survival strategies become a bedrock layer of our personalities and are not relinquished easily or quickly. Liberation from our CSSs is one of the most challenging and lasting features of the individuation process, requiring a good deal of courage, discernment, and endurance even into adulthood and elderhood.

Despite our having reached the Oasis and, consequently, some degree of psychosocial independence, the Loyal Soldier's ongoing strategies prevent us from forging more mature relationships, expressing personal potentials, or discarding childish identities. Our atavistic survival methods now form the core of our most self-defeating patterns: those that diminish our dreams and our healthy wildness, or that feed low self-esteem and troubles with intimacy. And, most irksome, these strategies are on automatic pilot, launched outside our awareness and without our consent or control. It's as if they were being masterminded by someone other than ourselves. Sometimes, we feel victimized by our own psyche.

In the Oasis, the Loyal Soldier's ongoing efforts to protect us from our early childhood wounds and fears become more of an obstacle to our growth than the original wounds themselves.

So what to do? Whatever your age, much of the following advice assumes you're in the Oasis, and that you're sufficiently healed emotionally, and mature enough, to perform the suggested self-assessments and action steps. If you're in the Cocoon or beyond, you'll most likely be able to do this work independently, but you might sometimes benefit from help. If, on the other hand, you're in an egocentric stage (3a or later) and/or are not sufficiently healed — likely for the majority of teenagers in America — then assistance will be needed from a skilled therapist or a mature parent or teacher, someone who is supportive, trusting, and loving. (Some ideas are suggested below.)

The preliminary step is to determine if your war is really over — specifically, the war of childhood survival that your Loyal Soldier has been fighting all along. Your Nurturing Parent is the dimension of your Self capable of making this assessment. The fact that you're in the Oasis does not guarantee that your war is over. It's over only when you're no longer prone to feeling like an emotionally abandoned child psychologically fending for yourself without the support of people who really love you and without your own mature psychospiritual resources.

All people of all ages possess a Nurturing Parent, but teenagers (and many older people) in an egocentric society are often not able, without the help of a mature mentor, to make contact with this fundamental resource. The ability to consciously access the Nurturing Parent is a normal outcome of the developmental processes of the Nest, Garden, and Oasis, but in an egocentric society, many people, and their parents, have done poorly with the tasks of these early stages. The war of emotional survival is rarely over for these children and teens, because most don't possess the emotional and social skills to nurture themselves in the face of harsh criticism or rejection by a parent or another dominant person in their life.

However, the war *does* end in your teen years or later if and when you develop both your inner and outer emotional resources. Your outer resources are healthy friends, mentors, and a dependable social network. Your inner resources are your authenticity; your skills in emotional integration, conflict resolution, status-assignment, and self-sustenance; and your skills in generating emotional safety, intimacy, and belonging — all capacities possessed by the Nurturing Parent dimension of your Self.

If you have not sufficiently developed these socioemotional resources, the war is *not* over and you really do still need the Loyal Soldier's old strategies for protection. Meanwhile, you also need help — from a psychotherapist, mentor, coach, or elder — in making contact with your Nurturing Parent and developing your social network.

Once the war is over for you, you — as your Nurturing Parent — can begin the same sequence of four steps the Japanese took with *their* loyal soldiers: they (1) welcomed them home as heroes; (2) thanked them deeply and sincerely for their loyalty, courage, and service; (3) told them, gently and lovingly and repeatedly, that the war was over (and showed them, too, that it was over); and finally, (4) helped them find new societal roles for employing their considerable talents.

It is not possible to stop your Loyal Soldier's childhood survival strategies by ignoring him, attempting to banish him, or rebuking him.

The first of these four steps requires that you identify your Loyal Soldier's CSSs, especially in those moments when he employs them. These CSSs are the things you say to yourself, or that you do, that keep you small (and "safe"). Whenever you catch yourself employing a CSS, compassionately turn toward your Loyal Soldier (using creative visualization) and, rather than criticize or reject him, welcome him "home" as the hero of your childhood that he truly was. The most effective times to welcome him home are the moments when he is active.

For example, say you just caught yourself turning down an attractive but risky invitation to attend a certain social gathering because you don't believe you could survive the potential humiliation if you came off as a fool. Begin by recognizing — from the perspective of your Nurturing Parent — that this is one of the methods your esteemed Loyal Soldier had successfully used to protect you in childhood. Instead of berating him or yourself for this defensive strategy, welcome him home as a hero. Let him know that you understand that he is still using this strategy in an attempt to keep you safe. Give him specific examples of your childhood circumstances in which you really did need such strategies to avoid criticism, rejection, punishment, or abuse. Show him, in other words, that what he did was a good thing under the circumstances.

The second step is to thank him for the intention, skill, and love behind his *current* strategy of keeping you safe by, in this case, advocating social isolation. Let him know how much you appreciate his courage, tenacious loyalty, and the intention behind this CSS. Specifically name this intention so he knows that you know. When you find tears of gratitude rolling down your face, you know you have fully accomplished this second step. It might take some weeks or months before you first succeed in this way, but it's essential to reach this milestone.

Third, gaze inside yourself and tell your Loyal Soldier that *the war is over.* Merely saying the words, however, is not enough. You must tell your Loyal Soldier as specifically as you can what the exact war conditions were during your childhood (for example, perhaps he chose social isolation for you because of a jealous, controlling, and critical older sibling who turned all the kids in the neighborhood against you) and in what sense you're no longer subject to those conditions. Then, to drive home the point that the war is really over, describe for your Loyal Soldier the relevant resources for relationship building and self-care that you now possess but didn't in childhood (for example, assertive self-expression, emotional skills, the ability to laugh at yourself, listening skills) and also your social resources (for example, name your existing true friends, guides, and mentors). If you have significant trouble with any of these components, the odds are that your war is not yet over.

As you enact these first three steps, it helps to remember that your Loyal Soldier has been functioning admirably for a very long time with extremely limited resources and information. He needs to be shown repeatedly that you — as your Nurturing Parent — are strong enough to take over his job. He's not going to turn over his post to just anyone. Even if the war is over, the subpersonality he has been protecting — your Wounded Child — is likely to be fragile (not tempered or strengthened or skilled). Your Loyal Soldier needs to know that you can protect this tender part of you, honor it, and allow it space to grow and develop. Your psychological integrity in the face of fear (of criticism or of your own strong emotions) needs to be confirmed to both your Loyal Soldier and yourself. The unconscious repetition of dysfunctional family patterns is not easily overcome.

These first three steps constitute the primary work of retiring your childhood survival strategies. Whenever possible, enact this sequence as soon as you recognize the reoccurrence of any of your old defensive patterns. This takes a good deal of courage, effort, and time.

In addition to taking these first three steps with your Loyal Soldier, there is another, essential thing you must do. At least some of the time, you must forge ahead and do the very thing your Loyal Soldier has tried to protect you from doing. In the example above, you will say YES to that attractive but risky invitation and attend the social gathering. In the worst-case outcome — say you end up feeling like a fool, or you get criticized — the most dreadful psychological damage that can occur, *if the war is truly over*, is that you will be embarrassed or hurt emotionally. But you will not be destroyed. You won't become suicidal or institutionalized. You won't find yourself psychologically or socially incapacitated. And the best-case outcomes are numerous and will result in much enjoyment and psychological growth.

Remember, these steps will work only if your war is over and if you're able to center your awareness in your Nurturing Parent, the dimension of your Self that is fully self-compassionate.

After many months, perhaps years, of this practice, you might be ready for the fourth and final step of Loyal Soldier rehab. This is when you'll reassign your Loyal Soldier to tasks that promote intimacy and fulfillment, thereby preserving and integrating his skills in a growth-promoting way. One person might, for example, ask her Loyal Soldier, whose capacity for vigilance is legendary, to watch for any and all opportunities to express love to new and old intimates, a tried and true (and positive) way to deepen relationships and make one's world safer, an intention any Loyal Soldier can fully get behind. Another person might ask his postwar Loyal Soldier to help him distinguish between people or situations that are truly dangerous emotionally and those that are both safe enough and risky enough to animate personal development.

Much of the best of contemporary psychotherapy is a collection of methods to help people identify their Loyal Soldiers' strategies, retire them, and develop a new set of strategies for fully feeling, imagining, and sensing, and for generating interpersonal intimacy and belonging. In the process, the war of emotional survival ends (if it hadn't already). This is the work that develops the essential resource of the Nurturing Parent. If your social environment is not healthy, then good therapy includes helping to make it so or, if that's not possible or likely, abandoning your former scene and creating a healthier one. As an innocent child in the Nest, you could not have done either of these things on your own, which is why you developed your Loyal Soldier strategies in the first place.

In doing this work of self-care and self-compassion, never reject, criticize, or attempt to get rid of your Loyal Soldier. When your Loyal Soldier's original purpose of self-preservation and survival is recognized and honored, you can begin to live increasingly beyond that purpose, shaping a life of imagination, exploration, courage, heart, and service.

In welcoming home your own Loyal Soldier, don't be surprised if you encounter a great deal of sadness. As you identify and then surrender your childhood survival strategies, you'll recognize how much you've lost or postponed — relationships, creative expression, personal fulfillment — as a consequence of those strategies employed so many years beyond their need. This grief can be so intense, so fearful in itself, that you might find yourself backing away from your Loyal Soldier rehab. Indeed, your Loyal Soldier himself will use strategies like self-criticism in an attempt to steer you away from this grief, which is terrifying to him, too. You might even be tempted to keep the war going — or convince yourself that it's still being waged when it's really over — in order to avoid facing the damage done.

Life is full of inevitable losses, including the lives of our loved ones and, eventually, our own vitality. Consequently, the ability to grieve is one of our most important psychological skills, and it is best cultivated during our time in the Oasis. When encountering the grief evoked by your Loyal Soldier work, you might remind yourself that within each loss are the seeds of a new life, just as, after a devastating forest fire, the seeds of a new forest wait in the soil. It helps to remember the archetype of destruction/creation: new life arrives only after the end of the old way, and grief is a necessary part of any deep transformation.

If you've made a good deal of progress with your own Loyal Soldier and the cultivation of your own Nurturing Parent, you might be able to help younger people (from their teens into, perhaps, their thirties) with *their* work. Say, for example, a girl or young woman, someone you know and care about, tells you there's something self-empowering she'd really like to do (for example, audition for a dramatic role), but she's afraid of failing or being criticized. Or say she tells you about a situation in which a CSS ended up hurting her (for example, she yielded to corruptive social pressure in order to be accepted).

The best way to help begins with listening without judgment. Then you might ask questions to help her thoroughly feel the emotions aroused by the situation and to discover what those emotions might tell her about herself (without judging herself). Your goal is for her to more fully and compassionately understand herself, her decisions, and the circumstances she found herself in. Talk her into — not out of — whatever emotions remain, so that she feels more accepted (by both you and herself) as the person she is. It's essential to remember that legitimizing her emotional reactions is not the same as endorsing the choices and actions she made *based* on those emotions. Many of those choices are the ones you're hoping she'll find alternatives to.

Let her know you understand the safety-generating capacities she's developed with the CSS she employed (for example, she avoided failure or social rejection). Then, more important, point out the capacities left *un*developed because of that CSS (for example, animated self-expression or poised self-esteem). Help her see that change is both possible and challenging, and that she'll need to make some effort to reach it. Let her know that true adults can offer her invaluable support, mediation, and guidance. Help her identify who those adults might be.

Following this, you might suggest that other scenarios are possible in the circumstances she found troubling even though the choice she made was logical and useful at one time. Give her examples of social risk-taking from your own life. If she seems ready for it, gently ask if she would consider trying different approaches in the future, something more mature, less defensive. If so, walk her through a few scenarios. Doing so is likely to bring her emotional woundedness to the surface. You can then explore with her why she might want to risk new behaviors and how she would know if she were ready to do that. Look for opportunities to evoke the kind of humor that often springs, at these moments, from self-recognition and self-compassion.

She might insist that any new approaches are out of the question. Continue the conversation nonetheless, looking for a place where the resistance might be small enough that some change is possible. Try to identify what resources or support she might need but doesn't yet have. If you find an opening, suggest an alternative course of action and let her know you're available for ongoing support. Portray the kinds of challenges she might experience were she to try a new approach, as well as how it could result in greater fulfillment. In the end, be a true ally and fully support her choice if it's not self-destructive. Remember that it's rare to fully understand what another person is struggling with.

If you note any signs of severe psychological disturbance (for example, suicidal or homicidal thinking, self-abuse, substance addictions, severe eating disorders, bizarre ideas, or emotional numbness), do refer her to a competent psychotherapist.

By assisting youth with their Loyal Soldier work, you help them discover and nurture their authentic qualities, even when these qualities are played out in shadowy ways, even, or especially, when they provoke your own shadow. (Shadow work is explored in the next chapter.) In your everyday interactions with youth, you can mirror back to them their admirable qualities, thereby supporting their progress toward a future soul-infused life.

EMOTIONAL HEALING IN NATURE

In both egocentric and soulcentric environments, Thespians overflow with mighty feelings. In our Oasis years, we often live with a sense of emotional vulnerability. Much of our psychological healing comes from embracing our Loyal Soldiers and our other wounded subpersonalities, with or without the help of psychotherapists or elders.

But one of the most potent allies we humans have always had in our emotional healing, in this or any stage of life, is the natural world itself. Time spent alone in nature, in which we offer our attention outward to the complex, mysterious, always fascinating wild, puts our troubles in perspective and allows us to re-root our awareness in self-sustaining and inspiring rhythms and cycles.

The contemporary American novelist and poet Jim Harrison tells a story from his teen years. Blinded in one eye at age seven, he underwent an operation in his senior year of high school to restore his sight. The operation failed and left him with terrible pain. About the same time, his first love abandoned him. On a warm day in April "heavy with the scent of dogwood buds," he sat alone in a woodlot.

> After a long time sitting on a log, perhaps an hour, my mind emptied out into the landscape and my preoccupations with the girl and other problems

leaked away. In the stillness garter snakes emerged to feed on flies that buzzed close to the ground among dead leaves and burgeoning greenery. Birds came very close because I had been so still in my sumpish reveries I had ceased to exist to the birds, and gradually to myself. I had become nature, and the brain that fueled my various torments had decided to take a rest by leaving my body and existing playfully in the landscape. The air became warmer and moister, so much so that it seemed densely palpable, swollen enough to touch. It did not so much begin to rain as the air quite suddenly became full of water. Given the circumstances the rain could not help but be a baptism. The natural world would always be there to save me from suffocating in my human problems.[23]

Of all the things we can and must do to create a healthier society, perhaps the easiest and most available step (even in the city) is to reintroduce children and teens — and adults, too — to the natural world.

GENDER DIFFERENCES
IN EARLY ADOLESCENCE AND BEYOND

The difference between men and women is a perennial topic of both acrimonious and amusing debate, but from the perspective of soul the sexes differ less than the controversy suggests. Soul itself has no gender. Traditions that embrace reincarnation generally hold that a soul can embody itself as either gender, the choice reflecting the soul's purposes.

And yet there are undeniable biological, psychological, and social differences between men and women, no doubt in every culture. In American society, the differences tend to be amplified and polarized, most likely due to egocentrism and developmental arrest in the Oasis and in the egocentric stages. In other cultures, gender identity is far more fluid and flexible. Gender-related personal qualities are not a simple matter of biology. For each individual, gender expression springs from a complex mix of genetics, anatomy, hormones, cultural customs and role models, education, parental influences, sibling dynamics, social feedback, and the soul's purposes.

Distinctions about gender expression are best made in terms of masculinity and femininity rather than in generalizations about men and women per se. Although most men are masculine and most women feminine, some men are mostly feminine and some women masculine, and others naturally androgynous.

We might ask: independent of cultural influence, what are the differences between human masculinity and femininity? I think of masculinity as an outward orientation, like that of male genitals. Masculinity is the tendency or capacity to move outward or forward; to seek progress; to see the problems, opportunities, and solutions at some distance and ahead of oneself in both time and space; to be competitive; and to probe into the world and into the future. Relative to the feminine, the masculine supports sharper distinctions and more clearly defined boundaries, which assist a person in moving forward and fabricating new things.

Genitalia notwithstanding, any given individual, male or female, can be more or less masculine at the core of the self. People who are feminine at their core can also develop their masculine capacities and sensibilities — and *need* to in the process of becoming whole, starting in the Oasis and continuing through the Wild Orchard.

Femininity is somewhat the reverse of masculinity. It is an inward orientation — like that of female genitals. Femininity is the tendency or capacity to be receptive, welcoming, cooperative, perceptually and emotionally attuned to what is already present. The feminine desire is to flesh out and enhance what already exists, to creatively adorn and praise it. Boundaries are more permeable, and similarities more important than distinctions, which supports receptivity and communion.

To become whole, women and men who are masculine at their core can and must develop their feminine capacities and sensibilities.

To be masculine or feminine at one's core is to possess the corresponding tendencies and capacities as givens.

Gender-based personality differences are most pronounced in the Oasis. One of the goals of maturation during this time, and especially in the next three stages, is to develop the weaker of our two gender orientations. As we do this, our personal expressions become less skewed toward the purely masculine or feminine, even though our cores remain what they were.

The Oasis task of creating an authentic and socially acceptable personality takes on a different flavor depending on core gender orientation. Teenage boys and girls with masculine cores must succeed as adolescent heroes. In the course of fashioning an authentic way of social belonging, they must prove themselves by rushing off into the world, slaying dragons and rescuing the oppressed. To fix what is wrong with themselves or their world, they need to perform outwardly heroic deeds. Win or lose, their authenticity and character are forged in the heat of "battle."[24] In leadership and negotiation, their proclivity is to make statements and stake out positions rather than ask questions.

All this is normal for adolescent boys and girls with masculine cores, but in a soulcentric setting this adolescent heroism runs its course by age fifteen or so. This is as it should be. If a man (or woman) at age thirty or beyond is still proving himself through dragon-murder, he might be a grave danger to himself and others. If he happens to be the leader of a sizeable army or corporation, he can wreak untold damage. If he is the commander of a nuclear superpower, he can destroy the world-as-we-know-it.

Feminine girls and feminine boys do not need to accomplish Herculean tasks in the world in order to socially individuate. They must, rather, learn to be receptive and present and to celebrate the spontaneities and allurements of the world. Their authenticity is forged not in the heat of battle but in the crucible of solitude and still-ness. They heal themselves and contribute to the healing of the world by summoning the remedy from their own depths. Their leadership and negotiation style is to ask ques-tions. All this is normal for adolescent girls or boys with feminine cores, but this pure femininity will have completed its essential contribution to a girl's (or boy's) authen-ticity and character by her midteens if she's had a soulcentric life up to that point.

To become whole, most Thespian men (namely, those with masculine cores) must learn to receive the world into the self and develop their feminine openness. Most Thes-pian women (those with feminine cores) must learn to thrust themselves assertively into the world and develop their masculine drive. After a few years of success with the tasks of Social Individuation, a man might continue to lead group activities in part by making assertive statements and taking strong positions, but he must also cultivate his ability to lead by asking questions. He must learn that the only positions worth tak-ing are those he discovers through the deep listening that his feminine qualities afford. Likewise, a woman might continue to lead in part by asking questions, but she must also learn to take firm stances, and she must learn to ask her questions with a mascu-line discernment, framing questions that open other people to whatever most needs attention.

In the Oasis, the differences between boys and girls, women and men, create consid-erable push-pull tensions and, in egocentric settings, mutual prejudice and gender wars. For mature adolescents and adults, however, gender differences, while sometimes exasperating, are a source of great enjoyment and celebration.

Soulcentric adults living in an egocentric society are well aware of and quite sen-sitive to sexism, in either direction, and support equal rights and opportunities for women. Yet they also see a larger issue: the greater goal is not to create a "healthier" egocentric society in which males and females have equal opportunities for patho-adolescent glorification, but rather to work to create a world that can support the de-velopment of all its members into soulful adults.

Although women have been terribly oppressed for five thousand years or more, and although femininity has been suppressed (especially in males) for as long, the prob-lem has not been masculinity but rather immaturity. The solution is not to make fem-ininity more important than masculinity but to create a soulcentric society in which mature men and women are more prevalent than lifelong adolescents.

COGNITIVE DEVELOPMENT IN THE TEEN YEARS

Between the ages of five and seven, most children, as we saw in the previous chapter, develop the capacity for concrete operations — the ability to think reasonably and logically about tangible objects. In the early to midteen years, approximately half of all young people experience another milestone of cognitive development, what Piaget called the capacity for "formal operations" — the ability to reason in the abstract world of possibilities.[25]

Using formal operations, not only can a person think about herself, but she can also think about herself thinking about herself. And she can think about many things at the same time, about the hypothetical, about things that don't exist, and about things that are contrary to fact. She can think with symbols and metaphors, allowing her to understand more fully what poets are doing. She can comprehend abstract principles of logic, being able, for example, to correctly answer questions like: "I have a coin in my hand. It is either a quarter or not a quarter. True or false?" Faced with a problem, she first considers all possible solutions and can systematically test each possibility, eliminating those that are wrong. She can foresee the consequences of contemplated actions, has some grasp of motivation, and understands that behavior has multiple causes. Compared to others, people with the capacity for formal operations can think in more complex, subtle, and sophisticated ways.

This watershed in cognitive functioning opens the way for the next steps in psychosocial development. Formal operations allow a person to envision ideals, create his own values, and understand himself, his motivations, and his relationships in a way not possible earlier. The ability to imagine ideals, for example, enables a teenager to form crushes and to develop his own way of being in the world distinct from that of his parents, two abilities essential to his creating a personality that is both authentic and socially acceptable. The ability to imagine possibilities enables him to wonder about his own possibilities.

We might wonder if the capacity for formal operations is necessary to progress beyond the Oasis, and whether a soulcentric upbringing is more likely than an egocentric upbringing to result in the acquisition of this capacity.[26]

CIRCLE OF IDENTITY: ETHNOCENTRISM

By the end of the Garden stage, the healthy ego's circle of identity had become sociocentric. The meaning of the word *mine* came to include family, closest friends, and the immediate neighborhood — in the sense of "what I belong to," not "what I own."

In the Oasis, although the circle of identity does not grow beyond sociocentrism, it becomes more complete and broader within that range. The healthy Thespian more consistently experiences the world sociocentrically, and she now does so from the perspective of her peer group, ethnic community, and larger society, in addition to that of her family. We might say that the circle of identity becomes ethnocentric, suggesting that now the individual usually chooses and acts, without deliberation, from the point of view of what's best for the larger community or nation. Although she is busy creating her own identity, this identity is broadening, becoming rooted in her societal or ethnic context. The circle of identity does not make its next significant leap (into worldcentrism) until the Cocoon stage.

SECONDARY EDUCATION
AND PERSONAL GROWTH FOR TEENAGERS

Given that the central task of early adolescence revolves around authenticity and belonging, we might ask: To what degree are our modern educational systems in line with the real needs of individual human development? Is compulsory schooling for teens a good idea? Is a classroom-based, academic education appropriate for all teens? As our society becomes more soulcentric and ecocentric, how might our approach to secondary education shift? In such a transitional, postindustrial society, in what ways would our educational goals and curricula change? What would daily life look like for teens if their years were no longer divided between nine months of hour-long classroom sessions followed by three months of work or play?

I have as many questions as answers here. Each soulcentric society would flesh out its educational and developmental approaches for teens in distinct ways. But it's high time we began to ask the questions.

For over one hundred years, mainstream American education has been systematically tuned to produce, on the one hand, blue-collar workers and soldiers, and, on the other, white-collar scientists, technologists, military officers, business managers, and career professionals. The idea has been to "keep America strong," which means more successful than other nations in competing for Earth's limited resources, on which all human economies are grounded. This has been accomplished in the United States and other Western societies by creating a large workforce of wage slaves and soldiers and a sizable cadre of sharp and ambitious minds capable of managing that workforce and of creating technological advances for the march of military-economic "progress." Consequently, we have a bifurcated educational system successfully designed to limit the options and dull the minds and aspirations of the first group while both sharpening and narrowing the minds of the second. The educational emphasis for the professional class is on thinking, but thinking in rather shallow and constricted modes. Independent, critical thinking and any kind of feeling, imagining, and sensing are minimized, marginalized, or discouraged because they are deemed irrelevant or detrimental to industrial development and personal fulfillment.[27] Another reason these innate human capacities are suppressed in Western societies (and *must* be) is because they easily expose the egocentric idea of "progress" for the self-destructive and world-devastating fantasy that it is.

Clearly, the agenda of mainstream Western education is not to engender authentic and relational adolescent personalities, to say nothing of visionary adults and wise elders.

Can we embrace both goals simultaneously — economic sufficiency and psychospiritual health — or are they mutually exclusive? In an egocentric world of warring nation-states addicted to conspicuous consumption, legions of soldiers, wage slaves, and computer programmers are a necessity. Many Americans would say our nation must, at a minimum, be able to defend itself against foreign aggression. But if we are too aggressive, either militarily or economically, too imperialistic, either culturally or religiously, too greedy, either materialistically or financially, we become — as we have — the primary sustainers and peddlers in the world of patho-adolescent egocentric culture, in which more stuff, more money, more security, is always better — and even necessary. And of course, the greedier and more aggressive we are, the more we need to defend ourselves. The more, as a society, we consume a lopsided share of the world's resources, the more we need slavery, sweatshops, and environmental plunder at home and especially abroad. Our national vulnerability is in inverse relationship to our tangible and concrete support of a just, compassionate, and sustainable world for all people, species, and habitats. "Looking out for number one," our nation's patho-adolescent agenda, encourages each American to personally adopt the same policy, thus sustaining national egocentrism and greed, which, in turn, feeds global egocentrism, slavery, and chronic war.

If American society is to mature — currently a prerequisite for global peace and justice — a larger proportion of individual Americans must mature. Toward that end, we must, as a society, fashion eco-soulcentric educational systems.

How much of what teens are forced to study in most of our middle and high schools is really relevant to the rest of their lives? Although Americans need to read, write, and count, most children find these fundamentals of literacy enjoyable and easy to acquire by the middle of the Garden stage, especially if they are allowed to learn in their own way and rhythm. Studies show that the astonishingly low literacy rate in our country is due not to a lack of schooling but to too much of the wrong kind of schooling. Most children become highly literate on their own if allowed to explore areas of genuine interest.

From an eco-soulcentric perspective, the skills that teenagers really need to acquire, beyond those of the Garden, are those discussed in this chapter: the skills of authenticity, emotional access and expression, conflict resolution, status assignment, sexuality, sustenance, human-nature reciprocity, and Loyal Soldier rehabilitation. The differences between this set of skills and those favored in contemporary American secondary education are telling. Some of the latter are subsumed under what I call "sustenance skills," but most of what is taught in American middle and high schools leads to no skills at all and to knowledge that is promptly forgotten after end-of-semester exams.

Most of the skills discussed in this chapter are best learned, not in a traditional classroom experience divided into one-hour intervals, but through more progressive educational models and in the course of genuine, wholehearted living outside of classrooms.

Is there really a large and standardized block of academic studies that all teens require? Given the basic knowledge acquired before puberty, and the basic skills of reading, writing, math, and computer literacy, what are the further academic studies that all teens need in order to become fully engaged members of a contemporary eco-soulcentric society? How much advanced study in math and science, for example, is relevant to most? In the process of growing whole, teens benefit much more from cosmology, mythology, and ecoliteracy than from algebra and physics. Should teen-year education, then, be much more individualized and varied than in our current American system?

Consider the following efforts currently being pursued in progressive educational circles in America and elsewhere to meet the eco-soulcentric educational and developmental needs of teenagers. There are now new teaching modes and methods being employed in homeschooling; Internet-based virtual classrooms; expeditionary learning programs; community internships; and innovative, personalized, small schools and learning communities. In the more progressive versions of these new approaches, all learning is ecocentric, which means that the central educational goal is to support each individual to become an integral member of the greater Earth community.

Independent, off-campus, community-based learning is a key feature of most of the new high schools. Even on days when students are in the school building, textbooks are rarely used. These students don't take tests, don't get conventional, daily homework, and don't get letter grades. Instead, they're encouraged to follow their interests and learn on their own, with guidance from teachers who have time for each of them. Journal writing and independent reading are common activities. Students who want to know something beyond their teachers' knowledge are encouraged to find experts either at the school or in the community.

The new range of educational choices allows students, parents, and teachers a wider selection to better match teens' individual needs with the learning opportunities available at particular schools. Some innovative secondary schools emphasize preparation for the sciences, some for business, some for the creative and performing arts, and others for the service professions (law, healthcare, architecture, engineering, education, and so on). In a science-oriented school, for example, entire curricula are based on having students learn science by *doing* science — by conducting actual research on the streets and in the businesses of their hometowns, in wild and semiwild places near the school, and in local parks.

In expeditionary learning schools, much of the academic work is accomplished

in the course of learning expeditions — extended, in-depth investigations of important real-world topics and themes. On a given day, student explorations may take them
out of the school building to do environmental research, conduct interviews at local
businesses, visit museums, or perform science or service learning projects. Reading and
writing are integrated throughout the curriculum and are not tiresome ends in themselves. Personal development and teamwork are not just emphasized but are embedded in school structures, practices, rituals, and academic studies.

In a soulcentric environment, all secondary education programs would give primary attention to the developmental tasks of the Oasis — and, later, of the Cocoon.[28]

Beginning no later than puberty, schools ought to encourage independent, out-
of-school learning opportunities, including service learning, especially for students for
whom the classroom is not the best place to learn. Youth who feel destined to become
scholars, academic educators, scientists, or service professionals might spend much of
their teen years in classrooms, but this ought to be the exception, not the rule it is now.

We might gradually do away with compulsory secondary education. Schools, as
we think of them now, really are not best for all teenagers, maybe not even most. But
if it's true that most teenagers are not well served by spending their youth in classrooms
studying typical contemporary curricula, what then are the alternatives? In addition
to independent study of, and being mentored in, the eight subtasks outlined in this
chapter, other possibilities for study abound: on-the-job learning of sustenance skills;
internships with local businesses and professionals; volunteer service-learning in the
community; cultivation of imagination, sensing, feeling, and thinking through art, music, writing, and craft projects supervised or coached by adult mentors (which to some
extent can also occur in classrooms); cultivation of friendships and responsible sexual relationships; physical and athletic development; games and sports; the enjoyment
of the natural world; and ongoing study of human-nature reciprocity and ecological
responsibility.

Currently, we think of secondary education as primarily a preparation for a job
or career. But although the acquisition of sustenance skills is an essential component
of teenage learning, it is only a small part. Besides, from a soulcentric perspective, how
you're really going to spend your life will not begin to become clear until the Cocoon
stage. Consequently, overemphasizing teenage investment in particular "employable"
skills might be largely a waste of time. On the other hand, if one's vision of human development extends no further than the Oasis, then, in fact, all teenagers might as well
begin, if not complete, training for jobs or careers that will carry them all the way to
retirement.

If the Oasis stage were to end in the mid- to late teens, as I believe it would in a
soulcentric setting, then multiyear training for a specific, lifelong career could justifi-
ably wait until the Cocoon stage (which might begin anywhere from the midteens to
the midtwenties) or even until the Wellspring.

Although mainstream America does not think soulcentrically about what is needed in stage-3 secondary education, this is even truer for stage-4 education, which merits no consideration at all in egocentric society. As we'll see in the next chapter, the Cocoon introduces yet another set of developmental and educational needs, as different from those of the Oasis as the latter are from the Garden.

CONFORMING AND REBELLING:
THE EGOCENTRIC COUNTERPART TO THE OASIS

... And we: always and everywhere spectators,
turned not toward the Open
but to the stuff of our lives.
It drowns us. We set it in order.
It falls apart. We order it again.
And fall apart ourselves.

Who has turned us around like this?
Whatever we do, we are in the posture
of one who is about to depart.
Like a person lingering
for a moment on the last hill
where he can see his whole valley —
that is how we live, forever
taking our leave.

— RAINER MARIA RILKE, "THE EIGHTH ELEGY"

When their early childhood took the form of Obedience or Entitlement Training (instead of the Nest) and their middle childhood took the form of Primary Socioeconomic Training (instead of the Garden), then teenagers undergo a version of stage 3 that I call Conforming and Rebelling. In this stage, parents and teachers continue employing (or attempting) age-adjusted methods of obedience and entitlement training (that is, punishments and rewards, respectively) and socioeconomic training, even as many of these teens attempt to resist such efforts.

In Conforming and Rebelling, it is not so much parents and teachers but mainstream egocentric society and peer groups that teens are either conforming to or rebelling against. In this stage, egocentric youth are attempting to find their own social, sexual, and economic way of belonging to the wider, postpubertal world inherited from their parents and society — in this case, a thoroughly and sadly egocentric world. Some teens will succeed at belonging to this world. These are the Conformists. Others will fail or will feel there is no point in trying. These are the Rebels.

The Conformists are, in general, the less imaginative, the less daring, the more fearful — the ones for whom egocentric parenting and education has "succeeded." Conformists keep the egocentric world functioning.

The Rebels are generally more creative, courageous, and angry. After having taken a good look at the mainstream social roles offered by egocentric society — and finding most all of them dismal, disheartening, or deadly — they respond with disbelief, despair, disdain, mockery, or rage, often resulting in depression or violence and sometimes suicide. Some Rebels just say no to joining mainstream egocentric society, and find a way, at least for a time, to live on the periphery. Other Rebels go through the motions of superficially belonging to the mainstream — perhaps even in model ways that appear, from the outside, to be genuine — but find no more heart, juice, or authenticity there than they would in any alien or anemic world. These Rebels are pragmatists and survivors, but the more "principled" Rebels in the former group consider them sellouts.

As in the previous two chapters, what I identify here as the egocentric counterpart to the Oasis is, for the sake of clear contrast, something like a worst-case scenario. Hopefully, you and your children experienced — or are experiencing — something far less extreme.

In a soulcentric setting, puberty is fully honored and celebrated by family and community. The new teenager is invited into a wider, more autonomous, more responsible, and more creative set of relationships within society and nature.

In contrast, in egocentric development, puberty is at best tolerated, more commonly dreaded, and most always met with attempts at control. In place of a healthy puberty, what egocentric parents and teachers see looks to them more like a tumult. From their perspective, all hell breaks loose. This is especially true in contemporary sixth- and seventh-grade classrooms. Hormones are now flowing wantonly, wreaking havoc on the pseudo-order imposed in earlier grades. The hormonal changes of puberty and their effects on social behavior make it more challenging (although still entirely possible) to prepare students for roles in a military-industrial society, a process begun in the previous stage of Primary Socioeconomic Training. Accordingly, as you can see in Diagram 3-6, p. 71) I refer to the egocentric counterpart to the transition at childhood's end as simply Riot.

Riot ushers the teenager into the stage of Conforming and Rebelling. At the same time that hormonal developments trigger a much-enhanced interest in the social and sexual world, many of the unresolved emotions of childhood erupt into consciousness. The first motivates the egocentric teenager, appropriately, to move well beyond the realm of his family. The second gives him plenty of emotional material to act out. While growing up in an egocentric society, he suffered a great deal of suppression and outright rejection of his authentic self. This left him with an array of unassimilated emotions, each of which now demands some sort of response: his anger about those rejections; his fear of more of the same; his shame at being flawed; his guilt for having broken the rules; and his grief over the loss of, for example, a loving family, intimate relationships, and an embodied membership in the natural world. The teen's egocentric education will have given him little or no training for coping with this sudden eruption of immense and complex feeling. In comparison, his soulcentric counterpart has considerably fewer unassimilated emotions and many more tools for integrating those that do arise.

Impersonators: Conformist, Rebel, Victim, and Prince or Princess

As mentioned earlier, most stage-3 teens in an egocentric world are not Thespians but Impersonators. Thespians, by experimenting with a variety of roles and styles, are in the process of deepening their authenticity. Impersonators, in contrast, have little or no idea who they are or how to find out: they're merely going through the motions. Conformists acquire a pseudo-identity by mimicking the styles and behaviors of the mainstream. Rebels achieve a pseudo-identity by adopting styles and behaviors that mock, negate, counter, or deconstruct the mainstream and, ironically, by conforming to the styles and behaviors of other Rebels.

Most Impersonators never achieve a fully sociocentric or ethnocentric circle of identity. Some are simply out for themselves; they have a narcissistic circle of identity. Others reach a limited version of sociocentrism in which they come to care for one or two others, perhaps a handful of friends, but these alliances tend to be unstable, often shifting suddenly and sometimes violently. Most Impersonators have a pervasive sense of being alone in a hostile or, at best, unpredictable world. It's no wonder that drug addictions, other escapes, and the final evasion, suicide, are so prevalent among Western people.

Throughout the sequence of egocentric stages (3a through 3f), neither the psychospiritual center of gravity nor the circle of identity progresses any further.

The egocentric stages are where most severe psychopathologies are found, especially major depression and personality disorders such as sociopathy (an inability to experience empathy, coupled with a generalized rage from childhood trauma, which is then acted out on others). When natural processes become arrested — in this case, the developmental unfoldings of the Nest, Garden, and Oasis — pathology results.

In order to enter the Oasis, most people in egocentric stages 3a through 3f need support from mature adults or psychotherapists in addressing the developmental deficits (the least-addressed tasks) of the first three stages. Once in the Oasis, additional help might be necessary to reach the Cocoon.

In addition to the Conformist and the Rebel, two other roles are common in egocentric society — the Prince or Princess and the Victim. Which one or more of these four an Impersonator embodies depends on her dominant emotional reaction to childhood psychological abandonment and her most effective available strategy for acquiring some degree of social security and acceptance.

If the Impersonator reacts primarily with fear — fear that she'll be abandoned again — then she'll be naturally motivated to do all she can to minimize future occurrences. She has two options: the Conformist and the Victim. If she has a reasonable amount of hope for obtaining the material or social rewards made available by egocentric society, she'll choose the Conformist route. If, on the other hand, her fear is partnered with a sense of ineligibility, she'll choose Victim.

If she reacts primarily with anger — anger at being abandoned — then her options are the Rebel or the Princess. If she's eligible for considerable social and material rewards, she'll select Princess. If her anger is joined by a sense of disenfranchisement, she'll opt for Rebel.

People in all four of these egocentric roles have largely failed at one or both of the nature-oriented tasks of the Garden and Oasis: the Garden task of discovering the enchantment of the natural world (both outer nature and their human nature: their emotions, imagination, and body), and/or the Oasis task of creating an authentic personality. Instead of achieving authenticity, they learned mere social and economic survival. Survival, of course, is much better than the alternative — death, prison, homelessness, or a locked psychiatric ward — and it's never too late for Impersonators to heal and mature.

The Conformist does whatever is necessary to meet the membership requirements of whichever group grants him the most desirable social status. More generally, he conforms to the values and roles of mainstream egocentric society. The more pleasing and impressive his self-presentation, the better the place he'll be granted by others. The Conformist is the most popular option for Impersonators in middle-class egocentric society, because, if the path to authenticity is unavailable, the most attractive alternative is one with egocentric rewards — security, comfort, money, consumer products, professional prestige, and power over others.

Everywhere we turn in mainstream egocentric society, we run into the same materialistic message: Life is about acquiring as much material wealth, physical attractiveness, and power as possible. As Rilke notes, we turn "not toward the Open / but to the stuff of our lives." A person's goodness or popularity is a matter of how much he owns and how good he looks. This is the most common message in Hollywood movies, popular books and magazines, TV programming, and other forms of advertisement, and this is the subtext in much of the conversation in egocentric society and in the choices made in the business world.

Like the Conformist, the Victim is also primarily motivated by fear of future abandonments but has little hope for obtaining the rewards of society. Victimhood is a common outcome for oppressed and poverty-class people in an egocentric society, but it happens in middle- and upper-class families, too.[29] Victims believe themselves to be ineligible for social or economic success either because of their class membership (in which case, it is often the egregious reality) or because of their self-image as loser, misfit, or oddball (possibilities for people of any class).

The role of Victim might not be as bad as it sounds. There are, after all, many Rescuers in egocentric society.[30] A Rescuer is a type of Conformist who finds his place in society by rescuing Victims. There are many kinds of rewards you can receive from a Rescuer when you are in the Victim position (we must keep in mind that those oppressed by racism, sexism, and classism often have little choice in the matter). Victim rewards include excessive sympathy from Rescuers; release from responsibilities; disability and workers' compensation for people who are not truly injured but can nevertheless manage a good semblance; underdog-type power over others; and, for those who succeed at suing the right person or organization, money.

In recent years, juries have awarded impressive judgments in personal injury suits to victims of such heinous crimes as spilled coffee or marred vacations. A jury of one's peers picked randomly from an egocentric society is likely to include a majority of Victims, Rescuers, and other Victim-sympathizers who will vote for their fellow Impersonator with the fantasy of being in that position themselves someday. What I call the "Myth of Innocence and the Cult of the Expert," an all-too-common egocentric pattern, operates as follows:

When something goes wrong in your life . . .

- it's not your fault (you're a Victim);
- it *is* someone else's fault (so find out who he is);
- he (the Perpetrator) should be made to pay for it, so sue him (the Victim becomes a Perpetrator himself, and the Perpetrator a Victim who can then proceed to the first step in this sequence);
- you do not possess the skill or knowledge to heal yourself or fix the problem (Victims are helpless);
- there is someone else out there (an Expert, a Rescuer) who does have the skill and knowledge you need (so find out who she is);
- if the Expert screws up in the course of healing you or fixing your problem, you can and will make her pay (thus transforming the Expert-Rescuer into a Victim who can then begin this sequence herself; this also transforms the Victim into a Perpetrator).

The Rebel and Prince or Princess have two things in common: their anger about the abandonments they've suffered and the fact that they end up shaping their lives around that anger. What distinguishes them is the disenfranchisement that the Rebel experiences (similar to that of the Victim). Not only is the Rebel angry, but he also doesn't believe he's eligible to get the rewards of society in any of the "legitimate" ways. (He's often correct.) His anger leads him to rebel against most everything his parents, teachers, and culture stand for. He might even rebel against some of his peers, for they, too, might have abandoned him at times. Rebellion is the most common Impersonator choice for angry people in the oppressed and poverty classes of egocentric society. It's also widespread among the angry middle class.

In essence, the Rebel says: I don't have a clue who I really am, but I'm not going to act or be anything like *them* — those corrupt sellouts with privilege, conventional power, or money. I'm going to be whatever they are not. And in spades.

Again, this is not all bad. The Rebel has a good deal of energy, self-respect, and freedom — certainly more than the helpless Victim or the chump Conformist. He's not a slave to a paycheck or "the man." He has his fellowship with other Rebels. He knows how to party and have a good time. He's eligible for rewards, such as special status within his clique or gang; opportunities to act out his anger in cathartic and violent ways against imagined or real oppressors and convenient scapegoats; a shadow form of notoriety and respect; a heady better-than-thou feeling; and all the loot he can steal or swindle, usually without guilt, especially if his victims are Conformists or Princes or Princesses in the wealthy mainstream.

Like Rebels, Conformists also don't know who they are, but they know how to act on the basis of what's acceptable — a solution opposite to that of the Rebels.

In common with the Rebel, the Prince or Princess too is angry, but, unlike the Rebel, is eligible to obtain and enjoy the material rewards of society. The Prince or Princess in fact feels entitled to those rewards. Prince- or Princesshood is the most popular stuck-Orphan path for angry people in the upper-middle and upper classes of egocentric society.

In essence, the Prince or Princess says: I don't have a clue to who I really am, but I'm angry and deserve benefits. I'm pissed off about my parents' attempts to get me to perform in humiliating ways — to be the cute or sexy Princess, for example, or the clever, on-the-make Prince. This is not really how I wanted to be, but I was willing to do it for the impressive bribery. I was given fabulous rewards in exchange for my Prince (or Princess) act. Although it felt like torture, I was well paid, and so I played along. Now I'm entitled to all I've been promised and then some. So whatever I'm going to be or do in life, I'll have plenty of privilege and power, money and possessions.

Being a Prince or Princess is clearly not so bad. Yes, they had to betray themselves to reap all those spoils, but as far as they can see, there wasn't a better option. In egocentric society, most people would exuberantly choose the life of a Prince or Princess (heiress, millionaire, sweepstakes winner, captain of industry, movie star) if they had the option. In addition to being angry and entitled, they might feel lucky.

Conformists, Rebels, Victims, and Princes or Princesses all betray themselves — their authenticity — in order to gain some degree of socioeconomic security (or excess) and some form of social acceptance. All remain stuck in the Orphan and Impersonator archetypes long past the time in life to move on to the Cocoon, the archetypes of the Wanderer and the Visionary, and the process of soul initiation, an option that is not facilitated or encouraged by an egocentric society.

Teenage Life and the Egocentric War against Human Nature

Through Obedience or Entitlement Training (stage 1) and Socioeconomic Training (stage 2), parents and teachers undermine the child's nature- and soul-centered life. By stage 3, the teenager has been sufficiently compromised — his innocence has largely been lost and his innate connection with nature severed — so that his alienation from self and world is now independently self-sustained. He perpetuates his loss by Conforming and Rebelling. He experiences little or none of the meaningful exploration of authentic qualities enjoyed in the Oasis process of Social Individuation.

Being more autonomous now — cognitively and socially — the stage-3 teenager does not need or want as much guidance as he received in childhood. Egocentric parents and teachers continue their attempts to control his life, but with generally diminishing success (this is as it ought to be). They attempt to make teenagers conform to their limited vision of what a human ought to be, but the stage-3 youth is now increasingly following his own agenda. This fact reflects a central aspect of stage 3 in both its egocentric and soulcentric versions. Namely, while the tasks of the earlier stages were initiated and/or overseen by others (parents and teachers), they are now increasingly self-directed and, within a few years, will be completely so for all but the most dependent.

This is one reason why the early years of stage 3 — the beginning of the teen years — are so difficult for both teens and parents in egocentric society. While the stage-3 youth is hormonally and motivationally ready to take full control of his own development, his parents are not ready to let him, and most often for good reason. He's not emotionally and economically ready for independence largely because of his egocentric upbringing, which has overlooked the development of his imagination, emotional skills, and capacity for economic self-reliance. As for his teachers, they're not going to endorse his autonomy in any significant way, in part because their closely supervised classroom jobs require otherwise. And his egocentric society, more generally, is not going to grant him sovereignty, because its very survival depends on the breaking or harnessing of his autonomous will and imagination.

Consequently, teenage life becomes one of the key battlegrounds on which egocentric society wages its war against human nature (and ultimately against greater nature). A teenager with much of his wildness left intact will want to cut a wide swath as he finds his way of belonging in the world. His egocentric society, however, needs him to accede to a limited number of socioeconomic roles. There the battle lines are drawn. With the vast majority of teenagers, egocentric society wins within a few years.

Most teenagers in an egocentric world give in to those demands, whether they conform to the mainstream or rebel against it. Actually, most do a mixture of both. Some

will conform to mainstream social groups and roles and act out their anger on minorities or gays; or boys and "men" will discharge their rage upon women or nature.
These acts of anger and violence do not undermine egocentric society but in fact
support it as often as not. Others, the Rebels, will fling their anger at icons and representatives of the mainstream, but will conform to the styles and mores of their own
Rebel groups and gangs as much as the Conformists conform to the mainstream.
Through their mostly symbolic protests, Rebels pose no threat to egocentric society.
(As we'll see, it's the Wanderers and Visionaries of stage 4 and beyond who are the real
subversives because they are the ones sowing the (r)evolutionary seeds of a soulcentric society.)

Most teenagers in an egocentric world, regardless of their version of the Impersonator, are largely impelled by their unresolved and unassimilated emotions from
childhood. Receiving little help with these emotions from the older generations — most
of whom have never achieved their own emotional integration — and finding little in
egocentric society that inspires them to belong and be faithful to it, many teens form
their own cliques, gangs, or realities. In their Rebel deportment, these teens will not
lend their fiery enthusiasm to sustaining or regenerating a society that offers them no
roles or ordeals worthy of their fidelity. Creating their own subsociety is their best alternative, but it's inadequate if it offers them no access to more mature humans —
mentors or elders who can help them with the tasks of Social Individuation and offer
a compelling vision of a society they might aspire to cocreate. Without the support of
genuine initiators, most teens in an egocentric society fail at fashioning an authentic
and culturally viable personality, and they remain stuck in stage 3 indefinitely.

Some teenagers react to egocentric society by withdrawing inside themselves,
sometimes through substance addictions. Others fall apart psychologically (their fall
often accelerated by drugs and alcohol) and are incarcerated in prisons or "therapeutic" institutions. (Some have the great fortune to connect with soulcentric therapists,
counselors, teachers, guides, or elders.) Due to their inability to understand teenagers'
genuine needs, egocentric parents, teachers, and other authorities merely demand more
discipline and more police. In effect, egocentric society judges, punishes, and shames
teens for how it has failed them.[31]

Teens who somehow manage to reach the Cocoon will then experience the bone-
deep longing for an initiation process that might effectively usher them into genuine
adulthood. How soulcentric guides, mentors, and elders in our society can support the
initiation process — and what happens to teens when this longing goes unmet — is
the topic of the next chapter.

Due to its multiple failures with the tasks of the Nest, Garden, and Oasis, egocentric society as a whole never progresses beyond the archetype of the Orphan. The
entire society takes on the qualities of a foundling fending for itself in a dangerous and
uncharitable world. Like an orphan, egocentric society is alienated from its own home

(nature), insecure, competitive, vigilant, defensive, aggressive when threatened, chronically hungry, and often depressed.

In an Orphan society like this, many teenagers (as well as older stage-3 people) turn to religion or psychotherapy for help, but a large proportion of psychotherapists and religious communities in such a society are themselves egocentric. Religion and psychotherapy — along with egocentric schools, workplaces, and politics — are, in fact, two of the major perpetuators of patho-adolescent society.

Egocentric Religious Communities

An egocentric religious community is one that, in practice if not dogma, is foremost concerned with promoting conformity to a narrow vision of social acceptability, a vision that is patho-adolescent, egocentric, ethnocentric, anthropocentric, and usually androcentric. The most obvious sign of religious ethnocentrism is the delusion that "our way is the only way." Egocentric religious communities tend to be aggressively imperialistic and often racist, although their terms for themselves are likely to be "missionary" and "redemptive."

A religious community is not the same as a religion. An egocentric religious community — a church, temple, congregation, or fellowship — can exist within the framework of any religion or spiritual path. The fact that a particular religious community is egocentric says nothing one way or the other about whether the religion or spiritual path itself is inherently egocentric.

Egocentric religious communities often promote a monotheistic god who is a sort of superparent, one who is harsh and critical and demands adherence to his rules or laws. Among his believers, such a god is feared above all else, in part because he has a war chest of increasingly severe punishments for the disobedient. A covert goal of egocentric religious organizations is to keep members in the position of dependent children or adolescents, stuck in Orphanhood, and consequently more easily controlled.

Socially, an egocentric religious community operates in the same way as the patho-adolescent society of which it is a component. Within the religious hierarchy, there is keen competition to occupy a limited number of high-status positions. Both within and outside the community, there is also the fundamental status differential of "the saved" versus "the damned" (the "in" versus the "out"). You acquire a favorable social status in the community by obeying a set of rules concerning social acceptability, rules that come from an immature parental figure — a religious leader — rather than your own conscience or uncorrupted human nature. You are educated to conform to those rules and discouraged from using your imagination or exploring your depths or, should you stray into those depths, from trusting anything you might inadvertently find there.

Egocentric religious communities treat you like a child and encourage you to treat yourself that way. You are reminded regularly, for example, that you cannot depend on yourself to know or discover what is morally right, and that you would be hopelessly lost without the guidance of the leaders, often referred to as "mother" or "father." Only the authorities are capable of interpreting the god's desires. The authorities are "mother" or "father" not in the sense of a true elder in relation to an initiate but in the sense of a parent in relation to a stage-2 child or immature stage-3 teenager.

To keep members in line, egocentric religious organizations employ a disciplinary system with a hierarchy of social punishments. At the top is expulsion from the religious community, perhaps not only for this life but for all future lives. This is the Orphan's ultimate fear, and egocentric religious leaders know how to exploit it. There is also the threat of eternal suffering — the ultimate stick for promoting conformity. People raised within egocentric religious communities, even sophisticated people who might otherwise understand social propaganda and the use of intimidation for control, might find it hard to dismiss the lurking fear that, if they act or speak in opposition to their egocentric religious community, they will suffer this ultimate banishment.

When leaders of an egocentric religious community feel they're losing control of their followers, they employ the threat of eternal damnation for an increasingly wider variety of "sins." Some add shame to the mix by identifying sinfulness as your original and deepest nature as a human being. In addition to invoking punishment, egocentric religious leaders attempt to bribe their followers into obedience. The ultimate bribe is some version of "heaven" in the afterlife. Egocentric heaven is a place of eternal peace and comfort where everyone and everything gets along famously. It is the absence of not just *some* bad things, but all of them, especially the chronic fear and repressed anger suffered by the religious Orphan. Heaven is where one need never again fear the sort of abandonment that was all too common in childhood.

Fear of a divine being is central to egocentric religious faith and is an extension and/or displacement of the Conformist's and Victim's earlier fear of their parents. The child in an egocentric family fears his parents because he believes that, if they get sufficiently angry, they might abandon him completely. His parents' good graces are in fact a requirement for survival. Egocentric religious authorities incite youth — those who are Conformists and Victims — to gradually shift the locus of their primary fear from their parents to a god, and to exchange their dutiful obedience to their parents for an absolute obedience to a god. (This is an instance of what psychologists call transference.) The result is to keep the individual developmentally arrested by preying on his fear of abandonment.

Egocentric Psychotherapy

Psychotherapy, too, even when it relieves suffering, can arrest development in stage 3 if the emphasis is placed upon what therapists often call "adjustment," upon helping people become more socially acceptable to egocentric society. In contrast, soulcentric psychotherapy cultivates authenticity, personal depth, and ecological responsibility — in addition to success with all the other tasks of the Nest, Garden, and Oasis — and, as a result, healthy personalities.

When a person's paramount goal is social acceptance, she is likely to be emotionally unstable and psychologically unhealthy despite being well regarded. She's unstable because, whenever the criteria for social acceptance changes, her personal expression must change, too. She's unhealthy because she defines herself externally — by how well she meets others' expectations — rather than internally, by how well she knows, likes, and actualizes herself. External self-definition leads to low self-esteem, shame, and depression due to the chronic implication that something is wrong with the self as it is.

Authenticity is half the task (the nature component) of Social Individuation. A healthy Thespian learns how and where her authentic self fits into the social world, and where it doesn't. She's not oriented toward gaining social acceptance at any cost. She regularly explores her inner life: What are my genuine interests and values? What do my emotions tell me about me? What personal and social styles best fit who I am on the inside? What are my hopes and dreams? What are my talents and gifts? What are my weaknesses and liabilities?

Encouraged by her initial discoveries about self, she turns her attention to the social world: Where do I best fit in socially and vocationally? How do I let my friends know how I am feeling and what I want? How do I respond to criticism? How will I express my personal style and talents? Who can I trust? Who truly loves me for who I am? With whom will I choose to make a life?

As she creates an authentic place within her social world, she also explores what she can do, not to adjust to her egocentric society, but rather to help transform it — to make it a more just, compassionate, emotionally alive, imaginative, wise, and sustainable society. A great deal of psychopathology is engendered by the pathological society to which egocentric psychotherapists help their clients adjust. In contrast, eco-soulcentric psychotherapy, which includes but goes beyond the client's relationship to self and society, addresses our relationship to the greater web of life. Rather than focusing primarily on the insulated self, the therapist better serves "mental health" by coaching his client to do his part to make the world a better place. Contributing to positive cultural change can be one of the most potent means of generating one's own positive personal change. These three interdependent domains — self, society, and planet — ought to inform the course of soulcentric psychotherapy with stage-3 clients in an egocentric world.

In contrast, the approach of the egocentric psychotherapist is informed by a thoroughly external question: how can I help my client achieve greater social acceptance and rewards? This agenda requires a keen understanding and appreciation for what the client's social world expects of him, especially his employer, spouse, insurance carrier, minister, or commanding officer. The egocentric psychotherapist helps her client develop behavioral strategies for conforming. Everything — the client, the social environment, even the psychotherapist herself — is viewed from the outside and no deeper than the surface.

Egocentric psychotherapy results in codependency, Impersonator patterns, and temporary, shallow self-esteem. The client might experience some relief resulting from the social acceptance he receives from the therapist and others, but before long, when the social expectations shift, he'll experience even lower self-esteem and even greater shame and depression. Engendering temporarily "happy" Conformists who are more alienated than ever from their authentic selves serves the central purposes of egocentric society — its businesses, bureaucracies, law enforcement, criminal justice systems, military, and managed-care corporations.

In recent years, managed care has placed enormous economic pressure on psychotherapists to become increasingly superficial and egocentric in their goals and methods. The goal of managed-care corporations, to enhance their own profits by generating savings for employers and insurance companies, is achieved by forcing therapists to adopt symptom-relief and social and vocational adjustment as the primary therapy goals, and to accomplish them as quickly as possible. The primary objective is not Social Individuation, but conformity. When managed-care corporations insist that therapists implement what is commonly termed "a treatment plan that is measurable, time-effective, and solution-focused," this is behavior-modification lingo for: "We want you to get this person functioning again at work as soon as possible. We want well-adjusted employees who minimize sick days and work inefficiencies."

A Society Stuck in Patho-Adolescence

The archetypes, values, and goals of the egocentric stage of Conforming and Rebelling illuminate the fabric of the patho-adolescence within which Western societies are mired — a way of life that emphasizes social acceptability, materialism, self-centered individualism, and superficial security rather than authenticity, intimate relationships, soul-infused individual service, and creative risk and adventure.

The egocentric standard for a healthy, full-functioning "adult" in Western society is a socially popular Conformist (Impersonator) who earns a lot and buys a lot, is religious (but not spiritual), is uncritically loyal to her country (but who exploits the natural world, on which her country depends), cares about the human children in her neighborhood (but is heedless of the plight of children of all species elsewhere in the world), and is vigilantly fearful for the security of her own people (but oblivious to the devastation perpetrated by her own society upon other peoples and other species). She's good-hearted within her social crowd, the life of the cocktail party, and a fashion trend-setter. At work, she ably and proudly does her part in creating or selling the products or services that keep egocentric society functioning — and, unbeknown to her, rolling toward environmental collapse. She does not suffer guilt or concern about her own or her society's way of life. She is married to her social counterpart, and their children are attending schools considered to be the finest. They attend an egocentric religious church or synagogue of their choice, and she volunteers with civic organizations. She reads the latest bestsellers, and her home is a Martha Stewart–inspired showcase. She is climbing social and professional ladders while building an impressive investment portfolio. She shops for the best bargains, giving no thought to toxin-producing processes or slavery-based practices involved in what she buys. She does not experience an intimate relationship with or sacred responsibility for the land she lives on, or the sky or waters, or any creatures other than the family pets. To her, nature is generally dangerous and dirty, but sometimes pretty. She does not wonder deeply or often about the meaning of her own or anyone else's life. She feels that politicians are not doing enough to protect her family's way of life. She does not intend any harm. She is doing her best, given her personal development and the lifestyle options her society offers.

A person seen by egocentric society as not so healthy, not so fortunate, and not so gifted would also be doing his best to achieve social acceptability, but not succeeding quite as well. His central goal in life, his primary struggle, is to enhance his socioeconomic standing, "to get ahead." He lives with lots of egocentric "if onlys": if only I could get a raise, move to California, live in a better neighborhood, join the club, find a desirable mate, win the lottery, look younger. He fervently seeks the American dream, which always seems a bit out of reach. Again, it's not all his fault that he has the desires and deficits he does; his society is equally responsible. Furthermore, if he is a member of an economically oppressed class, then his desire for basic socioeconomic well-being is in no way pathological: it is a necessary foundation for further personal development for him and his family.

The least functional person, by egocentric standards, also fully subscribes to the values of adolescent society but is failing in most of her pursuits. If she is working at all, she's barely making ends meet. She has few friends and has trouble maintaining relationships. She's moody much of the time and doesn't seem to have much fun. She's dominated by, and stuck in, the most negative dynamics of the Impersonator, whether Conformist, Rebel, Princess, or Victim. She feels abandoned, is angry about it, and fears even greater losses.

Egocentric society is sustained by all three of the above scenarios. Waking up from the egocentric trance, from the addiction to adolescent society and Western civilization, is exceptionally difficult.[32] Changing our lives after waking up is even more challenging. In order to contribute to cultural renewal, we must first recognize how we have been part of the problem. Then we can become the change we wish to see as we stride deeper into the world and deeper into our own lives.

All three portraits above pertain to Impersonators, not Thespians. A Thespian —

a healthy stage-3 person — is psychologically distinct from an Impersonator. A Thespian is an invaluable contributor and great boon to healthy society. The core problem in egocentric society is not stage 3 but egocentric *versions* of stage 3 and the relative rarity of healthy stage-3 people and those in later soulcentric stages. A healthy Thespian woman, for example, might create a stable domestic base from which her children, spouse, students, or she herself might someday leap into the Cocoon. She might grow her own organic food, take her kids camping so they'll develop a love of the natural world, recycle, and vote green. She might even drive a hybrid car, support local environmental groups, or become a working member of Amnesty International.

In contrast, the self-serving brand of individualism that America is known for, in cinema, business, domestic politics, foreign affairs, and so on, is a pathology that stage 3 often turns into, especially for masculine men and women who are Conformists and Princes or Princesses. This is an immature, each-man-out-for-himself individualism, one that drives people to push others aside in order to become king or queen of the hill, the adolescent hero. It has nothing in common with mature, partnership-based individualism, one that is expressed in the unique soul embodiment found in stage-5 and stage-6 adults, in which to be an individual is to be a particular node in the web of life, engaged in deeply fulfilling service to the whole, the collective, the universe. The adult hero's primary relationship is to the world, not to herself.

CREATING A SOULCENTRIC OASIS
IN YOUR TWENTIES OR LATER

Earlier in this chapter, we explored what teenagers can do to succeed at the tasks of Social Individuation, and what parents and teachers can do to support them. But what can you do for *yourself* in the Oasis stage after you've left your parents' home and completed school? What can you do to make progress with Social Individuation and prepare yourself for the transition into the Cocoon?

First, consider where you sit with the tasks of the first two life stages, the Nest and the Garden, especially the reclamation of your original innocence and your familiarity and comfort with the enchantments of wild nature. If full-bodied present-centeredness eludes you, or if you do not feel at home in nature, in love with the wild world, then achieving one or both of those would be a good place to start, or at least a major supplement to the following.

Next are all the subtasks of the Oasis outlined in this chapter. These challenging tasks are not just for teenagers! Working on them is the best thing you can do to move yourself deeper into, and eventually through, the Oasis.

When you run into difficulties with the tasks of the Oasis itself, you might find help from a psychotherapist proficient in healing emotional wounds and developing trust and intimacy, and/or a bodyworker specializing in emotional release and integration. Keep in mind, though, how difficult it has become to find a soulcentric psychotherapist in America, especially since the 1980s, when managed care systems began to undermine the mental health profession. But healthy therapists do still exist. Look for someone well trained and highly experienced who employs therapeutic methods that are authenticity-oriented, emotion- and body-based, and imagination-valuing, such as depth or existential psychotherapy, Gestalt, psychosynthesis, Hakomi, expressive arts, psychodrama, or Internal Family Systems.

Even after we move on to later developmental stages, we're never finished evolving the social vehicle we call personality. There is always opportunity, and sometimes need, for improved emotional access, additional healing work, and enhanced social, sexual, and relationship skills. We can always become more authentic and expressive.

In the Cocoon or beyond, we know it's time to re-attend to the developmental tasks of the Oasis when our self-esteem, relationships, or self-expression get in the way of our soulwork and personal fulfillment.

WHEN ARE YOU PREPARED TO LEAVE THE OASIS?

Regardless of their age, how can you tell when your children or students or your friends or clients (or you, for that matter) are on the verge of leaving the Oasis — whether or not they or you feel ready? (There is conscious readiness, and then there is what happens.) How can you tell when it's time to prepare for or create a rite of passage to mark or celebrate the transition into the Cocoon? How do you know when Thespians have had enough success with the task of creating a secure and authentic social self — enough to be primed for the next developmental shift?

We know it's not going to be a matter of age or academic grade. The Oasis can end as early as age fifteen and as late as . . . never. We also know that the timing is not up to the individual, her teachers, her parents, her therapist, or even her soul guide. No one chooses this (or any) moment of life-stage passage. As with all such transitions, it's up to the Mystery — or grace, if you prefer — to shift the individual's psychospiritual center of gravity from one location to the next. All we can do, if we wish to cooperate, is apply ourselves to the tasks of the stage we are in. But it helps if you can read the signs indicating that someone is nearing the passage. It helps because a rite of passage just might provide that last bit of energy needed to catalyze the shift. It also helps because the rite can formally mark the occurrence of the shift, thereby informing others in the community of the opportunity to support that person's entrance into the Cocoon.

There are two principal sets of signs to watch for. They concern the nature of the self that has been achieved, and the sorts of things the individual finds most compelling.

The person might not notice these signs himself or, if he does, might not understand their significance.

First, consider the self — the signs of a reasonably authentic and socially acceptable personality. When a Thespian (of any age) is ready to move on, most of the following will be true of her: She feels pretty good about herself — who she is in the world — most of the time, anyway. She has some friends who accept her, love her, and admire her for her sensitivities and talents even though she knows she's nowhere close to a finished product. She knows she has a lot more growing to do. She usually tells the truth about herself, and sometimes she's aware that she's attempting to deceive. Often she's able and willing to express her genuine preferences and emotions to people she cares about. When she finds herself in conflict with someone close to her, sometimes she can communicate her feelings and desires effectively and nonaggressively. She respects her own body and takes care of it. She makes some effort to respect and care for Earth's body in the place she lives. In her own way, she expresses love to her family and friends. When she screws up and realizes it, she's capable of apologizing. She can get around pretty well on her own. She has learned and accepted enough about her personality to know which sorts of people she gets along with and which sorts she doesn't. She's developed skills that allow her to earn a living. She knows the ways in which she learns best and recognizes many of her strengths and weaknesses. Although she hopes to round out her abilities, preferences, and learning styles, she doesn't feel it all has to happen tomorrow. She can celebrate when things go well, and grieve when she suffers a loss. She knows she belongs here on Earth and with her people.

A second sign is a germinal shift in principal interests — from society and peer group to the realm of mystery and soul. Her plane of focus begins to move from the breadth of everyday surfaces to the depths of the world and her own psyche. She begins to suspect there's something in life more alluring than making a big splash on the socioeconomic scene. She might find herself, for example, newly fascinated with poetry — not just because others think it's cool, but because she's discovering that the words point to a mystery, a beauty, an intimation of something at the heart of life that is sometimes enchanting, sometimes horrific, but always profound, even sacred. She might begin to feel this but have no words yet to express it. If extroverted, she might have a new interest in spending some time alone and perhaps less time with the crowd. Maybe she begins to feel that wandering in the natural world or tending to her art is more intriguing than another party night. She's definitely begun to suspect that there's a lot more to life than perfecting her personality or improving her social standing, even while those values remain. At times, she comes face-to-face with her mortality and wonders about death in a way she never has before. And perhaps she muses about divinity in a new way. What does the idea of spirit *really* imply? She wonders differently about romance, too, suspecting that it involves so much more than sex and social standing.

She's also likely to become exceedingly curious about her dreamworld, either for the first time or in an entirely new way. And her dream themes have shifted, too — the elders are certain to inquire about this — beginning now to revolve around symbols of the journey into the dark, the descent to the unknown. She might dream of leaving home forever, moving to a new apartment, her house in flames or ashes, journeys (or abductions) to the depths of canyons or oceans, her boat sunk, being murdered (perhaps by friends) or dismembered, beheaded, swallowed by a whale, eaten by bear, bitten by snake, lost in a cave, beckoned by an alluring and inscrutable stranger who turns into a devil.

In all these ways and others, she begins to peek over the edge of her life, peers down into the dusky abyss, and finds herself fascinated with the shadows. She commences to wonder what's hidden within or beneath the surfaces of everyday life. Like the Sun approaching the West, she's falling into the dark.

When these two signs appear — shifts in self and significance — the Thespian is drawing near a radical transformation in her being, even if she suspects nothing. But neither sign is necessary or sufficient. They don't trigger the shift; they are merely signs of its imminence. As often as not, the individual does not feel ready for the coming passage but, rather, feels rudely pushed into it by an invisible force (the Mystery) — thrust into it against her will with no option of turning back. It appears to be a general principle that we do not experience the passage between *any* two stages as entirely pleasant, if pleasant at all, as much as we might have desired the shift before it begins. If the Thespian notices anything as she nears the Cocoon, it might only be a vague sense of quickening.

But in a soulcentric environment, there are true elders who've been watching and noticing the signs. They will greet the Thespian at the threshold. She will not have to flounder alone. She will not have to invent her own methods for exploring the worlds that lie on the other side of that thin veil that separates normal from magical, common from extraordinary.

In an egocentric society, a rite of passage at this time has the additional value of proclaiming that the Thespian's strange new feelings and longings, which seem so antithetical to our culture, are in fact necessary, sane, and invaluable. The formal marking of this shift helps her align herself with what is happening at the core of her psyche. It says that her experience has some deeper meaning and is fully supported by trustworthy adults and elders.

Joanna Macy speculates that the stage 3-4 shift might be getting sped up in our time by our increasing anger and grief over the devastation of peoples, other species, and habitats.[33] These deep and deeply troubling emotions might catalyze personal maturation; they might trigger the ecocentric self slumbering at the core of the Thespian psyche. Joanna feels that this wave of individual awakenings might be Earth coming to its own defense in the form of maturing humans. More and more people are uncovering an immense and implacable sadness within themselves and recognizing that this is not a pathology but, to the contrary, a healthy and necessary response of our animal selves to the destruction of our world. Crisis consciously discerned is always a maturing influence for the psyche, summoning our deeper resources into action. The global crisis is calling us to extend our self-interest to embrace the whole.

There's another reason why people experience sadness as the Oasis comes to a close. What's being left behind is a stage teeming with social excitement, stylistic flash, erotic adventure unencumbered by an excess of meaning, wide-ranging value explorations, polymorphous relationship investigation, and adolescent heroic achievement. It was the first and last chance in life to be a kind of king (or queen) of the world. The Oasis was the best stage to be in.

CHAPTER SEVEN

THE WANDERER *in the* COCOON

Late Adolescence (Stage 4)

Not all those who wander are lost.

— J. R. R. TOLKIEN

Life is a mystery to be lived, not a problem to be solved.

— AUTHOR UNKNOWN

You are not surprised at the force of the storm—
you have seen it growing.
The trees flee. Their flight
sets the boulevards streaming. And you know:
he whom they flee is the one
you move toward. All your senses
sing him, as you stand at the window.

The weeks stood still in summer.
The trees' blood rose. Now you feel
it wants to sink back
into the source of everything. You thought
you could trust that power
when you plucked the fruit;
now it becomes a riddle again,
and you again a stranger.

Summer was like your house: you knew
where each thing stood.

Now you must go out into your heart
as onto a vast plain. Now
the immense loneliness begins.
The days go numb, the wind
sucks the world from your senses like withered leaves.

Through the empty branches the sky remains.
It is what you have.
Be earth now, and evensong.
Be the ground lying under that sky.
Be modest now, like a thing
ripened until it is real,
so that he who began it all
can feel you when he reaches for you.

— RAINER MARIA RILKE

Stage 4: Late Adolescence

Passage into this stage: Confirmation (confirms the adequate completion of
   the adolescent personality and consequently preparedness for the descent
   to soul)

Stage name: The Cocoon (the tomb for the adolescent and the womb for the
   adult)

Tasks: Leaving the "home" of the adolescent personality (the culture task) and
   exploring the mysteries of nature and psyche (the nature task)

Quadrant: West (soul, darkness, mystery, the hidden, the invisible)

Hemispheres: South and West (individual action)

Stage archetype: The Wanderer

Quadrant archetype: The Visionary

Gift to community: Mystery and darkness

Circle of identity: Worldcentric

Center of gravity: Mysteries of soul and nature, the underworld

Passage out of this stage: Soul Initiation

THE ENCHANTING AND DANGEROUS PORTAL

If you have been developing soulcentrically, a radical shift occurs for you at the southwest point on the Wheel. You feel a strong downward pull, and you fall increasingly

under the influence of the soul, like the inexorable tug of the full Moon upon the tides, like an autumn storm tearing leaves from tree limbs. Unable to resist the bewitching call from your own depths and from the mysteries of the wild world, you turn your back for a while on conventional society and, for the first time, fully face the West, the enchanting and dangerous portal that beckons you deeper into the world — though the fright of that turning is as great as its allure.

You are transiting, not between hemispheres of the Wheel, but from one quadrant (the South) to the next (the West). You are traveling from the domain of warmth and daylight to that of encroaching nightfall. Your center of gravity is shifting from your emotional and social life (South quadrant) to the life of your soul (West quadrant) — more specifically, from peer group, sex, and society (the Oasis) to the dark mysteries of nature and psyche (the Cocoon). Along with the Sun, you begin a descent, a plunge into the underworld.

The southwest point on the Wheel represents the life passage of Confirmation. So, too, it is the end of the primary influence of the archetypes of the Orphan and the Thespian, and the advent of the ways of the Wanderer (specific to the Cocoon) and the Visionary (common to both stages of the West quadrant). As a newly launched Wanderer, you turn away from the appetites of your Thespian personality (Rilke's "summer house") as you begin your arduous preparation for the passage of Soul Initiation sometime in the uncertain future.

These, then, are the two tasks of the Cocoon: leaving the adolescent "home" of your first personality (the culture task) and exploring the mysteries of nature and psyche (the nature task). The experiential encounter with soul is the constant intent of this stage. Soul Initiation is the final result.

In Western culture, the passage into the Cocoon, if reached at all, often occurs many years after we obtain the nominal status of "adult." Consequently, it might feel odd or offensive to have our years prior to Confirmation referred to as "adolescent." Jungian analyst James Hollis neatly resolves this awkwardness by making a distinction between our "first adulthood" and our "second adulthood." The latter commences with what I call the Wellspring (the stage after the Cocoon).[1]

As you enter the Cocoon — not at all a comfy haven, but a frightful place where caterpillar bodies disintegrate in the process of becoming moths or butterflies — your perspective on the meaning of life shifts. Where once you thought life was primarily about social, academic, economic, or religious projects, now you recognize it for the spiritual adventure it truly is. Now you begin to search for the shape of that greater story you're destined to live, the larger conversation you might have with the world, a conversation that is not only the ego's. Your foremost quest becomes your own soul, that unique psycho-ecological niche that only you can inhabit. You are like a dislocated species that must wander through the world until it once again finds a place it can call its own.

If you are developing soulcentrically, the southwest point on the Wheel is the moment your life departs radically from the way mainstream Western culture has come to think about human maturation.

CONFIRMATION: PASSAGE INTO SWEET DARKNESS

Confirmation marks your emergence from the long period of personal and social development that began in early childhood with the original appearance of a conscious self (at the time of Naming) and continued through both stages of the Wheel's South quadrant. Confirmation proclaims the adequate completion of an adolescent personality. At this passage, a soulcentric community confirms and celebrates your debut by acknowledging and welcoming a socially individuated person with a distinctive, even if provisional, identity, a person with a particular set of skills, ideas, sensitivities, styles, and values, an individual with a salient social cachet. But on this auspicious occasion, a second thing is confirmed, something with a dark as well as a joyful implication. Your psychosocial success in the previous three stages qualifies you for the formidable descent into the underworld in search of soul and destiny. A trapdoor has suddenly opened in the floor of your life, and whether you desire it or not, you are headed for the depths, which is to say, the greater significance of your own life. You have just been introduced to life's verticality, its third dimension, ending forever your slumbering existence in the flatland of the everyday social world. Now is the time to descend, and your preparedness has been recognized.

This is precisely the way human development proceeds — by periodic leaps into distinctive stages of being, each stage characterized by a unique psychospiritual center of gravity and worldview. You begin life with no consciousness of anything, and then, in what seems a sudden opening, you are vibrantly aware of this immense world and all its wonders, and you are sure life will forever remain an uncomplicated exploration of the world. And then puberty alters you at your core, and your social and sexual standing comes to mean everything to you. Several years later (at the earliest), just when you're finally getting used to society life, the world shifts again and terrifying mysteries beckon that were previously unsuspected and on which your life now depends. This sequence of periodic tectonic lurches is the way it has always been, and this is the way it will continue throughout the remainder of your life. Your center of gravity and your fundamental understanding of what the world is, keep shifting — if, that is, you keep maturing.

In a soulcentric setting, your transit into the West quadrant is facilitated and marked by a rite of passage, a Rite of Confirmation (an example of which is offered below). It might also be termed a Rite of Emergence, Completion, or Graduation — if, that is, the emphasis is placed on what's ending. Or your community might underscore the new destination and call it a Rite of Commencement, Departure, or Descent.

Confirmation contains loss as well as joy. Like all major life passages, it marks a death and a birth, both an emergence and a withdrawal. Emerging as an autonomous being from the social world that gave birth to you, you now withdraw into a time of wandering, either on your own or in the company of initiatory guides and fellow initiates. Confirmation marks the death of an engaged participant in everyday society and the birth of a wandering stranger encased in a transforming Cocoon.

In mainstream America, there are virtually no remaining traditions of a genuine adolescent withdrawal from familiar social life. We have the junior year abroad, or the post-high-school departure to join the military or attend a distant college, but all too often these are merely geographical relocations with little psychological or spiritual benefit.

Preparation for Soul Initiation requires that you be separated — psychologically if not physically — from the ordinary life of your community so that you might cease to define yourself according to the familiar rules and norms. During your Oasis time — the summer of your life — you gained some confidence in your personality and you came to trust the way that life unfolds. Now, as Rilke writes in his "Book of Pilgrimage," life becomes "a riddle again, / and you again a stranger" — to yourself and others.[2] You will have to relinquish your temptation to conform or to seek acceptance from others. You will have to go out on your own.

You will also have to move beyond any requirement to be "good," any obligation to be held back by shame about who you are. The primary time of being shaped by society is over. Together you and your community celebrate this ending — and surrender to it. At the time of Confirmation, the elders might introduce to you the nature of the next life stage using images like Mary Oliver's:

> You do not have to be good.
> You do not have to walk on your knees
> for a hundred miles through the desert, repenting.
> You only have to let the soft animal of your body
>   love what it loves. . . .[3]

Your task is not repentance for the sins of your past but a surrender to the desires of your truer human nature, that which "the soft animal of your body" loves. Oliver says this is *the only thing* you have to do, but she doesn't say it's easy. This is a surrender that takes some time and effort.

What's involved is actually both a surrender *of* and a surrender *to*: first a surrender of your beliefs about how you were supposed to be and how the world was supposed to work, and then a surrender to your deepest and wildest passions. These two surrenders correspond to the two tasks of the Cocoon.

At the time of Confirmation, you might physically leave your community and not return until the completion of the Cocoon. Alternatively, you might not leave until later in the stage and only for a few weeks or months. Either way, when you leave your physical and social home, the purpose is to prepare you for vacating your *psychological* home — your adolescent, or first-adulthood, identity.

It might seem cruel or unfair that your soul wants you to surrender your Thespian personality just after you completed the long and labored process of making it viable enough to take on the road. It's as if you had spent years building, from the foundation up, your first house, and now you're finally done. As you tack up the last piece of artwork on the living room wall and step back to admire the whole creation, you hear a knock and the front door swings open. There stand three strange angels, as D. H. Lawrence called them, motioning to you, informing you it's time to leave — forever. You begin to protest, but you know it's useless. It's time to go.

This knock on the door, the call to adventure, comes as soon as you have done enough work on your first personality that it is fully inhabitable. The greatest value derived from building that first house of personality comes from the building of it — not from the living in it. The angels — in the form of elders, initiators, dreams, immense feeling, tragic events or losses, or numinous experiences — arrive to summon you to the adventure for which you have longed. They are your guides to soul.

Rilke writes of the necessity of leaving home at the end of the South season of our lives:

> ... Summer was like your house: you knew
> where each thing stood.
> Now you must go out into your heart
> as onto a vast plain. Now
> the immense loneliness begins. . . .[4]

Why an immense loneliness? In surrendering the mainstays of your former worldview and separating yourself from everyday community life, you find that your old anchors and familiar reference points disappear. You have to rely on yourself more fully than ever before. You have to surrender the cherished belief that someone is going to protect you, save you, do the work of growing for you, or show you the way. Because many of these old pillars of support have disappeared for you, the descent necessarily begins with an immense loneliness. Only someone who possesses the skills required to create a viable first house of personality — only *that* person is going to be ready to survive and benefit from this degree and kind of loneliness. Although the knock on the door does not require you to be alone, it does require you to go your own way.

Leaving your summerhouse, however, does not mean you must betray your pre-existing responsibilities, especially if you are well beyond your teen years at the time of Confirmation. It doesn't automatically require you to quit your job, sell your house, leave your marriage, or end friendships, although one or all of these things might turn out to be necessary. Almost never would it mean abandoning your children. Most parents recognize their commitment to their children to be as sacred as their commitment to their own souls. The descent for a parent might be logistically different than it is for others, and probably a lot more challenging, but it can still be done. What leaving your summerhouse does require is that you surrender what no longer supports the exploration of your deepest nature. You will discover soon enough which roles, relationships, activities, and possessions get in the way of that exploration. You are being asked to radically simplify your life.

In a soulcentric community, the elders have their way of recognizing when your time of Confirmation is near, as discussed at the end of the last chapter. The elders see the signs that your paramount motivation in life has shifted from the further development of social identity to the primacy of spiritual adventure, or as Joseph Campbell puts it, from "society to a zone unknown."[5] The elders discern this moment directly, by *seeing* you, not by noting your chronological age or by assessing academic standing, physical development, or the results of personality tests. The elders know because they have been there themselves, and they understand the ecstasy and terror of what must happen next.

In an egocentric society — with few real elders and initiation guides — you might not have anyone to help you understand what is happening to you or to support you through this passage. But once your center of gravity shifts, there will be no turning back.

As a Confirmed individual, you enter the West quadrant of the Wheel and descend into psychospiritual darkness, the nightworld of mysteries, the womb of true character. David Whyte describes this moment, employing the intimate voice with which a wise and caring elder might speak to a frightened initiate:

> ... Time to go into the dark
> where the night has eyes
> to recognize its own.
>
> There you can be sure
> you are not beyond love.
>
> The dark will be your womb
> tonight.
>
> The night will give you a horizon
> further than you can see.
>
> You must learn one thing.
> The world was made to be free in.

Give up all the other worlds
except the one to which you belong.

Sometimes it takes darkness and the sweet
confinement of your aloneness
to learn

anything or anyone
that does not bring you alive

is too small for you.[6]

"The world was made to be free in": this you know in your bones, and this definitive and fearful knowledge is what supports you as you turn away from your secure but less-than-joyful first-adulthood life.

Any healthy high school student knows this, too. Once she has passed through Confirmation, it is this promise of freedom that inspires her. It is not the prospect of becoming a "responsible adult," as so many parents and educators wish for our youth. Responsible adulthood — holding down a job, paying the mortgage, getting the kids to school — is what we say we want for our youth, but the truth is, it's not even what we want for ourselves. Yes, most of us are responsible, but this is not what motivates us, excites us, or inspires us. Just like us, the majority of teens do not fantasize about becoming dependable grown-ups; they are not inspired by the prospects of a secure and predictable job and a pension plan. Selling out for a safe and banal existence is not what they have in mind for their lives. Healthy young people want to *live*, not survive. Spirited teens want to become, not "responsible adults," but animated, passionate, engaged, vital, alive, contributing, joyous adults — in love with the world, their lives, and others.

When we speak of responsibility, most of us probably mean that we want our youth to contribute to our communities — we want them to truly belong. But what empowers us to really belong is that we each do so in our own way. Their one true life is what we must help our youth find, and this discovery necessitates the underworld journey to soul.

In egocentric society, however, true life is denied in favor of socioeconomic success and conformity. When our Thespian youth exhibit signs that their center of gravity is beginning to slide West, those signs are ignored, disparaged, deflected, suppressed, or pathologized. Too often, the young man interested in art or poetry is told that he'll never support a family that way. The young woman who seeks solitude in nature or wants to talk about death might be referred to a mental health worker.

Young people, everywhere and in all times, sense, in their blood, the need for a passage, not directly into "adulthood," but into another and as yet unknown world. In our egocentric society, high-school-age and college-age youth are blindly attempting to access the mysteries and to uncover a loyalty to something greater than ordinary social life. Without elders or initiatory guides, they do whatever they can to shift their everyday frame of mind, to stretch their routine lives by risking them. The most popular pathways are alcohol, drugs, music, and sex, any one of which could actually help, especially with the support of elders or guides. But for our unmentored youth, these pathways usually go nowhere or worse. When youth attempt to self-initiate, they might wind up wounding themselves significantly — psychologically or physically — or ending their lives, perhaps intentionally. Some youth join gangs or cults. Some risk it all with extreme sports. Yet others attempt psychological border-crossings through spiritual practices borrowed from other cultures or based in self-designed rituals.

There are centuries-old college traditions of danger and irreverence, many of them rooted in an attempt to part the veils of mystery. In the Middle Ages, freshmen's noses were pressed to grindstones — literally — as their initiation into college life. In more recent times, Princeton sophomores get drunk and sprint nude through the snow. The freshmen at the U.S. Naval Academy at Annapolis attempt to slither up a greased granite monument. Sometimes such rites are just the crazy antics of the young. But other times they're genuine attempts at conducting the sacred business of initiation. These rites fail at their larger goal because they do not benefit from a conscious understanding of the underlying need, or from the guidance and wisdom of true elders.

In many of the self-designed rites of youth, the psychological and physical risks are exceedingly high, suggesting that what's at stake is something essential to human development. The participants — what we might call "normal, smart kids" — are willing to risk serious injury and death. In fact, fatalities are not uncommon. In the fall of 1999, twelve students were killed and many more seriously injured at Texas A&M University by the collapse of the traditional forty-foot-high pyramid of giant logs being built for the annual football game bonfire. Because youth, even in egocentric society, will always look for ways to lift the veil of ordinary (stage-3) reality, even when they don't understand what's calling them, such traditions and accidents will continue. Even more tragic than the occasional loss of life is the ineffectiveness of these rites at truly transforming the participants.

Although ultimately what moves a person from one stage to the next is the Mystery, there is still much we can do to help youth — and middle-aged people, too, for that matter — make the transition from the Oasis to the Cocoon. In the Oasis, Thespians prepare for this shift by working on the tasks of Social Individuation. Parents, teachers, mentors, and elders support them. Then, when the initiators or elders see that a Thespian is ready to wander, they employ a Rite of Confirmation that, in collaboration with the workings of grace, might tip the scales.

Possible features of a Confirmation rite include the following:

- A preparation time in which the initiate simplifies her life. She drops out of social scenes, roles, and jobs that would not support the underworld journey. She ties up loose ends, completes as much unfinished interpersonal business as she can, and says her good-byes.

- A community ceremony in which the initiate's social and psychological successes are affirmed. Her talents, achievements, unique styles, and sensibilities are noted. The community acknowledges her maturity and Thespian social contributions.
- Putting away, giving away, or ritually sacrificing objects and clothes associated with her early adolescence, or first adulthood.
- A ritual funeral for, or sacrifice of, the primary ego (the adolescent personality, which, in Western society, sees us through our first adulthood). This includes expressions of both grief and joy.
- The taking of vows, in which she dedicates this next stage of life to mystery, soul discovery, and the underworld journey.
- A ceremonial dedication or commitment to the initiation process that is about to begin. (The initiation process can span several years.)
- A ceremony of leave-taking, in which, perhaps, she changes clothes (symbolizing or embodying the shift from Thespian to Wanderer), performs purifications and/or exchanges gifts with family members and/or mentors. The ceremony might conclude with a symbolic leave-taking from the community or a literal departure for a few weeks or months, a year, or indefinitely.

A MID-TWENTIETH-CENTURY EXPERIENCE OF CONFIRMATION

In contemporary Western society, Confirmation rites are rare to nonexistent, but many people — a large minority — nevertheless go through the *passage* of Confirmation.

We find an illuminating example in Joanna Macy's memoir. In her teenage Oasis years, Joanna's social and religious life, and her vocational aspirations, revolved around Protestant Christianity. At age seventeen, she was a member of the Presbyterian Youth Caravan, and as part of that ministry, she led worship services at churches throughout the northeastern United States and taught Bible classes and organized church programs for all ages. In the fall of that year, 1946, she enrolled in Wellesley College, graduating four years later with a degree in biblical history. Joanna's relationship to the church was the linchpin of her early adolescent way of belonging to the world.

But in the winter and spring of 1950, during her final semester of college, when she was twenty-one, Joanna's psychospiritual center of gravity began to shift from Christianity toward the mysteries of nature and psyche: "I began to feel confined by the narrowness, the exclusivity with which [Christian theologians] set [the cross] against the world and all that was natural and instinctive. Feelings of mystical connection, yearnings to merge with God or nature, were viewed as intellectually sloppy and morally dangerous. That assumption had become so ingrained in me that I barely realized the toll that it took. If I questioned it, I felt silly and adolescent."[7] Nevertheless, Joanna started to explore new ways of conversing with the world. Sometimes, she attended Quaker meetings "and sat in the simple sufficiency of its silence." More generally, she discovered that "whole dimensions of life seemed to be left out [of Christianity]. Sunrise and the smell of wet soil[,] ... the way my body felt when I kissed Tony[,] ... the leaping joy in my legs as I danced. ... As a matter of fact, most of humanity was left out."[8]

Such revelations triggered for her the psychospiritual crisis of Confirmation: "I felt myself utterly unable to commune with what God had become for me. ... A jealous, righteous judge ... breathing down my neck, crowding me, sealing me in. ... Yet my refusal to pray brought no freedom; it only triggered a sense of hopelessness. I had hit a monumental dead end."[9] That dead end was Joanna's severance from the Oasis and the beginning of her Cocoon. In addition to the allure of the mysteries (nature, the sensual, the erotic, the spiritual), Joanna writes of the disorientation and hardships of leaving "home":

> The vocation that had for so long been the organizing principle of my life ...
> began to feel like a burden, even a trap, and half-consciously I hoped to be
> rescued from it. Incapable of saying "no" to the life purpose I had espoused,
> I drifted numbly, as if waiting for some *force majeure* to intervene — some
> man perhaps that would sweep me off my feet, anything to free me from the
> burden of self-knowledge and choice.[10]

The quintessential moment of Confirmation occurred for Joanna in early 1950, when she had her final interview with her primary college mentor, the chairman of the Department of Biblical History. Joanna spoke to her professor about the "spiritual desert" in which she had recently found herself. He responded by accusing her of dodging and fighting "the very faith at the core of your life." In an attempt to shock her back into the fold, he turned on her and barked, "Look, if you want to be an atheist, go ahead and be one."[11]

> But I chose to take his words at face value. For a long moment I stared at him,
> speechless with amazement. Of course, I didn't need to be an *atheist*. I had
> no interest in acquiring another label or defending another position. But the
> idea that I could simply loosen my grip on Christianity, relinquish it even, had
> never occurred to me. Why not? Perhaps I *could* just walk out. ... Open the
> door and walk out. I hardly dared believe that such freedom could be mine
> for the taking. "Oh," I breathed, "yes, of course."[12]

The professor's gambit was Joanna's knock on the door, providing her the opportunity to cross the threshold and enter the Cocoon.

LATE ADOLESCENCE AS A COCOON

A cocoon — that protective pouch of silk spun by the larvae of moths — serves as a womb for the pupal stage, in which the larva undergoes a complete metamorphosis, from juvenile caterpillar to flying adult. In the fourth stage of human life, the individual undergoes an analogous transformation, from an adolescent personality to an adult self — or from the first adulthood to the second.

What occurs in the human Cocoon is similar in scope and profundity to what occurred in the first stage of life, the Nest. During that stage we made a great sea crossing from the prebirth realm of spirit to the realm of human society and conscious self-awareness. Now we undergo a transmutation that is equally radical, mysterious, and momentous — we gradually make our way from a life centered in society and personality to a life centered in soul, from an individual whose goal is to improve his socioeconomic standing to one whose primary motivation is to discover his destiny and turn it into lived reality, a gift to others.[13]

From both the Nest and the Cocoon there ultimately emerges a being that flies. Unlike the Nest, however, the Cocoon is a psychologically perilous and tumultuous place and one that we must enter and inhabit on our own, without the support of parents or siblings. In the Nest, the family serves as a close, protective environment for the work of transformation. The Cocoon, in contrast, is as destructive as it is protective, and it comprises a much larger space, as big as the world. There can be no predetermined limits to our wandering. The whole world — the wild Earth, in particular — becomes our Cocoon. When we finally emerge, it will be Earth herself who gives birth to us this second time.

But we weave our Cocoon with more than just the things of nature. Other strands include our solitude, our deepest wounds from childhood and adolescence, our dreams, our greatest passions and allurements, our mortality, ceremonies, the dark, and our own shadow — all woven together to form an alchemical cauldron of change.

When the caterpillar enters his silk cocoon (for him, a tomb), he dies to his previous life and enters a liminal time of being neither Earth-crawling worm nor windborne flier. Likewise, upon entering our own Cocoons, we are neither adolescent Thespians nor initiated adults. We are betwixt and between. Within his cocoon, the caterpillar pupa, the chrysalis, does not feed, and within ours we do not draw further sustenance from society. Upon emerging from the Cocoon, the individual is reborn — as a true adult.

The Cocoon results in the disintegration of almost everything we know about the world and ourselves. The butterfly, of course, understands this.

There are four phases to the butterfly's life cycle: egg, larva (caterpillar), the pupa or chrysalis, and the imago (a mature adult, a butterfly). The transformational chrysalis phase is one of the great mysteries of biology. No one knows exactly how the caterpillar changes form in such a dramatic way. But this much *is* known: inside the caterpillar's body are clusters of cells called, of all things, imaginal buds. *Imaginal* refers to the imago, the adult phase, but it also means "of the imagination," and psychologists use the word *imago* to mean an idealized image of a loved one, including the self. The imaginal buds contain the idealized image, the blueprint, for growing a butterfly. While the caterpillar goes about its Earth-bound business, these cells, hidden inside, are imagining flight.

The caterpillar's immune system believes these imaginal cells are foreign and tries to destroy them, not unlike the way uninitiated human egos and egocentric cultures try to destroy the soul, nature, and the feminine. It's as if the caterpillar doesn't realize its destiny is to become a butterfly. Likewise, the uninitiated ego doesn't realize its destiny is to become an agent for soul. (It's no coincidence the Greek word for butterfly means "soul.") Once in the cocoon, the buds link up, the caterpillar's immune system breaks down, and its body literally disintegrates. The buds — essentially, stem cells — then build a butterfly from the chrysalis fluids. The caterpillar and butterfly are not really opposed to one another; the butterfly is not an alien organism within the caterpillar. They are, in fact, one and the same organism, with the same genetic code.

Inside the Cocoon, you come to understand what the butterfly knows: you are preparing to die in order for something new to be born — and to take flight.

What triggers the caterpillar's cocooning? During the larva stage, the caterpillar goes through four or five molts, each time shedding its skin for a new suit. But finally it gets to the skin that will not molt because biological sensors have detected that the skin has stretched as far as it is designed to go. This prompts the cocooning. It's as if the caterpillar knows in this moment that this is the end of the line for its old strategy of personal growth — this skin will not stretch or crack as the others have.

We humans go through several molts before the Cocoon — when the first personality finally loses its grip. These molts include Birth, Naming, and Puberty, and perhaps others within this time period. Confirmation signals that the first personality has taken us as far as it can.

The adolescent-to-adult transition (often the shift from the first to the second adulthood) is so radical and difficult that the entire life stage of the Cocoon serves as the middle phase of an extended passage — a passage that begins with a severance, or descent, at the time of Confirmation, and ends with a return at the time of Soul Initiation.

For some people, or in some cultures, the Cocoon might be divided into two stages: first, a period of preparation in which the individual continues to live in the general community; then a period in which he withdraws from all regular contact with everyday society. In nature-based cultures, the period of exile might last anywhere from a month to several years and might include components of both solitude and periods of instruction from elders. In contemporary Western culture, in which the journey of descent is not well understood, this exile might be experienced as a psychosocial banishment, an inability to fit in anywhere, and it might last decades or have no definitive ending.[14]

As the Cocoon stage commences, the initiate must move beyond his psychological dependence on others and on his previous social roles. He will no longer adopt, in whole or part, other people's identities or ways of belonging to the world. He will no longer sacrifice his one true life in order to make himself and others comfortable. He knows what he has to do. He must leave his old home and wander into the mysteries of nature and psyche.

THE WANDERER:
ARCHETYPE OF LATE ADOLESCENCE

In a soulcentric community, the underworld journeyer might be known as a seeker, an aspirant, a candidate for initiation, an exile, a pilgrim, a solitary, . . . in short, a Wanderer. This is the time in life when a person is most intensely in search of her most authentic self, a self she knows she will not find reflected back to her in the familiar arenas of her human village. She searches for the seeds of her destiny in the more diverse, wild, and mysterious world of nature. She no longer conforms to or rebels against society. She chooses a third way. She wanders — beyond the confines of her previous, early-adolescent (or first-adulthood) identity.

The Wanderer crosses and recrosses borders in order to find something whose location is unknown and unknowable. She will conclude she has found it not by its location in a certain place, or by its confirming a prior belief, but by how it feels, how it resonates within her upon discovery. She doesn't know where or when or how clues will appear, so she wanders incessantly, both inwardly and outwardly, always looking, imagining, and feeling.

The Wanderer cultivates an openness to mystery and offers her attention to the edge of thoughts, dreams, and feelings and to the borders between places and between events. She's aware that anything can happen at anytime, and that every moment is charged with the numinous. In her wandering, she makes her own path.

The task that lies before the Wanderer — uncovering her soul, her ultimate place in the world — is truly daunting. Although it is the very heart of her one true life, her soul is, at the outset of her wandering, something she has little or no conscious knowledge about. The elders have explained to her that this is an unavoidable feature of being human, a part of the rich drama that *makes* us human, a kind of hide-and-seek with

soul that prepares us for the challenges inherent in our individual destinies. By the time
her ego formed, at age three or four, she, like everyone else, had misplaced the image
with which she was born; she had forgotten her ultimate place in the world. During
childhood, after all, she needed to learn how to become a part of her human community and family, with their needs to define her in a more or less limited way. But now,
years later, having secured a good place in the village world, she strikes out on her own
in search of her lost soul, her authentic place, the stirring conversation that only she
can have with the world.

In American society today, there is very little support for true wandering during high
school or college. Yet this is when such support would be invaluable. At this time most
individuals' psyches are fully primed for border crossings. Many youth, even the
brightest, do not really want to go to college immediately after high school, and many
of those who believe they *ought* to go might not be best served by doing so. They need
to wander — and most colleges still do not encourage psychospiritual wandering in
any meaningful way.

The most progressive high schools and colleges, however, are designing and implementing initiatory curricula for youth who have entered what I call the Cocoon. We're
beginning to see initiated adults in the role of faculty members, and they are incorporating soul-discovery opportunities into their courses. They are offering experiential learning opportunities, including dreamwork, deep-imagery, and council process,
and embracing the study of soul poetry and initiatory literature, the arts as a means
to explore and embody the mysteries of soul, and guided wilderness experiences
aimed not at conquering nature but at an immersion in the wild and a surrender to
one's own deepest nature.[15]

The most valuable wandering, however, occurs outside of a school context. Most
Wanderers will need to roam far and wide geographically and culturally, and in and
out of wilderness, on their own. You might think that such a nomadic life would be
difficult for most to afford, but the fact is that true wandering requires little if any outside financial support. Self-reliance is an essential component of this life stage, whether
it occurs in a person's late teens or sixties or anywhere in between. When a person has
few material needs, subsisting with odd jobs along the way is not particularly difficult
to arrange.

If contemporary American youth manage to wander at all, they are generally left
to their own devices and have only the foggiest notion of what the journey is about or
what the goal might be. Yet if they are fortunate enough to hear and respond to the
soul's call, they will stumble, in their late teens or twenties or perhaps later, into one
way or another of wandering. As Theodore Roethke writes in "The Waking,"

...Great Nature has another thing to do
To you and me; so take the lively air,
And, lovely, learn by going where to go....[16]

Joanna Macy's time of wandering began the moment she left her professor's office in 1950. As with all Wanderers from all times and places, her initial companions were disorientation, angst, and a surrender to the present moment:

> Claiming my freedom pulled the linchpin from my life. My commitment to
> a Christian vocation had formed the core of my identity and self-worth
> since I was sixteen. Its loss left a hole inside me, even as I celebrated Com-
> mencement with my Wellesley classmates and sailed for Europe.... In some
> innermost dimension I felt at sea, without a rudder.
>
> While that was painful, it was also interesting, in a bleak sort of way. In
> my efforts to become an atheist, I was reading French existentialists. Camus
> and Sartre certainly showed how loss of meaning and direction was a char-
> acteristic feature of the world. Perhaps it was necessary to my growing up into
> a clear-eyed person of brave and honest intellect.
>
> These ponderings were hardly constant though. When you are 21 and on
> your own in Europe, there is plenty to divert you from existential angst. And
> so I practiced giving myself to the beauty of the moment.[17]

With a Fulbright scholarship, she studied political science for a year in Bordeaux, France. One morning, she passed a travel agent's shop, saw a sign that read "Students Half Price," and immediately decided she would go wandering, geographically and culturally. "No one will know where I am," she mused. "I can disappear into the world." And so she did — in Casablanca, Marrakech, and Tangiers. "And the world entered me as well."[18]

In Marrakech, the great square of Djemaa el F'naa, "the place of madness," kept drawing her back to wander among the kaleidoscopic colors, sounds, and scents of the hawkers, shops, and storytellers. There she fell fully in love with the world — and with her first lover.

> This wetness [of the fountains in the square] seemed to spring from the se-
> cret well of my own being, for I had been in the arms of my lover. I had given
> myself to him — the twin, the waiting one, whose face I had tried so long to
> imagine. And I knew I would open my body to his again, as I would meet him
> again and again in different faces and forms. The song of life was mine now.[19]

Like all people new to wandering, Joanna was in awe of the mysteries and ecstasies encountered in the Cocoon:

> I marveled...at what our lovemaking had revealed about the universe. Over
> the years I had come to believe that news about the nature of reality came

solely through the mind, in the shape of powerfully moving ideas. And now, totally independent of my views and judgments, this revelation, this breaking open, this falling through — into what? What were these currents and vortices that drew me down into them, as if everything else I've ever done were just dried sticks drifting on the surface of life?[20]

This is the universal experience of entering the Cocoon: You are drawn *down* (decidedly not upward). You fall through into currents that lead to never-before-seen places and never-before-experienced realms. You leave the flatland of everyday life — the middleworld — and break into the beauty and terror of the underworld.

Your Loyal Soldier will be mightily provoked by all these radical experiences, as was Joanna's in the midst of her first love affair: "My head rang with scolding voices. They sounded shocked and chagrined, as Mama would surely be. . . . These voices were my Presbyterian ancestors too, scornful of my weakness, my depravity. They even sounded like *me*: my inner guardian of personal integrity was horrified at what I was risking."[21] Loyal Soldier work is always a component of your time in the Cocoon.

My own experiences during my teens and early twenties provide another example of what American youth do in their unconscious attempts, sometimes successful, to wander. In my final two years of high school, in the late sixties, I differentiated my life from mainstream norms by adopting the dress, art, and manner of the hippie counterculture. I let my hair grow long and wore tie-dye and sandals. I bought an electric organ and joined a rock-and-roll band. I papered the walls of my bedroom with black-light posters. My parents, of course, were puzzled and sometimes alarmed. Each American generation, in the absence of genuine societal support for wandering, has found one way or another to be contrary, from flappers and beatniks, to punk, grunge, and goth.

But wandering is both different from and more than mere rebellion. I didn't start to wander in earnest until my first year in college. I experimented with psychedelics, studied Buddhist literature and practiced daily Zen meditation, read and listened to Taoists like Alan Watts and to psychedelic luminaries like Timothy Leary, and studied tai chi, martial arts, and Kundalini yoga. I bought a motorcycle and roamed with my friends increasingly greater distances from campus.

One summer, my friend Mark and I rode our motorcycles from North Carolina to California and back, encountering many exotic places and people along the way. We knew we weren't on the road just to see the country, but at the time we couldn't have said much more about our deeper goals. Nevertheless, encountering such a diversity of people and places surely loosened our attachment to our early-adolescent identities.

Graduate school in Colorado afforded me the opportunity to study other realities: sleep and dreams, hypnosis, tantric yoga, and astrology. I spent three summers at the Naropa Institute (now University) studying Tibetan Buddhism and other spiritual traditions and practices, and one summer at Esalen's Institute of Consciousness Studies.

There are so many ways to wander. Each individual finds ways that personally resonate. For me, technical rock climbing and mountaineering were additional avenues
that expanded the possibilities of my world, in this case through a conversation with
the vertical, the seemingly insurmountable, with questions of balance and rhythm, with
the limits of strength and finesse, with the need to surrender to what is, to crisis and
failure. Immersion in the mountain world, and wild nature elsewhere, nourished my
senses and imagination and intimated what it might mean to belong to a still larger
and more mysterious cosmos.

And romance is perhaps the most powerful and dangerous way of wandering in
our late teens and twenties. Like most youth, I learned much from both the agonizing
conflicts and the mind-blowing ecstasies, from both rejections and consummations,
in every case opening doors to the mysterious, dark rooms of the heart.

All of these border-crossing experiences in my teens and twenties offered opportunities to explore nonordinary social and spiritual realms, with the possibility of
uncovering some clues about soul. But in the absence of mature guides, I reaped only
occasional results of lasting significance.

THE VISIONARY: ARCHETYPE OF THE WEST

The Wanderer archetype has a defining relationship only to the Cocoon. The Visionary,
on the other hand, is the archetype of the entire West quadrant and consequently illuminates two stages, both late adolescence and early adulthood. (See Diagram 3-4, p. 68.)

The Visionary is one who sees well — with imagination and feeling as well as with
clarity and precision. She sees the potentials as well as the actual, and she sees how to
get from one to the other. She sees *into* people, places, and possibilities and cultivates
a relationship with the invisible realms as much as with the visible. She is in conversation with the mysteries of the world, on the lookout for signs and omens. She attends
especially to the edges, those places where one thing merges with another, where consciousness shifts and opens, where the world becomes something different from what
it initially appeared to be.

Of the four windows of knowing (thinking, feeling, imagining, and sensing), imagination is the Visionary's most potent tool, her way of seeing into the dark of the underworld, her way of illuminating the shadows, of dropping deeper into soul.[22]

I chose the Visionary as the archetype of the Cocoon and the Wellspring because
the darkening West is where we cultivate the ability to see into the unknown.

Visionary action entails three component skills. First, the Visionary is able to access and retrieve the images and stories waiting for her in her soul: these are the images
and stories she was born to celebrate and live as her gift to the world. Second, the Visionary is capable of understanding the world clearly, profoundly, and compassionately.

She is sufficiently independent, confident, and mature to set aside her immediate desires so as to recognize what the world needs, what the world wants from her. Third, the Visionary can connect up the results from the first two steps. She has the creative and synthetic ability to see how her personal soul images and stories can be effectively embodied in the world. She has a keen understanding of both her unique gift and the world's need, and she can imaginatively bridge the gap between the two. In this century, doing this serves the Great Turning.

The Visionary is able to borrow concepts and images from one discipline or field of study and apply them to another. She is able to see, for example, that a physicist's talk of holograms can help a psychologist understand the nature of the self. Or she sees, like Joanna Macy, how the teachings of the Buddha can empower the work of environmental activists. Being able to carry a concept from one discipline to another requires an open and wild imagination, a type of poetic consciousness capable of making leaps of perception and understanding.

The Visionary creatively ventures into the dark depths — like Orpheus searching the underworld for Eurydice — to retrieve something mysterious and precious (his soul) and bring it back to the middleworld of everyday society. Only someone who has had sufficient success at the tasks of the Oasis and passed through the transition of Confirmation can do this. The rules and conventions of society do not help the Visionary do his work; new possibilities and patterns must be unearthed. Like the Wanderer, the Visionary is neither a Conformist nor a Rebel. He allows his vision and the dream of the Earth to take precedence over tradition.

THE CALL TO ADVENTURE

Around the time of Confirmation, we hear what Joseph Campbell referred to as "the call to adventure" — the realization that it is time to inherit a greater life, to plunge ourselves into the limitless expanse and depth that the world affords. This moment is both a great crisis and an unsurpassed opportunity. Our old way of life has been outgrown. Our familiar goals, attitudes, and patterns of relationships no longer fit our sense of who we are.

The call to adventure might be heard several times in a life. During the Cocoon, each call signifies the opportunity to go deeper, to withdraw further from everyday society and enter that extended time of passage that leads to rebirth.

Most people, even in egocentric society, first hear the call sometime in their midteens, and I believe we're genetically predisposed in just that way. Around the age of fifteen or sixteen, we naturally begin to wonder about the more mysterious and enigmatic dimensions of life. We begin to ask the big questions about love, meaning, destiny, death, and transcendence. But our patho-adolescent society does all it can to discourage such exploration. We're expected to stay in school and prepare for a job, career, or marriage and family.

But the door to the mysteries can and does open again after our teens. For example, most people I've asked say they heard the call to adventure between the ages of twenty-seven and thirty (whether or not they remember hearing it earlier). They felt an overwhelming urge then to leave behind the life they had so carefully composed and go off in search of a greater destiny.[23] Some found the courage to do so. Others didn't. Some had the courage but not the opportunity, especially if they had young children or others who depended on them as caregivers.

Jungian analysts (and Jung himself) say that it's rare to be ready for the descent to soul (and, consequently, our second adulthood) until midlife, until, say, our midforties. They're probably correct — about modern Euro-Americans, that is. But many nature-based people say *their* youth are ready at puberty. This is quite a range of opinion about the ideal timing of the descent — from age thirteen to forty-five. Based on my own observations, I'd say that the call can be heard and heeded anytime from puberty on, but that, for contemporary people, the door to soul opens most commonly and emphatically in our midteens, our late twenties, and our midforties.

In the soul-suppressing environments of Western society, however, the call may never be heard — or answered — in an entire lifetime, or perhaps not until one's deathbed. The vast majority of midlife crises might be better understood as overdue calls to adventure, as spiritual opportunities triggered by a personal crisis — an affair, severe job dissatisfaction, an empty nest, or the simple realization one day that you're not going to live forever.

Midlife crises often begin like this: Your life has been humming along for some time, fairly secure in its basic socioeconomic qualities, and then *wham!* Suddenly the roof caves in, and everything about your life seems wrong. Your job has become a dull cage, your social scene an unremitting replay of the same characters and conversations, and your family a lifeless mockery of intimacy — sometimes polite, sometimes seething with hostility. Or at least, so it seems at the outset of the crisis. This is the soul appearing on the scene — with an attitude and a comment about the course of your life.

In egocentric society we tend to think of midlife crises as something to simply get through, to work out of our systems in short order so we can resume our routine lives. Rather than really leaving our routine lives and embracing our neglected wildness, we simply act out for a few weeks — with a younger lover, a sports car, or an exotic adventure — and then settle down again.

Others hear the call to adventure before the advent of a midlife crisis. Perhaps *you* had the great good fortune of finding a teacher or guide who understood the necessity and joy of the descent. Perhaps, as a young adult, you encountered a true elder and were spiritually adopted. Or maybe you suffered a terrible calamity: a terminal diagnosis, a near-death experience, a physical accident that left you disabled, the loss of a loved one, a divorce, the destruction of your home or homeland, a suicidal depression, or the utter loss of your religious faith.

However and whenever it happens, when you hear the call, you find your nose suddenly pressed up against previously avoided existential questions: What is my life about, anyway? What do I live *for*?

Joseph Campbell writes,

> That which has to be faced, and is somehow profoundly familiar to the unconscious — though unknown, surprising, and even frightening to the conscious personality — makes itself known; and what formerly was meaningful may become strangely emptied of value.... This first stage of the mythological journey — which we have designated the "call to adventure" — signifies that destiny has summoned the hero and transferred his spiritual center of gravity from within the pale of his society to a zone unknown.[24]

It is always possible, however, to refuse the call entirely and to turn the ear back to the egocentric interests of unrewarding work, relationships, and pop culture. Refusing the call turns our flowering world into a wasteland of open-pit mines, clear-cuts, strip malls, and billboards.

Families, communities, and societies that are nature-based and soul-oriented provide ritual opportunities — Cocoons — for those who have heard the call and are properly prepared. The Australian walkabout, for example, is a component of the preparation for adulthood. The aboriginal youth wanders off into the bush alone for an extended period of time, avoiding the company and conversation of other humans. He goes in search of the one place where he belongs, a place that's part of him and of which he is a part. In finding this place, he finds himself.

What might a genuine, contemporary walkabout look like in Western societies?

THE QUEST FOR AUTHENTIC IDENTITY

The Wanderer (of any chronological age) seeks to discover her ultimate place in life. Not just any place will do. Her authentic place is not simply one that someone will pay her to occupy, such as a job. Nor is it a task she happens to have the talent to perform, such as an art or a craft, or a career that a vocational counselor recommends for her, such as banking or social work. Nor is it a social role, such as caregiver, student, parent, servant, leader, whore, or rebel, that other people will accept her in. It's got to be *her* place, one that is in keeping with her vital core. It's a place defined not by the deeds she performs but by the qualities of soul that she embodies; not by her physical, social, or economic achievements but by the true character she manifests; neither by her capacity to conform to the masses, nor by her ability to creatively rebel against the mainstream, but by the unique way she performs her giveaway for her community. Her ultimate place is identified not by *any* social forms or roles but, rather, by the symbols, stories, and archetypes unearthed from the deep structure of her psyche and by the way the world invites her to belong to it.

Consequently, the Wanderer must now go off in search of the one life she can call her own. Joseph Campbell says it this way:

> The differentiations of sex, age, and occupation are not essential to our character, but mere costumes which we wear for a time on the stage of the world. The image of man within is not to be confounded with the garments. We think of ourselves as Americans, children of the twentieth century, Occidentals, civilized Christians. We are virtuous or sinful. Yet such designations do not tell what it is to be a man, they denote only the accidents of geography, birth-date, and income. What is the core of us? What is the basic character of our being?[25]

In her poem "The Journey," Mary Oliver suggests that, in Western society at least, when a person finally leaves the home of her first adulthood in search of her greater destiny, it is psychologically if not chronologically "already late enough" in her life. Furthermore, this decisive leave-taking doesn't happen in a quiet, sunlit, or easy life moment, but rather in the middle of a "wild night."[26] At such a moment, the Wanderer's greatest need is for the company of her own true voice, but she is not likely to hear that voice until she has progressed some distance down the road. She must enter the dark night of her life with blind faith or not at all.

The Wanderer is, in Oliver's words, "determined to save the only life [she] could save." This is not a recommendation for selfishness. This savable life is identified only by "[striding] deeper and deeper into the world" until she discovers the place where her life and the life of the world are one.[27] She finds the place where, as theologian Frederick Buechner says, "our deepest gladness and the world's hunger meet."[28] That place, that way of being in relationship with the world, is what I mean by *soul*. The life she saves is what Campbell calls (in the quote above) "the core of us, the basic character of our being," which leads to a life of fulfilling service. This salvation is an act of love, love of both self and world.

The primary purpose of the Cocoon is to prepare the individual for this radical transformation. As terrifying as it is to leave home, and however much the old wounded and wounding voices of childhood keep pleading that we not go, there comes the time when we hear the call, open the door, and step out.

In our society, the late teens and early twenties are often thought of as our one chance in life to sow wild oats. This way of thinking belies an unconscious co-optation of our innate wildness — our true, abiding, and sustainable vitality. Something in us is truly wild and wants to stay that way through our entire life. It is the source of our deepest creativity and freedom. When we say about youth, "Let them have their day, their wildness, their fun; soon enough they'll settle down like we all do," we're betraying the fact that we've made our human world too small for soul. We've abdicated a critically important part of our human nature.

Even the phrase "sow wild oats" suggests that, like oats, our wildness is doomed to domestication. Egocentric society believes these human oats (and their sowers) are not meant to remain wild. Young people might briefly be allowed their "freedom," but it's rare that they are encouraged to uncover, celebrate, and claim their full wildness for a lifetime. Soul — our authentic identity — is a dimension of that wildness.

THE WANDERER'S CONTRIBUTION TO SOCIETY:
MYSTERY AND DARKNESS

The gift that the Wanderer contributes to her world — simply and amply through her presence — is the aura of mystery, darkness, the unknown, the emerging future. The Cocoon is the time of life when we are most "other," most enigmatic, least defined. The Wanderer becomes a foreign thing, embodying and imparting to those of other stages the ambience of the wild, the imaginable, the anomalous, the dream . . . the possible human and the future of human society.

The Wanderer is the early-phase Visionary who is mythically and often literally sent by the village out into the wilderness with the charge of gathering a piece of the unknown and bringing it back — the unknown that is at once a threat to the customs and routines of the village and the village's only hope for cultural sustainability. "Without vision, the people shall perish."[29] She brings back tidings and talismans from the edge, from the periphery, the psychospiritual realms beyond the borders. She is both admired and somewhat feared.

It's as if she has been conscripted for a type of warrior service, as if she is paying her debt to society by risking it all in her search for a visionary boon for her clan. Among soulcentric people, this is their counterpart to military service. This is what their youth are doing instead of — or if necessary, in addition to — defending their communities. They are not serving as missionaries for the church, the corporation, or the government. This wandering in the darkness is a wrestling with angels, a struggle the healthy ego hopes to lose. As Rilke writes,

> . . . Whoever was beaten by this Angel
> (who often simply declined the fight)

went away proud and strengthened
and great from that harsh hand,
that kneaded him as if to change his shape.
Winning does not tempt that man.
This is how he grows: by being defeated, decisively, by
constantly greater beings.[30]

Whether she dwells within the village, lives in a remote enclave with fellow initiates and teachers, or wanders alone in some wild hinterland, the inhabitant of the Cocoon generates a psychic turbulence in her community. Her people know that she's out
there, and they know what she's doing. She is somewhat dangerous to herself and others (in just the right ways), and yet she is an embodied affirmation that the darkness
must be embraced if community life is to remain vital and sound. Her very existence
inspires others to have faith in the unknown, to seek innovation and vision in hidden
and unexpected places.

I recall a young psychotherapist, Paula, a whirlwind of energy who joined the staff
of a mental health center where I worked in the mid-1980s. She was very much in the
Cocoon stage at that time and was constantly bringing a fresh and radical perspective
to her therapeutic interventions. Short on experience and polish, but long on originality and irreverence, she inspired us all to reconsider our own approaches and try
out new ways of helping our clients. Although we might not have admitted it, her example gave us pause and roused us to reconsider the very meaning of psychotherapy
and why we were in the profession in the first place. For some of us, this examination
ultimately deepened our practice and enhanced our enjoyment of the work. And for
one or two others, I suspect, it might have been a significant factor that led to an appropriate career change.

The Wanderer — she who prepares for Soul Initiation — ventures beyond the
borders of the village to retrieve something new, something postconventional, so that
human culture and consciousness can continue to evolve. The existence of the Wanderer is an invaluable reminder to everyone else that the village is a tiny spot of light
in a vast field of fruitful darkness, and that the village exists both in opposition to that
darkness and because of it.

THE DEVELOPMENTAL TASKS OF THE COCOON

...I said to my soul, be still, and wait without hope
For hope would be hope for the wrong thing; wait without love
For love would be love of the wrong thing; there is yet faith
But the faith and the love and the hope are all in the waiting.
Wait without thought, for you are not ready for thought:

So the darkness shall be the light, and the stillness the dancing.
Whisper of running streams, and winter lightning.
The wild thyme unseen and the wild strawberry,
The laughter in the garden, echoed ecstasy
Not lost, but requiring, pointing to the agony
Of death and birth....

— T. S. ELIOT, "EAST COKER"

As a Wanderer, you apprentice to the unknown, to mystery. You long to be initiated into the fully embodied life of your soul, but you will have to wait. The fallow time of the Cocoon, the time between death and (re)birth, cannot be dodged. To catch up to your soul, you'll have to learn, as T. S. Eliot writes, to place your faith and love and hope in the waiting. But you will be anything but idle. You will undergo a multifaceted and lengthy preparation and metamorphosis.

Two essential tasks must be addressed: saying good-bye to the old and making yourself ready for the new. More specifically, you must gradually leave the home of your former identity, and you must explore the mysteries of nature and psyche in preparation for Soul Initiation. (See Diagram 3-3, p. 61.)

As with every other stage, here too there is a dynamic, mutually beneficial tension between the culture task (leaving home) and the nature task (exploring the mysteries). As you roam farther from home, you increasingly crave security and you feel less courageous about entering the mysteries, a destabilizing experience whether those mysteries are fearsome or alluring. Human culture — even a healthy one — seems to say to you, "Oh, for heaven's sake, join me as you are now. Pick a social role, any role, and learn to occupy it. We need you now. You belong with us."[31] But nature counters, "*I* am your true home. Enter me deeply."

This is the nature-culture tension in the Cocoon. In their dispute, both nature and culture are correct. You do belong to both. But your personal development requires that you not choose a side, that you simultaneously hold the opposing claims and withstand the tension between them. This conscious holding of the opposites will, itself, constitute a significant stimulus to your maturation within the Cocoon. It might even be one of the primary factors that create the Cocoon in the first place, and your pain and longing as you hold the tension might be necessary to dissolve your caterpillar body, allowing a butterfly to one day take form.

In the Cocoon, the fear evoked by the mysteries urges you to turn and run — back to your early-adolescent, or first-adulthood, way of belonging. But if you've had enough success with Social Individuation in the Oasis, you'll find the courage and fortitude to proceed. Then, the fear evoked by the mysteries will goad you to further hone your skills of self-reliance and to relinquish your familiar identity (these are the two components of the culture task).

Notice that you wouldn't have to work so hard at the Cocoon's culture task (leaving home) if the nature task (exploring the mysteries) weren't so fearsome. Roaming far from home is not so challenging when new places turn out to be predictable, benign, and easily manageable. The nature task of the Cocoon consequently benefits the culture task. And yet you wouldn't *want* to work so hard at the culture task if your longing to enter the mysteries of nature and psyche were not so strong. Your passion to learn something about your soul gifts and your soul path (your true nature) evokes the strength and courage to undertake the often-harrowing practices involved in leaving home, practices that require you to look fiercely and compassionately at your addictions, your wounds, your childhood survival strategies, and the monsters lurking in your personal shadow. Likewise, it is the joy springing from your initial discoveries of soul that sustains your ongoing experiential exploration of the old wounds and of the fragmentations inherent in your former Thespian life.

Dissatisfaction with the life that you lived in the Oasis does not by itself provide you nearly enough motivation to embark on the underworld journey. Stronger, more sustainable motivation derives from your longing for a deeper connection to soul and to the world, a longing to live the one life you were born for and to claim the joy that leaps within that life.

This is why the culture task of the Cocoon — leaving home — and its associated practices would not have been possible in the Oasis. It's not just because your personality wasn't yet strong enough; more important, your motivation to stride deeper into the world, as Mary Oliver puts it, was not yet ripe.

The further you explore the enigmas and raptures of life, the more enthralled you become with them despite the dangers, and the more you are determined to leave your old home forever. Again, the nature task propels the culture task. And the more you relinquish your attachment to your former identity, the farther you're able to wander, unencumbered, into the world. The culture task propels the nature task.

Although I refer to the culture task as the "first" one and the nature task as the "second," you must actually work on the two simultaneously. Every success with one enables you to take the next step with the other. As you progress with the two tasks, you more fully embrace your life, and new, unimagined realms of experiences become available to you, experiences that are necessary if the Cocoon is going to alter your consciousness as required. This is one of the gifts of the tension between the apparent opposites of nature and culture, which, in the end, are not opposed but complementary.

After some time, you discover that the nature and culture tasks of the Cocoon blend and fold into one another, as if in a dance. Every step of leaving becomes a step of arriving. As you separate from your former society-centered identity, you claim more of your nature-and-soul-centered identity.

LEAVING HOME

This first task — the culture task — is to acquire the skills and practices that support you to wander in the most profound way. As we've seen, this departure involves a whole lot more than changing your address or saying good-bye to your hometown. As you relinquish your old ways of belonging, you enter a fruitful spiritual darkness that becomes your new habitat as you make progress by descending.

There are two subtasks involved in leaving home: (1) honing your skills of self-reliance, and (2) relinquishing attachment to your adolescent, or first-adulthood, identity.[32]

Honing the Skills of Self-Reliance

As with the passages of birth and death, you journey alone through strange and unfamiliar realms on your way to a soulful, or second, adulthood. You must learn to conduct yourself boldly and to make difficult and critical choices without the comforting presence of a life partner, guide, or teacher at your side. You must sharpen your skills of physical, social, psychological, and spiritual self-reliance. Undoubtedly you lack certain of these skills, and you'll need them if you are going to truly wander. These are skills that may never have been necessary had you remained in the Oasis your whole life.

For example, if your wandering will take you into wilderness or foreign cultures, you'll need the practical skills of travel, navigation, language, and self-care. Even more important and challenging, you'll need psychological and spiritual skills. You must be proficient at making friends and allies, defending yourself against enemies, and resolving conflicts. You'll need to know what to do when you lose heart, when you feel more intensely than you thought possible, when you want to run, when you need to let go of whatever is dear to you but holds you back, when you get stuck, and when you suddenly break through. You'll need to know how to access strength and courage during times of danger or difficulty or when you lose faith.

How will you acquire these skills? You'll learn from mentors and peers, from books and courses, but mostly you'll learn through experience, through trial and error. You'll learn by courageously choosing new experiences with unfamiliar places, people, activities, and relationships.

But you won't be in control of the learning process as much as you'd like. Tension between the nature and culture tasks will provoke experiences you could not have chosen for yourself — and often wouldn't have. Support you didn't know to ask for will show up. Challenges you would never have wanted will appear.

Should you encounter any impasses while honing your self-reliance skills, you'll seek counsel and instruction from initiation guides, elders, and your own inner guides and resources.

Harley Swift Deer, a Native American teacher, says that each of us has a survival dance and a sacred dance, but that the survival dance must come first. Our survival dance, a foundational component of self-reliance, is what we do for a living — our way of supporting ourselves physically and economically. For most contemporary people, this means a paid job. For members of a religious community like a monastery, it means social or spiritual labors that contribute to the community's well-being. For others, it means creating a home and raising children, finding a patron for one's art, or living as a hunter or gatherer. Everybody has to have a survival dance. Finding or creating one is our first task when we leave our parents' or guardians' home.

Once your survival dance is established, you can wander, inwardly and outwardly, searching for clues to your sacred dance, the work you were born to do. Your sacred dance sparks your greatest fulfillment and extends your truest service to the world. Discovering the deep structure of your sacred dance is your goal in the Cocoon. Committing to this sacred dance is the essence of Soul Initiation. You know you've found it when there's little else you'd rather be doing. Getting paid for it is superfluous. You would gladly pay others, if necessary, for the opportunity.

This points to the importance of self-reliance, not merely the economic kind implied by a survival dance but also the social, psychological, and spiritual kinds. To find your sacred dance, after all, you must take significant risks. You might need to move against the grain of your family and friends. By honing psychological self-reliance, you'll find it easier to stay focused on your goals in the face of others' resistance or incomprehension, your own initial failure or setbacks, or economic or organizational obstacles. And spiritual self-reliance will maintain your connection with deepest truths and what you've learned about how the world works.

Swift Deer says that, once you discover the nature of your sacred dance and learn effective ways of embodying it, life will support you in doing just that. What your soul wants is what the world also wants (and needs). Some segment of your human community will say YES to your soulwork and will empower and help you to do it. Gradually, in the Wellspring (the following stage), your sacred dance becomes what you do, and your former survival dance is no longer needed. Your sacred dance and your new survival dance become one and the same. You are supported in doing what you find most fulfilling.

How do you get there? The first step is to create a foundation for self-reliance: a survival dance of integrity that allows you to be in the world in a good way — a way that is psychologically sustaining, economically adequate, socially responsible, and environmentally sound. Cultivating right livelihood, as Buddhists call it, is essential training and a foundation for your soulwork; it's not a step that can be skipped.

Relinquishing Attachment to Your Adolescent Identity, or First Adulthood

Leaving home means casting off the provisional identity you developed in early adolescence and have been refining (or not) ever since. That identity was primarily focused on social standing, psychological and economic security, interpersonal and physical comfort, and, especially in egocentric society, the sort of personal power that is *power over* rather than *power with*. A soul-rooted identity, in contrast, is primarily focused on discovering and offering the gifts of soul to the world.

The Wanderer's separation from her adolescent identity is a gradual and challenging process that culminates at the time of Soul Initiation. During the Cocoon stage, she adopts several practices that loosen her hold on the old way. These particular practices vary from one cultural context to another, but there are common themes that can be identified. What follows are six examples.

Addressing Developmental Deficits from Earlier Stages

There's always some remedial work to complete in the Cocoon. No matter how wholesome your childhood and teen years, no matter how loving your parents and teachers, no matter how well you avoided the major traumas of this human life, some tasks from the Nest, Garden, and Oasis will have been neglected. Now, in the Cocoon, there's both time and need for some catch-up, otherwise these developmental deficits might imprison you in your adolescent identity. At the ends of chapters 4 through 6, we explored methods for addressing those deficits, including ways to reclaim your innocence, wonder, communion with nature, and the wildness of your own emotions, imagination, and body. We also considered how you might become adequately ecoliterate and conversant with mythology and the new cosmology.

Your success in the Cocoon also requires an adequate emotional and interpersonal foundation established in the Oasis, as well as a balance between your masculine and feminine capacities and sensibilities. If you have significant difficulties with any aspects of emotional or social competence, it would be wise to seek guidance or mentoring from soulcentric psychotherapy, support groups, relevant workshops, or an emotionally mature friend or family member. If you're not sure where to begin, review the chapters on the Nest, Garden, and Oasis while holding that question.

As you do this work, it's important to understand that addressing developmental deficits is not the same thing as healing your wounds from past emotional traumas. If you look at the list of tasks and subtasks from the first three stages (see appendix), you'll note that emotional healing is not among them. There are, of course, related tasks — such as cultivating your skills with emotional access and expression, conflict resolution, status assignment, and Loyal Soldier work — but none of these tasks have the specific goal of resolving emotional traumas, understanding or healing childhood relationships, or helping you to generally feel better. Some or all of these goals might be realized along the way — and this is always salutary — but these do not form the central objective of soulcentric development in the first three stages.

At least as far as back as Freud, our egocentric society has placed excessive emphasis on emotional healing *for the purpose of the adolescent ego's comfort.* This emphasis might very well subvert the more vital personal development that enables us to progress beyond the Oasis (or any of the egocentric stages). With no vision of personal development beyond stage 3, egocentric society steers people toward egocentric life goals centered on socioeconomic comfort and, for the therapeutically minded, conclusive emotional healing of the past.

But, given that you'll never be healed of all of your emotional wounds, there's no need to become fixated there! An obsession with stage-3 psychotherapy can arrest your development. In the course of attending to the tasks of the first three stages, you'll be sufficiently healed to enable further maturation. Once you reach the Cocoon, one of your goals is to become less attached to decisively healing your past (without, of course, compromising your full capacity to feel and express your emotions, which is one of the tasks of the Oasis).

Consequently, this first practice within the subtask of relinquishing attachment to the adolescent personality — namely, addressing your developmental deficits — does not specifically address the emotional healing of past wounds and relationships. Instead you cultivate some degree of nonattachment to that agenda. In the Cocoon — but not before — you must adopt a different attitude to your past woundings. They are no longer the major identifiers of your life but are only some defining components of the smaller story that characterized your childhood and early-adolescent existence. And your goal in the Cocoon is to eventually leave behind that smaller story, in part by cultivating some Nurturing Parent compassion for your inescapable human fragility, as well as a healthy sense of humor concerning it. Even as your wounded subpersonalities and traumas occasionally shape your behavior in hurtful and even humiliating ways, even as unmet emotional needs can provoke pain that sometimes feels as if it will kill you, in the Cocoon you must accept some of this suffering as one element that supports your maturation. While you always hope to feel more, not less, your goal is to do so without becoming mired in the past.

But here, the difference between being in the Oasis (or any of the egocentric stages) and being in the Cocoon makes all the difference in the world. In any version of stage 3, trying to distance yourself from emotional healing is a form of psychological self-obstruction. In the Cocoon and beyond, however, although emotional suppression is never the goal, it's time to progress beyond the emotional therapies that aim to comfort or decisively heal the adolescent ego.

As we'll see in a few pages — in the discussion of the sacred wound — the goal of emotional work in the Cocoon is not the ego's comfort but its death and rebirth. Such a goal would be either ill advised or impossible in stage 3.

Giving Up Addictions

In stage 3, you might have avoided some emotionally painful precincts of your life by numbing yourself through addictions. The most damaging addictions are chemical, creating a primary neurological impairment of your capacity to feel and a secondary behavioral impairment — by altering what you attend to and how you spend your time.[33] But there are many other addictions, such as food, impersonal sex, TV, gambling, and work, and these too, by distracting and deadening you, can effectively cut you off from your full range of feeling, sensing, remembering, and imagining.

Even though you've reached the Cocoon, some addictions might have come along with you. As you prepare for the encounter with soul, you'll have to leave behind any substances or activities that might distance you from the mysteries of nature and psyche. And you will have to replace them with positive habits of presence and self-encounter. This can be an arduous task — addictions can be exceedingly difficult to kick. People with substance addictions especially will need help — from friends and family, psychotherapy, twelve-step and other recovery programs, acupuncture, and/or other mainstream and alternative health-care approaches.

Sooner or later, we each have to address the paramount addiction in the Western world: our psychological dependence on the worldview and lifestyle of Western civilization itself. Ecopsychologist Chellis Glendinning makes this point brilliantly in her book *My Name Is Chellis, and I'm in Recovery from Western Civilization*.[34] The Western worldview says, in essence, that technological progress is the highest value, and that we were born to consume, to endlessly use and discard natural resources, other species, techno-gadgets, toys, and, often, other people, especially if they are poor or from the global South. The most highly prized freedom is the right to shop. This is a world of commodities, not entities, and economic expansion is the primary measure of progress. Profits are valued over people, money over meaning, our national entitlement over global peace and justice, "us" over "them." This addiction is the most dangerous one in the world, because it is rapidly undermining the natural systems of Earth.

The more we live this way, the more alienated we become from something more meaningful, and the more we need this way of life to keep us from experiencing that alienation. Our addiction to Western civilization can linger even into the Cocoon and beyond. Each of us must carefully examine our own lives and uncover the ways in which this addiction remains.

Relinquishing attachment to the adolescent identity is a primary means of overcoming our dependence on the cultural worldview within which this identity formed.

Exploration of the Sacred Wound

When the Wanderer has eliminated all substance addictions and other notable dependencies, and has made significant progress with the Oasis task of welcoming home her Loyal Soldier, she finds one branch of memory that is particularly and uniquely painful. This is an early psychological wound, a trauma so great she formed her primary survival strategies of childhood in reaction to it, so hurtful that much of her personal style and sensitivities have their roots there.

If she grew up in the worst sort of egocentric setting (in which family dysfunction is common), she might have been emotionally abused or neglected. Perhaps an alcoholic father blamed her for his own misery or acted as if she were his girlfriend, or an insecure and jealous mother saw her as a threat to her marriage. Maybe an older stepsister tormented her, or a strict and demanding parent told her she would never measure up.

She need not come from a dysfunctional family, however, to have wounds. Her core wound may stem from birth trauma or a birth defect, or the death of her mother when she was three, or a pattern of innocent but shattering betrayals at the hands of her older brother. Maybe it was her father's absence due to illness, or her guilt at surviving the car wreck that claimed her younger sister, or her own childhood bout with a potentially deadly fever.

Although personal histories often include injurious events such as these, the core wound rarely stems from a single traumatic incident. More often it consists of a pattern of hurtful events or a disturbing dynamic in one or more important relationships.

Even in the healthiest families, each person suffers from a core wound. From the perspective of the Cocoon, this is not an accident, nor is it unfortunate. Some say that the soul orchestrates the wounding, to catalyze a special type of personal development not possible until the Cocoon, one that requires a trauma for its genesis.

By experientially exploring your core wound, you can render it sacred. Your wound holds a key to your destiny.[35] By surrendering to the grief and frightful memories at the heart of the wound, no longer distancing yourself from what you uncover there, your psyche is torn open so that new questions can be asked about who you are at your roots. These fomenting questions facilitate the death of your old story and the birth of a larger story, a soul story, one revealed by the wounding itself. The goal in sacred-wound work is not to patch up your small story, or to heal the adolescent ego, but to disidentify from both. The wound becomes sacred when you are ready to release your old story and become the vehicle through which your soul story can be lived into the world.

By courageously diving into your core wound, patiently allowing the suffering to do its work, neither indulging nor repressing the pain, you reach the bedrock of your psyche, where the most profound truths of this lifetime await. But you must avoid making sense of your pain too soon, finding relief too quickly, blaming someone for your anguish, or seeking revenge. Don't cave in and seek refuge in self-blame, self-pity, or playing the role of the victim or martyr; or through denial, cynicism, abandoning your own dreams and values, or paranoid confidence in a never-ending series of further woundings. Allow the wound to do its work on you even if you descend into a pit of hopelessness. If you remain there long enough, you'll be shorn of the personal patterns and attachments that must die so you can be reborn into a greater life. Sacred-wound work should not be attempted before the Cocoon stage.

Rumi says, "Wherever there is a ruin, there is hope for treasure — why do you not seek the treasure of God in the wasted heart?"[36]

In the contemporary West, conscious investigation of the sacred wound, when attempted at all, most commonly takes place in those rare psychotherapies that journey deep into the psyche to encounter the demons and monsters of our greatest fears. These wounds can also be approached through exceptional forms of bodywork or through ceremonies that expose our grief and allow its full experience. In a soul-centered setting, the elders, who know we all carry sacred wounds, offer rituals and nature-based practices that help us uncover and assimilate the lessons and opportunities, the treasures, hidden in our wounds. In whatever way we go about it, a thorough acquaintance with our sacred wounds loosens our attachment to our former identity and becomes a vital component of the metamorphosis that occurs within the Cocoon.

Learning to Choose Authenticity over Social Acceptance

As a Wanderer, you must be true to yourself. You cannot continue to follow the crowd.

As a Thespian, you learned the basics of authenticity. Within the bounds of what your Loyal Soldier would permit, you learned to distinguish what is true about yourself from what is not. When push came to shove, however, you probably treated social acceptance as more essential to your life than authenticity. It was. As you were acquiring social skills, you needed to fit in with your peers and establish a social identity that worked. Even when you weren't afraid of being rejected, you often went along with the crowd because it was easier or because you didn't know what you really wanted.

Now, in the Cocoon, you must take up the practice of prioritizing authenticity over acceptance. Authenticity and integrity become your foundations for asking the deeper questions of soul.

Distinguishing authenticity from deception — at *any* stage of life — requires the ability to access and understand your attitudes, interests, desires, values, and emotions. But the more advanced practice of choosing authenticity over social acceptance requires something more: you must tell yourself and your intimate others the truth, all of it, as thoroughly as you can, especially when it's difficult. What you express is from the heart and intended to serve both yourself and others. You must adopt the practice of making all your actions align with what you know to be emotionally and spiritually true.

A key authenticity practice is to stop pleasing others at the expense of your own integrity. If the important others in your life — at home, at work, at play, in your spiritual community — want you to be someone you are not (for example, a carefree confidant, a charmer, a rescuer, a victim, a bad boy, a scholar, a hometown hero, a pleaser, a homeboy, a loser, or everybody's mother), you will have to surrender your impulse to keep living your life for them. You will have to relinquish your willingness to make major life decisions just to take care of them emotionally or to win their approval.

You will, in essence, have to learn the difference between shallow and deep loyalty, between doing what another wants or asks and doing what your heart tells you is best for all concerned — yourself and others. Shallow loyalty is ultimately selfish if your goal is to increase your acceptance or socioeconomic security through compliance. It is both selfish and destructive if your goal is to give others what they want despite your knowing the "gift" is harmful. If a parent, for example, wants her grown son to live forever at home (physically or psychologically), it would be emotionally harmful to both the son and the mother for the son to comply. Supporting a person's weakness, psychopathology, or addiction is always a case of shallow loyalty, otherwise known as enabling, caretaking, or codependency.

Making Peace with the Past (the Death Lodge)

The Wanderer knows that, in entering the Cocoon, she's preparing to die (psychosocially) in order to be reborn. She must abandon her old home to set out for the new. She longs for the journey but is understandably terrified by the prospect. To help her approach the edge, the elders or initiation guides might suggest some time in the death lodge once she has made progress with the preceding practices.[37]

The death lodge is a symbolic and/or literal place, separate from the ongoing life of the community, to which the Wanderer retires to say good-bye to what her life has been. She might dwell there for a full month or, during the course of a year, for an hour on most days or for several long weekends. Some of her death-lodge work will take place in the cauldron of her imagination and emotions, while at other times it will occur face-to-face with friends, family, and lovers. She will wrap up unfinished emotional and worldly business to help release herself from her past.

In her death lodge, she will say good-bye to her accustomed ways of loving and hating, to the places that have felt most like home, to the social roles that gave her pleasure and self-definition, to the organizations and institutions that both shaped and limited her growth, and to her parents or caregivers who birthed her and raised her and who will soon, in a way, be losing a daughter.

She might choose to end her involvement with some people, places, and roles. In other cases, she might need only to shift her relationship to them. Although she must surrender her old way of belonging, she need not violate sacred contracts. Some contracts might have to be renewed at a deeper level. It is essential that she does not fool herself: embarking on the underworld journey is not a legitimate justification for abdicating preexisting agreements or responsibilities to others.

Whether ending or shifting relationships, she will feel and express her gratitude, love, and forgiveness. She will say the difficult and important things previously unsaid. She may or may not visit with each person in the flesh, but she will certainly have many poignant and emotional encounters.

If her parents were not criminally abusive, she will forgive them for not being who she wanted them to be. If they are still alive, she will attempt this in person. This could be the most important and difficult part of her death lodge. She knows by now no parents are perfect nurturers and all have their own wounds. She knows that surrendering her former identity requires her to release her fantasy that her human parents will somehow become perfect (or merely healthy or responsible), or that she will find someone else — a lover or therapist — to be her perfect parent. As with her Loyal Soldier work, she must become a Nurturing Parent to herself.

In her death lodge, the Wanderer also mourns. She grieves her personal losses and the collective losses of war, race or gender or class oppression, environmental destruction, community and family disintegration, or spiritual emptiness. Not only does she cease to push the painful memories away, but she invites them into her lodge and looks them in the eye. She allows her body to be seized by those griefs, surrendering to the gestures, postures, and cries of sorrow. She grieves in order to let her heart open fully again. She knows at the bottom of those grief waters lies a treasure, one of the sources of her greater life.

In the Cocoon, we surrender our comfortable lives above those waters. We enter depths so dark we fear we will die, and in a way, we will.

To relinquish your former identity is to sacrifice the story you were living, the one that defined you, empowered you socially — and limited you. This sacrifice captures the essence of leaving home.

Toward the end of the Cocoon, you begin to live as if in a fugue state. Imagine: after developing an adequate and functional identity, you now have become as if amnesiac, dissociated from your prior life. But unlike the victim of amnesia, you seek to discover not who you used to be but who you really are.

Your time in the death lodge grants freedom. Untied from the past, you dwell more fully in the present, better able to savor the gifts of the world. You find yourself projecting less and seeing the world more clearly and passionately. You experience an enhanced gratitude for the richness of life, for the many opportunities that await you.

Learning the Art of Disidentification through Meditation

Meditation practice develops the alertness of a centered mind, the ability to stay focused and calmly present. Meditation also guides you to disidentify from the small self, "the self that says, 'Not me, I'm not gonna die,'" as Buddhist author Natalie Goldberg puts it.[38] Through meditation practice, you learn to distinguish your personal consciousness — your beliefs about yourself, your ego — from the vast stillness of consciousness, the calm observing witness at the center of the storm of your life.

Within the Cocoon, it's essential to loosen your grip on the small self, the self that *is* going to die in this stage. A meditation discipline will help you open up to your larger self, or what Goldberg calls your "wild mind." As you experience your wild mind more regularly, your attachment lessens to any particular way your ego might constellate itself. Your capacity for soulful shape-shifting increases correspondingly. Your ego becomes more fluid, more adaptable to the desires of soul, spirit, and nature.

. Your underworld journey will be greatly facilitated if you practice the art of centering and disidentifying. Readers who are ready to begin or reanimate their meditation practice are encouraged to enroll in a course with a qualified teacher.

These, then, are six practices for leaving home. None of them are common components of high school or college curricula in the contemporary Western world (as they ought to be), none are high on the agendas of our youth themselves or of most of their parents, none are staple practices of our mainstream religious communities. We might long for what these practices facilitate (a soulful or second adulthood), but might have little idea how to get there. But it *is* possible, and with these practices to help you shed your former identity, it might not be as difficult as you imagine.

EXPLORING THE MYSTERIES
OF NATURE AND PSYCHE

The Wanderer's second task in preparing for Soul Initiation is to explore the mysteries of nature and psyche. Where his first task is to leave his accustomed home, in the second he meanders toward a new abode and a second birth. He will find his new place — his soul-rooted way of belonging to the world — by exploring the mysteries of his own human consciousness and its relationship to Earth and cosmos, which is to say the natural world.

This second task has two components: (1) learning and employing techniques for soul encounter, practices that will help the Wanderer approach the soul and gather what he finds there, and (2) cultivating a soulful relationship to his life and to all life.[39]

Soul Encounter versus Soul Initiation

Before discussing the specific pathways to soul, it's important to appreciate the distinction between *soul encounter* and *soul initiation*. A soul encounter is an experience, while Soul Initiation is the transition between two specific developmental stages (which is why I capitalize it in this book along with all the other life-passage names). More specifically, a soul encounter is an experience of an image, symbol, or story — something numinous or sacred at the very core of an individual life, and which communicates something of the person's ultimate place in the world. Soul Initiation, in contrast, is the transition from psychological adolescence to true adulthood, from the Cocoon to the Wellspring.

By *the process of soul initiation* (not capitalized), I mean the developmental unfolding that takes place over the entire course of the Cocoon, includes one or more experiences of soul encounter, and is consummated at the *passage* of Soul Initiation.

During your time as a Wanderer, the experience of soul encounter opens your consciousness to the central mysteries of your life, an opening that will guide the most creative choices of your adulthood and immeasurably deepen your appreciation of the world and all life. Your goal in the Cocoon, however, is not just a single glimpse of soul but a developing relationship, an ongoing conversation with those mysteries. Through that conversation, your life, in later life stages, becomes mature art — the engaged, active embodiment of your deep imagination in service to an evolving world. In the twenty-first century, that art is your contribution to the Great Work.

Soul encounters are rare before the midteens, but there is no reason they cannot occur in childhood. The Lakota holy man Black Elk (1862–1950) received his first and most profound vision when he was nine years old. Later in this chapter, we'll reflect on what Thomas Berry identifies as the principal soul encounter of his life, an event that occurred when he was eleven.

Soul encounters also happen *after* Soul Initiation. There is always more to discover about our ultimate place in the world. We'll explore some examples of postinitiation soul encounters in the following chapters on the Wellspring and Wild Orchard.

During a soul encounter, you learn something about your destiny, which can be variously phrased as: why you were born, your mystical calling, what gift you're meant to bring to the world, your one true life, the larger story you might live, your particular way of belonging to the Earth community, the largest conversation you can have with the world, your unique psycho-ecological niche in the web of life, or your ultimate place.

Soul encounters take a variety of forms. One of the most common is a perception (visual, acoustic, or kinesthetic) of the mysterious image you were born with, your soul image. Another is a revelation of the shape of your soul story — the story you were born to live in the world. A third is a numinous meeting with a being or place that communicates something of your destiny through language, gesture, emotion, image, or dream.

These three versions of soul encounter are, of course, related. First, note that to embody your soul image is to enact a certain story. Second, at the heart of your soul story is an image (or symbol or idea or quality) that you incarnate by living your life in a soul-infused way. Finally, a numinous encounter with a Sacred Other — a being or place — most always reveals either your soul story or image (or both).

A soul image is often multifaceted and complex, like an elaborate tapestry with many smaller component images. A single soul encounter might be a glimpse of only one or more facets of that soul image. At times in your life, you could be simultaneously drawing on several soul images, and you might not yet be able to understand their relationships to one another. Eventually, the puzzle comes together, perhaps when you experience a deeper image — one more central to your soul — that holds all the others as specific instances.

Woven into the fabric of your soul image is a mysterious symbol or theme that holds the secret of your life purpose. Through one or more soul encounters, you discover how that symbol or theme reveals the gift you were born to carry to others, and how your soul powers are vehicles for doing so. The fact that you have *your* particular soul qualities, and not others, is the truth at the center of your soul image.

Your soul story might be unveiled to you in a single revelatory experience — through a dream, a vision, the voice of the sacred, or a sudden insight. On the other hand, the shape of your soul story might be only gradually revealed as you weave together the themes and symbols from the soul encounters you've had up to that point in your life.

At the time of my first soul encounter, at age thirty, I was given the image of a cocoon.[40] Although the meaning of that image was mysterious to me at the time I received it, I immediately recognized that weaving cocoons would in some way be a central task of my life. I understood a cocoon as a place of extraordinary transformation, but other than that, I couldn't have said what the image meant or how I might go about embodying it. I only knew that creating conditions and settings for personal transformation was a core element of my calling. That particular soul encounter did not identify any delivery systems — cultural means by which I would weave cocoons. I was not told to become a vision-quest guide, a psychologist, or a writer. Later events fleshed out the meaning of the experience and the forms for living it.

You might glimpse your own soul image only once in your life, or you might observe it, and variations of it, many times. You might encounter somewhat different images on different occasions. I believe that each new encounter elaborates on the previous ones, offering further differentiation, clarification, or extension. Soul images are most commonly experienced visually — we humans are markedly sight-oriented, both behaviorally and neurologically — but, for many people, the image is auditory, kinesthetic, or emotional. The image might occur as a sensation in your body, a song you hear with every cell, or a powerful feeling coursing through you. You may or may not be able to put words to it. The image might be an "inner" one (like a dream image or one from your waking imagination), or it might be something you perceive with your senses. Sometimes it combines both imagination and sensing. Or you might not know whether it derives from imagination, sensing, or both, since that distinction often loses its significance when it comes to the soul.

Each person's soul image or soul story is as unique and mysterious as his or her destiny. I've had the great privilege of hearing the accounts of many soul encounters and witnessing how those revelations have been imaginatively embodied. These numina include a sacred chalice from which others might drink; a heart that mirrors other hearts; a glistening web spun over the waters of life; a woman with a sparkling heart who walks the path of a bear; a strong and nurturing tree; a geyser; healing hands offered to the world; a pathfinder; the heart song of a raven; and an undersea overseer. Others I know have discovered that the kernel of their soul story is to stand at the edge of the waters and help those who are ready to cross; to walk rainbows; to shine the light of the north; to sing the song that calls the Divine Beloved; to stalk the heart like a wolf; to sing the songs of the soul; or to echo the cry of Earth.

Malidoma Somé, the African shaman and teacher from the Dagara tribe whom I mentioned earlier, learned during his initiation process that his soul story was about making friends with strangers or enemies.[41]

At age eleven, Thomas Berry ventured out for the first time behind the site where his family was building a new home in North Carolina. He came to a creek and crossed it. It was an early afternoon in late May. There he beheld a meadow covered with blooming white lilies.

A magic moment, this experience gave to my life something that seems to explain my thinking at a more profound level than almost any other experience I can remember. It was not only the lilies. It was the singing of the crickets and the woodlands in the distance and the clouds in a clear sky.

...As the years pass this moment returns to me, and whenever I think about my basic life attitude and the whole trend of my mind and the causes to which I have given my efforts, I seem to come back to this moment and the impact it has had on my feeling for what is real and worthwhile in life.

This early experience, it seems, has become normative for me throughout the entire range of my thinking. Whatever preserves and enhances this meadow in the natural cycles of its transformation is good; whatever opposes this meadow or negates it is not good. My life orientation is that simple. It is also that pervasive. It applies in economics and political orientation a well as in education and religion.[42]

In her memoir, Joanna Macy recounts two experiences nine years apart that seem to me to be soul encounters. The first occurred when she was twenty-eight, at the birth of her second child, Jack. After delivery, the physician administered ether before

closing her birthing tear with stitches. In the resulting trance, woven of both the anes-
thetic and the mysteries of childbirth, she had a life-changing vision:

> I am lifted up, high over the world, which is so far below that I cannot see it.
> Yet I am also at the heart of the world, and a giant wheel is turning — and
> the manner of its turning is the secret of all things. I am on it, spread-eagled
> across its spokes, my head near its open center. Sometimes it seems I could
> *be* the wheel, I'm so inseparable from it. I feel the spokes shudder through my
> body with alternating and intensifying sensations.[43]

At first she feels warmth, and it is very pleasant. But then the warmth slowly increases until it reaches intolerable heat. Then the heat slowly turns to its opposite —
a relieving coolness, which gradually intensifies into a terrifying frigidity. Then it's
slowly back to warmth. Next the warmth turns into slow movement that gradually
grows to an agonizing frenzy followed by a gradual slide to its extreme opposite of sta-
sis. The wheel keeps turning, each sensation giving birth to its opposite. Additional
paired opposites were freedom and order, and reason and passion. "Each of the opposites becomes intolerable without the other. Each, when clung to, gives rise to its an-
tipode.... I accept, as if I have always known, the inevitability and accuracy of what
now is revealed. But I am frightened and pray for ignorance."[44]

This terrible and ecstatic vision of a great wheel became a guiding force for
Joanna. During the next several years, the wheel gave her the fortitude to continue her
courageous explorations of world and psyche: "In a way that I could not explain, even
to myself, the turning wheel betokened an order at the heart of reality. It erased my fear
of the hole inside me.... If a hole appears, just walk through it, see what's on the other
side."[45] This last statement could be taken as an articulation of the Code of the Wanderer. A slightly expanded version might be: celebrate mystery, explore the dark and
the depths, and trust in the order, magnificence, and meaningfulness of the universe.

An experience of soul encounter allows us to see the thread of meaning that runs
through our life like an underground stream. Several years later, Joanna was living in
India and had a brief audience with the Dalai Lama. There she saw a painting of an
eight-spoked wheel, the sacred Buddhist symbol of the Wheel of the Dharma, which
immediately recalled her vision: "The memory of the great wheel on which I had hung
and turned had never dimmed in the seven years since.... It let me glimpse a vast, underlying order that connected and made sense of all things, and left me with the hope
that I might someday be able to understand.... Had the Dharma been in store for me
all along? This time, instead of fear, I felt only awe and promise."[46]

As it turns out, Joanna has devoted much of her life to understanding the great
wheel of her vision and to sharing what she has learned. She has done this through the
lenses of the Buddha Dharma, general systems theory, and deep ecology.

What seems to me to be a second soul encounter occurred for Joanna when she was thirty-seven and still living in India. She had recently begun a Buddhist meditation practice under the guidance of an elder, Freda Bedi, and was experiencing the disorienting yet exhilarating sensation of having no solid "I" that she could hold onto.

> To my inner eye appeared a bridge, slightly arching, made of stone. I could see
> the separate rocks of which it was built, and I wanted to be one of them. Just one,
> that was enough, if only I could be part of that bridge between the thought-
> worlds of East and West, connecting the insights of the *Buddha Dharma* with
> the modern Western mind. What my role might be — at the podium of a col
> lege classroom? at a desk in a library tower? — was less clear to me than the con
> viction possessing me now: I would be a stone in the building of that bridge.[47]

Here was another glimpse of a soul image, this time a bridge that she might embody in acts of service. She was not yet able to identify her cultural delivery system for soul — would she be a professor? a librarian? — but she *knew* she would become a stone in that bridge. It would be a few more years before she made the decisive commitment to embody the great wheel and the bridge stone. But I believe that commitment was, for Joanna Macy, her Soul Initiation.

Soul Initiation is that extraordinary moment in life when we cross over from psychological adolescence to true adulthood, from our first adulthood to our second. It is when our everyday life becomes firmly rooted in the purposes of the soul. The embodiment of our soul qualities becomes as high a priority in living as any other. Because Soul Initiation signals the start of the Wellspring, we'll discuss it further in the next chapter.

Acquiring and Developing a Set of Soulcraft Skills

This is the first of the two subtasks in the Wanderer's exploration of the mysteries of nature and psyche. What I call "soulcraft skills" are a set of practices, found in cultures everywhere, that expedite the experience of soul encounter. These skills are employed in accessing, exploring, and comprehending the deep structure of our individual relationships to the world, by opening the door to experiences that lie outside our everyday cultural frame of reference.

Soul encounters can, of course, occur independently of the exercise of any skills. Sometimes, even without effort and when we least expect it, the soul shows up, pulls the rug of ordinary life from beneath us, and showers us with its confounding radiance. We hear our true name spoken for the first time, or an angel appears and invites us to wrestle, or we awake in the wilderness at midnight to a deer licking our forehead, or, out of nowhere, God says, "Take off your shoes!" Revelation *can* occur without conscious preparation for it. But more commonly, we must make deliberate and courageous steps in the soul's direction, using practices that open the way to the mysterious and the veiled.

In nature-based cultures, there are a great variety of these soul-oriented practices, techniques, and ceremonies taught by initiation guides and elders to the Wanderer youth of their communities. These soul-encounter skills are essential at this time of life, every bit as important as the skills involved in hunting, horticulture, food preparation, and shelter building.

For Western teenagers, too (those who have reached the Cocoon), developing soulcraft competence is more vital to their genuine personal development than math, science, soccer, and business know-how. But in egocentric society, exceedingly few youth, in their teens or twenties, ever gain proficiency in soulcraft skills.

Every culture has, or once had, many soul-discovery practices. Some of the most common, each explored in considerable detail in *Soulcraft*, are as follows:

- Soulcentric dreamwork: experiential processes for facilitating transformation, personal deepening, and initiation through the rich landscapes of our nocturnal visions. Soulcentric dreamwork diverges from other, more common dream approaches in its premise that every dream is an opportunity to develop our relationship to the undercurrent identities beneath our surface personalities and routine agendas. Each dream provides a doorway into the unfolding story, desires, potentialities, and invitations of the soul, and a chance for the ego to be further educated and initiated into that underworld story and those underworld desires and possibilities. The purpose of soulcentric dreamwork is not to heal, improve, flatter, or entertain the personality but rather to destabilize it and create an opening to the mysteries of nature and psyche. With such an approach, we do not work on our dreams but help our dreams to do their work on us.

- Deep imagery or active imagination: inner journeys in which we interact, while awake, with the other-than-ego inhabitants of our own psyches or Earth's psyche. There are many approaches, but among the most effective are those that involve imaginal animals as inner guides to personal wholing and initiation.[48]

- Self-designed ceremony: a means of conversing with soul and nature in the Mystery's own language of embodied symbol and image.

- Discovery, fashioning, and use of symbols and objects: for attracting or embodying soul images or universal, transpersonal qualities.

- Skillful use of hallucinogenic or entheogenic substances as a component of ceremonies and soul-discovery processes: for the purpose of guided, ritual explorations of the underworld of soul.[49]

- Symbolic artwork: for the purpose of both discovering and expressing soul qualities.

- Journal work: creative writing as a way to connect with our own depths and to cultivate a relationship with the Mystery.

- Vision questing: fasting for three days or more in wilderness solitude and crying for a vision that reveals how we might serve our people and the world.

- Apprehending and responding to signs and omens in nature.
- Body practices for altering consciousness: to perceive actualities and imagine possibilities that we might otherwise overlook, and in doing so helping us weave the subtle and unseen forces of the world into form, making the unconscious conscious. Examples:

  - Fasting
  - Breath work: consciousness-altering breathing techniques
  - Practices involving extreme physical exertion
  - Yoga postures and movement

- Council work: a way of empowering people to speak from their hearts, an ancient practice transforming the experience of contemporary group process. Council work enables us to open to the radical otherness of our fellow humans, in that way knitting together true community, and supports us in accessing and expressing our most vital truths.
- Trance drumming and rhythms: for entering trance states, opening the door to the otherworld, and unearthing the mysteries or numina beneath our surface lives.
- Ecstatic trance dance: surrendering to the images and entities, inside and out, that want to move us and be danced by us.
- Ceremonial sweats and saunas: for altering consciousness, communing with the Others, and evoking visions and revelations.
- Enactment of traditional or contemporary ceremonies, rituals, and nature festivals: examples are equinox and solstice ceremonies, and observations of sunrise, sunset, and new and full Moons. Purposes include aligning ourselves with the cycles of nature, altering consciousness, facilitating communion with the Others, and helping us experience ourselves and the world from an ecocentric perspective, which is always resonant with that of the soul.
- Talking across the species boundaries: dialogues with other-than-human beings for the purpose of becoming more fully human.
- Animal tracking and other methods of sensitive and skillful nature observation: to learn about and from the Others, to enhance our own wildness and ecocentricity, and to explore the mysteries of both nature and psyche.
- Telling, retelling, and study of myths and other sacred stories: awakening consciousness to the archetypal and numinous.
- Composing a personal myth: understanding the events of our own lives from a larger, deeper, symbolic perspective.
- Storytelling: recounting our personal journeys, including the stories of our woundings, told within a compassionate, ceremonial container that embraces the transpersonal dimension of all narratives.
- Sensitive listening and clear reflection ("mirroring") of other people's stories.

- Sacred speech: conversation that deepens our presence with other people, self, and place.
- Ritual silence during initiatory group processes.
- Sacred sexuality: a doorway to the mysteries of nature and psyche.
- Soulful music, poetry, and chanting: altering and aligning consciousness with the Mystery.

This is just a partial list, exemplifying the many possibilities. From the beginnings of the human story, we have generated countless methods to cross the borders from mundane consciousness to a sacred and intimate communion with the world.

Several themes are common to this diverse collection of soulcraft practices. Many, for example, entail the deliberate alteration of consciousness. In order to encounter the soul, the uninitiated ego must be shorn, at least temporarily, of its familiar beliefs about self and world. The defended confines of ordinary consciousness must be temporarily breached or radically shifted. The conscious self must be able to look at its own psyche from a different perspective, from a unique angle, from a position of altered awareness — similar to a person viewing Earth from outer space or someone returning home after a month in an exotic culture. Most soul-encounter practices induce liminal states of temporary ego dissolution that release us from the usual rules and norms of our personality and culture, opening the way to fresh observations and creative adventures.[50]

Upon entering the Cocoon, the Wanderer has a natural and implacable thirst for consciousness-altering knowledge and skills. If there are no initiation guides to teach such methods, she will attempt to find her own way. Most un-eldered teenage Wanderers in Western society, for example, end up using mind-altering chemicals — including alcohol — which, outside a ceremonial context and without spiritual guidance, are unlikely to lead to successful encounters with soul, and which might be physically, psychologically, and spiritually harmful. Indeed, many of the soulcraft methods listed here can be dangerous. Mature guidance and adequate preparation are crucial.

In addition to nonordinary states, soulcraft practices have other common themes. Many of these techniques, for instance, are rooted in metaphor and symbol, such as dreamwork, deep imagery, ceremony, responding to signs and omens, poetry, and art. No surprise: symbol is the currency of imagination, and imagination is the primary window to soul.

Many soulcraft practices evoke powerful emotion. When we cross beyond our ordinary relationship to the world, we provoke experiences from which we had formerly been "protected." Some terrify us. Others give rise to joys and ecstasies. Sometimes we're flooded with sadness, for losses suffered and unclaimed dreams now irretrievable. Other times we stumble into unhealed wounds and the hurt, anger, guilt, shame, and grief waiting there. In every case, emotions encountered on the descent provide the opportunity for a more vibrant alignment with the world and with our souls.

Another common theme is conversation with the Sacred Other, the exotic presence appearing as a frog or a raven, the wind or silence, a saguaro cactus or a blade of grass, our lover's face in the midst of lovemaking, the voice of God, a dying child, or a poem or painting. The conversation may or may not be verbal, but its medium is always the intimate interaction between the conscious human self and another being distant from our surface lives. Ardently encountering that Other changes us as might a profound conversation with a person from a wholly different culture. The Sacred Other is found in many terrains, in dreams, deep imagery, ceremony, states facilitated by psychotropic plants, trance dancing, the wilds of nature, sexual ecstasies, and the great mythologies of the world.

Entering the conversation with the Other ushers us to the edge of our world, where we might gain an astonishing and invaluable perspective. The conversation invites us to think and imagine outside the box, to enter the unknown, to cross borders, to descend into dark mysteries.

Another common thread is that soulcraft practices stimulate a profound bonding, not just between people, but also between humans and the other beings of nature. Bonding across the species boundaries helps us overcome the conflicts and disparities between nature and culture and within human culture. By amplifying our identification with all life-forms, with ecosystems, and with the planet itself, we cultivate what the deep ecologist Arne Naess calls the "ecological self," or what James Hillman terms "a psyche the size of the Earth," or what I refer to, in the next chapter, as the "ecocentric self."[51] This is the broader and deeper human self that is a natural member in the more-than-human community.

Wandering in nature is yet another common theme of soul-encounter practices, nature being a mirror of soul (and vice versa). And finally, story, rhythm, music, and the arts in general are regular features. Some say all arts originally arose as methods for approaching or celebrating the sacred.

Cultivating a Soulful Relationship to Life

This is the second of the two subtasks in exploring the mysteries of nature and psyche. A soulful relationship to life is cultivated through a set of practices and disciplines with a scope larger than merely the acquisition of specific skills or techniques, as was the focus with the soul-encounter practices discussed earlier. The goal with this second subtask is a radical, soul-centered shift in the Wanderer's orientation to life.

A similar distinction between technique and lifestyle is found, for example, in Buddhism, where the practitioner not only learns specific skills such as meditation but also cultivates an approach to everyday living, the noble eightfold path, which includes the practices of right speech, right action, right livelihood, and right thinking.

The Wanderer must adopt methods for reclaiming and embodying her soul every day. The more she and others in her community learn to live soulfully, the more her community itself shifts from egocentric to soulcentric. These lifestyle practices assist the Wanderer not only in discovering her soul gifts but also in changing the world. This is one way the Wanderer, before Soul Initiation, participates in the Great Turning.

These lifestyle practices have a common theme: giving one's life over to something *other*, the desires of nature and the soul, something distinct from the familiar Western, egocentric goal of "getting ahead."

What practices cultivate a soulful existence? What follows are thirteen examples applicable to women and men from any culture or tradition.[52]

The Art of Solitude

Solitude does not come naturally to many people in egocentric society. Even when not socializing, most Westerners avoid true solitude through a myriad distractions — TV, the Internet, computer games, newspapers, crossword puzzles, solo sports, busywork. Solitude might threaten us with boredom or an anxiety that could lead to difficult truths, unfinished emotional business, and the shadow side of our human nature. Although true solitude — alert aloneness without diversions — can be challenging, it is often the necessary gateway to our deepest passions.

The Wanderer learns to look discerningly into the face of her aloneness and discover what truly brings her alive and what doesn't. Practicing the art of solitude, she spends hours alone, awake, unoccupied with everyday routines, letting what comes, come. She works her way up to several days alone. She practices true aloneness, not with her dog, her music, or a book, and mostly not in her house — just her, unprotected from the immensity of her psyche and the miraculous, animate world.

Through the practice of solitude, you too can discover how you are alienated from yourself and the world. You will come to grips with one of the most profound and implacable facts of the human condition: that in an essential way we all are, in fact, alone. We were born alone and will die alone. In solitude you will learn how to live as a mortal human. You will learn to comfort yourself. You will learn how to move your attention from one event or experience to another, neither avoiding nor indulging in the painful ones.

As a Wanderer, you must develop a communion with your aloneness, one that is as profound and sacred as any other relationship in your life. You will come to belong to your aloneness as much as to any place, job, or community.

Solitudo is Latin for nature. In true solitude, you remember yourself as a part of everything, as a native of the natural world. You rediscover ease, inspiration, belonging, and wisdom in your own company.

Discovering Nature as a Mirror of the Soul

Our relationship to the natural world evolves as we progress through the stages of soulcentric development. In a healthy childhood, nature holds great fascination and

wonder; it is the wide arena in which we discover and explore the world of our inheritance. By imitating the animals, birds, and trees, we acquire a rich vocabulary of
gestures that we assemble into our own way of being human.

In early adolescence, the natural world becomes a mirror of our developing adolescent personality, a screen on which we project our fears and hopes for belonging.
Sometimes we know we're projecting, and sometimes we don't. We experience some
of our emotions as if they were qualities of nature rather than our own. But gradually
we become conscious of our projected emotions and learn to directly embody and assimilate our feelings. The terrifying forest reveals our fear of our own shadow side or
of our inscrutable future — or both. The dreary day of rain opens the door to our own
unclaimed sadness. The majestic mountain rings out our hope and aspirations.

Then, in the Cocoon, an astonishing change happens. We begin to detect not just
our emotions but also the hidden and mysterious qualities of our own psyches reflected
back to us by nature. Unearthing our souls is an endeavor distinctly different from projecting our emotions and personalities onto nature.

On her vision fast in the summer mountains of southern Utah, one young
woman's attention was regularly drawn to the aspens on the edge of her camp. Rhiane
was particularly beguiled by the markings on the bark that looked to her like eyes looking back at her. Through imaginative conversation with these aspen eyes, she felt, on
the first day, as if the aspens saw her — *really* saw her. In particular, she felt seen as a
spiritual being grounded in the truth of her heart. On the second day, she recognized
that she herself had the capacity to see others in the same way that she felt the aspens
saw her — as heart-centered spiritual beings. By the third day, Rhiane accepted that
this way of seeing others was central to her destiny, something that had never occurred
to her before.

One might wonder whether the aspens literally told Rhiane these things or
whether it was a projection of her ego. I see it a third way. I believe that our souls —
not our egos and not the beings of nature — are the most active element in these
encounters. The soul wants us to know it. When our minds are sufficiently clear and
receptive — as on a vision fast — our attention is naturally drawn to aspects of nature that most resonate with our souls. The aspens, then, were, for Rhiane, more likely
passive mirrors than active ones. In other words, the aspens were not choosing to tell
Rhiane about her. Rather, Rhiane was noticing a quality of the aspens that resonated
with her own soul qualities or potentials. Our souls want us to wake up and see ourselves more clearly, like a mentor pointing out essential things for his student to discern and revere.

It's important, then, to distinguish ego projection from soul reflection. The latter surprises us, even stuns us; it's not what we were expecting or hoping for. It's not
an answer we would have given ourselves. A soul reflection, unlike a projection, seems
too big for us and too difficult to embody. It feels as much like a burden as a blessing.

In the Cocoon, then, we begin to encounter nature's reflections of our own depths. Our souls, after all, are elements of Earth's soul. Like poets, we begin to detect in the patterns of the wild our own capacities for courage, love, sacrifice, desire, faith, belonging — all the possibilities of our own humanness in their primary and most vital forms. Eventually, we might detect, for the first time, our individual soul story or our ultimate place in the world. We come to understand that sometimes what we observe in nature reflects aspects of our own unique essence. Nature announces who we might become. And so we begin to enter nature as a pilgrim in search of his true home, a wanderer with an intimation of communion, a solitary with a suspicion of salvation.

Human ecologist Paul Shepard portrays how a healthy adolescent begins to experience nature. On the Wheel, this transition corresponds to the commencement of the Cocoon:

> Thenceforth natural things are not only themselves but a speaking. He will not put his delight in the sky and the earth behind him as a childish and irrelevant thing. The quests and tests that mark his passage in adolescent initiation are not intended to reveal to him that his love of the natural world was an illusion or that, having seemed only what it was, it in some way failed him. He will not graduate from that world but into its significance. So, with the end of childhood, he begins a lifelong study, a reciprocity with the natural world in which its depths are as endless as his own creative thought. He will not study it in order to transform its liveliness into mere objects that represent his ego, but as a poem, numinous and analogical, of human society.[53]

Archetypal forms and patterns exist not only in the human psyche but also in the natural world. Wind, water, fire, mountain, rainbow, bird, butterfly, fish, snake, bear: Earth archetypes. In shamanic traditions, the apprentice learns his craft by using the powers of his imagination to become the various animals and nature elements. In so doing, he "re-members" himself in the course of remembering he has always been nature. In *The Once and Future King*, T. H. White's retelling of the King Arthur legend, Merlin educates young Arthur by changing him, for short periods, into various creatures — a falcon, ant, badger, and wild goose. Gautama Buddha is said to have had many previous lives as a number of different animals. Moving from one archetypal nature identity to another: this is the genius of the shape-shifter within each of us. By imaginatively merging with the many forms and forces of Earth, we regain a conscious relationship with our souls.

Wandering in Nature

The Wanderer seeks the hidden, the mysterious, the wild. He knows that the changes in consciousness and identity that he goes through while searching are as important as finding what he seeks. He is not in a hurry. Wandering is as valuable as anything else he might do.

Where will he wander? "Through hollow lands and hilly lands," says W. B. Yeats in "The Song of Wandering Aengus."[54] Like Aengus — the Irish god of love, beauty, and poetry — the Wanderer might find himself in an enchanted hazel wood, by a stream, beneath the stars and Moon and Sun, among white moths and long, dappled grass or within sight and scent of apple blossoms. But in addition to wildlands, he will roam through diverse states of consciousness and have serendipitous communions with remarkable people. He will adopt meandering as his way of life.

The Wanderer explores the interweaving of psyche and nature, how a dream or a myth, for example, suggests a landscape or waterscape through which to wander, or a *way* to wander, or an image to seek in his ramblings. Or he might stroll into the wild and run smack into a repeating dreamscape from childhood. *Now* what will he do? Inner and outer wanderings support, extend, and enrich one another.

The Wanderer might start out on a forest or desert trail, but it won't be long before he meanders off the beaten track. Because he is stalking a surprise, he attends to hunches, feelings, and images as much as he does to the landscape. He heeds the edges of sight and hearing. Sometimes he'll be called to crawl into a low cave, to dance on top of a knoll, to swim to the center of a lake, to roll in the tall spring grasses, or to fall asleep by a bubbling spring. Sometimes he will trade music with a songbird. Often he will sit with beings he meets — a flower, lizard, rock, pika, wind, or the Moon — and begin a conversation.

Sometimes he will wander into the wilds with the expectation of finding one thing, one thing in particular, material or not, that calls him most strongly. Other times he will go out without an intention to find anything at all.

He will wander often, and often for an entire day, sometimes for several days with his home upon his back. His initial agenda will fall away as he picks up new tracks, scents, and possibilities. He will smile softly to himself over the months and years of his wanderings as he notices how he has changed, how he has slowed down inside.

Through his journeys, he cultivates wonder and surprise, rekindling the innocence that got buried in his adolescent rush to become somebody in particular. Now he seeks to become nobody for a while, to disappear into the woods or the canyon so that the person he really is might find *him*.

Wandering in nature is perhaps the most essential soulcraft practice for contemporary Westerners who have wandered so far *from* nature. Earth speaks to us with a manner and might unlike anything in town. What nature has to say is the necessary complement to what we hear all day long from news, ads, and social chatter. To save our souls, we need *nature's* news.

Wild wandering can serve as the hub from which all other soulcraft practices radiate — for example, the art of solitude, of self-reliance, of befriending the dark, or of shadow work. And obviously, natural landscapes are the best places to practice track-ing, ecological observation, attending to signs and omens, and talking across the species boundaries. Our wanderings might provide the seeds for dreams, deep imagery work, self-designed ceremony, storytelling, sacred-wound work, symbolic artwork, council processes, or soul poetry — any one of which will eventually lead us back into the hollow lands and hilly lands.

Living the Questions of Soul

In 1903, Rainer Maria Rilke famously advised a young poet to live the questions of soul. Rilke counseled his friend that no one else could answer for him his most ur-gent questions, and that he would have to wait before he could answer them for him-self. Rilke also recommended that his young friend spend time in nature, offering his careful and loving attention to "the simple in Nature, to the little things that hardly any-one sees, and that can so unexpectedly become big and beyond measuring."[55] Rilke's primary advice to those seeking their true work in the world was "to go into yourself and test the deeps in which your life takes rise."[56] The essence of this time of life, he wrote, is in the questions:

> I want to beg you, as much as I can, dear sir, to be patient toward all that is unsolved in your heart and try to love the *questions themselves* like locked rooms and like books that are written in a very foreign tongue. Do not now seek the answers, which cannot be given you because you would not be able to live them. And the point is, to live everything. Live the questions now. Per-haps you will then gradually, without noticing it, live along some distant day into the answer.[57]

Confronting One's Own Death

A courageous encounter with the unalterable fact of mortality supplements and extends the activities of the death lodge. In the death lodge, you made peace with your past and prepared to leave behind an old way of belonging to the world; you prepared for a "small death." Now you have the opportunity to prepare for your inevitable and final death, look your mortality in the eye, and make peace with the cruel fact that, ul-timately, you will have to loosen your grip on all of life, not just a life stage.

You're not likely to uncover and embody your soul if you are living as if your ego and body are immortal. Put more positively, your Soul Initiation will be rich to the ex-tent that you can ground yourself in the sober but liberating awareness of limited time. This very moment could be your last.

The confrontation with death is an unrivaled perspective-enhancer. In the com-pany of death, most desires of early adolescence fall away. What are the deepest long-ings that remain? What are the surviving intentions with which you might enter a soul-filled adulthood? The confrontation with death will empty you of everything but that kernel of love in your heart and your sincerest questions. Empty and open, you approach the central mysteries of your life.

You might practice vividly imagining your own aged, diseased, or mortally wounded body. You might look carefully at photographs of decaying corpses, of people dying of wasting diseases or starvation, of autopsied cadavers. Remind yourself regularly that you, too, like all flesh, will one day leave behind your body and all else, and that it will happen on a day very much like this one, maybe in a place, if you are fortunate, like the one you're in this very moment. Visualize your own earth burial, sky burial, fire burial, or water burial, or perhaps all four.

Perhaps you will volunteer at a hospice and spend hours gazing into the eyes of those who lie at death's door, your heart stretching ever wider, both your eyes and your companion's peering over the edge of life's cliff. In the hospice, you will witness the dying process, life ebbing away, and the moment of death itself. You will see people die well and not so well. You will see how families accept death or refuse to deal with it. You will see some people embrace their deaths and celebrate their lives, and others die bitter and angry, never having acknowledged they were dying.

Discuss death with your companions. While alone, wonder about death, wander with it, wrestle with it. Feel its presence, both emotionally and physically. Ask yourself and others questions about death and share your feelings and speculations.

As the Yaqui sorcerer don Juan instructed Carlos Castaneda, ask death to be your ally, to remind you, especially at times of difficult choices, what is important in the face of your mortality. Imagine death as ever present, as accompanying you everywhere but remaining just out of sight behind your left shoulder.

In these ways, make peace with your mortality. One day you might find you are less attached to the particular form you have made of your life. Then you'll be better prepared to converse with soul and its outrageous requests for radical change.

With any soulcraft practice, the Wanderer seeks to put his ego in a double bind, a checkmate that makes it impossible to continue the old story of adolescence or the first adulthood. Confronting the inevitability and ever presence of his death loosens his grip on his routines, dislodges his old way of obtaining his bearings, and ushers him to the threshold of the unknown. Horrified, he discovers he must give up everything in order to get what he *really* wants — the one life he can call his own — with no guarantee of success or even of survival.

The Art of Shadow Work

The candidate for initiation knows that the portal to the underworld is guarded by demons, and that monsters even more fierce lie beyond the threshold. She has come to understand, at least intellectually, that many of these demons and monsters reflect unconscious elements of her own psyche. The ego has rejected them and labeled them "not me" and as "evil" or "bad." Carl Jung refers to these unknown or unrecognized aspects of self as components of the archetype he calls "the shadow." Beginning in the Cocoon, the Wanderer has the opportunity to search out and reclaim these distressing shades. Hidden within them are essential components of her wholeness, and wholeness is what she's after.

Most elements of the shadow — wildness, say, or carnality or selfishness — were disowned and repressed during childhood and early adolescence as an attempt, successful or not, to win acceptance from family and peers. Our Loyal Soldiers were in charge of this downsizing operation. Far from being a mistake, this was necessary in order to form a socially adaptive personality, a first identity. Now, uncovering a soul-rooted identity requires a descent into those dark realms to retrieve the lost pieces. Therein lie key elements of our destiny.

Although the shadow cast by the ego contains perverse and socially unacceptable qualities, it also contains traits we would see as too *positive* to be ours — selfless generosity, perhaps, or eloquence, or creative urges like spontaneous public singing. The shadow is always the converse of the ego, and the ego includes some destructive, self-deprecating, and antisocial attitudes. We might have been abandoned or punished as children, for example, if we had embodied positive qualities our parents considered inappropriate to their social standing or that made them uncomfortable or envious. The shadow contains all aspects of the psyche inconsistent with the ego, whether judged good or bad.

Before being reclaimed, the negative elements of the shadow appear to the ego as disagreeable and frightening. They show up as scary or unpleasant dreamworld characters and as dayworld people onto whom we project our own negative traits, such as greed, cowardice, rage, weakness, arrogance, or cruelty. We project our negative shadow onto nature, too: hairy beasts, dark forests, swamps, tornadoes, bats, snakes, and volcanoes.

The positive elements of our shadow — qualities we consider highly virtuous, elevated, or otherwise exemplary — are also projected onto others. These are the exemplary traits we see in others but can hardly imagine for ourselves.

Negative-shadow work goes deeper in the Cocoon than in the Oasis. In the Oasis, the goal of shadow work, when attempted at all, is to uncover our unacknowledged negative traits, take responsibility for them, learn to soften or eliminate them, and cease to project them so that we no longer unconsciously undermine our relationships and opportunities. The objective is a neutralized or "fed" shadow and a healthier and better-functioning personality.

In the Cocoon, however, an additional goal in shadow work is to get to know our shadow elements intimately — so thoroughly that we uncover at their hearts some of the psychospiritual resources we need for the embodiment of our souls. For example, say you harbor a negative stereotype of people of a particular race, nationality, religion, or personality type. The odds are that, in your Cocoon-stage shadow work, you will discover that people of that description often possess a certain positive quality — say, sensuality, assertiveness, or joy — that is considerably underdeveloped in you, and without which you cannot mature beyond your current plateau. But maturing in this way is exactly what your Loyal Soldier fears, because your doing so will expose you to social risks and potential psychological losses. This is one of the reasons why your Loyal Soldier had arranged for you to unconsciously judge those others as wholly negative.

Often we discover that our negative shadow holds something sacred: our deepest passion. This might be a longing to dance, to create magic, to sing, or to love with abandon. When we are young, we name our passion something else — so we can suppress it. We name it foolish, selfish, odd, crazy, or evil. This misnaming protects us from social injury, from being rejected or marginalized by our family or peers.

In both its negative and positive aspects, the shadow contains values and perspectives needed to round out our conscious personalities. It contains personal powers we'll need when we befriend or wrestle with the inner and outer dragons and angels met on our underworld journey.

The second phase of your shadow work in the Cocoon is to determinedly cultivate the positive resources uncovered in both your negative and positive shadow projections. As you do so, your adolescent way of belonging will *not* be reinforced: it will instead be further undermined. Each element of the shadow incorporates strengths, unique perspectives, and sensitivities that we could not have imagined at the start of our shadow work. Without these qualities, our personalities remain unbalanced, fragmented, or otherwise incomplete.

Because this advanced form of shadow work profoundly challenges the adolescent personality, undertaking it is either impossible or unwise before the Cocoon stage.

As a Wanderer, however, you'll find it necessary to adopt the regular practice of identifying and engaging the shadow. Take careful note, for example, when you find yourself with a strong charge — positive or negative — around another person, especially someone you don't know well. Which of their qualities do you like or dislike? Look for these same qualities in yourself, perhaps expressed in subtle or unexpected ways, or only occasionally but with a vengeance or a flare. Wonder about the other qualities of that person, too, the ones you didn't notice at first. Then imagine how you might be changed if you embraced that person as an ally or assimilated their qualities. Whether the other is from your everyday life or the nightworld of dreams, engage in imaginary dialogues with this shadow figure. Or imagine yourself merging with the shadow, and then allow it to express itself through drawing, painting, writing, movement, music, or dance.

The Art of Romance

During the previous stage of the Oasis, the Thespian acquired the basic skills of sexual relating and social bonding. This was foundational and necessary. Now, within the Cocoon, romance is approached as an art — for romance is a royal road to soul as much as it is a path to genuine, conscious loving.

The Wanderer learns that when she falls in love, she will project not only the most noble qualities of her own soul but also, before long, her most negative shadow qualities. She knows eventually she'll see her own shadow in her lover's face, and, when she does, it will be disheartening, frightening, possibly repulsive. Knowing this, she'll say yes to love anyway. Unveiling the shadow is as valuable a gift of romance as any other — and as dangerous.

The Wanderer knows her love affair has the potential to reveal mysteries both joyous and painful. Intense feelings and nonordinary states of consciousness will challenge and possibly erode her understanding of what life is, and who she is. She hopes for this as much as she fears it. If, in the rapture of love, she should feel like her true self for the first time in her life, she will know that her partner is only a catalyst. If she does not learn how to praise the Mystery when it shows up as love, the experience will fade and she will blame her lover for the loss as much as she had once given him or her the credit.

The candidate for Soul Initiation discovers that soulful romance keeps her in direct communication with the unknown, uncovers her sacred wound, reveals her shadow, and opens the door to ecstasy and union with the beloved of the soul. She discovers that sexual love is a spiritual experience as well as a carnal one. She learns to look into her lover's eyes and see not just her friend and sexual partner but also a reflection of her own animus or anima (that is, the inner man or woman who serves as her guide to soul) and also, perhaps, a reflection of the divine lover.

She will also learn how romance and a surrender to her innate sexual nature usher her into a more robust membership in the natural world. Our sexuality, after all, is one current in the great streaming of nature. In a soulcentric approach to romance, we revere sex as a celebration of the nature both within us and without.

Mindfulness Practice

Mindfulness and developing a personal relationship with spirit (the practice discussed next) are central features of the upperworld half of spirituality. Yet these two practices are also essential to the Wanderer and to soul discovery, in that our individual relationships to consciousness and spirit are core elements of our souls.

Mindfulness is calm presence with what is, whether joy or pain, ease or difficulty, boredom or ecstasy, life or death. It is both a specific skill and an all-embracing approach to life, and it is most commonly developed through a discipline of meditation, prayer, or contemplation.

The Wanderer knows the underworld will afford physical, emotional, and spiritual challenges. She will encounter personal demons. There will be beauty so stunning it hurts. In the midst of ecstatic ordeals, she might weaken and find it difficult to stay awake or present. The mind will try to slip away. A vital presence during such intensity might be difficult to sustain, though this is when it's most valuable. Mindfulness practice gradually cultivates courage, wholeheartedness, and the capacity to remain present with all experiences.

For the Wanderer to succeed in her quest to uncover her soul, she will need to return, continuously, to where soul waits for her — in this very moment, in the image emerging from her depths, in the emotion moving through her like liquid heat, in the truth she is making with her own body, in the glistening drop of water caught in the spider's web spun between the blue-green needles of *this* spruce in *this* snowy meadow.

Mindfulness practice supports the Wanderer in developing the mental control she needs to stay faithful to her most ardent intention — to retrieve and embody her soul's desires.

In quieting the mind, she also learns to temporarily withdraw support from the everyday agendas of the personality, all the hopes, worries, desires, fears, dreams, and plans, even the personality's desire to act as an agent for soul. Eventually, she experiences what remains of consciousness after the mind comes to rest. She recognizes the Observer or the Witness, that empty, crystalline point of awareness that awaits after the everyday self has fallen away in the fire of the now. She experiences her personal filament of sentience unified with the consciousness that pervades and constitutes all of creation. As she opens to the mysterious nature of psyche, she comes closer to knowing spirit and so, too, her soul.

Developing a Personal Relationship with Spirit

The Transcendent Other — God, Tao, Buddha, Allah, Goddess, Great Mystery — has been named and understood in as many ways as there are cultural, religious, and spiritual traditions. Each individual, too, interprets divinity from a unique perspective. In the Cocoon, we each discover our particular path to spirit, within or outside the framework of existing traditions. We each come to our own way of praying — or of rejecting prayer — and to our own conversation with All That Is.

The Wanderer, as she relinquishes attachment to her first identity, finds herself asking questions about spirit: If I am not simply my body or my ego, then what am I? If I am a spark of consciousness in the universe, what is the larger consciousness of which I am a part? How am I to be in relationship with this greater consciousness?

The Wanderer's goal is to begin a personal conversation with spirit, something more than just listening. By what means will she speak back? What things are acceptable to express? Can spirit make mistakes? Is it okay to argue with spirit? Is spirit wrathful? All loving? Both? Is spirit male? Female? Both? Neither? Does spirit prefer we refer to it in capitalized words — Spirit, Him, Her, It, God? Or is "goddess" okay with Him? Does spirit have a sense of humor? Does spirit personally need or want something from *us*? Does spirit itself grow, evolve, or transform? In developing a personal relationship with spirit, perhaps these questions are best answered through conversation with spirit as opposed to asking others for their opinion.

We must be willing to engage in the conversation. How will we do it? With what ceremonies, metaphors, symbols, religious objects, or texts? Through prayer or song? Which language? Alone or in community? In relation to Earth as well as heaven, or only one or the other — or neither? How will the body be involved, if at all? The emotions? Will we dance our prayers? Are we willing to question religious or spiritual authority as to how it is "supposed" to be done? Are we willing to trust our own experience? Are we eligible for a direct relationship with spirit without the intercessory services of priests or priestesses?

However understood and embodied, a personal relationship with spirit cultivates humility, a sense of meaning and love in the hidden heart of the universe, a bone-deep knowing that one is an integral member of an evolving cosmos. We are inspired to create a life founded on a sense of interconnectedness and interdependence with all.

Service Work

While in the Cocoon, the Wanderer longs for two things: deep fulfillment (the experience of truly belonging to the world) and the ability to provide a genuine, soul-infused service to his more-than-human community. Perhaps he understands that these two things — fulfillment and service — cannot be obtained separately. True fulfillment arises out of service. He knows, however, that he won't be fully eligible for either on a deeply felt or sustained basis until after Soul Initiation. He must first discover the essence of his soul's desires, make a commitment to those desires, and then acquire the skills to embody them in the world.

But the Wanderer recognizes that his preparation for Soul Initiation requires that he cultivate the attitude, spirit, and temperament of service — the mind-set that will make his life a gift, a giveaway. Performing service will help draw soul to him — and him to soul. Doing so is what contemporary society generally calls volunteering, the performance of good works for the opportunity to be of service.

In the Cocoon and earlier, what counts as service is usually identified by others, not by the soul. (After Soul Initiation, the nature of your service *is* primarily identified by your soul.) The Wanderer might consult initiated adults and elders for suggestions. In the twenty-first century, contributing to the Great Turning is naturally the objective of most service work, but this hardly limits the possibilities, which include projects in the realms of social justice, peace, reviving local economies, nature conservation, political reform, creation of true democracies, global market and economic reform, housing, homelessness, hunger, health care, and many other areas.

In addition, as the Wanderer goes about his everyday life, he will encounter opportunities to be of assistance, to engage in "random acts of kindness." True service,
as opposed to fixing or rescuing, is performed with gratitude and surrender to outcome.

Service work during the Cocoon is a way of wandering more deeply into the world
as well as into our own hearts. By immersing ourselves in community assistance, we
draw closer to the mysteries of our true (soul) work.

Praising the World

Why, if it's possible to come into existence
as laurel, say, a little darker green
than other trees, with ripples edging each
leaf (like the smile of a breeze): why, then,
do we have to be human
and keep running from the fate
we long for?...

— RAINER MARIA RILKE, "THE NINTH ELEGY"

The natural world, the arts, the wild and sacred in each individual person, and
healthy human culture are all extraordinary beyond measure — if only we have the
eyes to see and the ears to listen. The Wanderer cultivates such eyes and ears, as well
as the mouth, nose, skin, sensibility, and heart that go with them. The Cocoon stage
is the time to fall hopelessly in love with the world.

Toward that end, the Wanderer takes up the practice of praising the particular
things and beings of the world that he encounters each and every day — the flower,
rabbit, Moon, light on the meadow, the storm, symphony, people's care of the commons, the theater, the infant's innocence, the child's wonder, the teenager's fire, the
adult's creative passion, and the elder's wisdom. Like Rilke, he praises mortality, too.
The Wanderer learns to praise with his whole being — using verse, song, gesture, dance,
tears, sketches, sculpture, ceremony, and performance. He does not keep his wonder
and praise to himself.

Rilke continues:

...Is it not the secret stratagem
of our unspeaking Earth
to have lovers express her abundance
as she drives them into each other's arms?...

By acclaiming the extraordinary features and the very existence of every landform
and life-form, the Wanderer falls ever deeper into a consciousness of blessing and miracle. If he persists, an astonishing surprise awaits him: one day, it will dawn on him that
he himself could not be an exception to the rule of resplendence. At this revelation, he

will grasp — beyond all explanation — that he, too, is a wild and miraculous thing. The universe then opens more fully for him, and he finds himself at home in the world to a depth he had never imagined possible. Now he runs into the fate he longs for.

> ... Earth, isn't this what you want? To arise in us, invisible?
> Is it not your dream, to enter us so wholly
> there's nothing left outside to see?
> What, if not transformation,
> is your deepest purpose? Earth, my love,
> I want that too. Believe me,
> no more of your springtimes are needed
> to win me over — even one flower
> is more than enough. Before I was named
> I belonged to you. I seek no other law
> but yours, and know I can trust
> the death you will bring.... [58]

Advanced Loyal Soldier Work: Walking into the Fire

In the Oasis, our Loyal-Soldier work focused on learning to recognize our childhood survival strategies — in the moment they were deployed, or even beforehand — and then welcoming home the Loyal Soldier. We learned how to let him know that the war of childhood survival was over, to thank him for his devoted service, and to relinquish his old strategies. We learned how to care for ourselves in more mature ways. This work, although commenced in the Oasis, continues throughout our lives.

But in the Cocoon, we become eligible for a more advanced form of Loyal Soldier work, another practice that wouldn't have been advised, even if it were possible, during the Oasis: *the Wanderer walks directly and proactively into the fire from which the Loyal Soldier had been keeping him safe in earlier stages.*

Our childhood survival strategies were designed to make us feel and act small in order to keep us psychosocially safe. Our foundational Loyal Soldier work (in the Oasis) renounced that sort of safety, but this did not, by itself, usher us into the initiatory cauldron. Now it's time to do just that — to determine which sorts of actions and settings most alarm our Loyal Soldier and to make a habit of choosing precisely those actions and settings.

For example, if a man had been punished in childhood for being too exuberant, bold, or imaginative, his Loyal Soldier might have used harsh self-criticism to save him from severe social consequences. He might have learned to keep a lid on his undomesticated creativity by telling himself that his ideas and intuitions were pedestrian, impractical, or crazy. During the Oasis he would have learned to embrace his Loyal Soldier and to help him relax those survival strategies. Now in the Cocoon, he has the opportunity to go out on a limb and launch his wildest artistic projects. In addition to the immediate rewards of unfettered creativity, those projects will also bring him face-to-face with precisely the symbols, impulses, places, and people that will most effectively intensify his journey of descent to soul. They will open the door to experiences that will undermine his old story and reveal the passions, images, and greater stories that wait in his depths.

His Loyal Soldier, of course, will react with ridicule, predictions of humiliation and ruin, and other old tricks. But by now the Wanderer expects this and will, as often as he can, respond with love and gratitude, as well as with his next step into that burning fire.

Conscious Development of the Four Dimensions of the Self

By *Self* I mean our personal wholeness, a totality that holds all the original capacities, potentials, and resources of our humanness. The Self can be further described by dividing it into four dimensions corresponding to the four cardinal directions of the human psyche.

I've already mentioned in these pages the North aspect of the Self, which I call the Nurturing Parent or the Generative Adult. This is the facet of Self capable of providing genuine, loving care to both oneself and others, competently offering empathy and service. Also, with the North Self, we contribute our best and most creative parenting, leading, teaching, directing, producing, and healing. Contemporary courses and programs for developing the North Self include those on leadership development, democracy, nonviolent communication, negotiation skills, parenting, conscious loving and intimacy, creative expression, sensitivity training, and social artistry.

The South dimension is the one I call the Wild Self. It is fully at home in the human body and in the natural world. The Wild Self has a sensual, erotic, and enchanted relationship with the world. It is the indigenous and instinctual self, every bit as wild, natural, and at home in nature as any animal, tree, or habitat. Opportunities for enhancement of the Wild Self include wilderness programs and experiential courses on natural history, massage training and other somatic practices (such as Rolfing and Feldenkrais), sensory awakening and Gestalt awareness, sacred sexuality (such as tantra), yoga, music, rhythm, and dance.

The West Self is variously known as the anima or animus, the Guide to Soul, or the Muse. This facet of the Self revels in the mysteries and qualities of the soul, the underworld, night, darkness, dreams, destiny, and death. In its West aspect, the Self wants to lead us down — and can — and wants us to be continuously dying to our old ways while giving birth to the never-before-seen. Support in developing the West Self can be found through studies of dreamwork, the artistic process, myth, ritual, poetry, deep imagery, mystery traditions, depth and archetypal psychology, creativity, and (of course) soulcraft.

The East dimension of Self is the Sage, Fool, Trickster, or Innocent, or more generally, the Guide to Spirit. This component of the psyche is most at home with the mysteries of the divine, with the upperworld, light, enlightenment, laughter, eternity, and the nondual. It wants to lead us up — and can — to the realm of pure consciousness beyond distinctions and striving. This dimension of the Self is awakened and ripened through study of meditation, prayer, yoga, Taoism, Buddhism, Kabbalah, Sufism, humor or comedy, and clowning.

The East dimension of Self is not itself spirit, nor is the West dimension soul. The East is the doorway to spirit, and the West the portal to soul. Self is our wholeness. Soul is our center, or core. Spirit is the immanent and transcendent unity that contains all.

Each society generates its own methods and traditions for cultivating the four dimensions of wholeness, but in egocentric society it is rare to find a single curriculum that covers more than one or two.

In the Cocoon, we require some degree of conscious access to all four dimensions of the Self in order to both enter the underworld of soul and fully benefit from our encounters there. We need our South wildness to fire the adventure, and our competent North nurturance to care for ourselves during these emotionally, physically, and spiritually challenging journeys. We need the East's capacity for presence and equanimity in order to fully open to and absorb the experience, and we need the West's love of and familiarity with darkness to guide us.

Through the first three stages of life, we might have gained conscious access to one or more of these four dimensions of the Self, but it would be rare indeed if we had developed a workable relationship with all four. Now, in the Cocoon, it's time to engage this task, which, like other developmental labors, will be ongoing for the rest of our lives. The tasks of the Cocoon — leaving home and exploring the mysteries of nature and psyche — are greatly facilitated by conscious access to all four facets of the Self.[59] At times this will be necessary.

These, then, are a baker's dozen of lifestyle practices for the Wanderer. In *Soulcraft*, I explore three additional practices: the art of being lost, befriending the dark, and withdrawing projections. Even in egocentric society, people of any age naturally gravitate toward these sixteen kinds of practices once the adolescent personality is sufficiently developed and prepared for the descent to soul.

SOULCRAFT VERSUS PSYCHOTHERAPY

In the Cocoon, the Wanderer's primary focus is soul encounter, not psychotherapy. In this section, I explore why psychotherapy by itself will not enable the Wanderer to encounter his soul or to become an initiated adult. Therapy, in fact, might distract him from his soul. For the Thespian, soulcraft practices might be dangerously countertherapeutic. For the Wanderer, soulcraft practices might be *appropriately* and *beneficially* countertherapeutic.

As mentioned earlier, by *soulcraft* I do not refer to any techniques invented by me, but rather to the vast set of practices, both ancient and modern, found in the mystery traditions of every culture for facilitating the experiential encounter with soul. To distinguish it from soulcraft, I use the word *psychotherapy* to mean interpersonal practices aimed at helping the conscious self (the ego) improve its adjustment to its social world and its emotional life. Its goal is ego growth — namely, to produce a person more in touch with himself emotionally and bodily, more centered and calm, less conflicted in his social relationships, more capable of empathy and intimacy, and adequately secure economically. These goals are significant and vital, especially in the Oasis and any later stages when we need to develop the personality's basic capacities or to address emotional meltdowns or relational culs-de-sac. In addition, ego growth is foundational to our spiritual development — in both the underworld and upperworld senses of *spiritual.*

But psychotherapy itself (in the way I'm defining it here) rarely helps us penetrate the veil of the often illusory life of the middleworld, nor does it develop our relationship with the transpersonal mysteries of soul and spirit.[60] Psychotherapy, when successful, helps us interpersonally and intrapersonally, but it does not directly help us to mature into the transcultural visionaries needed to support the Great Turning from egocentric to soulcentric culture. As James Hillman and Michael Ventura put it in the title of their 1992 book: *We've Had a Hundred Years of Psychotherapy and the World's Getting Worse.*

Hillman and Ventura do not mean to imply that psychotherapy has no value. Given egocentric society's multiple obstacles to successful ego-growth, psychotherapy is needed now more than ever. But the goals of a *soulcentric* psychotherapy are not job satisfaction or improved adjustment to a pathological society but refined social and emotional skills and enhanced personality-level authenticity — the goals of the Oasis — which provide the foundations for the soul-rooted development of the more mature life stages of the Cocoon and beyond.

Hillman and Ventura are making another point too: psychotherapy, no matter how effective it might be, has clearly not made the world a better place. While the popularity of psychotherapy increased exponentially during the course of the twentieth century, the world got dramatically worse. It's likely in fact that egocentric psychotherapy contributed to the degradation of the world by encouraging a focus on narrowly defined personal desires rather than the greater world's critically urgent needs. Sometimes and in some ways, psychotherapy has encouraged complacency, conformity, and narcissism.

Hillman and Ventura suggest — and I agree with them — that sometimes the most effective therapy is active involvement in making the world a better place through the kinds of activities I call "service work." Not only does service work — social, political, or environmental activism — contribute to a better world, it also engenders better, healthier people. First, it provides a respite from the self-obsession encouraged by many schools of therapy. Second, it builds self-esteem through the experience of being useful, helpful, and a part of a meaningful effort larger than one's own life. Third, if it is true that our emotional troubles are, at least in part, and maybe substantially, sourced in our recognition that our world is threatened, then service work reshapes us as part of the solution. When we engage in activities that address a significant problem, we feel better and less helpless, and usually right away.

Beyond service work, soul-encounter practices (whether called "soulcraft" or any other name) help make the world a better place in a yet more foundational way. These practices, when successful, engender true visionaries whose efforts are our primary resource for creating a soulcentric society. Genuine social transformation is not facilitated by well-adjusted conformists but rather by actively engaged visionaries who are both sad and angry about the state of our world, and who are also deeply hopeful as they create and implement new cultural forms — new ecocentric ways of conducting trade, health care, education, architecture, agriculture, politics and government, psychotherapy, and soulcraft.

Unlike that of psychotherapy, soulcraft's aim is neither for nor against saving our marriages, cultivating our social skills or friendships, enhancing performance or enjoyment in our current careers, ending our depressions, helping us understand or express our feelings, gaining insight into our personalities or personal histories, or even making us what we would ordinarily call "happier." Any one of these outcomes might result from soulcraft, but they are not its goal.

  The goal of soulcraft — in all its diverse cultural forms — is to help people, in the Cocoon or later stages, cultivate the relationship between the ego and the soul. This is underworld business, business that might, at first, make our surface lives more difficult or lonely, or less comfortable, secure, or happy. Soulcraft practices prepare the ego to *abandon* its social stability and psychological composure and to become an active, adult agent for soul, as opposed to maintaining its former role as an adolescent agent for itself.

Soulcraft can be countertherapeutic, because it often involves — even requires — dissolution of normal ego states, which can traumatize stage-3 people who have fragile or poorly developed egos, further delaying, impeding, or reversing basic ego development and social adjustment. A good foundation of ego growth in the first three stages — sometimes with the help of psychotherapy — is required if a later soul initiation process is going to fulfill its ultimate promise of soulful service to community (and, with it, cultural evolution). A well-balanced ego is the necessary carrier of the soul's gifts.

Soulcraft at the wrong time can undermine the ego's viability. Shadow work, for example, which helps us recover rejected parts of our selves, may not be the best idea for people in the early stages of recovery from substance addictions, sexual abuse, or other emotional traumas. A vision fast would not be advisable for a clinically depressed person. The soulcraft use of entheogens, even if they were legal, would not be wisely recommended for children, most teenagers, or chronologically older people with poor ego boundaries.

At the same time, psychotherapy can interfere with soulcraft. To move closer to soul, a Wanderer might need to leave a relationship, job, home, or role. Some therapists might discourage such changes, fearing an abdication of "adult responsibilities," a lost opportunity for deepened intimacy, or economic self-destruction. Or a therapy client ready for a soul-uncovering exploration of her sacred wound might be counseled that such a journey is unnecessary. Some soulcraft practices — wandering alone in wilderness, practicing the art of being lost, or a solo vision fast — might be deemed nontherapeutic, too dangerous, or even suicidal. Or an egocentric therapist might discourage efforts to make soul-rooted cultural changes, thinking his client is merely projecting personal problems onto the greater world.

Although sometimes therapists would be wise to counsel against soulcraft work, at other times, if the individual *is* ready for the descent, or if a sacrifice, psychological dying, or social-cultural risk *is* necessary to encounter or embody the soul, then such counsel would impede the soul journey. Without an appreciation of the soul's radical desires, psychotherapy can interfere with psychological and spiritual maturation and promote a nonimaginative normality.

Malidoma Somé gives us an extreme example of how the goals of therapy and what I call soulcraft can diverge.[61] His people, the Dagara, realize that, when their thirteen-year-old boys undergo their initiation ordeals, a few boys will never return; they will literally not survive. Why would the Dagara be willing to make such a sacrifice? For the boys who die, this is certainly not a therapeutic experience. Although the Dagara love their children no less than we do, they understand, as the elders of many cultures emphasize, that without vision — without soul embodied in the lives of their men and women — the people will perish. And, to the boys, the small risk of death is preferable to the living death of an uninitiated life. When we compare Dagara society with our own, we find that an even greater percentage of our teenagers die — through suicide, substance abuse, auto accidents, gang warfare, and military service — in their unsuccessful attempts to initiate themselves. For the Dagara, a few boys perish while the rest attain true adulthood. For us, a larger portion of teens perish and very few ever attain true adulthood. Which approach is more barbaric?

CIRCLE OF IDENTITY AND SENSE OF COMMUNITY:
FROM ETHNOCENTRIC TO WORLDCENTRIC

By the end of the Oasis, the Thespian's circle of identity was fully ethnocentric — the individual experienced himself, first and foremost, as a member of his nation or his ethnic or cultural group. He became, as it were, fully enculturated. Now, through the experiences afforded by the Cocoon, his circle of identity expands beyond his cultural boundaries: it becomes worldcentric. The Wanderer begins to experience all of humanity ("the whole world") as the realm that informs his existence and merits his greatest loyalty. He no longer identifies himself exclusively in terms of the cultural roles that he happens to occupy. He still acts within those roles, but now he's able to assess their appropriateness and genuineness from the perspective of humanity. He has truly become a global citizen.

Whether or not conscious of it at any particular moment, the worldcentric person is disposed to treat all of humanity as "mine" — what she loves and defends. Her choices and actions, in other words, are generally sourced in what is best for humanity as a whole. What's more, her compassionate regard is not just for people currently alive but also for the people of the future. Like the Haudenosaunee, the indigenous Americans whom the French called the Iroquois, the Wanderer considers the impact of her actions, for ill or good, on the children of the seventh generation.

In addition to having the ability to think from the point of view of humanity, the worldcentric individual instinctively *experiences* life from that perspective. Merely being able to think worldcentrically is an academic, and important, exercise that is relatively easy. The truly worldcentric person, however, takes the perspective of humanity reflexively without any external prompting or incentives. She values the needs of humanity as a whole more highly than those of any particular racial or national groups, including her own, whenever those needs or perspectives are in conflict. Although she is proud of and devoted to the wholesome qualities of her own culture, she understands that her people embody only one way of being human, and that her community's conception of divinity or sacredness is not the only valid one. She wants to know what is fair and morally right for humanity as a whole, not just for the people of her culture. Her position is not "my country, right or wrong," but "global human justice, comfortable for me or not."

A worldcentric circle of identity corresponds to the stage of moral development that psychologist Lawrence Kohlberg refers to as "postconventional," in which the individual is able to criticize her own culture. She's no longer limited to or identified with her nation's traditional beliefs, attitudes, and norms. She might still agree with most or even all of them, but now she possesses the critical distance necessary to transcend them when her expanding sense of self demands it. She has a much freer and wider field of choice. She is approaching true adulthood.

Worldcentrism (also called "universal pluralism") does not mean that the Wanderer necessarily considers the rights of, say, a foreign-looking stranger to be as important as, or more important than, his own. Rather, he has the ability to empathize with that stranger or with an ethnic group other than his own, and he's now able to consider the possibility that he might better serve humanity as a whole by giving the stranger's immediate needs or desires greater priority than his own. For a worldcentric individual, this would not be a multiculturally altruistic act. It is something more mature: an act of self-love or, as Arne Naess argues, following Kant, an act of Beauty.[62] In principle, this is comparable to the sociocentric person concluding at times that he would better serve his family by putting his sibling's needs before his own immediate ones. At other times, the worldcentric individual might conclude that his immediate personal needs, or those of his own ethnic group, have priority because this would serve humanity best. For the worldcentric person, this would not be a selfish conclusion.

When people discuss international or multicultural ethics, they often talk past one another when their individual circles of identity are at different levels of maturity. Consider, for example, what happens when a worldcentric person tries to convince an ethnocentric middle-class American of the value of global economic equality and justice. The most the worldcentric person can hope to accomplish is to get the other to agree out of compliance, compromise, or morality — but not as an act of worldcentric self-love or Beauty.

SECESSION:
THE EGOCENTRIC COUNTERPART TO THE COCOON

The egocentric and soulcentric Wheels diverge radically in the fourth stage of life. During each of the first three stages, the psychospiritual centers of gravity were the same on both Wheels even though the nature-oriented tasks were minimized or ignored in the egocentric sequence. The hub of a young person's life moved from spirit (stage 1) to family and nature (stage 2) to peer group, sex, and society (stage 3). Even in an egocentric world, the genetic and biological imperative, combined with family and social support, are almost always sufficient to carry us through these developmental shifts even if we fail significantly at some of the tasks of the first two stages. Many people do not embody stages 2 and 3 as fully as they might have in a soulcentric setting, but most everyone's center of gravity advances nevertheless to that of stage 3.

However, beginning with stage 3 (the Oasis in the soulcentric setting, Conforming and Rebelling in the egocentric), biology and egocentric society are often not sufficient to move our center of gravity any further.

On the egocentric Wheel, an individual's center of gravity never progresses beyond the stage-3 sphere of peer group, sex, and society, while on the soulcentric Wheel, an individual's center of gravity moves on with each additional stage. Likewise, the ego-centric circle of identity never grows beyond the ethnocentric. Nationalism, chauvin-ism, and xenophobia remain more common than not.

Unlike the soulcentric sequence, the egocentric stages can be at least roughly co-ordinated with chronological age. Stage 3a (Conforming and Rebelling) usually spans from age twelve or thirteen to sixteen or eighteen. Then, somewhere toward the end of high school (or the corresponding age range, if she drops out), the egocentric teenager undergoes a transition we might call Exodus, in some ways the opposite of Confirma-tion. (See Diagram 3-6, p. 71.) Whereas Confirmation marks the adequate completion of a first personality, Exodus signifies the essential failure of Social Individuation.

At Exodus, the older teenager emotionally confronts the fact, more fully than be-fore, that she will leave home soon, that she longs to do so, and that she is not psy-chosocially prepared for it. Unlike the soulcentric "leaving home" at Confirmation, which is a profound shift in one's way of belonging to the world, here it will only be a change in address, a psychosocial leave-taking from family life, and a greater re-sponsibility for her day-to-day affairs. However, for the teenager doing poorly with the tasks of stage 3 (in part due to difficulties in stages 1 and 2), the prospect of true au-tonomy is especially frightening. At Exodus, the teenager emotionally separates from what she experiences as the bondage of her family life, but where she's headed does not differ in any real way — namely, into an adolescent society that simply sustains Rebelling and Conforming in new contexts: social group, marriage, the military, college, and work.

I think of this egocentric version of late adolescence — which begins in the late teens and spans through most of the twenties — as Secession, stage 3b. The "young adult" now emotionally and socially secedes from family affairs. In the previous stage (3a), although sometimes she rebelled against her parents, she was still very much hooked into her family's social life. Now, in Secession, she emotionally exits — at least, on the surface (in her depths, she is still entrenched in family dynamics even though there remains very little meaningful communication or intimacy with her parents). Early in Secession, she usually departs physically too, leaving for college or a job and a home of her own.

During Secession, many youth suffer a profound ambivalence about having left home. Often parents act out one pole of this ambivalence and their child acts out the other. The parents might attempt to control her economically or morally, or they might tell her she's not really prepared to be on her own or that she'll be a failure (both of which are often true). She often acts out the opposing position: that her parents are incapable of understanding her (most often true), that it is inconceivable that she could ever have been born to such people (not at all true), and that the sooner she completely severs herself from them the better (maybe true, maybe not).

In other families, the roles are reversed, with the parents in a hurry to fully emancipate their child and the terrified child dragging her heels. Some families flip-flop between the two extremes.

Youth who succeed at the egocentric tasks of Secession manage to change their physical address no later than their early twenties. The unsuccessful ones maintain a lifelong dependency on their parents and stay home in one way or another. For most, however, Secession ends by the late twenties.

But there's no need to wait for Secession to end and turn into the subsequent ego-centric stage of Capitulation. To move from Secession to the Oasis, a person must turn to the least addressed or least accomplished tasks of the Nest, Garden, and Oasis, especially the nature dimensions of those tasks.

A THIN COCOON

In egocentric society, people who manage to reach the Cocoon often embody this stage in a way that looks and feels indefinite, watered down, or insubstantial. Their center of gravity has shifted to the mysteries of nature and psyche, but their focus seems to waver and they might be unclear about how to proceed. This is most likely due either to a lack of wandering support from elders, mentors, initiators, or the larger society, or to significantly incomplete tasks from the first three stages, or both. These people have progressed developmentally, but the Cocoon they inhabit is thin.

People in a thin Cocoon do what they can to disidentify from the adolescent per-sonality and to wander more deeply into the world, but they might have doubts about the value of what they're doing or what their destination might be, even in the most general terms. They might succumb to pressure from their egocentric friends and family who are worried, exasperated, or critical of their priorities, and who appeal to them to settle down, "make some real money," and plan for their retirement and old age. They probably feel like strangers in a strange land. (They are.) They are likely to have difficulty reaching the next passage on their own. A thin Cocoon might last for many years, possibly decades.

As an example, consider a married, forty-two-year-old college-educated mother of three with a full-time job at a bank and several deep friendships. She's an ardent sup-porter of the environment, is politically active, makes anonymous donations to sev-eral charities, is passionate and educated about the rights of citizens in developing countries, and is doing her best to instill these values in her children.

She's captivated by the mysteries of nature and psyche. She attends a dream group, practices yoga, and has an on-again, off-again Buddhist meditation practice. She's in love with the natural world and goes for walks in nearby wildlands. There's a small organic garden in her backyard, and she has solar panels on her roof. In her quiet time, she reads poetry and mythology, but this often leaves her feeling empty and sad.

This woman is a Wanderer in a thin Cocoon, and has been for many years. She has not yet had an encounter with her soul (as far as she can tell, at least). She has no idea about the deeper meaning of her life. When this truth hits her, she's depressed for long periods. She sometimes sees a therapist and considers leaving her family, but then gives up and finds a project to occupy her mind. She's lonely in a profound way because she has not yet found herself.

If she were to find an underworld guide, or were to suffer the right kind of major loss, or if she somehow were to become willing and able to cross the borders into the mysteries of nature and psyche, she might plunge immediately and fully into the work of the Cocoon — including some remedial work on the tasks of the first three stages — and rapidly progress toward Soul Initiation.

TIMES OF WANDERING AFTER THE COCOON

The Cocoon is by no means the only time in life when we wander psychospiritually. It is simply the first significant period when we do so and the only stage in which wandering is the very substance and center of our lives. In subsequent stages, there'll be times (relatively brief) when we need to once again wander and reassess our lives — for example, when we near the transitions of Induction, Crowning, and Surrender, and in times of spiritual crisis within each stage. Such times provoke a self-confrontation, a dying and a letting go, in preparation for a deeper understanding and embodiment of our lives.

Regardless of our age or developmental level, the Wanderer archetype operates within us whenever we need greater depth or meaning or purpose in our lives. The Wanderer within is always ready to both search for soul and generate new ways of embodying the qualities of soul we have already uncovered.

THE DISTINCTIVENESS OF ADOLESCENCE

A question at the heart of this book, one that launched my original inquiry into the nature of human development, and which seems to have no clear answer in contemporary society, is this: What is the essential distinction, if any, between adolescence and adulthood? Can we identify differences more meaningful than age, self-confidence, or economic self-reliance?

The Wheel proposes an answer. The differences between adolescence and adulthood are radical indeed and can be expressed in terms of archetypes, developmental tasks, centers of psychospiritual gravity, inherent contributions to community, and circles of identity. Furthermore, not only is adolescence distinct from both childhood and adulthood, but there are *two* stages of adolescence, which I call the Oasis and the Cocoon, each distinct from the other, and with opposite trajectories.

The long progression from childhood to adulthood is a movement in and out of ordinary community life. Puberty is a rite of incorporation into the larger social community, where teenagers learn to create an authentic social presence. Confirmation is a rite of separation *out* of that community and into a time of mostly solitary wandering, there to prepare for true adulthood. Soul Initiation once again incorporates the individual back into society as an adult who becomes "visible / while carrying / what is hidden / as a gift to others."[63]

If we compare the Oasis with the Wellspring (two stages later), the dissimilarities between adolescence and adulthood become particularly striking. While the Thespian defines himself in terms of society, either in conforming to it or rebelling against it, the Apprentice differentiates himself in terms of his relation to soul and the more-than-human community of the natural world.

WHEN DO YOU EMERGE FROM THE COCOON?

During the Cocoon stage, through one or several encounters with soul, the Wanderer discovers something of the image or gift that is his to bring to the world, or of the larger story that he's meant to live, or of his ultimate place of belonging in the world. He understands this place ecocentrically: it's his place in the more-than-human world, as opposed to a culturally defined vocation or social role. Coming to know this place is as joyous as any accomplishment in his life.

Then one day it dawns on him that he cannot devote the rest of his life solely to exploring the underworld mysteries. He cannot remain forever on the periphery of society as a student of soul. He realizes, with some shock and grief, that the time is coming when he must gather what he has learned (and has become) in the Cocoon — however inadequate this might feel — and fully return to his community. He must now contribute something of consequence to his people. His student-wandering days are over.

There's an immense sadness in leaving the exotic wandering life of the Cocoon. It was the best stage of life to be in.

CHAPTER EIGHT

THE SOUL APPRENTICE
at the WELLSPRING

Early Adulthood (Stage 5)

...out of the silence
you can make a promise
it will kill you to break,

that way you'll find
what is real and what is not....

— DAVID WHYTE, "ALL THE TRUE VOWS"

...To be human
is to become visible
while carrying
what is hidden
as a gift to others....

— DAVID WHYTE, "WHAT TO REMEMBER WHEN WAKING"

The job is to seek mystery, evoke mystery, plant a garden in which strange plants grow and mysteries bloom. The need for mystery is greater than the need for an answer.

— KEN KESEY

Stage 5: Early Adulthood

Passage into this stage: Soul Initiation

Stage name: The Wellspring (Soul-Rooted Individuation)

Task: Learning to embody soul in culture — acquiring and implementing delivery systems (the culture component) for soul qualities (the nature component)

Quadrant: West (soul, darkness, mystery, the hidden, the invisible)

Hemispheres: North and West (collective action)

Stage archetype: The Soul Apprentice

Quadrant archetype: The Visionary

Gift to community: Visionary action, hope, and inspiration

Circle of identity: Ecocentric

Center of gravity: Cultural depths (the embodied mysteries of nature and psyche)

Passage out of this stage: Induction (confirms mastery of a delivery system)

SELF-ACCEPTANCE

At sunup, my girlfriend and I soak in a hand-fashioned hot-springs pool, big enough for four or so, in the Mojave Desert in the middle of nowhere. We are in an immense sandy basin, no less than a long day's drive from anywhere, down a seldom-used dirt road. A small cluster of car camps are scattered among the sparse and spiny creosote bushes that grow seven feet tall at most. We sit alone in hot waters and the cool breezy air beneath the fanning fronds of palm trees, gorgeously green in a land of grays and browns. The early February morning is beginning to warm now that the Sun has peeked over the ridge of one of the mountain ranges that surround us and soar nearly two vertical miles above our heads.

A remarkably fit and youthful couple in their sixties amble over, shed their terrycloth robes, and join us in the small pool. They are companionable and well spoken. She turns out to be a nurse, he an astrophysicist. The conversation warms up as quickly as the day, and soon we hear the scientist say that, for him, self-acceptance is the true sign of maturity. My girlfriend glances at me, knowing my devotion to the possibility of a deeper form of maturity. I am in fact thinking that, although true self-acceptance is rare in our world and an essential feature of maturity, it is not what *defines* maturity — at least not authentic adulthood. It seems to me that some measure of self-acceptance is actually what we first achieve in a healthy adolescence.

Before I manage to respond, the affable scientist has somehow moved on to the crusty question concerning nature and nurture — how much of each accounts for our choices and behavior. Implicit for the scientist is the assumption that, together, the influences of nature and nurture add up to a hundred percent. I however think, in resonance with the depth psychologist James Hillman, that perhaps there is a third factor — soul — that is reducible *neither* to nature nor to nurture, and that our choices, at least those arising from our deepest selves, are not determined or even constrained by either our genetic makeup *or* our life histories. Perhaps soul exists before sperm and egg meet, and soul might have an agenda neither created nor limited by what we experience in life. "I believe we each carry true wildness," I say at last to the aging scientist, "and, thanks to that wildness, our lives need not be determined by our biological inheritance or our prior experience. Perhaps our lives are most creative and fulfilling when we have accessed and embodied that wildness, our deepest individual potentials, the destinies for which we were born … our souls."

As I utter the last word, the scientist and the nurse, in unison, draw back a bit in what seems like an involuntary movement. There is a sudden pause in the conversation and an ever-so-slight wave appears in the water between us. Politely shaking their heads, they softly avow that this idea of soul and nondetermined freedom is not acceptable. I take an in-breath, but before I can respond, the local hot-springs loudmouth wanders over and hijacks the conversation. My girlfriend and I take the opportunity to slip away, but this brief exchange keeps eating at me. What defines true adulthood, I wonder, and what is the relationship between the adult ego, self-acceptance, and the soul?

One day, several years later, I abruptly realize that, while I was there at the desert hot springs wondering about the nature of adulthood, I was sitting the whole time smack in the middle of one of nature's best metaphors for adulthood — a wellspring.

EARLY ADULTHOOD AS A WELLSPRING

A wellspring is the source of a stream, the fount of the precious waters of life. From the invisible depths, cool, clear elixir percolates and purls, astonishing us as it flows into our perceivable world, nourishing and sustaining all and everything. Our deeper life is like a wellspring — welling up from below, invisible (unconscious) at its source but rippling into our palpable existence, galvanizing our imagination and endeavors.

Mythologies around the world overflow with springs, those dependable abodes of generativity, nourishment, holiness, magic, and the numinous.

The newly initiated adult dwells at a kind of wellspring, tends to it, apprentices there. Having discovered in the Cocoon the underworld source of her one true life, she now resides where that underground gift surfaces, where it becomes visible and valuable to her people. She abides at the interface between the mysteries and the manifest in order to decipher the manner in which the transformational enigmas emerge into form. In the course of her exploration, she becomes a wellspring herself. In apprenticing to soul, she learns to embody in everyday enterprises subterranean secrets in service to the Earth community.

In nature, there is always new and tender growth around wellspring edges. These damp districts are fertile and wholesome places where pollination and procreation abound. Animals are drawn in, both for food and for the magic, here where life is prolifically sprouting, concentrated like the first morning of creation.

In all these ways, early adulthood is a Wellspring. In no other stage of life does the human more carefully and passionately study the workings of creativity, the maneuvers by which the invisible becomes visible. Following Soul Initiation, the Apprentice's greatest desire is to become a wellspring herself. Accordingly, the newly initiated adult apprentices herself to the creative process itself and to a discipline through which she can learn the particular magic to which her soul has summoned her.

At the Wellspring, there is a mentor of mystery, perhaps several. These mentors are the adults and elders who have mastered crafts for rendering the invisible visible, for carrying to others the same sort of gift the new adult has been called to manifest. At the Wellspring, the initiate apprentices to one or more such artisans — sorcerers, Merlins and Morgaines, artists of cultural renaissance.

As suggested by such an animated word as *spring*, the accent at the Wellspring is on action, on getting the business of the world done, but in every moment staying sourced in the mysteries, rooted in the enigmatic creativity of the unfathomable depths. And, as suggested by *well*, the Wellspring is a stage of life that conveys abundant health, well-being, and wholeness to the Earth community. The people look to the Wellspring as well as to the wellsprings for something simultaneously natural and mystical, the elixir of life.

After many months of sitting with the assertion of the scientist at the desert hot springs, I ended up both agreeing and disagreeing with him: Adult maturity, I believe, is in fact marked by self-acceptance, but, I insist, the important thing is soul-acceptance, not mere ego-acceptance. Initiated adulthood is primarily about embracing, honoring, and doing right by our soul gifts, and not at all about an acceptance — whether self-admiring or resigned — of our genetic endowments, our personalities and personal histories, or our current life circumstances.

SOUL INITIATION:
PASSAGE INTO AUTHENTIC ADULTHOOD

Soul Initiation occurs at the West point on the Wheel, halfway round the circle of life. The West, the place of the setting Sun, is where the light of everyday ego consciousness sinks below the surface toward the depths. There your personality becomes rooted firmly in the soul's desire that you belong to the world in the way that only you can. This way of belonging — inhabiting your ultimate place in the world — is something quite particular. Your place has been waiting for you since the beginning, and now you can no longer deny it. Embodying your soul — its qualities, images, and story — becomes a first-tier priority for you. To embody your soul is to engage in visionary action, ways of doing and being that breathe new life into the world with or without your intention to do so. To manifest your soul's desires in the world is a political act, one that contributes, in the twenty-first century, to the Great Work.

But at Soul Initiation it's not so much that you independently *choose* to make soul embodiment a top priority; it's more that the Mystery, sensing you're ready enough, *commands* you to that task, and you assent.

At the West point on the Wheel, although you're diving beneath the horizon, you remain in the West quadrant. Consequently, in the Wellspring, you continue under the primary influence of the West's mysterious and fruitful darkness, as you did in the Cocoon. But what *does* change at Soul Initiation — and this is an enormous shift — is the hemisphere you inhabit. You depart the South half of the Wheel and enter into its North. This will be the only time in life you'll move in either direction between these hemispheres, from the half of life focused on your individual existence to the half devoted to the collective life. Your personal development is no longer your primary concern — at least not the way it was when you were a child or student, as an Explorer, Thespian, or Wanderer. Now, every day, you are keenly mindful that you live on the same boat as all other Earth creatures; you all float or sink together. The evolving life of the collective — the more-than-human community — matters as much to you now as your individual trajectory because, after all, they are inseparable. You are now more an agent for the Mystery — for soul and spirit — than for your narrowly defined self.

Because the North hemisphere represents the night half of the Wheel, the Wellspring is also the stage in which you first fully get to know the dark. You come to understand that the dark is not defined by the absence of light (as you had inevitably believed in childhood and adolescence) but has its own vital qualities and inherent values wholly independent of the light.

In addition to remaining in the West *quadrant* (soul, darkness, mystery, the hidden, the invisible) while in the Wellspring stage, you also abide, of course, in the West *half* of the Wheel, where you have been since puberty and will be until the end of adulthood. Your life, in other words, is still more about action than being. You are in the heart of the half of life in which you get things done, accomplish, go somewhere, manifest — regardless of how much or little your awareness might also be rooted in the eternal present.

In that your life is now about the collective as well as about action, your psychospiritual center of gravity has shifted from your individual exploration of the mysteries of soul and nature (the Cocoon) to your active embodiment of those mysteries in a life of service to your community (the Wellspring). The hub of your life has moved from the transcultural back to the cultural as you learn, in David Whyte's words, to "become visible / while carrying / what is hidden / as a gift to others." Two stages earlier, in the Oasis, your life was also centered in culture, but then from the surface perspective of personality rather than from the depths of soul, as it is now.

"Tell me, what is it you plan to do / with your one wild and precious life?" the poet Mary Oliver asks.[1] Soul Initiation is the moment, not when you decide for yourself, but when an answer wholly claims you. It is the moment when you fully accept your calling, your own particular mission in life.

William Wordsworth wrote of such a moment when he was a young man in college, after a night of summer revelry. As he walked home at dawn in the hills of northern England, the world showed *him* what he was going to do with his life:

> ...Ah! need I say, dear Friend! that to the brim
> My heart was full; I made no vows, but vows
> Were then made for me; bond unknown to me
> Was given, that I should be, else sinning greatly,
> A dedicated Spirit. On I walked
> In thankful blessedness, which yet survives....[2]

As discussed in the last chapter, the answer that claims you often takes the form of an image or a story, a motif burned into your soul before birth, a song in the presence of which your heart fully opens. This pattern or symbol is the gods' way of sending you off to life with a destiny and a task, with a template of how to *be* in this lifetime. Your soul image or story shows you your ultimate place and the nature of the gift you were born to bring into the world.

Once you've been shown your soul image or story, you must learn how to enact it within your particular culture, time, and place. This is the central developmental task of the Wellspring. Determining an effective form of embodiment and learning the necessary skills are more the ego's tasks than the soul's. The form of embodiment is the *delivery system* for your soul image or story. The delivery system may be art, architecture, raising children, psychotherapy, gardening, teaching, politics, healing, poetry, dance, or any other cultural practice.

A soul image might be a single image, but if so, it's a highly symbolic and extraordinarily rich image, like a dream or a landscape or an intricate painting. "One picture is worth ten thousand words," the Chinese say. Resting in that single image is enough inspiration for a lifetime. Unfolding and discerning the multiple layers takes time. It is a treasure of great sacredness and value, emanating a type of noetic antiquity and sanctity, your personal Dead Sea Scroll.

Soul Initiation transforms your life by virtue of the truth at the center of your soul image or story — something you encountered one or more times in the Cocoon or earlier. Your commitment to that truth results in a radical simplification of your life. Upon making that covenant with soul, you suffer the disintegration of the identity you so carefully built for yourself through childhood and adolescence. It feels like dying. It *is* a type of death. As David Whyte writes in "Revelation Must Be Terrible," "You are leaving everything / and everyone you know behind. . . . When you open your eyes to the world / you are on your own for the first time."[3] Most activities and relationships that do not support your soul purpose fall away. Your former life agenda is discarded, half-completed projects abandoned. Some of your former personal problems are not solved but outgrown. Old ways of presenting and defending yourself become less appealing.

Although the ego undergoes a profound change at Soul Initiation, it's not what we'd normally call a change in personality. What shifts in this moment is not your personal style, strengths, weaknesses, traits, attitudes, abilities, or knowledge. Rather, what changes is your status or place in the world. You're now living closer to your ultimate place. Although Soul Initiation itself does not alter your personality, your personality will begin to mature in often surprising ways following your initiation.

The transformation in your life at Soul Initiation is irreversible. You have, in effect, made "a promise / it will kill you to break," as Whyte writes. You now have an obligation both joyous and terrible. There is a sacred responsibility to fulfill. No excuses. Following initiation, it is

> . . . as if your place in the world mattered
> and the world could
> neither speak nor hear the fullness of
>
> its own bitter and beautiful cry
> without the deep well
> of your body resonating in the echo.
>
> Knowing that it takes only
> that one, terrible
> word to make the circle complete,
>
> revelation must be terrible
> knowing you can
> never hide your voice again.[4]

Having uncovered your soul image or story, you long to embody your soul in a way that engenders genuine and intimate communion between people, the land, and the other-than-human beings. This is the way you'll participate in the unfolding of the *world's* soul. You know the world cannot flower into its full potential without each person, including you, playing the part each was born to play.

The author and Mayan initiation guide Martín Prechtel writes, "For there to be a world at all, every indigenous, original, natural thing must start singing its song, dancing its dance, moving and breathing, each according to its own nature, saying its name, manifesting simultaneously its secret spiritual signature."[5] Every person alive today descended from nature-based peoples. We evolved within the rich tapestry of the natural world. Every one of us has something unique to contribute to that tapestry. This knowledge waits within like buried treasure, a soulful seed of quiescent potential. Some may be here to bring light into the world; others to retrieve the infinite treasures of darkness. Some may celebrate the miracle of existence by inspiring us through song, others through dance, or through the visual arts, or science. Some may be here to give form to a certain range of ideas, or cultural practices, or stories. Others are here to heal, to understand, to nurture.

After Soul Initiation, when you awake most mornings, your first inspiration for the day will concern your soulwork. Soul embodiment becomes far more meaningful and fulfilling to you than career advancement, buying a new home, or going on a tropical vacation. It can also be more challenging and maddening!

What ultimately confirms your initiation is neither your soul encounter(s) nor the blessing of a community authority — even an elder — but rather the depth of fulfillment you derive from living your soul into the world, and the contribution your soulwork makes to the wholing of the world.

Before Soul Initiation — in the first half of life, the South half of the Wheel — the relationship between your ego and soul is like that of a child to his guardian angel. Your soul is an invisible presence doing its best to guide you. You might sense a benevolent being watching over you, but your awareness of that angel tends to be sporadic at best, and you do not yet understand that it will become your job, your destiny, to carry out the angel's desires, or even what those desires might be. Soul *encounters* are conscious experiences of that angel and its desires. Following those encounters, the soul seems less like an angel and more like a shimmering place in the world waiting for you to occupy it. Soul *Initiation* is the moment you commit yourself utterly to embodying the specific desires of your soul, or place, as revealed in one or more soul encounters.[6]

Following Soul Initiation — in the second half of life, the North hemisphere of the Wheel — the relationship between ego and soul is like that of prime minister to king, first mate to skipper, handmaiden to queen, or worker bee to queen bee. You accept your true place as the soul's agent and commit yourself to actualizing the image or story at your core.

In the Wheel's South, the soul serves the ego. In the Wheel's North, the service flows more in the other direction. At Soul Initiation, you understand that the soul (or, alternatively, spirit) has been preparing you during the first half your life to serve *it* (and the world) during the second half.

In contemporary, egocentric culture, we have to be careful with the word *initiation*. Many people associate it with elitism, secret societies, flaky or nefarious cults, and oppressive, hierarchical organizations. For some people, the word evokes, on the one hand, a sense of their own inadequacy (if they have not undergone an initiatory experience and believe they ought to have) and, on the other, suspicions of arrogance, ego inflation, or naïveté on the part of those who participate in initiatory rites. Because of the word's considerable charge, it's probably best to avoid public declarations of being initiated. Soul Initiation is not something to be worn like a badge or status symbol; it is to be quietly embodied through a life of soulful service.

For this reason, it might be best, in our egocentric culture, to forgo public passage rites that formally mark and celebrate Soul Initiation. A wiser choice might be to enact a ceremony in solitude or perhaps with a small group of intimates who are moved more by the profound responsibility you're embracing than by a higher status they might imagine you've acquired. You and they will experience the event as being as much like a funeral (for a cherished way of life that has come to an end) as a wedding, one between the ego and the soul.

That said, contemporary Soul Initiation rites might look quite different from those of indigenous peoples, both ancient and contemporary, for a few reasons. First is the danger of self-aggrandizement, just discussed. Second, Soul Initiation in egocentric culture is not only rare but also, when it does occur, likely to happen much later in life (in our twenties or anytime afterward) than it did, or still does, for indigenous peoples (who are more likely to undergo this passage in their teens). Third, we have lost our own traditions of Soul Initiation and must now imagine new ones that fit who we have become.

Several people I know have enacted Soul Initiation rites in the form of a marriage ceremony between the ego and the soul, or between the ego and the anima or animus, the Guide to Soul. Vows are taken, prayers are offered, rings or other symbols are consecrated, and gifts are given and received. Human witnesses are present or not. The relationship between ego and soul is celebrated for now having a primary position in the individual's life.

ADULTHOOD AND SOUL-ROOTED INDIVIDUATION

In contemporary society we tend to think that adulthood is, at its core, all about hard work and practical responsibility — earning a living, developing a career, getting married, and rearing children. Although these are in fact components of life for most of us after our early twenties, they don't yield an incisive or inspiring portrait of adulthood. All these things, after all, can be, and often are, enacted by teenagers and older adolescents.

I think, instead, of David Whyte's image quoted at the beginning of this chapter: "To be human / is to become visible / while carrying / what is hidden / as a gift to others." As an adult, you're in the process of claiming your full humanity by the way that you embody soul — by the way you express your love for the world through engaged actions inspired by your particular way of belonging to life. You are incarnating the vision revealed during your time in the Cocoon. But you are not trying to heroically fix or save the world; you are simply participating in the world as fully as you can and in the way only you can. This is the most you can do for the world, and it is sufficient.

The Wheel suggests that true adulthood is rooted in something transpersonal, a revelation that is then embodied in practical responsibility and deeply fulfilling work. These mystical roots of adulthood are acknowledged in healthy, ecocentric societies past and present. Thomas Berry suggests a similar definition for *adult*, namely, a person with a practical way of carrying out a vision or a dream. "The dream," Thomas says, "inspires, guides, and drives the action."[7] In a similar vein, the cultural anthropologist Angeles Arrien speaks of "walking the mystical path with practical feet."[8] In the 1960s, the humanistic psychologist Abraham Maslow introduced the concept of "self-actualizing people," another idea that richly resonates with what I mean by an initiated adult:

> Self-actualizing people are, without one single exception, involved in a cause outside their own skin, in something outside of themselves. They are devoted, working at something, something which is very precious to them — some calling or vocation in the old sense, the priestly sense. They are working at something which fate has called them to somehow and which they work at and which they love, so that the work-joy dichotomy in them disappears.[9]

As I suggested in the first chapter, all true adults are artists, visionaries, and leaders, whether they live and work quietly in small arenas or very publicly on grand stages. The most potent seeds of the Great Work of cultural renaissance come from the uniquely creative work of initiated adults.

In order to embody the gifts of your soul, you must cultivate the skills, sensibilities, and values that support such an intention. For this reason, the Wellspring might also be called the stage of Soul-Rooted Individuation, during which you shape a social presence and a personality that can most effectively embody soul.

In early adolescence — the stage of *social* individuation — you differentiated your personality in relation to society; social popularity and economic security were your principal concerns. Now your primary developmental opportunity is to root your ego in the dark and rich humus of your destiny. What lifestyle, relationships, training, knowledge, and work will best accommodate this desire?

True service to community and deep personal fulfillment are the twin and inseparable aspirations of adulthood. Soul-rooted service is the adult's way of loving the world. Sometimes this service takes the form of a career or raising a family. But, more generally, soulful service is what the adult aspires to perform in every action every day, whether or not he is a parent, whether or not he has a job, and, if he does have one, irrespective of his job description.

The process of soul-rooted individuation necessitates the further cultivation of the Self, our human wholeness. In the Cocoon, the Wanderer developed a conscious relationship with each of the four dimensions of the Self, as described in the previous chapter. Now, in the Wellspring, the Apprentice must learn to balance the strength of these four intrapsychic resources so that he can employ them equally. Whichever of the four are weakest deserve the most attention.

Soul-rooted individuation catalyzes a third phase in your relationship to authenticity and self-acceptance. Two stages earlier, in the Oasis, you learned to distinguish between acting authentically and deception-for-the-sake-of-acceptance, but when push came to shove, acceptance by your peers was more important than being impeccably real. Artifice and duplicity were sometimes worth the price. Then, in the Cocoon, you learned to prioritize personal authenticity over social acceptance, wholeness over self-protection.

Now, in the Wellspring, authenticity takes an even more mature form, an allegiance to something greater and deeper than your emotions, opinions, and everyday desires. Now the soul's call takes precedence. Soul embodiment becomes not only more important to you than social approval but also more important than your situational personal comfort (in those hopefully rare moments when you must choose between them). This priority ushers you toward a deeper form of genuineness — a soul-rooted authenticity. The desires of your everyday personality are not sacrificed or suppressed but subordinated to the desires of your soul.

THE SOUL APPRENTICE:
ARCHETYPE OF EARLY ADULTHOOD

The transition from ego-acceptance to soul-acceptance both signals and exemplifies the transition from adolescence to adulthood. Ego-acceptance strives for a good fit between personality and human community. Soul-acceptance seeks a good fit among *three* parties: personality, soul, and the *more-than-human* community. The adult aspires to effectively embody his gifts of soul in the mysterious and complex web of people, other creatures, and ecosystems.

The Thespian developed a society-rooted way of being human as he apprenticed himself to the roles and enterprises afforded by his family and culture. The Wanderer left behind this first social way of defining himself and sought a deeper way as he apprenticed himself to the mysteries. Now the initiated adult becomes an apprentice to his soul and to a discipline that enables him to live those mysteries into the world. Although a Soul Apprentice has diverse life interests, the center of his existence is his longing to make manifest his soul's desires.

During this stage, the Apprentice's understanding of his soul image or story often deepens, broadens, or shifts. His soul apprenticeship is anchored not by a particular version of an image or story but by an approach to life in which his fundamental inspiration for living comes from the mysteries. He's tuned into the subterranean currents of the world and grasps the vital importance of aligning his daily life with the truth and potentials at those depths. He has accepted the terrifying and ecstatic responsibilities of a true artist — making the invisible visible, the unconscious conscious. He recognizes that to live his soul story into the world is both a blessing and a burden. The vision he's received undermines his former security, and he must accept this inevitable vulnerability. The invitation to apprentice to soul is experienced, in part, as a violation, a pain, something he is first tempted to flee. But the Soul Apprentice assents to his responsibility to lead from his depths. He is growing toward his full humanity.

THE VISIONARY, PART II

The archetype of the Visionary rules both stages of the West quadrant — the Cocoon and the Wellspring. But Soul Initiation ignites the adult phase of the Visionary, she who not only sees the soul-infused possibilities but also possesses means to make them manifest.

In contemporary culture, we tend to think of the Visionary in a limited way, as an archetype that lives only through men and women generating the grandest innovations in art, science, technology, or government. But in fact a Visionary's deep creativity is as likely to manifest more quietly — say, in her garden or in her way of loving or her poetry. We must abandon the self-defeating belief that only the most extraordinarily gifted people are destined to be Visionaries. *All* initiated adults are Visionaries. Each one of us is meant for a life of creative and engaged artistry. We each have the capacity to uncover astonishing new possibilities and to bring them into form for the benefit of the Earth community.

As she enters the postsunset shadows of the West, the Soul Apprentice learns to make bridges between the underworld of vision and the middleworld of society. This is the adult Visionary undertaking. She sees both the world's need and how her soul meets it, how her soul's desire fits in the world like a piece of a jigsaw puzzle. She comes to understand the relationship between her soul and the world as like a marriage. By giving herself to the largest conversation she can have with life, she helps the world actualize its potentials, and simultaneously, she takes the place that is hers alone, a place that has been waiting for her, drawing her to it. When she finds her ultimate place, she falls into it with joy and trembling.

THE APPRENTICE'S CONTRIBUTION TO THE WORLD: VISIONARY ACTION, HOPE, AND INSPIRATION

The Soul Apprentice at the Wellspring is gifted with vision in its most concentrated form. Although we continue to be visionary as we grow, in no other stage does revelation move through a person with such animation, freshness, and on-the-ground engagement. Even people in later developmental stages marvel at the Apprentice's capacity to detect the invisible and to give it an initial shape. During the previous stage, the Wanderer was only learning to be in relationship to the mysteries. And in comparison to the Artisan of the next stage, who is focused more on blossom than seed, the Apprentice resonates more fully with the possible, the imaginable, the conceivable, the hidden, and the not-yet-formed. All others in a soulcentric community are grateful for, and perhaps a bit envious of, the profundity and originality of the Apprentice's embodied imagination.

The Apprentice's life is also a testament to the hope that springs from sacred gifts retrieved from inscrutable darkness, gifts that allow the human community to heal or become more vital and sustainable. Václav Havel, playwright, visionary, and former president of Czechoslovakia, thinks of this kind of hope

> as a state of mind, not a state of the world. Either we have hope within us or we don't; it is a dimension of the soul, and it's not essentially dependent on some particular observation of the world or estimate of the situation....
>
> Hope, in this deep and powerful sense, is not the same as joy that things are going well, or willingness to invest in enterprises that are obviously headed for early success, but, rather, an ability to work for something because it is good, not just because it stands a chance to succeed. The more unpropitious the situation in which we demonstrate hope, the deeper that hope is. Hope is definitely not the same thing as optimism. It is not the conviction that something will turn out well, but the certainty that something makes sense, regardless of how it turns out.[10]

Implicit here is the distinction between what I think of as mature and immature hope. The latter believes there's nothing we can do to change the outcome; we can only sit helplessly and hope for the best. Mature hope, however, motivates action until the outcome is achieved or abandoned. It inspires us to become the change we seek. Author and activist Rebecca Solnit writes:

> Hope is not like a lottery ticket you can sit on the sofa and clutch, feeling lucky.... Hope is an ax you break down doors with in an emergency;... hope should shove you out the door, because it will take everything you have to steer the future away from endless war, from the annihilation of the earth's treasures and the grinding down of the poor and marginal. Hope just means another world might be possible, not promised, not guaranteed. Hope calls for action; action is impossible without hope.[11]

In addition to visionary action and hope, the Apprentice offers the gift of inspiration. She spurs us to be courageous and to take risks, to believe (or remember) that the Mystery can be made manifest, that soul is continuously birthed into the world. To *inspire* means to breathe into or to draw in by breathing. It also means to be filled with spirit, the breath of life or of the divine. If inspiration, then, carries new breath and spirit into the world, the Apprentice possesses the purest form of it.

THE DEVELOPMENTAL TASKS OF THE WELLSPRING

To realize her visionary potential — to render it of value to her people — the Apprentice must discover practical means to embody her soul in the more-than-human world. This is her developmental task. She must develop one or more culturally viable delivery systems (this is the culture component of the task) for her soul gifts, about which she is always learning more (the nature component).

Exactly how she will embody her soul qualities depends in every way on her physical and psychological strengths and weaknesses, her constitution and disposition, her character and personality type more generally, her gender and age, and on her language, culture, epoch, and the geographic region in which she lives. No two people, even with nearly identical soul qualities, will embody their gifts in the same way. The form of embodiment partly depends on the materials, technology, and art forms that she might be able to access and utilize, and on the traditions and disciplines available to her. Which existing delivery systems she might learn from Artisans or Masters will depend, of course, on the established traditions of her people as well as on the exotic arts she might encounter during her travels or studies.

Nature and culture, as always in human life, are in a push-pull relationship within the Apprentice, her stage, and her task. For the Apprentice, this is a continual dance between form and essence. Nature says she must be faithful to essence, to that spark of cosmic mystery she was born to manifest. Culture says she must be loyal to form, to the practices and traditions by which the people recognize and shape value and meaning.

She must practice a type of double vision. If she focuses excessively on established form, she might get lost in the minutia of her delivery system, trying to get it just right or even to perfect it. She might succumb to the customs or critiques of "professionals" or "established artists" in her field who insist that only they know the authentic way. This is especially likely if — no, when! — she begins to lose touch with her original motivating vision. In such moments, to which we are all susceptible, she might abandon her soul's intent in favor of an impressive or "correct" appearance. Or she might become overly enamored of the allure of technique, method, famous or charismatic personalities in her art or craft, or possibly her own developing fame or wealth. If form comes to mean too much to her, she'll become an empty shell. She must never wander far from the Wellspring, the place where the soul waters emerge from below.

On the other hand, if she places too much emphasis on essence or purity, she'll fail to craft a form effective for delivery of the gift. The Mystery will remain just that, never to become part of this world in a functional way. She might fear becoming too much of this world, of tainting the Mystery, and consequently herself, by translating it into worldly form. She might also succumb to the understandable fear, even terror, of the responsibility inherent in carrying what is hidden as a gift to others. She could find herself overwhelmed by the immensity or burden of the task. She might be so doubtful of her capacity to do it well — or at all — that she finds herself paralyzed and unable to begin.

And yet the nature and culture tasks of the Wellspring serve one another. By always keeping her inner eye on essence, her chosen cultural forms can deliver her true gift. Conversely, endowed with the knowledge and techniques of previous generations of innovators, she is enabled to hone her craft so that the merely possible becomes more fully and effectively grounded in this world for her people.

The key then is to live with one foot each in nature and culture. The Soul Apprentice must, as Angeles Arrien puts it, walk a mystical path with practical feet. She must remain mindful of what she's delivering (nature) as she acquires and hones her craft for delivering it (culture). Her mission, after all, is sacred — marrying essence and form, mystery and matter.

The Apprentice's developmental task can be divided into four subtasks:

- identifying one or more cultural settings for her soulwork
- developing the skills of her soulwork (acquiring a delivery system) and performing that work in her community
- further explorations of her soul image or story and of the nature of her soul powers
- the soul-rooted individuation of the personality (differentiating the self in relation to soul, as opposed to the earlier differentiation in relation to society)

These subtasks are generally performed concurrently.

Identifying One or More Cultural Settings for Soulwork

The soul doesn't say, "Be a writer or an artist" or "Become a physician" or "Go into politics or business." It certainly doesn't declare, "Make lots of money." We might imagine a memo from the soul to the ego: "You were born with a certain image or story line, one that you've begun to uncover, and you possess certain soul powers (core abilities, knowledge, and values).. These are your gifts to bring to the world and your tools for embodying them. Now you must determine which settings and roles, among those available to you in your time and place and culture, will allow you to carry these gifts to your people. You might even have to invent a new role. My primary task has been and remains to help you discover your ultimate place and your true gifts. Your task is to embody them."

Soulwork, in other words, does not correspond to a job title. There's no requirement that you have a job at all, or if you do, that it be the best place to embody your soul. And if you have a conventional job within Western society, there's not much chance your job description makes any reference to your soul qualities. Think of your job as merely a setting for soul embodiment. Two people might have the same job and embody very different soul qualities. Perhaps they are both psychotherapists, but one has the soul task of recovering buried treasure, while the other's is to celebrate inner gardens or to help people open their hearts like blossoming flowers.

The Apprentice will not identify an appropriate cultural setting for her soulwork by consulting a vocational guidance counselor or searching the want ads. She might take a job to keep herself and her family fed, but she won't confuse a job with her real work. She knows she can perform her soulwork, to some extent, at *any* job, because her true work is as much about her way of being as it is about her way of doing.

Initiated adults desire to perform their soulwork as often and in as many settings as possible. For example, a woman whose soul gift is to evoke people's enchantment in the natural world might do so during chance encounters with children in her neighborhood or with people in the park, even though she might make her living as an accountant. A man whose soulwork is to embody innocence and the loving qualities of spirit will hope to radiate this gift whether at work or at play, with family or with friends. A woman whose gift is to inspire wonder, and who does so primarily through her paintings, might make her living as a shop manager. Most Apprentices, at least early in the Wellspring, do not get paid for their soulwork.

Recall the distinction between the sacred dance and the survival dance discussed in the previous chapter. The latter is what you do to make a living. The former is your way of offering your life to the world. With years of effort and good fortune, your survival work and soulwork become one and the same, as they did for Robert Frost:

> ... But yield who will to their separation,
> My object in living is to unite

My avocation and my vocation
As my two eyes make one in sight.
Only where love and need are one,
And the work is play for mortal stakes,
Is the deed ever really done
For Heaven and the future's sakes.[12]

The Soul Apprentice seeks arenas within which to offer his soul gifts. Sometimes he finds clues and openings in the most unlikely places, even when he isn't looking. He takes leaps even when doing so terrifies him. He chooses projects, training, jobs, and life paths that resonate with his soul's desires. Intuition is an essential ingredient in his choices. He lets go of expectations and preconceived notions, and he opens to unexpected opportunities. Sometimes he receives suggestions from an elder. Signs or omens might appear.

At any given point in the Wellspring, he might ask himself, "Of the opportunities currently presenting themselves, which path would offer the right amount of challenge (great enough but not too great)? Which choice would test me in the right ways? What decision would my soul suggest?" Rather than relying on his strategic (conscious) mind to figure out answers, he will instead clear an inner space into which imaginative answers might fall.

In 1969, after living in Asia and Africa for several years, Joanna Macy and her family returned to the United States and settled in Washington, D.C. It was the time of the Vietnam War, and Joanna became active in the antiwar movement. My impression is that Joanna had recently gone through the passage of Soul Initiation. Now she was seeking cultural settings in which to embody what she had learned during her soul encounters. She began by taking a part-time job with a civil rights organization and became a speechwriter for a Black politician. She writes, "The civil rights work and these anti-war actions helped me take even more seriously than before the mystical openings I had experienced."[13] Meanwhile, she actively lived the question of how she might embody the intention of being a stone in the bridge spanning the Buddha Dharma and the modern West: "I still wanted to do graduate studies in world religions, with a focus on Buddhist philosophy. Maybe I could find a way to translate the Buddha's understanding of self — or non-self — into a Western mode, to help my countrypeople come home to each other and play their part in building a world not based on fear."[14]

Consequently, at age forty, Joanna began graduate school. Her evolving ideas about a delivery system broadened as a result of her active, ongoing conversation between self, soul, and society: "I assumed that [my vision] was a bridge between East and West and that to serve as one stone in it, I should become a scholar of Asian religions, particularly the Buddha Dharma. But then the civil rights and anti-war movements made me look afresh at my own society, with questions that extended beyond interpretations of ancient scriptures."[15]

In her graduate studies, she uncovered some axial patterns in the work of progressive Western poets and thinkers,[16] one of which was "a loss of belief in that pillar of Western thought: the autonomy of the individual self. . . . How delusory was the separate, Cartesian ego, and how imprisoning its pretensions. So I began to see my own response to the Buddha Dharma as part of a larger paradigmatic shift in the West, as an urge arising within the Western mind — the urge to reconnect."[17]

Through her personal blend of visionary experience, compassionate action, work, wondering, intellectual inquiry, and a great desire to be of service, Joanna gradually focused on a cultural setting for her soulwork. She would become a scholar both of Buddhism and of the germinal Western urge to move beyond the delusion of an unembedded self and to reconnect with the world and a greater identity.

Soon afterward, Joanna came across a Buddhist scripture that became the conceptual hub of her work ever since. This is the teaching known as Prajna Paramita, or the Perfection of Wisdom, a core insight that, because of its pivotal position in Buddhism, has been personified as the Mother of all Buddhas: "Wisdom is not about bits and pieces, she [the Mother of all Buddhas] said, it's about relationship. It's about the compassion that comes when we realize our deep relatedness. In this fashion, she brought forth in new words the Buddha's central teaching: the dependent co-arising of all phenomena."[18]

This insight — that everything is what it is by virtue of its relationship with everything else (and, consequently, of its place) — became known as the Second Turning of the Wheel (of the Buddha Dharma). Likewise, in the evolution of Joanna's soulwork, her discovery of Prajna Paramita was the second turning of the wheel that she first saw as a vision at her son's birth, some fifteen years earlier. This second turning was a key event in her identification of an early delivery system for soulwork, namely, a scholarly exploration of the fruitful resonance between Buddhist thought and contemporary Western science.

Acquiring a Delivery System for Performing Soulwork

Through his early explorations in the Wellspring, the Soul Apprentice settles on a cultural setting (or two) in which he can embody his soul's desires, a delivery system that fits his capabilities and sensibilities. Next he needs to acquire the relevant skills by apprenticing in a specific discipline. He might find or meet an accomplished craftsman who embodies a similar soul quality, someone who can teach him a suitable form.

This is the second subtask of the Wellspring: developing the skills that enable the Apprentice to perform his soulwork in his community. He will apprentice himself either to a person (an Artisan or Master, or several) or in a discipline — a craft, trade, science, profession, or art. In the contemporary world, in addition to or instead of a face-to-face apprenticeship, he might create a self-structured course of study, increasingly possible with advances in communication technology and information sciences.[19]

In the Wellspring, the Apprentice does not simply acquire academic information or a serviceable trade. More important, she develops the knowledge and skills that enable her to perform a type of magic, to make manifest in beneficial forms a mystery retrieved from the underworld. Soul apprenticeships are not to be confused with stage-3 training in business, academics, or craft. What makes an experience a soul apprenticeship is that it's an ongoing conversation between vision and work, between essence and form.

Furthermore, the soul apprenticeship is decidedly not about learning a craft that will be utilized only sometime later, after the Wellspring. As an initiated adult, the Soul Apprentice's first responsibility and opportunity is to serve the more-than-human world through her soulwork. She learns by doing, and her failures are as valuable as her successes, because she learns from both.

As we've seen, Joanna Macy acquired her first delivery systems for soulwork in part through her study and practice of Buddhism, civil rights, and antiwar activism. But in the fall of 1974, she stumbled upon another essential strand: general systems theory, a then-emerging field of Western science that describes patterns of energy, matter, and information that give rise to everything from cells to galaxies.

For her dissertation, she explored the mutual resonances between general systems theory and Prajna Paramita, thereby serving as a stone in the bridge between the modern West and the ancient East. Her scholarship became a means for her to both acquire a delivery system and implement it (for example, through a book she wrote and several experiential programs she created).

Meanwhile, Joanna was also engaged in her personal practice of Buddhism, including meditation and the cultivation of compassion, under the guidance of Buddhist teachers in both America and India. The spiritual discoveries from this practice were as significant to the development of her soulwork as the intellectual discoveries from her scholarship.

Another aspect of Joanna's soulwork has been environmental activism, especially concerning the nuclear power and weapons industries. She has assisted citizen's legal interventions against nuclear polluters, participated in nonviolent occupations of reactor sites, and chaired conferences on environmental dangers and responses. Her dedication to this work came out of her deepening grief in the 1970s as she learned how industrial growth society was rapidly devastating the living systems of Earth.

In our times, most everyone in the Wellspring is becoming increasingly concerned about the environment. As our center of gravity turns to the embodiment of soul (our ultimate place in the world), we naturally grow more aware of the very world that evokes our soulful passions. In such an egocentric era as ours, Soul Apprentices can expect intense waves of emotion — sadness, anger, fear, guilt, despair — arising from the awareness of what we humans are collectively turning loose on our planet.

As of this writing, Joanna has been a leading activist for over thirty years in movements for peace, justice, and a safe environment. We might wonder what allows for such sustained engagement. My belief is that the most effective activism is both motivated and sustained by being consciously connected to the individual's deepest purpose, her soul story or image, as has been true for Joanna.

Further Explorations of Soul Image or Story and of the Nature of Soul Powers

The Apprentice deepens her ongoing experiential exploration of soul. She understands that Soul Initiation is only that — an initiation, a beginning, one that places her on a path. She must further clarify and differentiate her vision. She begins adulthood with little more than an image or a story and lots of inspiration and passion. The variety of tools available to her for ongoing soul exploration — those that I call "soulcraft practices" — are those she learned and used as a Wanderer in the Cocoon.

Soul exploration is a labyrinthine journey of many turns, occasional dead ends, startling discoveries, and challenging episodes. Sometimes, for example, soul first appears in disguise, as shadow, illness, or setback. If more benign efforts fail to get our attention, soul might try something more drastic. What at first feels to the Apprentice like a misfortune might turn out to be just the ego shake-up she needed to enable a deeper entry into the mysteries of nature and psyche. As she opens to the promptings and urges from the depths, she uncovers additional themes and motifs of her soul story. She is on a risky and compelling adventure of self-discovery, often arriving in places she would never have suspected or chosen.

One of her most fruitful avenues of exploration is her sacred wound, always a guide to soul. In the Cocoon, she made her first expeditions into the underworld terrain of her wound. Now, by probing deeper, she discovers additional seeds of destiny.

More generally, much of what is learned about soul at the Wellspring derives from the Apprentice's ongoing conversation with the world, the back-and-forth between the Apprentice's performance of her soulwork (the second subtask) and the way the world responds, whether with interest, indifference, support, obstacles, success, or failure.

Although soul encounters can and do occur in any of the eight stages, their greatest concentration is in those two shadowy stages that form the West quadrant, the Cocoon and Wellspring. Before the Cocoon, the immature ego is mostly unprepared to open to the numinous. After the Wellspring, the initiated ego focuses more on leadership (the Wild Orchard and Grove) and on spirit (the Mountain Cave) than on further soul discovery.

Joanna Macy's soul encounters continued during her Wellspring years. In 1974, for example, she asked for and received a blessing from a Tibetan Buddhist sage, His Holiness Karmapa. While the Karmapa held her head in his hands, she felt an electric charge shoot through her. "That's all — except that I barely slept for the next three weeks." Instead, she sat awake as words and images and thoughts resounded in her psyche, "a torrent of revelation.... Two visual themes predominated. One was the tree, with its branching limbs and roots. The other was the neuron in the neural net, with its intricate dendrites and synaptic connections. In their continual self-transformations there wasn't one stable point, nothing to hang on to, but I felt no fear — just wonder and a kind of exultation."[20]

It was during the time of those sleepless nights that Joanna walked into a graduate seminar and first learned about general systems theory. "Almost immediately I saw that the systems view of reality fit the patterns that I had been seeing all those wakeful nights since the Karmapa's blessing."[21] In this way, a Wellspring revelation led Joanna to a key element of her evolving soulwork delivery system.

The Soul-Rooted Individuation of the Personality

The Apprentice's fourth subtask is the more general differentiation of the personality in relation to both soul and society. This process of soul-rooted individuation was discussed earlier in this chapter. The focus of this task is broader than the form of soulwork we choose: Here we ask what lifestyle best accommodates the urgings of our souls — which friendships, community roles, philosophies, spiritual practices, creeds, dress, diet, living arrangements, climates, environments, and politics.

In her Wellspring, there were several ways Joanna Macy differentiated her life in relationship to soul, her guide being the truth of her own experience. In 1974, for example, she underwent the Buddhist refuge ceremony, in which one commits to spiritual awakening, to the Buddha's teachings, and to the spiritual community that preserves and practices those teachings. She took this step as a response to the "gladness and gratitude" she felt for Prajna Paramita, the hub of her first delivery system.

Although her marriage to Fran remained strong and grew in mutual trust, she had to admit to herself, and then to him, that she did not believe in monogamy. (It turns out neither did he.) "The social norm of sexual exclusivity," writes Joanna, "did not conform to the truth of my own experience — nor to my increasingly strong views about the limits of ownership. People cannot own each other any more than they can possess air, sun, or wind. Along with Friedrich Engels, I came to see monogamy as a patriarchal institution whose original motives had to do with economic control."[22]

In uncovering their deeper values, Joanna and Fran rejected and replaced additional aspects of the standard American lifestyle. Seeing the waste and bondage of Western consumerism and how it led to foreign wars and environmental devastation, they began to live more frugally and simply. And the nuclear family seemed to them to be unnecessarily isolated, to be wasteful due to the duplication of goods in each household, and to be burdensome to parents raising children. They created a communal home, a cooperative living arrangement for their family and four additional adults.

SCULPTED BY WIND AND RAIN

Being the second half of the Wheel's West quadrant, the Wellspring, like the Cocoon, rumbles with mysterious images and underworld encounters. Much of our psychospiritual development in this stage is catalyzed by periodic numinous encounters.

During my own Wellspring, my soulwork mostly took the form of guiding vision fasts and working as a psychotherapist. But this was not a period of uniform confidence in my life direction. There were distressing times when I doubted I was on the right path. Often it took a solo retreat in wilderness to provoke a confrontation with mystery that allowed me to see my way through the impasse. The following encounter occurred in southern Utah in the early 1990s.

I sit facing an odd-looking boulder on a red sandstone ledge, some three hundred vertical feet above the thin stream that trickles through the depths of this narrow and remote desert canyon. High above, a lone raven rides a thermal that rises off hot redrock, his guttural calls echoing in the parched amphitheater scooped from the canyon wall. The sun burns my back and draws moisture from my brow and from under my arms. The sedimentary canyon layers, color-coded in gradations of earth tones, have eroded over eons into flowing tiers of irregular benches like an ancient crumbling coliseum. The bird glides back and forth through flawless fields of red and blue, as if sewing earth to sky. In the moment, it seems odd to me that his undulating shadow moves upon the red but is imperceptible against the blue. Then he soars close to me and the soughing pulse of his wings sounds like an earnest act of resuscitation, quick labored exhalations, as if someone is trying to blow wind into me.

I am afraid I have utterly failed with my life.

The boulder is what lured me here. It's about the size of a short, chunky human, a rounded lump of sandstone shaped like a twisted and dented cauldron and perched lonesomely up near the back wall of this canyon pocket that otherwise holds only occasional scatterings of stone, a few courageous desert flowers, and here and there a small spare juniper or piñon. This particular rock is mostly white, splashed with swirls of red, buff, gray, and lavender. It squats comically on the bare bedrock, reminding me of how a dog or coyote sometimes sits, tilted onto one haunch, tongue dangling, eyes wide and bemused.

I am drawn by the boulder's curious ugliness. It has stubbles and pimples on its eroded head. Its jaw is crooked, misshapen. It gazes at me cockeyed.

I introduce myself. Out loud. I start with the name I received at the time of my first vision fast, a dozen years earlier, and then progress through my given name and the various nicknames my parents and friends have assigned me at one moment or another, ending with the name I now use every day. Then, for good measure, I throw in the Hebrew name I was given at birth (never used) and also what my lover calls me when she's happy with me (not used enough). I skip over what she calls me at other times. I tell the boulder what I know to be the significance of, and the connotations of, and the personas that go with, each name. And because the rock hasn't answered yet, I say that what I seek today is to learn more about my true place in this world.

Looking up, I spot Raven, who cocks a glossy black wing, a suspicious dark eye, a smirky beak in my direction.

"So, Rock," I sigh and continue, "when I first saw you, I found you, quite frankly, to be . . . well . . . ugly. In this place, you know, you really *stand out* in your ugliness. There are no other rocks quite like you. You seem, in fact, to be somewhat of a misfit."

I pause, something clutching at my heart and bringing tears. "Well . . . I guess that's how I've been feeling about *myself* — somewhat of a misfit."

I sit with the rock, gazing at him. I notice some features I had previously missed. He has something like jewels on his top, like he's wearing a crown.

How can it be that I've sat with this rock for over an hour and I'm just now beginning to really see it? Embedded in his upper surfaces are iridescent bits of minerals, some — perhaps mica — flashing tiny rainbows, others affording splashes of turquoise or jade. Circling his head are several erosional protuberances that look like the turrets of a castle.

"As a matter of fact," he says suddenly, startling me, "I am Little Rock King."

Apparently, he's going to talk to me after all.

I risk telling him more about myself and why I've wandered up here. I try to explain how death — my unremitting awareness of mortality — has defined much of my life, has been a teacher to me . . . and a tormenter. Constant questions about death have been with me, since early childhood.

"The truth is I'm afraid of dying without making any difference in the world — a difference, that is, that *makes* a difference. I'm afraid of failure, of big mistakes, of wasting my life as a psychologist or a wilderness guide when maybe I ought to be an environmental activist...or a monk...or who knows what. I'm afraid of not being enough. And I'm afraid of my anger, my intolerance and impatience, and my fear of really going for it.

"Sometimes I'm afraid I'm just going to get old and erode, get ugly like I thought *you* were at first. Why strive so hard to be of service when we're all going to end up soon enough as ash and dust?"

I take a deep breath and try to calm myself down. I'm surprised by the intensity of emotion.

I pause, peering at Little Rock King, searching for a clue. Raven calls, *cor-ac cor-ac*, as he slips behind a sandstone ridge near the Sun. I feel a familiar hollowness in my belly, a flash of heat in my face, a sudden dizziness.

After a while, Little Rock King speaks, again surprising me, "I'll tell you this. I take the form that I do as a gift of wind and rain. I'm not afraid of erosion, although it means death for me. Indeed, I seek it. In fact, if you'd be so kind as to pour some water on me, it might help me erode today."

I look at my half-filled bottle, feel the heat and dryness of the day, wonder how far away in space and time I might be from more water. I wonder why I'm sitting here talking to a rock. I reach for the bottle, pull up the spout, and squeeze out a couple of meager streams, flicking them in his general direction.

"Come on," says Little Rock King, shouting at me now, "like you really mean it!"

I get up, walk the few feet over to Little Rock King, respectfully now, and slowly pour out the entire contents of my bottle, all of it, on his top, on his sides, and especially beneath him — around his legs — where erosion can do its greatest work, perhaps toppling him one day. I imagine him tumbling crazily down over the hard bare slope, joyously exploding into a thousand fragments, gleefully surrendering in the midst of the last spectacular gesture of his life, dust billowing everywhere, scattering himself over reef, sand, yucca, and prickly pear cactus, coming to rest against juniper trunks, sagebrush, chamisa, leaving various hues of himself smudged on the bedrock and caked in windrows like miniature moraines.

This image of ecstatic surrender revives me. Suddenly my whole being has shown up. I have arrived at last, coming into a more conscious relationship with this place and this time and this rock. My head clears.

The water has deepened the boulder's stunning colors and made his jeweled crown shine all the more brilliantly. His elegance and magnificence now take my breath away.

"Yes," Little Rock King affirms, as if reading my thoughts, "erosion has uncovered whatever uniqueness and beauty I have. For me, erosion is not a failure. This journey through life, toward death, sculpts me into greater individuality. My ultimate goal, though, is to blend in fully with my world. The more I erode, the more completely I take my place here, continuously surrendering my current form in order to become a more integral part of the life of this canyon. Perhaps it's time for you to surrender your current form. Rather than concluding that you've been a failure or a misfit, perhaps it's time to allow the world to have its way with you and to carve you into something more essentially you.

"At this point in my existence, it's my place to be Little Rock King. It's not who I've always been or who I'll always be. The less I defend myself from the world, the more I erode and the more I become myself. So I fully surrender to erosion. I am sculpted by life, by wind and rain. I rejoice in being shaped by the world of which I am part. I collaborate with death, and you have helped me today with the gift of your water. Perhaps you'll find your own way to surrender to erosion."

I sit on the hot surface of a petrified sand dune, slack-mouthed, gazing at an oddly shaped rock, sweat and tears in my eyes. Little Rock King's words resonate deeply with something essential, something I had learned many years before: at my core I am not a psychologist or a wilderness guide, although those settings are appropriate for my work. Nor is my life defined by the possibility of becoming a monk, an activist, or anything else. These are all passing forms. Rather, I am here, like everyone, to bring a certain promise into the world, to perform a certain soul task. By surrendering to erosion, I allow that promise to be embodied most effectively. Erosion, truly, is no failure.

Raven soars by again, quite close, his head tucked beneath his wing, flashing a wink. Crossing to the other side of the canyon, he disappears.

Since my time with Little Rock King, I have come to see that, as a human, I am like him in some ways, and I am different as well. Our similarities arise from the fact that the journey through life holds the promise of a developing uniqueness and a contribution of self to community and place, being sculpted by life as we are exposed to the powers of the world, to the forces of love and death, like the erosion of sandstone by wind and rain. Then, toward the end — and yet through the same process of erosion — something of our essence rejoins our original home. I have come to understand life as a journey from spirit, through the realms of soul, to an eventual return to spirit.

Yet we humans — with our psyches split between conscious and unconscious elements — are different from Little Rock King in at least one respect: if we are going to be shaped beautifully by the world of which we are a part, we need to do more than simply surrender to erosion. Unlike Rock, we must also actively and consciously participate in that shaping. We must undertake a complex and demanding journey of individuation. We will not find or take our true places in the world without effort, without occasional ordeal and sacrifice, without failure. Only through such effort will we embody the life of our souls and reveal the shining form beneath, a form both unique and beautiful.

CIRCLE OF IDENTITY AND SENSE OF COMMUNITY:
FROM WORLDCENTRIC TO ECOCENTRIC

In the previous stage, the Cocoon, the individual's circle of identity became world-centric: "mine" or "ours" came to encompass human strangers and people from other ethnic groups. The Wanderer learned to consider the impact of his and others' decisions on humanity as a whole, and not merely on those presently alive but also on the future seven generations.

Now, at the Wellspring, the Soul Apprentice's circle of identity matures further and becomes *ecocentric*. His discernment and appreciation of community comes to embrace more than his family, more than the members of his clan or religion or nation, and even more than the human species. He begins to instinctively identify with all species and landscapes, all animals, plants, and ecologies. He acts empathically with the entire web of terrestrial life.

The ecocentric self, what deep ecologist Arne Naess calls "the ecological Self," is a hallmark of an initiated adult: "If reality is experienced by the ecological Self, our behavior naturally and beautifully follows norms of strict environmental ethics.... We must find and develop therapies which heal our relations with the widest community, that of all living beings."[23]

Ecocentrism develops as a matter of course during the Wellspring precisely because the Apprentice is now learning to embody soul. In that the human soul is inseparable from nature, the soul-rooted adult increasingly experiences himself as a full member of the natural world. He experiences his existence as an expression, first and foremost, of Earth and secondarily as an expression of his culture. He re-members himself in his original fidelity to Earth. He recomposes his life in that light. As an imperfect human, of course, he will have misunderstandings and blind spots concerning what that fidelity entails, but as he continues to mature, his ecocentrism will evolve.

Another way to understand why ecocentrism appears in the Wellspring is that the Soul Apprentice has recently made a promise it will kill him to break — a commitment to serve the Mystery in the Apprentice's unique way, a service that nurtures all of life. The Apprentice's commitment, therefore, is premised on his interdependence with all beings.

In addition to developing the ability to "*think* like a mountain" — ecologist Aldo Leopold's celebrated phrase[24] — the Apprentice comes to *act* from an ecocentric perspective, every day and instinctively. He values the needs of the terrestrial web more highly than those of any single species within it (including humanity). But he understands that humanity's real needs are never in conflict with those of the web, because anything that harms the planet-as-a-whole harms humanity, spiritually as well as physically. Beyond mere intellectual understanding, the Apprentice begins to live from his awareness that the planetary ecosystem is humanity's home — that Earth provides our food, shelter, companions, healing, beauty, and fulfillment. Earth is literally where we stand, the limb on which we perch.

An ecocentric person does not merely ask whether another species' needs are more important than humanity's. (To do so is ecological altruism.) For the Apprentice, acting on behalf of another species is not necessarily an ecologically altruistic act. It is something even more mature. His efforts on behalf of that other species demonstrate self-love as much as love for humanity because his circle of identity embraces the entire web of life.

For example, a person with an ecocentric self doesn't necessarily consider the needs of wolves to be more important than the needs of the local human village or ranchers. Rather, he has the ability not only to empathize with the wolves but also to conclude that the ecosystem that he shares with them might be better served by giving the immediate needs of the wolves a higher priority than his own, the village's, or the ranchers' (even if he's one of the latter). For the Soul Apprentice, standing in support of the wolves would be standing in support of his ecosystem, the more-than-human community. At other times, from the same ecocentric perspective, the Apprentice might conclude that his family's needs or the needs of the village take priority because this serves the ecosystem best. For the ecocentric person, this would not be a selfish conclusion.

We live in and as part of an immensely complex web that has evolved over many millions of years, and every member of this web has its essential place and gift.

Joanna Macy and Molly Brown note that all ecocentric people, at this time of environmental devastation, feel a great distress on behalf of the larger whole that we are each a part of. "It is the pain of the world itself, experienced in each of us."[25] Being individual cells in the living body of Earth, every person feels the pain of the planet, although many do not understand the source of their melancholy. "That pain is the price of consciousness in a threatened and suffering world."[26] Experiencing this distress is natural. It is an essential component of our collective healing. The purpose of pain, after all, is to warn us to take remedial action.

BOTH ROOTED AND FLOWING:
THE LIFE OF THE APPRENTICE

What does the day-to-day life of a Soul Apprentice feel like? Is it possible to generalize? How does the experience of self and world change after Soul Initiation?

A metaphor emerges. Imagine being a sea plant growing from the ocean floor. You are both rooted and flowing, solidly anchored in something immense and unfathomable — Earth itself — yet also a part of a vast liquid medium that sways and whirls. You roll and surge with deep-sea currents, neither resisting nor insisting. Submitting to the push and pull of ocean tide and current, you trust this larger being to animate you in a way that best serves your unfolding. Your roots, sunk in bottomless sands, draw up nutritive elements that energize your life. The water supports your limbs, graciously.

Likewise the more-than-human world supports the embodiment of the Apprentice's life. By virtue of her soul, she is rooted in the web of the natural world, *and knows it*. Her most significant choices flow from the urgings of her soul.

The Apprentice is aligned with forces that are like sea currents or tides. Whether or not she sees or fully understands them, she recognizes these forces as agents of her destiny. She is nudged into her soul life, and sometimes yanked. She knows that the world soul — what we more commonly call nature or the universe — has fashioned a unique place for her. She allows herself to fall into that place like rainwater into a streambed.

When the Apprentice acts in alignment with his soul qualities, he experiences synchronicities, events that appear to be coincidences but are more accurately understood as resonances between ego, soul, and world. The world responds to the Apprentice's choices of soul-aligned actions with an echo, a reverberation, confirming his understanding of his soul and supporting his choices.

Some soul-aligned actions create tipping points, big changes engendered by small events. When enough water collects behind a dam formed by a glacial moraine, the dam is breached and the entire lake bursts through. That last drop of water is what triggers the rupture. When the right kind of seed crystal is added to a supersaturated solution, a mineral instantly solidifies. Soul-resonant choices are sometimes like inserting the last piece in a puzzle, enabling the whole to take form and become evident.

On my first vision fast, in 1980, I learned that my soulwork was to weave cocoons — ceremonial spaces where old forms die and new ones are birthed. I began my apprenticeship to this calling by studying with several teachers — Roger Strachan, Steven Foster, Meredith Little, Dolores LaChapelle, and Elizabeth Cogburn, among others — and by offering wilderness-based rites for people in my community. Although I seldom spoke of it, the image of the cocoon was central to my life and was the seed image around which I designed the programs I guided. The world seemed to support my efforts. Word spread and people came. I had the good fortune to find extraordinary wilderness sites for my programs in the Southwest deserts and mountains. And despite my fumbling efforts as a guide, people returned from the wild with astonishing reports of life-changing encounters with the mysteries of nature and psyche. Moreover, in guiding these rites, I experienced the greatest fulfillment I had ever known, a sense of fully being in the right place.

In what felt like further confirmation, the world reflected back to me in startling ways the symbol of the cocoon, as if my life had become part of a fabric woven with that theme. For example, on that first vision fast, I invented an odd backcountry shelter, both a floor and roof fashioned from a single tarp, thirty feet of cord, three small metal rings, and the assistance of three small trees alongside my tarp. I ran cord from a grommet at the corner of the tarp, through a ring tied to a tree trunk, then back to another grommet, and so on. In this way I was able to sleep under the stars and, when rain came, simply pull the cord and tie a knot to set the roof in place. Weeks later, while glancing through a book on camping gear and methods, I found a diagram of a nearly identical structure. The author labeled it "the cocoon."

The cocoon image showed up in other, considerably more challenging ways. A few years after my first vision fast, I was on a backcountry ski tour with two friends. We got caught in an avalanche. Phil was buried and did not survive. For many weeks, I was tormented by survivor guilt, hounded by the feeling that there was something more I could have done to find Phil before it was too late.

Seeking help, I went to see a spiritual counselor in a distant city, a woman of unusual insight and compassion. Morgan Farley and I had never before met, and she knew nothing about me other than the fact of Phil's death. And yet she told me that, beneath the surface of consciousness, Phil and I had had an agreement that I would assist him in his death. I would not have believed something like that — it would have seemed too predictable an attempt to console me — if it weren't for the way Morgan expressed it. She said our specific agreement was that I "would help him weave a cocoon for his transition out of this life." She said the snow was his cocoon.

Her assertion was all the more poignant in light of what had happened only minutes before the avalanche. Phil and I were standing together in silence, shoulder to shoulder, on the summit, well above timberline, taking in the vast expanse of mountains, snow, and sky. Although no words were spoken between us, I know that he, like me, was overcome in that moment with the beauty of the world, the miracle of life, and the spiritual bond that connected us to each other and both of us to the world. Just before we left the summit, Phil and I turned to face one another, looking deeply into each other's eyes, and a silent but profound understanding passed between us, something so intimate and powerful that it staggered me. We had never before shared a moment anything like that. There were no words then or now to adequately describe it, but I felt both bewildered and blessed.

Before I could respond to Morgan's statement, she also declared that my work in this lifetime was, in fact, to help others weave cocoons to facilitate their major life transitions. Most of these transitions would be from one stage of life to the next, she said, but sometimes they would be from this life to what lies beyond.

Synchronicities and resonances such as these are confirmations that the Apprentice is on the right path. Although sometimes unwelcome, they are always experienced as grace — divine love and guidance freely bestowed.

While some events confirm the Apprentice's soul-rooted way of belonging to life, others remind him that the world will no longer support him in his old way despite his attempts to the contrary. A few months after enacting his vision fast, an organizational consultant wrote to me about his new life direction:

> Before I committed myself to this new mission and vision of my work, my business was on the way to having the best financial year in the eleven of its existence. As soon as I made a commitment to the new direction, business opportunities dried up. Clients had to cancel scheduled assignments because of budget cuts. Prospective assignments that, before, I would easily secure were awarded to competitors. Gradually, I realized that those assignments were congruent with my previous focus but not with my new mission.

Faith is an essential companion for the Apprentice and an indispensable facilitator of his life path. In order to embody his vision, to make it real, he must have the faith to live it. This is especially difficult at first, when the vision seems so mysterious and cryptic. No one can help the Apprentice until he has journeyed quite a way down the road on his own. It's only by walking that his path becomes clearer. The way the world responds will either confirm or disconfirm (and redirect) his initial understanding of his soul image or story.

After Soul Initiation, an *interactive field* exists between the ego, the soul, and the world, a field that deepens the Apprentice's understanding of his soul qualities. The Apprentice progresses on his path not through mere contemplation of his vision but by means of the conversation he enters with the world through his actions.

The soul asks the initiated adult to put his faith in something immaterial and yet bigger than his everyday self. The organizational consultant quoted earlier wrote:

> As difficult as circumstances are right now, I also sense that I am where I need to be. The learning opportunities abound.... The material struggle has made me aware of how ingrained in me are the norms of the culture in which we live. This has prompted me to question how I define success, how I define myself. I have a deeper experience of the interconnectedness that underlies all creation.... Each day is a new learning experience. I am afraid and excited at the same time. The old is dying and the new has not yet fully revealed itself. I am in a time of outer and inner chaos.... I know I must trust the process and remain in it. To try to escape the present circumstances would be to deny my call and thereby deny who I am.

Despite the inevitable trials and fatigue, the Apprentice must continue acting on his vision. In doing so, he changes the world and he changes himself.

After Soul Initiation, gratitude flows into and through the Apprentice's life in a new manner and a greater measure. He is boundlessly grateful for the conscious relationship he now has with soul, with the Mystery more generally, and with the web of life.

He embraces the vision granted him as a blessing to both himself and his community. His gratitude motivates him to offer his gift at every opportunity, no matter how tired he gets and no matter how unappreciated he might feel. Gratitude becomes a wellspring flowing out of him in passion, creativity, and engaged action, each day his heart opening more to the world in both grief and joy.[27]

The Apprentice's gratitude moves him to give his life to the world through his soul-work even when social, political, and/or environmental circumstances are unbearably difficult. At such times, he is especially likely to learn more about his gift and his way of delivering it. When the world is dismal, when most politicians seem clueless, when people are killing their neighbors, when nations are waging wars of aggression in foreign lands, and when the environment that sustains us is being ravaged, the Apprentice prays that he be enabled to shine his life like a light.[28] This is his way of loving the world and, in the twenty-first century, his way of participating in the Great Turning.

The Apprentice also learns to love more deeply in his individual relationships. After Soul Initiation, he is capable of greater intimacy because he knows *himself* at a deeper level, and he can bring more of his wholeness and authenticity to his relationships. There is more of him available to *be* in relationship. Discovering his particular way of belonging to the world allows him to be in fuller and more satisfying relationships with everything else *in* the world. But his discovery of soul provides only an opportunity. It is up to him to follow through.

The Apprentice also has the opportunity to deepen his experience of romance. With practice, he might become better at owning his projections of shadow and of his anima or animus. He's better able to surrender to the inevitable dismemberment of romance. He seeks to be stretched and shape-shifted by bumping up against the ways he unnecessarily defends himself from loving and being loved, his Loyal Soldier still stubbornly trying to protect him from what it imagines to be complete annihilation. The apprentice to soul is also an apprentice to love.

He also discovers that his relationship to the wild world of nature mirrors his romantic relationships, and, even more, that nature becomes the context within which he experiences his loving. His longing for his lover resonates with his love of nature. Perhaps they become indistinguishable.

STRANDS OF A PERSONAL SOUL STORY:
A WEB OF NUMINA

It often feels like our soul is in hiding, but in fact it's beckoning wildly to us in our relationship to nature and in the nature of our relationships. To become better acquainted with soul, we must track its enigmatic signs. The signs are everywhere, but it takes practice to spot them. Uncovering them is part of the third subtask of the Well-spring. The more we follow the signs, the better we understand our soul image or story and the nature of our soul powers.

Composing a soulful life requires an appreciation of story — of plot, character, symbol, relationship, conversation, and meaning. Our destiny, after all, is a story to be lived into the world. As Soul Apprentices, we gather together our most extraordinary experiences until they assume the shape of a unified story whose central theme is our unique way of belonging to the world. As I have suggested, many of the principal strands of our soul story are likely to arrive in the Cocoon and Wellspring.

A person's soul story braids together many diverse elements of life, but not just any elements. The threads of a soul story are, as a rule, numinous — supernatural, mysterious, filled with the presence of the holy or sacred. Numinous experiences grip or exalt, as if by a spell. They evoke the deepest emotional responses as though a window had suddenly opened to the otherworld, a veil lifted. They are often marked by synchronicities, encounters that reveal or confirm a resonance between symbol, myth, dream, or vision, on the one hand, and our embodied life or destiny, on the other, between current experience and that of long ago or not-yet-lived. A soul story gathers numina and synchronicities from both waking and sleeping, from ordinary ego states and the most altered, from recent days and earliest childhood, and weaves them into a luminous fabric.

Ultimately, a soul story connects the fabric of one's own life with the greater tapestry of the world or universe. As illustration, I offer a few strands of my own soul story and the shape of the web that holds them together:

After a long day's hike into the arid rock desert of southern Utah, my companion and I reached the bottom of Labyrinth Canyon[29] and took off our heavy packs. The early evening sky was clear, and so we set out our sleeping bags beneath the sky in a parched meadow of sagebrush, barrel cactus, and bunchgrass growing up through the sandy and encrusted red soil.

The meadow had been cleared many years earlier by a Mormon rancher, a brave and stubborn man who had managed somehow to push a wagon route down into this remote and rugged slickrock canyon, where vertical walls rise a thousand feet above the valley floor. There was little evidence left of his efforts to eke out a living here one hundred years ago, except for the remains of an ancient one-room log cabin in the middle of the meadow.

The evening wind whistled through the cabin's doorless entry, down the stone chimney, and out the unglazed windows. Shaggy remnants of the mud-and-thatch roof hung in random sheets from the remaining beams and rafters above the small living space. A few yards from the cabin, on the far side of our unfurled sleeping bags, hunched the desiccated skeleton of the rancher's buckboard, only three wheels remaining.

Behind the cabin, an old barbed-wire fence strung on unmilled juniper posts ran off to the east toward a low sandstone reef of barren red-and-brown rock. The reef gradually grew in height as it ran south and then east, joining with the main eastern wall of the canyon that now blazed crimson red and lavender in the roasting hues of sunset. A gust spit brick-red sand at the scarlet blooms of the barrel cacti, unable to dull their glow. In front of the cabin, the leaves rustled on the large, lone cottonwood standing on the high, sheer bank above the arroyo. Down below, the creek ran full, and from a hundred yards upstream to the south came the soft roar of the falls that tumbled through this desert oasis. Tamarisk and willows choked the green world below us as we searched with our eyes for a plausible route to cross the creek in the morning.

Although this was my first visit to this canyon, it felt as much like home as any place I'd ever been, as if I belonged here, as if I had a history here or a destiny, or both.

It was May 1981. We were here on a reconnaissance, seeking a location suitable for fasting rites. We sought a lonely and magical arena, a place where people could get lost from the world and yet find their way back to camp after three or four days of crying and dying and giving birth to themselves. It would have to be a remote spot rarely traveled by other humans. It would have to have water despite the lack of rainfall. It would have to be accessible to men and women not necessarily in the best physical shape — or used to carrying their homes on their back. Yet most important were the elements of mystery and wildness. The chosen location would have to evoke both light and shadow, and offer a doorway to an underworld in which seekers could learn to writhe out of skins grown too tight.

In the morning, we hiked up a dry wash that joined the main canyon on its east side. This long and narrow defile intrigued us, its multicolored walls carved sinuously in sloping sandstone strata. Around a bend, a lone and twisted juniper grew from red bedrock on a broad and barren terrace. One bare and weathered limb seemed to point farther up the canyon like the gnarled arm of Death. Inexplicably, I felt I was being summoned by a horror or a holiness — I didn't know which — that I would have to encounter whether or not I was ready. Continuing on, we were drawn to a high, rounded amphitheater carved into the upper reaches of the canyon. Climbing to the back wall of the horizontal bowl, we turned and looked down into the canyon bottom.

We sat. The sun beat upon our backs through an azure sky. The wind stirred mightily, careening through the amphitheater like a runaway ghost train. A lone raven cackled high above. We gazed out over a convoluted maze of redrock country to the west, into the main canyon and beyond.

On the high western wall of the Main Fork, a mile or two distant, a large and striking rock formation dominated the landscape, roundly lit by the long light of morning, its profile unequivocally male and humanoid — and eerily familiar. A feeling of both doom and hope swirled up from my belly, almost toppling me. Nausea mixed with a sparkly giddiness.

The rock formation's head and neck formed one of the higher points on the distant ridge. From shoulder to crown alone, he must have towered more than two hundred vertical feet. He stared back at us, his gaunt red visage topped by close-cropped brown hair, his eyes lost deep inside elongated sockets, his long nose casting a shadow across half his face. He had an intelligent and alien look, perhaps due to his large, thin ears with their extended upper edges. His blocky chin was solidly set in a gaze of great gravity. On his broad shoulders lay grayish brown epaulets, giving him the look of a commanding officer of an unknown and inscrutable force.

But I did know him. I knew him well. This was not our first meeting.

Ten years earlier, in 1971, when I was in college in North Carolina, I was a student of extracurricular states of consciousness, as well as of the lessons of the classroom and of friendships and romances. My wide-ranging exploration of the mind included states I experienced through yoga, meditation, music, dreams, hypnosis, and a handful of psychedelic journeys.

Although not extensive, my experiences with entheogens were significant. They opened for me "the doors of perception," to use William Blake's phrase, made famous by Aldous Huxley's book of that title. After passing through those doors a few times, I found that the parochial beliefs of my youth as to what did and did not constitute reality were permanently toppled. I was enabled — required, in a sense — to hold the world more loosely, to embrace the symbolic and numinous treasures inherent but rarely appreciated in everyday affairs.

Although mind-shifting substances taught me much about being in the world — about reality and perception — they revealed nothing about my soul qualities or desires, at least nothing I was able to recognize during that period of my life. To be sure, they deepened my sense of how spirit moves in everything, provided a glimpse of ecstatic union with the divine, and tutored me in the relativity of ego states and the existence of other realities, but they did not reflect back to me my own singularity in a way that I could assimilate.[30]

There was one psychedelic experience, however, that had in fact offered me a piece of my soul story, something that at the time made no sense to me, and doubtless never would had it not been for my time in the Cocoon, which led me to wander into Labyrinth Canyon in the first place.

On that day in 1971, the catalyzing ally was mescaline, the primary psychoactive agent of the hallucinogenic peyote cactus native to Mexico and the American Southwest. Not knowing any better, my two college roommates and I spent the day within the walls of our small apartment several miles from town. One particular experience on that day stands out vividly, even now, more than thirty-five years later. For reasons unknown, my psyche — or was it the world soul? — assaulted me with the image of a colossal humanoid figure, just the head and shoulders.

At the time, it didn't feel like a mere image; I felt like I was being accosted by a revelation. This being, holy and terrifying, would not let me go. It blasted me with rumbling sound, blinding colors, and a furious exhortation that I obey its command, of which I had no comprehension. For an eternity, it seemed, I sat trembling at the feet of an unknown and immense power. I could not escape. Desperate to respond in some way, I searched through the apartment for something I could do with my hands. I found a set of multicolored sculpting clays.

I had never sculpted before that day (nor since), but I sensed, or hoped, that I could somehow appease this god if I could shape its figure with my hands, as if I might convince it that I had received its message, that I had submitted, that it would be all right to let me go. I worked the clay for hours. This helped me calm down, center myself, and eventually return, more or less intact, to my everyday world. And it turned out I fashioned a decent likeness of that mysterious being, the finished piece standing a mere four inches high, from shoulders up. It had brown hair; a red face, neck, and shoulders; and grayish brown epaulets.

For several years, that little sculpture lived on a windowsill or a bookshelf as it accompanied me through my twenties and a succession of rented apartments and homes that stretched from one side of the country to the other and back again. I suppose I thought of it as a souvenir from an anomalous experience and perhaps as a decent artistic creation. A couple friends wondered if it was Spock from the original *Star Trek* series. The truth is I didn't have a clue what it was.

Until that day in Labyrinth Canyon. The shape, colors, facial features, and expression of that rock formation were identical to my vision and the replica I created ten years prior. I doubt an accomplished sculptor could have produced a likeness more precise than my little amateur statuette. And more to the point, I felt the same overwhelming mystery and fear that took hold of me the first time — and had the same impression that some entity was calling me and demanding I do . . . something.

Since 1981, I've returned many times to Labyrinth Canyon, mostly to guide vision fasts. During the long hike to base camp, there is one spot where you can see the giant rock-being on the western skyline. I referred to him as the Rock Guardian because it seemed as if he watched over this complex of canyons and knew its secrets. I was determined to visit him one day. There had to be a reason the Guardian had appeared to me in that vision and then, years later, appeared again in this canyon, as if he had called me here.

On the vision fasts I guided in Labyrinth Canyon, we spent eight days there. During three of those days and nights, the fasters were alone in their solo spots. On one of those solo days, if there were others to watch base camp and the weather was decent, I would run up the Main Fork with the intention of visiting the Rock Guardian and perhaps discovering something of what he knew.

Finding him, however, was anything but easy, even for an accomplished orienteer with a topographic map. Despite his colossal size, the Guardian cannot be discriminated on the map from numerous other lumps and knobs that colonize that ridge. Before I could get halfway to where he stood, he'd disappear behind canyon walls, and I'd get lost and snarled in thick bottomland vegetation along the main wash or one of its many tributaries. There was simply no way to tell from the ground how best to approach him. The terrain surrounding him is an eroded labyrinth of immense complexity, with at least five secondary canyons radiating like fingers toward his province from the Main Fork. I felt like Theseus in his quest to find the Minotaur in the Cretan Labyrinth, but without a thread to unravel and follow back.

Short of hiring an aircraft, I had no recourse but to try each side canyon one at a time. It was all I could do in a full day just to reach the head of one such canyon and return to base camp by dark. Several years passed before I found the right combination of turns.

When we finally came face-to-face, I was dumbstruck by his immensity, despite years of anticipation. I stood at the feet, nay the toes, of a giant, Buddha-like being rising several hundred feet above me, a complete torso now visible beneath the head and shoulders. His feet rested in the sands of the wash and his head pierced the heavens. He presided over a court of solemn rock-ministers who towered above me in two long lines forming the walls at the head of the canyon.

For years, I had imagined myself climbing up to one of his shoulders to stand on an epaulet and shout my long-standing questions into one of his ears. Who are you? Why did you call me? What can you teach me or show me? How might I serve you? But, alas, it was evident that his precipitous lower body was unclimbable, nor was there any other realistic route by which to approach his shoulders from within his canyon.

But now, at least, I could mark the Guardian's location on my map.

Another two years passed before I found a route up the western wall of Labyrinth Canyon. The sandstone strata of these regions erode into vertical series of shallow benches separated by sheer escarpments. With patience, however, one can usually find a spot in which the wall has partially crumbled, creating a steep but negotiable slope with which to gain the next higher bench. Other times, one can find side ridges that project from the main wall like flying buttresses, affording a path to higher ground. After several dead ends, I managed to put together a circuitous and convoluted route of ramps and traverses that ultimately reached to the top, nearly a thousand vertical feet above the canyon floor. From there it was an easy, but airy, scramble south to the Guardian's shoulder.

With great excitement, I approached the Guardian's left ear in anticipation of finally unleashing my many questions. But when I reached him I no longer had questions, only wide-eyed wonder.

From his shoulder, I looked down for the first time into the canyon that he stood guarding, the one behind him, now stretched out below me to the west. I had known from my maps, of course, that there was another canyon there, one nearly as extensive and complex as the one from which I had ascended, but I had no idea that it would look like it did, no idea that *this* was what he had been guarding all along.

I stood transfixed by a canyon so remote and so difficult to access that there were no records of its exploration. The guidebooks did not make even passing reference to it. Yet this landscape was bewilderingly familiar, impossibly personal. I had seen and passed through this very terrain in a series of repeating dreams that had haunted my early childhood, from perhaps age four or five, dreams I hadn't recalled for a dozen years or more.

Spread out below me were fiendish badlands, a surrealistic valley of grotesquely eroded rock formations populated by herds of mushroom-shaped knobs and domes, an army of sandstone spires and needles, a forest of collapsing monoliths, all in earth-tone shades of reds, browns, and purples. The far western wall of this canyon was an immense slope covered with a multitude of lofty rock towers that looked like a packed stadium of hushed aliens that had just risen to their feet in awe as the ultimate moment of a sacrificial rite played out below them. Through the center of the valley curved a dry streambed of tan sand, like a tree-lined drive to nowhere, except this one was bordered not with stately conifers but with demonic stone monuments.

This was the very landscape through which I had walked — no, floated — during those enigmatic dream-visions of childhood, dreams that haunted me with an aura of terrible holiness, an atmosphere of impenetrable mystery, wild power, and death.

At the time of the dreams, I wouldn't have had words such as *mystery* or *holiness*, but these notions are now the only ones that can convey what I felt. The dreams disappeared from memory around the start of my school years, but then I began to remember them in my midteens — perhaps when my center of gravity first began to shift toward the Cocoon — at which time I began to think of this dreamscape as the Cemetery.

In the dreams, I am floating along a dusty road in a strange, hilly landscape — dry, colorful, hot, rocky — a striking contrast to the verdant New England of my childhood. This is an ancient place, and I am alone. I move like a disembodied spirit, like a soft breath of wind. On either side of the road are irregular rock walls in reds and browns, vertically streaked in places with black. They are as tall as two-story buildings, topped occasionally with stunted shrubs or vinelike growth. There are bright red flowers here and there along the roadsides. Over the top of the left-hand wall, I can see a high, steep slope covered with a mass of monoliths like huge tombstones.

There is something that feels odd and frightening about this place, particularly due to its stale, musty odor, like old books, temples, or churches. But there is also a fragrant scent of flowers. Whatever this place is, it is not part of my family's religious tradition. It feels foreign, even alien. As a teenager, the memory of this dreamscape felt Christian to me — something to do with Christ's death and transformation.

I reach a place on the road at which there is an opening, a green-wreathed archway, in the left-hand wall. I enter. Tall, blocky objects like giant tombstones and crypts loom everywhere in dense stands with a labyrinth of paths leading among them in all directions. I sense spirits hovering about. Lingering ghosts.

Now I hear a sound, an unearthly chanting, a chorus of muted voices arising from a location ahead of me. I follow, winding through alleys and passages, between burial chambers and catacomb entrances.

As I round the corner of a tall crypt, the chanting grows louder. Down a flight of stairs and to the left is a dark opening that leads into an underground vault. I'm scared. Yet it feels as if I am being summoned. I step down toward the opening. There, another short flight of stairs descends into a cool, dark room, humid compared with the blazing day outside. Entering, I smell damp stone mixed with pungent incense.

Inside, several figures are slowly moving about and gesturing methodically with their hands and heads. They are robed and hooded, and surround a stone table. Chanting solemnly in low tones, they make gestures with small objects in their hands, as if ritually signing in some ancient cryptology.

There is a body, a dead person, on the slablike table. The chanting grows louder. The hooded figures now glance my way and reveal to me the strange objects in their hands — metal instruments and wooden implements, relics of mysterious origin and use, some of them long and thin like wands, some short with rounded ends, all elaborately wrought with a variety of emblems and adorned with the characters of an exotic syllabary.

They are showing me something about death.

As I stood on the Guardian's shoulder, flooded with image, emotion, and bewilderment, I resolved to return and look for a route down into the Cemetery. It took five years and three attempts before I succeeded. On that third journey, I fasted alone in the Cemetery for four days and nights.

My encounters with the Guardian and the Cemetery illustrate several points about soul stories. The soul speaks most powerfully through emotion-laden images found in dreams, visions, nature, and meetings with remarkable beings. A soul story weaves together these numinous and synchronistic events from all stages of life and from both waking periods and sleep. Each experience sheds some light on one or more others. Often the experiences are deeply mysterious, puzzling, or terrifying, but always compelling and ultimately inspiring.

But most important, perhaps, is that we must courageously and creatively act on these experiences. We must initiate projects and embark upon journeys that are symbolically significant, like finding a way to the Guardian's ear to shout impassioned questions. In so doing, we uncover additional strands of our soul story, layers we might never have uncovered otherwise, and we discover unsuspected linkages between the strands, resonances that lend dimension and animation to the narrative. Our numinous experiences serve as signposts and emissaries along our soul path, enabling us to eventually uncover the deepest mysteries of our souls.

My discovery of the Guardian, for example, occurred while searching for a first location to conduct passage rites. Meeting the Guardian served as an early confirmation that I might be on a valid track with my life-work. My soul had left a calling card ten years earlier, a sign I did not understand at the time, but so disturbing I responded by sculpting it, in this way assuring its place in memory until something of its significance was revealed.

Discovering the Guardian also validated that Labyrinth Canyon would be a fitting environment for wilderness rites, location being a primary consideration for such undertakings. Underworld guides know that they are relatively minor players in the extraordinary events that unfold during their work. The specific location, as well as the power of the ceremonies themselves, are far more significant factors.

Then there is the Guardian's link to the landscape of my childhood dream-visions and what took place in the dream crypt. For me, this correlation was a validation that my soulwork would embrace the realities and sacred mysteries of death and dying, both the psychological and physical varieties. The monks in the crypt seemed to be welcoming me as a student of Death.[31] My path led down into cryptic underground realms, suggesting I was to serve as a bridge between the middleworld of society and the underworld of symbol and soul.

During my quest to address the Guardian and unearth his secrets, I came to understand that, like the Guardian, I was to be a defender of wildness and mystery, an emissary of shadowy secrets, a custodian of hidden pathways, a steward of the canyons, a guide of human passages.

I believe that each one of us has a unique relationship with at least one particular place on the planet, a place where we feel completely at home and in which our soul's story can unfold most fully, a place in which we can be most successful in consciously accessing soul, a place that serves as a personal doorway to the underworld — the sort of place that Labyrinth Canyon and the Cemetery are for me.

The Australian Aborigines have a similar conviction. They believe that, for each person, there is a "place on earth where he most belongs, and his essence, his deepest self, is indistinguishable from that terrain."[32] Although it is a place from which he draws great strength and inspiration, it is also a place for which he carries a profound responsibility, a responsibility to help preserve the vitality of the land.

The cultural ecologist David Abram tells us that "we are situated in the land in much the same way that characters are situated in a story... along with the other animals, the stones, the trees, and the clouds, we ourselves are characters within a huge story that is visibly unfolding all around us, participants within the vast imagination, or Dreaming, of the world."[33] This "huge story," I believe, is the world story or the universe story. Our personal soul stories reveal the particular ways we, as individual humans, belong to the greater story.

Perhaps the most important aspect of a soul story is that it attests to the fact that we are characters in a greater unfolding. The most significant events of our lives form a pattern, reveal essential themes, and carry a meaning. The complex and eloquent connection between these numinous events, when recognized, inspires us by confirming that we are participants in a larger drama linking us with everything else — the web of the world — a drama with direction and meaning.

SOUL EMBODIMENT IN AN EGOCENTRIC WORLD

Learning to embody soul through a culturally relevant delivery system takes some time even in the best of circumstances, even in a soulcentric environment. The first half of authentic adulthood, the stage of the Apprentice, overflows with challenges, adventures, false starts, and victories. It's like starting over in life with a new identity.

Living in an egocentric society, however, makes soul embodiment even more difficult. Vocational choice in contemporary America, for example, is rarely based on a true calling uncovered through encounters with the soul. It's more likely to stem from a desire to please a parent or to follow in a sibling's footsteps, or be based on aptitude tests administered by a guidance counselor, serendipity, what's fun, what religious or social leaders recommend, or the intention to get rich or at least make an adequate living.

So, when you first arrive at the Wellspring, you might already have years invested in a survival job that you chose when you were quite a bit less aware, one that might have no obvious compatibility with your soul story. Meanwhile, you probably have a household to maintain and perhaps kids to raise or elderly parents to look after.

Early in the Wellspring, these obligations seem like a distraction from your apprenticeship. At first, perhaps they are, but you must remember that you don't need the right job to do your soulwork. Every moment is an opportunity to sing your unique note, once you have discovered what that note is, and if you are in the Wellspring you have made that discovery. So, yes, it's entirely possible to perform your soulwork at your survival job — and when you're with your family.

There are other significant challenges to being an Apprentice in an egocentric society. You must learn to resist, for example, the constant exhortations and temptations to create a life of safety, conformity, or material excess. After Soul Initiation, you must remind yourself daily of the image or story that is yours to embody, and you must remain faithful in your efforts to do so. It will help immensely if you can isolate yourself as much as possible from the trivializing and soul-numbing dimensions of mainstream popular culture while you continue to do what you must to put food on the table and keep a roof over your head (if you need one).

In an egocentric world, due to its lack of soul-orientation in education, cultural practices, and spirituality, you might be uncertain how to act on your soul's desires, even after your Soul Initiation. Or if you know what to do, you might be afraid to go out on a limb. But that's what you must do. You might not feel ready for your next step without the psychological momentum of additional soul encounters, but if you are in the Wellspring, that's probably just a Loyal Soldier story you're telling yourself.

You might make it your highest priority to find an Artisan or Master with soul powers similar to yours. When you've tracked down such a person, you can apprentice to him or her and plunge into your first delivery system for your soul gifts.

A PARCHED WELLSPRING

As I've suggested, it is the Mystery (or grace) that makes the final determination as to when our center of gravity shifts from one developmental stage to the next. But in egocentric society, due to the lack of cultural support for soul-rooted individuation, many people who cross the threshold of Soul Initiation might find themselves in a somewhat parched Wellspring.

Even though the Mystery has already enabled the Apprentice to make that pivotal promise it would kill him to break, he might be a bit foggy about the image or story he's to embody or the place in the world he's to occupy. There might be few elders, social groups, or spiritual practices to support him in clarifying his soul story or exploring it further. He might know without doubt that he has a particular destiny to realize, and that great unseen forces guide his life, but he might not yet have crystallized ideas about how to proceed. He hears the call and feels the tug of soul and is doing his best without out a map or the cultural support that would facilitate progress.

But, if this description seems to fit you, it's important that you not fool yourself. You might not actually be in the Wellspring. I believe that Soul Initiation does not occur, even weakly, until you understand enough about your destiny — on the deep-structure level of soul mysteries, as opposed to the surface level of cultural delivery systems — to make a conscious commitment to it with full recognition of what this commitment demands of you. If this is not true of you, you're probably in the Cocoon (and that's not at all a bad place to be).

How can you tell which of the two stages you're in? Take a look again at the bottom of page 73, where you'll find a list of clues, the most definitive being your psychospiritual center of gravity. To assess the latter, ask yourself this: When your thoughts, imagination, and emotions are given free rein, where do they end up more often then not? Do you find yourself musing about the particular mysteries of nature and psyche that you have encountered? If so, you're probably in the Cocoon. Or do you find yourself in reveries about specific imaginative ways to *embody* those mysteries among your people? The latter is characteristic of the Wellspring.

If you are in the Wellspring and you stall out, you would benefit from the help of an elder or soul guide to deepen your exploration of soul, further develop your soulcraft skills, and, if you have not yet done it, identify a suitable delivery system for your soulwork. Psychotherapy might be of help, too, but you probably don't need the sort of therapy that facilitates ego growth or social adjustment through ego support. More beneficial for you at this moment in life are the rare soul therapies that aim at personal transformation through ego death and rebirth.

CAPITULATION: THE EGOCENTRIC COUNTERPART TO THE WELLSPRING

Recall that, in the egocentric Wheel, the center of gravity never progresses beyond its stage-3 location of peer group, sex, and society. So although the Wellspring's egocentric counterpart (Capitulation, stage 3c) is a type of developmental movement beyond stage 3b (Secession), it nevertheless is a further expression of being stuck in the Orphan-Impersonator archetype.

Toward the end of the teen years, young men and women in a soulcentric society are experiencing their first encounters with soul through soulcraft practices introduced by elders and initiators. In contrast, most late-teen youth in egocentric society have recently entered the stage of Secession, in which they have emotionally and socially seceded from their families. They might also be attempting to create an initiation process of their own, but as we've seen, the results are most always inconclusive or tragic.

By the time they reach their mid- to late twenties, most egocentric women and men are no longer fighting their families and the mainstream. They have developed a lifestyle of conformity (social and occupational), superficial entertainment, and self-numbing that successfully suppresses the soul and its painfully poignant desires. Egocentric young adults learn to place a tight lid on their own depths, the grandeur and sacredness of the natural world, and their experience of connectedness with all other beings. This is why, as shown in Diagram 3-6 (p. 71), I've chosen Soul Suppression as the name for the transitional event at the West point of the egocentric Wheel — in contrast to Soul Initiation on the soulcentric Wheel. Soul Suppression eventually leads to a soul depression, the chronic and implacable emptiness of an endless string of colorless days.

Soul Suppression can also lead to what we might call "shadow eruptus," in which the ego is overtaken by shadow elements it cannot yet assimilate. An individual experiencing this finds himself acting out formerly repressed and misunderstood impulses (the opposite of the ego's skewed position) that both terrify and seduce him —

the cross-dressing he-man, for example, or the clergyman who acts out sexually, the raging and violent peace activist, or the child-abusing psychologist. Or the shadow enactments might be relatively subtle — the hamburger-craving hunting opponent, the affair-prone "family values" proponent, the gambling accountant, or the bingeing exercise coach.

In any case, the transitional event of Soul Suppression is the start of the egocentric stage of Capitulation. Now that the individual's social and emotional Secession from his family of origin has run its course, whatever societal rebellion he might have engaged in and whatever wild oats he might have sown, he now surrenders to the values, goals, and styles of egocentric society. That society constantly broadcasts and embodies the message that life is about the pursuit of eternal youth, safety, security, and material possessions. The egocentric young "adult" capitulates to these goals. He settles down.

In one version, he loses all hope, and even memory, that there might be more to life. He shrugs his shoulders and, eventually, hunches them. He apprentices himself to a life of unfulfilling productivity within the industrial-consumer machine. He learns a trade, a profession, or a domestic role that will afford him adequate amounts of hollow security, money, and social attractiveness.

In a second variation, however, he does not give up hope. It nearly kills him to hold on to the possibility of a more fulfilling life, but he does. He just doesn't know specifically what to hope for and what to do with his longing. This fills him with grief. Sometimes, though, he can go weeks in denial. Often, he tries one New-Age program or remedy after another. Or he might look for balm in a mainstream religion or a self-help program. Living in an egocentric society, he does not know that what he most needs is the personal development that comes from revisiting his least-addressed tasks of the Nest, Garden, and Oasis. Meanwhile he has a job, a relationship, a mortgage, and maybe children.

The stage of Capitulation begins by the late twenties and usually lasts through the thirties.

While the soulcentric young adult in the Wellspring is apprenticing to his soulwork, his egocentric counterpart is capitulating to a life of survival work and survival roles. (A third group remains in an extended soulcentric Oasis. A fourth has reached the Cocoon.)

It's also possible that the individual in an egocentric society might not get as far as Capitulation. He might instead remain in the earlier stage of Secession — as a Rebel, a Prince, or a Victim. Capitulation is available only to Conformists, which accounts for the majority of postpubertal egocentric people in contemporary American society. But it's always possible — and this, of course, is the hope — that any of the four types of Orphan-Impersonators will wake up and re-enter the stream of soulcentric life at whatever point in stage 3 they left off. Surely, nature and the soul are conspiring to help them.

You can help, too. If you or others you know are in Capitulation, have not given up hope, and desire a more authentic life, you can help them or yourself turn gradually from a conformist lifestyle and, in its place, embrace the tasks of the Nest, Garden, and Oasis, especially the nature dimensions of those tasks. In due time, this will lead to a healthy Oasis, which is, in turn, the portal to the Cocoon and soul-rooted individuation.

SOUL EXPLORATION AFTER THE WELLSPRING

Even after completing your soul apprenticeship, there will be intermittent need for further soul exploration and for greater soul acceptance. There's always more to discover about your destiny and core powers. Sooner or later, each new and expanded understanding of your path becomes a limitation to further growth. Dark-nights-of-the-soul do not cease once and for all. Nor do the occasional periods of self-doubt and moments of losing your way. From time to time, you must descend into the underworld, shedding old skin. Even after moving past the West quadrant of the Wheel, there'll be times you must crack the shell of the ego and hatch a more effective vehicle for soul embodiment.

Our lives are like crabs, who lose their shells periodically and at great risk. They nevertheless shed their old homes in what amounts to a great leap of faith, a sudden, frightening departure and a movement toward a glimmering unknown.

WHEN ARE YOU DONE WITH YOUR SOUL APPRENTICESHIP?

Let's say you've honed a delivery system for your soul, one that has succeeded admirably in carrying your gifts to the world. Let's say you've been doing this soulwork for several years, and that your society even supports you in doing so. If you participate in a monetary economy, this means you're getting paid for it. If so, your survival work and soulwork have become one — an exceptional event, but not a necessary one for completing your soul apprenticeship.

In any case, there'll come a day when you realize that the continued performance of your soulwork through your familiar delivery system is no longer deeply fulfilling. This awareness evokes a crisis. Perhaps you've become bored or burned out with what had been your most creative conversation with the world. You might even have developed some significant doubts about your life direction. Or maybe you still derive satisfaction from your work, but a growing unease suggests your delivery system needs altering in some way. You hear the world calling you as strongly as ever, but you're no longer sure how to respond.

But you also know that the opportunity here is not simply a matter of exchanging forms. The world is actually calling you in a bigger way. With all your focus on mastering your delivery system, you might have lost sight of just what it is you'd been delivering — the gift of your soul. It occurs to you that you're now being asked to understand your soulwork more deeply, closer to the bones, to see it independently of any particular delivery system. You're being asked to surrender your current understanding of your soul powers so that you might comprehend them more fundamentally, more in accord with the themes and symbols of your soul image or story. You know there's a greater commitment you must make, and a greater risk you must take.

The odds are that the Mystery is responsible for this impasse, and that you are about to be launched into a major life passage. Like all passages, this one, too, will begin with a dying — an often-wrenching period of confusion, disorientation, and loss. There's a great sadness in leaving the Wellspring, as full as it was with mystery, soul discoveries, artistic tradition, and the fulfillment of making an authentic and meaningful difference in the world. Let's face it, the Wellspring was the best stage to be in.

CHAPTER NINE

THE ARTISAN *in the* WILD ORCHARD

Late Adulthood (Stage 6)

I am certain of nothing but the holiness of the heart's affections and the truth of the imagination.

— JOHN KEATS

You walking, your footprints *are*
the road, and nothing else;
there is no road, walker,
you make the road by walking.
By walking you make the road,
and when you look backward,
you see the path that you
never will step on again.
Walker, there is no road,
only wind-trails in the sea.

— ANTONIO MACHADO, "PROVERBS AND TINY SONGS"

Stage 6: Late Adulthood

Passage into this stage: Induction (confirms mastery of a delivery system for embodying soul powers)
Stage name: The Wild Orchard
Task: Creating and implementing innovative delivery systems (the culture component) for soul (the nature component)
Quadrant: North (giveaway)
Hemispheres: North and West (collective action)
Stage archetype: The Artisan
Quadrant archetype: The Warrior-Martyr
Gift to community: Seeds of cultural renaissance
Circle of identity: Holistically ecocentric
Center of gravity: Cultural giveaway as art form
Passage out of this stage: Crowning

IMPOSSIBLE DREAMS

Finally, in May 1996, I found my way into the Cemetery, that wild, underworldly landscape of my early-childhood dreams (from the 1950s) to which the Rock Guardian had led me by way of a mescaline-assisted vision (in 1970) and by a series of numinous day-world encounters in southern Utah (between 1980 and 1994). The Cemetery sits in the protected heart of a convoluted maze of redrock canyons. When I arrived at last in the precincts of the Cemetery, I was in the company of two friends, Steve Zeller and Annie Bloom. Steve and I had come there to enact our own four-day vision fasts, and Annie to support us, her role being the psychospiritual equivalent of both hospice counselor and midwife.

Getting even close to the Cemetery wasn't easy. Never having been there in the flesh, I knew it only as a dreamscape, although I'd also glimpsed it from a great distance — from the Guardian's shoulder, standing a thousand feet above it and a mile to its east. I'd attempted to reach the Cemetery on two previous occasions, by two different routes, both times with groups I was guiding. I'd failed both times. This third time, we tried yet another approach, one that seemed more likely to succeed but which was a lot longer. Significantly, on this attempt I assumed not the role of guide but the more appropriate posture of supplicant.

After several hours of enjoyable backpacking through canyoncountry, we passed through a region where the going was exceedingly difficult, frustrating, even maddening. This was a quarter-mile section of saturated canyon bottom choked by ten-foot tall willow brush growing as thick as hair. There was no circumnavigating the willows: they were boxed in on either side by sheer canyon walls. Crashing and stumbling through the pollen-choked thicket, I cried out my misery in maudlin, overwrought phrases that, even in the moment, I knew epitomized the existential plight of a person approaching the death-birth ceremony of a vision fast. "This is hopeless!" "It's a dead end!" "I'm lost!" "I can't find my way through!" Only later could I laugh about that.

When we finally emerged on the other side of the willows, our reward was a three-mile, backbreaking slog up a side canyon through bone-dry, shifting sands and wind-blown dunes.

Despite these trials, I was fully aware that we were journeying through a landscape as stunning as ever a person could hope to visit — a wildly eroded sandstone other-world of towering rock pillars, domes, terraces, and vertical cliffs painted pink, rose, mauve, cinnamon, and vermilion.

Late in the day, we made camp by a spring, a spot I guessed to be within a half mile of the Cemetery.

After a restful evening together and then a tender early morning ceremony of severance, Steve and I trekked off in our separate directions with backpacks now nearly empty, apart from our four-day supplies of water. Despite the extraordinarily complex topography, I found the hidden opening into the Cemetery without difficulty, as if summoned there. The primary feature of the Cemetery is a steep, five-hundred-foot slope colonized by hundreds of sandstone minarets, cabin-sized mushrooms, and giant tombstones. This fantastic hillside is intimately enclosed by a red-walled cirque formed on three sides by precipitous ramparts topped with enormous monoliths. I slowly picked my way up the slope to the horseshoe-shaped ridge rimming the Cemetery bowl. There, on a high, narrow pass overlooking both the Cemetery and a canyon to its north, I made my camp — not much more than a sleeping bag on a pad, three gallons of water, and a few ceremonial items.

My emotions were running strong. While trekking through the Cemetery up to its ridge, I had wept much of the way. Here, I was finally entering a holy place that had called me since age four, an exceedingly remote locale with no sign of previous human visitation, at least not since the thirteenth century, when the Ancestral Pueblo People mysteriously disappeared from this region of the Southwest. And, for me, this was not just another canyon pocket. I had intentionally placed myself in the midst of a grave-yard in which, I imagined, my death was as likely as any other conceivable outcome.

And then there were the thorny reasons I had chosen to fast this time, reasons that had brought me to this particular place in this moment and not to some other. As ful-filling as my life had been for many years, I had felt in recent months that I had reached the end of the road I had been traveling, and I didn't know where to go next. An immense sadness had claimed me. I had found myself in my midforties, having realized most of the dreams of my early adulthood. For fifteen years, I had been immersed in the aura of those bewitching dreams, which, as I entered the Cemetery, still swirled around me. It was an aura of heartrending hope and unbearable sadness for a world embroiled in madness and of personal visions invested with the greatest longing. As a young man, I had dared to want something passionately.

Sitting in my solitary camp, a deep grief claimed me, a lament really. I vividly recalled the yearnings of my youth — aspirations to have meaningful work that might contribute to a more sane and just world; a loving, playful, and fulfilling relationship; a caring community of friends; an aesthetically pleasing and ecologically valid home; and joyful ways to immerse myself in, explore, and celebrate the natural world. Having achieved these things, I now found myself with the melancholy that arrives with the fulfillment of long-held dreams. It would be easy enough now to sit back and enjoy the fruits of my labors. But that prospect left me thoroughly downhearted. Would I listen to the voices saying there wasn't any more to achieve in life, that anything else was a romantic illusion? Or would I accept the risk of once again leaving the home I had built for myself?

During those four days, I lived with heat and cold, blasting ridge-top winds, lizards, the staccato flutter of bat wings at dusk, stars and galaxies, blooming claret cup cacti, and ever-present hunger. Many birds came in close. A canyon wren whistling her melodious aria of descent. Sudden swallow jettings and explosive hummingbird invasions. Raven croaks and soarings. Silent vulture circlings.

On the first afternoon, I sat with my journal and made a list of all the as-yet-unrealized potentials of my life: proficiency with flutes, hospice volunteering, sailplane piloting, astronomy, and several others. Then I took a good look at the list. Although they were all true potentials, I supposed, none were ardently inspiring. I could have added each item to my life without any fundamental changes in my way of belonging to the world.

Then I thought that maybe what I needed was to drop everything and go find a master in some art or discipline, someone I could study with. Become an apprentice again. Yes, *that* seemed like the right thing to do, and I latched onto the idea. If I had gone as far as I could with my early-adulthood dreams, I reasoned, then it must be time to become a student again. It didn't seem to matter so much what I would become a student *of*.

At the time it didn't occur to me that anything my everyday strategic mind could think during my fast could not possibly be the answer. With hindsight I can certify that these lists and plans were just the ego attempting to save itself by throwing me bones — which is all it had to throw.

Meanwhile, dreams arrived unbidden, as well as emotions, reveries, memories, wind, night, and critters. These were, as usual, the much more significant encounters. In one, my father comes to me while I'm in a dreamlike state late one evening and admonishes me not to fall into the traps that he had, which he describes as self-doubting and being one's own worst enemy. I weep for the poignancy and gracious generosity of his counsel.

Then I dream of visiting a large mining operation in the desert run by a very attractive woman. Ore is successfully being extracted and moved on conveyor belts, but the mine hasn't made a profit yet. But there's still hope it will.

In another dream I wander through a small shop in the home of an older middle-aged couple who are enthusiastically selling what they advertise as "distinct items" or "curios." But all the things on their shelves seem to me very ordinary despite each being displayed like a little treasure. The woman shopkeeper draws my attention to a set of old, leather-bound books, green with gold lettering. I don't purchase anything.

Several people came to visit in my imagination. First was Dorothy Wergin, my earliest spiritual mentor, who had tutored me in many things, had been deeply nurturing, and had believed unquestionably in my potential. She had died several years earlier. I missed her dearly. There in the Cemetery I sent love and gratitude to her for helping me heal, grow, and see myself more clearly, and ultimately, for helping me leave the home of my early-adolescent belonging.

My oldest sibling, Ricky, came — as a fine young man. He had died as an infant before I was born. I had never been to his grave. I vowed to go someday.

My friend Phil, who died in the avalanche.

Another friend, Richard, who had passed away a few years before.

My father's father and both my grandmothers, all departed.

I had come to the Cemetery fearing I might physically die there but ended up being visited by the spirits of departed loved ones. I felt each one of them helping me to open my heart and risk it all.

But by doing what?

As I looked out on the sea of towers and giant toadstools, each one seemed to be a deceased being, each rock-person its own separate tomb or crypt, yet all joined like ocean waves or the branches of a tree.

Each day, my ridge-top camp felt increasingly more like an as-yet-unlit funeral pyre or a sacrificial altar at the top of the colossal, high steps of an Aztec temple.

Consequently, I once again avowed Death as my teacher and ally. And Death then turned to me and asked, "Who are you? For what do you live? What will you bring your people?"

The wind blew all day, each day, driving me even crazier than I might have been anyway. I named my camp Windy Gap. My lament grew stronger. I wept. I felt extraordinarily weak. I moaned, grunted, cried out.

Midmorning of the fourth day, a giant yellow-and-black swallowtail butterfly fluttered by, its wingspan at least six inches. The day before, I thought I'd seen it at a distance but then concluded I'd only imagined it. I had never seen one so huge in all of canyoncountry. Now it danced around my camp for several minutes before coming very close to my left cheek and circling round my head. It said, "Cocoon Weaver, Impossible Dreamer of Windy Gap," an elaboration on what another, smaller yellow butterfly had told me sixteen years earlier.

I prayed the rest of the day, "May the wind carry me home to my self."

That night I dreamed again. My wish to study with a master is granted in the night-world. I'm a teenager, not yet driving age. There's an exceptionally large yellow-and-black school bus. I had once heard of a kid who took it for a spin. I decide to do the same. I get in and head into town, driving down the moderate slope of a broad avenue, scared and exhilarated, almost out of control (the brakes are shot), but I manage not to hit anything. I drive to the workplace of a man I know, perhaps to show off. He's a strong, wise, and kind man in his early mature-adulthood. He is a workingman, what we would think of as a blue-collar artisan, and very much alive and able. He seems to feel I did well to get there in the big bus. He offers me a job loading heavy sacks of material on a cart and then delivering them to a factory where the material is used to make things, perhaps food. He shows me in detail how to balance the sacks on the cart, seven maximum, he cautions, or it will tip. As a special treat for me, he makes a run of sacks that have a drawing of me on them (like a logo) instead of the usual one. I am thrilled.

In the morning, I packed up and walked, teetering, out of the Cemetery and re-joined Steve and Annie for a wholesome and wholehearted breakfast feast.

I returned home ready to take the big, risky, yellow-and-black ride and to be guided by the mature workingman (of me) toward a new task of carrying what is hidden as a gift to others. To truly become such a man myself, I understood I would have to remain faithful to a mining operation (and the woman who runs it) and to learn to recognize the treasure in seemingly ordinary things, especially old leather-bound, green-and-gold things that might contain wisdom. Above all, I would have to rely on my heart, be grateful for friends, family, and teachers who have gone before, and trust my impossible dreams, the ones from layers of the psyche even deeper than the yearnings of a young adult.

It did not occur to me at the time, but looking back it's clear that my fast in the Cemetery marked the end of my soul apprenticeship and the commencement of the Artisan stage of the Wild Orchard. I believe that my initial fantasy of apprenticing to another master was my ego's (and/or Loyal Soldier's) attempt to avoid the death of my Wellspring way of belonging to my life and to dodge the risks and responsibilities of mining the deeper ore of soul.

I began to design new programs (which I called "soulcraft journeys") that were, in both intention and form, distinct from what I had been taught by the many extraordinary teachers with whom I had had the privilege of studying during my Cocoon and Wellspring years. I developed my own nature-based innovations with dreamwork, shadow work, psychotherapy, council work, poetics, sacred wound work, and self-designed ceremonies. Innovating in this way was a good deal riskier than seeking another teacher. It felt as if I were going a long way out on a limb. (I was.) I stopped thinking of myself as a vision-fast guide or a psychotherapist and became a soulcraft guide, a creator of new forms for the ancient art of weaving cocoons of soul initiation. I feared that some of my psychology and rites-of-passage colleagues thought me deranged. (They probably did, maybe still do.)

In hindsight, I would say that I had, in fact, begun mining that soulcraft ore a few years before my Cemetery fast. Those early attempts at new forms, however, had not yet been "profitable" in the sense that I had not yet been ready or willing to fully trust that I could manifest a mystery in my own way, that I could truly create an innovative form. My psychospiritual center of gravity had not yet shifted from form to art, from tradition to renaissance.

Upon returning from the Cemetery, I shared with my closest colleagues my impossible dreams for shaping new practices for a genuinely contemporary and Western version of nature-based soul initiation. Several gifted and courageous guides joined me in imagining new forms. I began to write the book you hold in your hands. Thirty inspired dreamers and I designed and incorporated a new Animas Valley Institute, which grew from eight programs a year and five guides to forty programs and twenty guides.

I gradually learned to trust my impossible dreams.

INDUCTION: PASSAGE INTO ADULT ARTISTRY

The Wellspring ends when you've mastered one or more delivery systems for your soul image or story and you stop looking outside yourself for instruction or role models for embodying soul. You begin to fashion novel and creative forms that arise out of your own depths — or the depths of the world, you're not sure which. In a soulcentric setting, your community has already recognized for some time the performance of your vision in service to your people. And your soul-rooted individuation has progressed to the point that, more often than not, you behave socially as the person you experience yourself to be privately.

As a Soul Apprentice, you gradually understood your soul qualities in deeper ways, and you honed your skills at embodying those qualities through a particular craft. It is the former — your understanding — that is fundamental and essential and that you now carry with you into the second half of adulthood. After all, from time to time you need to change the cultural context in which you embody soul, or you might need to learn an entirely new craft. Soul is the constant; its form and sphere of embodiment varies.

The end of the Wellspring is marked by the transition of Induction — your incorporation into a circle or guild of Artisans. Whether or not you undergo a formal or ceremonial initiation at this time, Induction is the spiritual passage your psyche experiences. The Mystery's opinion of your readiness takes precedence over what you or others might think or do.

But this is not an occasion for ego inflation. As with all major life-stage transitions, this one entails as much dying as birthing, as much burden as blessing. Your success with soul-rooted individuation at the Wellspring is being celebrated, but you're also being asked to step up to a position of greater responsibility, challenge, and risk. Your student and apprentice days are over. Now is the time to assume the full obligations of cultural leadership, as well as the fulfillment and joy inherent in that status. The success of the Great Turning depends on you — and millions of others — doing just this.

In a soulcentric setting, Induction into the Wild Orchard might be marked and celebrated by a Rite of Induction. This rite of passage might include the following:

- the ritual surrender of the role of Apprentice, including a sacrifice or giveaway of symbols, objects, or clothing specific to your apprenticeship
- an affirmation, by elders, of the personal qualities you have exhibited as an Apprentice, and a recognition of the signs of your readiness for the next stage of the Artisan
- formal reminders, by elders, of the responsibilities of the Artisan and the nature of the Wild Orchard
- the taking of vows
- the bestowal of symbols, objects, and clothing representing the Artisan
- a three- or four-day fast in wild solitude

At Induction, you stand at the northwest point on the Wheel. You are taking your leave of the West quadrant and making your first appearance in the North. You are moving from the domain of sunset and nightfall to full-on night. You are migrating from a West life focused on the enigmatic depths to a North life centered on leadership and giveaway. As an Apprentice, you were, of course, already enacting your soul-work, but you still lived more in the mysteries (West quadrant) than in the manifest (North quadrant). Now as you move from the Wellspring to the Wild Orchard, your center of psychospiritual gravity — the hub of your life, your greatest longing — shifts to the art of cultural giveaway.

In a sense you're moving from essence to form, but this is essence-infused form and you have no attachment to the particular form. The form delivers the essence (soul). The form shifts in whatever way necessary. In the Wild Orchard, form fully follows function.

Moreover, you're exiting the time of life in which the Visionary archetype has its greatest influence and entering the quadrant of the Warrior-Martyr and, more specifically, the stage of the Artisan.

Although you're coming into a new quadrant of life, you're not transiting between hemispheres. You remain in the North half of the Wheel (the hemisphere of collective orientation) as well as the West half (the hemisphere of action). Consequently, as in the previous stage, you're in your adulthood, the time of collective-centered action.

As you approach the passage of Induction, your world begins to fall apart in one way or another. In Joanna Macy's memoir, we see the first sign of impending Induction in May 1977, when she was forty-eight. She was in Boston for a weekend, visiting her son Jack, who was attending college there. They went to hear the French ocean-explorer Jacques-Yves Cousteau speak as part of an all-day symposium on threats to the biosphere. Cousteau decried the many forms of relentless ocean pollution, including garbage, oil spills, sludge, and plutonium. Most alarming was the dying of the plankton, the microorganisms needed not only as food for other ocean creatures but, even more fundamentally, for the production of the oxygen most Earthlings need for survival. The whole symposium was "an immense bazaar of apocalyptic information" backed up with reams of scientific data. On that day Joanna fully awoke to the fact that "we all, in the ways we lived and consumed, [were] wasting our world."[1]

Late that afternoon, while riding the "T" (the commuter train), "something gave way inside me." This, I believe, was the first shifting of her center of gravity toward the Wild Orchard.

I found myself looking at the faces across the aisle through tears that I was powerless to stop or hide. It felt like the collapse of some inner scaffolding that for years had been holding the kind of information I had harvested all day, holding it up and out of the way, on a shelf in my mind. As that scaffolding crumbled, years of stored knowledge about what we were doing to our planet — to ourselves — cascaded into my heart and body, bringing a realization I could no longer keep at bay: yes — we can succeed now in destroying our world.

... I had no idea how to live with it. Over the coming days and weeks and months it would return at odd moments, like a blow to the solar plexus.[2]

Induction *is* a blow to our solar plexus. There *is* no way to live with it — as a Soul Apprentice, that is. As our center of gravity begins to shift, we are seized by a new and painful awareness of our responsibilities. Something in us recognizes that we are being summoned by the world to a deeper creativity, commitment, and action.

The dying phase of Induction's death-rebirth process had begun for Joanna on that May day in Boston. By the fall, it was still churning:

Below the surface, a dark, obsessive labor continued to grip me. It seemed to have taken hold of both my mind and my body, emerging as sensations and feeling states that activated intense thought. Since it did not *start* on the cognitive level, as a philosophical problem, I could not say with any precision what this labor was. I only knew that it had to do with the meaning of life in a world that humans were destroying.[3]

That fall, Joanna had the intuition that humanity itself was in the midst of a death-rebirth process. Her description of this process, framed in general systems terms, is an equally apt identification of what she was personally going through in the throes of Induction: "I remembered how open systems restructure themselves in response to challenge. In order for new values, new organizing principles to emerge, they undergo 'positive disintegration.' In our evolution, we have been through this process many times; it is inevitably disorienting. To survive, the system just needs to stay open to feedback."[4]

Induction (like all major life passages) entails a positive disintegration, in this case an erosion of the Apprentice's way of belonging in order to allow for reconfiguration as an Artisan. The disintegration is "positive" because it makes possible a more evolved or mature state, like the dissolution of the caterpillar that leads to a butterfly.

LATE ADULTHOOD AS A WILD ORCHARD

Michael Pollan, in *The Botany of Desire*, notes that every apple seed contains not only the prospect of a unique apple tree but also a one-of-a-kind apple. Apple growers are able to harvest crops of homogenous apples only by propagating trees by means of a form of cloning called grafting. If each seed were allowed to have its way, no two apple trees would bear identical apples. Their color, shape, texture, and taste would be as singular as snowflakes and fingerprints.

Ripe adulthood is like a wild apple tree. If we grow as nature and soul would have it, each of us blossoms peerlessly in adulthood. Our fruit — our giveaways — are without equal, never before seen.

The second half of adulthood is a Wild Orchard in the midst of an encultured human village, each adult begetting his or her own unique fruit, an unrivaled bestowal. The distinctive fruit that each adult bears is truly a boon as well as a feast for the people. Through her soulwork, the Artisan provides a singular nutriment essential to the community's wholeness, an element no one else could duplicate. The celebrated dancer and choreographer Martha Graham puts it this way: "There is a vitality, a life force, a quickening that is translated through you into action, and because there is only one of you in all time, this expression is unique. And if you block it, it will never exist through any other medium and be lost. The world will not have it."[5]

To become or remain healthy, every ecology — including each human community — must be resilient, diverse, fruitful, and ever changing. The growing edge for any particular human ecology is composed of the deeply creative gifts of Artisans. The Wild Orchard is a matrix of cultural possibilities, an artist's studio of social generativity, a weaver's loom of human evolution.

The second half of adulthood also becomes something like an alchemist's laboratory. The base personality undergoes transmutation into a precious element of the greatest cultural value: the distinctive psyche of a mature servant-leader with a matchless contribution for the more-than-human community. And, because all adults are ecocentric — fully aware of and respectful of humanity's dependence on the web of creation — each one helps lead us toward sustainability and vitality, the Great Work of our time.

THE ARTISAN: ARCHETYPE OF LATE ADULTHOOD

The development of the ego, the conscious self, can be divided into four phases, which together span a lifetime (and eight life stages). In the first phase, corresponding to the first life stage (the Nest), there's no ego. The second phase comprises the next three life stages — from middle childhood through adolescence, the stages of the *primary ego*. The distinguishing qualities of the primary ego are two: it is anchored in society, and it understands itself to be an agent for itself, including when it is being generous and altruistic. The Cocoon foments great change for the primary ego as its self-centeredness loosens. At Soul Initiation, the ego transforms. Entering the collective (North) half of the Wheel, it experiences itself as being anchored in, and as an agent for, soul. This *secondary ego* carries us through the next three life stages, from early adulthood through early elderhood, the Wellspring through the Grove. Early elderhood is, again, a transitional stage. By the time of Surrender, the ego has relinquished all desire to accomplish. The *tertiary ego* of the Mountain Cave experiences itself no longer as an active agent (for anything) but as a space in which certain things unfold.

In devising a framework for understanding and naming the archetypes for the three stages of the secondary ego, I was drawn to the medieval guild model because it conceives of a developmental progression in capacities and responsibilities within a specific craft. One starts out as an apprentice, later earns the status of an accomplished artisan (or journeyman), and finally becomes a master of the craft. The guild sequence helped me understand how soul embodiment develops through these three life stages.

As an Artisan in the Wild Orchard, you create never-before-seen forms for embodying soul in the world. The delivery system in which you apprenticed while in the Wellspring guided you as you acquired the art and craft of soul embodiment. Your apprenticeship was essential and foundational. Now it's time to let your creativity run wild, to imagine as grandly as you can, to let no perceived limitations impede you. You begin to avidly live the following questions: "If my only criterion were to deliver my soul gift to my people as magnificently and fully as possible, how would I do it? Through what forms? With what voice? In which settings?"

After your many Wellspring years of performing your vision, you've not only mastered a form but, more important, you've acquired a deep-rooted familiarity with what your soul qualities feel like as they pour forth from you. On countless occasions, you observed your soul powers at work in the world. You saw the ways your best efforts affected others, how you changed the lives and experiences of people you've served, perhaps how you shifted the collective field, or how certain human or natural habitats were rendered more wild, diverse, or vital.

In these ways, you've acquired a nuanced feel for the results that your soul desires. Now, in the Wild Orchard, you intend to engender *those* kinds of results regardless of how you get there, and often enough you in fact no longer know how you'll get there. You can no longer assess how well you're doing by your faithfulness or prowess at employing the form(s) of your apprenticeship years. Now, like Machado's walker, "you make the road by walking... / and when you look backward, / you see the path that you / never will step on again."

In the Orchard, as you enact your soulwork, you feel inexorably drawn toward the outcome your soul longs for. It's as if the future causes you. Your intellect — more generally, your everyday strategic mind — plays little or no part in your choice of form or of timing. Your inner eye seeks out the significance, the meaning, or the unknown that the world is calling forth and for which you serve as an agent of manifestation.

With the tools you've acquired and honed during your apprenticeship — as well as the tools and methods you never knew you had or never even knew existed — you fashion new, on-the-spot delivery systems for soul. Sometimes you use a given form or approach only once. Other times you hone a new delivery system over a period of months or years. Sometimes it feels like a new medium has chosen *you*.

Quite frankly, there are moments when you feel like a wizard, a magician, a sorcerer or sorceress. You astonish yourself, and yet, at the same time, you know you can personally take almost no credit for what flows through you. You are an instrument, an agent for the Mystery or the Muse. Perhaps the most essential talent you can claim as personally yours is the ability to get out of the way of your own soul. That's when you feel most alive. At your best moments, it doesn't even feel like you're making choices. You're simply assenting to what wants to emerge into the world through you. Your soulwork requires increasingly less effort. You're in the flow.

Author Ursula Le Guin writes, in *A Wizard of Earthsea*: "As a man's real power grows and his knowledge widens, ever the way he can follow grows narrower: until at last he chooses nothing, but does only and wholly what he must do."[6] This surrender to destiny and this creative wizardry with delivery systems is the core of the Artisan's life. It is the mature poet discovering a new voice or a new style of verse, or the psychotherapist devising a new intervention in the moment, perhaps a new approach for each client. It is the musician who discovers, to his astonishment and delight, a novel rhythm, musical form, or vocal style being drawn from him. It is the architect envisioning a new vernacular, or the businessman recognizing an original way to meet a genuine social need without creating pollution, waste, poverty, or injustice. It is a politician intuitively grasping a deep but unconscious aspiration of the majority and having the courage to go out on a limb, publicly declare it, and work for its realization no matter what the political risks.

The Artisan is an initiated adult fully embodying the fact that she is an artist, that she has a sacred responsibility to her art, and that her soulwork — and her life more generally — is her art. She is discovering what it means to give her life to the world as an expression of her art. She is seeing, probably to her surprise, how many competing agendas, priorities, and desires she is willing to sacrifice for that art.

The Artisan learns that any pretension gets in the way of her soulwork. Her challenge is to remain authentic, loyal to her soul, while being responsive to the world's needs. She surrenders any ambition she might once have had to be a great or acclaimed artist in any conventional sense, because her intent is community vitality, not personal fame or aggrandizement.

And yet she knows she cannot do without a certain soul-rooted boldness — a belief in the gifts she has to offer, a confidence that the world wants her to do her part. She needs that boldness to risk going out on the limbs the world calls her to.

At times, of course, she feels inadequate or fears failure. But she reminds herself that her work, her life, is not about personal success but about the health of the collective. She understands, especially at this stage of life, that self-criticism and self-pity are as self-centered as self-indulgence and self-promotion. The Artisan's true reward is not public acclaim or approval but the fulfillment that comes from the performance of her vision.

THE WARRIOR-MARTYR: ARCHETYPE OF THE NORTH

While the Artisan is the archetype specific to the Wild Orchard, the Warrior and Martyr are the archetypes active throughout the North quadrant of the Wheel and consequently both the Orchard and the Grove. (See Diagram 3-4, p. 68) The Warrior and Martyr speak to what both late adulthood and early elderhood are like at a depth well beneath the qualities of their individual archetypes (the Artisan and Master).

Recall that the quadrant archetypes at first seem more mysterious than the stage archetypes, and that this is because they must hold more meaning. To hold more, they must operate on deeper levels. This appears to be a general principle of psyche. The deeper we understand ourselves, the more of the world we identify with and, as a result, the wider our circle of identity.

The Warrior and Martyr are actually two facets of a single archetype. It's not as if some people in the North are Warriors and others Martyrs. Every person in these stages embodies the qualities of both. The Warrior and the Martyr share an extraordinary capacity for leadership and service; the difference between them is their mode of contribution. The Warrior is a defender of the community's well-being. The Martyr nurtures the community through caregiving — a giveaway that entails a certain degree of suffering. Both are courageous architects of new cultural realities. Both lead with the heart.

The Warrior archetype I have in mind is not, of course, the adolescent masculine hero or soldier, or the politician or corporate executive whose ambition is economic and political power over others. Rather, here in the North stages, we find the more evolved, mature Warrior, the spiritual Warrior, who is as likely to be a woman as a man. In addition to fulfilling her role as a creator of new forms, the Warrior is also a passionate guardian of the sacred. She protects, for example, the ceremonies, sacred objects, land, water, sovereignty, and diversity of her people and their environment. And she inspires and rallies others to these causes.

The spiritual Warrior understands there are connections between all species and habits, and that human life is thoroughly interdependent with the larger natural environment. Therefore, when the Warrior defends the life of her community, she thinks, feels, and acts on behalf of the entire biosphere, not merely the human dimension of it.

As for the Martyr half of the North archetype, we must be careful with the word itself because of the unappealing connotations that *martyr* has accrued in recent centuries — someone who chooses to suffer death rather than renounce religious principles, or someone who makes a great show of suffering in order to arouse sympathy.[7] I considered substituting here the more modern *Caregiver*, but in the end I stayed with the symbolically rich and mythically charged *Martyr*.

The genuine Martyr is clear about what he holds sacred — namely, that which he discovered during the two stages of the West quadrant. He's willing to sacrifice and suffer, if necessary, in order to protect or sustain the sacred. But what defines him is not his suffering but his loving and his nurturing. The Martyr knows what he'd be willing to die for, but more important, he knows what he lives for. Any sacrifices he makes are not means to an end — they are not his way of performing his giveaway. Rather, they're a price he's willing to pay in order to perform his soulwork and nurture the life of his people.

One of the ways our soul powers develop as we mature is through an increasingly opened heart, a stretching that inevitably entails a kind of suffering. Spurred by our love for the world, we go to the very depths of our psyches to find and bring back gifts we would not have been able to carry were it not for our time in the underworld. We care so much about the world that we're willing to endure this expansion of the heart. This pain, occasioned by loving, is the kind of suffering implied by the archetype of the Martyr.[8] The original meaning of *compassion* is "to suffer with," an experience that derives from our deep knowledge of interconnectedness, an insight that grows keenest in the North quadrant.

There is a second sort of suffering encountered in the North. In both their Warrior and Martyr aspects, Artisans and Masters bear great responsibilities. They're being asked by the Mystery to consciously embody the sacred in the world — more so than in any other life stage. They become vehicles for archetypal energies much more powerful than the human personality. Regardless of their level of personal development, this responsibility is at times more than they can gracefully bear. Emotions become overwhelming; the body breaks down; projections by others, both negative and positive, distract or disempower; or the will waivers. Artisans and Masters might succumb to these pressures and projections, and regress to the sort of pettiness and vengeance that we see exhibited even by the gods and goddesses of Greek mythology. No matter how brave and gifted a person might be while carrying the archetypes of the Warrior and Martyr, there will be times when the personality is overcome and suffers.

In Buddhism, the Warrior-Martyr is a single, blended archetype called the bodhisattva, the hero or heroine who refuses enlightenment until all sentient beings are saved from suffering.[9] One of the bodhisattva's qualities is his great compassion for all beings. He suffers *with* other beings, which implies his Martyr facet. He does not remain aloof from the distress of others, because he knows all too well that there is no private salvation. His identity is ecocentric.

But the bodhisattva is also portrayed as a warrior. In an eighth-century Tibetan Buddhist prophecy, for example, there is a bodhisattva known as the Shambhala warrior, referring to people who will not appear until the twentieth and twenty-first centuries. More than twelve hundred years ago, Tibetan Buddhists accurately predicted that our present time would be an era of global crisis and danger. Joanna Macy explains that the Shambhala warriors were foreseen as people of great courage, both morally and physically, whose task would be to go into "the very heart of the barbarian power," the corridors of dominator power, and dismantle the weapons there.[10] Buddhists understand that all weapons are made by the human mind through decisions and action, and that they can be unmade in the same way.

The Shambhala warriors have "weapons," too, but they are compassion and insight. Compassion motivates us to act. But compassion alone can lead to burnout. We also need ecocentric insight into the radical interdependence of all things, which informs us that "the line between good and evil runs through the landscape of every human heart,"[11] and that any action stemming from compassion will benefit the web of life beyond what we could predict or perceive.

I like to imagine that the Shambhala warriors of our time, envisioned so long ago,

are our Artisans and Masters, those who serve in true leadership positions at this time
of the Great Turning. In the Orchard, the Warrior-Martyr — who is also an Artisan
in this stage — serves in part through his passionate creation of innovative forms and
new social practices or ways of life. These new forms and practices might be in any of
the realms of human endeavor, such as art, science, technology, health care, governance,
economics, literature, education, spirituality, and soul development. In the next chapter (on the Grove), I discuss how the Warrior-Martyr, as a Master, serves life through
an even more mature form of compassion.

Although suffering is an element of the North, it hardly defines this quadrant. To
the contrary, the performance of our giveaway brings great joy and fulfillment, perhaps the greatest in life.

Ultimately, the Warrior-Martyr is a Lover. She has found a way of manifesting the
love she has for the world. She fulfills herself through the love embodied in her giveaway.

The reason the Warrior-Martyr archetype resonates so strongly with the North quadrant is because winter and the middle range of the night are the times we're most in
need of the giveaways of the most capable, courageous, compassionate, and nurturing
leaders among the people.

Regardless of our age or stage, however, both the Warrior and Martyr archetypes
are always available to us. The Martyr is operative whenever we are compelled by our
souls to suffer a greater opening of our hearts and to care for our loved ones and loved
places. Likewise, the Warrior archetype operates within us whenever we feel bound to
defend and protect life.

THE ARTISAN'S CONTRIBUTION TO THE WORLD:
SEEDS OF CULTURAL RENAISSANCE

The Artisan's soul-infused creativity sows seeds of cultural renaissance. Every human
culture, to remain healthy, sustainable, and vibrant, requires a constant renewal of ceremonies, crafts, cultural practices, and the arts. Each society must generate new
knowledge, skills, self-understanding, and modes of self-transcendence. To evolve, a
human community must have available a diverse set of authentic and viable social
forms that enables it to respond to shifting times, long-term weather patterns, food
sources, spiritual needs, cultural longings, and relations with other human groups.

Artisans are the primary spawners of these new creations. Their singular inventions, their unique ways of embodying soul, are each a seed for innovative cultural possibilities. Some seeds will sprout into practices or traditions that eventually occupy a
central place in the culture. Other seeds will serve only one or two people or for a fleet-
ing moment or in a transitory setting. But all Artisan seeds ultimately serve the entire

biosphere, not just the human village. The Artisan's seeds are sourced in soul and thus in nature. When the Artisan is creating from her depths, she is manifesting what nature birthed her to do.

The Artisan lives day-to-day with one eye on the illimitable unmanifest possibilities of soul and the other on the infinitely variegated materials and modes with which to manifest those promises. She is a womb of the world, an interface between the Mystery and humankind.

THE DEVELOPMENTAL TASK OF THE ARTISAN

As once the wingéd energy of delight
carried you over childhood's dark abysses,
now beyond your own life build the great
arch of unimagined bridges.

Wonders happen if we can succeed
in passing through the harshest danger;
but only in a bright and purely granted
achievement can we realize the wonder.

To work *with* Things in the indescribable
relationship is not too hard for us;
the pattern grows more intricate and subtle,
and being swept along is not enough.
Take your practiced powers and stretch them out
until they span the chasm between two
contradictions.... For the god
wants to know himself in you.

— RAINER MARIA RILKE

Building Unimagined Bridges

As we've seen, the task of the Artisan is to create and implement innovative delivery systems for soul, in this way providing his community with the abundant fruit of life-giving service. Embodying soul is the nature component of his task, and creating new delivery systems that are effective in his society is the culture component.

With hands and heart, the Artisan is shaping new forms that he will fill with gold. With voice and deep imagination, for example, he is fashioning poems and songs to praise the world. With love and cunning, he is sculpting original social technologies to liberate human creativity and cooperation. He is a design artist molding vehicles for the Mystery — distinctive channels for spirit and artful arrangements for soul. In Rilke's image, the Artisan is building "the great / arch of unimagined bridges" between the Mystery and the phenomenal world.

Every day, the Artisan feels the tension between nature and culture with every move. He lives, in fact, at an ecotone — the interface of the wild and the weal, at the pivot point of essence and form. He learns that he can fully serve his people only by surrendering wholly to nature as it flows through him. He desires to contribute to society (the commonweal) while being faithful to soul's wild intentions. He discovers that if he puts either goal above the other, he ultimately disappoints both.

The new delivery systems created by the Artisan are not necessarily tangible and do not necessarily result in material objects such as works of art. The desired result is service, not things, even when things are a means for delivering the gifts of soul. As was true for the Apprentice, an Artisan's delivery systems might be in any arena of culture, including education, healing, food production, the economy, leadership, spirituality, science, and the arts.

Whether his service is tangible or intangible, the Artisan's task does not require the invention of new cultural traditions such as original art media, political philosophies, educational methods, or economic systems. His service is just as likely to flow through a new voice expressed within an existing tradition like poetry, jazz, medicine, ecology, agriculture, ecopsychology, cybernetics, democracy, or journalism or other media.

Whatever delivery systems he employs, the Artisan is doing something new within that form, or stretching that form's envelope, or applying it to a novel context. At the Wellspring, the Apprentice found his voice and embodied something unique (soul) with preexisting forms. In the Orchard, the Artisan imaginatively offers his voice in ways that transcend allegiance to the old forms or the means of utilizing them.

Furthermore, some Artisans function more by doing and some more by being. The "be-ers" perform their soulwork more through their style of interacting with or inspiring others than through specifically identifiable products or projects, the latter being the approach of the "doers." The "be-ers" focus on relationship building more than on the achievement of measurable goals. Some would say that the being mode of soulwork is more feminine and the doing more masculine.

In either case, the Artisan oversees the cross-fertilization of soul and world. The world longs for the singular productions of the soul, and the soul is in love with the forms and forces of the world. The soul knows that the world provides an infinite field of potential for the manifestation of the Mystery. The world desires to be made complete through each soul (human and otherwise). The soul and the world are fulfilled in one another. Facilitating this mutual fulfillment is the core of the Artisan's task.

Not much can be said about *how* the Artisan accomplishes his task, because his giveaway is so intuitive, imaginative, and creatively performed. There are as many ways to create or use innovative delivery systems as there are Artisans. Like Keats, the Artisan becomes certain "of nothing but the holiness of the heart's affections and the truth of the imagination." By the latter, Keats means not the relatively shallow imagination under the strategic mind's control but the mysterious imaginings that arise unbidden from the depths, like spring waters.

The Muse — the goddess who inspires creative acts — makes her strongest appearance in the Wild Orchard. The Muse, in this stage, often suggests specific delivery systems for the soul's desires, and the job of the Artisan's conscious personality is to become a receptive field for those suggestions and then to actualize them with aplomb. The Artisan must forge a conscious alliance with his Muse and learn to trust her, to seek her counsel, and to honor her with praise and gratitude. He would do well to make ritual offerings to her.

The Muse appears in many realms and guises. For me, while writing the final drafts of this book, the Muse has made her blessed and astonishing appearances through dreams, waking "voices," and the counsel of a gifted visionary, Geneen Marie Haugen.

In her invisible form in my waking life, the Muse most often shows up first thing in the morning (immediately upon my arising or while I'm brushing my teeth), as well as during yoga, while I'm hiking in wild places, and on long bike rides in the Animas Valley. When the flow of my writing bogs down at an impasse or a conundrum, I ask her for advice — despite the fact that she rarely responds directly to my requests. At the start of a mountain ramble, for example, I might ask her about a quandary I have regarding, say, stage 2, and, usually within a few minutes, she'll begin advising me about stage 4 or 6.

Sometimes there'll be a rush of brilliant ideas, and there I am several miles from home without pen or paper. I've had to develop some skill at mnemonics (the original Muses were, after all, the nine daughters of Mnemosyne by way of Zeus), so that there's something to write down at the end of my hike.

The Muse has a sense of humor. Sometimes I paranoidly wonder if she's just teasing or mocking me or trying to get me to embarrass myself. Once, for example, when I had asked her something about stage 7, she told me I should title chapter 2 "The Power of Here." She seemed to be having fun by suggesting an underworld complement to Eckhart Tolle's decidedly upperworld book *The Power of Now*. But she didn't stop there. She added that I should be sure to note that, "after Soul Initiation, wherever you go, *Here* you are." "Look," I responded, "I'd like readers to take me seriously!" "Just do it," she said. I didn't tell her at the time, but I thought, "Okay, I'll do it, but my editor will rescue me later by deleting it."

The Muse also shows up regularly in my dreams. On my Cemetery fast, for example, there she was, running a mining operation in the desert.

While in the midst of the most concentrated writing for this book, I had one of the most significant Muse dreams of my life: I am visiting a large residential institution for women that feels somewhat like both a college and a convent. I am here because, on the next day, I am to begin guiding a four-day experiential program for them. The women — young, middle-aged, and older — all seem rather interesting, well-spoken, and attractive. The rooms are intimate, carpeted, and softly lit, with art- and book-lined walls. I am standing in the foyer outside a meeting room where women are moving in and out, some alone, some in pairs or small groups. One woman explains to me that everyone has been "working creatively" with their personal responses to what I will be presenting in the coming days (based on materials sent earlier). There appear to be two approaches. About half of the women are walking around with armfuls of papers and books and discussing ideas. The other half are carrying large rectangular trays packed with seedlings in small containers of soil. The cultivation of these plants is their way of developing an imaginative relationship with the subject matter of the upcoming program.

The morning after this astonishing dream, I made offerings and performed ritual observances of gratitude to those whom I now call the Muses of the Sacred Academy of the Feminine. I resolved to be responsive not only to the elegant ideas of the Muses but also to the tender green sprouts they cultivate.

Although the Artisan cannot be provided with specific guidelines for accomplishing his task, he might find valuable some advice from Rilke, who addresses his readers at the same deep-structure level on which the Artisan must learn to operate. Rilke says that working with things (form) is, itself, easy enough, but one discovers that "the pattern grows more intricate and subtle, / and being swept along is not enough." The Artisan must concede that he possesses "practiced powers" (acquired in his Wellspring years), and that he must now use them (and further develop them) in order to "span the chasm between two / contradictions."

What are the two contradictions? Essence and form? Nature and culture? The invisible soul and the visible world? Or perhaps the oppositions and paradoxes of which Carl Jung writes — such as mind and body, male and female, or human and god — or others such as ideas and seedlings, Buddhism and Western science, despair and hope. What Jung calls the "transcendent function"[12] is the intrapsychic reconciliation that emerges after opposites have been consciously identified and the tension between them patiently held in awareness. The Artisan is the person in the human community most capable of spanning the chasms between such opposites.

Another paradox: in the Wild Orchard the Artisan is simultaneously at the peak of his talent and a mere instrument of soul. There is a great advantage to such an arrangement. Knowing so clearly that the role of the conscious self — the strategic mind — is only to implement the soul's creativity, and having honed his skill to the point that it can be applied instinctively, the Artisan is now free to give his full attention to what he's delivering. Liberated from self-consciousness about form, he can give himself entirely to essence. We can witness this, for example, in the virtuoso musician whose awareness, during a performance, is fully devoted to the feeling or soul of the music, with no worry whatsoever about notes or technique.

In addition to carving new channels in the familiar landscapes of his soulwork, the Artisan learns to manifest his soul qualities in domains novel to him. Let's say, for example, that a man's soul powers feature an extraordinary sensitivity to the vitality of the natural world, that he senses a radiant presence in nature that most people largely overlook. Imagine that, as an Apprentice, he learned to awaken others to this dimension of nature through landscape painting. Now as an Artisan, he might learn to embody this same soul power by guiding people on wilderness journeys or through healing work with plant medicines. "Now beyond your own life build the great / arch of unimagined bridges."

From the perspective of egocentric society, it might be said that Artisans at midlife often make radical changes in their careers or professions. With a soulcentric view, however, we'd say they are doing precisely the same work utilizing new delivery systems. The Artisan learns to manifest his soul gifts most everywhere he goes, in most environments and social settings in which he finds himself. His giveaway becomes the very warp and woof of his life. His soulwork is essentially who he is in the world.

Joanna Macy's first innovative delivery system, in her Wild Orchard years, was what she came to call "despair and empowerment work." She traces its beginnings back to the summer of 1978, one year after the start of her Induction process (as I see it) in Boston. At a conference at Notre Dame, she was about to chair a week-long working group on "The Prospects for Human Survival." In the face of all the dreadful data of environmental devastation, she wondered where in their lives people could find hope and the courage to act. Rather than rely on the typical dispassionate delivery of a scholarly paper, she wanted to set a different tone. So she invited participants to introduce themselves not in terms of their academic positions but by sharing personal experiences of how the global crisis had affected their lives. Emotions were stirred, "touch[ing] some raw nerve connecting us all. . . . I learned two things that week: that the pain for the world which I carried around inside me was widely and deeply shared; and that something remarkable happened when we expressed it to each other. Instead of miring ourselves in doom and gloom, the opposite had happened. We had turned some key that unlocked our vitality."[13]

In the middle of her last night at Notre Dame, Joanna was awake and wondering what that key might be. Suddenly, she began furiously scribbling notes. Here she gives us a rare glimpse of the soul and ego of an Artisan working together to create something genuinely new, to "build the great / arch of unimagined bridges":

As with the turn of a kaleidoscope, my thoughts and dreams of the past year, since riding the T from the Cousteau symposium, reassembled themselves. A new pattern emerged, and in it I saw the logic of despair work. I named it that — "despair work" — because I knew about grief work and the need to validate anguish over the loss of a loved one. This was different, of course, because the full loss hadn't occurred yet and we hardly wanted to resign ourselves to it. But it was similar in the energy released by our willingness to feel inner pain.

The liberation which that willingness brings — the clarity of response as the feedback loops are unblocked — made total sense to me now, in terms of both systems theory and the Dharma. I remembered the first "weapon" of the Shambhala warrior: *karuna*, or compassion . . . [which] meant to be unafraid of the suffering of the world and its beings — even our own.[14]

In that singular moment, several elements of Joanna's Wellspring experience connected up for her, including her revelation in Boston, her studies of Buddhism and general systems, her own grief and despair, and her environmental activism. The result was the kind of creative breakthrough that is characteristic of the Wild Orchard.

A year later, she led her first weekend workshop, titled "From Despair to Empowerment." Within a few weeks, invitations to lead programs began pouring in. Colleagues appeared from all directions, bringing their own wisdom and skills. Together they created a network called Interhelp and began publishing a journal. She wrote a book, *Despair and Personal Power in the Nuclear Age*. The world said YES to Joanna's sacred dance.

Integrating the Self

If the Artisan has a second developmental task, it is the advanced cultivation and integration of the four dimensions of the Self — the generative and nurturing leadership of the North; the playful, emotionally vibrant, instinctive, and sensual wildness of the South; the imaginative depths and visionary capacities of the West (one of the West's aspects is the Muse); and the innocence, wisdom, and chicanery of the East.[15] In the Cocoon, the Wanderer developed a conscious relationship with these four intrapsychic resources. In the Wellspring, the Apprentice learned to balance them — to employ them equally in his life. Now, in the Wild Orchard, the Artisan learns to fully integrate them so that he can employ all four simultaneously in an interwoven, mutually enhancing way. This integration of the Self can be thought of as a second task or, alternatively, as a component or feature of his primary task of manifesting novel delivery systems.

If the Apprentice's soul embodiment relied too much on one or two dimensions of the Self, as is typical, now the Artisan must integrate the other two or three in his giveaway. With this balanced integration, he'll be able to manifest his soul qualities in ways and in places he had previously never dreamed of.

Carrying Archetypal Energies

Although perhaps not a formal task, an additional challenge of the Wild Orchard is learning to carry the archetypal energies of this stage without identifying with them. The Artisan, Warrior, and Martyr archetypes generate potent emotional charges in society. These charges attract powerful projections — both positive and negative. People will sometimes treat you as if you *are* those archetypes — godlike, dangerous, all-providing. Believing you own an archetype on a personality level is always hazardous to self and others. The archetypes represent the qualities flowing through you. The conscious self is not the origin of these qualities.

But for a time, you borrow these capacities from the collective unconscious to help you serve your more-than-human community. You must learn to carry them with grace, dignity, and humility. Deep gratitude is essential. In fact, in the Wild Orchard one of your most important practices is to cultivate gratitude for the archetypal support you receive, for the opportunity to serve, and for the fulfillment derived from serving.

Despite the archetypal support you receive — and partly because of it — your task as the Artisan is highly demanding and arduous. Throughout this stage, you must find, over and over, the inner reserves of strength, courage, and persistence that will allow you to continue being a vehicle for manifestation and service.

Your challenge is to become more ordinarily human at the same time your role in society becomes more archetypal and charged. Becoming more human in the Wild Orchard requires, in part, that you tend to the most incomplete tasks of earlier stages. In addition to carrying out your Artisan tasks, you might also, for example, continue exploring new depths and realms of soul, reclaiming your shadow, exploring your sacred wound, welcoming home your Loyal Soldier, opening to nature's enchantment, and cultivating your capacity for innocence and present-centeredness. Continuing or deepening your meditation practice will help you disidentify with the archetypes and projections and cultivate humility.

CIRCLE OF IDENTITY AND SENSE OF COMMUNITY: HOLISTIC OR BIOREGIONAL ECOCENTRISM

In the Wellspring, your ecocentric perspective began to bloom, enabling you to instinctively choose and act from the point of view of other species and the planetary biosphere as a whole. Now, as an Artisan, your circle of identity deepens and grows more complex within this ecocentric perspective.

As your ego becomes a more refined vehicle for your soul story or image, there's also a further refinement in your relationship to your bioregion. Both become more differentiated — in intricacy and subtlety. You become ecocentric, not merely species by species, but also in relation to whole ecologies. In the Wellspring, you came to think and act from the perspective that each individual species has rights just as humanity does. But in the Wild Orchard, you begin to intuit — and then grow assured — that bioregions themselves are types of individuals and that their rights are above and beyond those of their member species. You not only *think* eco-holistically (this is relatively easy, and the odds are you've already been doing it for years) but you also begin to instinctively *act* eco-holistically.

Now that you are in the North of the Wheel (the place of the giveaway), you more fully grasp the opportunities you've been given to contribute to a vital more-than-human community right where you live. Just as you are learning to use whichever delivery systems most effectively embody your unique gifts, you are also learning to act in whatever ways most effectively contribute to the health of your unique bioregion. In relation to your place on Earth, you become more Martyr-like (compassionate) and more Warrior-like (insightfully and fiercely protective). Your circle of identity, in short, deepens from the generic ecocentric (all beings have rights) to the holistically ecocentric. This entails a more nuanced grasp of the interconnections between the species, weather, and habitats of your watershed.

As your identity evolves, you feel increasingly like an apple tree: every seed of each of your apples holds a unique opportunity for manifesting appleness. What's more, you understand that your soul-rooted creations are not so much yours as the land's. Your bioregion manifests itself and fulfills itself in part through you. Your felt sense of who you are naturally roots itself more deeply *where* you are.

In 1985, Joanna Macy conceived a second innovative delivery system in collaboration with Australian rainforest activist John Seed. The Council of All Beings grew out of their evolving and shared holistic ecocentrism.

Joanna was in Australia conducting despair and empowerment workshops for environmental activists. John attended one of her workshops, after which he offered to show her what remained of one of Australia's great primordial rainforests. They spent the day together in an area in which John and other activists had once managed to stop a logging operation. John told Joanna his life-changing story of how, when he was standing there facing the police and the bulldozers, what he sensed above all else was the forest rising up behind him. In that moment, he experienced himself as the rainforest protecting itself through its one small part that had recently (in geologic terms) emerged into human thinking. He "felt himself rooted again in that which had brought him forth," and he tapped into his "vaster and truer identity" — what deep ecologist

Arne Naess terms the "ecological Self."[16] Since that day, what has sustained John's forest activism has been his recognition that he is simply part of the forest protecting itself.

Joanna describes what happened after John told her his story:

"How can we adapt despair and empowerment work to free us from the notion that we humans are the crown of creation, that we have claims on the rest of life?" John challenged me. We were squatting on the bank of a forest pond, . . . absently watching the waterbugs and considering a swim.

"The work we did on the weekend was powerful," he told me. "It blasted away our numbness, uncovered our passion for life. But it's missing a piece. We're still prey to the anthropocentrism that's destroying our world."

So what would it take, we wondered, as we stripped and dove into the pond. What kind of group work could move us beyond our shrunken human self-interest? The question turned in my mind as I swam down into the brown water. . . .

The answer that emerged was the Council of All Beings. By the time we dried off and dressed, it was taking shape in our minds: a simply structured ritual, in circular form, where people would step aside from their human identities and speak on behalf of other life-forms.[17]

Joanna and John co-led the first Council of All Beings a few days later. The ritual caught on and soon they were leading councils all over the world.[18] Through their instinctive Artisan ecocentrism — experiencing their membership in particular ecosystems — Joanna and John created a way to help people of any developmental stage begin to think and feel ecocentrically.

THE ALCOVE OF DEATH

In the Wild Orchard, soul-rooted individuation, including integration of the four dimensions of the Self, is often catalyzed or amplified by numinous experiences. More than once, this has occurred for me through encounters with Death.

Sometimes we're granted the chance to meet with Death as a perceptible and embodied presence, an experience above and beyond that of confronting our own mortality. The first time I spoke directly and tangibly to Death was in a redrock canyon in southern Utah not long after entering the Wild Orchard.

Some years earlier, Steve Zeller and I had taken our first hike down Grotto Canyon[19] to look for base-camp sites for future vision-fast groups. We came to the mouth of one of Grotto's tributaries and decided to have a look. After a minute's trek up the side canyon, Steve sat down without explanation and said he'd wait there. He waved me on with an odd smile. As I continued, the chasm began to feel a bit creepy, but it was nothing I could identify specifically — just a sense of foreboding. Deciding it didn't feel so good up there, I turned back and told Steve what happened. He said, "No kidding. There was no way *I* was going up there." We didn't speak about it further.

A few years later, another friend, Dave, returned from a solo hike in Grotto Canyon. He told me he'd ventured into a side canyon and up a steep south-facing slope to a giant alcove in the upper wall. He said he'd felt strongly pulled by something. He peered into the dark interior of the alcove. When his eyes adjusted, he recoiled. He wouldn't tell me exactly what he saw but said, with eyes wide, that his name for that place was "Death Alcove." He had not gone in.

I found the topographic map of Grotto and asked Dave to identify the alcove's location. He pointed to the north wall of the same side canyon Steve and I had entered.

Within a year, Judy, another friend (who does not know Dave), took a winter hike down Grotto Canyon with her dog, Lucky. She said there was one place in particular that really got her attention. It had scared her — no, terrified her. It was an alcove high on the wall of one of the many side canyons. The hair on the back of my neck stirred. I asked her what was frightening about it. She said there was something odd on the back wall, but emphasized that it was really the whole *feeling* of the place. Lucky wouldn't go any nearer than several yards from the alcove's mouth and had barked wildly when Judy started to. Judy had grown frightened, and she and Lucky had fled. She told me that she came to think of that place as "the Alcove of Death." I pulled out my topo map. Same place.

Two years later, in May, I was camped in the lower end of Grotto Canyon leading an eight-day soulcraft program. There were twelve of us. We had not planned to be in that canyon that week, but my intended destination, the Cemetery, was unreachable that spring due to heavy winter snows still blocking the access road. I had planned a group exercise in the Cemetery that involved a ritual encounter with Death. I told the group about my aborted plans. They wanted to enact the ceremony anyway and asked if there wasn't an appropriate location in Grotto Canyon. I said no, it needed to be done in the Cemetery. They insisted I must know a spot that would work.

Then, in midsentence, while assuring them a second time that there couldn't possibly be another site, I remembered the Alcove. So I told them that maybe I did know of a place that could work, but that it was too far, that I had never actually been there, that there was no trail between here and there, and that I wasn't even sure I could find the place. Besides, it would take half a day to hike that far up the main canyon and another half to return by nightfall. To my chagrin, they all wanted to go and wouldn't hear otherwise.

The real reason I didn't want to go was because of what I had promised myself I would do in the Cemetery ceremony. For several months, I had been feeling a need to commit myself more fully to my soulwork. Any of my friends, if asked, would have said that this was ludicrous, but on some level I really believed I was still holding back. So I decided to return to the Cemetery — a place where the presence of Death was, for me, palpable — and to make a sacred vow in Death's presence. Given how I intended to frame that vow, the prospect of actually doing it was intimidating.

The next day we arose before dawn, loaded our daypacks for a full day on the trail, brought along our drums, and headed upstream. I grew more anxious by the step. After five tiring hours, we reached the mouth of the side canyon. Looking high on its north wall, I immediately saw the alcove with its dark entrance yawning into the bright day. There were also two smaller alcoves on the same wall farther to the east, lower and closer to where we stood. I turned around to the person behind me, a highly intuitive and compassionate man. I pointed to the alcove farthest to the east, and said, unconvincingly, that that must be our destination. Michael laughed, put his arm around me, and said he knew I knew otherwise, and that there was no way of getting out of this.

Resigned, I told the group that we'd hike up the slope until we found the right spot to prepare ourselves, a place where we'd ask each person two very poignant and difficult questions. When the ceremony had come to me several weeks earlier, I knew only that this staging area would be known as the Place of the Questions. There we would enact a ceremonial group-consensus process to determine who was and who was not psychologically prepared to climb to the Cemetery ridge (now the alcove) — based on each person's answers to the two questions. Only those who received unanimous consent would go the rest of the way, and they would go alone, one at a time.

Ascending the narrow chasm of stream-polished red sandstone, we climbed steeply, threading our way through a massive tumble of boulders on petrified sand dunes until we came to the base of a house-sized rock. Climbing left around the shadowed base and then to the top of the rock, we found that it had a flat roof just large enough for the twelve of us to gather there in a circle. Only a few feet from where we stood, in the direction of the alcove high above, was a giant yucca — a "century plant" that sends up a twelve-foot stalk of blossoms. This particular yucca stalk had grown and then dried into the exact shape of a giant question mark. With a wry smile, I remarked that we had apparently found the Place of the Questions.

It was midday, the sky was flawlessly blue, and it was hot on that jumbled slope of baking rocks. When I was granted permission to go, I pulled off my T-shirt and scrambled full speed, hands and feet, up the incline as the others drummed below. The aerobic effort briefly kept my fear in check. My primary objective was to look Death in the eye — if he was really there — and make a solemn declaration of my soulwork, and ask him to take my life anytime my commitment should falter.

Reaching the alcove, I stopped, heart beating wildly, feeling very small on the edge of such an immense space. The shadowed cavern was about a hundred feet deep and at least that high, and twice as wide at its mouth. A mostly undisturbed slope of pure tan sand ran steeply up from my feet toward the back wall. A single large clump of sacred datura, whose large white flowers are sometimes used as a hallucinogen and can be lethal, once grew in the center of the sand slope, but it was long dead, its gray branches now a mass of desiccated bones two feet high. There were no other signs of previous life or habitation in this place.

Then I saw, on the back wall, a thin, ten-foot-tall humanoid figure in high relief, apparently formed from minerals leaching from water seeps in the soft sandstone. Dressed in a long, flowing emerald, gold, and black robe, he gazed down at me with hollow eyes and a terrible aura of omniscience. Involuntarily I dropped to my knees in the sand. If I were really going to do it, this was the moment. Trembling, breathless, I began to describe my soulwork, my commitment to it, and my request that he be my most fierce ally by holding my life as a surety for my vow.

As I spoke, Death nodded, but with what seemed like an air of impatience and indifference, perhaps some amusement. Uncertain, I kept speaking. He began pointing to his left without ever shifting his gaze from me. When I finished, he said, "You can make whatever promises you want, but they're of no interest to me until you make a commitment to *her.*" He gestured again to his left.

Only then did I see her, a similarly robed figure, not quite as tall, standing next to him, his left arm embracing her shoulders. Dumbfounded, I looked back at him and he said, "This is my wife, Joy."

In that moment, my understanding of Death and of my own life shattered. It was as if a cathedral had crumbled around me and I stood in billowing dust. This was the last thing I could have imagined hearing from Death. The old symbols had abruptly fled, there were no scriptures to consult, no questions to ask, and the only possible actions were meaningless.

"She is as much a presence in eternity as me," Death continued. "You have some awareness of mortality and a beginning relationship with me, but you have little affiliation with Joy. Your soulwork will not progress further until you surrender to *her.* Don't come back until you have."

As he spoke, my perceptual experience of the alcove was shifting radically. Upon arrival, it felt like I had imagined it would — a foreboding place that only heroes or fools would visit. Now it emanated a sweet aura, a sanctified glow, something like I'd expect of a honeymoon cottage. The alcove now felt more like a marital abode for Death and Joy, a playground for their eternal romance.

Overwhelmed and disoriented, I turned and staggered slowly down the slope. I felt both ruined and gifted by an encounter I would not have known how to imagine. On that day, I began my apprenticeship to Joy — a teacher who stands partnered with Death.

An embrace of joy truly had not been my strong point. I tend to be overly earnest.

I had expected Death to help me become even more assiduous, but in fact he directed me toward what I now see was my least developed virtue — the capacity for light-heartedness, playfulness, and simplicity, the capacity to surrender to joy. I needed these things not merely to round out my personality and humanity but also because they're essential ingredients for growing deeper into my soulwork.

Since that first visit to the Alcove of Death, I have come to think of it as, in truth, the Alcove of Love, a celebration of the alchemy between Death and Joy who, joined, exist as Love. A dark and foreboding place becomes a doorway to our true home. We are irrevocably altered by walking ceremonially toward what we most fear.

CULTURAL ARTISTRY IN AN EGOCENTRIC WORLD

As an Artisan in an egocentric world, you have no guarantee that society will welcome your gifts. It's possible that people will look upon your innovations or your original voice as odd, irrelevant, or crazy, or perhaps as subversive or immoral. Or you might do your work in complete obscurity and frustration, at least for a while. You're attempting to bring mystery, wildness, deep imagination, and praise of the sacred (the natural) to a society obsessed with security, comfort, material wealth, and the ownership of things. The culture you live in consists mostly of commodities and objects, while all things *you* encounter are entities and subjects.

A soulcentric society understands that culture must be continually renewed; it welcomes seeds of organic, wild innovation. Egocentric society, in contrast, wants an unrocking boat, preferring the predictability of genetically modified organisms and other human-controlled, synthetic forms.

As an Artisan in an egocentric world, you must persevere in fashioning and offering your innovations. You must remind yourself that there are people and places that need exactly what you were designed to create. Yes, in our society there aren't so many people who are receptive to soul-rooted gifts, but then there are also few people like you manifesting such gifts. It just might take longer for you to find each other. Don't give up.

In our March 2006 conversation, Thomas Berry told me he had always felt it necessary to do his work and express his perspectives regardless of the reactions he received, and regardless of whether anyone was even listening. He noted that he in fact had not had much of a following until the late 1980s (his midseventies), even though he had been giving talks and publishing books and articles since the early 1960s: "I had developed a certain confidence that I was contributing something needed and something worthwhile, and that I could say things that were challenging. I felt I was doing something right and something that was authentic." Thomas's soulwork, like that of all genuine adults and elders, has consisted of his ongoing conversation with the world, a conversation not widely noticed by society until relatively late in his life. Thomas's life is, in part, a teaching about the necessity of soulful self-acceptance in adulthood, especially in an egocentric world.

In my April 2006 meeting with Joanna Macy, she too spoke of the challenges of cultural artistry in an egocentric world:

> One of the real hardships of being an innovator is that you don't know how to honor what's really good about what you're doing, because it's all so strange. And then you just proceed. Sometimes I am so grateful, looking back, that I had the courage to persist in doing things that no one else was doing. There was nobody else legitimizing it.
>
> I remember when I did the first despair and empowerment workshop in Washington, D.C. [This was in the spring of 1982, during Ronald Reagan's first term as president.] I put up notices — [*she laughs heartily in self-amazement*] in *Washington*! I made a flyer and put it out in the *post office*! You know there's something very touchingly innocent about that. I would sort of walk in where angels feared to tread.
>
> I'm impressed by this quality of innocence that goes along with innovating anything. You can't stop to think how silly it can look. Because it can *really* look very silly. If you are easily daunted by that, you'll not get far. So the [inner] child helps you do it. You go to the child for innocence.

In an egocentric society it's easier to become discouraged in the always difficult work of creative innovation, because it's easier to convince yourself that no one cares about what you have to offer. But this is just a strategy of your Loyal Soldier, who is still attempting to keep you safe by making you feel small. Thank him for his kind intentions, and stay on your course. The fact is that, in an egocentric world, your soul gifts are needed even more than in a healthy one. Remember that self-doubt is as self-centered as self-inflation. Your obligation is to reach as deeply as you can and offer your unique and authentic gifts as bravely and beautifully as you're able.

Another danger for Artisans is archetypal projection, mentioned earlier; this minefield is even more hazardous in egocentric society. Due to the relative scarcity of genuine adults and elders, there are few people embodying the archetypes of those stages. Consequently, the initiated adults and elders end up holding those archetypal energies for many more people than in soulcentric society. The dangers and pitfalls are correspondingly amplified.

Many Thespians and Orphan-Impersonators (together, the majority of people over age twelve) will have a profound reaction to the archetypal energies you embody as an Artisan. Some will greatly admire you. Others will scorn and ridicule you because of their fear of those same archetypes within their own psyches or their envy of your ability to embody them, or both.

It's a privilege to carry the archetypes of the Artisan, Warrior, and Martyr, but with these potent energies pulsing through you, your social presence becomes distinctive, palpable, and unsettling — even if people have no idea who you are or what you do.

Some of the people who do know you will become furious or disillusioned when you exhibit ordinary human frailties such as anger, doubt, moodiness, carelessness, favoritism, or indecision. (And you will.) Or conversely, they might interpret your ordinary human qualities of shyness, charm, aggressiveness, or joy as further evidence of the archetype, in this way intensifying the projection. Many people will want you to take the role of a god or goddess so that you can do the work of embodying the necessary archetypal energies, which are so rare in their world.

In our patho-adolescent society, there's a tendency to want to sabotage or exalt anyone who's crossed beyond the adolescent life and reality. If you're not careful and skillful as an Artisan, either reaction will destroy you. This is one of the means by which an egocentric society keeps itself stuck — by undermining those who manage to mature.

For an Artisan in an egocentric society, balancing the archetypal with the human is a lot more challenging than in a soulcentric society. But the projections provide you with additional opportunities to cultivate your compassion for self and others, your capacity to take things less personally, and your ability to disidentify from the archetypes working through you. The projections remind you to embrace your humanity — to grow deeper into your heart, your vulnerability, and your enduring incompleteness. Your humility must grow in proportion to your uniqueness and beauty.

A SPARSE ORCHARD

It may happen that the Mystery has reasons for moving a person into the Wild Orchard before he has truly mastered a first delivery system. If so, it will be a thin or sparse Orchard — or one not so fecund or wild. He may end up creating and implementing new delivery systems without the benefit of capacities he would have developed in a more vital and complete Wellspring.

The Mystery might have pushed him into a sparse Orchard because it was aware of opportunities to sow certain seeds of cultural renaissance that might not have been possible had it waited longer. Better a sparse Orchard than none at all. If and when possible, the Artisan in a sparse Orchard will return to the tasks of earlier developmental stages in order to flesh out his presence in his current stage.

MANAGEMENT: THE EGOCENTRIC COUNTERPART TO THE WILD ORCHARD

In the previous egocentric stage of Capitulation (3c), a person stalled in the Conformist version of the Orphan-Impersonator sold out to the values, goals, and styles of superficial, egocentric society: the pursuit of security, safety, comfort, everlasting youth, and, sometimes, wealth.

At the end of Capitulation, the Conformist, now thoroughly assimilated and resigned to his egocentric role, undergoes the transition of Promotion, usually at midlife (in the early forties). He receives an advancement to the rank of manager (or supervisor, administrator, or director), the primary leadership role in egocentric society. He's arrived at the height of his egocentric powers. He's now eligible to make his share of the decisions that, often unwittingly, further extend and enhance the dominance of the industrial growth society, decisions with repressive and destructive effects on himself as well as others. He is financially rewarded, sometimes amply, for his work.

This, then, is the egocentric stage of Management (3d), the counterpart to the Wild Orchard. On the egocentric Wheel (Diagram 3-6, p. 71), Management is the sixth stage, but from the perspective of the soulcentric Wheel, this is another Conformist version of stage 3a. Most people in Management are between the ages of forty and sixty.

As in previous chapters, my intention in portraying this egocentric stage is to maximize the contrast with soulcentric development by describing something like a worst-case scenario. With good fortune, the reader's experience and perspective will not be so extreme or, better, will be completely different. Remember, there are at least three possible stages that forty- or fifty-year-olds might be in, each of them distinct: Management, the Oasis (a soulcentric stage), and the Wild Orchard. (The Cocoon and Wellspring are also possibilities.)

In Management, the Conformist-Impersonator is, in essence, a prisoner who's been promoted to a position of control over the lives of other prisoners. The new prisoner-manager has a higher-level manager over *him*, and so on. The patho-adolescent society — the egocentric system itself — has ultimate control over all the prisoners. In this scenario there is no single person or cartel — no evil dictator or junta, no god or devil — that occupies the decisive role of warden, Big Brother, or insecure wizard behind the curtain. There are only managers of various rank, organized in egocentric hierarchies built on the principle of domination over others, as opposed to partnership power *with* others or service *to* others. Those at the top of the hierarchies receive the most egocentric rewards but, psychospiritually, are as much victims and prisoners of the system as those lower down. No one in the system actually *wants* to destroy the biosphere that supports us all. Everyone is as bewildered as the next about what can be done to change the system. Meanwhile, it's business as usual. (Few in the system recognize that the primary means to transform the system is a society-wide cultivation of individual maturity — which would result in the necessary shift in collective consciousness.)

The egocentric system perpetuates itself through a set of regulations, laws, and unspoken agreements to which most everyone adheres (unnecessarily). One of the most destructive laws gives corporations the same rights as individual persons, in this way creating monstrously powerful sociopathic institutions with the legal right to eschew the ethical sensibility and environmental responsibility we might expect from mature humans. The unspoken agreements include the tenets that land, forests, water, airwaves, genetic codes, and numerous other elements of the commons (or commonwealth) can be privately owned, that money has value and can be exchanged for things of real value, and that governments can create money.

There is a special class of prisoners — law enforcement officers — whose job, in addition to maintaining genuine public safety, is to marginalize those who resist patho-adolescent conformity. Within egocentric hierarchies, there are no true leaders — no genuine adults or elders — only managers, only lords of the flies.

In Management, many Conformists are motivated to genuinely serve their community, but it is difficult for them to succeed in a meaningful or fulfilling way, because they don't truly understand what they have to give or what would count as true life-sustaining service. Without meaningful progress in personal individuation, their efforts to serve are unlikely to provide substantial benefit to others or significant fulfillment for themselves.

Two styles of egocentric management are the pseudo-Warrior and the pseudo-Martyr.[20]

Pseudo-Warriors

On the surface, pseudo-Warriors appear to be successful. They might achieve impressively in business, finance, government, science, the arts, health care, or education. They might generate fantastic profits or pioneer new educational methods. Perhaps they have passed consequential legislation, are raising money for a worthy cause, or are accomplishing significant medical or technological advances.

But the pseudo-Warrior did not come to her work by way of an initiation process, and consequently her intentions and labors are not sourced in the Earth's unfolding or rooted in the soul's desires. Her career choice is derived not from her depths but from family pressure or inheritance, vocational guidance, financial or social ambition, or arbitrary life circumstances.

Often, at the end of the workday, the pseudo-Warrior returns home with a sense of emptiness or despair. And despite her achievements and good intentions, her labors — especially if she's employed by a large corporation or egocentric government — might cause significant harm to individuals, communities, or environments. Like most people in egocentric society, she has little training in or awareness of ecological relationships. Some pseudo-Warriors sense that their work does not benefit the whole and that it might even be detrimental, but they're not aware of alternatives. They're embedded in the egocentric and anthropocentric system like most everyone they know. Some pseudo-Warriors, those with limited moral development, experience no guilt for how their efforts plainly damage the world. Foremost for them are personal pleasure, wealth, and power.

Two specific versions of the pseudo-Warrior are the Robber Baron and the Tyrant. Both are Conformist-Impersonators and sometimes Prince- or Princess-Impersonators. The Robber Baron is an unethical capitalist, a captain of industry who achieves great success at the expense of humanity and the environment shared by all species. He is often a sociopath (has no conscience), but, on the other hand, he might be simply and genuinely unaware. The Robber Baron exploits the labor of poor and oppressed people at home and abroad. He assaults the Earth to extract and use or sell the planet's "cheap" (to him) resources. He pollutes the land and water and air as a by-product of his business. He peddles toxic, useless, or exploitative products and services such as soft drinks, baby formula, contemporary television programming and advertising, child pornography, junk food, crack cocaine, pesticides, or chemical fertilizers. Despite his or his company's constant marketing efforts to generate this desire, he'll tell you that it's not his fault that people want and buy these things. Partly, he's correct. He's providing people with the products and services they demand and that afford some acceptance, pleasure, convenience, or success. And what egocentric person would blame him for doing what pays so well, in dollars, prestige, or power? In the end, what motivates most Robber Barons is the same thing that impels all Orphans. He wants to be accepted, he wants a comfortable place in society, and he doesn't want to be alone or to have to "leave home." He is, in essence, a Conformist doing what he's been taught.

Due to the way egocentric society functions, it's difficult for any one of us to completely avoid occupying the role of the Robber Baron — or his customer. At least at times. At least unconsciously.

While the Robber Baron is bent on profits, the Tyrant is hooked on power. The Tyrant leads in a harsh, cruel, and oppressive manner. His interest is not service or leadership but domination or personal triumph (or revenge). His usually hidden motives constitute a variation on the egocentric Orphan theme of greed and security. Beyond reaping whatever material rewards he can, he wants to safeguard his insecure place in the world. Unlike other Orphans, he acquires his safety by force; he cannot be thrown out unless he's overthrown. Instead of gaining his place by pleasing the authorities, he *becomes* the authority. He winds up isolated in his fortress and soon enough realizes he has plenty of power but no friends.

The Tyrant has more opportunities than most Orphan-Impersonators to act out his anger at the early abandonments and betrayals he suffered as a child. He can show the world (and especially his parents) that he will no longer be pushed around, that others can no longer control his place in the world. *He* will do the deciding and the controlling now. With sufficient military power at his command, he can enjoy the perverse catharsis of acting out his childhood rage through state-perpetrated terrorism, unprovoked invasion of sovereign nations, genocide, or world war.

In addition to the world-class Tyrants who terrorize their own people and/or other nations, there are also the countless Petty Tyrants encountered every day in an egocentric society. The Petty Tyrant possesses relatively little destructive force, but his mischief can be harmful nonetheless. None of us are immune to becoming Petty Tyrants when our unmet Orphan needs are stirred up — when something triggers our fear and anger over real or imagined abandonments.

Pseudo-Martyrs

Pseudo-Martyrs represent a second style of egocentric management. They manage not from the position of organizational boss or supervisor but from the role of helper or servant. From a distance, it looks like they're contributing to their families and society, but on closer inspection it turns out they take more than they give.

Pseudo-Martyrdom is common in egocentric society, so much so that we have several well-known terms for it. These include the Caretaker, the Rescuer, the Enabler, and the Codependent. In one version of the pseudo-Martyr, a person provides services to others with the hidden agenda of carving out a place of acceptance for herself, a place safe from abandonment. She accomplishes this by making herself indispensable. As long as others depend on her, they won't throw her out. She believes, at her core, that she has little worth as a human being, and that nobody would really want to be with her if they didn't have to.

In another variation, the pseudo-Martyr does not question her worth but believes she'll not get what she needs and deserves unless she sees to it herself, which she does by indulging others until she's made them dependent on her. At this point, she's in control because others need her to get what *they* want. If she encounters resistance, she blackmails them, either emotionally by evoking guilt, shame, or fear, or materially by withdrawing money or privileges.

With the Caretaker version of the pseudo-Martyr, the individual achieves a safe place by helping others, but his "care" comes at a high price for both the recipient and the provider. The recipient must pay through her collateral emotional caretaking of the Caretaker, as well as through her guilt for taking so much, and through her consequent lack of development and loss of autonomy. The Caretaker pays by never truly feeling loved or worthy. He's needed for what he does, not loved for who he is. Every act of caretaking digs his hole of low self-esteem a spadeful deeper. He also pays by enslaving himself to a life of service from which he derives little fulfillment. He's buying superficial acceptance, not true belonging. Unlike the genuine Martyr, the Caretaker is indeed a taker, not a (care) giver.

Rescuers are pseudo-Martyr Conformists who specialize in relationships with Victims.

Enablers are in relationships with alcoholics or other chemically dependent persons.

The Enabler enables the addict by supplying her with substances or covering for her when she's too wasted to meet her obligations.

A Codependent is also partnered with an addict, whether that addiction is chemical or behavioral. More generally, a Codependent exchanges his authenticity for acceptance. In codependent relationships, two people are enmeshed in an emotionally abusive alliance. They stay together because it gives them each a place, even though it's often a miserable one.

By whatever name, the pseudo-Martyr substitutes his or her real self and authentic relationships for a place of temporary, precarious safety.

Although we should hold pseudo-Martyrs and pseudo-Warriors responsible for their behavior, it's essential that we do not blame them for being the way they are. In egocentric society, many people who reach the stage of Management have never seen other options. If you or others you know are in Management and would prefer soul-centric individuation, the best thing to do (and it works) is to turn to the least addressed or least accomplished tasks of the Nest, Garden, and Oasis, especially the nature dimensions of those tasks.

WHEN DOES ADULTHOOD END?

Compared to the pseudo-Warrior and pseudo-Martyr, the Artisan in the Wild Orchard has little interest in security and no illusions of invincibility.[21] But she enjoys an authentic and rich relationship with her heart, her soul, her work, her people, the other-than-humans, Earth, and ultimately, the universe.

Still, one day she notices a waning in the fulfillment she derives from her soulwork, even while remaining brilliant as a channel for her giveaway. She begins to notice she's less interested in accomplishing, in getting things done. She's not excited about arriving somewhere other than where she is, or interested in making where she is any different from what it is. She's still performing her soulwork with a variety of delivery systems, but the work is becoming increasingly effortless. She's no longer motivated to generate new forms of embodiment for her particular set of soul powers. Something new now calls. It's not so much about doing as it is about being.

This Artisan is nearing the North point on the Wheel, the ending and fulfillment of the West hemisphere, the doing half of life. Another crisis of identity looms on the horizon.

It's sad to leave the Wild Orchard, with all its imaginative and fulfilling busyness, with all its magical, soul-infused inventions of things, ideas, crafts, and expressions never before seen or heard. The Wild Orchard surely was the best stage to be in.

CHAPTER TEN

THE MASTER
in the GROVE *of* ELDERS

Early Elderhood (Stage 7)

Dear darkening ground,
you've endured so patiently the walls we've built,
perhaps you'll give the cities one more hour

and grant the churches and cloisters two.
And those that labor — maybe you'll let their work
grip them another five hours, or seven,

before you become forest again, and water, and
    widening wilderness
in that hour of inconceivable terror
when you take back your name
from all things.

Just give me a little more time!
I want to love the things
as no one has thought to love them,
until they're real and ripe and worthy of you.

I want only seven days, seven
on which no one has ever written himself —
seven pages of solitude.

There will be a book that includes these pages,
and she who takes it in her hands
will sit staring at it a long time,

until she feels that she is being held
and you are writing.

— RAINER MARIA RILKE

Stage 7: Early Elderhood

Passage into this stage: Crowning
Stage name: The Grove of Elders
Task: Caring (the culture component) for the soul of the more-than-human
     community (the nature component)
Quadrant: North (giveaway)
Hemispheres: North and East (collective being)
Stage archetype: The Master
Quadrant archetype: The Warrior-Martyr
Gift to community: Wholeness
Circle of identity: From ecocentric to cosmoscentric
Center of gravity: The soul of the more-than-human community (the web of
     life)
Passage out of this stage: Surrender

PLAYED BY UNSEEN HANDS

Toward the end of my years fashioning this book, I realized that, in order to legitimately write about elderhood, I would need, in addition to the conceptual structure of the Wheel (with its psychological and ecological implications about the final two life stages), some instructive time with actual elders. After all, I wasn't able to write of this life stage from my own experience. I wanted to ask elders directly about their experience of elderhood and how their current life stage differs from their adulthood.

With input from friends, I drew up a list of a dozen well-known people who seem to exemplify authentic elderhood — a life station rarely attained in Western culture.[1] After a good deal of musing, I settled on two people, a man and a woman I felt were exceptional contemporary elders in the fullness of what such a status implies — Thomas Berry and Joanna Macy. I chose these two also because, in concert, their written work provides the most elegant and comprehensive means I've found for understanding humanity's current crisis and opportunity — in particular, their inspiring images of the Great Work and the Great Turning, respectively. I wrote to them, and to my delight both agreed to meet with me, Thomas in March 2006 at his home in Greensboro, North Carolina, and Joanna the following month at her home in Berkeley, California.

In this chapter, you'll find several selections from my interview with Joanna (who I believe was in the Grove when we met) as well as a few strands of my conversation with Thomas (who I believe was in the Mountain Cave). Much more of the latter interview will be found in the next chapter.

Joanna, as noted earlier, is an internationally renowned eco-philosopher; activist for peace, justice, and a safe environment; and scholar of Buddhism, deep ecology, and general systems theory.

From the beginning of my conversation with Joanna, I was moved by how emotionally and biographically candid she was willing to be with me, a stranger. She told me, for example, that she had recently, at age seventy-six, been experiencing some confusion about the value of the work she had done in her life. Given how deeply she has influenced the lives of millions around the world — through her books, talks, and workshops — I found this startling and poignant, almost heartbreaking. I asked her to explain.

JOANNA MACY: How to put it? . . . This may have to do with the diminishment of powers that comes with aging, and it may have to do with the genuine loss of agility and quickness of mind and body and the kind of erosion of self-regard that that brings — but there are times that I think that, if someone were to ask me, "What did you do with your life?" I wouldn't have any idea what to say.

BILL PLOTKIN: In what sense?

JM: I don't know. It just seems . . . there's a movement into formlessness that I feel about myself and my work. I don't have any definition. I just get some people together in a workshop and help them love life.

There's a feeling of being inadequate as I hurry along, because I feel burdened by having more to do than I have time or capacity to do it. So many communications. So much to handle. And I'm not getting to it. I have a cloud of feelings that I ought to be able to manage my time better.

BP: Well, here's another angle I wonder about. In the model I've developed, when a person moves from the Wild Orchard to the Grove of Elders, which means moving from the Wheel's West half of *doing* to the East half of *being* — something of that transition is experienced as "It was never really me doing it, anyway." It's a recognition that, "although I once took credit for the contributions I made, I now realize I was actually just a vehicle. Perhaps I knew that before, intellectually, but now I'm really getting it in my bones, a direct experience that I was actually just a channel for something rather grand and mysterious."

JM: Oh, yeah, that's it.

Part of the syntax I'm developing for myself and for my work has to do a lot with the preposition *through*. "To allow this to be spoken *through* you" or "to allow this to happen *through* you." Redefining power that way. So, that's true. I think that that's part of it.

Another thing I've noticed, too, is that it seems there are many more syn-chronicities happening — oh, my, hugely! — for which there is no way I can take any credit. I don't feel I can take credit for anything. Maybe that's part of it. But there are things that come up — people come into my life, and things come in, and things happen that I could not have orchestrated. And if I had thought, "Oh, this is something that can happen," I wouldn't have known how to get there. But they can only happen if there had been some larger power. For example, often I have the image of large, unseen hands weaving things together. And the word *grace*, which has always been very precious to me, seems more and more appropriate.

BP: That resonates with the way I've thought about the Grove of Elders, in that it seems there would be a process in this stage of letting go of striving. But there's a lot that's been earned through the previous six stages, especially the stages I call the Wellspring and the Wild Orchard, during which you've performed your authentic adult work in the world. Through that work, you've become a more dif-ferentiated or defined node in the net, in the web of life. You've become more your true self, and you've embodied your essence in the world. And you've done this through your striving, through intent, through your actions.

So, one aspect of the Grove of Elders is that you become like a seed crystal placed in a supersaturated solution. Just your presence causes your whole envi-ronment to crystallize in a certain way. The possibility had been there all along, but it needed you, the seed crystal, to materialize. So, just your presence as a Mas-ter — a stage-7 elder — allows certain things to happen that have to do with who you've become in your life. And you — your conscious self — you just look and notice that it's happening and realize that you didn't specifically have an inten-tion to orchestrate it. It just happened around you. And I suppose that would be experienced as synchronicity. It's as if, after so many years of creating a soul-infused self, your authentic presence in the world is on automatic pilot.

JM: Oh, lovely. Yes. This is very moving to me to think about, as you talk about that. As I think about it, it makes emotion come up — tears in my throat.

BP: Gratitude for the world?

JM: Happiness.

BP: Perhaps a release from having to try so hard, after all those years?

JM: Yeah, that's right. The trying so hard, which I seem less good at now. The striv-ing that I'm less good at. But, actually, what you're pointing out, helping me see again, is that the best things have nothing to do with my striving. Nothing! They just come in — it's amazing — in such a way that this happens and that happens. And of course it says something so astonishing about the nature of reality, the way systems self-organize. I mean, it's what I have taught, but still, to experience the truth of what you've believed and taught is astonishing! Isn't it?

BP: Yes, indeed. Perhaps this is similar to the contrast between "I have to make it happen" and dependent co-arising [the Buddha's teaching of mutual causality or interbeing — everything is shaped by everything else]. "I have to make it happen" implies that it all starts with me, and if I don't do it, it's not going to happen. Whereas, the truth is that I'm just one element in the mix, or that I'm an agent for the intentions of something mysterious, like soul or spirit or nature.

JM: Yes. It's so beautiful! So beautiful.

So, I put down words here [in her previously written notes on her experience of elderhood] like "less controlling." And I wasn't a control freak, anyway. But it's certainly less now.

Another thing is that there's more spontaneous expression of intuition, or a readiness to go by the seat of my pants for the group, to say what comes up and to find that I might say something offhand that's just what needs to be injected. So it's almost like letting myself be played by these unseen hands.

Joanna's experience of being played by an invisible force echoes Rilke's poem that begins this chapter. Rilke asks Earth for seven final days to love the things of the world and to write his love into a book that a woman might read, until she feels held and feels that Earth itself did the writing. Rilke experiences Earth as working through him, and through his reader as well, just as Joanna speaks of some larger power or grace — unseen hands — working through *her*.

CROWNING: PASSAGE INTO ELDERHOOD

As explained in chapter 3, I adapted the term *Crowning* from *Croning*, a contemporary word for a woman's rite of passage into elderhood, the stage of the crone.[2] By adding a "w" to make it "crowning," it says the right thing for both genders. With its implication of royalty, Crowning marks the transition into the most esteemed social and spiritual quarter of life.

Crowning occurs at the North point on the Wheel. The North, which corresponds to midnight on the diurnal cycle, is where your ego consciousness completes its adaptation to the dark, so that you are able now to see keenly into the hidden dimensions of the world and to conduct yourself in the "light" of that knowledge.

In the seasonal cycle, the north compass point corresponds to the winter solstice, which is when your consciousness completes its acclimatization to the cold (in addition to the dark) by honing the competency that allows you to thrive in challenging conditions and contribute to the common good. Crowning, then, represents your achievement of mastery in the enactment of your soulwork.

At the North hour in life, your personality becomes firmly rooted in true character — your soul-infused expression of Self. More and more, you instinctively embody your character in your everyday behavior without deliberate intention to do so.

At Crowning, you relinquish your conscious attachment to the embodiment of your soul powers — the attachment that was the very definition of your adulthood — as you turn your attention to domains much wider than your individual soul life, namely, the soul of the more-than-human community. But it's not so much that you *choose* at this moment to make the web of life your top priority; it's more as if the Mystery, sensing you're ready, commands you to take up that task, and you assent.

At the North point on the Wheel, although you pass from the West half of the Wheel to the East, you remain in the North quadrant. This means that, in the Grove of Elders, your life is still centered in the North qualities of leadership, giveaway, and service (the manifestation of your soul gifts), just as it was in the Wild Orchard.

But what *does* change at Crowning — and this is a huge shift — corresponds to the movement from the West hemisphere of the Wheel to its East. You are transiting from the half of life focused on *doing* (striving, aspiring, convincing, insisting, struggling, competing, contending) and manifesting your uniqueness (West, soul) to the half devoted to *being* (accepting, enjoying, celebrating, receiving, submitting, enduring) and reflecting the universal (East, spirit).

This movement, then, is opposite the one you made at puberty — from childhood's spiritual innocence (and, consequently, being) to the adolescent quest for identity and uniqueness (and, consequently, doing). In other words, you are returning to a state similar to childhood, when you were last in the East hemisphere. Worldly accomplishment is no longer your primary conscious focus — at least not the way it was when you were a student and adult, as a Thespian, Wanderer, Apprentice, or Artisan. The biblical metaphor is that life leads from the garden of innocence to the world of knowledge-pain-freedom and then returns to the garden, now a place of wisdom, which is the matured embodiment of innocence.

In elderhood, you find yourself every day more astonished by what already *is* than by what could be. Like Rilke, who writes, "I want to love the things / as no one has thought to love them," you want to celebrate, nurture, and love all of life more than you want to get some place different or create something new. You begin to feel more like an expression of life than a conscious fashioner of it.

In our interview, Joanna echoed this theme of transiting from doing to being, from accomplishment to celebration:

> For me, moving into elderhood has been a movement from informing or arguing or persuading or telling...to evoking. From informing to evoking. From arguing to blessing. From proving — I don't have the slightest interest in proving anything anymore, and not so much in telling, either — to hinting, waiting, blessing, or evoking. And I have greater gratitude and greater comfort in not knowing. This is the don't-know mind, which is recognized more in Buddhism than in other major religions.

The elements of the don't-know mind of elderhood are perhaps constellated at the moment of Crowning, which is akin to Rilke's "hour of inconceivable terror / when" Earth takes back her "name / from all things." When Earth takes back her name from *you*, you grasp that what you have accomplished in your life was not so much your doing as it was Earth's.

After Crowning, in addition to remaining in the North *quadrant* (leadership, competence, knowledge, giveaway), you also continue to abide, of course, in the North *half* of the Wheel, where you have been since Soul Initiation and will remain till the end of your days. Your life, in other words, is still much more about the collective than the individual. You're in the middle of that half of life in which you focus on your cultural and ecological context more than on individual goals separate from your relationship to the whole.

In that your life in the Grove of Elders is now about *being* (in addition to the collective), your center of psychospiritual gravity has shifted from your giveaway as art form (the Orchard) to the web of life (the Grove). The hub of your life, in other words, has moved from the depths of your own soul to the depths of the community soul, from the innovative performance of your art to the integrity and well-being of the world.

Your soul-infused contribution to the world continues, but now you allow it rather than push it. You find that you manifest your soul qualities without having to do anything in particular to make this happen. You become an observer-recipient of the gifts of your soul, as if witnessing the artistry of another person. Your soulwork happens *through* you. You can't help it.

Although you can retire from a job (especially a survival job), you cannot retire from soulwork. Your soulwork, once you discover it, is a constant strand of your life. It is always evolving into new forms, but its essence does not end until this life does.

Your transition into true elderhood might be marked by a rite of passage, a Rite of Crowning. Because Crowning takes place at the end of the Artisan stage and consequently celebrates your soulwork mastery, your community (if it is soulcentric) might at this time express its gratitude to you for all you have offered as an adult. But in contrast to a merry and unmomentous retirement party, this would be a sincere public recognition of your true character and an initiatory passage into the final quadrant of the Wheel.

A Rite of Crowning might also help you to bear, brave, and suffer through the significant loss inherent in your passage out of the Wild Orchard. Although Crowning brings an increase in psychosocial status and maturity, there is also the loss of a familiar and comfortable mode of being and its sources of enjoyment and fulfillment. You are surrendering nothing less than your unquestioned belief in your own personal agency, your sense of individual accomplishment. This triggers a great crisis of identity. The nascent elder realizes deep in her bones, as did Joanna, that the ego cannot take any central credit for what has been accomplished through her.

Although the transition into elderhood might be marked by a formal, community-implemented rite of passage, such a rite is not nearly so important at this season of life as it was at earlier stages. As a perhaps more fitting alternative, an elder might mark her own Crowning by a period of withdrawal, an interval of solitude that might allow the metamorphosis of this passage to unfold in its own way.

This is what Joanna did. In 2004, she took what she called "a sabbath year," a whole year without commitments "to see what would happen to my mind" when not so busy. During that year, she devoted much of her time to her meditation practice, "letting the practice inform me." She also played the recorder. And she did a lot of looking. "I got to looking and staring at things. Staring at the sky. I was doing that this morning. I can look at things for *so* long. There's no end to it! It's sort of the best thing I do. [*laughter*] I just want to..." [*tears...of grief? ecstasy? both?*] I am reminded again of Rilke's seven pages, his book of solitude in which he has written of his love of the things of the world: "and she who takes it in her hands / will sit staring at it a long time."

IN THE GROVE OF ELDERS

Consider a mature-growth redwood or cedar forest. Picture a grove of ancient trees in the midst of that forest. Those colossal trees are the crown jewels of the ecosystem. Not only do they, in their lofty presence, constitute evidence of a healthy forest community, but they also are a principal factor in generating and maintaining the health of their biome. Those elder trees provide shelter and a stable environment of air, soil, and water for the growth of other trees, bushes, flowers, and grasses, and consequently, food and home for a great variety of animal species.

Mature trees sustain their world — sustain *our* world. Maintaining the world's integrity, they are unsurpassed preservers and nurturers. Human elders like Joanna Macy and Thomas Berry fulfill this same role. Their very presence — like old-growth trees, so rare now — grants us hope for a healthy human community sometime in the future, a climax culture. Elders play an essential role in engendering a healthy cultural environment for children, adolescents, and adults, and in enabling those adults to one day become elders themselves.

Having returned to the source of their own innocence and wonder, elders celebrate these same qualities in children even more effectively than most parents can. Knowing the source of their true life in the mysteries, they recognize when an adolescent is ready to begin her own exploration of hidden dimensions, and they help guide that essential journey. Having spent an abundant adulthood embodying their soul gifts, they mentor those adults whose work lies in a similar vein. And most important, they possess the wisdom and perspective that animate the big questions and that allow the long view by which they guide their human society in relationship to the greater world.

In a soulcentric society, and where possible in egocentric society, stage-7 elders meet together in council from time to time, like ancient trees gathered in a grove. This is one of their essential roles. In every human community, in every place and time, questions arise that are so big that no single elder (and no assembly of mere adults) can hope to answer them. With such decisive concerns, there is no substitute for the Council of Elders. These matters require too much scope and depth to be left to adult leaders, or even worse — as we do in Western and Westernized society — to adolescent kingpins and warlords. The Council of Elders must assure that the ventures of human society benefit the greater Earth community. Never before has the guidance of true elders been more urgently needed. The achievement of the Great Turning largely depends on their wisdom and leadership.

If and when Western society matures, a true Council of Elders will supersede what we now call the United Nations.

THE MASTER: ARCHETYPE OF EARLY ELDERHOOD

The archetype of the Master represents the third and final step in the guild sequence of apprentice-artisan-master. The Master has achieved virtuosity in his soulwork. Now he no longer strives to perfect his craft, not because further improvement isn't possible, but because his conscious focus in life has progressed from artistry to mentoring, from innovation to caring for the web of life.

In our interview, Joanna affirmed that this tending to the web of life had in fact become the center of her conscious sensibility.

JM: I've written about the web of life and taught about it for the last thirty years, but it's becoming more *real* to me.

BP: It's more where you live now?

JM: Yes. Like I pray to it. Or I listen to it. And I do a lot of noodling about how, philosophically and metaphysically, the web of life can be a more-than-human intelligence, almost endowing it with personality. The Mother of All Buddhas [the Buddha's central doctrine of mutual causality] blends in my mind with Gaia, and with the web of life, and with the goddess of all the little animals.

The Grove stage is characterized by a gradual shift from doing to being, from the honing of skill to the development of a centered nonstriving. Previously, life had been defined by personal initiative and an energetic promotion of the ego's agenda — whether that ego was a child's, adolescent's, or soul-rooted adult's. Now, for the Master, the challenge and opportunity is to get out of the way of the magic, to surrender to the way in which life — the Mystery, or the Tao — wants to manifest through the individuated self. The Master learns to release her personal ownership of her soulwork.

When the Master thinks about the particular form of soulwork she performed as an adult — say, health care, education, or agriculture — her primary concern is that work's relationship to community, culture, and nature. Her interest, in other words, shifts from discovering how to most innovatively perform her work to assuring that this particular genus of work finds its balanced place in the greater web of life.

A person cannot enter the Grove without having undergone the development that takes place in the Orchard. A Master, in other words, is not merely an old person — and not even necessarily an old person. If he did not develop mastery of his soulwork as an Artisan, his understanding of that work would not be deep enough to enable him to clearly see its significance from the perspective of the whole. This understanding is one dimension of true elderhood.

Masters are the community members who have the wisdom, scope, and perspective to assess the balance between the human world and the larger web of life that we're part of. As we are seeing now in our world all too plainly, if the human is not in balance with the whole, everything suffers and eventually dies.

THE WARRIOR-MARTYR, PART II

In the Orchard, the Warrior-Martyr's qualities of fierceness and compassion were manifested through the Artisan's creation of innovative delivery systems for soul. Now, in the Grove, the Warrior-Martyr archetype functions through the Master's fierce defense and impassioned nurturing of the more-than-human world. More keenly than others, the Master feels her interdependence with all life and how she is, in essence, summoned into existence through her relationships with all other beings. As a Warrior-Martyr, then, her heart naturally breaks open in response to the suffering of others, and she will go to whatever lengths necessary to protect life, especially at the species and habitat levels.

In our interview, Joanna spoke of the Warrior and Martyr facets of the bodhisattva archetype as she experiences them in her own elderhood:

JM: In opening to his pain for the world, the Warrior lets himself be broken. The bodhisattva who has been evoked for me more and more recently is the one called Ksitigarbha or Jizo. He is the one who voluntarily descends into the deepest levels of hell because he can hear the crying there. And what just moves me so is that he goes down *not* necessarily to rescue and bring them up — not like on a cowboy journey — but rather, "*If* there are people there, I will be with them." And that is just so big ... [*weeps*] ... it's just so moving to me. "If my brothers and sisters are there, I'm going to go be with them. I'm not so arrogant to believe I know how to deliver them, but at least they won't be alone. I will own that part of human experience."

BP: It's not altruism.

JM: Yeah, *altruism* is much too weak of a word. *Martyr* always has this connotation in our culture of self-righteousness, altruism, and piety.

But Jizo or Ksitigarbha — there's nothing sentimental there. "If this is the reality that spawned me, if this is what the web of life contains, then I will embrace it." It's really the recognition of *sarvodaya* — Pali for "we all wake up." If there's any waking up, we wake up together.

I am reminded of Joanna's decades-long work on behalf of future generations through such endeavors as the Nuclear Guardianship Project. Cosmologist Brian Swimme once introduced her to an audience by saying, "She has lots of friends. Most of them aren't born yet."

THE MASTER'S CONTRIBUTION TO THE WORLD: WHOLENESS

The gift that the Master is to her people goes beyond her leadership, mentoring, and tending to the community soul. Her very being is a gift of wholeness, and in at least three ways. First, the core value in her life, which arises from her psychospiritual center of gravity, is the desire that every thing and every creature be allowed its true place, so that the world functions in its fullness, in accordance with its comprehensive destiny. She appreciates that each species, each habitat, and each social issue is related to all others. She understands that everything is alive, that it all fits together, and that we are all participants and reflections of the whole. Like a grove of old-growth trees, her vital presence holds the world together. She radiates wholeness.

Second, through her soul-rooted individuation in the Cocoon, Wellspring, and Orchard, the Master has consciously cultivated her own wholeness: she has, in other words, accessed, strengthened, and integrated the four dimensions of the Self — the Innocent-Sage, the Wild Self, the Anima- or Animus-Muse, and the Generative Adult. Her Crowning confirms her wholeness, in this sense, in addition to her mastery of her soulwork. Although she is neither perfect nor normative — her personality has become more particular, not more universal — she is as close as humans get to being fully human, to embodying and bestowing all the possibilities of humanness.[3] Even when others can't name it, they can sense this wholeness in her presence.

Third, through her specific actions, through her devoted tending of the web of life, and by her advocacy of the rights of all beings, the Master lends to the human village an air of completeness, rightness, tolerance, compassion, and forgiveness — all these being close cousins of wholeness. The rarity of these qualities in our world today speaks both to the scarcity of true elders and our compelling need for them.

THE DEVELOPMENTAL TASK OF THE MASTER: CARING FOR THE SOUL OF THE MORE-THAN-HUMAN COMMUNITY

Although a momentous shift from doing to being is under way in the Grove, as a Master you still have a task to perform: caring for the soul of the more-than-human community.

You couldn't truly do this, however, without being able to *perceive* the soul of the community. But, of course, as a Master, you *can* do this. This discernment comes from your years of conscious, soul-rooted membership in the world, your Apprentice and Artisan years, during which you developed and implemented your soulwork. The essence of your giveaway, after all, derives from your ultimate place in the world, which is to say your place in nature. Your soulwork, in other words, had its roots not only in a human community but also in the larger Earth community. The latter membership — and not your family, job, social network, nation, or religion — was your primary allegiance in your adult years. Through your consciously lived Earth membership — your ecocentric identity — you beheld and fathomed the soul of the more-than-human community.

The soul of the Earth is the essence or the psyche of the being called Gaia. To truly know another individual at her depths is to perceive and to know her soul, the ultimate way she fits into the web of life. The Earth, too, can be known this way. To perceive the soul of Earth requires a sense of what Taoists call the way of life, the fact that everything in our world is in relationship to everything else, that nothing is itself without everything else, and that anything that seems to be a distinct thing is actually an element or strand in a larger pattern. It is to sense what the Chinese call *li*, the dynamic patterning of nature, the web of relationships within and throughout the planet.

To truly care for the Earth community, then, a person must sense or intuit the soul of the Earth, the underlying pattern of nature expressed through an astounding diversity of forms and species. This understanding — beyond the powers of language to adequately express — comes through years of adult soulwork and the resultant personal development. When your discernment of Earth's soul crystallizes, you undergo the transition into elderhood. The apprehension of Gaia's soul might in fact be the very thing that catalyzes Crowning or that informs the Mystery of your readiness.

To care for the soul of the more-than-human community is to help maintain an equilibrium between the human village (culture) and the larger world (nature). The nature-culture tension in this stage, therefore, is woven into the very fabric of the Master's task. If the culture dimension (cultivating a viable society) is ignored, the people perish from starvation, disease, exposure, or war (civil or otherwise). If the nature dimension (preserving ecological wildness and diversity) is ignored, the people (and many other species) perish from the degradation or loss of habitat. Throughout the twentieth century, and now at the beginning of the twenty-first, we have witnessed the grievous neglect of *both* dimensions — by most national governments and most large corporations. Our hope currently lies in the leadership and efforts of individuals, grassroots networks, nongovernmental organizations, and the more local and smaller-scale governments and businesses.

Caring for the soul of the more-than-human community has at least five components: (1) defending and nurturing the innocence and wonder of children, (2) mentoring and initiating adolescents, (3) mentoring adults in their soulwork, (4) guiding the evolution or transformation of the culture, and (5) maintaining the balance between human culture and the greater Earth community. In doing these things, the Master embraces and engenders wholeness.

Defending and Nurturing the Innocence and Wonder of Children

As part of their delight in all forms of Earthly life, Masters — whether or not they are grandparents — derive immense joy from observing and interacting with children, both Innocents and Explorers. Perceiving and appreciating the soul of the Earth more keenly than most people in earlier stages, Masters are adept at recognizing wild nature in human children, in particular their natural innocence and wonder, essential foundations for all that follows in life. Masters, then, do all they can to defend these qualities in children from whatever elements of their society might compromise child-nature.

But Masters do more than defend these qualities; they also directly nurture them through personal interaction with children and through promoting nature-culture-balanced curricula and child-rearing practices. For example, Masters lobby for and model (as needed) the importance of touch, play, nature, and stories in the Nest. For children in the Garden, they champion, for instance, their need for free play in nature, the celebration of the imagination and senses, the thorough exploration and embrace of emotions, and the enjoyment of sacred stories (mythology and cosmology).

Earth elder Thomas Berry reminds us that children must understand that their home is not the industrial world but the world of "woodlands and meadows and flowers and birds and mountains and valleys and streams and stars."[4] Thomas tells us that children must also be enabled to directly experience the universe. In fact, he believes the child is our guide to how the universe ought to be experienced by *all* of us.

When they're with children, Masters might look like they're playing — laughing together, gardening, fashioning things, exploring the natural astonishments of the world. They are. But they're also celebrating innocence and wonder, nurturing the imagination, senses, and emotions, and, in all these ways, caring for the soul of the world.

Mentoring and Initiating Adolescents

In the role of mentor, Masters might tutor Thespian youth in the Wheel of Life or its cultural counterpart, teaching them about life stages and passages, tasks and archetypes, subpersonalities, human wholeness, and psychological types. In this way, Masters help Thespians appreciate the unfolding stages of growth as well as their own developing uniqueness and wholeness. More generally, Masters support youth finding their way through the maze of challenges as they approach the Cocoon — for example, through value exploration, emotional access and expression, Loyal Soldier relations, and the minefields of authenticity, personal conflicts, and sex.

Even more vitally, as we saw earlier, it's primarily the Masters who have the time and the knack to recognize when particular Thespians are ready to enter their Cocoon time of initiatory instruction and wandering. And Masters play a central role in training and initiating Wanderers, helping them disengage from their early adolescent way of belonging, teaching them soulcraft skills and practices, and preparing them to assume their unique roles in the community and, more generally, on Earth.

Masters are naturally the village authorities on the initiation of youth because, in addition to having undergone the descent themselves, they possess the long view allowing them to fully appreciate where initiation leads, and they hold a thoroughly nature-based perspective on life. The Masters' ecocentric outlook informs them that, if their culture is going to remain vital and continue to evolve, the adolescents must be initiated into their individual destinies. They appreciate the big picture of human development and see the deeper significance of the social and psychospiritual struggles of youth.

Mentoring Adults in Their Soulwork

In caring for the soul of the more-than-human community, a Master often mentors Soul Apprentices who've been called to the same craft as hers. She might also impart to those Artisans of her soulwork "clan" the knowledge, skill, and wisdom she's gathered about embodying their shared brand of wildness and mystery, and, in so doing, deputize the next generation and bestow on them the scepter of leadership.

Although the Master has known since the Garden that she is mortal, in the Grove she begins to see, more specifically, the end of her soulwork days. She lives with the knowledge that she will relinquish her place to others. What does she wish them to comprehend? What aspects of her soulwork will she choose to pass on? Which tools and techniques? Which principles and perspectives? Naturally her orientation now leans more toward training and mentoring and less toward innovating and producing.

JM: I spend more time now with people who come to consult me. The mentoring part, on an individual basis, happens more.

I also have a heightened appreciation in elderhood for redundancy. I'm using that as a systems term. In any evolution or development, whether embryonic or cultural, there are many paths to the same goal. If one is blocked, then another is taken. There are many people doing things similar to what I'm doing. My delight in that fact increases with elderhood because I am moving away from competitiveness.

I never was possessive about the work. I was always giving it away. I'm just concerned about quality. People do some of the more charged and significant pieces of my work, and they'll do it without even bothering to read my book. They'll just hear someone describe it. That *does* annoy me.

BP: What can be done about it?

JM: Complain!

A Master desires that the emerging adult leaders fully grasp the deep structure of their soulwork, understanding both the nature of the mystery from which that work springs and the nuance of form that allows it to sing.

Guiding the Evolution or Transformation of the Culture

A fourth way to care for the soul of the more-than-human community is to oversee, individually and as part of a council of elders, the evolving direction of the culture. Technical advancements, environmental changes, and social and cultural shifts can require significant modifications in the organization, agenda, or values of society. With the multidimensional global crisis of this century, this is especially true, perhaps more than ever in the human story. We are in great need of Masters to guide us through the terribly difficult times to come, to see the need for specific cultural corrections, to design the appropriate responses, and to oversee their implementation.

In our interview, Joanna distinguished between the biological status of old age and the social or psychospiritual status of elderhood: "Eldering is a relational function that has both instructional aspects and inspirational aspects — the elder as a holder. In so many cultures, the elder holds the tradition." To this I would add that the elder holds not so much the surface forms of the tradition but, more importantly, its deep-structural essence, from which depths new forms might emerge to serve cultural evolution.

The elder leads and teaches partly through stories. Joanna sees the elder as carrying the collective stories of cultural memory, the universal and mystical stories, the stories of vast realms.

One of the ways that Joanna, as an elder, is influencing the evolving direction of our culture revolves around what she calls "deep-time work." This is a collection of perspectives and exercises that help people experience their present lives within much larger temporal contexts, nourishing a strong, felt connection with both past and future generations. The experience of deep time utterly contrasts with the sense of time unique to — and all too prevalent in — contemporary society. "[Our] economy and technologies depend upon decisions made at lightning speed for short-term goals, cutting us off from nature's rhythms and from the past and future as well. Marooned in the present, we are progressively blinded to the sheer ongoingness of time. Both the company of our ancestors and the claims of our descendants become less and less real to us."[5]

In her work with deep time, Joanna invites us to bring both our forebears and the future beings into our awareness in order to help us comprehend, from a suitably vast perspective, the choices we must make in this century.

Joanna explains that the ultimate purpose of deep-time work is to "save life." Saving life — the life of all species — is a central goal for the Master as she guides the evolution of the culture. This became an explicit intention in Joanna's work early in her adult years, but she has grown increasingly passionate about it since her center of gravity shifted to the web of life.

Joanna's deep-time work began in the 1980s with the Nuclear Guardianship Project, a network of citizen groups monitoring the inconceivably deadly by-products of nuclear technology. At that time, she and her colleagues were confronting the mind-boggling span of a quarter million years — the time it takes for plutonium to decay. More recently, they have been looking at depleted uranium, which is deadly far longer.

Because of uranium, our karma extends into the future 4.5 billion years, which is mythic by its very nature because it's the assumed age of Earth. We have manufactured munitions that are lethal that long. And the U.S. administration insists upon making even more because of the military advantage — even if they kill and mutate our own troops!

The deep-time work is an additional resource in experiencing our identity as Gaia, our life as Gaia. This can help us hold the horror — in a way, the darkness — that we have been creating for ourselves ever since the Second World War with our policies of political and economic control. But it's gotten so much more blatant. Now we are ready to nuke Tehran. This is disastrous in the extreme and evidence of a psychopathic, self-destructive element in our culture.

Rabbi Zalman Schachter-Shalomi, founder of the Spiritual Eldering Institute, offers additional ideas for how elders today might serve cultural evolution.

I'm thinking of an elder corps. Instead of sending young soldiers into the world's trouble spots, we would send in elders. They would meet with those who had lost grandchildren on both sides of the conflict and grieve with them. I think that with such conversations, the aggravated political climate would yield to wisdom and compassion.

. . . We're inhabitants of a planet that is trying to save its life. Earth needs a cadre of conscious elders who are aware of their task for healing the planet.[6]

Another component of Joanna Macy's culture-guiding Master work is to reassure people that they can openly face the horrors of our current global situation and be empowered by the consequent grief, despair, and strategic challenges:

> One of the ways I care for the soul of the community is to offer reassurance. In many ways, it comes without deliberation. I'm often saying, "You can make it. You are going to be able to make it. It's going to be a hard time, you know, but you can make it. You belong to the Earth and you can make it."

> To reassure is one of the things that I do so constantly and so spontaneously in my work because we're all looking at "Ahhhh!" [*uttered as an expression of fright*] We *dare* to look at our dark sister Erishkigal.[7] You know, when Inanna went down into the underworld, she pulled back the curtain and looked! At the same time, there must be this constant reassurance: "See how tough you are! You see what's going on, and you are doing what you are because you *love* this world, and that love is reciprocal love! You're *born* for this time. The whole Earth, for all these billions of years, has conspired through all these conditions to bring you up to this point."

> Early on, the work that I initiated with despair, which is probably the most central feature of it all, was to trust, to demand, that you *can* face this even if you think you're going to die, because you *won't* die. It's positive disintegration, not death.

As underworld guides know, personal maturation, especially in the Cocoon, often begins with a dying (a "positive disintegration"), always a necessity before the rebirth of Soul Initiation. Likewise, the twenty-first-century Masters know that the transformation of culture, which they are charged to oversee, requires something like a collective descent into our inescapable grief and despair over the real possibility of our self-inflicted extinction, a descent that empowers our will to act and our capacity to respond imaginatively and effectively. The Great Turning is our cultural rite of passage, perhaps the Soul Initiation of the human species. The Masters of our time must assume the role of underworld guides for the human collective.

Maintaining the Balance between Human Culture and the Larger Earth Community

This fifth subtask is perhaps the most vital component of the Master's guardianship of the soul of the world. The Master must take his place as one of the trustees of the culture. His charge includes the long-term sustainability of the human-wild interface and consequently of the vitality of the land, waters, and air. He becomes a defender of the diversity and integrity of all life.

"Defender of life" is an accurate characterization of the work of Thomas Berry since the beginning of his elderhood in the early 1980s. On his own initiative, as well as in collaboration with many organizations and groups around the world, Thomas has led the way in expressing the urgency of refashioning all human affairs to conform with the larger functioning of our planet. He tells us that elders must now help the younger generations reinvent culture in all four of its "great establishments that control our lives — the government/legal establishment, the economic/corporation establishment, the education/university establishment, and the religious/church or synagogue or mosque establishment."[8]

Connecting this fifth subtask of the Master with each of the other four — they are, of course, not truly separable — Thomas writes that "the coming generation, the generation now being educated in high school and college, needs to have something that will fascinate them [task 2: mentoring the youth], that will inspire them to do heroic things [task 3: mentoring adults in their soulwork]. They must gain a vision of a mutually enhancing human/Earth relationship [task 5: maintaining the culture-nature balance]. . . . [This] is the integral way into the future [task 4: guiding the transformation of the culture], but it must rest upon an experience. That is why I think the child analogy or the child reference is so important [task 1: nurturing children's innocence and wonder], and it's why I dedicated *The Great Work* to the children, by which I mean *all* the children" — the children of the fish, flowers, birds, mammals, trees, and so on.[9]

The core themes of the Master's most vital work are eloquently expressed in the Earth Charter (2000), a worldwide, cross-cultural people's treaty, a Declaration of Interdependence embodying the hopes and aspirations of the emerging global society. From the Earth Charter:

> We stand at a critical moment in Earth's history, a time when humanity must choose its future. As the world becomes increasingly interdependent and fragile, the future at once holds great peril and promise. To move forward we must recognize that in the midst of a magnificent diversity of cultures and life forms we are one human family and one Earth community with a common destiny. We must join together to bring forth a sustainable global society founded on respect for nature, universal human rights, economic justice, and a culture of peace. Towards this end, it is imperative that we, the peoples of the Earth, declare our responsibility to one another, to the greater community of life, and to future generations.[10]

In an eco-soulcentric society, a majority of politicians, community leaders, and judges — people elected or appointed to positions of cultural leadership and service — are Masters, genuine elders. This is what we find in Lao-tzu's Taoism (from sixth-century-BCE China) — the leader or ruler as a person of considerable wisdom and selflessness, qualities that emerge only after decades of soulcentric maturation. A true politician's job is not so much to rule the human community; it is more to oversee the balance or interface between the human realm and the rest of creation, between the village and the greater Earth community. This is a holistic approach to governance in which the foremost principle is right-relationship with the whole, as found, for example, in the traditions of the Haudenosaunee Nation (Iroquois), from whom the eighteenth-century founders of the United States learned and adopted many of the principles of democracy.

The history of politics in Western civilization is replete with stories of patho-adolescent power grabbers or, at best, well-intentioned Thespians. Genuinely adult politicians are rare; truly *elder* statesmen are even more so. Currently, the United States appears to be leading the way, among the "developed" nations, in patho-adolescent politics, in which too many leadership choices are motivated by greed and fear and enabled by immaturity, paranoia, and lack of moral development. With a majority of voters in stage 3, these politicians, despite their records, continue to get elected (or appointed by the Supreme Court).

Social and ecological health, therefore, depends on the collective personal development of all voters, in fact of all people — of all races, ages, genders, and classes — and on the establishment of cultural forms and practices that allow for equitable and genuine human maturation. Masters are the people most qualified for overseeing this essential project of enhancing individual and collective maturation, which is, in turn, critical for maintaining the balance between human culture and the larger Earth community.

More generally, Masters are the ideal candidates for civic leadership. They ought to be the foundation upon which cultural and political governance rests.[11]

In our interview, Joanna expressed her profound admiration for the Onondaga tribe of the Haudenosaunee Nation, a people who exhibit the genuine elder's ability to defend the balance between humanity and the Earth.

> The Onondaga people in upstate New York model an extraordinary human capacity. They recently [March 2005] made a land rights claim. They're the last of the Haudenosaunee Nation to do so. And the astonishing thing is that they're seeking *nothing*. They will let everybody stay where they are — white families, white businesses — they just have to clean up, environmentally, because it's become very toxic there. They are asking *only* that people clean up. There has been no legal claim like that before.[12]
>
> They are also preferring to stay poor rather than to have a casino, because they have seen what that does — the Mafia comes right in with the casino.

Along with Joanna, we can all learn from the Onondaga. We can, for example, learn how to help our own people endure economic and environmental devastation (as did the Onondaga), toward which we, too, are now headed. We can learn how to help people "measure up," as Joanna put it, "to something that's going to be a huge, huge challenge" and in many ways already is. In the soil of the human heart, how do we grow the psychological and spiritual resources we'll all need?

CIRCLE OF IDENTITY: FROM ECOCENTRISM TO COSMOSCENTRIC CONSCIOUSNESS

A human being is a part of a whole, called by us "universe," a part limited in time and space. We experience ourselves, our thoughts and feelings as something sep-arated from the rest — a kind of optical delusion of consciousness. This delusion is a kind of prison for us, restricting us to our personal desires and to affection for a few persons nearest us. Our task must be to free ourselves from this prison by widening our circle of compassion to embrace all living creatures and the whole of nature in its beauty.

— ALBERT EINSTEIN, *IDEAS AND OPINIONS*

As we've seen, a significant psychospiritual crisis takes place during the Grove, and, as in all previous stages, this crisis is the ego's. Literally or figuratively, the Master awakes one morning to the terrible revelation that he was never the origin of his own give-away, that, all along, the Mystery or the Tao was manifesting the soul's qualities through him. The ego feels like it's being left behind, discarded. (Soon enough, at death, it will be.) The Master might fall into a profound depression or a deep grieving.

But by entering this crisis and weathering it, the Master's circle of identity will widen from holistic ecocentrism (his differentiated identity as Gaia) toward cos-moscentrism. In other words, as the Master's sense of individual identity is worn away, he gradually comes to experience the entire universe as the realm that informs his ex-istence. The cosmoscentric ego is emblematic of one who experiences the universe, all of space and time, as "mine." The Master loses his previous sense of autonomous per-sonal agency and acquires a new sensibility, a keen appreciation of his partnership with the cosmos. His cosmoscentric (or spirit-centered) choices, actions, and awareness arise from the perspective of the whole and of eternity. The cosmoscentric ego regularly ex-periences perfection in all that is beheld, and it marvels at the endless play of spirit — the Mystery — lighting up all forms and forces of manifestation.

Although the formation of the cosmoscentric ego begins in the Grove, it is not completed until the Mountain Cave.

WIDENING CIRCLES: THE LIFE OF THE MASTER

I live my life in widening circles
that reach out across the world.
I may not complete this last one
but I give myself to it.

I circle around God, around the primordial tower.
I've been circling for thousands of years
and I still don't know: am I a falcon,
a storm, or a great song?

— RAINER MARIA RILKE

As we've seen, Joanna Macy is one of those rare people who has truly lived her life "in widening circles / that reach out across the world." Now in her elderhood, she finds herself, like Rilke, merging, in a way, with the astonishing phenomena of nature and culture — in gratitude and amazement.

There's more wonder in my life now. Astonishment. The sky, the clouds floating in it, the trees, the birds, the hummingbirds, the bugs. There's a lovely self-evaporating into the incredible beauty of this world, and wanting to let it be seen and loved while we still can, before we lose that capacity. I often quote Rilke's poem from *The Book of Hours*. Remember, when he says, "Dear darkening ground..." [She recites, from memory, the poem that begins this chapter.]

Like Rilke, "I want to love the things as no one has thought to love them." I feel this in the work I do now in the workshops. That's cause enough. If we can just love.

When I wrote *Coming Back to Life*, in 1997 and 1998, I realized what had been coming into the work. There were more and more gratitude practices. Gratitude became the way to take your place in the world. And because things are so bad, if people are going to open up to their intuitions of mega-death and loss, they need to be holding, and be held by, this world more. And gratitude is a royal road to that. This is profoundly reassuring.

The emphasis on gratitude may be also reflecting something of the character of my shift from adulthood to elderhood.

I feel this in my marriage, too. I'm just blown away by my husband. It's amazement. I think that amazement at life is close to mystical awareness. I'm blown away by just the *fact* of Fran. I think that would be true with any human. There's such an incredible mystery at the heart of any being.

So in the workshops, in the practices I use, I do a lot to help people look in that way — with gratitude and astonishment — or even see each other that way.

It works, too.

Joanna also spoke of her elderhood in terms of an increasing joy, lightness, and laughter, and a physical awareness of her heart:

When I was in Boulder last week, I saw a friend who knew me in this work twenty-five years ago. And he said, "I can't get over the joy in you." And here I was actually talking about apocalypse! But there was so much lightness and joy in me that he was just amazed. And I thought, Well, that is true, there's a certain lightness in the way I do my work. And part of that is feeling very dispensable. Earlier in life, there's a sort of arrogance — "There's no one like me" — that you need, in a way. Along with the innocence of the child, you need a lot of crazy confidence to be an innovator. And so one of the characteristics that can come with that is, not self-importance, but taking the task seriously. You have to, because nobody else is. You have to be ready to *die* for it.

But then I've been noticing this change — there's a lightness and laughter now. More laughing at myself. Maybe that's part of what I was hinting at with the word *indispensability*. In the adulthood work, you can't afford to consider yourself dispensable. You *have* to take it seriously.

Another thing I have noticed is that I've become much more aware, almost physically, of my heart. In my teaching, I have always talked about the heart-mind, because the heart is where the Buddhists locate the mind. We really need this. So, in talking with people or writing, I'll often refer to the heart as the thinking organ.

And what I've been experiencing is that there are physical sensations around this — warmth, especially. Heat. The heart can really hurt, like it's received a blow or been bruised or cut open. The phrase I used in a practice I taught was "breathing through" — how to be with the pain in the world. You breathe in the pain of the world and then breathe it out through your heart, I say, "If you have an ache in your chest when doing this, as if your heart could break, it's okay, because your heart is not an object that can break. But if it were, the heart that breaks open can hold the whole universe." And that phrase has been quoted more than anything else I've said or written.

So, it's interesting that in my elderhood, more than before, there's a physical sensation reflecting that. "When the heart breaks open, it can hold the whole universe." In that phrase is the major thrust of the work: redefining pain for the world as compassion, instead of pathologizing it as a sign of personal neurosis or personal failure.

Thomas Berry is best known for his deeply instructive commentaries on the human-Earth relationship. What most people don't realize is that his first book on the subject, *The Dream of the Earth*, was not published until he was seventy-four years old (in 1988).

Thomas's Earth-centered work is the labor not of his adulthood but of his elderhood, his Master years in particular.

Looking back at his career, we can see that his interests, consciousness, and conscience, like Joanna's, evolved in widening circles, as these do in all people who continue to mature. During what I imagine to be his Wanderer years, Thomas was a Catholic (Passionist) monk living in a monastery (he's still a member of the Passionist order) and was a student of Western intellectual history. During his Apprentice and Artisan years (Wellspring and Wild Orchard), he was a scholar of worldwide cultural history and religion, with a focus on the civilizations of China, India, and pre-Columbian America. In 1970 (at age fifty-six), possibly around the time of his passage of Induction, he founded the Riverdale Center for Religious Research.

Then in the early 1980s, Thomas's life changed course after he discovered the newly released United Nations World Charter for Nature, a largely ignored document that was the forerunner of the Earth Charter, and which speaks of the environmental causes of our global crisis. The UN Charter for Nature made Thomas realize that humanity must learn to live in balance with the greater Earth community, a realization that, I imagine, propelled him into his elderhood. As a Master, he wrote and published *The Dream of the Earth* (1988), *The Universe Story* (with Brian Swimme, in 1992), and *The Great Work* (1999). At the start of his elderhood, he left behind the religion-and-cultural-historian work of his adulthood, even though it remained as the foundation of, and a strand within, his elder, Earth-centered work.

CARING FOR THE EARTH
IN AN EGOCENTRIC WORLD

Caring for the soul of the more-than-human community is challenging even in a soul-centric culture. But it's particularly arduous in an egocentric society, especially one like ours, in its advanced state of cultural decline. To make matters worse, there are few Masters in our society to do the all-important work that only they can do well. A much-diminished cadre of elders must now oversee the most extensive and urgent Earth-care in human history.

The current state of the world evokes great anguish and despair for anyone paying attention, but this is especially true for the Masters who, by virtue of their mature hearts, feel the world's degradation all the more acutely. And yet, as Warrior-Martyrs, Masters are able to behold and hold all this dying and loss, including their own, and still act to preserve and protect what they can.

In her efforts to preserve life and diversity in an egocentric world, mature anger can be one of the Master's greatest resources. Mature anger is part of a healthy reaction to the many unconscious people in power causing suffering, death, and extinction for so many individuals, species, and cultures. Anger of this kind promotes clarity and motivates constructive and corrective action, as well as compassion for those who are suffering.

Joanna Macy has been an activist for over thirty years. The value of mature anger was confirmed and amplified for her during one of her visits to Tashi Jong, a Tibetan Buddhist monastery in northern India. One of the monks pointed out to her a large statue of Yamantaka, the wrathful bodhisattva, whom Joanna described to me:

> Yamantaka is the embodiment of rage. He has three heads, and his hair is on fire, and he is garlanded with skulls. He's strung also with heads that have been just cut off. These are not even skulls; they're live heads. He's draped with venomous serpents. He's got three right hands holding *vajra* daggers. He holds a heart in each of his three left hands. He's cutting out the hearts. The hearts are those of greed, hatred, and delusion. He's cutting out the roots of suffering. That's one of my favorite teachings in the Buddha Dharma. It's not about *evil*. You don't need to posit an evil force. It's just the suffering we create when we get caught in greed, hatred, and delusion. And these roots of suffering are mutually reinforcing, like a positive feedback loop. So, this bodhisattva, Yamantaka, is very, very fierce.

After pointing out to Joanna these features of Yamantaka, the monk exclaimed in tones of great awe and reverence, "Oh! So great anger! Oh, straight from the heart of pure compassion!" This did not seem to be the common "spiritual" view of anger as something necessarily negative or destructive. I asked Joanna if that was her perspective, too.

> Yes, and this is the thing. Even the Dalai Lama and even Thich Nhat Hanh often use the word *anger* instead of *hatred* in referring to the roots of suffering, thus betraying the patriarchal fear and condemnation of anger. It's very comfortable when you're in the driver's seat to say that there's something wrong with people who are resentful and discontent. Condemning anger can be a form of oppression.

"Anger straight from the heart of pure compassion!" I needed to hear that.

There are additional aspects of our egocentric world that make the Master's work exceptionally challenging. In an age-stratified society, elders (and older people, more generally) have fewer interactions with both children and adolescents. And, even when they do have time with young people, there are many impediments faced by the Master. Innocence, wonder, and authenticity are difficult to foster in children and youth when training in consumerism and computer technology begins so early in life, when there is so much TV and so little free time in nature, when educational systems ignore or suppress sensing, feeling, imagination, and critical thinking, and when many religious institutions foster fear, hatred, and/or disregard of nonmembers.

The Master's efforts are also hampered by adolescent politics and military adventurism; the loss of respect for older people; society's failure to distinguish elderhood from old age; an immature, youth-worshipping culture; and the rapidly accelerating destruction of the environment.

The work of the Master today is daunting. Yet we have never needed Masters more. It is essential, everywhere in the world, that we entrust them with leadership and that we support them in forming local, regional, national, and global Councils of Elders.

A SPARSE GROVE

Some people might be ushered from the Wild Orchard to the Grove of Elders prematurely — either at a younger age than usual or simply before they are fully ready developmentally. Again, the Mystery has its reasons. If it had waited longer to shift their center of gravity to the soul of the more-than-human community, there might not have been a chance for them to provide the elder-services they're capable of — or to experience the fulfillment that comes in the Grove.

But when someone becomes a Master prematurely, she might not have a fully conscious appreciation of the soul of the more-than-human community, an appreciation that, under more favorable circumstances, would have developed through a more sustained and fruitful adulthood of soul encounter and embodiment. Without a vivid sense of Earth's soul, a Master cannot clearly discern what Thomas Berry calls "the dream of the Earth," the inherent dynamics and directions in the unfolding of the planet's existence. These dynamics and directions are either directly apprehended (through a mature, deep imagination), or revealed by the deep-structure themes uncovered in experiences such as deep time, interspecies interconnectedness and cooperation, climate change, and the dynamic patterning of nature suggested by the Chinese word *li*. To the Master, these patterns and themes communicate Earth's desires for itself and the most realizable of sustainable futures.

Sensitivity to the dream of the Earth enables the Master to most effectively contribute to a mutually enhancing relationship between humanity and the greater Earth community. She accomplishes this by catalyzing Earth-resonant cultural changes. These are the tasks of the Master that require the greatest subtlety, depth of perception, and intuition.

But the Master in a sparse Grove can still mentor adults whose soulwork has an essence similar to hers. And she can still usher youth into the mysteries of the Cocoon and defend and nurture the innocence and wonder of children. These activities, by themselves, are enormous contributions.

There are now many millions of people in their old age who have little sense of the personal value they might contribute to their world, and who consequently bear a great emptiness and sorrow. Older people represent perhaps the greatest untapped human resource in the world. But this is an opportunity that can be embraced. I believe it's possible to transit from old age to true elderhood by cooperating with the Mystery and addressing the most incomplete tasks from previous life stages.

PASTURE AND PLAYTIME: THE EGOCENTRIC COUNTERPART TO THE GROVE OF ELDERS

At the time of life when Artisans are undergoing the passage of Crowning, those who have been Orphan-Conformists following the egocentric sequence reach the rueful milepost of Retirement, which, in our society, usually occurs between ages sixty and seventy. This marks the end of Management and the commencement of Pasture and Playtime, stage 3e, as seen in Diagram 3-6 (p. 71). *Retirement* itself is a rather sad term, because it implies something dreadful — that a person has become essentially useless to a society that measures value in terms of economic productivity and defines progress in terms of the gross national product.

Many look forward to Retirement, while others dread its arrival, but in either case, everyone knows it's not considered the threshold to a higher status. Despite the common celebrations — office parties, gold watches, pension plans, and extravagant kick-off vacations — depression often follows within a few months as the retiree confronts the reality that he is no longer valued by society, and that he does not know how to value himself independently of his former job.

A person's psychological loss at Retirement is significant, entailing not only the loss of a respectable if not esteemed place in industrial growth society but also, more poignantly, his recognition in some corner of his psyche that he did not live the deeper, richer, more meaningful and fulfilling adulthood that he might have — and now it's too late. The resulting grief can be enormous, and few retirees in egocentric society have learned how to access, experience, and assimilate so powerful an emotion. Because they do not know how to grieve, their sorrow gets stuck within the psyche, mostly below consciousness. And this is precisely what depression is — stagnant, unassimilated emotion. With no other avenue of release, those emotions seep out as physical symptoms, disease, or nightmares, or result in addictions or relationship dysfunction.[13]

What I am portraying here is, again, a worst-case scenario, even if all too common. With good fortune, you and your friends and loved ones are experiencing or will experience something less extreme. For people in their sixties and seventies, there are at least three developmental possibilities in our society: Pasture and Playtime, the Oasis (a drawn-out, ongoing, soulcentric stage 3 begun at Puberty), and the Grove of Elders. (The Cocoon, Wellspring, and Wild Orchard are also possibilities in this age range.)

Most retired persons who are developmentally in the Oasis do enjoy a fulfilling life. They have a warmhearted and pleasurable family life and social network, and they have found or created ways to remain active in their civic, recreational, professional, academic, religious, or spiritual communities. Because it is a soulcentric stage, the Oasis is always a psychologically healthy one; and Thespians of any age contribute to the well-being of society. The tragedy of remaining in the Oasis while in one's sixties and later is not what happens in that stage, but what doesn't — someone who might have become a true elder has not, and this represents a significant loss to self, society, and the Earth community.

But both an old-age Oasis and the Grove of Elders contrast enormously with the egocentric Pasture and Playtime (stage 3e). At Retirement, Orphan-Conformists (and/or their spouses) stop working a regular job, as they are generally deemed by both self and others as too old to contribute significantly. As they retire from Management, it's often said, darkly, that they are, like an aged horse, "put out to pasture" to live out their remaining days. The pasture might look like an RV, a city park, or a retirement community in Florida, Arizona, or Southern California.

In egocentric settings, older people often make their retirement into what they think of as a second childhood, sometimes perhaps to distract themselves from emptiness. This is a sorrowful commentary on both childhood and elderhood. Many retired persons intend to spend the rest of their days playing inconsequential games. Recently I heard a radio interview with an older man from Mississippi who spent much of his time at a local casino. Asked why, he responded, "Well, I'm retired now, and you can watch TV only so long." It is tragic that life would end with a vision no grander than such triviality and cultural marginality.

Equally sorrowful, a person's physical health in old age often is not robust enough to allow much opportunity for enjoyment.[14] The promised playtime, which the Orphan-Conformist anticipated during so many decades of hard work and raising a family, often turns out to be short lived or unattainable. What he might discover after years of soul-numbing work and saving for retirement is that he's been deposited on a dreary and barren shore. In that moment, he might recognize all too poignantly the opportunities he missed in youth to wander into a mysterious world and discover the one life he might have called his own. He might find himself enraged at the society that failed him.

But even in egocentric society, life need not end in such sadness, anger, and despair. If you or others you know are in Pasture and Playtime *and* desire something more fulfilling, you can help yourself or them belatedly embrace the tasks of the Nest, Garden, and Oasis, activities that are likely to be preferable to other visions of retirement.

Growth-enhancing activities for seniors include meditation, yoga, quiet time in nature, creative and expressive arts, tai chi, time with infants, experiential (outdoor) study of natural history, wandering in nature, dancing, gardening, poetry, emotional skill development, and learning and practicing relationship-enhancing skills.

WHEN IS IT TIME TO LEAVE THE GROVE?

In contrast to many contemporary retirees, the Master in the Grove of Elders has a full heart, knowing she's lived a long life as a conscious, engaged, and grateful member of the more-than-human community. She knows that the Mystery has used her well, that it has for many years worked through her to benefit the ever-unfolding life of the planet and even the universe. She is filled with gratitude for the world and for the life she has been granted, even when she suffers doubts about how much she really accomplished and how much of her success she can really call her own. (These questions are a component of her gratitude for the world.)

Gradually, through the course of her Grove years, she becomes increasingly content to just look and listen and feel, to marvel at the evolving world with the wonder and innocence — the presence — of a child. The urge to do more begins to wane. She might sense that it's time to give up her seat at the Council of Elders. Cultural leadership no longer feels like her task. She is prepared to surrender to spirit and to re-enter the East quadrant of the Wheel, which she left so many years before, at the dawning of her conscious life at age three or four.

It's sad to leave the Grove, with its countless opportunities to be so centrally involved in the evolution of culture and so intimately and dynamically engaged in the everyday lives of children, adolescents, adults, and other elders. Undoubtedly, the Grove is the best stage of life.

CHAPTER ELEVEN

THE SAGE *in the* MOUNTAIN CAVE

Late Elderhood (Stage 8)

What we call the beginning is often the end
And to make an end is to make a beginning.
The end is where we start from....

    ... And any action
Is a step to the block, to the fire, down the sea's throat
Or to an illegible stone: and that is where we start.
We die with the dying:
See, they depart, and we go with them.
We are born with the dead:
See, they return, and bring us with them....

    We shall not cease from exploration
And the end of all our exploring
Will be to arrive where we started
And know the place for the first time....

        — T. S. ELIOT, "LITTLE GIDDING"

Stage 8: Late Elderhood

Passage into this stage: Surrender
Stage name: The Mountain Cave
Task: None, but what happens (without deliberation) is: tending the universe
Quadrant: East (spirit, cosmos, light, innocence, wisdom)
Hemispheres: North and East (collective being)
Stage archetype: The Sage
Quadrant archetype: The Fool
Gift to community: Grace
Circle of identity: Spirit-centered or cosmoscentric
Center of gravity: The cosmos (spirit)
Final passage: Death

GAZING INTO THE HEART OF THE WORLD

On my first vision fast, at age thirty, I camped alone in remote, trailless wilderness high in the northern Colorado Rockies. For five early-fall days, I dwelled in silence at a jewel of a lake set in a blue-green spruce forest a few hundred feet below timberline. Above the trees, craggy granite peaks soared into the sky like silver arrows.

Several precious hours each day, I sat in a small meadow and gazed out on the lake and at a particularly majestic spruce on its shore. The spruce stood with astonishing grace and serenity. It, too, gazed upon the lake but also, it seemed, far beyond it — deep into the heart of the world. It seemed to comprehend the world, and to belong to it, in a manner I had previously not known possible. I became aware that I was in the presence of a consciousness both wild and wise.

During the first three days of my fast, my emotions and imagination progressively opened to my new home of rock, water, forest, sailing hawk, elk song, and stars. By the afternoon of the third day, my perception had shifted dramatically. Each thing — each mountain, wildflower, marmot — had grown radiant with a vibrant loveliness, ablaze with its own peerless character.

On the third day, I noticed for the first time that the lakeshore spruce was clothed in a vivid and luminous blue-green robe. The tree's entire form now appeared fully fleshed out as if its branches had enlarged and its needles thickened. And, in an extravagant act of generosity, the spruce revealed to me its true identity. At last I could see this was no mere tree — in fact, not a tree at all, at least not in the way we normally think of trees. Here was a monk, a sage and solitary contemplative who had been living for decades at this mountain lake and emptying himself into the world. I watched the monk hail the beavers of the lake with a nod, his gesture returned by the splash and slap of a beaver tail.

The astonishing thing at the time was not that the spruce appeared to be a monk, but that I had previously mistaken it for merely a tree.

Stage-8 elders are very much like that tree-monk — graceful, wise, serene, wild, and generous. Among the very few such elders I have met, Father Thomas Berry stands out as a vivid example. Like the tree-monk, he seems to have accomplished the task Einstein recommended to us all: "to free ourselves from this prison [of imagined separateness] by widening our circle of compassion to embrace all living creatures and the whole of nature in its beauty."[1] I have come to understand late elderhood as the stage in which human compassion blossoms most fully.

In the spring of 2006, when Thomas was ninety-one, I had the great privilege of spending two days with him at his residence in Greensboro, North Carolina. A lifelong cultural historian, ecotheologian ("geologian," he says), and Christian monk, Thomas is one of the leading environmental thinkers and authors in North America. My goals in meeting with Thomas were to better understand the nature of true elderhood and our current time of planetary transformation.

A quarter-century before meeting Thomas — on my fourth day at that high mountain lake — the tree-monk lifted his arm and pointed to his left. Following his gesture, I turned to see a yellow butterfly meandering in my direction. When it reached me, the butterfly brushed my left cheek and whispered my name, my true name, revealing something of the gift that is mine to carry to others.

In a similar way, I have come to understand Thomas as a monk who, for more than thirty years, has been speaking the truth of our collective human name. A genuine Earth elder, Thomas has illuminated our responsibilities to this world and the sacred gift we, as a species, might contribute to the universe. Like an emissary from the heart of the world, he has welcomed us home to our true community on an enchanted blue-green planet within a boundless universe, after an exile, not of thirty years, but of perhaps five thousand or more — since the beginnings of Western civilization. This, I believe, is what the stage-8 elder does. He celebrates the mysteries of the universe and reminds us of our collective place in the cosmos.

In Thomas's words — both spoken and written — we find a discerning and inspiring portrait of human potential and an ardent articulation of the splendors of the Earth and cosmos. Nowhere have we been given a more fierce description of the perils and sorrows of humanity's current course, or a more hopeful portrayal of the fulfillments of a future human-Earth partnership that we might yet create together.

As would be true of any genuine elder, Thomas's wisdom and leadership are recognized cross-culturally. Years ago, after having spoken to a gathering of native peoples in Canada, one of the tribal leaders said he had never before heard a white man speak with such understanding of and compassion for indigenous peoples. At the end of the gathering, they turned to him and called him "Grandfather." Thomas told me, "I always thought of that as one of the most wonderful moments in life — to be called Grandfather."

For many indigenous peoples, the words *grandfather* and *grandmother* evoke the spirit of what I mean by *elder*. It's not a reference to a person of a certain age. It doesn't require that a person have grandchildren (Thomas, a monk, does not). Any adult in any culture recognizes a true elder. If you're a grandfather in one culture, you're a grandfather in any. Grandfathers and grandmothers belong to Earth and cosmos first, a particular culture second.

A genuine elder possesses a good deal of wildness, perhaps more than any adult, adolescent, or child. Our human wildness is our spontaneity, our untamed vitality, our innocent presence, our resistance to oppression, and our rule-transcending vivacity and self-reliance that societal convention can never contain. We are designed to grow deeper into that wildness as we mature, not to recede from it. When we live soulcentrically, immersed in a lifelong dance with the mysteries of nature and psyche, our wildness flourishes. A wild elderhood is not a cantankerous old age or a devil-may-care attitude, nor is it stubbornness or dreamy detachment. Rather, the wildness of elderhood is a spunky exuberance in unmediated, ecstatic communion with the great mysteries of life — the birds, fishes, trees, mammals, the stars and galaxies, and the dream of the Earth.

During my long conversation with Thomas, the wildness, passion, and mystery of his thinking at first surprised and delighted me. Later I remembered that such mystical motifs are strewn like exotic seeds throughout his books and talks.

The pleasure of Thomas's company arose as much from his warm and gracious presence as it did from the provocative ideas he shared with me. Having suffered a stroke two and a half years earlier, Thomas had moved into an assisted-living community. Arriving for our first visit, I climbed a flight of stairs, turned toward his room, and there he was, ambling with his cane in my direction, despite his advanced years and the pain entailed in walking. Mindful of our meeting, he was on his way to greet me, which he did with a beaming smile, a melodic "Hello!" and a hearty laugh conveying the sort of delight one might have imagined to be reserved for old friends.

My first question for Thomas was: "What's the difference between old age and elderhood? What makes a person a genuine elder as opposed to an adult?"

After chuckling a bit at the scope of such a question, Thomas began by distinguishing scientific thinking from cosmological thinking, the former having "lost" the universe — "a sacred communion of subjects," in his words — and having replaced it with a mere "collection of objects." Cosmology, in contrast, *celebrates* the universe. Then he defined adulthood as "the capacity for conscious presence to the universe and for a human personal response to the universe." He told stories about coming of age in early-twentieth-century America, noting that he "grew up with the universe," whereas now children grow up without one because neither science nor religion "have a universe." He then segued to thirteenth-century Europe and the profound significance, at that time, of Thomas Aquinas's embrace of Aristotle over Plato. Then an explanation of why "the difficulty of the modern American world is that only humans have rights," and some additional points about the Bible, the loss of cosmology, the nature of childhood, and the significance of imagination. All these and other ports along the way were organic components of his final summation of elderhood — seventy minutes later — as "the easing of the tension of opposites in favor of identity or the serenity of fulfillment."

His answer to each of my questions had a similar quality, a vast perspective I believe to be characteristic of people in late elderhood. It was as if he received my question, extracted its essence, filled the entire room with the kernel of my inquiry, and then infused the whole building with it, in fact all of the Carolina piedmont and, finally, the universe. He held my questions in such a boundless context — as if each answer began among the galaxies — that at times I wondered if he had understood what I had asked. But soon enough it became evident he was simply starting with the big picture, and gradually he would return to the heart of my question. By then, I knew he had not only understood my query but had understood it in a bigger way than I had asked.

Thomas emanated warmth and humor throughout our time together despite troubling stretches of pain, difficulties finding the right word or remembering a name, and initial bewilderment over my challenging questions. His easy laughter, often at himself, wove in and out of our conversation. Yet, although humble and gracious, Thomas is not falsely modest. At one point, in the midst of his explanation of the role of sacrifice in Buddhism, he interjected, "My book on Buddhism, I claim [*laughter*] as a *really good* book. I'm not always proud of my books, but my book on Buddhism, I *like* that book!"

I was reminded — and am again now — of the stage-8 elder's distinctive blend of guilelessness and wisdom, and of his easing of the tension between the apparent opposites of enthusiasm and nonattachment.

SURRENDER: PASSAGE INTO NONATTACHMENT

The Master's time in the Grove ends with the transition of Surrender — a relinquishment of effortful striving, a cessation of the usual attachment to outcome. Following this passage, the elder no longer has a personal agenda of projects to accomplish

in this lifetime. From moment to moment, she surely has desires and preferred outcomes, but they are no longer consciously framed as items on a grand "What I Must
Achieve" list. Her desires are simply a path to enhanced fulfillment in the moment.

Along with a winding down of striving, Surrender is the commencement of
something new — the final stage of life, the tenure of the Sage. (Keep in mind that the
stage of late elderhood is not at all equivalent to advanced old age. The Mountain Cave
is a stage rarely reached in egocentric society.)

Upon reaching Surrender, you stand at the northeast point on the Wheel. You're
taking leave of the North quadrant and making your return to the East, the quadrant
you left almost a lifetime ago, at Naming — at age three or four. While your acquisition of an ego was celebrated at Naming, now you release your attachment to ego at
Surrender. In a sense, Surrender is the undoing of Naming; it is when you *forget* your
name, your way of self-designation that separates you from other things.

On the diurnal cycle of the Wheel, the stage of late elderhood is the final wedge
of night. The night, the top half of the Wheel, began with sunset (at the west compass
point) and will end at the first slight graying of the eastern horizon, corresponding to
your return to the east point. As the light returns, you will enter it.

As you commence late elderhood, you are returning to the first half of the quadrant in which you began this life, the half always reached last. You have come around
again to the most enigmatic of the four directions, the one you share with stage-1 children, who have not yet fully separated from the Mystery out of which we all emerge.
Now, at the end, you return to that Mystery, but this time with full consciousness of
the journey and its destination. As T. S. Eliot writes, you arrive where you started, and
know the place for the first time. Due to the fact that life is a cycle, not a linear progression, the end is where you start.

You are moving into late winter. (Winter began at the North point of the Wheel.)
You are migrating from a life focused on leadership and giveaway to an existence centered in the present moment and the eternal.

As a Master, you already possessed and shared a good deal of wisdom, but your
life was still more about using your knowledge and skills to intentionally lead and guide
(North) than it was about a full embrace of the moment and a spontaneous expression of wisdom (East). Now, as a Sage, your propensity is to celebrate the wondrous
and numinous.

As you move from the Grove to the Mountain Cave, your center of psychospiritual gravity, the hub of your life, graduates from the soul of the more-than-human
community (the nurturing of all Earthly life) to the entire cosmos and the presence
of the Mystery moving among and through all things. This does not mean you hold
any less of an ecocentric view, or that you care any less about the Earth community.
Rather, your consciousness simply becomes centered in an even vaster realm, one that

integrates terrestrial life as a (very) special case. As this takes place, you also release attachment to the particular shape your soul might take.

In relation to the quadrant archetypes, you're leaving the primary influence of the Warrior-Martyr (North) and reentering the quadrant of the Fool (East). In terms of individual stage archetypes, you are moving from Master (a Warrior-Martyr) to Sage (a Fool).

Although you're changing quadrants, you're not transiting between hemispheres. You remain in the North half of the Wheel (the hemisphere of collective orientation) as well as the East half (the hemisphere of being). In other words, you're still in the time of collective-centered being, otherwise known as elderhood.

Surrender is one of the four most radical transformations of human consciousness. These four are Naming (the birth of the conscious ego), Soul Initiation (the achievement of the second-stage, or soul-rooted, ego), Surrender (the attainment of the third-stage, or cosmoscentric, ego), and Death (the final release of the individual self). (See Diagram 3-3, p. 61.)

The transition at this time of life might be marked and celebrated by a Rite of Surrender. Perhaps the community assembles at the Master's home and celebrates with a feast of thanksgiving for the many gifts the elder has bestowed on the people and the land throughout his long life. Prayers are offered that the elder might live many more years and grace the community with his presence, wisdom, and love.

The passage of Surrender might sometimes be triggered by changes in health, events that might support the release of striving. For example, it's possible that Thomas entered late elderhood at the time of his stroke in November 2003. He suffered a fall in August, underwent surgery three weeks later for the resultant broken shoulder, and suffered another fall just before the stroke. What we in contemporary society think of as afflictions of old age might often be initiations into later life stages, commencements that we have forgotten how to appreciate. From the perspective of an adolescent-egocentric society, all losses are dreadful and deplorable. From the perspective of soul and spirit, many losses are gains — and many gains are actually losses.

The psychospiritual shift that occurs at Surrender is a version of those transcendent moments — such as the Zen Buddhist satori or the Hindu samadhi — sought by many spiritual adherents during earlier stages of life. But here it is not a temporary state achieved through psychospiritual disciplines but rather an abiding mode of being attained by virtue of a lifelong progression through the soulcentric stages of the human life cycle.

Although the foundation for Surrender is established in earlier life stages — for example, with the relinquishment of the adolescent ego during the stage of the Cocoon, and with the release of egoistic ownership of soulwork at Crowning — transcendence at last becomes the Master's primary reality. At this milestone, the elder turns ardently toward the Mystery, the inscrutable spiritual force that moves in, through, and as the universe. He relinquishes the second-stage, soul-rooted personality, now no longer his vantage point from which to observe, appraise, understand, or act. Completing the passage from doing to being, he advances from his previous psychospiritual identification with the Earth community to a consciousness centered within the universal and the eternal — again, without any loss of his compassionate connection to people and planet.

THE MOUNTAIN CAVE

In the final stage of life, the elder, in a certain sense, departs the human community while remaining a full member of it. Although in most cases he still engages in everyday village life and relationships, he is no longer *of* the village. He sees both into and beyond the village. He is more a member of the cosmos than the county, even while he continues to love, enjoy, and contribute deeply to village life. In the midst of the human world, he embodies the universe, the present moment, and eternity. It's as if he has risen to a higher plane while remaining very much among us. (Again, late elderhood must be distinguished from advanced old age.)

Late elderhood is less about physical mobility and more about passage into the marvels of the cosmos, especially those right here on Earth. The Sage stays close to home, a place identifiable not only by geography and ecology but also by mystery and mythology. Whatever roof might be over his head, his residence is like a Mountain Cave.

Time spent with a Sage is like a visit to a mountain hermitage, a simple place high above the dust and clamor of the village, a spare room like a monk's cell but a locale awash in intimations of wildness, vastness, silence, and cosmos. In his presence, the world feels full of cascading water, pine forests, fresh air, wild creatures, the innocence and wonder of the first day of creation, the miracle of existence, the music of the spheres, the all-pervading, star-filled breath of the cosmos. In a sense, the Sage dreams all the time, as Thomas told me he does. He sees the stars and galaxies even in the day.

At the very end of the Sage's life, the Mountain Cave functions also as a death lodge where the Sage completes his time in this world, and where family and community members come to express their gratitude and love and make their final farewells.

THE SAGE: ARCHETYPE OF LATE ELDERHOOD

When a person moves from the North quadrant of the Wheel into the East quadrant, the image of the Sage assumes the dominant archetypal influence. Having left behind the everyday life of familiar endeavors, the Sage cannot properly be said to have a developmental task, because, for the Sage, personal accomplishment no longer holds great importance. Although there is no task, much nevertheless happens in this stage, including many developmental unfoldings and inestimable cultural offerings.

For example, the Sage brings many gifts of wisdom to her people. Having lived through all other stages, the Sage sees the life cycle from a mountaintop perspective. And, as a former Warrior-Martyr, she has honed a particular way of contributing to the life of her community. This contribution does not end as she returns to the East quadrant. Rather, her very being constitutes the gift. People around her notice that life-serving events regularly occur in her presence even though she does not specifically attempt to cause them.

Whereas Artisans and Masters (that is, Warrior-Martyrs) are energetic community leaders, the Sage moves beyond active leadership to become more of an oracle, prophet, or humble consultant, one you must seek out because she's not going to knock on your door or sell herself to you.

The Sage's cultural function, if you can call it that, is to help us appreciate and live in resonance with the cosmological patterns, to educate us with her wisdom, her love, her humor, her way of being still. As she completes the process of letting go in preparation for the final surrender, she inspires the rest of us to let go of the lesser things in our lives and to ask ourselves to consider more deeply what is of true and lasting value.

I asked Thomas how people can identify a true elder, a Sage, and how we should think of the leadership role of an elder in contrast to that of an adult. He told me, "The first thing is that it would be more in the bearing of the person rather than in what he says. It should be an immediate identification of someone who has an integral life appreciation, and whose thinking deepens a person's own experience. It's a kind of grace, I think, that goes with a style of presence to others. It's not something that needs to be approved by having some official position."

My favorite exemplar of the Sage archetype is the Taoist master Lao-tzu, whose philosophy has been described as "common-sense mysticism" and "creative quietism" and, by Lao-tzu himself, as the way of the "simpleton" or the "do-nothing."[2] Lao-tzu was a legendary Chinese teacher and mystic from the sixth century BCE. The only remaining record of his wisdom is the small book titled the *Tao Te Ching*, translated as *The Way of Life*. Following are two excerpts from the collection of eighty-one sayings found in the *Tao Te Ching*.[3] The crystal clear qualities of the East shine through here — both the East of the Orient and the East of the Wheel — as Lao-tzu evokes several qualities that, in the human realm, are embodied most clearly by the Sage.

Here he writes of humility, graciousness, and transcendence of the separate, finite self —

The universe is deathless.
Is deathless because, having no finite self,
It stays infinite.
A sound man by not advancing himself

> Stays the further ahead of himself,
> By not confining himself to himself
> Sustains himself outside himself:
> By never being an end in himself
> He endlessly becomes himself.

And here, of action rooted in essence or being —

> There is no need to run outside
> For better seeing,
> Nor to peer from a window. Rather abide
> At the center of your being;
> For the more you leave it, the less you learn.
> Search your heart and see
> If he is wise who takes each turn:
> The way to do is to be.

Thomas, too, in our interview, spoke of a Taoist-like simplicity in elderhood:

> Childhood and elderhood go together. They seem to be mirror images of each other. There is the simplicity of the child and the simplicity of the elder. One is at the beginning, the other at the end. There's a phrase that's used a great deal by Thomas Aquinas [the thirteenth-century Italian philosopher and theologian]: "All things tend to return as to their end to that whence they came in the beginning." We often say that the older you get the more you see things like a child.

Although wise, the Sage does not personally experience himself that way. As his identity merges with the universe, it's the universe that seems wise to the Sage. The Sage himself feels like he does nothing. Carl Jung, at the end of his long life, expressed these sentiments in the final pages of his autobiography:

> When people say I am wise, or a sage, I cannot accept it. A man once dipped a hatful of water from a stream. What did that amount to? I am not that stream. I am at the stream, but I do nothing. Other people are at the same stream, but most of them find they have to do something with it. I do nothing. I never think that I am the one who must see to it that cherries grow on stalks. I stand and behold, admiring what nature can do.[4]

As the Sage merges with nature, he simply admires nature's way.

THE ARCHETYPE OF THE FOOL (REVISITED)

The Fool does not play by the rules or norms of everyday society. He's neither for nor against commerce, social niceties, or accepted morality. He's not interested in getting somewhere other than where he is or in avoiding what the conventional mind considers to be dangerous or immoral. He is beyond or prior to custom, etiquette, propriety, protocol, and safety. In card zero of the Tarot we see him strolling blithely ahead, seemingly unaware that he's about to walk off a cliff.

As the archetype of the Wheel's East quadrant, the Fool presides over both late elderhood and early childhood, itself a seemingly impossible stunt. He encompasses and merges two ostensibly divergent qualities: the innocence of the child and the wisdom of the elder.

But innocence and wisdom, in truth, are not so far apart. Both draw on the capacity to perceive simply and purely, to be fully present to the moment and to all things happening within it. Wisdom takes in the big picture, but then innocence does as well, although without the capacity to explain it or even comment on it.

The Sage, then, is a rendering of the Fool. In common parlance, the sage and fool appear to be contrasting personas, even opposites, one connoting wisdom and the other ignorance. At their sacred depths, however, these are fully aligned archetypes. Both exhibit a nonattachment to form or outcome. The Fool often acts from what seems to be innocence, humor, or lampoonery but is no less wise for it. We often think of a sage, in contrast, as strictly sober; but having journeyed beyond striving and the offices of social leadership, the true Sage has neither investment in sobriety nor compulsion to comply with rules. In the behavior of the Sage, we also see the Fool.

The Fool helps us grasp the big picture by poking fun at himself (and, in so doing, at all of us) or by making fun of us directly. He also might respond to our solemn questions and conceptions with perspectives that reject or reframe our most cherished assumptions.

With great earnestness, I asked Thomas if he would tell me about some of the moments in his life when he experienced personal vision, revelation, or major transformation. Laughing heartily at my question, he responded: "About all of them! I transform every half hour!"

Among his countless cultural forms, the Fool shows up in myth and ritual as the Sufi's Nasruddin, the familiar Native American tricksters Coyote and Raven, the Heyoka of the Navajo, and the Mudheads of the Hopi. The Fool is at once an artless clown, sly trickster, and wise teacher.

There's also a long and complex tradition of fools in Western literature. In Shakespeare's plays, the fool's madness or innocence, real or feigned, gives him license to mock the pretensions and self-deceptions of his social "superiors." The bard's fools take advantage of their unique position to speak unwelcome or comic truth, providing us with wise and insightful commentary on both tragic and comic events. The Sage, as sacred Fool, does all these things as well.

In a more contemporary context, the Fool makes a brilliant and hilarious appearance as Chauncey Gardiner, played by Peter Sellers in the 1979 film adaptation of

Jerzy Kosinski's novel *Being There*. The childlike simpleton Gardiner (who is a guile-less gardener) becomes Washington's new political messiah. The story exposes a variety of excesses and pathologies of adolescent pseudo-warriors and their political machinations.

Although the archetypal presence of the Fool is most pronounced in early child-hood and late elderhood, it can operate anytime in anyone's life when, against all odds, we suddenly lighten up about matters we had taken so seriously. When the Fool breaks through, we're able to laugh at ourselves, appreciating our immediate circum-stances from a larger perspective.

The Fool is the archetype of the East because his brilliance, lightheartedness, sim-plicity, and transcendent overview remind us of what we each experience at dawn, especially in the presence of the rising Sun.

THE SAGE'S CONTRIBUTION TO THE WORLD: GRACE

As we've seen, a healthy individual of any life stage adds a special and particular qual-ity to his community just by being a part of it. In the case of the Sage, his presence affords the gift of grace — not only to the human village but also to the more-than-human world. By *grace*, I mean the influence or agency of the Mystery. The presence of a Sage evokes in others a visceral experience of the Mystery at work in the world, including intimately right here among us. When we are with a Sage, we're more likely to intuit a coherent and meaningful pattern in life, something we are part of, a feel-ing that things ultimately make sense even if we can't begin to articulate it. We are re-generated and strengthened by the living presence of a Sage, who renders our world less confusing, ambiguous, chaotic, or daunting.

Within the sphere of the Sage, we feel graced not only by an elder but by the uni-verse itself, for which he is, after all, humanity's principal representative and evocator. The Sage merges with the transformational nature of the universe, becoming an evo-lutionary force in his community — without any need (or method, for that matter) to intend it.

Grace is one face of love — a love that pervades the cosmos. The Sage embodies and emanates an inspiring and heart-opening affection, both innocent and wise, that sweeps every being into its orbit.

Death, too, as the final passage of life, is a gift of grace. When death arrives for the Sage, there is no resistance, because he has already merged with grace. The Sage's dy-ing is a final concentration within his being of the presence of grace. For the Sage, death is a celebration, a final joining with the Mystery.

In addition to grace emanating through Thomas Berry's work, grace is also one of the regular topics *of* his work. He writes in *The Great Work*, "We need to experience the sequence of evolutionary transformations as [of the universe] moments of grace, and also as celebration moments in our new experience of the sacred."[5] These moments are the extraordinary turning points that are so miraculous as to seem ultimately inexplicable, moments like the initial expansion of the universe or the dawning of life on Earth.

DEVELOPMENTAL NONTASKS IN THE MOUNTAIN CAVE

Although the Sage has no developmental tasks — at least not in the way she did in earlier stages — this does not mean, of course, that she doesn't *do* anything, but rather that her doing rarely has a conscious intent reaching beyond the moment. Neither does her intent reach beyond her current circumstances. In making choices, in other words, she no longer begins with a conscious review of the larger context of her actions — the more-than-human community, the Earth, the universe. This is because she has, in a sense, merged with the universe and, consequently, there is no need to assure herself that her choices are aligned with it. Her way of being is instinctively in tune with the cosmos. This is one of the paradoxes of the East quadrant. Lao-tzu's aphorism "The way to do is to be" becomes a lived reality for the Sage.

In the Mountain Cave, the tension remains between nature and culture, but it is no longer a presence within the Sage herself. She transcends the nature-culture dichotomy because she has literally become a force of nature — one embodied in culture. The nature-culture tension of the Mountain Cave is, however, borne by the human community in which the Sage lives. Swirling around the Sage is the eternal tension between life and death, but the Sage herself does not resist her mortality. She has entered a friendship, perhaps a love affair, with death. Nature — and the Sage herself — says that, like all life, she must die when her time comes. However, the human community (the culture component of the nature-culture tension) cherishes the presence of the Sage and wishes her to live vibrantly forever. The Sage, then, dwells in the center of the nature-culture tension of her stage, unaffected by it. The death-life struggle is an immutable, necessary, and cosmic conflict that the Sage amplifies for others by her very presence.

Although the Sage has no tasks, something essential does take place in the Mountain Cave, something we might call "tending the universe." The presence of each Sage allows the rest of us to consciously inhabit a universe of indeterminate size and duration, as opposed to a mere city, state, bioregion, nation, decade, century, or even planet. Each Sage is like a hologram of the universe. The presence of each Sage is a tending of the universe.

There are at least four categories of things that happen in the Sage's sphere that nourish and even sustain the world: (1) wisdom sharing, (2) the coordination of the human realm with the cosmological realm, (3) mentoring by means of an enduring imaginal presence, and (4) preparation for death.

Wisdom Sharing

Wisdom is not to be confused with knowledge. There's no doubt that the Sage has learned a lot of facts in her long lifetime, but more essentially she has acquired wisdom, a vast perspective that allows her to recognize, value, and support what truly sustains life, the life of the whole.

No longer pushing pet projects, she has no conflicting interests or hidden agendas. Therefore her wisdom represents a pure take on the integrity and needs of the whole. Her wisdom, like her presence more generally, is a tending of that whole — the universe.

During our conversation, Thomas shared with me some wisdom about the nature of wisdom itself. He told a story from ancient China, from the fourth century BCE, the era known as the Period of Warring States. Mencius, a Chinese philosopher and author of the time, tells the tale of an esteemed elder's hazardous journey from one warring state to another. Upon arrival, the ruler notes that the elder traveled a long distance and asks what he brought that will profit the kingdom:

> The elder answers, "Why speak of profit? If your people profit, your subordinate is going to ask. 'What's in it for me?' It will take only 10 percent of the people to disrupt the whole process. So, why speak of profit? I come to teach wisdom, not profit. If you teach justice first, profit will follow. But if you start with profit, then it will disrupt everything."
>
> In light of America at this time and its preoccupation with profit, this is a very significant statement.

The wisdom Thomas shared with me those two days was both magnified and concentrated when he handed me a single page of his recent writing. It was titled simply "Notes on the Universe." On it were seventeen numbered statements, each only a line or two long. Thomas explained,

> It's just a few thoughts about what to be conscious of when you start probing things. It's more a kind of a guide to *how* to do it rather than just *what* you do.
>
> For instance one of the statements on this page is "Always be aware of what you lose as well as what you gain." This points to a terrible flaw in the contemporary world. We know what we gained with the automobile, for example, but we don't know what we lost. We gained a lot by printing, but we

lost memory. Before printing, we carried whole volumes of books in memory. And we also lost spontaneity. And children are losing imagination . . . and literature.

These statements are guides to how to think about things. They provide context, you might say. For instance, one of the best things you can do in developing your thinking is to think in terms of the twentieth and twenty-first centuries. [This is another of the seventeen statements.] In other words, not to talk simply about "the future." Talk about the twenty-first century. Particularly for children, it's important to identify what's going to happen during their lifetime. It's important to be, not a twentieth-century person, but a twenty-first-century person. Because that's where you are. The twentieth century is finished in more ways than one.

Another item is, "What is done for profit, and what is done for itself," which is terribly important.

Another one is, "The universe is a communion of subjects, not a collection of objects."

Or, "Why is there a universe?" [*laughs*] Because existence communicates itself. That's a good one. People don't think about that at the present time.

To know *how* to approach something is so terribly important. But generally people don't learn that until later in life. And that's part of the elder's role — knowing not only what is needed but the conditions under which it can be carried out.

The Sage in the Mountain Cave cannot help but take the long view or invoke the big picture. He lives in and from that perspective. He serves each being by serving the universe.

The Coordination of the Human Realm with the Cosmological Realm

A second function of the Sage, as Thomas explained it to me, is to personally represent and embody "the correspondence of the human process with the natural process." For a society to be healthy, it is essential that all its members experience themselves "in integral relationship with the surrounding forces of the universe."[6] The presence of the Sage expedites and coordinates this experience. Again Thomas illustrated his point with a reference to ancient China.

The residence of the emperor, Thomas explained, was arranged to correspond to the four cardinal directions. As part of an annual cultural process, which Thomas termed "a cosmological ritual,"[7] the emperor was required to move from one of the four sections of the palace to the next in sync with the changes of seasons. In addition, distinctive music was performed during the different seasons, particular colors were used, and members of the court wore special clothes. The distinctive robes donned by the emperor himself displayed the unique colors, designs, and symbols of the current season. Every ritual performed at the royal residence was carefully coordinated with the seasonal sequence. The emperor, for example, inaugurated the spring planting by plowing the first furrow. All these measures were necessary to keep the human affairs of the kingdom in correspondence with the cycles of nature.[8] Thomas continued:

> The whole mood of the society was determined by mythic forces, you might say. These cosmological forces were manifested differently in the different periods of the seasonal cycle. So the Chinese ruler was primarily someone who coordinates the human with the cosmological, the human with the universe and with the rhythms of the universe. Mencius describes the perfect ruler as the one who merely sits on the throne and faces south. He doesn't *do* anything. He's just a coordinating presence that enables everything to function.
>
> A society needs this — and this is a role of the elder. So to go deep into the cosmological functioning of the planet, the primary elder of the society has to be the organizing reference about which everything moves. He's moving from place to place according to the season. In this manner, he controls the whole process. And this is an ultimate principle in human-Earth relationships. A human is an integral member of the planet Earth, is guided *by* the planet Earth, and is *controlled* by the planet Earth, bound in a transphysical relationship.

For the ancient Chinese, the natural order and the human order "constituted an interwoven existence. The ruler was the linchpin holding the two together, or the interpreter who negotiated the bonding of the two. This he did through the power of his personhood as moral leader. That is why the ideal ruler needed only to sit on his throne and face south and the entire cosmic-human order would be affected by his moral presence."[9]

This ultimate principle in human-Earth relationships — that a human being has existence, vivacity, and meaning only as a conscious participating member of the Earth community — is most fully embodied in the life and being of the Sage, whose integral membership in the Earth community is consciously lived. In his very being and presence, each Sage holds and emanates the wholeness and integrity of Earth and the Earth community. In doing so, he tends the universe.

My own first experience of this function of the Sage was not through an encounter with a single elder but rather with an elder-designed ritual encompassing a whole village. During a frigid February in the early 1980s, I traveled with Steven and Jessica Zeller to the Hopi Reservation, in the American Southwest, at the time of the Hopi's annual Kachina Night Dances.

One evening, as uninvited guests, the three of us walked into the Second Mesa village of Shongopovi, a traditional Hopi pueblo of small adobe homes. In a large open plaza, there were five or six kivas.

A kiva is a small, underground ceremonial chamber, a sacred space for rituals performed in an annual cycle. The Hopi kivas are rectangular and built a half story underground and a half above. They are accessed primarily by means of a ladder that leads down through a small square hole in the roof. The kiva symbolizes the universe for the Hopi people and is the focal point of Hopi life.

The three of us seemed to be the only white people in the village, but there were hundreds of native men, women, and children out in the streets and plazas, most of them gathered in the vicinity of the kivas. It was a windy and bitterly cold night. Standing near one of the kivas, we could hear rhythmic chanting inside and occasional shouts. Every half hour or so, the chanting would stop and a group of a dozen or more kachinas — otherworldly, human-sized beings — would ascend the ladder and disappear into the night. After a while, another band of kachinas would appear and descend into the kiva.

The kachinas are deeply respected ancestral spirits — intermediaries or messengers between the gods and the Hopi people. There are over three hundred varieties of kachinas. When they are on Earth, they manifest themselves in physical form. That night in Shongopovi, each of the Hopi men who took on the role — as well as the identity and consciousness — of a kachina was dressed uniquely, colorfully, and, to us, wildly (also quite minimally, their bare arms and legs and thin garments contrasting dramatically with our winter hats and multiple layers). Most wore masks and some assortment of feathers, skirt, sash, deer antlers, ears of corn, sprigs or ruffs of spruce, daubs of mineral paint, and necklaces. All held rattles in their right hands and had additional rattles tied behind their right knees. Some wore carved masks of wolf, snake, badger, or other animals. Other kachinas, unidentifiable to us, had a blue, tubular snout or a long, red tongue protruding over a black beard, or a yellow beak, green squash-blossom ears, or upcurved horns.

The kachinas are popularly believed to live half the year atop the Kachina Peaks, many miles to the west near present-day Flagstaff. But in Hopi cosmology, the kachinas actually come from quite a bit farther away — from distant stars and galaxies. Each year at the time of the winter solstice, they begin to return to the Hopi mesas for the purpose of helping humanity continue its evolutionary journey. The Hopi community comes out to ceremonially welcome back the kachinas during the Kachina Night Dances.[10]

It's tempting for me now to think of the kachinas as performing, for the Hopi people, one of the functions of the Sage — namely, the coordination of the human realm with the cosmological realm. If the kachinas are tending the universe, it is fitting that they come from the distant reaches of the cosmos.

After an hour or so in the village, during a pause between dances, we walked up onto the roof of one of the kivas. A few other people also stood there. We looked down into the kiva and saw the empty dance floor. Privately, the three of us were each wishing we could descend the ladder. Apparently reading our thoughts, a Hopi man gestured and said it would be okay to go down if we wished. It still surprises me today that we simply took his word for it.

Promptly descending the ladder, we found ourselves at the east edge of the unoccupied dance area, approximately twelve or fourteen feet square. But the kiva was far from empty. Just behind the ladder was a crackling wood stove providing a bit of heat. Standing near the stove was a Hopi elder who, as we arrived, uttered a sound we took to be a greeting. This was the kiva chief. Behind him, filling the east half of the kiva, which we had not been able to see from above, were two dozen Hopi women and children sitting in tight rows of chairs facing the dance area, which is to say they faced, at that moment, the three of us Anglos.

The Hopi people looked at us quietly and blankly but not with reproach. Although we did not feel unwelcome, there was not a single unoccupied seat or a single square foot of standing room in the "audience" half of the kiva. We seemed to have two choices — go back up the ladder or sit on the untenanted *bancos* — shallow built-in ledges at seat height — lining the three sides of the dance area itself.

Again, it's hard for me now to believe we did it, but we did. We sat on the *banco* along the north wall.

We heard no sound of protest. Although the air was charged with portent, it did not seem wrong to be there. Improbably, we seemed welcomed — an act of cross-cultural generosity and graciousness that astounds me even more now than it did then.

We settled in, intoxicated by the scent of earth, incense (probably sage and juniper), wood smoke (probably piñon), and the exotic spice of human — or semihuman — exertion. The space was bathed in a warm golden glow.

After a while, the ceiling rumbled and we heard rattles and a falsetto shout announcing a kachina presence above and a demand for admittance. The kiva chief responded in assertive tones of honoring and welcome. Then a band of twenty kachinas streamed down the ladder in a rush of color and otherworldly aura. They were accompanied by a Hopi clown impersonating a Spanish conquistador, with whom the kiva chief traded comic banter of feigned disrespect. The Hopi audience of women and children chortled.

The kachina dancers took their positions in the open area in front of us. At a signal, they simultaneously began their dance with a single powerful stomp. Perfectly synchronized, accompanied by their own rattles and chanting, they moved earthwise (counterclockwise) around the dance area in simple, slow steps while chanting in loud, low tones that reverberated hypnotically in the earth-and-stone-walled chamber.

The three of us sat only inches from the dancing kachinas, who seemed unaware of our presence. We took care to keep our feet tucked in and our backs and heads pressed against the kiva wall.

In just this way, we spent most of the night, thoroughly entranced. Wave after wave of kachinas flowed down the ladder, danced, and ascended, their presence both ancient and vital. The sight, sound, and scent of the dancers penetrated us profoundly. In the dizzying hours of that night, the kiva felt to me like a great ship crossing a vast ocean, sometimes a caravan traversing a great desert, sometimes an earthen vessel sailing through the cosmos.

What we witnessed was a traditional ritual in the cosmological sense of which Thomas speaks. The Hopi people have been observing the seasonal cycles in this manner for millennia. This was not mere entertainment but sacred observance.

It became clear to me sometime in the heart of the night that these ceremonies were precisely what kept the universe running. This thought did not arrive as a conjecture open to debate. I did not wonder if it was true. It was simply incontrovertible. It was the only way my mind could describe to myself — and later, others — the experience of being in that kiva.

In the end, the most fitting phrase my Anglo mind could summon was that we had spent a night in "the engine room of the universe." The Hopi people were stoking the fires of the cosmos. Or, in the words that Thomas offered me a quarter century later, they were "coordinating the human realm with the cosmological realm."

And by doing that, they were tending the universe.

In addition to community rituals like those enacted by a Hopi village, a Chinese imperial court, or a band of dervishes in the Middle East, each individual Sage, through his or her presence, gestures, and expressions, assures that the universe remains a universe.

The implication — that without such ritual observances and without Sages, the universe ceases to exist — might seem hyperbolic to the Western mind. But remember that the universe is not merely a collection of physical objects. It is a communion of subjects, as Thomas puts it, a living entity that must be tended. If any component of our animate world — the human species, for example — fails to fulfill its role, refuses to take its true place, the universe is correspondingly diminished. And if humanity plays a *defining* role in the universe, as Thomas believes, then our collective failure to fulfill our role does indeed imperil the universe. This helps us grasp the awesome responsibility that rests on each Sage, and that rests more generally on the eldering function of each society — in particular, the responsibility to continue the cosmological observances. Each society, then, must remain vital enough to engender Sages, whose presence in the culture is one requirement for the very cultural vitality that makes Sages possible.

In our interview, Thomas spoke about the cosmological role of the human:

The human is a mode of being of the Earth rather than a distinctive being *in* the universe. A universe is not a universe until the humans are present. You couldn't have a universe without humans. It would have no meaning. It would exist merely physically, which is hardly to exist at all. What it needs is to exist in a consciousness of community. The human, in a sense, brings the universe to itself. The human is the being in whom the universe is fulfilled. So, the human has a profound cosmological role. Human consciousness provides a way in which the universe can reflect on itself and celebrate itself in a special mode of conscious self-awareness.

The human enables all the other modes of natural beings to exist in a universe, because it's the human that identifies the whole as a unity. The other modes know in part but don't know the universe as a unity.

Although it is humanity in general that has this "profound cosmological role," it is the Sage, in particular, whose presence inspires and guides human society in this role.

Due to the gradual loss, over the past two or more millennia, of the majority of Sages and ritual cosmological observances, we have been, in effect, shirking our responsibilities as humans, and we have been losing the universe, bit by bit. We have correspondingly become less human. Thomas, in fact, began our interview by saying, "To my mind, we no longer have a cosmology. We no longer have the universe. There's a tendency to think that the basic division in thought is between scientific insight and religious-moral insight. If it's not scientific, it must be religious. But both religion *and* science have lost cosmology and hence the universe."

Later, he returned to this topic:

The flaw throughout the whole human process right now and the difficulty of executing the life stages you mention is primarily due to the lack of a universe. Science does not have a universe, and science does not tell you how to *use* science. Science offers no guidance, so that when we start using science destructively, science has no way of helping us to deal with that. And we pass it over to religion, but religion is as incompetent as science, in regard to cosmology, because religion abandoned cosmology after the thirteenth century.

[True] adulthood is heavily involved with cosmology. Cosmology is an understanding of the human role in the universe and the human role in society. A society is normally structured to establish a special relationship that humans have with a particular time, place, and heritage within the larger dimensions of existence. So, our sense of adulthood is distorted in our time due to a lack of integral relations with a functional society and with a functioning Earth-Universe.

Mentoring by Means of an Enduring Imaginal Presence

The Sage continues to sustain the human community even after he has left the scene of everyday commerce and village life, even, in fact, after he dies. This is the third way that he, as a vital force, tends the universe. His image flourishes in individual psyches and in collective memory. In this way, his legend and his mythological aura exert a continuing and substantial influence on the life of the village, in both the local and the global senses. Depth psychologist James Hillman comments, "What is left once you have left the stage is an idiosyncratic image, especially the one presented in later years.... One's remaining image, that unique way of being and doing, left in the minds of others, continues to act upon them — in anecdote, reminiscence, dream; as exemplar, mentoring voice, ancestor — a potent force working in those with lives left to live."[11]

In Western societies, the word *ancestor* is invariably uttered in reverent tones, even when one's forebears were of questionable moral character or when one knows nothing about them. We must distinguish between true elders from earlier times and people who simply went before.

In many cultures people say that, although the elder-ancestors are no longer embodied, they have not disappeared. They are still experienced as tangibly present in the fluttering leaves, the overseeing clouds, the desert dust-devil roaming the sandstone cliffs, the roaring geyser, or the stars presiding over all things at night. These elders do not depart; they simply change form or shift shape. They merge in an enduring way with our world so that their presence is always available to teach and advise.

Rather than "ending" in this stage, the Sage is extending himself backward, forward, down, and up, until he becomes identified with so much more than the small self.[12] He becomes eternal and universal. His presence goes on in the world and his image endures in the minds of others. His image and presence tend the universe.

Preparation for Death — the Death Lodge

A fourth feature of the Mountain Cave is the death lodge, discussed earlier in connection with the Cocoon, the stage that occurred exactly half a lifetime earlier. But then, it was a metaphor for a psychospiritual practice that helped the initiate prepare for the demise of the adolescent personality. Now the death lodge is an actual domicile — with material as well as psychospiritual reality — in which the Sage prepares for the end of life.[13]

In the death lodge phase of the Mountain Cave, the Sage undertakes a grand review, a way of putting his life in order, of making a final peace with everyone and everything, of forgiving self and others as needed. The Sage does this naturally and instinctively, not as a chore or obligation. From his Mountain Cave vantage point, the Sage sees the wholeness and integrity of his life story in a way not possible earlier. With the relinquishment of the second-stage (soul-rooted) ego's ownership of that story, the Sage appreciates his life in a new light — one that is nonattached and, consequently, at peace.

This peace flows from the fact that the Sage understands his life story as part and parcel of an evolving universe. He sees that, through his embodiment of soul, he has participated fully in the life of the cosmos. He appreciates that his life has always been merged with the unfolding of a greater mystery.

Rabbi Zalman Schachter-Shalomi, in his discussion of the end of life, suggests a way for the dying process to be conducted and observed by the elder, his family, and his community, an approach resonant with the consciousness of the Sage. Preparation for the final passage is done in such a way that

> a child can come to the bedside of a dying grandparent and say, "Oh, wow, so that's how it goes." A good completion would take away much of the fear associated with death....
>
> ...Imagine if people who are not afraid of dying would tell the truth to their children and grandchildren and work with them consciously when a will is written.
>
> ...A good death would be one that says, "I'm not hungry for more life, and I don't think I've over-stayed my time here."
>
> ...Instead of being in intensive care, with tubes in you, strapped to the bed, can you imagine being surrounded by loving people as you prepare to die? Can you imagine having a chance to once again glimpse what life is about and to give thanks for the privilege of having had the chance to live?
>
> ...If the right [dying] work is done, the work of grieving, for those left behind, is easier. Taking the sting from death would help us to live in greater harmony with the process in which life recycles itself for further growth and consciousness.[14]

The Sage might even choose the particular day of his death, desiring to end his life consciously and cleanly rather than to linger after his purpose, his loving, and his good-byes are completed. The Sage has already journeyed beyond death in the way the rest of us think about it. Death, for him, is not an ending but a phase-shift. He has merged with the universe. As Lao-tzu puts it, "The universe is deathless. / Is deathless because, having no finite self, / It stays infinite."

By concluding his life in a good way, with and among loved ones, the Sage makes a statement, beyond the power of words, that death is an essential part of life and of an evolving cosmos. Even his death and his way of dying tend the universe.

CIRCLE OF IDENTITY:
COSMOSCENTRIC CONSCIOUSNESS

... I entered the life of the brown forest,
And the great life of the ancient peaks, the patience of stone,
    I felt the changes in the veins
In the throat of the mountain, a grain in many centuries, we have
    our own time, not yours; and I was the stream
Draining the mountain wood; and I the stag drinking; and I was
    the stars,
Boiling with light, wandering alone, each one the lord of his own
    summit; and I was the darkness
Outside the stars, I included them, they were part of me. I was
    mankind also, a moving lichen
On the cheek of the round stone ... they have not made words
    for it, to go behind things, beyond hours and ages,
And be all things in all time, in their returns and passages, in the
    motionless and timeless center. ...

— ROBINSON JEFFERS, "THE TOWER BEYOND TRAGEDY"

The spirit-centered or cosmoscentric circle of identity that begins to form in the Grove is completed in the Mountain Cave. This means that the Sage experiences all of creation as "hers" in the sense that the universe is her primary felt membership. She has gone "behind things, beyond hours and ages, / [to] be all things in all time," as Jeffers writes. Or as Einstein puts it, she has widened her "circle of compassion to embrace all living creatures and the whole of nature in its beauty."

The vitality and ongoing evolution of the whole — for example, of Earth as a living being — has for the Sage a distinctly higher value than the survival of any of its components, including any of its particular peoples, institutions, or nations. To some, this position might seem to lack compassion, but the Sage lives from the awareness that all things suffer or perish if the whole is harmed. Thomas writes, "We have to get used to the idea — and this is bothersome for many of us — that the integral Earth is more important than single humans; in other words, the community of the planet Earth is primary and the humans are derivative. If we do not base our way into the future on this insight, we will not survive."[15]

As I imagine any Sage would, Thomas embraces the universe — the natural world in its widest expanse — as the primary guide in life and as the principal source of personal revelation. Throughout our interview, Thomas — a Catholic monk for more than seven decades — spoke cosmoscentrically. For example:

The Christian world has been focused on the Jesus experience. And since the discovery of printing and the availability of Bibles, it has been focused on the biblical revelatory tradition. Now, however, we need to move from that to the revelation of the natural world. In fact, I think the universe is the primary guide for everything *in* the universe, and particularly for the human project. The planet Earth, for example, is the primary source of food, the primary source of intellectual development, the primary guide in government. It's basic to everything and all the professions. It's the primary educator, the primary religious experience. So, everything from here on needs to be seen in this new context.

When I talk about the Great Work of the twenty-first century, it is to restore the significance of the universe in the human project and the meaning of the human project within the universe project.

Thomas Aquinas has a wonderful passage where he says, "The universe is the ultimate and noblest perfection in things." He also tells us that "the good of the species is greater than the good of the individual." In other words, the community is a greater reality than each individual in the community. And that's something that's central. "Hence, a multiplicity of species adds more to the goodness of the universe than a multiplicity of individuals of one species." It's so obvious, you hardly think it needs to be said.

The individual human ego does not disappear until death, but, for the Sage, the ego experiences itself, consciously and persistently, as an agent or handmaiden not merely for soul but for spirit, which is to say, for the universe. The Sage's existence is informed by the cosmos.

THE LIFE OF THE SAGE: A TIME OF FULFILLMENT

To describe his experience of elderhood — specifically, of the stage I call the Mountain Cave — Thomas began by contrasting it with adulthood. He said that one of the key characteristics of genuine adulthood is the capacity to appreciate the complementarity of opposites, which are different but harmonious expressions of a single thing. He gave two examples of complementarities appreciated by adults:

Religion, particularly at the present time, holds a difference between the revelatory communication that we have through scripture and the revelation we have through our experience of the natural world. There's a tendency to diminish one in favor of the other. But this is a *qualitative* difference, not a contradiction.

Another example is men and women. They're the same species but qualitatively different. It's their difference that attracts. So, opposites fulfill each other, or attract each other.

So things rightly understood tend to be complementary rather than contradictory. And the capacity to appreciate the complementarity of opposites, rather than the contradiction of opposites, is a characteristic of adulthood.

I think of elderhood, on the other hand, as the easing of the tension of opposites in favor of identity or the serenity of fulfillment. That's why we have the expression "To understand fully is to forgive." Elderhood is a time for fulfillment and forgiveness. It's a time for peace.

The Sage, then, has moved from an appreciation of the complementarity of opposites to a personal identification with all things, the latter experience defining late elderhood.

Carl Jung, in the last two pages of his autobiography, written in his early eighties, also spoke of experiencing in his final years an easing of the tension of opposites — in particular, between meaning and meaninglessness. He also spoke of a growing identification with the world, "a kinship with all things," and a falling away of his sense of individuality.

The world into which we are born is brutal and cruel, and at the same time of divine beauty. Which element we think outweighs the other, whether meaninglessness or meaning, is a matter of temperament. If meaninglessness were absolutely preponderant, the meaningfulness of life would vanish to an increasing degree with each step in our development. But that is — or seems to me — not the case. Probably, as in all metaphysical questions, both are true: Life is — or has — meaning and meaninglessness. . . .

When Lao-tzu says: "All are clear, I alone am clouded," he is expressing what I now feel in advanced old age. Lao-tzu is the example of a man with superior insight who has seen and experienced worth and worthlessness, and who at the end of his life desires to return into his own being, into the eternal unknowable meaning. . . . Yet there is so much that fills me: plants, animals, clouds, day and night, and the eternal in man. The more uncertain I have felt about myself, the more there has grown up in me a feeling of kinship with all things. In fact it seems to me as if that alienation which so long separated me from the world has become transferred into my own inner world, and has revealed to me an unexpected unfamiliarity with myself.[16]

THE DISAPPEARANCE OF THE SAGE
IN THE EGOCENTRIC WORLD

In addition to the catastrophic loss of species and habitat in recent centuries, we have witnessed the correlated disappearance of authentic elders.

I asked Thomas why so few of our senior citizens become true elders. For him, deficits in human development and environmental devastation both are tied to our individual and collective alienation from the natural world.

One reason for the lack of personal development is that we live in a society where there's almost universal effort to be what a person is *not*. There's constant effort to adapt to the circumstances in which we find ourselves. And this diminishes the capacity for authenticity.

The times have changed so much. It's almost impossible now to grow up with any integral sense of who we are. We have to adapt to so many situations that are to some extent not natural. We don't have contact with the natural world. We don't know what the natural world *is*. We are adapting to an invented world, to a manipulated world. We learn manipulation, and we *are* manipulated, and we learn to manipulate in order to survive. And much of our education is learning how to survive in a world of mutual manipulation and mutual exploitation, all under the guise of assisting people to advance their careers or to develop a way of life.

Due to our society's inauthenticity, nature-alienation, social manipulation, and economic exploitation — the impacts of which begin at birth and reach their pinnacle in early adolescence — few people attain *either* true adulthood or elderhood. The effect on society of having so few elders, Thomas told me, is "artificiality and the inability to deal with the most basic realities of existence."

A SHALLOW MOUNTAIN CAVE

It's possible the Mystery might nudge a Master from the Grove of Elders into the Mountain Cave before he has accomplished much of what he could have otherwise as a community leader caring for the soul of the world. If he enters the Mountain Cave prematurely, he might find himself in a somewhat shallow Mountain Cave, perhaps one not so mystical, effortless, or insightful. Yet he will still have wisdom to share, his presence will help coordinate the human realm with the cosmological, and his psyche will nevertheless have the time to prepare itself for a good and graceful death.

One reason among many that the Mystery might rush him into a shallow Mountain Cave is because it knows death is coming, and the time has come to prepare for the final crossing. Experiencing the passage of Surrender (the release of striving) some months or years before death — this can be understood and received only as a generous bestowal of grace.

FAILURE:
THE FINAL STAGE OF EGOCENTRIC DEVELOPMENT

At the northeast point on the Wheel, the person who, since puberty, has been stalled in an egocentric stage 3 (that is, in stages 3a through 3e) does not experience Surrender and does not enter the Mountain Cave. Rather, he takes his leave from Pasture and Play-time, suffers the transition I call Withdrawal, and enters a final life stage that might frankly be termed Failure (stage 3f). Withdrawal most commonly takes place between the late seventies and late eighties.

In this section, I am portraying the extreme egocentric pole of the end of life, a portrayal that serves as a stark contrast to that of the Mountain Cave. For any particular person, the final season of life might not — and hopefully *does* not — look so bleak. Also, remember that, in addition to Failure and the Mountain Cave, the Wheel identifies other possibilities for the final stage of life, including an old-age version of the Oasis (the soulcentric stage 3). The latter can encompass plenty of joy and fulfillment. An Oasis that extends all the way to the end of a long life is not itself a misfortune; the tragedy lies in what the individual and his community fails to benefit from, namely, the Mountain Cave.

The previous egocentric life-stage of Pasture and Playtime (stage 3e) ends when a senior citizen can no longer physically or cognitively manage the recreational and social activities of the aged. Most sports, even bowling, become too rigorous. Driving a car becomes too dangerous. Card games and board games become too confusing. Many hobbies and crafts are no longer possible due to a loss of dexterity, balance, strength, or visual acuity. Many friends and family members have passed on, and it might be too much of a chore, anyway, to make social visits.

The fact that Retirement leads to the Pasture is not entirely baneful, because at least Playtime is part of the package. After Withdrawal, however, there is little left but loss and decrepitude. The individual in the stage of Failure is overwhelmingly cognizant of what is over, much more than she is aware of what remains. With little wisdom attained and little left for her to do, her transition into this final egocentric stage is a Withdrawal from life without the finality of death.

Withdrawal is a retreat from a society and world that have failed the individual, and to which he has in turn failed to offer anything of substance. It is truly the threshold of Failure. And this is exactly how we speak of it. We say, "Grandfather is failing," and we mean primarily his health; but whether we acknowledge it or not, we might also be alluding to his failure emotionally, interpersonally, soulfully, and/or spiritually. We're admitting that his life — and the lives of so many others — will end, alas, in defeat. Perhaps our own will as well.

Some people welcome their own Failure, feeling that death will soon bring a release from the pain and anguish of life, and perhaps a new beginning. Some believe that on the other side of the veil they'll be reunited with loved ones and find the peace that eluded them in this life.

For those of us who are younger and still have our health, this is an exceptionally painful and despairing reality to grasp — that egocentric life often ends with depression, loss, confusion, pain, disability, and regret. This is a terribly sad thing for me to write and for so many of us to acknowledge, especially for those of us with aged parents experiencing Failure rather than the Mountain Cave or a late-life Oasis. We want to shield them from such an end, but what can we do if their entire lives followed the Orphan-Conformist sequence? We feel we should be as upbeat as we can, because it seems ruthless and unfeeling to tell the truth or even admit it to ourselves. Besides, if we acknowledge the terrible sadness of so many elderly lives in an egocentric society, then implicitly we also acknowledge this as our own possible fate. We don't want to believe this is possible — and whether it is or not, we don't want to think about it much.

Gradually, we might grasp the cruel fact that the path to a denouement other than Failure should have begun in childhood, not in old age. Further, we might realize that genuine elderhood will not become the rule until we create eco-soulcentric societies. The generations whose elder years we can truly enhance are today's children and adolescents, as well as those not yet born.

Many people in advanced old age suffer an increasing restriction in their experience of time. There's so much unfinished business, so many emotions unfelt, so many traumas and failures never addressed or resolved, and so much personal potential never realized that many older people simply learn to blot out the past. It's just too painful to look back. Meanwhile, there's not much to look forward to, other than one's continued decline and death. And so the future can be denied as well. This leaves the individual in a present moment shrunk to a minimal span, a mere instant with no roots or branches. There's little memory or anticipation, because both are too painful. Such a state might be diagnosed as geriatric dementia or depression, and sometimes as a feature of Alzheimer's disease. Mainstream medicine commonly thinks of it as a neurological disorder with psychosocial consequences, but it is just as likely a psychosocial disorder with neurological consequences.[17]

These geriatric disorders, however, might sometimes be the only way the Mystery can dissolve an older person's egocentric ego before death, perhaps enabling some of the intrapsychic work to take place that the ego had held at bay.

The senior citizen in Failure is experiencing a dizzying restriction in both time and space. Soon there will be only *this* moment of time, uprooted from the past and future, and only this small cubicle in this retirement home or hospital.

In the Mountain Cave, in contrast, the Sage moves deeper and more fully into the world, into the universe. And his sense of time actually *expands* into what Joanna Macy calls "deep time" — a growing awareness of our relationship to the beings of the distant past and a communion with the generations of the measureless future.

Gerontologists, psychotherapists, and geriatric social workers have made valiant progress in improving the day-to-day experience of those in Failure (and most likely some in the Mountain Cave, too), and this is to be applauded. But the tragic fact remains that too often the best anyone can do for those in Failure is to diminish their suffering and offer them a series of momentary distractions. Many people now live years longer than they might have in earlier centuries, but with little hope or joy. Some pray daily for death. Many have become a burden to family and the health-care system.

The Mountain Cave is a blessed reward for both the Sage and her people, while Failure is a tragedy for both the senior citizen and her community. In both cases, something of our ending is prefigured in our beginning. The most likely people to become Sages are those whose lives begin as Innocents in a soulcentric Nest. Likewise, an advanced old age of Failure begins with the loss of innocence in infancy and with the seeds sown in Obedience and Entitlement Training.

But it's never too late in life to heal, grow, and individuate. If you are, or a loved one is, in the stage of Failure, the best response might be a belated turn toward the tasks of the Nest, Garden, and Oasis.

FAILURE AND GRACE

Despite the prevalence in our society of Withdrawal leading to Failure, a certain blessing, a grace, can nevertheless accompany advanced old age for many people in egocentric stages (including Failure). In our last years, it seems possible for the Mystery to take hold of our psyches much more readily than in our younger days, irrespective of what our earlier life might have been, even without our having had a postadolescent, imaginative life.

There comes a time, in other words, when many people can no longer biologically or neurologically sustain an egocentric agenda. At the very end of life, the Mystery is going to reclaim us one way or another. As we approach death, the ability to maintain separation from the world diminishes. No matter how self-centered we might have been, even into our eighties or beyond, the world has its way to soften us up — our minds and hearts, as well as our bodies. We begin to psychologically merge with the world as we lose our ability to maintain the dividing walls.

Should this happen, others will notice (even if we don't) that our old attitudes and fixed positions have mellowed or disappeared. Somehow our hearts will have broken open, and we'll have fallen in love with the world, both with our people and with greater nature. We'll find ourselves rejoicing in our memberships — in our human community, in Earth, and in the universe.

Perhaps this homecoming is the world's way of saying that, after all our struggle and striving, now at last is the time, regardless of how much we have individuated, to experience peace and to share with others our natural astonishment at the spontaneities and miracles of this world.

This intercession of grace or the Mystery in the midst of Failure, when it occurs, allows for another significant and redemptive possibility — the making of a good death despite the regrets of the life that preceded it. Because imminent death, when not denied, is a most severe challenge to the ego, the dying process can result at long last in a soul encounter even after a life dedicated to soul suppression. But this assumes a person willing to sit in the death lodge and open his heart to both the sorrows of his life and the love that nevertheless still infuses that life. Here is an opportunity to forgive and ask forgiveness, to express our love, and to complete our final worldly business in a good way. This takes a good deal of courage, consciousness, and, probably, ample support from loved ones with a soulcentric perspective. But it can be done, and the modern hospice movement is proof of it. Although it's a shame that a soul encounter must often wait till the very end, it is better late than never.

DEATH: RETURN TO MYSTERY

For the Sage — a woman or man with a third-stage, or cosmoscentric, ego — the prospect and process of dying is experienced as a natural and joyful return to spirit, a merging with the Mystery from which we sprang. Buddhists say it's a release into Buddha-nature or sky-mind. It is in fact an ascent, a merging with the light, an enlightenment. This is, of course, why death — along with birth — sits at the East on the Wheel, the place of sunrise, the place from which the light arrives and from which it rises.

In our interview, Thomas spoke of his experience of the proximity of death. Characteristically, his attitude toward his fellow elders was positive and benevolent.

> Elderhood is a time of fulfillment. You are abandoned by anxiety — at peace. This is a place here [his assisted-living residence] where I have an experience of older people who have a few years to live. I'm impressed here by the general upbeat mood of the place. It's not a place of particular anxiety. There's a sense of people who are good to each other. They take care of each other. Sometimes you have religious people talk about the anxiety of dying. But dying is actually a simple, natural process.

At the end of the process of dying, in the very last moments of conscious life, the Sage is keenly aware of the passage he is undergoing. Having already completed most of his merger with the Mystery, he is not sad to go, even while he might be sad to leave loved ones behind or to never again see autumn aspen leaves or greet the morning mountains. Ready to go, he embraces his death as an arrival as much as a leaving. With consciousness and gratitude, he is yielding to the final surrender, undergoing the last passage. As he takes the concluding step that brings him back to the East point on the Wheel, he enters the light of the rising Sun, there to return home, to the place from which he began so many years before.

Toward the end of his time in the Mountain Cave, although the Sage is not sad to go, the people in his community most certainly are sad. They are not only sad to lose the embodied presence of a beloved Sage but also sad *for* the Sage that his time of profound fulfillment and happiness is drawing to a close. Each time they are with him, they recognize and are graced by his joy, humor, and delight in creation (in addition to his wisdom, kindness, and compassion). Consequently, along with their joy in beholding the peaceful or rapturous completion of the Sage's life, they are bound to feel some grief to see him depart from such a blessed state. The Mountain Cave, after all, was certainly the best stage of life to be in.

CODA

THE EYES *of the* FUTURE

The eyes of the future are looking back at us and they are praying for us to see beyond our own time. They are kneeling with hands clasped that we might act with restraint, that we might leave room for the life that is destined to come. To protect what is wild is to protect what is gentle. Perhaps the wildness we fear is the pause between our own heartbeats, the silent space that says we live only by grace. Wilderness lives by this same grace. Wild mercy is in our hands.

— TERRY TEMPEST WILLIAMS,
RED: PASSION AND PATIENCE IN THE DESERT

IT TAKES A VILLAGE: THE INTERDEPENDENCY OF SOULCENTRIC STAGES

The Wheel illuminates why soulcentric human development, if it is to be a common achievement, requires an intact, vital, eco-soulcentric community, a village in which people of all stages and ages interact daily.

We've seen, for example, that early childhood is healthiest when parents, before starting a family, have matured into stage-5 adults (Soul Apprentices at the Wellspring). Wellspring parents are best equipped for carrying out the delicate and vital tasks of the Nest (stage 1).

However, most parents are not likely to have reached the Wellspring without the help of stage-7 elders (Masters) and stage-5 and stage-6 initiation guides (Soul Apprentices and Artisans) when those parents-to-be were in their final months of stage-3 adolescence (the Oasis). Those elders and guides, discreetly yet eagerly watching, would have spotted young women and men in their first signs of Confirmational "molting" — signs such as a staggering curiosity about poetry, symbols, or the Mystery, or a certain eloquence or ardor in romantic courtship. Seeing the signs, the elders and guides would have assisted those youth in the always arduous and sometimes harrowing transition into the Cocoon (stage-4 adolescence) and, from there, through the Wanderer's extended odyssey (typically several years) that culminates in the threshold of Soul Initiation, the Wellspring portal.

Also, in a life-enhancing village, stage-7 and stage-8 elders (Masters and Sages) — in addition to parents — are intimately involved in raising stage-1 and stage-2 children (Innocents and Explorers). Masters and Sages, with their spiritual presence ripened far beyond mere biological grandparenthood, provide a developmental resource for children that even stage-5 parents cannot offer. This is the difference between children embraced only as beloved human offspring, and children also perceived and constantly held to be progeny of Earth and as mysteries of the cosmos.

Stage-5 and stage-6 teachers, aunts and uncles, and other community members (Soul Apprentices and Artisans) are also essential cofacilitators of a healthy childhood and adolescence. Fully infused with the Mystery, these individuated adults instinctively draw out and celebrate the essential innocence and wonder of children and the wildfire of teens.

Meanwhile, all Artisans in the village are regularly retrieving from the mysteries of nature and psyche new cultural practices and knowledge, some of which inspire new modes of childhood education. *Every* Artisan creation, for that matter — in any cultural realm — brings beauty, wonder, and vitality to the community like a whirling spring breeze filled with flower fragrance, rainfall, and birdsong.

And all of these multiform village blossomings and hatchings can burst forth only within the shimmering realm of numinous interdependency orchestrated by the mysterious presence and ceremonial observances of the stage-8 elders, the Sages.

Concerning the initiation of youth, the traditions of the eco-soulcentric Tuareg people of the Sahara offer us a specific cultural glimpse of the interdependency of developmental stages.[1] Every day, in their tribal groups of seventy to a hundred people, Tuareg adults and elders are keenly observing each child and teen in order to intuit what soul qualities or soul story might be emerging out of the patterns and flowering mysteries of those individual lives. This is not so the elders can reveal to a youth her destiny and, in doing so, rescue her from the tasks and trials of her own soul-discovery, but rather to help her see what soul qualities are emerging and to shape opportunities for her to consciously discover her particular way of belonging to the world. Amazing to us in the West, even the child's and teen's peers have input, enabled by the fact that they have never lost their innocence and consequently their ability to listen deeply and observe discerningly. Still, the elders' voices count most. Eventually, there will be a second communal name-giving ceremony for the youth (the first having occurred eight days after birth) and an initiation ordeal. Among the Tuareg, there is strong cultural pressure discouraging youth from marrying or starting a family before these events unfold. In this way, the Tuareg assure that only initiated adults (stage-5 men and women) conceive and raise children.

It takes a village — a whole, eco-soul-centered human community — to raise a child well, but it also takes a whole village to produce a parent capable of raising a child well. And it takes a healthy more-than-human community to have a healthy village. As Thomas Berry points out, it takes a whole, blooming planet and a wild universe to generate a sound human community. The health of the whole is the foundation of health for each individual.

MYSTERY DOORS

Although we can never really know the fine points of how the Mystery propels us from one stage to the next, we might nevertheless suppose that we encounter at each major life transition a particular door through which the Mystery enters into time. Some of these doors take the form of other people. Some are physiological events. Some pertain to the web of life or our destined place in it. All are incarnations of the Mystery. Perhaps the doors for the nine major life passages are as follows:

- Birth — mother
- Naming — a culminating neurological development
- Puberty — sexual flowering
- Confirmation — the elders or initiators (or an illness, injury, trauma, or crisis)
- Soul Initiation — the soul image or story itself
- Induction — the Master (in recognizing the Apprentice's mastery of a first form)
- Crowning — the more-than-human community (web of life) as a morphic-field presence
- Surrender — a culminating decline in health
- Death — Death (as an archetypal presence)

SECRETS OF THE WHEEL

In broad overview, the Wheel reveals the following attributes or "secrets" of our human life cycle: We are born innocent in the East, experience our woundedness in the South, uncover the mysteries of our souls in the West, fully embody those mysteries in the North, and surrender them in full consciousness upon our return to the East. With a bit more detail:

- *East*: Our original innocence contains, in its specific qualities, the particular and intricate patterning of our destinies. We were each born to occupy a unique place in the world, the only place from which we can be in fully authentic and interdependent relationship with all things.
- *South*: Our embarrassing, confounding, and painful personal wound is something sacred. At the heart of that wound we find one of the essential keys to the riddle of our soul gift, image, or story, and a catalyst for the cultivation of our soul powers.
- *West*: We must die (to our adolescent personality) in order to be reborn (to soul). Our destiny or gift lies both at the core of our psyche and at the heart of the world. We fully recover this treasure only by devoting ourselves to a conversation between the two (psyche and world), a communion that dissolves our adolescent personalities and forms a soul-rooted ego.
- *North*: Our foremost contribution to the world and our greatest personal fulfillment are realized through the enactment of the vision we received in the West.
- *East*: At the end of all our exploring, we arrive where we started and know the place for the first time.

THE GIFTS OF THE STAGES

With a closer look at the specific gifts of each of the soulcentric life stages, we can learn more about the mysteries of the human life cycle. The gifts of the stages form an unfolding archetypal sequence in eight steps, in which each gift gives birth to the next:

- *The Nest*: It's the parents' responsibility and joy to preserve the child's original innocence, her unique human nature, which is ultimately her particular way of being in relationship with all things. It will eventually blossom as her gift to the world.
- *The Garden*: Wonder is what innocence grows into. Innocence does not disappear; it gives birth to wonder as the child more actively engages her world. Relative to innocence, which is receptive, wonder is active, an exploration, an entering *into*.
- *The Oasis*: Wonder gives birth to creative fire. The intense focus contained in wonder, like the South's sunlight concentrated through a lens, eventually ignites the teenager's world. Her creativity consumes old forms and forges new.
- *The Cocoon*: The adolescent's fire eventually transforms the ego itself, sparking a romance with the mysteries of the world. The incinerated self, or ego, reduced to ashes, transforms into a phoenix (or butterfly) that mates with the world.

- *The Wellspring*: Our romance with the world gives birth to the love child of our soulwork (which inspires others and generates hope).
- *The Wild Orchard*: Our soulwork sows seeds of cultural renaissance. (The love child grows up and serves the world.)
- *The Grove of Elders*: Cultural renaissance engenders and sustains wholeness of the more-than-human world. (For the Earth community to be whole, humanity must maintain integrity in its relationship to the web of life.)
- *The Mountain Cave*: Wholeness in the world supports the presence of grace — the mysterious, unimaginably creative unfolding of the universe.
- We begin in innocence and end in grace.

NATURE, CULTURE, AND PERSONAL DEVELOPMENT

The Wheel of Life helps us appreciate the inseparability of personal development and cultural vitality. A society is mature only when — and because — it includes a sufficient proportion of mature members. Inversely, individual maturity is most effectively fostered by mature societies. The interdependence of the individual and society is a guiding principle of the Great Work of our time.

The personal is political. Soulcentric individuation leads to, and is necessary for, positive cultural change. Positive cultural change is the single most effective facilitator of personal individuation. The two are necessarily and intricately interwoven. As a person matures into a soul-rooted adulthood, she naturally becomes a sustainer of her culture (if her culture is already healthy) or a transformer of it (if it is not). She sustains or transforms her culture directly through her soulwork and indirectly by way of the ecocentric field she generates while doing that work. (An ecocentric field is a complex of psychosocial forces that make it easier and more natural for people to act as members of the Earth community.) Through her being as well as her doing, she contributes imaginative new fibers for the fabric of a vital culture, a tapestry mutually and concurrently woven by all soulcentric members of her society, especially the true adults and elders.

As her circle of identity expands, the personal becomes increasingly political for her, and vice versa. The food she chooses to eat, for example, has everything to do with the environmental costs of growing that food and getting it to her. By the time of the Wellspring, the life and health of the more-than-human community (the commons) has become her immediate, personal concern and fulfillment.

In terms of its *effects*, the political is personal in all stages of life — even an infant is affected by the public affairs (politics) of his culture — but we usually don't become reliably aware of this reality until we reach a healthy Oasis. In terms of its *causes*, the political is not effectively sourced in the personal until the Wellspring, when our individual soulwork deeply serves the collective. (It's in the Wellspring that we enter the North half of the Wheel, the hemisphere of the collective.) In a society with few adults and elders, the personal is not generally recognized as political, and vice versa.

In the modern world, there's mostly an inverse relationship between individual human development and the so-called development, or industrialization, of what are thought of as poorer, or "undeveloped," countries. On average, the least psychologically developed humans (those who are most adolescent and patho-adolescent) appear to be in the self-described "developed" countries (the First and Second Worlds). The most developed (mature) humans appear to be, on average, those in the traditional and indigenous Fourth World societies — those very few cultures, that is, that have so far escaped the social and ecological pillage of industrial "development" and "progress." I suspect that in the "developing" countries (the Third World, consisting mostly of the global south), the level of moral and psychological development depends on the extent of industrialization there.

Economic-industrial development in these "underdeveloped" nations, when conducted by egocentric corporations, governments, and religious organizations, destroys the cultural integrity of the traditional peoples who live within the borders of those nations. Cultural devastation results in the loss of the cultural resources that support the people in maturing into true adulthood and elderhood. The loss of genuine adults and elders (psychological, social, and spiritual leaders) further degrades the culture.

Helena Norberg-Hodge gives us an example from Ladakh, a high-altitude Himalayan desert province in northern India often called "Little Tibet":

> Ladakh ... is a place of few resources and an extreme climate. Yet, for more than a thousand years, it has been home to a thriving culture. Traditions of frugality and cooperation, coupled with an intimate and location-specific knowledge of the environment, enabled the Ladakhis not only to survive, but to prosper. Everyone had enough to eat; families and communities were strong; the status of women was high.
>
> Then came "development." Now in the modern sector [of Ladakh] one finds pollution and divisiveness, inflation and unemployment, intolerance and greed. Centuries of ecological balance and social harmony are under threat from the pressures of Western consumerism.[2]

This story has been played out all over the world for five thousand years or more, with the result that very few intact, indigenous cultures now remain on the planet. Martín Prechtel, in *Long Life, Honey in the Heart*, gives us a late-twentieth-century example of the devastation of an indigenous people, the Tzutujil Maya of Guatemala. John Perkins, in *Confessions of an Economic Hit Man*, tells how he served as a U.S. government agent of socioeconomic destruction in several locations around the globe.[3]

What, in egocentric society, we call "economic development" undermines individual human development, and the sabotage of human individuation in turn serves the interests of industrialization. Immature people (children and adolescents of any age) are much more exploitable as workers than are true adults and elders. If at all possible, mature people organize effectively, resist oppression, and create for themselves imaginative socioeconomic alternatives. Adults and elders defend the integrity of their culture and the ecosystems within which they live. Children and adolescents, in contrast, are often unaware of what is being done to them, their culture, and their homeland by the powerful, benign-faced forces of foreign corporations and egocentric religious organizations.

The destruction of traditional and healthy cultures serves egocentric economic interests. In the case of most Third World countries, the only people economically served by industrial development are a small urban elite within those countries and a larger urban elite in the developed countries that sponsor the industrialization, commercialization, and privatization of natural resources. The majority of the local population is displaced from their land, impoverished, and largely forced to move to where the factory jobs are.

Measured solely in terms of individual psychospiritual maturity, the United States is arguably the most culturally degraded society in the world, despite the fact that it is one of the technologically and scientifically most advanced. The depravity of American society is apparent in human horrors such as the institutionalized use of torture only sixty years after the Third Reich, a U.S. administration engaged in a variety of war crimes punishable by death in the World Court, and a society-wide pandemic of suicides and severe psychopathologies.

The good news, however, is that individual development and socioeconomic development need not be opposed. In fact, each can serve and amplify the other. In a healthy (eco-soulcentric) society, this happens as a matter of course. The Great Turning wholly depends on our ability to create a diverse, planetwide web of eco-soulcentric societies.

Norberg-Hodge, who is the founder and director of the Ladakh Project, has been demonstrating since 1975 that another path into the future is possible, for us as well as the Ladakhis. Her work shows that, compared to what we are accustomed to in the modern West, there is an older, more fundamental pattern of living available to us, "a pattern based on a coevolution between human beings and the earth"[4] — that is, between culture and nature. This is the same pattern underlying the Wheel of Life, in which both individual development and cultural practices are attuned to natural rhythms and cycles.

In Ladakh, Norberg-Hodge has shown that some kinds of technological and economic development can enhance, or at least be compatible with, healthy individual and cultural development. For example, she and her colleaques have developed and introduced solar greenhouses, enabling villagers to grow vegetables year round; solar heating systems for homes, water, and cooking; photovoltaic power for lighting; micro-hydro-electric and small wind turbines; and a seed-saving program for the cultivation and protection of indigenous grains and legumes. For over thirty years, the Ladakh Project has been helping the Ladakhi people to transform their society from preindustrial to *post*industrial, leaping over many of the devastating social, economic, and environmental impacts of colonialism, misguided "development," and industrial monoculture.[5]

As another example, Joanna Macy learned about and participated in an alternative approach to development in Sri Lanka. Sarvodaya is a Buddhist-inspired community-development movement that, at the time Joanna was there (1979–1980), involved thousands of Sri Lankan villages. She writes:

> In my mind, I still hear the local Sarvodaya workers in their village meetings and district training centers: Development is not imitating the West. Development is not high-cost industrial complexes, chemical fertilizers, and mammoth hydro-electric dams. It is not selling your soul for unnecessary consumer items or schemes to get rich quick. Development is *waking up* — waking up to our true wealth and true potentials as persons and as a society.[6]

Socioeconomic and personal development can be aligned, integrated, and mutually reinforcing. In both the personal and social senses, development is a matter of waking up — to our true potentials, our destinies, and our ultimate place in the world.

> Sarvodaya means … "everybody wakes up." "Everybody" includes the landless laborers as well as the farmers; the school dropouts as well as the university trained; the women and children and old people along with the merchants, managers, and civil servants. What they call "awakening" happens when, prompted by local Sarvodaya organizers, they meet together, plan, and carry out joint community projects. They wake up to their real needs, to their capacity to work together, and to their power to change.
>
> … [Sarvodaya] asserts that development can only be meaningful in terms of human fulfillment. While this fulfillment involves the production and consumption of goods, it entails a great deal more — such as unfolding the potential for wisdom and compassion. … It denotes the awakening of the total human personality. Indeed, the transformation of personality — "the building of a new person" — is presented as the chief aim.[7]

Individual maturation and cultural development have a third essential partner: the natural world. A healthy natural environment (and access to it) is necessary for ecosoulcentric individual development, which is central to the endurance and evolution of a healthy human society. A healthy society, in turn, is necessary for a healthy natural environment of which that society is a member. The latter relationship has especially been true since the industrialization of the nineteenth century, but there are many stories from millennia ago of societies that were wiped out or forced to relocate due to the ecological damage they wrought.

Meanwhile, a healthy natural environment is an essential foundation for healthy human societies. If our environment is sick, degraded, or uniform, the same happens to us. And as we've seen, healthy societies naturally facilitate individual maturation. Moreover, because healthy children grow into adults that revere nature, sound personal development supports the maintenance of a vital environment. The eco-psycho-social cycle of dependent co-arising is complete.

The growing worldwide people's movements for peace, just societies, and sustainability are inseparable, because a healthy society must be peaceful, just, and sustainable. None of these movements, however, can succeed unless the movement for a healthy environment succeeds. And all four of those movements are doomed unless there is significant progress in psychospiritual maturation for a majority of all peoples. None of these five movements come first. All must be addressed simultaneously. Each fails or succeeds hand in hand with the others.

The Great Work of our time consists of the dynamic, complex interweaving of these movements for justice, sustainability, peace, environmental health, and eco-soulcentric human development.

CONSCIOUSNESS CHANGE
AND HUMAN DEVELOPMENT

Lack of personal meaning and fulfillment is endemic to contemporary Western and Westernized societies. Why are depression, anxiety, and suicide increasingly common? Social analysts point to the stresses and strains inherent in modern life. But I believe the cause has more to do with what we bring — or don't bring — to life than with what we encounter *in* it.

My observations of human nature, summarized in the Wheel, suggest that, other than socioeconomic oppression, the primary cause of individual distress is pervasive failure in human development (in the first three life stages) as found in, and caused by, contemporary egocentric society. The good news is that, once we understand this, we can begin to make the changes that lead to a positive future, the deep structure of which is proposed by the Wheel.

In the 1960s and 1970s, American society began making some of these cultural changes, as seen in the human potential movement and the consciousness revolution, both of which emphasized achieving nonordinary states through spiritual paths, humanistic and transpersonal psychology, music, art, entheogens, and social and political consciousness-raising. Through these practices, much of a whole generation shifted from the Oasis to the Cocoon, although perhaps a rather thin Cocoon.

By themselves, these movements did not bring about a lasting or sufficient cultural shift, because they did not possess the means to support people in the passage from the Cocoon to the Wellspring, from late adolescence to adulthood. Consciousness change, especially in the Cocoon, is part of what's needed for personal development, but it's surely not enough. What was missing in the 1960s and 1970s (and remains so) was a widespread societal embrace of the tasks of the Cocoon, which requires the cultural presence of a sufficient number of adult initiation guides and elders. And a *thin* Cocoon calls for remedial attention to the under-addressed nature-oriented tasks of the Nest, Garden, and Oasis. Also missing was (and is) a widespread understanding of the soulcentric developmental needs of children and teens in those first three life stages. This understanding, when implemented, enables most youth to reach a healthy Cocoon — healthier than that which most Wanderers experienced in and since the 1960s.

The Wheel suggests that optimal human development begins not in adolescence but in infancy. The child's well-being and potential, from her very first days, are deeply served by her family's intimacy with the natural world — a natural world that includes the infant's own nature, her original innocence. The Wheel proposes that healthy development requires a balancing of nature and culture in every stage, including plenty of free-ranging nature-play in childhood along with cultural instruction. And the Wheel suggests that the principal catalyst of true adulthood is what it has been for tens of thousands of years: a dream, vision, or other numinous experience occurring during "a descent," as Thomas Berry puts it, "into our pre-rational, our instinctive resources."[8]

HUMANITY'S SACRED WOUND

For billions of years, billions of creatures
have made a home on this jeweled planet
of water and stone. Wild love affairs
— Sun and Earth; fungi and algae; bacteria
and mitochondria — preceded and spawned us,
our ancestral lineage recorded in the original eyes
of trilobites, in undulating muscle of jellyfish,
in ancient skeletal minerals sketched first
in the dark heart of stars.

Peering billions of years backwards in time,
we probe deep space and cosmogenesis,
decipher the unfurling story of life,
yet barely perceive the future hurtling
toward us, even as it's shaped

by our ambitious grasping hands and filled
with the stuff of human imagination —
however impoverished or vast.

Billions of creatures already know
their perfect place in the cosmic dance —
their specific genius expressed in relation
to nectar or coral reef, sequoia or hawk.
Millions of unlettered species already answer
questions we have barely begun to ask —
the oldest mystery school apparent in ones
who commune without cults, communicate
without language, migrate without combustion,
or — without brains or hands — couple with the Sun,
birthing energy from endlessly streaming photons.

What must they think of us — hungry ghosts,
hooked up to plasma TV, gathering faraway food
in packages, drinking from bottles of plastic,
razing forests for scented tissue and catalogues,
slicing our own flesh for pleasure or perfection,
pouring poison into the faultless bodies of children,
loading the tender arms of young men and women
with bombs and guns, exploding their minds
with the dismembered bodies of their own kind
before they know how to wallow with a lover
in wildflowers, beneath the holy Moon
and burning eyes of the gods, before they know
what genius smolders in them, awaiting fire,
before they know how to pluck a columbine
and offer cool nectar to the lover's tongue?

This is the way it's always been:
Billions of creatures co-arising, fading in and out
of the irreversible cosmic symphony. Do they regret
living as they must, cued to primal harmonics
of tide and storm, phytoplankton
and oak, lion and vole?

And what of us?
In the last green flash of consciousness,
before we are swallowed by the great night sea,
will we wonder if we have left a wake of ruin

or of celebration — an offering
of reciprocal magnitude
to the billowing imagination
and wild cosmic womb
from which we first emerged
as spark, as seed,
as a fragile embryo
of possibility?

— GENEEN MARIE HAUGEN, "QUESTIONS FOR CREATURES
WITH FORWARD-SEEING IMAGINATION (FOR THOMAS BERRY)"

At the outset of this book, I suggested that humanity as a whole has an innate vulnerability, a "sacred wound," and that this vulnerability arises from our uniquely human mode of consciousness. This wound predisposes us to getting lost, both individually and collectively, failing to flower, and getting stuck in stage 3. Sometimes it leads some of us to engage in truly deranged conduct, like "slicing our own flesh for pleasure or perfection" or "loading the tender arms of young men and women / with bombs and guns," as poet Geneen Marie Haugen writes, or, ultimately, destroying our biosphere.

Our human mode of consciousness is self-reflexive, which is to say that we know that we know. In other words, there's a small part of our consciousness, the ego, that is aware of itself as being aware. This confers a tremendous behavioral advantage but also a potentially fatal liability. Although the ego knows that it knows, there is a whole universe of things that it does *not* know (especially before maturity), things that the larger, nonegoic portion of the human psyche *does* know and that are necessary for its own survival. These are things like how to keep a heart beating and how to be a healthy member of the more-than-human community — how to make "a home on this jeweled planet / of water and stone."

The immature (early-adolescent) ego is capable of making conscious choices that are, in the long run, inadvertently ecocidal and therefore suicidal — for example, "gathering faraway food / in packages, drinking from bottles of plastic, / razing forests for scented tissue and catalogues." A mature ego, in contrast, learns how much it does not know and how much it depends on sources of knowledge and wisdom that come from outside its realm, namely from the deep imagination, the Mystery, myth, nonordinary states of consciousness, archetypes, dreams, vision, ritual, nature, and elsewhere. A society with few genuine adults is racing blind and hell-bent toward a cliff.

Yet, just as is the case with our individual wounds, there is also an inestimable benefit that comes with our species' collective wound, a boon made possible by our distinctive human mode of consciousness. Geneen suggests that this is the gift of our "forward-seeing imagination." Coupled with our opposable thumbs and our uniquely human symbolic language, our forward-seeing imagination grants us the capability to create a viable future, not only for ourselves, but also for all Earthly creatures. In the twenty-first century, this capacity has become a necessity for survival.

Others say that the gift of our collective wound is the ability to consciously rejoice in the grandeur of the universe, a capacity that might have everything to do with our collective human destiny. The conscious celebration of the universe might be "an offering / of reciprocal magnitude / to the billowing imagination / and wild cosmic womb / from which we first emerged / as spark, as seed, / as a fragile embryo / of possibility."

By recovering and reclaiming the power of our human deep imagination and our capacity to celebrate the universe, we render sacred our species' wound. We become *Homo imaginens*.

CIRCLE AND ARC REVISITED

A more evolved human or society is not necessarily a more mature human or society — and vice versa. It's possible, for example, that the human species has been evolving over the past five thousand years, while at the same time most individual humans and societies have become increasingly immature. If this is true, then we have fallen further and further behind our potential, and yet our potential has grown despite the fact that we have not.

The evolution of our species — of anything, actually — is an arc, a one-way, non-repeating trajectory, while the maturation of individuals within that species takes the form of a circle, an ever-renewing cycle. The circular pattern described by the Wheel, however, is only one frame in a long evolutionary unfolding of circular patterns of human maturation, each frame lasting perhaps several thousand years or more.

I suspect that individual development (the circle) and species evolution (the arc) are essentially independent processes. The evolution of our species does not force individuals to mature psychospiritually, and individual maturation, in general, does not cause our species to evolve.[9] But, in our time, if we do not mature as individuals (and consequently as societies), the entire arc of human evolution might soon come to an end. We are in danger of extinction — along with the extinction we have already wrought upon thousands of other species. The continuation of our human arc depends wholly on which circle — egocentric or soulcentric — we embrace.

GLOBAL CULTURE CHANGE

Most everyone knows by now that global climate change, resulting from greenhouse-gas-induced global warming, is the most immediate threat and challenge we face at this time. But the primary difficulty in responding to this crisis is not technological. The knowledge and means already exist to reverse the still-escalating increases in greenhouse gas emissions. What we are lacking is the political and social will to do it. Reversing global warming requires a transformation in the values and lifestyles of all Western and Westernized societies, a shift from patho-adolescent consuming to mature, ecocentric communing. In this book, I've characterized this necessary change as a change from egocentric to soulcentric society, the Wheel being, in two of its facets, a perspective on deep cultural therapy and a design tool for creating healthy human communities and life-sustaining societies.

This suggests that what underlies the crisis of global climate change is a deeper crisis we might call *global culture change*, which significantly predates our current climate crisis. While the latter began only two centuries ago, the former has been in process for about five thousand years. Global warming is the result of a millennia-old unfolding in which our human cultures have become increasingly egocentric and pathological — that is, increasingly alienated from nature and soul.

It seems reasonable to suggest that global culture change is our bigger and most immediate crisis — and opportunity. We must redesign all our major cultural institutions — education, governments, economies, and religions — to be in partnership with Earth systems. We must learn to raise all children and teens in alignment with nature and natural cycles. In particular, we must preserve the innocence of early childhood; we must refashion middle childhood as a time of wonder and free play in the natural world; we must assist young teens to be as authentic and creative as they can, with themselves and others. And we must engender full societal support for late teens (and young and middle-aged people, as necessary) as they explore and are transformed by the mysteries of nature and psyche. And we must do this for all people, in all socioeconomic classes, in all societies.

Is this possible? No. But let's not let that stop us...

IMPOSSIBLE DREAMS

"There is no use trying," said Alice, "one can't believe impossible things." "I dare say you haven't had much practice," said the Queen. "When I was your age, I always did it for half an hour a day. Why, sometimes I've believed as many as six impossible things before breakfast."

— LEWIS CARROLL

As Albert Einstein notes, "No problem can be solved from the same level of consciousness that created it." When we're operating in our everyday, conundrum-generating mode, any real solution, should we encounter one, will seem impossible.

And yet genuine solutions exist and are often offered to us by our own psyches —
often by the soul or the Muse. These solutions arise from a level of consciousness decidedly different from our ego's. Unless our own consciousness shifts, the soul's and
Muse's suggestions will seem to us like impossible dreams and we'll dismiss them out
of hand. But these solutions are impossible only from the perspective of the ego that
has not yet awakened to a larger story and a more mysterious and numinous world than
it has yet imagined. All dreams, visions, and revelations come to our conscious minds
from a greater domain.

Humanity — in fact, the entire Earth community — currently exists in such dire
circumstances that the most significant, viable, and potent solutions will seem like impossible dreams to most everyone (at first). But this is apparently the way it has always
been in our universe. At the greatest moments of transformations — what Thomas
Berry calls "moments of grace" — the "impossible" happens. Like it did 2 billion years
ago, when a certain bacterium (eukaryote) learned how to metabolize oxygen (that is,
breathe) and how to reproduce by meiotic sex. Or perhaps like the big bang itself, some
14 billion years ago, creating something out of nothing. Or the appearance of an Earth-
ling with conscious self-awareness. More generally, "wild love affairs," Geneen writes,
"— Sun and Earth; fungi and algae; bacteria / and mitochondria — preceded and
spawned us. ... This is the way it's always been."

The idea of a soulcentric society living by an ecocentric sequence of developmental
stages — to most people, this will seem an impossible dream.[10] In the face of the mind-
boggling casualties and depravities of contemporary Western societies, the Great
Turning, too, might seem like an impossible dream, sometimes even to us impossible
dreamers. Yet at this critical hour, any dream worth its salt *ought* to seem impossible
to mainstream society and to the mainstream elements of our own minds. In George
Bernard Shaw's play *Back to Methuselah*, the serpent says to Eve, "You see things; and
you say 'Why?' But I dream things that never were; and I say 'Why not?' "[11] Great wisdom, this, from the iconic underworld emissary — counsel that we ourselves would
do well to heed in this hour of radical crisis and opportunity.

If you consider the data on such things as current wars, environmental destruction, and political-economic corruption, there seems to be little hope for humanity and
most other members of the biosphere. But if, alternatively, you look at the fact of miracles — moments of grace — throughout the known history of the universe, it will
dawn on you that there is and always has been an intelligence or imagination at work
much greater than our conscious human minds. Given that we cannot rule out a moment of grace *acting through us* in this century, we have no alternative but to proceed
as if we ourselves in fact can make the difference — if, that is, enough of us uncover
and enact our soulwork. It is vital that we each believe in and perform our impossible dreams, those with roots in the Mystery. In the end, I am quite certain, we will not
be rescued by anything other than ourselves. If we are saved by a miracle, it will be the

miracle of enough of us maturing into artists of cultural renaissance and imaginatively putting our shoulders to the wheel of the Great Turning.

Perhaps the process of catching up to our human potential will unfold in two steps. First, we must learn to engender a healthy adolescent society, one in which we take good care of our environment and each other — largely motivated by our fear of what would be our own human losses otherwise. A desire to save ourselves by becoming wiser consumers and more loving neighbors might be enough to stem the tide of destruction we are currently witnessing, even if this desire is anthropocentric. A transitional society such as this will be a major advance beyond what we have now, and I believe we can (and must) realize such a society in a matter of a few years. The most progressive contemporary trends suggest to me that we're well on our way — with tens of thousands of visionaries leading us on.

The second step will be to make the quantum leap from a healthy adolescent society to one that is truly mature (eco-soulcentric). A mature society desires a lot more than to save itself physically and economically. It seeks, for example, to save the rainforest for the rainforest's sake, not just because it mitigates global warming or because it might contain plants that could someday provide medicines for humans. In addition to protecting the habitat of *all* species, a mature society has a shared visionary awareness of where we're going as a people and a planet. As Thomas Berry says, such a society experiences the world not as a useful collection of objects but as a sacred communion of subjects. This requires a radical change in the values of our current consumer culture. Although it might take several generations to grow a mature society, I believe we are entirely ready to piece together its infrastructure. In this book, I have attempted to outline what such an infrastructure might look like. It all begins with the way we raise children and mentor teenagers.

My impossible dream is simply this: in this century, we each will learn to mature, live, and love in a way that enables us to succeed as Great Turners, someday regarded as honored ancestors in the "eyes of the future."

APPENDIX

Summary of Eco-Soulcentric Development

EAST (STAGES 1 AND 8)
(ARCHETYPE: THE FOOL)

STAGE 1: The Innocent in the Nest (early childhood)
Passage: Birth
Gift: Innocence, luminous presence, and joy
Circle of Identity: None/infinite to selfcentric
Center of Gravity: Spirit
Tasks (managed by parents or caregivers): The preservation of innocence and the formation of a healthy, intact, culturally viable ego

SOUTH (STAGES 2 AND 3)
(ARCHETYPE: THE ORPHAN)

STAGE 2: The Explorer in the Garden (middle childhood)
Passage: Naming (celebrating the emergence of conscious self-awareness)
Gift: Wonder
Circle of Identity: Sociocentric
Center of Gravity: Family and nature
Task: Learning the givens of the world and our place in it
Subtasks:
    1. Discovering the enchantment of the natural world. The four realms of nature:
        a. Wild nature (the other-than-human world)
        b. The human body (including the five senses)

       c. Imagination (especially dreams and spontaneous imaginings)

       d. Emotions

  2. Learning cultural ways: the social practices, values, knowledge, history, mythology, and cosmology of our family and culture

STAGE 3: The Thespian at the Oasis (early adolescence; Social Individuation)

Passage: Puberty (specifically, when we begin to experience ourselves primarily as members of a peer group and community beyond our membership in family and nature)

Gift: Fire

Circle of Identity: Ethnocentric

Center of Gravity: Peer group, sex, and society

Task: Creating a secure and authentic social self (one that generates adequate amounts of both social acceptance and self-approval)

  Subtasks:

    1. Exploring values and learning the skills of social authenticity

    2. Emotional skills: emotional access, insight, action, and illumination

    3. Art of conflict resolution (with both outer and inner conflicts)

    4. Status-assigning skills

    5. Skills in sex and sexual relationships

    6. Sustenance skills

    7. Studying human-nature reciprocity and ecological responsibility

    8. Welcoming home the Loyal Soldier

WEST (STAGES 4 AND 5)
(ARCHETYPE: THE VISIONARY)

STAGE 4: The Wanderer in the Cocoon (late adolescence)

Passage: Confirmation (of our adequate completion of an adolescent personality and consequently of our preparedness for the descent to soul)

Gifts: Mystery and darkness

Circle of Identity: Worldcentric

Center of Gravity: Mysteries of soul and nature, the underworld

Task 1. Leaving home (relinquishing our adolescent identity)

  A. Honing the skills of physical, psychological, and social self-reliance

  B. Relinquishing attachment to our adolescent identity

    1. Addressing developmental deficits from earlier stages

    2. Giving up addictions

    3. Exploring the sacred wound

    4. Learning to choose authenticity over social acceptance

5. Making peace with the past (the death lodge)

6. Learning the art of disidentification through the practice of meditation

Task 2. Exploring the mysteries of nature and psyche

A. Acquiring and developing a set of soulcraft skills (examples: dreamwork, the way of council, self-designed ceremony, nature dialogues, deep imagery, trance drumming and dancing, sensitivity to signs and omens, soul poetry, symbolic artwork, use of plant allies, fasting, tracking)

B. Cultivating a soulful relationship to life

Practices and disciplines that support Task 2B:

1. The art of solitude
2. Discovering nature as a mirror of the soul
3. Wandering in nature
4. Living the questions of soul
5. Confronting our own death
6. The art of shadow work
7. The art of romance
8. Mindfulness practice
9. Service work
10. Advanced Loyal Soldier work: walking into the fire
11. Developing the four dimensions of the Self
12. Praising the world
13. Developing a personal relationship with spirit
14. The art of being lost
15. Befriending the dark
16. Withdrawing projections

STAGE 5: The Soul Apprentice at the Wellspring (early adulthood; Soul-Rooted Individuation)

Passage: Soul Initiation (the moment when we commit, utterly, to the embodiment in the world of our soul image, soul story, or soul powers)

Gift: Visionary action, hope, and inspiration

Circle of Identity: Ecocentric

Center of Gravity: Cultural depths (the embodied mysteries of nature and psyche)

Task: Acquiring and implementing delivery systems for embodying soul in culture

Subtasks:

1. Identifying one or more cultural settings for soulwork
2. Developing the skills of soulwork (acquiring a delivery system) and performing that work in our community
3. Further explorations of soul image or soul story and of the nature of soul powers
4. The soul-rooted individuation of the personality (differentiating the ego in relation to soul, as opposed to its earlier differentiation in relation to society)

NORTH (STAGES 6 AND 7)
(ARCHETYPE: THE WARRIOR-MARTYR)

STAGE 6: The Artisan in the Wild Orchard (late adulthood)
  Passage: Induction (confirms mastery of at least one form of soul embodiment)
  Gift: Seeds of cultural renaissance
  Circle of Identity: Holistically ecocentric
  Center of Gravity: Cultural giveaway as art form
  Task 1. Creating and implementing innovative delivery systems for soul
  Task 2. Advanced cultivation and integration of the four dimensions of the Self
STAGE 7: The Master in the Grove of Elders (early elderhood)
  Passage: Crowning (initiation into true elderhood)
  Gift: Wholeness
  Circle of Identity: From ecocentric to cosmoscentric
  Center of Gravity: The soul of the more-than-human community
  Task: Caring for the soul of the more-than-human community
    Examples:
      1. Defending and nurturing the innocence and wonder of children
      2. Mentoring and initiating adolescents
      3. Mentoring adults in their soulwork
      4. Guiding the evolution or transformation of the culture
      5. Maintaining the balance between human culture and the larger Earth
          community

EAST (STAGES 8 AND 1)
(ARCHETYPE: THE FOOL)

STAGE 8: The Sage in the Mountain Cave (late elderhood)
  Passage: Surrender (of the goal-oriented ego; primary life orientation returns to
    spirit)
  Gift: Grace
  Circle of Identity: Spirit-centered or cosmoscentric
  Center of Gravity: The cosmos (spirit)
  Nontask: Tending the universe
    Examples:
      1. Wisdom sharing
      2. The coordination of the human realm with the cosmological realm
      3. Mentoring by means of an enduring imaginal presence
      4. Preparation for death: the death lodge
  Final passage: Death

ACKNOWLEDGMENTS

The maps and ideas in these pages emerged from insights gathered and crystallized during a twenty-five-year apprenticeship to nature and the human soul, an opportunity for which I am profoundly grateful. Central to this apprenticeship was the education received from guiding hundreds of group programs — experiential, multi-day immersions into the mysteries of nature and psyche. While it was always my foremost desire that each participant ripen from his or her experience, there is no question that I myself benefited immensely. I am grateful for the vital things I learned from these courageous women and men who yielded to their indigenous vulnerability, plunged into nature's depths, and trusted their longing for a wilder and more meaningful life. Also instructive have been my own challenging moments of personal unfolding provoked by uncommon encounters with people, other creatures, wild landscapes, and archetypal presences.

Equally vital have been the countless conversations and creative collaborations with colleagues and co-guides concerning the most effective ways to model what we have observed in nature and human nature. Several times, following such discussions, one draft of this model abruptly ended and another began.

For the final form of this book, I am most indebted to three people:

Geneen Marie Haugen offered generous and deeply imaginative suggestions on innumerable occasions. In particular, she encouraged me to rename each of the developmental stages for a natural habitat or setting; and it was from our imaginative collaboration that the new names emerged. Geneen was also my writing coach and one of my editors on the final drafts of this book as well as my first, *Soulcraft*. Geneen — either in person or as her imagined presence just behind my left shoulder — stood faithfully with me during the final months of this project, advising about idea coherence, word choice, sentence construction, and many other writerly matters. I only wish I had been a better student. Her brilliant editing of the first chapter was invaluable in enabling me to adequately articulate the book's overarching frame. Equally important, Geneen supported me in moments of doubt; she never lost faith that I would complete this project in good form; and her playful, wild, and sensual companionship engendered joy throughout the adventure.

Donna Medeiros has been a loyal friend and colleague through at least a dozen years of the evolution of this model of human development. She has wrestled with every feature of the model as it applies to her own individuation as well as that of the many people she has tenderly and adeptly mentored. I have benefited immeasurably from her ideas, questions, suggestions, support, and encouragement. She reviewed and critiqued every chapter in this book, lovingly and fiercely advising changes and selflessly contributing her own understandings, many dozens of which I have gratefully incorporated in these pages. She has cared about the growth of this model as much as I have.

Sabina Wyss, another dear friend and cherished colleague, has co-taught with me an annual four-day program on the Wheel. She reviewed and offered detailed responses to each chapter, and contributed innumerable ideas, inspirations, and stories.

Through the years, many other friends and comrades have offered significant ideas, invaluable critical comments, editing, field-testing of the model, and heartfelt encouragement. These include, especially, Peter Scanlan, Annie Bloom, Kerry Brady, Rob Meltzer, Steve and Jessie Zeller, Len Fleischer, Bill Ball, Tom Lane, Michael Thunder, Laura Sewall, Molly Young Brown, and Mary Gomes. Many others assisted with concepts, images, stories, editing, inspiration, and moral support, including Mitchell Alegre, Jeffrey Allen, Ro Babcock, Jasmin Bloch, Wes Burwell, Barry Chaloner, Lauren Chambliss, Laura Cooper, Cristin Culbreath, Ann DeBaldo, Michael DeMaria, Deborah Demme, Julia Dengel, Gene Dilworth, Peggy Dulany, Barbara Fairfield, Lynn Goodwin, Judy Hall, Christina Hardy, Steven Hart, Jeff Hood, Trebbe Johnson, Lily Kaplan, Louden Kiracofe, Steffi Lahar, Amy Levek, David Levine, Susanna Maida, Jim Marsden, Mary Marsden, Dorothy Mason, Peggy McCauley, Ed Muller, Mary Lou Murray, Chelle Nagle, Julian Norris, Ron Pevny, Dan Popov, Rachel Posner, Tony Putman, Jamie Reaser, Mado Reid, Patti Rieser, Ann Roberts, Grace Ross, Jade Sherer, Roger Strachan, Dianne Timberlake, Rebecca Wildbear, Joe Woolley, and Stephanie Yost-Mentzell.

During my final two years working on this book, Mary Karis, Animas Valley Institute's executive director, offered deeply appreciated friendship and support, and adroitly managed the affairs of the institute, affording me the time and stillness to complete this project.

I am grateful for the support and encouragement of the AVI board members during the final years of completing this project, including Bill Ball, Cathy Edgerly, David Ellisor, Martin Goldberg, Deb Kenn, Ron Margolis, Jim Marsden, Chris Moulton, Tony Putman, Jamie Reaser, and Beverly Winterscheid.

I thank New World Library editorial director Georgia Hughes for her careful reading of the manuscript, her wise and perceptive suggestions, and her benevolent tending of all phases of the book's development and production. Thanks, as well, to my literary agent, Anne Depue, and to editors Bonnie Hurd and Kristen Cashman.

I am indebted to Thomas Berry and Joanna Macy for their profoundly inspiring lifework and their guiding eldership in this time of global crisis and awakening. I am grateful, too, for their gracious willingness to be in conversation with me, their heartfelt support of my project, and their generous permission to use portions of my interviews with them in these pages.

My everlasting appreciation goes to the Muse.

And thanks to Hermes, who warmly sat on my lap during much of the writing and dug his underworld claws into my legs, keeping me focused, grounded, and amused.

Finally, to all the forms and forces of wild nature, I owe the greatest gratitude, especially for the enduring love affair between Earth and Sun, a romance that makes possible the rhythms of every day and year as well as each of our lives and destinies.

NOTES

CHAPTER 1: CIRCLE AND ARC

The chapter epigraphs are from Thomas Berry, *The Dream of the Earth* (San Francisco: Sierra Club Books, 1988), pp. 207–8; and Drew Dellinger, "hieroglyphic stairway," *YES!* (Summer 2006): 47.

1. We find similar definitions of adulthood articulated by Joseph Campbell (namely, the hero who has descended to the underworld, experienced ego death and rebirth, and returns with, or as, a gift that helps restore his community to wholeness), Abraham Maslow ("people . . . devoted to . . . some calling or vocation . . . which fate has called them to"), Angeles Arrien ("walking the mystical path with practical feet"), Thomas Berry ("a person with a practical way of carrying out a vision or a dream"), and others. These quotes come from Campbell, *The Hero with a Thousand Faces* (New York: Pantheon, 1949); Maslow, *The Farther Reaches of Human Nature* (New York: Viking, 1971), p. 43; Arrien, "Walking the Mystical Path with Practical Feet" (a talk presented at the Institute of Noetic Sciences conference, 2001, Palm Springs, CA); and Berry, personal communication, March 16, 2006.

2. Macy attributes the formulation of the term "Industrial Growth Society" to the Norwegian eco-philosopher Sigmund Kvaloy, as does Dolores LaChapelle. See Macy and Molly Young Brown, *Coming Back to Life: Practices to Reconnect Our Lives, Our World* (Gabriola Island, British Columbia: New Society Publishers, 1998), p. 15; and LaChapelle, *Sacred Land, Sacred Sex: Rapture of the Deep* (Silverton, CO: Finn Hill Arts, 1988), p. 50. "Life-sustaining Society" is Macy's term. David C. Korten, *The Great Turning: From Empire to Earth Community* (San Francisco: Berrett-Koehler, 2006). Thomas Berry, *The Great Work: Our Way into the Future* (New York: Bell Tower, 1999).

3. For *ecocentric* people, their primary conscious membership is not in a family, ethnic group, or nation, but in the more-than-human Earth community. Synonyms for *ecocentric* include *nature-centered*, *biocentric*, and *nature based*.

4. For many more examples and much inspiration, see Paul Hawken, *Blessed Unrest: How the Largest Movement in the World Came into Being and Why No One Saw It Coming* (New York: Viking, 2007).

5. David Abram, *The Spell of the Sensuous: Perception and Language in a More-Than-Human World* (New York: Random House, 1996).

6. Macy and Brown, *Coming Back to Life*, pp. 17–24.

7. Ibid., p. 21.

8. Thomas explains further: "The new cultural coding that we need must emerge from the source of all such codings, from revelatory vision that comes to us in those special psychic moments, or conditions, that we describe as 'dream.' We are, of course, using this term not only as regards the psychic processes that take place when we are physically asleep, but also as a way of indicating an intuitive, nonrational process that occurs when we awaken to the numinous powers ever present in the phenomenal world about us, powers that possess us in our high creative moments. Poets and artists continually invoke these spirit powers, which function less through words than through symbolic forms." *The Dream of the Earth*, p. 211.

9. The final two quotes in this paragraph are from Thomas Berry, personal communication, March 16, 2006.

10. A related Einstein quote is, "We can't solve problems by using the same kind of thinking we used when we created them." Quoted in Margaret Wheatley, *Leadership and the New Science* (San Francisco: Berrett-Koehler, 1999), p. 7.

11. With the development of agriculture, a new form of adolescent pathology became possible (in fact, inevitable), a pathology that begins with greed and eventuates in hoarding, domination, and violence. Before agriculture, there was little to hoard because there was little material surplus. Among hunter-gatherers, no one within the tribe was significantly wealthier (in a material sense) than anyone else. The tribe's survival depended primarily on cooperation among its members. Extreme or pathological selfishness was not tolerated. However, with the advent of agriculture and farming (the domestication of selected animal and plant species), came the inevitable pathogenic notion of personal property and the possibility of some people deciding that hoarding things for themselves might be a good idea.

Once an agriculture-based tribe produces a single individual determined to hoard — and able and willing to use lethal force to do so — the cultural fabric of that society begins to disintegrate. To protect themselves, other individuals begin to hoard as well. The tribe becomes increasingly materialistic, competitive, anthropocentric, and violent. Economic-class structure and slavery soon follow.

Before long, the ruler of such a tribe (a patho-adolescent individual, usually male) decides that raiding *other* tribes for their crops, animals, women, and other "wealth" would be another good idea. This is the beginning of empire. As historian Andrew Schmookler explains in *The Parable of the Tribes: The Problem of Power in Social Evolution* (Albany: State University of New York Press, 1995), the neighboring tribes now have four options: be exterminated, be conquered and assimilated, become aggressive and warring themselves, or flee (migrate a sufficient distance from the violent tribes). And that, in a nutshell, is the history of our world over the past several thousand years.

Most societies eventually came under the control of pathological (sociopathic) adolescent leaders (tyrants, usually male) who systematically altered cultural traditions to enhance their ability to dominate. Among the alterations were (and are) anthropocentric, androcentric forms of religion; an emphasis on hostile competition over cooperation; land "ownership"; suppression of nature-honoring and nature-based rituals; class stratification and slavery; racism; sexism; militarism; plutocratic forms of governance; the systematic murder of true adults and elders (shamans and other cultural and spiritual leaders); compulsory egocentric education and the resulting ecological illiteracy; and perhaps the ultimate modern subversion of healthy society: the creation of corporations bestowed with the rights of persons.

A primary result of these and other cultural changes was the suppression of the human's innate ability to mature into true adulthood and elderhood, further undermining the cultural resources that support human development. This disruption of the natural course of human maturation is a central aim of dominator societies for the simple reason that children and developmental adolescents (of any age) are much easier to control and dominate than are true adults and elders.

In the twentieth century, this process of cultural degradation and greed-rooted empire-building reached its inevitable culmination, and in two ways. First, most every "tribe" in the world has now been assimilated within the modern dominator model of culture: the global industrial growth society. There is virtually nowhere left on Earth for healthy, partnership societies to live in peace. (There might be a few yet remaining in the most remote corners of the planet.) Second, the industrial growth society now threatens the entire human species with extinction.

As a consequence, we find ourselves faced with the global necessity to cooperate and form partnerships with all beings (human and otherwise) with whom we share our small planet — or perish.

12. I am indebted to Geneen Marie Haugen for helping me grasp the full significance of this wound.
13. See, for example, Thomas Berry, *The Great Work: Our Way into the Future* (New York: Bell Tower, 1999), pp. 162–63 and 198–99.
14. It was Geneen Marie Haugen who first pointed this out to me.
15. Berry, *The Dream of the Earth*, p. 133.
16. Indeed, as mathematical cosmologist Brian Swimme has noted, humanity is itself now a geological force.
17. Geneen Marie Haugen, "Cultivating a Planetary Imagination" (working manuscript, 2006). Original italics.
18. "But human beings are imagining people. I'd call my book on culture *Homo Imaginans, The Imagining Human.*" Thomas Moore, "Songs of Unforgetting," *Parabola* (Winter 2003): 8.
19. Berry, *The Dream of the Earth*, pp. 132–33.
20. Making ourselves whole again is a lot more than mere healing. Healing resolves deficits, while wholing cultivates invaluable psychological resources.
21. Ruth Wilson writes, "Early experiences with the natural world have been positively linked with the development of imagination. The work of Edith Cobb (1977) is perhaps the most noteworthy in this regard. Her work, based in large part on a search for the creative principle in the human personality, involved a careful analysis of a wide variety of autobiographical recollections of highly creative adults. Many of these recollections reflected an 'early awareness of some primary relatedness to earth and universe' (Cobb, 1977, pp. 17–18). Based on these and similar findings over her 20 years of research, Cobb concluded that childhood represents a special phase in life 'during which the most actively creative learning takes place' (Cobb, 1977, p. 17).

"Early experiences with the natural world have also been positively linked with the sense of wonder. Wonder, as described by Cobb (1977), is not an abstract term or a lofty ideal. It is, instead, a phenomenon concretely rooted in the child's developing perceptual capabilities and his or her ways of knowing. This way of knowing, if recognized and honored, can serve as a life-long source of joy and enrichment, as well as an impetus, or motivation, for further learning (Carson, 1956)." Ruth A. Wilson, "The Wonders of Nature: Honoring Children's Ways of Knowing," *Early Childhood News* 6, no. 19 (1997). This article can also be found at Early Childhood News, www.earlychildhoodnews.com/earlychildhood/article_view.aspx?ArticleID=70 (accessed September 18, 2007). The references Wilson cites in this excerpt are Edith Cobb, *The Ecology of Imagination in Childhood* (New York: Columbia University Press, 1977); and Rachel Carson, *The Sense of Wonder* (New York: Harper & Row, 1956).
22. Some differences between contemporary and traditional human development have already been mentioned: a new approach to and further differentiation of adolescence; a universe story that incorporates the time-developmental perspective as well as ever-renewing cycles; universal visionary capacity; and the emergence of *Homo imaginens.*

23. For this understanding, I am grateful to depth psychologist and wilderness guide Peter Scanlan.
24. Rupert Sheldrake, *The Presence of the Past: Morphic Resonance and the Habits of Nature* (London: Fontana/Harper Collins, 1989).
25. R. Buckminster Fuller, *Synergetics: Explorations in the Geometry of Thinking*, vols. 1 and 2 (New York: Macmillan, 1975, 1979); David Bohm, *Wholeness and the Implicate Order* (London: Ark Paperbacks, 1984).
26. Mary Oliver, *New and Selected Poems* (Boston: Beacon Press, 1992), p. 114.
27. Berry, *The Dream of the Earth*, p. 206.
28. Berry, *The Great Work*, p. 165.
29. Ibid., p. 196.
30. Ibid., p. 199.
31. Ibid., p. 200.
32. Ibid., pp. 200–201.

CHAPTER 2: THE POWER OF PLACE

The chapter epigraph is from David Wagoner, "Lost," in *Traveling Light: Collected and New Poems* (Champaign: University of Illinois Press, 1999), p. 10. A section epigraph that appears later in the chapter is from David Whyte, "The Sun," in *The House of Belonging* (Langley, WA: Many Rivers Press, 1997), p. 90.

1. I am indebted to psychologist Peter G. Ossorio for his lucid articulation of the concept of "place" within the methodology he names "status dynamics." See Ossorio, *Place: The Collected Works of Peter G. Ossorio*, vol. 3 (Ann Arbor, MI: Descriptive Psychology Press, 1998).
2. Buddhist scholar Joanna Macy tells us that this is, in essence, the central teaching of the Buddha. Commonly referred to as *dependent co-arising*, this observation affirms that a thing has the qualities that it has because of its relationship to everything else. The "arising" or "being" of anything depends on its relationship with all other things. Every thing, that is, comes into being in relationship to everything else. Or, a thing is what it is because of the *place* that it occupies. Thomas Berry says it this way: "Nothing is itself without everything else" (personal communication, March 16, 2006). The universe is like a giant web, and what we call things can be conceived as nodes (places) in that web. When the relationship between any two things changes, everything changes. By virtue of dependent co-arising, everything has its unique place. From this perspective, you could say that the Buddha's central teaching is about soul.
3. Brian Swimme and Thomas Berry, *The Universe Story: From the Primordial Flaring Forth to the Ecozoic Era — a Celebration of the Unfolding of the Cosmos* (New York: HarperCollins, 1992), p. 40.
4. From David Whyte, "The Sun," in *The House of Belonging*, p. 90.
5. Another common term for conscious self-awareness is *self-reflexive consciousness*, which means, in essence, "I am conscious of my self." The object (self) refers reflexively to the subject (I). To know that we know is to be conscious of ourselves as knowers.
6. No one has been more articulate, systematic, or lucid in writing about the concept of *person* than psychologist Peter G. Ossorio. See, for example, his *The Behavior of Persons* (Ann Arbor, MI: Descriptive Psychology Press, 2006). And cultural ecologist David Abram has given us our most thorough and eloquent understanding of the intimate relationship between mind and Earth, of "the rootedness of human awareness in the larger ecology." He elucidates mind or psyche not as something within our brains or bodies but as an actual landscape within which we are immersed and through which we wander. See, for example, his *Spell of the Sensuous* (New York: Pantheon, 1996), pp. 237–57 and pp. 261–62 (the quote in this paragraph is from p. 261).

7. The reductionist's question, "How does neural activity become a thought?" is as absurd as "How does the molecular structure of a bird's wing become flight?" or "How does the geological structure of the Moon make some of us crazy once a month?" Neural activity is part of the process of human thinking, but the firing of neurons is not the same thing as thought anymore than a hormone is the same thing as love.

8. From David Whyte, "All the True Vows," in *The House of Belonging* (Langley, WA: Many Rivers Press, 1996), p. 24.

9. Robert A. Johnson, *Inner Work* (San Francisco: Harper and Row, 1986), p. 7.

10. Thomas Berry, foreword to *Soulcraft: Crossing into the Mysteries of Nature and Psyche*, by Bill Plotkin (Novato, CA: New World Library, 2003), p. xiii.

11. Geneen Marie Haugen, personal communication, January 7, 2007.

12. Ossorio, *The Behavior of Persons.*

13. From Whyte, "All the True Vows," p. 24; from Mary Oliver, "The Journey," in *Dream Work* (New York: Atlantic Monthly Press, 1986), pp. 38–39; from Whyte, "What to Remember When Waking," in *The House of Belonging*, p. 28.

14. With apologies to Jon Kabat-Zinn.

15. Thomas Berry, *Evening Thoughts* (San Francisco: Sierra Club Books, 2006), p. 149.

16. Eckhart Tolle, *The Power of Now: A Guide to Spiritual Enlightenment* (Novato, CA: New World Library, 1999).

17. There is much more to say about the differences and relationship between spirit and soul, but rather than repeat what's in *Soulcraft*, I refer the reader to chapter 2 of that book and/or the website of Animas Valley Institute (www.animas.org), where you can find updated versions of the chapter.

18. Riane Eisler, *The Chalice and the Blade: Our History, Our Future* (Harper and Row, 1987), p. xvii.

19. David Korten, *The Great Turning: From Empire to Earth Community* (Bloomfield, CT: Kumarian Press; San Francisco: Berrett-Koehler, 2006), p. 21.

CHAPTER 3: OVERVIEW OF THE WHEEL OF LIFE

The chapter epigraph is from William Stafford, "The Way It Is," in *The Way It Is: New and Selected Poems* (Saint Paul, MN: Graywolf Press, 1998), p. 42.

1. Aniela Jaffé, "Symbolism in the Visual Arts," in *Man and His Symbols*, ed. C. G. Jung (New York: Doubleday, 1964), p. 240.

2. Quoted in T. C. McLuhan, *Touch the Earth: A Self-Portrait of Indian Existence* (New York: Promontory Press, 1971), p. 42.

3. For example, Jungian analyst Marie-Louise von Franz tells us that "symbolic structures that seem to refer to the process of individuation [that is, psychological development] tend to be based on the motif of the number four." "The Process of Individuation," in *Man and His Symbols*, ed. C. G. Jung (New York: Doubleday, 1964), p. 200.

4. Von Franz, for example, notes: "There is a Jewish legend that when God created Adam, he first gathered red, black, white, and yellow dust from the four corners of the world, and thus Adam 'reached from one end of the world to the other.' " "The Process of Individuation," p. 200.

    Concerning the universal nature of the fourfold, Jaffé tells us that "an Indian creation myth relates that the god Brahma, standing on a huge, thousand-petal lotus, turned his eyes to the four points of the compass. This fourfold survey from the circle of the lotus was a kind of preliminary orientation, an indispensable taking of bearings, before he began his work of creation.

    "A similar story is told of Buddha. At the moment of his birth, a lotus flower rose from the earth and he stepped into it to gaze into the 10 directions of space. (The lotus in this case was eight-rayed; and Buddha also gazed upward and downward, making ten directions.)...

"The spatial orientation performed by Brahma and Buddha may be regarded as symbolic of the human need for psychic orientation. The four functions of consciousness described by Dr. Jung... — thought, feeling, intuition, and sensation — equip man to deal with the impressions of the world he receives from within and without. It is by means of these functions that he comprehends and assimilates his experience; it is by means of them that he can respond. Brahma's four-fold survey of the universe symbolizes the necessary integration of these four functions that man must achieve." Jaffé, "Symbolism in the Visual Arts," p. 240.

5. For example, Black Elk is quoted as saying, "Everything an Indian does is in a circle, and that is because the Power of the World always works in circles, and everything tries to be round. In the old days when we were a strong and happy people, all our power came to us from the sacred hoop of the nation and so long as the hoop was unbroken the people flourished. The flowering tree was the living center of the hoop, and the circle of the four quarters nourished it. The east gave peace and light, the south gave warmth, the west gave rain, and the north with its cold and mighty wind gave strength and endurance." McLuhan, *Touch the Earth*, p. 42.

6. Writing of the pancultural sacred circle, Joseph Campbell notes: "The dome of the heaven rests on the quarters of the earth, sometimes supported by four caryatidal kings, dwarfs, giants, elephants, or turtles. Hence, the traditional importance of the mathematical problem of the quadrature of the circle: it contains the secret of the transformation of heavenly into earthly forms." *The Hero with a Thousand Faces* (1949; reprint, Princeton, NJ: Princeton University Press, 1968), p 42.

7. See, for example, Hyemeyohsts Storm's *Seven Arrows* (New York: Ballantine, 1972); Angeles Arrien's *The Fourfold Way* (New York: Harper Collins, 1993); Four Worlds Development Projects' *The Sacred Tree* (Twin Lakes, WI: Lotus Light Publications, 1985); and Howard Isaac's *The Wheel of Life* (n.p.: Sudden Impressions Printing Service, 1994). Several other models I studied are unpublished or were presented orally.

8. Since the early 1980s, Foster and Little have further developed their work in many ways. See their *The Four Shields: The Initiatory Seasons of Human Nature*, (Big Pine, CA: Lost Borders Press, 1999).

9. Other four-directions maps are anchored to the twelve signs of the zodiac (and the circling of the planets), or to the phases of the Moon.

10. When we northerners face the midday Sun, we are facing the south, and the Sun appears to move in a clockwise direction around us, rising in the east, moving through the south, and setting in the west. In contrast, for people of the Southern Hemisphere, the Sun appears to move counterclockwise, still rising in the east, of course, but passing through the northern sky during the day.

   Nevertheless, everything in this book holds for both hemispheres. People of the Southern Hemisphere need only remember that (1) everything said here about the direction of north is true for your direction south, and vice versa, and (2) the movement of your Wheel goes counterclockwise instead of clockwise. Notice, however, that for *both* the Northern and Southern Hemispheres, the Wheel moves sunwise. (People of the Northern Hemisphere invented modern clocks; they naturally chose to make the hands of their clocks move in the same direction that the Sun appears to move.)

11. McLuhan, *Touch the Earth*, p. 42.

12. Joseph L. Henderson, "Ancient Myths and Modern Man," in *Man and His Symbols*, ed. C. G. Jung (New York: Doubleday, 1964), p. 110.

13. Campbell, *The Hero with a Thousand Faces*, pp. 19–20.

14. Also see Mark Levon Byrne, "Heroes and Jungians," *San Francisco Jung Institute Library Journal* 18, no. 3 (1999): 21.

15. See Carol S. Pearson, *The Hero Within: Six Archetypes We Live By* (San Francisco: HarperCollins, 1989).
16. An imageneer is a pioneer who explores the frontier of human imagination.
17. Marilyn Busteed and Dorothy Wergin, *Phases of the Moon: A Guide to Evolving Human Nature* (Tempe, AZ: American Federation of Astrologers, 1982).
18. In this book, I refer to the second half of childhood as "middle childhood" rather than "late childhood." This seems to be the most common current practice. For adolescence, adulthood, and elderhood, on the other hand, I refer to the second half as "late."
19. *Soul Initiation* can mean two different things in this book: (1) the moment of passage from the Cocoon to the Wellspring, and (2) the *process* of initiation, which, depending on how you think about it, starts anywhere between Birth and Confirmation and ends at the *passage* of Soul Initiation. In this second sense, initiation is quite a long process, not a weekend ceremony!
20. I derived the phrase "psychospiritual center of gravity" from Joseph Campbell's almost identical "spiritual center of gravity." He writes that "the 'call to adventure'... signifies that destiny has summoned the hero and transferred his spiritual center of gravity from within the pale of his society to a zone unknown." See *The Hero with a Thousand Faces*, p. 58.
21. Ibid.
22. John Seed, Joanna Macy, Pat Fleming, and Arne Naess, *Thinking Like a Mountain* (Philadelphia: New Society Publishers, 1988), p. 36.
23. It's possible in stage 3, for example, to go through the motions of working on the tasks of stage 4 — sacred wound work, for instance. But in stage 3, working with those wounds would not be a way of leaving the home of the adolescent personality or entering the mysteries, and *those* are the true tasks of stage 4. Or, in stage 3, 4, 5, or 6, you could devote time to the stage-7 activity of mentoring the youth of your community, but doing so wouldn't be caring for the soul of the Earth in the way you could in stage 7. And *that* is the true task of stage 7. Being able to work on a given developmental task requires the foundations established in the previous stages and having your psychospiritual center of gravity located in the realm that enables that task. However, what you *can* do in any given stage is to cultivate your relationship with the archetypes associated with later stages and also with the four dimensions of the Self (corresponding to the four cardinal directions). (An in-depth discussion of the four dimensions of the Self is beyond the scope of this book; it will be the subject of a later work.)
24. I believe it's best not to share with another person your opinion, if you have one, about what stage he or she is in. Although every stage is the best one to be in if you embrace its challenges and gifts, people in egocentric societies tend to think hierarchically and feel that later stages are better than earlier ones.

CHAPTER 4: THE INNOCENT IN THE NEST

The chapter epigraph is from Rainer Maria Rilke, *Rilke's Book of Hours: Love Poems to God*, trans. Anita Barrows and Joanna Macy (New York: Riverhead Books, 1996), p. 88.

1. Terry Tempest Williams, *Refuge: An Unnatural History of Family and Place* (New York: Vintage, 1991), p. 50.
2. All quotes from Laura Cooper in this chapter are from personal communication with the author, 2006.
3. See Arnold Van Gennep, *The Rites of Passage* (Chicago: University of Chicago Press, 1960), chaps. 4 and 5, for many examples from cultures around the world.
4. Other ceremonies might be performed during the child's first four years — stage 1 — including ritual observances of the first haircut, the first meal with the family, the first tooth, the first walk, the first outing, and weaning.

5. Personal communication, 2006, with Sabina Wyss, who has spent much intimate time living with the Tuareg.

6. Thomas Berry notes a similar ceremony enacted by the Omaha people of North America. "The infant is taken out under the sky and presented to the universe and to the various natural forces with the petition that both the universe and this continent, with all their powers, will protect and guide the child toward its proper destiny. . . . In this manner the infant is bonded with the entire natural world as the source, guide, security, and fulfillment of life." *The Great Work: Our Way into the Future* (New York: Bell Tower, 1999), p. 39.

7. This fact underscores a key feature of the East quadrant of the Wheel — because they are spirit-infused, individuals in these two stages (1 and 8) have no conscious tasks at all. In the first stage of life, the tasks are someone else's, and in the final stage, there *is* no task — no conscious striving.

8. Jean Piaget, *Language and Thought of a Child* (London: Kegan Paul, Trench and Co., 1932).

9. Elisabet Sahtouris, *EarthDance: Living Systems in Evolution* (Lincoln, NE: iUniverse, 2000). Healthy interspecies competition can be thought of as a type of cooperation; it cultivates the strengths and unique characteristics of both species and, in that way, also enhances the health of the ecosystem.

10. Sigmund Freud, *New Introductory Lectures on Psychoanalysis* (New York: Norton, 1969), p. 100.

11. In an egocentric society, it might be necessary for some of this wildness to be kept hidden from the mainstream, shared openly only with family members and other intimates.

12. Theodore Roszak, *The Voice of the Earth: An Exploration of Ecopsychology* (New York: Touchstone, 1992), pp. 289 and 290.

13. For references on childbirth, see Birthing the Future, www.birthingthefuture.com.

14. See William and Martha Sears, *The Baby Book* (New York: Little, Brown, and Co., 2003), and *The Attachment Parenting Book* (New York: Little, Brown, and Co., 2001); Katie Allison Granju with Betsy Kennedy, *Attachment Parenting* (New York: Atria, 1999); Jean Liedloff, *The Continuum Concept* (Boston: Addison-Wesley, 1985); Meredith F. Small, *Our Babies, Ourselves* (New York: Knopf, 1999).

15. We'll consider boundary-setting and positive discipline in greater detail in the next chapter (stage 2).

16. Buddhist monk Thich Nhat Hanh suggests a similar statement as a regular practice in nonviolent communication and for loving more deeply: "I know that you are here, and it makes me very happy." (Thich Nhat Hanh, *True Love* [Boston: Shambhala, 2004], pp. 14–15). This is a potent statement to use regularly in a family. It can elicit tears and open guarded hearts when spoken at key moments.

17. Dolores LaChapelle, *Sacred Land, Sacred Sex: Rapture of the Deep* (Silverton, CO: Finn Hill Arts, 1988), p. 132.

18. Ibid., p. 137.

19. Ibid., p. 118.

20. Judy Hall, personal communication, December 15, 2005.

21. Bruno Bettelheim, *The Uses of Enchantment: The Meaning and Importance of Fairy Tales* (New York: Knopf, 1977), dustjacket.

22. Many psychologists refer to this earliest sense of identity as "primary narcissism." *Narcissism* refers to autoeroticism and an excessive fascination with the self. In relation to infancy, it's a misleading term with derogatory connotations, despite the fact that those who use the term in relation to infancy consider narcissism to be entirely normal and appropriate in this first stage of ego development. My speculation is that the use of *narcissism* in relation to infants reveals a misunderstanding or devaluing of early-childhood innocence.

23. Carolyn Zahn-Waxler, "Becoming Compassionate: The Origins and Development of Empathic Concern," *Shift*, no. 13 (December 2006–February 2007): 20–23.

24. Alan Watts, *The Wisdom of Insecurity* (New York: Vintage, 1968).

25. From Wikipedia, http://en.wikipedia.org/wiki/James_Dobson#Views_on_corporal_punishment _and_authority (accessed January 11, 2007).

26. Traci Pedone, "The Essentials of a Healthy Home: It's Best to Start Disciplining Your Children When They're Young," 2005, Focus on the Family, www.family.org/parenting/A000001549.cfm (accessed January 11, 2007). Italics in the original.

27. James Dobson, *Dare to Discipline* (New York: Bantam, 1982), p. 7.

28. James Dobson, *The Strong-Willed Child* (Borden, Saskatchewan: Living Books, 1992), p. 235.

29. Psychoanalyst Alice Miller has written extensively in this area. See her *The Drama of the Gifted Child: The Search for the True Self* (New York: Basic Books, 1981).

30. Although opposite in obvious respects, OT and ET are equally effective methods for shaping people to experience themselves as consumers. With OT, the reward for obedience is active participation in the egocentric, materialistic society. In the case of ET, the consumption of people and things is explicitly what one has been trained to do. In both cases, the child is learning to be a shopper rather than a human being. He's being taught that the world is made up of commodities rather than entities, and that he is a consumer rather than a communer.

31. I first learned this from Dr. Peter G. Ossorio, during his course on advanced personality theory at the University of Colorado at Boulder in 1973.

32. Alfie Kohn, *Unconditional Parenting: Moving from Rewards and Punishments to Love and Reason* (New York: Atria, 2005).

33. Some stage-1 educational programs, of course, are beneficial, designed to help kids catch up with basic social skills rather than compete academically.

34. Michael Gurian, *The Soul of the Child* (New York: Atria Books, 2002).

35. Robinson Jeffers, "From The Tower Beyond Tragedy, final scene," *The Selected Poetry of Robinson Jeffers*, ed. Tim Hunt (Palo Alto, CA: Stanford University Press, 2001), p. 114.

36. For additional help and inspiration, consider the books, tapes, and programs by Michele Cassou and Stewart Cubley (*Life, Paint, and Passion* [New York: Tarcher, 1996]), Julia Cameron (*The Artist's Way: A Spiritual Path to Higher Creativity* [New York: Tarcher/Putnam, 1992]), Aviva Gold (*Painting from the Source: Awakening the Artist's Soul in Everyone* [New York: Harper Perennial, 1998]), and Jane Seaton (*Artlife: Creative Journeys for Life Healing* [Boulder, CO: Sounds True, 2001], audio cassette).

CHAPTER 5: THE EXPLORER IN THE GARDEN

The chapter epigraph is from Richard Lewis, *Living by Wonder: The Imaginative Life of Childhood* (New York: Touchstone Center Publications, 1998), p. 137. A section epigraph that appears later in the chapter is from Rainer Maria Rilke, "The Eighth Elegy," in *In Praise of Mortality: Selections from Rainer Maria Rilke's Duino Elegies and Sonnets to Orpheus*, trans. Anita Barrows and Joanna Macy (New York: Riverhead Books, 2005), p. 49.

1. Children are, of course, typically named at birth, and naming rites are often performed at that time as well. See Arnold van Gennep's discussion of naming rites in *Les Rites de Passage* (1908; reprint, Chicago: University of Chicago Press, 1960), pp. 50–64.

2. In that this passage represents the child's conscious arrival from the upperworld of spirit, it might alternately be called Landing or Arrival. Or, in that this is the time of leaving the Nest, it could be called Fledging.

3. Soulcentric societies are imaginative, cooperation based, just, and ecocentric. A more complete definition and portrait of soulcentric societies is found in chapter 2.

4. I am indebted to Carol Pearson for the image of the Orphan archetype. See her *The Hero Within: Six Archetypes to Live By* (New York: HarperCollins, 1989).

5. An egocentric society is one that is materialistic, competition based, violent, and anthropocentric. A more complete definition and portrait of an egocentric society is found in chapter 2.

6. Some speculate that the soul, before birth, chooses its parents, but my point here is that the conscious stage-2 child does not make these choices.

7. Dolores LaChapelle, *Sacred Land, Sacred Sex* (Silverton, CO: Finn Hill Arts, 1988), p. 144.

8. Paul Shepard, *Nature and Madness* (San Francisco: Sierra Club Books, 1982), p. 10.

9. Joanna Macy, *Widening Circles* (Gabriola Island, BC: New Society Publishers, 2000), pp. 2–3.

10. Ibid.

11. Richard Louv, *Last Child in the Woods: Saving Our Children from Nature-Deficit Disorder* (Chapel Hill, NC: Algonquin Books of Chapel Hill, 2005), p. 28.

12. Ibid., p. 31.

13. Ibid., book jacket.

14. A. Faber Taylor, F. E. Kuo, and W. C. Sullivan, "Coping with ADD: The Surprising Connection to Green Play Settings," *Environment and Behavior* 33, no. 1 (2001): 54–77.

15. Ingunn Fjortoft, "The Natural Environment as a Playground for Children: The Impact of Outdoor Play Activities in Pre-Primary School Children," *Early Childhood Education Journal* 29, no. 2 (2001): 111–17.

16. A. Faber Taylor, A. Wiley, F. E. Kuo, and W. C. Sullivan, "Growing Up in the Inner City: Green Spaces as Places to Grow," *Environment and Behavior* 30, no. 1 (1998): 3–27; R. Moore and H. Wong, *Natural Learning: Rediscovering Nature's Way of Teaching* (Berkeley, CA: MIG Communications, 1997).

17. Robert Pyle, "Eden in a Vacant Lot: Special Places, Species, and Kids in the Community of Life," in *Children and Nature: Psychological, Sociocultural, and Evolutionary Investigations*, ed. P. H. Kahn and S. R. Kellert (Cambridge, MA: MIT Press, 2002).

18. Nancy M. Wells and Gary W. Evans, "Nearby Nature: A Buffer of Life Stress among Rural Children," *Environment and Behavior* 35, no. 3 (2003): 311–30.

19. Ann Coffey, "Transforming School Grounds," in *Greening School Grounds: Creating Habitats for Learning*, ed. Tim Grant and Gail Littlejohn (Toronto: Green Teacher / Gabriola Island, BC: New Society Publishers, 2001).

20. William Crain, "How Nature Helps Children Develop," *Montessori Life* (Summer 2001).

21. Robin Moore, "Compact Nature: The Role of Playing and Learning Gardens on Children's Lives," *Journal of Therapeutic Horticulture* 8 (1996): 72–82.

22. Louv, *Last Child in the Woods*, pp. 107–8.

23. David Sobel, *Beyond Ecophobia: Reclaiming the Heart in Nature Education* (Great Barrington, MA: Orion Society, 1996), p. 13.

24. Organizations such as Hooked on Nature are inspiring and empowering parents and teachers to help children experience the wonder of nature. See www.hookedonnature.org. See also Genesis Farm, and Jane Goodall's international work with her Roots and Shoots program.

25. Sobel, *Beyond Ecophobia*, p. 19.

26. In many communities across America, nonprofit organizations arrange for adult volunteers to accompany children into nature in a variety of settings, returning to childhood the elements of belonging, empathy, rootedness in the wild world, the play of the senses, natural learning, and wonder.

27. Sobel, *Beyond Ecophobia*.

28. Ibid., p. 39.

29. Thomas Berry, "The Universe Is Our University," *Timeline*, no. 34 (July–August 1997): 22.

30. Dan Acuff, *What Kids Buy and Why* (New York: Free Press, 1997), p. 174; B. Patterson, *Build Me an Ark* (New York: Norton, 2000).

31. Edith Cobb, *The Ecology of Imagination in Childhood* (1977; reprint, New Orleans: Spring Publications, 1993). Cobb based her conclusions on her extensive observations of children at play and on her analysis of some three hundred autobiographical recollections of childhood by creative people from many cultures and periods.

32. James Hillman, *The Soul's Code: In Search of Character and Calling* (New York: Random House, 1996), pp. 86-87.
33. Richard Lewis, *Living by Wonder: The Imaginative Life of Childhood* (New York: Touchstone Center Publications, 1998), p. 106.
34. Ibid., p. 107.
35. From a letter written to the Reverend Dr. Trusler, dated August 23, 1799, *The Complete Poetry and Prose of William Blake*, ed. David V. Erdman (Berkeley: University of California Press, 1982), p. 702.
36. Culture is a given in childhood, but beginning in early adolescence (stage 3), the individual becomes a cocreator of culture — in partnership with her fellow humans, the other creatures of their place on Earth, and the images and archetypes of the collective unconscious.
37. John Leo, "C Is for Character," *U.S. News and World Report* (November 15, 1999): 20.
38. See Linda Kavelin Popov's *The Family Virtues Guide: Simple Ways to Bring Out the Best in Our Children and Ourselves* (New York: Penguin, 1997).
39. A culture's social practices, values, and stories are, in addition, rooted in extracultural elements of nature — emotions, imagination, and the people's relationships to the other-than-human beings.
40. Colleen Cordes and Edward Miller, eds., *Fool's Gold: A Critical Look at Computers in Childhood*, 2001. See Alliance for Childhood, www.allianceforchildhood.net/projects/computers/computers _reports_fools_gold_download.htm (accessed June 12, 2007).
41. See Michael K. Stone and Zenobia Barlow, eds., *Ecological Literacy: Educating Our Children for a Sustainable World* (San Francisco: Sierra Club Books, 2005).
42. See, for example, Paul Shepard's *Nature and Madness*.
43. When we've lost the sacred myths of our ancestors, we find ourselves, before long, creating or adopting new ones. Perhaps this explains the astonishing popularity of J. K. Rowling's *Harry Potter* series, J. R. R. Tolkien's revived *Lord of the Rings*, modern film versions of ancient myths, such as *Star Wars* and *The Matrix*, and film presentations of inspiring and vital indigenous myths, such as *Whale Rider*, about the Maori people of New Zealand, and *Fast Runner*, about the Inuit of the circumpolar North.
44. Thomas Berry, *Evening Thoughts: Reflecting on Earth as Sacred Community* (San Francisco: Sierra Club Books, 2006), p. 59.
45. And there are many such versions. See references for this chapter in the resource section in the back of this book.
46. Berry, *Evening Thoughts*, p. 145.
47. John Gatto, *Dumbing Us Down* (Gabriola Island, BC: New Society Publishers, 1992), back cover.
48. Ibid., p. 68.
49. I haven't been able to find the original source of this quote, but I can tell you this: for over thirty years, these words of Watts's have been pinned to the wall over my desk, handwritten by me on an old scrap of paper.
50. Although the discovery of nature's enchantment and the acquisition of cultural membership are the primary tasks of the Garden, there are other developmental milestones during this period, each of which supports one or both of the primary tasks. A partial list might highlight the following: the learning of rules (that is, those that govern games and social practices, as well as those involved in linguistic skills and math), learning cultural age norms, developing peer relationships outside the family, acquiring the skills of cooperation as well as amicable competition, taking on responsibilities at home and school, adopting sound physical exercise habits, learning how to make or fix things, learning how to interact in groups, and learning gender roles.

    Are these developmental milestones as important to childhood development as learning the givens? In my view, all these competencies are components or complements of — and therefore are subordinate to — the child's unpressured exploration of the natural and social worlds around and within him. You could say that the above list of developmental milestones constitutes some of the trees of the forest of learning the givens.

51. Eligio Stephen Gallegos, *Animals of the Four Windows: Integrating Thinking, Sensing, Feeling, and Imagery* (Santa Fe, NM: Moon Bear Press, 1991).

52. Ibid., p. 6.

53. Jean Piaget, *The Construction of Reality in the Child* (New York: Basic Books, 1954).

54. True sociocentrism (beyond social altruism) is the developmental precursor of adult ecocentrism, in which the well-being of the more-than-human environment is the highest priority, above that of both the human village and any other single species. Clearly, ecocentrism is a rare quality in contemporary business, politics, education, and religion. Indeed, it's rare enough in environmental circles.

55. Chris Suellentrop, "Are Video Games Evil?" *Wilson Quarterly* (Summer 2006), www.wilsoncenter.org/index.cfm?fuseaction=wq.essay&essay_id=193155 (accessed June 13, 2007).

56. Quoted in Amy Beare, "In Search for Signs of Hope," *Timeline*, no. 32 (March-April 1997): 13. See Mary Pipher, *The Shelter of Each Other: Rebuilding Our Families* (New York: Grosset/Putnam, 1996).

57. See Randy White, "Young Children's Relationship with Nature: Its Importance to Children's Development and the Earth's Future," 2004, White Hutchinson Leisure and Learning Group, www .whitehutchinson.com/children/articles/childrennature.shtml (accessed December 16, 2005).

58. "Authentic Movement is a completely self-directed form in which individuals may discover a movement pathway that offers a bridge between the conscious and the unconscious." See Authentic Movement Institute, www.authenticmovement-usa.com (accessed June 13, 2007). Five rhythms is a movement meditation practice devised by Gabrielle Roth in the 1960s. See Gabrielle Roth, *Sweat Your Prayers* (New York: Tarcher/Penguin, 1997).

59. I know of no better resource in this regard than Brian Swimme's *The Hidden Heart of the Cosmos* (Maryknoll, NY: Orbis Books, 1996).

CHAPTER 6: THE THESPIAN AT THE OASIS

The chapter epigraph is from Jelalludin Rumi, "The Guest House," in *The Illuminated Rumi*, trans. Coleman Barks (New York: Broadway Books, 1997), p. 77. A section epigraph that appears later in the chapter is from Rainer Maria Rilke, "The Eighth Elegy," in *In Praise of Mortality: Selections from Rainer Maria Rilke's Duino Elegies and Sonnets to Orpheus,* trans. Anita Barrows and Joanna Macy (New York: Riverhead Books, 2005), p. 51.

1. Joanna Macy, *Widening Circles* (Gabriola Island, BC: New Society Publishers, 2000), p. 21.

2. All quotes from Lauren Chambliss in this chapter are from personal communication with author, April 2006.

3. Kia Woods, *Art and Soul Teen Initiation Rite: A Community and Family Rite of Passage Enactment* (New York: Kiamesha Studio, 1997).

4. L. Mahdi, N. Christopher, and M. Meade, eds., *Crossroads: The Quest for Contemporary Rites of Passage* (Chicago: Open Court, 1996).

5. Carl G. Jung, ed., *Man and His Symbols* (New York: Doubleday, 1964), p. 161.

6. Marie-Louise von Franz, "The Process of Individuation," in *Man and His Symbols*, ed. C. G. Jung (New York: Doubleday, 1964), pp. 161–62, 164.

7. In egocentric societies, there is no need to modify the term *individuation* with the qualifier *social*, because there is no widespread conception of an ego stage beyond that which begins in childhood.

8. Those who permanently stall in the Oasis (the soulcentric version of stage 3) also go through a sequence of substages lasting approximately one decade each, but I don't describe these substages in

this book. Such an effort is, in essence, what modern developmental psychology has accomplished with its many stage models based on empirical investigation of average, "healthy" people in contemporary egocentric societies.

9. From this brief description of gender differences, most people would say that Western society is far more masculine than feminine, and that, collectively, we would greatly benefit from moving in the feminine direction. I agree. But Western society does not simply tend toward masculinity; it tends toward *adolescent* masculinity — in fact, an egocentric and pathological version of it. The larger goal of social transformation is not merely a more gender-balanced society, but one that is more mature (less adolescent, pathological, and egocentric, and more soulcentric).

10. Adventure programs can help people explore risk-taking through experiential, team-based adventures in nature — ropes courses, rock climbing, walking on thin ice, or running whitewater rivers. Well-designed programs also familiarize participants with the psychological and social risks and benefits involved in team building, cooperation, leadership, emotional expression, and conflict resolution.

11. Macy, *Widening Circles*, pp. 30–31.

12. Ibid., p. 30.

13. Ibid.

14. I've borrowed the phrase "the full catastrophe" from the movie adaptation of Nikos Kazantzakis's novel *Zorba the Greek* (screenplay by Nikos Kazantzakis and Mihalis Kakogiannis).

15. Mary Oliver, "The Summer Day," in *New and Selected Poems* (Boston: Beacon Press, 1992), p. 94.

16. A later section of this chapter, "Egocentric Psychotherapy," offers a brief look at why competent therapists are becoming increasingly rare in egocentric society, and a few tips on how you might spot one nonetheless.

17. There are four kinds of depression, each a result of some thwarted dimension of human nature. The four kinds correspond to the four cardinal directions of human nature. Emotional depression is a South depression, one in which our emotions are blocked from being felt, understood, and expressed. Emotional depression is not itself a type of emotion (like sadness), but rather the frustration of an emotion, its incomplete assimilation. The other three kinds of depression result from the thwarting of soul (West), creative service (North), and spirit (East).

18. See David Levine's *Teaching Empathy: A Blueprint for Caring, Compassion, and Community* (Bloomington, IN: Solution Tree, 2005).

19. For a definitive discussion of status assignment and status dynamics, see Peter G. Ossorio, *The Behavior of Persons* (Ann Arbor: Descriptive Psychology Press, 2006); and Raymond M. Bergner, *Status Dynamics: Creating New Paths to Therapeutic Change* (Ann Arbor: Burns Park Publishers, 2007).

20. See, for example, Michael K. Stone and Zenobia Barlow, eds., *Ecological Literacy: Educating Our Children for a Sustainable World* (San Francisco: Sierra Club, 2005); and David W. Orr, *Earth in Mind: On Education, Environment, and the Human Prospect* (Washington, DC: Island Press, 2004).

21. I was first introduced to the image of the Loyal Soldier in 1981 by psychosynthesists Morgan Farley and Molly Young Brown.

22. From David Whyte, "The Fire in the Song," in *Fire in the Earth* (Langley, WA: Many Rivers Press, 1997), p. 35.

23. Jim Harrison, *Off to the Side* (New York: Grove Press, 2002), p. 33.

24. In pathologically egocentric societies, this fact about masculine teenagers is regularly exploited by military recruiters, hawkish politicians, football coaches, salespersons, advertisers, and gang leaders.

25. Piaget postulated that only about half of teenagers in Western societies acquire the capacity for formal operations. Some people do not develop this cognitive capacity until their early twenties. Many *never* get there. Apparently there is a cutoff point after which it will not happen. A bit more than half of all Western people are abstract thinkers and the rest concrete thinkers.

26. The capacity for formal operations is also a requirement for critical thinking: the ability to think for oneself, to weigh information, experience, and observation, and to compare, clarify, choose, and discern. The capacity for critical thinking has become increasingly rare in Western society. "Critical thinking is that mode of thinking — about any subject, content, or problem — in which the thinker improves the quality of his or her thinking by skillfully taking charge of the structures inherent in thinking and imposing intellectual standards upon them." Michael Scriven and Richard Paul, "Defining Critical Thinking," n.d., at Critical Thinking Community, www.criticalthinking.org/aboutCT/definingCT.shtml (accessed August 1, 2007).

27. In fundamentalist religious settings, too, independent critical thinking and deep imagination are actively suppressed.

28. A good example of educational design that embraces many of the developmental tasks of the Oasis can be found in Outward Bound's approach to expeditionary learning. Outward Bound's design principles include the primacy of self-discovery, the cultivation of curiosity, self-responsibility for learning, empathy and caring, risk taking and learning from failures, collaboration as well as competition, cultural diversity and inclusion, learning about nature and human-nature reciprocity, time for solitude and reflection, and the importance of service and compassion. See Expeditionary Learning Schools, Outward Bound, www.elob.org/.

29. This is not to blame the poor for being poor. When a poor or oppressed person is as retarded in his personal development as most egocentric middle- and upper-class persons, a likely factor is societal or class oppression and the resulting lack of opportunities. We are in great need of initiated adults whose soulwork leads them to address public policy and social welfare in order to enhance the opportunities of the disadvantaged. Equally we need adults able to generate diverse pathways to Soul Initiation effective for young people in each social class and subcultural group.

30. Our egocentric society functions largely as a system of Victims and Rescuers (and Perpetrators). Witness our dysfunctional tort system and our disempowering approach to welfare, to name just two examples.

31. See Andy Fisher's *Radical Ecopsychology: Psychology in the Service of Life* (Albany, NY: State University of New York Press, 2002), pp. 148–49.

32. See Chellis Glendinning's *My Name is Chellis and I'm in Recovery from Western Civilization* (Boston: Shambhala, 1994).

33. From my interview with Joanna Macy, April 18–19, 2006. Also see her *World as Lover, World as Self* (Berkeley, CA: Parallax Press, 1991), pp. 183–92.

CHAPTER 7: THE WANDERER IN THE COCOON

The chapter epigraphs are from J. R. R. Tolkien, *The Fellowship of the Ring* (1954; reprint, New York: Hougton Mifflin, 2004), p. 207; and Rainer Maria Rilke, "The Book of Pilgrimage," *Rilke's Book of Hours: Love Poems to God*, trans. Anita Barrows and Joanna Macy (New York: Riverhead Books, 1996), pp. 95–96. Section epigraphs that appear later in the chapter are from T. S. Eliot, "East Coker," in *Four Quartets* (New York: Harcourt, Brace, and Co., 1943), p. 28; and Rainer Maria Rilke, "The Ninth Elegy," in *In Praise of Mortality: Selections from Rainer Maria Rilke's Duino Elegies and Sonnets to Orpheus*, trans. Anita Barrows and Joanna Macy (New York: Riverhead Books, 2005), p. 57.

1. See James Hollis, *The Middle Passage: From Misery to Meaning in Midlife* (Toronto: Inner City Books, 1993).

2. Rilke, *Rilke's Book of Hours*, pp. 95–96. "The Book of Pilgrimage" is the third of four "chapters" in *The Book of Hours*.

3. Mary Oliver, from "Wild Geese," in *Dream Work* (New York: Atlantic Monthly Press, 1986), p. 14.

4. Rilke, *Rilke's Book of Hours*, pp. 95–96.

5. Joseph Campbell, *The Hero with a Thousand Faces* (Princeton: Princeton University Press, 1949), p. 58.

6. David Whyte, "Sweet Darkness," in *The House of Belonging* (Langley, WA: Many Rivers Press, 1997), p. 23.

7. Joanna Macy, *Widening Circles* (Gabriola Island, BC: New Society Publishers, 2000), p. 50.

8. Ibid.

9. Ibid., p. 51.

10. Ibid.

11. Ibid., p. 52.

12. Ibid., pp. 52–53.

13. Cocoons and nests are similar places. In both, a profound change in form takes place. In fact, in my first book, *Soulcraft*, I referred to the first stage of life as the Family Cocoon and the fourth stage as the Second Cocoon.

14. For example, in the countercultural 1960s and 1970s, something extraordinary happened: much of an entire generation heard the call to adventure, said YES, and entered the Cocoon. The hippies recognized that there had to be more to life than the American, or Western, dream. They employed a great variety of methods to lift the veil — psychedelics, music, dance, and Eastern spiritual practices — and most succeeded in one way or another. But with few elders and initiators to guide the way, and with the constant pressure from mainstream society to submit and conform, most were unable to effectively embody what they found in their wanderings. Relatively few reached the far shore of Soul Initiation and genuine adulthood.

15. Examples of progressive colleges that have begun to espouse soul-discovery for their students: Prescott College in Arizona, Naropa University in Colorado, Sonoma State College in California, and, on the graduate level, Pacifica Graduate Institute in California and the California Institute of Integral Studies.

16. Theodore Roethke, *The Collected Poems of Theodore Roethke* (New York: Doubleday, 1953), p. 108.

17. Macy, *Widening Circles*, p. 56.

18. Ibid., p. 61.

19. Ibid., p. 61.

20. Ibid., pp. 61–62.

21. Ibid., p. 62.

22. These are the four modalities of consciousness described by Stephen Gallegos and discussed in chapter 5.

23. Astrologers say the call we hear in our late twenties corresponds to our first Saturn return. It takes about twenty-eight years for Saturn — which, astrologers say, insists that we take our true place in the world — to make a full revolution around the Sun, thereby returning to the position it occupied at the time of our birth. Whether the opening to soul in our late twenties is incited by Saturn, the progressed Moon, or our genes, or directly by grace, or by some combination, I couldn't say, but it seems to be a common phenomenon.

24. Campbell, *The Hero with a Thousand Faces*, p. 58.

25. Ibid., p. 385.

26. Mary Oliver, "The Journey," in *Dream Work* (New York: Atlantic Monthly Press, 1986), p. 38.

27. Ibid., pp. 38–39.

28. Frederick Buechner, *Wishful Thinking: A Theological ABC* (San Francisco: Harper, 1993).

29. Bible, Proverbs 29:18.

30. Rainer Maria Rilke, "The Man Watching," in *Selected Poems of Rainer Maria Rilke*, trans. Robert Bly (New York: Harper and Row, 1981), pp. 105, 107.

31. Egocentric society's version of that message is less appealing, more undermining, and ultimately more addicting: "If you get the right job, have the right friends and hobbies, and contribute to

consumer culture, you *might* belong someday. But you must keep buying, doing, getting more attractive, and playing better all the time. Your belonging is just around the corner." We are never told that we belong just as we are.

32. What follows is a relatively brief summary of these two subtasks. See my book *Soulcraft* for greater detail and many illustrative stories.

33. In the Western world, alcohol and marijuana have been among the most commonly abused substances. When used addictively, they create a barrier between our egos and our core selves, including our emotions, in somewhat opposite but equally consequential ways. Alcohol, a central nervous system depressant, disinhibits us in small to moderate doses. If used to excess, it simply numbs us, and we become zombies unable to access our selves to any depth. Marijuana, on the other hand, provides something like experiential binoculars — wherever we turn our attention, we experience what's there in greater detail. We're drawn in. When used compulsively, however, these binoculars can turn into blinders, concealing the painful emotional areas so much in need of our attention.

34. Chellis Glendinning, *My Name is Chellis and I'm in Recovery from Western Civilization* (Boston: Shambhala, 1994).

35. This perspective is best articulated by psychologist Jean Houston in *The Search for the Beloved: Journeys in Mythology and Sacred Psychology* (Los Angeles: Tarcher, 1987).

36. Quoted in Annemarie Schimmel, *Mystical Dimensions of Islam* (Chapel Hill: University of North Carolina Press, 1985), p. 191.

37. Steven Foster and Meredith Little introduced me to the death lodge as a practice in preparing for a vision quest. See their *Roaring of the Sacred River: The Wilderness Quest for Vision and Self-Healing* (Big Pine, CA: Lost Borders Press, 1997), p. 34.

38. Natalie Goldberg, *Long Quiet Highway: Waking Up in America* (New York: Bantam, 1994), p. 93.

39. What follows here, too, is a relatively brief summary of these subtasks. See *Soulcraft* for more.

40. I recount the full story of this experience in the prologue to *Soulcraft*.

41. Malidoma Somé, *Of Water and the Spirit* (New York: Arkana, 1994).

42. Thomas Berry, *The Great Work: Our Way into the Future* (New York: Bell Tower, 1999), pp. 12–13.

43. Macy, *Widening Circles*, p. 74.

44. Ibid., p. 75.

45. Ibid., p. 76.

46. Ibid., p. 91.

47. Ibid., p. 106.

48. See Eligio Stephen Gallegos, *The Personal Totem Pole: Animal Imagery, the Chakras, and Psychotherapy*, 2nd ed. (Santa Fe: Moon Bear Press, 1990).

49. *Entheogenic* is an alternative term for *psychedelic*, but whereas the latter means "mind- (psyche) manifesting (delic)," the former means "engendering (genic) a god (theo) within (en)."

50. *Liminal* refers to a transitional state during which an individual is no longer who he was and not yet who he will be.

51. Arne Naess, "*Self* Realization: An Ecological Approach to Being in the World," in *Thinking Like a Mountain: Towards a Council of All Beings*, by John Seed, Joanna Macy, Pat Fleming, and Arne Naess (Philadelphia: New Society Publishers, 1988); James Hillman, "A Psyche the Size of the Earth," in *Ecopsychology: Restoring the Earth, Healing the Mind*, ed. Theodore Roszak, Mary E. Gomes, and Allen D. Kanner (San Francisco: Sierra Club Books, 1995).

52. The first nine of these practices are explored in greater depth in *Soulcraft*. The tenth (service work) and eleventh (praising the world) were not included in *Soulcraft* but are essential practices in the Cocoon. The final two (advanced Loyal Soldier work and developing the four dimensions of the Self) are introduced here for the first time.

53. Paul Shepard, *Nature and Madness* (San Francisco: Sierra Club Books, 1982), p. 9.

54. Richard J. Finneran, ed., *The Collected Poems of W. B. Yeats* (New York: Scribner, 1996), pp. 59–60.

55. Rainer Maria Rilke, *Letters to a Young Poet* (1934; reprint, New York: Norton, 1954), p. 34.

56. Ibid., p. 20.

57. Ibid., p. 35.

58. All verse in this section is from Rilke, "The Ninth Elegy," in *In Praise of Mortality: Selections from Rainer Maria Rilke's Duino Elegies and Sonnets to Orpheus*, trans. Anita Barrows and Joanna Macy (New York: Riverhead Books, 2005), pp. 57–60.

59. This topic, the four dimensions of the Self, is the subject of a future book.

60. Certainly there are exceptions to this generalization. Applied depth psychology is an example of a discipline that combines what I call psychotherapy and soulcraft.

61. Somé, *Of Water and the Spirit.*

62. Naess, "*Self* Realization."

63. This is David Whyte's phrase from his poem "What to Remember When Waking," in *The House of Belonging* (Langley, WA: Many Rivers Press, 1997), p. 27.

CHAPTER 8: THE SOUL APPRENTICE AT THE WELLSPRING

The chapter epigraphs are from David Whyte, "All the True Vows" and "What to Remember When Waking," in *The House of Belonging* (Langley, WA: Many Rivers Press, 1997), pp. 25, 27; and Ken Kesey, quoted in "The Art of Fiction," interview by Robert Faggen, *The Paris Review* 130 (Spring 1994).

1. Mary Oliver, from "The Summer Day," in *New and Selected Poems* (Boston: Beacon Press, 1992), p. 94.

2. From "The Prelude: Book Fourth: Summer Vacation," in William Wordsworth, *The Complete Poetical Works*, lines 333–38, found at Bartleby.com, 1999, www.bartleby.com/145/ (accessed July 12, 2007).

3. From David Whyte, "Revelation Must Be Terrible," in *Fire in the Earth* (Langley, WA: Many Rivers Press, 1992), p. 32.

4. Ibid., p. 33.

5. Martín Prechtel, *Secrets of the Talking Jaguar* (New York: Tarcher Putnam, 1999), p. 282.

6. With full respect to those Buddhist teachers who suggest otherwise, I believe the spiritual challenge in life is not to rid ourselves of desire but to distinguish egocentric desires from soul desires, to extinguish the former (primarily through personal maturation), and to cultivate nonattachment to the latter. Soul desires are to be embraced, celebrated, and embodied (although with nonattachment to outcome).

7. Thomas Berry, interview by author, March 16, 2006.

8. Angeles Arrien, "Walking the Mystical Path with Practical Feet" (a talk presented at the Institute of Noetic Sciences conference, 2001, Palm Springs, CA).

9. Abraham Maslow, *The Farther Reaches of Human Nature* (New York: Viking, 1971), p. 43.

10. Vaclav Havel, *Disturbing the Peace: A Conversation with Karel Huizdala* (New York: Vintage, 1990), pp. 181–82.

11. Rebecca Solnit, *Hope in the Dark: Untold Histories, Wild Possibilities* (New York: Nation Books, 2004), p. 5.

12. Robert Frost, "Two Tramps In Mud Time," in *A Further Range* (New York: Henry Holt and Company, 1936), p. 16.

13. Joanna Macy, *Widening Circles* (Gabriola Island, BC: New Society Publishers, 2000), p. 128.

14. Ibid.

15. Ibid., p. 132.
16. Joanna writes, "I was impressed by the particular courage with which the Western mind faced the bankruptcy of its own self-belief. Two contemporary figures became for me emblematic of that kind of lonely valor: the American poet Theodore Roethke and the Argentinean writer Jorge Luis Borges." Ibid., p. 133.
17. Ibid., pp. 132–33.
18. Ibid., p. 135.
19. As we make the transition to a more soulcentric society, our colleges, art institutes, and vocational and technical schools will offer expanding opportunities to apprentice to Artisans and Masters. Too many of our egocentric institutions of higher learning have become clusters of lecture halls where people are fed information derived from mutually disconnected disciplines and delivered by teachers as uninitiated as their students.
20. Macy, *Widening Circles*, pp. 141–42.
21. Ibid., p. 142.
22. Ibid., p. 149.
23. Arne Naess, "*Self* Realization: An Ecological Approach to Being in the World," in *Thinking Like a Mountain: Towards a Council of All Beings*, by John Seed, Joanna Macy, Pat Fleming, and Arne Naess (Philadelphia: New Society Publishers, 1988), p. 29.
24. Aldo Leopold, *A Sand County Almanac* (1949; reprint, New York: Ballantine, 1970), p. 140. Italics are mine.
25. Joanna Macy and Molly Young Brown, *Coming Back to Life: Practices to Reconnect Our Lives, Our World* (Gabriola Island, BC: New Society Publishers, 1998), p. 27.
26. Ibid.
27. I am grateful to Annie Bloom for teaching me about gratitude.
28. Thanks to the Indigo Girls for their song "Let It Be Me" on their 1992 *Rites of Passage* album. Also to Abe Lincoln, who has frequently been quoted as saying, "I am not bound to succeed but I am bound to live up to what light I have."
29. Not its actual name.
30. I've discussed this topic with hundreds of psychedelic journeyers, and most of them have come to this same conclusion. However, given the evidence of ethnobotanists and cultural anthropologists, I believe this finding has less to do with the true potential of psychoactive substances in the facilitation of soul encounter than with our culture's loss of the knowledge and ritual foundations that would enable such substances to serve as one component of a soul-revealing experience. The modern-day explorer of consciousness should keep in mind that psychoactive substances constitute only one element in one version (that is, substance-assisted) of one component (that is, ego-destructuring) of a process of soul encounter that, to be successful, must involve extensive preparation, social support, and a wisely designed ritual context.
31. These monks were dressed in the same manner as the tree-monk I met on my first vision fast, a story recounted in my first book, *Soulcraft*. I return to this story in chapter 11 of this book.
32. David Abram, *The Spell of the Sensuous: Perception and Language in a More-Than-Human World* (New York: Vintage, 1996), p. 167.
33. Ibid., p. 163.

CHAPTER 9: THE ARTISAN IN THE WILD ORCHARD

The chapter epigraphs are from John Keats, letter of November 22, 1817 to Benjamin Bailey, in *The Complete Poetical Works of Keats* (1899; reprint, Boston: Houghton Mifflin, 1958), p. 274; and Antonio

Machado, *The Soul Is Here for Its Own Joy*, ed. and trans. Robert Bly (New York: Ecco, 1999), p. 248. A section epigraph that appears later in the chapter is from Rainer Maria Rilke, *The Selected Poetry of Rainer Maria Rilke*, ed. and trans. Stephen Mitchell (New York: Vintage, 1982), p. 261.

1. Joanna Macy, *Widening Circles* (Gabriola Island, BC: New Society Publishers, 2000), pp. 169, 170.
2. Ibid., pp. 170–71.
3. Ibid., p. 173.
4. Ibid.
5. Quoted on Zaadz, http://quotes.zaadz.com/Martha_Graham, p. 1 (accessed July 14, 2007).
6. Ursula Le Guin, *A Wizard of Earthsea* (New York: Bantam, 1975), p. 87.
7. *Martyr* is by no means the only sacred term that egocentric culture has turned around, often into its opposite meaning. *Myth* and *ritual* are two of the most obvious instances. My favorite example of reversed meaning, however, is *hoodwinked*. According to current usage, it means "to deceive by false appearance, to dupe." Many people do not know that *hoodwinked* originally referred to the ultimate moment in an initiation ceremony: The initiate is led into the most sacred room or site of the culture or religious society. A hood has been placed over his head in order to protect him from the spiritual power of the objects in that space; to gaze too long would be harmful. The veil will be lifted for just a moment so that he may briefly view the *sacra*. To be hoodwinked, then, is to receive a great blessing. For us moderns, however, who know better, there is no such thing as a sacred reality that powerful; accordingly, a hoodwinking could only be a swindle.
8. The meaning of *martyr* might have gotten so turned around as a result of egocentric society's loss of its connection with soul. If you remove the dimension of soulwork from the concept of the martyr, what remains is someone for whom principle is more important than mission or calling, and for whom form is more important than substance or depth. In the worst case, a martyr is someone who makes a show of suffering in order to wring sympathy from others.
9. Joanna Macy writes, "The heroes and heroines of the Mahayana Buddhist tradition are the bodhisattvas, who vow to forswear nirvana until all beings are enlightened. As the *Lotus Sutra* tells us, their compassion endows them with supranormal senses: they can hear the music of the spheres and understand the language of the birds. By the same token, they hear as well all cries of distress, even to the moaning of beings in the lowest hells. All griefs are registered and owned in the bodhisattva's deep knowledge that we are not separate from each other." *World as Lover, World as Self* (Berkeley, CA: Parallax Press, 1991), p. 22.
10. Ibid., pp. 179–80.
11. Ibid., p. 180.
12. Carl Jung, *The Archetypes and the Collective Unconscious*, trans. R. F. C. Hull, vol. 9, pt. 1 of *The Collected Works of C. G. Jung* (Princeton: Princeton University Press, 1969), p. 289.
13. Macy, *Widening Circles*, p. 180.
14. Ibid., p. 181.
15. Again, the full exposition of the four dimensions of the Self will be the subject of a forthcoming book.
16. Macy, *Widening Circles*, p. 222.
17. Ibid., pp. 223–24.
18. See John Seed, Joanna Macy, Pat Fleming, and Arne Naess, *Thinking Like a Mountain: Toward a Council of All Beings* (Gabriola Island, BC: New Society Publishers, 1988).
19. This is not how the canyon is named on any maps.
20. I am following here Carol Pearson's terminology in her *The Hero Within: Six Archetypes We Live By* (San Francisco: Harper, 1989).

21. Alan Watts writes, "There is a contradiction in wanting to be perfectly secure in a universe whose very nature is momentariness and fluidity. But the contradiction lies a little deeper than the mere conflict between the desire for security and the fact of change. If I want to be secure, that is, protected from the flux of life, I am wanting to be separate from life. Yet it is this very sense of separateness which makes me feel insecure. To be secure means to isolate and fortify the 'I,' but it is just the feeling of being an isolated 'I' which makes me feel lonely and afraid. In other words, the more security I can get, the more I shall want." *The Wisdom of Insecurity* (New York: Vintage, 1968), p. 69.

CHAPTER 10: THE MASTER IN THE GROVE OF ELDERS

The chapter epigraph and a section epigraph later in the chapter are from Rainer Maria Rilke, *Rilke's Book of Hours: Love Poems to God*, trans. Anita Barrows and Joanna Macy (New York: Riverhead Books, 1996), pp. 91–92 and 48, respectively. An additional section epigraph is from Albert Einstein, *Ideas and Opinions* (New York: Crown Publishing, 1954), quoted in Reneé Weber, ed., *Dialogues with Scientists and Sages* (London: Routledge and Kegan Paul, 1986), p. 203. Emphasis added.

1. In addition to Joanna Macy and Thomas Berry, the list included Marion Woodman, Gary Snyder, Jane Goodall, Robert Johnson, and James Hillman.

2. Due to many centuries of misogyny in Western culture, *crone* in popular usage has come to mean "an ugly, withered old woman; a hag" (according to *American Heritage Electronic Dictionary,* 1992). But in recent years, women have begun to remember, retrieve, and restore the word's original, sacred, and archetypal meaning — a mature woman of wisdom and power.

3. You might think that in the final stage of life, the Mountain Cave, one is most fully human, but the Sage is, in a sense, *trans*human — of spirit as much as human.

4. Thomas Berry, *Every Being Has Rights* (Great Barrington, MA: E. F. Schumacher Society, 2004), p. 7.

5. Joanna Macy and Molly Young Brown, *Coming Back to Life: Practices to Reconnect Our Lives, Our World* (Gabriola Island, BC: New Society Publishers, 1998), p. 135.

6. Rabbi Zalman Schachter-Shalomi, "Respecting Elders, Becoming Elders: Can Elders Save the World?" *YES!* (Fall 2005): 41–44.

7. In the ancient Sumerian initiation myth, Erishkigal is the goddess of the underworld, and her sister Inanna is the goddess of heaven and Earth. Inanna courageously journeys into the underworld to confront her sister, who kills Inanna and hangs her corpse on a peg. Inanna is later reborn.

8. Berry, *Every Being Has Rights*, p. 9.

9. Ibid.

10. From the Earth Charter website, www.earthcharter.org: "Created by the largest global consultation process ever associated with an international declaration, endorsed by thousands of organizations representing millions of individuals, the Earth Charter seeks to inspire in all peoples a sense of global interdependence and shared responsibility for the well-being of the human family and the larger living world." The drafting of the Earth Charter was catalyzed by the 1992 Earth Summit held in Rio de Janeiro. As of August 2007, the United Nations has not yet endorsed the Earth Charter. However, the Earth Charter International Council is spearheading the effort to persuade the U.N. to do so, as well as engaging in many other projects to raise awareness about the charter and increase engagement with the principles and practice of sustainable development.

11. Some Sages (stage-8 elders) might also serve as politicians or judges, but I imagine this would be rare. It's more likely that they would be consulted by civic leaders, rather than filling those roles themselves.

12. "The Onondaga people wish to bring about a healing between themselves and all others who

live in this region that has been the homeland of the Onondaga Nation since the dawn of time," said Sid Hill, Tadadaho (spiritual leader) of the Onondaga Nation. "We want justice. New York State took our land illegally and needs to acknowledge this injustice and our rights to the land. But we will not displace any of our neighbors — the Onondaga know all too well the pain of being forced to leave our homes and do not wish that on anyone.

"... In asserting our land rights, we insist that polluted areas be cleaned up and that the lands and waters be protected for generations to come.

"... [Our] Nation and its people have a unique spiritual, cultural, and historic relationship with the land ... This relationship goes far beyond federal and state legal concepts of ownership, possession, or other legal rights. The people are one with the land and consider themselves stewards of it."

From "Onondaga Nation Announces Land Rights Action Promising No Evictions and No Casinos," at Peace 4 Turtle Island, March 10, 2005, www.peace4turtleisland.org/pages/onondaga pressrelease.htm (accessed June 21, 2007).

13. A person in such circumstances would benefit greatly from some sessions with a talented psychotherapist specializing in emotional access and expression (increasingly difficult to find), or sessions with a massage therapist trained in emotional release work.

14. Of course, a true elder is as likely to suffer the challenges of poor health, loss of family and friends, or financial ruin, and these terrible losses must be grieved. The difference for the genuine elder, the Master, is that the tasks of the Grove can usually be performed despite such losses, and his community (if soulcentric) will support him economically in his elder role because he is one of their greatest assets. In contrast, the Orphan in Pasture and Playtime, having suffered the same losses, might no longer be capable of his favored pastimes whether or not his society deems those activities valuable.

CHAPTER 11: THE SAGE IN THE MOUNTAIN CAVE

The chapter epigraph is from "Little Gidding" in T. S. Eliot, *Four Quartets* (New York: Harcourt, Brace, and World, 1943), pp. 58–59. A section epigraph later in the chapter is from Robinson Jeffers, "The Tower beyond Tragedy," in *The Selected Poetry of Robinson Jeffers* (New York: Random House, 1959), pp. 138–39.

1. Albert Einstein, *Ideas and Opinions* (New York: Crown Publishing, 1954), quoted in Reneé Weber, ed., *Dialogues with Scientists and Sages* (London: Routledge and Kegan Paul, 1986), p. 203.

2. Witter Bynner, trans., *The Way of Life* (1944; reprint, New York: Perigee Books, 1980). The first two descriptions are from Bynner's introduction, pp. 12 and 11, respectively. Lao-tzu's self-descriptions are from his twentieth "saying," p. 36.

3. Ibid., pp. 28, 55.

4. Carl G. Jung, *Memories, Dreams, Reflections* (New York: Random House, 1965), p. 355.

5. Thomas Berry, *The Great Work: Our Way into the Future* (New York: Bell Tower, 1999), p. 170.

6. Thomas Berry, *Evening Thoughts: Reflecting on Earth as Sacred Community* (San Francisco: Sierra Club Books, 2006), p. 50.

7. Thomas noted in our conversation that the origin of *all* rituals is cosmological. "Even in Christianity, we celebrate the parts of the day" with morning and evening prayers, for example. "There is a qualitative difference between the morning and evening," and this temporal difference reflects a cosmological difference. "It's not just a time difference but a profound psychological difference."

8. In this regard, the Wheel of Life is a set of guidelines for coordinating human development with natural cycles.

9. Berry, *Evening Thoughts*, p. 84.

10. See Frank Waters, *Book of the Hopi* (New York: Ballantine, 1963).

11. James Hillman, *The Force of Character and the Lasting Life* (New York: Random House, 1999), p. xxx.

12. Ibid., chap. 1.

13. Scott Eberle, a hospice physician and rites-of-passage guide, has written an exceptional book, *The Final Crossing*, about the death lodge, in which he recounts the final days of his beloved teacher and friend Steven Foster. Through the final three decades of the twentieth century, Steven and his wife, Meredith Little, did more than any others to restore to the contemporary Western world the ancient, cross-cultural ceremony of the wilderness vision fast and its associated body of practices, including that of the death lodge.

14. Rabbi Zalman Schachter-Shalomi, "Respecting Elders, Becoming Elders: Can Elders Save the World?" *YES!* (Fall 2005): 41–44.

15. Thomas Berry, *Every Being Has Rights* (Great Barrington, MA: E. F. Schumacher Society, 2004), pp. 10–11.

16. Carl G. Jung, *Memories, Dreams, Reflections* (New York: Random House, 1965), pp. 358–59.

17. Undoubtedly, some cases of dementia and Alzheimer's are truly neurological disorders and can be experienced by people in the Mountain Cave as well as in other stages.

CODA: THE EYES OF THE FUTURE

The chapter epigraph is from Terry Tempest Williams, *Red: Passion and Patience in the Desert* (New York: Vintage, 2002), p. 215. Section epigraphs that appear later in the chapter are from Geneen Marie Haugen, "Questions for Creatures with Forward-Seeing Imagination" (manuscript, 2007); and Lewis Carroll, *Through the Looking Glass* (1872; reprint, London: Penguin, 1998), p. 174.

1. Sabina Wyss, personal communication, June 15, 2006.

2. Helena Norberg-Hodge, *Ancient Futures: Learning from Ladakh* (San Francisco: Sierra Club Books, 1991), dustjacket.

3. Martín Prechtel, *Long Life, Honey in the Heart* (New York: Tarcher/Putnam, 1999); John Perkins, *Confessions of an Economic Hit Man* (New York: Plume, 2005).

4. Norberg-Hodge, *Ancient Futures*, p. 2.

5. See the website of the International Society for Ecology and Culture at www.isec.org.uk/pages/ladakh.html (accessed September 18, 2007).

6. Joanna Macy, *World as Lover, World as Self* (Berkeley, CA: Parallax Press, 1991), p. 132.

7. Ibid., pp. 132–34.

8. Thomas Berry, *The Dream of the Earth* (San Francisco: Sierra Club Books, 1988), pp. 207–8. These words of Thomas's about the necessity of the descent are part of the chapter 1 epigraph in this book.

9. There might be a "tipping point" at which the psychospiritual maturation of a critical mass of individuals *does* influence a species jump. But this is a kind of maturation beyond any we have yet known collectively; it requires us to fully recognize ourselves, first and foremost, as inhabitants and expressions of Earth and the cosmos.

10. A few other impossible dreams, past and present: putting a human on the Moon; the end of the cold war; the end of apartheid in South Africa; and John Seed's dream of stopping the destruction of the rainforests despite the data and socioeconomic trends showing it to be hopeless.

11. George Bernard Shaw, *Back to Methuselah,* act 1, *Selected Plays with Prefaces,* vol. 2 (New York: Dodd, Mead, 1949), p. 7.

RESOURCES *for* PARENTS, TEACHERS, TEENAGERS, *and* VISIONARIES

CHAPTER 4 (STAGE 1: EARLY CHILDHOOD)
Childbirth Resources

See www.birthingthefuture.com.

Resources for Parents of Stage-1 Children

Attachment Parenting International (see www.attachmentparenting.org, including the organization's list of suggested books).

Baldwin, Rahima. *You Are Your Child's First Teacher.* Rev. ed. Berkeley, CA: Celestial Arts, 2000.

Bettelheim, Bruno. *The Uses of Enchantment: The Meaning and Importance of Fairy Tales.* New York: Knopf, 1977.

Chilton Pearce, Joseph. *The Magical Child.* Reissue ed. New York: Plume, 1992.

Granju, Katie Allison, with Betsy Kennedy. *Attachment Parenting: Instinctive Care for Your Baby and Young Child.* New York: Atria, 1999.

Gurian, Michael. *The Soul of the Child.* New York: Atria, 2002.

Kohn, Alfie. *Unconditional Parenting: Moving from Rewards and Punishments to Love and Reason.* New York: Atria, 2005.

Liedloff, Jean. *The Continuum Concept: In Search of Happiness Lost.* New York: Addison Wesley, 1986.

Patterson, Barbara, and Pamela Bradley. *Beyond the Rainbow Bridge: Nurturing Our Children from Birth to Seven.* 2nd ed. Amesbury, MA: Michaelmas Press, 2000.

Sears, William, and Martha Sears. *The Attachment Parenting Book: A Commonsense Guide to Understanding and Nurturing Your Baby.* New York: Little, Brown, 2001.

Sears, William, Martha Sears, Robert Sears, and James Sears. *The Baby Book: Everything You Need to Know about Your Baby from Birth to Age Two.* Rev. ed. New York: Little, Brown, 2003.

Small, Meredith F. *Our Babies, Ourselves: How Biology and Culture Shape the Way We Parent.* New York: Anchor, 1999.

CHAPTER 5 (STAGE 2: MIDDLE CHILDHOOD)
Guides for Raising Children Ecocentrically and Soulcentrically

Chiras, Dan. *EcoKids: Raising Children Who Care for the Earth.* Gabriola Island, BC: New Society Publishers, 2005.

LaChapelle, Dolores. *Earth Festivals: Seasonal Celebrations for Everyone Young and Old.* Silverton, CO: Finn Hill Arts, 1974.

Nahban, Gary, and Stephen Trimble. *The Geography of Childhood: Why Children Need Wild Places.* Boston: Beacon Press, 1995.

Pipher, Mary. *The Shelter of Each Other: Rebuilding Our Families.* New York: Grosset/Putnam, 1996.

Popov, Linda Kavelin. *The Family Virtues Guide: Simple Ways to Bring Out the Best in Our Children and Ourselves.* New York: Penguin, 1997.

Sobel, David. *Children's Special Places: Exploring the Role of Forts, Dens, and Bush Houses in Middle Childhood.* Detroit: Wayne State University Press, 2002.

Philosophical, Psychological, and Ethnological Background

Barrows, Anita. "The Ecopsychology of Child Development." In *Ecopsychology: Restoring the Earth, Healing the Mind,* ed. Theodore Roszak, Mary E. Gomes, and Allen D. Kanner. New York: Sierra Club/Crown, 1995.

Cobb, Edith. *The Ecology of Imagination in Childhood.* New York: Columbia University Press, 1977; New Orleans: Spring Publications, 1993.

Gallegos, Eligio Stephen. *Animals of the Four Windows: Integrating Thinking, Sensing, Feeling, and Imagery.* Santa Fe, NM: Moon Bear Press, 1991.

Kahn, Peter H., and Stephen R. Kellert, eds., *Children and Nature: Psychological, Sociocultural, and Evolutionary Investigations.* Cambridge: MIT Press, 2002.

LaChapelle, Dolores. *Sacred Land, Sacred Sex: Rapture of the Deep.* Silverton, CO: Finn Hill Arts, 1988.

Louv, Richard. *Last Child in the Woods: Saving Our Children from Nature-Deficit Disorder.* Chapel Hill, NC: Algonquin Books of Chapel Hill, 2005.

Mander, Jerry. *Four Arguments for the Elimination of Television.* New York: Harper Perennial, 1978.

Shepard, Paul. *Nature and Madness.* San Francisco: Sierra Club Books, 1982.

———. *The Others: How Animals Made Us Human.* New York: Island Press, 1997.

Ecocentric and Soulcentric Education

Gatto, John. *Dumbing Us Down: The Hidden Curriculum of Compulsory Schooling.* Gabriola Island, BC: New Society Publishers, 1992.

Levine, David. *Teaching Empathy: A Blueprint for Caring, Compassion, and Community.* Bloomington, IN: Solution Tree, 2005.

Lewis, Richard. *Living by Wonder: The Imaginative Life of Childhood.* New York: Touchstone Center Publications, 1998.

Orr, David W. *Ecological Literacy: Education and the Transition to a Postmodern World.* Albany: State University of New York Press, 1992.

Resurgence magazine, no. 226 (September–October 2004).

Sobel, David. *Beyond Ecophobia: Reclaiming the Heart in Nature Education.* Great Barrington, MA: Orion Society, 1996.

Stone, Michael K., and Zenobia Barlow, eds., *Ecological Literacy: Educating Our Children for a Sustainable World.* San Francisco: Sierra Club Books, 2005.

Mythology and Fairy Tales

Brothers Grimm and Josef Scharl. *The Complete Grimm's Fairy Tales*. New York: Pantheon, 1976.
Campbell, Joseph. *The Hero with a Thousand Faces*. New York: Pantheon Books, 1949.
———. *Historical Atlas of World Mythology*. 5 vols. New York: Harper and Row, 1989.
———. *The Masks of God: Creative Mythology*. 4 vols. New York: Arkana, 1995.
——— with Bill Moyers. *The Power of Myth*. New York: Anchor, 1991.
Suzuki, David, and Peter Knudtson. *Wisdom of the Elders: Sacred Native Stories of Nature*. New York: Bantam, 1992.

The Universe Story

Swimme, Brian. *The Hidden Heart of the Cosmos: Humanity and the New Story*. Maryknoll, NY: Orbis Books, 1996.
Swimme, Brian, and Thomas Berry. *The Universe Story: From the Primordial Flaring Forth to the Ecozoic Era — A Celebration of the Unfolding of the Cosmos*. New York: HarperCollins, 1992.

Children's Books on the Universe Story

Decristofano, Carolyn Cinami. *Big Bang! The Tongue-Tickling Tale of a Speck That Became Spectacular*. Watertown, MA: Charlesbridge, 2005. Read aloud, ages six to eight; read by yourself, ages eight and up.
Liebes, Sidney, Elisabet Sahtouris, and Brian Swimme. *A Walk through Time: From Stardust to Us— The Evolution of Life on Earth*. New York: John Wiley and Sons, 1998. Read by yourself, ages twelve and up.
Maddern, Eric. *Earth Story*. London: Frances Lincoln, 1998. Read aloud, ages four to six; read by yourself, ages seven to ten.
Morgan, Jennifer. *Born with a Bang: The Universe Tells Our Cosmic Story*. Nevada City, CA: Dawn Publications, 2002.
———. *From Lava to Life: The Universe Tells Our Earth's Story*. Nevada City, CA: Dawn Publications, 2003. Both books by Morgan are to be read aloud, ages six to eight; read by yourself, ages nine and up. The third book in this trilogy continues with mammals and the human.

For Family Councils and Meetings

Baldwin, Christina. *Calling the Circle: The First and Future Culture*. New York: Bantam, 1998.
McGarvey, Suzanne, and Kim Leon, "Family Councils: The Key is Communication." http://muextension.missouri.edu/explorepdf/hesguide/humanrel/gh6641.pdf (accessed August 6, 2007).
Zimmerman, Jack, and Gigi Coyle. *The Way of Council*. Las Vegas, NV: Bramble Books, 1996.

Principles of Ecoliteracy and Ecocentric Education

Here are a few highlights of ecocentric educational methods and principles (see the references listed above):
• Project-based and place-based learning: Children select projects to work on as a team. Through their participation in the project, they develop their skills in imagination, independent thinking, feeling, math, reading, writing, cooperation, conflict resolution, leadership, planning, problem solving, craftsmanship, and so on, and their proficiency in the integrated and coordinated use of these diverse skills. Knowledge acquired can be in most any field, including biology, physics, psychology, zoology, ecology,

agriculture, business, sociology, economics, and politics. The projects worked on are place-based — they address real-world problems in the school and community and allow the students to create real-world solutions that make a difference.

Place-based learning allows children to spend significant time in habitats and communities as they exist outside the classroom — farms, gardens, wetlands, forests, rivers, and mountains. Some place-based project examples: an edible school yard (a child-created and -maintained organic garden that supplies the school cafeteria, which is partly "staffed" by the students as apprentice chefs); the ecological restoration of a creek; creation and maintenance of a fish pond; school interior decoration; transformation of the school grounds into a sustainable permaculture system; tree planting; establishment and maintenance of a seed bank; beekeeping; and the creation and landscaping of a small lake. Research confirms that we learn best what we experience directly, and learn least what we merely read about.

- Ecoliteracy, or "Education for Sustainable Patterns of Living" (the latter phrase was coined by Fritjof Capra, Zenobia Barlow, and their colleagues at the Center for Ecoliteracy in California): Ecoliteracy is understanding the principles of organization that ecosystems have developed to sustain the mysterious and intricate web of life. Sustainable human communities are best modeled after nature's ecosystems, which themselves are sustainable communities of plants, animals, and microorganisms. Writes Capra, "We need to teach our children — and our political and corporate leaders! — the fundamental facts of life: for example, that matter cycles continually through the web of life; that the energy driving the ecological cycles flows from the sun; that diversity assures resilience; that one species' waste is another species' food; that life, from its beginning more than three billion years ago, did not take over the planet by combat but by networking." [In "Landscapes of Learning," *Resurgence*, no. 226 (September–October 2004): 8.]

- The way to sustain life is to build and nurture a more-than-human community. The great question of our time is how we will live in light of the fact that all humans, other species, and all habitats are bound together in a single community of life that is now threatened by human numbers and carelessness.

- Learning is most effective when the whole school is transformed into a learning community. Teachers, students, administrators, and parents work together to support learning by each member of the community. Everyone is both a teacher and a learner.

- To be effective, education must engage the entire human community, not only the schools.

CHAPTER 6 (STAGE 3: EARLY ADOLESCENCE)
General

Gatto, John Taylor. *The Exhausted School: Bending the Bars of Traditional Education.* Berkeley, CA: Berkeley Hills Books, 2002.

Glendinning, Chellis. *My Name Is Chellis and I'm in Recovery from Western Civilization.* Boston: Shambhala, 1994.

Johnson, Julie Tallard. *The Thundering Years: Rituals and Sacred Wisdom for Teens.* Rochester, VT: Bindu Books, 2001.

Mahdi, L., N. Christopher, and M. Meade, eds. *Crossroads: The Quest for Contemporary Rites of Passage.* Chicago: Open Court, 1996.

Mahdi, L., S. Foster, and M. Little, eds. *Betwixt and Between: Patterns of Masculine and Feminine Initiation.* Chicago: Open Court, 1987.

Woods, Kia. *Art and Soul Teen Initiation Rite: A Community and Family Rite of Passage Enactment.* New York: Kiamesha Studio, 1997.

Resources on Ecology, Design, and Biomimicry

Bailey, Jill, ed. *The Way Nature Works*. New York: Macmillan, 1997.

Benyus, Janine. *Biomimicry: Innovation Inspired by Nature*. New York: Harper Perennial, 1997.

Bioneers. See www.bioneers.org.

Hoagland, Mahlon B., et al. *Exploring the Way Life Works: The Science of Biology*. Boston: Jones and Bartlett Publishers, 2001.

Orr, David W. *The Nature of Design: Ecology, Culture, and Human Intention*. New York: Oxford University Press, 2004.

Wann, David. *Deep Design: Pathways to a Livable Future*. Washington, DC: Island Press, 1996.

CHAPTER 7 (STAGE 4: LATE ADOLESCENCE)

See my book *Soulcraft: Crossing into the Mysteries of Nature and Psyche* for a full exploration of the Cocoon stage and for a comprehensive set of resources for visionary Wandering. A few additional, favorite references are listed below:

Abram, David. *The Spell of the Sensuous: Perception and Language in a More-Than-Human World*. New York: Vintage Books, 1996.

Berry, Thomas. *The Great Work: Our Way into the Future*. New York: Bell Tower, 1999.

Bosnak, Robert. *A Little Course in Dreams*. Boston: Shambhala, 1998.

Foster, Steven, and Meredith Little. *The Roaring of the Sacred River: The Wilderness Quest for Vision and Self-Healing*. Big Pine, CA: Lost Borders Press, 1997.

Goldstein, Joseph. *The Experience of Insight: A Simple and Direct Guide to Buddhist Meditation*. Boston: Shambhala, 1987.

Houston, Jean. *The Search for the Beloved: Journeys in Mythology and Scared Psychology*. Los Angeles: Tarcher, 1987.

Korten, David. *The Great Turning: From Empire to Earth Community*. Bloomfield, CT: Kumarian Press and San Francisco: Berrett-Koehler, 2006.

Levoy, Greg. *Callings: Finding and Following an Authentic Life*. New York: Three Rivers Press, 1997.

Macy, Joanna, and Molly Young Brown. *Coming Back to Life: Practices to Reconnect Our Lives, Our World*. Gabriola Island, BC: New Society Publishers, 1998.

Whyte, David. *Crossing the Unknown Sea: Work as a Pilgrimage of Identity*. New York: Riverhead Books, 2001.

PERMISSION ACKNOWLEDGMENTS

Grateful acknowledgment is given to the following sources for permission to reprint previously published material:

CHAPTER 1: CIRCLE AND ARC

From *The Dream of the Earth* by Thomas Berry, copyright © 1988 by Thomas Berry. Used by permission of Sierra Club Books.

Excerpt from "hieroglyphic stairway" by Drew Dellinger. Copyright © 2006 by Drew Dellinger. Used by permission of the poet. www.drewdellinger.org.

From *The Great Work* by Thomas Berry, copyright © 1999 by Thomas Berry. Used by permission of Bell Tower, a division of Random House, Inc.

CHAPTER 2: THE POWER OF PLACE

From *Traveling Light: Collected and New Poems* by David Wagoner. Copyright © 1999 by David Wagoner. Used with permission of the poet and the University of Illinois Press.

From *The Universe Story* by Brian Swimme and Thomas Berry. Copyright © 1992 by Brian Swimme. Reprinted by permission of HarperCollins Publishers, Inc.

Excerpts from "The Sun," "All the True Vows," and "What to Remember When Waking" in *The House of Belonging* by David Whyte, copyright © 1997 by David Whyte. Reprinted by permission of Many Rivers Press, Langley, Washington, 360-221-1324.

Excerpt from "The Journey" from *Dream Work* by Mary Oliver, copyright © 1986 by Mary Oliver. Used by permission of Grove/Atlantic, Inc.

From *The Great Turning: From Empire to Earth Community* by David C. Korten. Copyright © 2006 by David C. Korten. Reprinted with permission of Berrett-Koehler Publishers, Inc. All rights reserved. www.bkconnection.com.

CHAPTER 7: THE WANDERER IN THE COCOON

"Dich wundert nicht.../You are not surprised..." from *Rilke's Book of Hours: Love Poems to God* by Rainer Maria Rilke, translated by Anita Barrows and Joanna Macy, copyright © 1996 by Anita Barrows and Joanna Macy. Used by permission of Riverhead Books, an imprint of Penguin Group (USA) Inc.

Excerpt from "Wild Geese" in *Dream Work* by Mary Oliver, copyright © 1986 by Mary Oliver. Used by permission of Grove/Atlantic, Inc.

Excerpts from "Sweet Darkness" in *The House of Belonging* by David Whyte, copyright © 1997 by David Whyte. Reprinted by permission of Many Rivers Press, Langley, Washington, 360-221-1324.

From *Widening Circles* by Joanna Macy. See acknowledgment under chapter 5.

Excerpt from "The Waking," copyright © 1953 by Theodore Roethke, from *The Collected Poems of Theodore Roethke* by Theodore Roethke. Used by permission of Doubleday, a division of Random House, Inc.

Campbell, Joseph; *The Hero with a Thousand Faces*. See acknowledgment under chapter 3.

From "The Man Watching" by Rainer Maria Rilke, from *Selected Poems of Rainer Maria Rilke*. Edited and Translated by Robert Bly. Copyright © 1981 by Robert Bly. Reprinted by permission of Harper-Collins Publishers, Inc.

Excerpt from "East Coker" in *Four Quartets* by T. S. Eliot, copyright © 1940 by T. S. Eliot and renewed 1968 by Esme Valerie Eliot, reprinted by permission of Harcourt, Inc.

From *The Great Work* by Thomas Berry. See acknowledgment under chapter 1.

From *Nature and Madness* by Paul Shepard. See acknowledgment under chapter 5.

"The Ninth Elegy," from *In Praise of Mortality* by Rainer Maria Rilke, translated by Anita Barrows and Joanna Macy, copyright © 2005 by Anita Barrows and Joanna Macy. Used by permission of Riverhead Books, an imprint of Penguin Group (USA) Inc.

CHAPTER 8: THE SOUL APPRENTICE AT THE WELLSPRING

Excerpts from "All the True Vows" in *The House of Belonging* by David Whyte. See acknowledgment under chapter 2.

Excerpts from "Revelation Must Be Terrible" in *Fire in the Earth* by David Whyte, copyright © 1997 by David Whyte. Reprinted by permission of Many Rivers Press, Langley, Washington, 360-221-1324.

From *The Farther Reaches of Human Nature* by Abraham H. Maslow, copyright © 1971 by Bertha G. Maslow. Used by permission of Viking Penguin, a division of Penguin Group (USA) Inc.

From *Disturbing the Peace* by Václav Havel, copyright © 1990 by Václav Havel. Used by permission of Vintage, a division of Random House, Inc.

From *Hope in the Dark* by Rebecca Solnit, copyright © 2004 by Rebecca Solnit. Used by permission of Nation Books.

Excerpt from "Two Tramps in Mud Time" in *A Further Range* by Robert Frost, copyright © 1936 by Robert Frost. Reprinted by permission of Henry Holt and Company, Inc.

From *Widening Circles* by Joanna Macy. See acknowledgment under chapter 5.

From *The Spell of the Sensuous* by David Abram, copyright © 1996 by David Abram. Used by permission of Pantheon Books, a division of Random House, Inc.

CHAPTER 9: THE ARTISAN IN THE WILD ORCHARD

Excerpt from "Proverbs and Tiny Songs" by Antonio Machado, in *The Soul Is Here for Its Own Joy*, edited and translated by Robert Bly. Reprinted by permission.

CHAPTER 10: THE MASTER IN THE GROVE OF ELDERS

CHAPTER 11: THE SAGE IN THE MOUNTAIN CAVE

CODA: THE EYES OF THE FUTURE

INDEX

E

ABOUT *the* AUTHOR

BILL PLOTKIN, PHD, has been a psychotherapist, research psychologist, rock musician, river runner, professor of psychology, and mountain-bike racer. As a research psychologist, he studied dreams and nonordinary states of consciousness achieved through meditation, biofeedback, and hypnosis. The founder and president of Animas Valley Institute, he has guided thousands of people through initiatory passages in nature since 1980. Currently an ecotherapist, depth psychologist, and wilderness guide, he leads a variety of experiential, nature-based individuation programs. He is the author of *Soulcraft: Crossing into the Mysteries of Nature and Psyche.* His doctorate in psychology (1976) is from the University of Colorado at Boulder.

ANIMAS VALLEY INSTITUTE

ANIMAS VALLEY INSTITUTE — founded in 1980 by Bill Plotkin — offers a rich assortment of journeys into the mysteries of nature and psyche, including experiential immersions and training intensives derived from the Eco-Soulcentric Wheel, the model of human development featured in this book. For more information on courses based on the Wheel, as well as larger-format versions of the diagrams in this book and exercises that help you experience each of the eight life stages, visit:

www.natureandthehumansoul.com

For over twenty-five years, Animas has been designing and guiding nature-based programs that evoke the life-shifting experience of soul encounter — the revelation of a larger personal story that whispers to us in moments of extraordinary aliveness. This story reveals the path to our deepest personal fulfillment as well as our essential gift to the world, a world urgently in need of the transformative contributions of consciously engaged adults — visionary artists of cultural renaissance.

Individually and collaboratively, Animas Valley Institute's guides have created and shaped dozens of practices that assist people of Western cultures in their quests for more meaningful and fulfilling lives aligned with both nature and soul. These soulcraft practices spring from wilderness rites, depth psychology, the poetic tradition, nature-based peoples, and the wild world itself — to comprise a contemporary, Western, and nature-rooted path to soul discovery and initiation.

Animas currently offers forty annual programs for adults and young adults in various locations and ecosystems in the United States and Europe.

To learn more about Animas programs,
visit our website: www.animas.org,
email us: soulcraft@animas.org,
call: 800-451-6327 (U.S.A. only) or 970-259-0585,
fax: 970-259-1225,
or write:
Animas Valley Institute
P. O. Box 1020
Durango, CO 81302
U.S.A.